EUROPEAN TRAVEL LAW

Wiley Series in
EUROPEAN LAW

Barnard/EC Employment Law (Revised Edition)
0–471–96665–7 624 Pages

Burrows/European Social Law
0–471–96537–5 484 Pages

Caiger/1996 Onwards: Lowering the Barriers Further
0–471–95768–2 338 Pages

Cross/Electric Utility in the European Union
0–471–96668–1 288 Pages

Emiliou/The European Union and World Trade Law
0–471–95552–3 420 Pages

Farr/Harmonisation of Technical Standards, Second Edition
0–471–95926–X 516 Pages

Goyder/EC Distribution Law, Second Edition
0–471–96122–1 360 Pages

Hervey/Sex Equality Law in the European Union
0–471–96436–0 458 Pages

Lonbay/Remedies for Breach of EC Law
0–471–97109–X 300 Pages

Forthcoming titles

Holder/Impact of EC Environmental Law in the UK
0–471–97535–4 300 Pages

Kaye/European Case Law on the Judgments Convention
0–471–94089–5 512 Pages

EUROPEAN TRAVEL LAW

Edited by

Zahd Yaqub

Barrister

and

Becket Bedford

Barrister

Foreword by
Michael Lipton QC
Past-Chairman of Tourism, Travel and Hospitality
Law Committee, IBA

JOHN WILEY & SONS
Chichester • New York • Weinheim • Brisbane • Singapore • Toronto

First published in 1997 by   John Wiley & Sons Ltd,
Baffins Lane, Chichester,
West Sussex, PO19 1UD, England

National 01243 779777
International (+44) 1243 779777
e-mail (for orders and customer service enquiries): cs-books@wiley.co.uk
Visit our Home Page on http://www.wiley.wiley.co.uk or
http://www.wiley.com

Other Wiley Editorial Offices

John Wiley & Sons Inc., 605 Third Avenue,
New York, NY 10158-0012, USA

VCH Verlagsgesellschaft mbH, Pappelallee 3,
D-69469 Weinheim, Germany

Jacaranda Wiley Ltd, 33 Park Road, Milton,
Queensland 4064, Australia

John Wiley & Sons (Asia) Pte Ltd, 2 Clementi Loop #02-01,
Jin Xing Distripark, Singapore 129809

John Wiley & Sons (Canada) Ltd, 22 Worcester Road,
Rexdale, Ontario M9W 1L1, Canada

British Library Cataloguing in Publication Data

A catalogue record for this book is available from the British Library

ISBN 0–471–94354–1

Typeset in 10.5/12pt Baskerville by Footnote Graphics, Warminster, Wilts
Printed and bound in Great Britain by Bookcraft (Bath) Ltd, Midsomer Norton, Somerset

This book is printed on acid-free paper responsibly manufactured from sustainable forestation,
for which at least two trees are planted for each one used for paper production.

Contents

CONTENTS

CONTENTS

CONTENTS

Foreword

The Europe of today is a huge market of over 425 million consumers, organised into 15 members of the European Union (EU) and three additional members of the European Economic Area (EEA). Tens of millions of Europeans travel each year for business and pleasure. As in the rest of the civilised world, tourism and travel has become one of the major industries in the modern European economy. In terms of gross output, this industry is the largest in the world and continues to grow.

The tourism and travel industry in Europe employs tens of thousands of people and serves the needs of millions for travel, accommodation and related services. The needs of international trade are growing and the technologies of transport and communications are continuously developing. These combine to produce an industrial environment characterised by dynamic expansion in capability and complexity.

The law governing this rapidly expanding industry is necessarily diverse and complex. As part of the increasing co-operation on a Europe-wide basis, there has been added a broad European legal dimension to this industry, exemplified by the EC Directive on Package Travel, which impacts on the travel plans of almost every traveller whose trip originates within the European Union.

The chapters of this book provide succinct descriptions of the travel law in the Member States of the European Union. Whether one encounters legal problems in Belgium, Ireland, Spain, England or Germany this reference book will become the touchstone of the tourism and travel industry. In its uniquely broad coverage and straightforward, clear style, this work lays a solid foundation of information and knowledge upon which the industry will be able to rely as it moves forward into the twenty-first century. As a North American, I envy the practitioners of European tourism and travel law who now have available this powerful tool to assist them in guiding representatives of the industry through the complex web of law which governs the ever expanding European travel industry.

The creation of this compendium of legal information from across the breadth of Europe is due to Mr Zahd Yaqub. He conceived the idea for such a work, enlisted the authors, all recognised experts in their home countries and both co-ordinated and encouraged the completion of their chapters. When he requested that I write the Foreword to this book several months ago, I soon realised that he had undertaken a very onerous task. Certainly all members of the Tourism and Travel industry, be they travel agents, tour operators, hoteliers, or transportation companies will be indebted to Mr Yaqub and Mr Bedford. As chairman of the Tourism,

Travel and Hospitality Law Committee (Committee Y), one of the sections on Business Law of the International Bar Association, I am delighted and honoured to be associated with this unique and useful contribution to the understanding of travel law in modern Europe.

Michael D Lipton QC
Toronto, Canada
January 1997

About the IBA

The International Bar Association (IBA) is the world's foremost international association of lawyers, with a membership of over 17,000 individual lawyers in 173 countries, as well as 156 Bar Associations and Law Societies. Its principal aims and objectives are:

- to encourage the discussion of problems relating to professional organisation and status;
- to promote exchange of information between legal associations worldwide;
- to support the independence of the judiciary and the right of lawyers to practise their profession without interference;
- to keep abreast of new developments in the law, and help in improving and making new laws.

Above all, though, it seeks to provide a forum in which individual lawyers can contact and exchange ideas with other lawyers.

The IBA has three Sections: the Section on Business Law, the Section on General Practice and the Section on Energy & Natural Resources Law which has over 13,000 members. Within the Section on Business Law there are 27 Committees, each specialising in a particular area of business law.

Section on Business Law

The Committees of the Section on Business Law aim to study and discuss the legal and practical aspects of issues relating to their particular topic from an international viewpoint.

Members are typically partners of law firms practising in national and international business matters, or in-house corporate lawyers of companies active in international business. Members of the judiciary and academics also join and participate in the activities of the Committee.

Committee Y

Committee Y was formed in response to the need to provide a forum to discuss legal issues relating to Tourism, Travel and Hospitality Law. It meets annually as part of either the Biennial Conference of the Section on Business Law or the Biennial Conference of the International Bar Association. Some areas covered by Committee Y at these meetings are:

the legal status of time sharing in different countries, the responsibilities of tour operators and their ability to impose surcharges and to cancel/vary holidays and the law relating to tour operators and travel agents in Latin American countries. Membership of a Committee enables lawyers to become personally acquainted with qualified colleagues in other countries specialising in the same or similar areas, to whom they may turn for professional assistance in their own international practice.

Preface

The expansion of travel with the acceleration of new Member States joining the EC, will see an increase in inter-Europe travel.

Tourism is the largest industry in Europe, accounting directly for[1] 6.5% of the Community's gross domestic product; an equivalent proportion of total employment, comprising 8 million jobs; 7.5% of capital investment; and 17% of consumer spending.[2] Tourism's gross turnover is estimated world-wide at $3.4 trillion.

The tourism industry has the potential to create sustained economic growth and jobs, thus contributing to the Community initiative for relaunching the European economy.

This book aims to give an overview and analysis of the activities of the EC in the sphere of travel and consumer protection measures to assist the tourism consumer.

A body of case law has developed pertaining to tour guides and tourists as recipients of services. European Union legislative provisions deal with the free movement of persons, goods and services, consumer protection measures, and judicial control, etc. These measures facilitate the free movement of travellers, whilst affording them comprehensive protection.

The book discusses the Package Travel Directive, including a consideration of the *Dillenkofer* judgment, and also contains contributions from the individual Member States reviewing the implementation of national measures governing the tourism industry, the establishment of travel agencies, and measures to assist consumers.

We are indebted to all those who provided the inspiration for this project, especially the IBA Travel, Tourism and Hospitality Law Committee.

Postscript

The preliminary ruling of the ECJ in *Dillenkofer*[3] confirms, to the chagrin of the UK and others, what we, the editors, have long suspected, namely that Article 7 of the Package Travel Directive 90/314/EEC

---

[1] A3–0352/93 European Parliaments Tourism Committee
[2] World Tourism Organisation
[3] Joined Cases C–178/94, C–179/94, C–188/94, C–189/94 and C–190/94 *Erich Dillenkofer and Others* v *Federal Republic of Germany* (8 October 1996). The judgment is reproduced in Appendix 24.

requires Member States to guarantee that "money paid over by purchasers of package travel will be refunded and a guarantee that they will be repatriated in the event of the insolvency of the organiser".[4]

The ECJ ruled that Article 7 "would not have been fully implemented if, within the prescribed period, the national legislature had done no more than adopt the necessary legal framework for requiring organisers by law to provide sufficient evidence of security".[5]

It follows that the Member States will be liable to package holiday-makers if tour operators become insolvent without having sufficient security. It is not enough for the Member States to require tour operators to provide sufficient evidence of security by the imposition of civil, or even criminal, sanctions. It would appear that the Member States are required to set up or support existing guarantee funds with state backing.

Should the Member States fail to do so, they will themselves be liable to compensate package holiday-makers for breach of a Community law obligation, namely failure to implement the Package Travel Directive within the prescribed period.[6]

We are indebted to the publishers for enabling us to include a mention of *Dillenkofer*. The book is now complete. We hope that it will be judged to be not only an aid to practitioners, but also, and perhaps more importantly, as a guide to travel agents, tour operators, regulators and consumers.

Zahd Yaqub
Becket Bedford
January 1997

---

[4] *Ibid.*, Questions 1 and 2.
[5] *Ibid.*, Questions 3 and 4.
[6] *Francovich; Brasserie du Pêcheur and Factortame; British Telecommunications; Hedley Lomas.*

Acknowledgements

I would like to thank the following for their continued support and assistance: Marinus Vromans; Takis Kommatas; Cedric Guyot; Pim WH de Vos for writing the chapter on Principles of Travel Law at the eleventh hour, Martin Briggs, RCI Europe Ltd, for his work on behalf of the IBA Tourism, Travel and Hospitality Law Committee; Nassos Christoyanno-poulos DG XXIII at the Commission Tourism Directorate; Keith Hale from LACOTS; Dr Jose Fosman, president of the IFTTA, and John and Maureen Robertson. Thanks to the contributors for their patience and hard work, without which this would not have been possible.

Thanks are also due to my chambers' clerks for retrieving faxes and letters and for taking phone messages, to my colleagues in chambers Réné Wong and George Papageorgis, and in particular to Elisabeth Linden, a very special lady, for all her support, encouragement and inspiration.

Many thanks to David Wilson, our long-suffering Publishing Director, for his unreserved patience and commitment to the project.

Special thanks are due to Michael Lipton QC for agreeing to write the Foreword, to everyone at the IBA, and to Brenda and Quinton Gerwat-Clark and Clive Parrish AETA.

Finally I would like to thank Farha, Sara, Sommyya and my family for their inspiration, love and support.

Zahd Yaqub
January 1997

List of Contributors

Ahola, Pentzin, Rantasila & Sokka Oy	Ahola, Pentzin, Rantasila & Sokka Oy, Helsinki, Finland.
Ulrik Andersen	Dragsted & Helmer Nielsen, Copenhagen, Denmark.
Walter Beatty	Vincent & Beatty, Dublin, Ireland.
Becket Bedford	Barrister, London, England.
Hector Díaz-Bastien & Paloma Peman Domecq	Díaz-Bastien & Truan, Madrid, Spain.
Stefano Dindo	Studio Legale Dindo, Verona, Italy.
Cedric Guyot	Derks, Star Busmann, Hanotiau, Brussels, Belgium.
Guy Harles	Arendt & Medernach, Luxembourg.
Dr Christoph Hasche	Wessing, Berenborg-Gossler, Zimmerman, Lange, Hamburg, Germany.
Marc Jobert	Avocat à la Cour, Paris, France.
Dr Mario A Kakabadse	World Trade Organisation, Geneva, Switzerland.
Takis G Kommatas	Takis G Kommatas Law Offices, Athens, Greece.
Michael Lipton QC	Past-Chairman of Tourism, Travel and Hospitality Law Committee (Committee Y), IBA.
David Parratt	Bishop, Robertson and Chalmers, Glasgow, Scotland.
Henrique dos Santos Pereira	M P Barrocas & Associados, Lisbon, Portugal.
Iain Taylor	Bishop, Robertson and Chalmers, Glasgow, Scotland.
June Turkington	McKinty & Wright, Belfast, Northern Ireland.
Pim W H de Vos	de Vos & Steinz, Amsterdam, The Netherlands.
Marinus Vromans & Caroline Bleeker	Barents & Krans, Brussels, Belgium.
Zahd Yaqub	Barrister, specialist in EC law, London, England.

Tables

PROPOSED DIRECTIVES AND RECOMMENDATIONS

CASES

EUROPEAN LEGISLATION

NATIONAL LEGISLATION

STATUTORY INSTRUMENTS

Part I

EC and International Travel Provisions

General European Community Law Provisions Pertaining to Travel

Chapter 1
General European Community Law Provisions Pertaining to Travel

Zahd Yaqub
Barrister

1.   Introduction

(i)   The EC Treaty

The EC Treaty (The Treaty of Rome as amended by the Single European **1.1** Act and the Maastricht Treaty) confers on any national of a Member State the right to move and stay freely within the territory of another Member State other than that of his residence, on simple presentation of an identity card or passport.

(a)   Article 7a

Article 7a of the EC Treaty provides: **1.2**

> The internal market shall comprise an area without internal frontiers in which the free movement of goods, persons, services and capital is ensured in accordance with the provisions of this treaty.

The internal market is intended to operate in the same way as a national market; there must be no controls at the frontiers between Member States on the movement of goods, services, capital or persons, just as there are no controls between regions within a state. As checks at internal frontiers are done away with, measures must also be taken to eliminate the reasons for them, whether by harmonising the legislation of Member States, by setting up or reinforcing co-operation between Member States, or by bringing in an effective system of controls at external frontiers.

Measures are required to be taken in a number of fields: right of asylum; **1.3** visas; controls at external frontiers; police co-operation; judicial co-operation in criminal matters; and so on. However, Member States had not eliminated controls on individuals by 31 December 1992, as required by Article 7(a).

(b)   Article K

Article K. 1 of the Maastricht Treaty on European Union ("the Maas- **1.4** tricht Treaty") provides that Member States must regard certain areas as matters of common interest.

The areas referred to in Article K.1(1) to (6) are:

(1) asylum policy;

(2) rules governing the crossing by persons of the external borders of the Member States and the exercise of controls thereon;

(3) immigration policy regarding nationals of third countries:

   (a) conditions of entry and movement by nationals of third countries on the territory of Member States;

   (b) conditions of residence by nationals of third countries on the territory of Member States, including family reunion and access to employment;

   (c) combating unauthorised immigration, residence and work by nationals of third countries on the territory of Member States;

(4) combating drug addiction . . .

(5) combating fraud on an international scale . . .

(6) judicial co-operation in civil matters.

1.5   Member States must inform and consult one another within the Council with a view to co-ordinating their action in the areas referred to above. Pursuant to Article K.3(2) the Council may act on the initiative of any Member State or of the Commission in these areas, and the Council may, *inter alia*:

   (a) adopt joint positions and promote, using the appropriate forum and procedures, any co-operation contributing to the pursuit of the objectives of the Union;

   (b) adopt joint action in so far as the objectives of the Union can be attained better by joint action than by the Member States acting individually on account of the scale or effects of the action envisaged; it may decide that measures implementing joint action are to be adopted by a qualified majority.

(c) Article 100c

1.6   These matters remain in the inter-governmental arena pursuant to Article 100c(1), which provides that:

> The Council, acting unanimously on a proposal from the Commission and after consulting the European Parliament, shall determine the third countries whose nationals must be in possession of a visa when crossing the external borders of the Member States.

This provision brings visa policy within the Community sphere of action. It provides for the determination of which third countries shall require visas for its nationals before they may cross the external borders of the Community. Such harmonisation of visa policy is considered essential to permit opening up of internal frontiers in order to achieve a degree of consistency between the different Member States.

1.7   All decisions under Article 100c(1) will be taken by unanimous vote in Council until 1 January 1996, when qualified majority voting will commence.

Under Article 100c(3), the Council was obliged, before 1 January 1996, acting by a qualified majority on a proposal from the Commission and after consulting the European Parliament, to adopt measures relating to a uniform format for visas.

(ii) The External Frontiers Convention

The Commission has published a "Convention of controls on persons **1.8** crossing external frontiers", ("the External Frontiers Convention") (COM (93) 684), tabled in accordance with Article K.3(2)c of the Treaty, and a proposal pursuant to Article 100c on visas. The revised Convention on controls on persons crossing external frontiers replaces an earlier draft instrument negotiated within the framework of inter-governmental co-operation. The text takes account of the conclusions of the EC Treaty establishing the EC, and the adoption of a Council Regulation in 1991 and 1992 regarding baggage controls.

Article 3 of the Convention provides that the European Court of Justice has jurisdiction over the Convention.

The External Frontiers Convention sets out a list of those countries **1.9** whose nationals require visas when crossing the external frontiers of the Community. It is intended that at a later stage the Council should complete the harmonisation of this matter by drawing up an exhaustive and binding list of countries where nationals are to be exempted from visa requirements. Pending this full harmonisation, Member States will remain free to require a visa or not in the case of nationals of non-community countries which are not listed in the annex.

(iii) The Schengen Convention

The list is based on work already carried out by nine Member States **1.10** within the framework of the Schengen Agreement. In 1985, five Member States, Germany, France, Belgium, the Netherlands, and Luxembourg, signed the Schengen Convention on the gradual abolition of checks at their common borders. This Convention entered into force for these countries in September 1993, whilst Spain, Portugal, Greece, and Italy, acceded to the Convention in March 1994. The three states not signing the Agreement were the United Kingdom, Ireland and Denmark (which has now applied for observer status).

One of the major aims of the agreement is the pusuit of a common visa policy. Since there is no supranational judicial control there may be variations in the implementation of this policy from one contracting state to another. A binding implementing convention was signed on 19 June 1990 which required ratification and was implemented in March 1995 via the Schengen computer system in all of the nine countries listed above. Austria has now applied to join the Convention.

(iv)   Proposed Council Directive on the right of third-country nationals to travel in the Community

1.11   The purpose of this Directive (OJ C306/5) is that Member States shall grant third-country nationals who are lawfully in a Member State the right to travel in the territories of the other Member States in accordance with this Directive.

The proposed Directive provides in Article 1(3) that it will not affect provisions of community or domestic law on:
–   stays other than for a short time, and
–   access to employment and the taking up of activities as a self-employed person applicable to third-country nationals.

Article 3 provides that Member States shall grant the right to travel to third-country nationals who hold a valid residence permit issued by another Member State. Any such person may travel in the territories of the other Member States for a continuous period of not more than three months, provided that he meets the following requirements:
–   he must be in possession of a valid residence permit and a valid travel document;
–   he must have sufficient means of subsistence, both to cover the period of the intended stay or transit and to enable him to return to the Member State which issued the residence permit, or to travel to a third-country into which he is certain to be admitted.

1.12   The Directive permitted Member States to expel a third-country national who holds a residence permit issued by a Member State and who is exercising the right to travel, but who does not meet the requirements laid down in paragraph 1 above.

The Directive provides that Member States shall confer the right to travel on third-country nationals who are exempted from visa requirements by all the Member States.

Member States may authorise a third-country national to stay in their territory beyond three months.

1.13   The implementing convention deals with immigration and asylum, as well as with police co-operation, extradition, narcotic drugs and judicial co-operation. The mechanisms for exchanging information on persons and goods through the Schengen Information System (SIS) have not yet been made operational.

The Schengen Convention, whilst aiming for free circulation within the contracting states, allows the maintenance of those controls which the contracting states consider necessary.

The ratification of the External Frontiers Convention and the regime it will establish, will do much to strengthen the perception of Europe as a single tourism destination.

The mutual recognition of visas and the equal recognition of residence papers and visas as regards the crossing of internal frontiers and short stays are not yet covered by legislative initiative.

(v) The economic and social effects of tourism

The free movement of nationals between Member States, raises the question of tourism and its importance for the European economy.

Tourism is of great economic importance both at European and world level. Tourism represents one of the Community's main sources of income, accounting for an estimated 5.5% of G.N.P. Tourism is clearly much more important for some Member States than for others, as regards both income and expenditure. The percentage of G.N.P. represented by tourism is almost double the Community average in Spain and France, and above the Community average in Greece, Ireland and Portugal.

In terms of employment tourism-related activities account for one million jobs, representing around 6% of the total number of jobs in the Community.

An additional aspect which demonstrates the vitality of tourism is its ability to generate major investment, not only in the industry itself but also in other areas of the economy. Tourism has a dynamic and diversifying effect, which acts as a boost for other sectors of the economy.

Finally, tourism is a particularly effective way of bringing together individuals and the cultures of which the tourists are ambassadors and representatives, and also a means of affirming European identity through tourists and local populations meeting one another.

2. Tourism and the Community

The Commission, supported by the European Parliament and the Economic and Social Committee, has been working since the early 1980s towards giving this field its rightful place in the range of Community activities.

(i) The legal and institutional framework

(a) Declaration (No 1) on Civil Protection, Energy and Tourism

The Declarations attached to the Treaty of European Union are not an integral part of the Treaty. Further, they are not enforceable in the European Court of Justice. In Declaration (No 1) on Civil Protection, Energy and Tourism the Commission declared that Community action in those spheres will be pursued on the basis of the present provisions of the EC Treaty and the Treaty on European Union.

The Member States declared that the question of introducing into the EC Treaty, Titles relating to energy, civil protection and tourism, will be examined in accordance with the procedure laid down in Article N(2) of the Treaty on European Union, on the basis of a report which the Commission will submit to the Council by 1996 at the latest.

1.17   Article N(2) of the Treaty on European Union provides "that a conference of representatives of the governments of the Member States shall be convened in 1996 to examine those provisions of this Treaty for which revision is provided".

Article 3 of the EC Treaty sets out the activities of the Community (at Article 3(t)): "measures in the spheres of energy, civil protection and tourism". Tourism is thus in the position of being included in the list of Community objectives, without any corresponding operative provisions in the Treaty itself. The declaration provides for their potential inclusion as Titles within the Treaty. We will have to wait until 1996 to see what further developments occur in this area.

(b)   European Tourism year

1.18   Community action to assist tourism really began with the proposal by the Commission, declaring 1990 as European Tourism year. (Council decision 89/46/EEC of 21 December 1988 (OJ 1989 L17/53).)

This was the first opportunity to exploit the potential of the economic and social importance of tourism, while establishing close relations between the public and private sectors throughout the Community. The discussions held at informal meetings of the Ministers responsible within the Community all suggested that the Commission should draw up an action plan to assist tourism. The discussions highlighted the following points of concern:

(i)   a diversity of views on what action the Community should take on tourism;

(ii) the lack of transitional co-operation between decision-makers in the various fields of activity relating to and affected by tourism, and between public authorities, economic generators, trade associations and consumers; and

(iii) a fragmentary structure for consultation within the Commission as a major concern.

A form of co-operation between the various Commission departments which supplements the standard internal consultation procedures, thus will make it easier to take the specific nature of tourism into account in all Community activities.

(c)   The Community Action Plan

1.19   The Commission adopted a three year action plan by Council Decision 92/421/EEC of 13 July 1992, being a Community Action Plan to Assist Tourism (OJ 1992 L231/26). This is the most significant measure reached at Community level on tourism. There are two types of measure:

(i)   general measures strengthening the horizontal approach to tourism in Community and national policies, providing information and promoting exchanges and co-ordination;

(ii)   specific measures which allow the Commission to act as a catalyst in certain fields of tourism activity.

The duration of the action plan is three years from 1 January 1993.

Article 4(2)c of the Action Plan to Assist Tourism provides for measures to improve the quality of Community tourist services. Article 6 provided for a report to be published by June 1995 evaluating the success of the measures in the Community by the Commission.

The annex to this Council decision provides that Community action should support initiatives which improve the provision of information to tourists, and their protection, in areas such as existing classification systems; signposting, symbols, time share arrangements, overbooking, and procedures for redress.

The main Community measures affecting the tourist are those aimed at: **1.20**

(i)   making it easier to pass the Community's internal frontiers;

(ii)   improving information for tourists and their protection as consumers; and

(iii)   promoting tourism as a basis for social integration.

Since the European year of Tourism, which finished in 1991, the Commission has co-financed a number of pilot projects relating to encouraging new tourism activities and products, and promoting sustainable tourism. Some of the important measures are:

(i)   rural and cultural tourism (OJ 1991 C128/10)

(ii)   sustainable tourism (OJ 1992 C51/16)

(iii)   transnational actions and cultural tourism (OJ 1993 C128/09).

(ii)   Freedom of movement

The EC Treaty confers on any national of a Member State the right to   **1.21** move and stay freely within the territory of a Member State other than that of his residence, on simple presentation of an identity card or passport. This was one of the first rights acquired by citizens of the Community as tourists. Article 8 of the EC Treaty provides for citizenship of the Union:

(1) Citizenship of the Union is hereby established.
Every person holding the nationality of a Member State shall be a citizen of the Union.

(2) Citizens of the Union shall enjoy the rights conferred by this Treaty and shall be subject to the duties imposed hereby.

Declaration No. 2 to the Treaty on the nationality of a Member State's citizen states that:

the question whether an individual possesses the nationality of a Member State shall be settled solely by reference to the national law of the Member State concerned.

The immigration laws of each Member State will therefore decide who is a citizen of the Union.

The problem revolved around Member States' sovereignty and the Community institutions over the common determining conditions for nationality.

1.22 Article 8(a) provides for the free movement of citizens in the Union, and gives a right to free movement for Union citizens.

(1) Every citizen of the Union shall have the right to move and reside freely within the territory of the Member States, subject to the limitations and conditions laid down in this Treaty and by the measures adopted to give it effect.

(2) The Council may adopt provisions with a view to facilitating the exercise of the rights referred to in paragraph 1; save as otherwise provided in this Treaty, the Council shall act unanimously on a proposal from the Commission and after obtaining the assent of the European Parliament.

The introduction of this article into the EC Treaty, covers individuals who were not already covered in the Directives on students, retired workers, and self-employed persons. It follows on from the "non-economically active persons" Directive 90/364/EEC (OJ 1990 L180/26), that all Union citizens are covered. Members States may derogate from the provisions, on the grounds of public health and national security.

1.23 The Citizenship of the Union provisions in Article 8 are all subject to Article 8(e), which provides that the Commission shall report to the European Parliament, the Council, and the Economic and Social Committee every three years on the application of the provisions of this part. It provides that the Council, (acting unanimously on a proposal from the Commission and after consulting the European Parliament), may adopt provisions to strengthen or to add to the rights in these articles, which it shall recommend to the Member States for adoption in accordance with their respective constitutional requirements.

Abolition of controls at internal frontiers

1.24 While many problems remain regarding border controls on individuals, the Commission has noted some advances under the Schengen agreements which aim to abolish all controls on people crossing common borders. Seven of the Member States of the Union (Germany, Belgium, Spain, France, Luxembourg, the Netherlands and Portugal), have applied the Schengen Convention between them, in an irreversible way, as from 1 July 1995. (France has however applied the safeguard clause – allowing the temporary reinstatement of border controls for reasons of public order and national security.) The implementation of the Convention represents an important stage in the completion of the objective of Article 7A of the EC Treaty.

In parallel, on 12 July 1995 the Commission adopted three proposals for Directives aimed at the abolition of controls on people crossing internal borders throughout the European Union as a whole. In the opinion of the Commission, the internal market must function under the same conditions as a national market, where intra-community journeys should be undertaken just like journeys between regions or provinces of a Member State. But until the internal frontier controls are abolished, the internal market will not be a reality for Community citizens. Of course, the abolition of the internal frontier controls should in no way involve a reduction in the safety of the European citizen. On the contrary, it is specifically provided for in the proposals that the abolition of the controls will not enter into force unless the essential supporting measures to ensure the maintenance of a high safety level in the area without frontiers is definitively adopted and satisfactorily implemented. All these measures are on the Council table.

The first of the new proposals gives concrete expression to the aim of **1.25** abolishing controls, and clarifies the scope of the prohibition on carrying out controls and on imposing formalities at internal borders (OJ 1995 C306). This proposal confirms that all persons, whatever their nationality, are the beneficiaries of the abolition of internal frontier controls. A "safeguard clause" exists that may be invoked when a Member State is confronted with a sufficiently serious material threat to public order or safety.

A second proposed Directive aims to modify secondary legislation in the field of free movement of people, so as to eliminate from these texts any provision making it possible to carry out controls on persons at the time of crossing an internal border (OJ 1995 C289).

Lastly, a third proposal aims to grant to nationals of third countries, **1.26** who are legally in a Member State, the right to make a short visit to the territory of the other Member States if they are equipped with a residence permit or a visa valid for all the Member States of the Union (OJ 1995 C307). This is also an inseparable supplement to the proposals that the Commission submitted in December 1993 as regards crossing external borders, by envisaging equivalence between a residence permit and a visa delivered by a Member State, as well as the mutual recognition of visas. By this measure, several million foreign residents will be able to go to different countries of the Union without being forced to equip themselves with a visa beforehand, which will encourage tourism and cross-border acquisition of goods and services.

In 1996 the Council adopted two regulations – that of 29 May 1995 establishing a model type of visa (Reg (EC) 1683/95), and that of 25 September 1995 determining the list of third countries whose nationals must have a visa to enter Community territory (Reg (EC) 2316/95).

Format for visas

1.27   The introduction of a uniform format for visas is an important step towards harmonisation of visa policy in accordance with Article 7A of the Maastrict Treaty. This Article stipulates, that the internal market shall comprise an area without internal frontier, in which the free movement of persons is ensured in accordance with the Treaty.

The Council has produced Regulation (EC) No 1683/95, which lay down a uniform format for visas. The Regulation sets out those specifications which are not secret, but these need to be supplemented by further specifications which must remain secret to prevent counterfeiting and falsification, and which may not include personal data or references to such data.

These Regulations apply to visas where the intended stay is no longer than three months in all, and lay down the specifications for such visas with regard to security features etc.

1.28   In accordance with Article 7A of the Treaty, the Council has published Council Regulation EC No 2316/95, determining those third countries whose nationals must be in possession of visas when crossing the external borders of Member States. The third countries are listed in the Annex. Member States are left with discretion in the following circumstances only:

(i)   They may determine the visa requirements for third countries not on the common list, and the Regulations do not prevent a Member State from deciding the conditions under which nationals of third countries lawfully resident within the State's territory may re-enter the State after leaving it.

(ii) They may determine the visa requirements for persons who produce passports or travel documents issued by a territorial entity or authority which is not recognised as a state by all Member States only if that entity or territorial authority is not on the common list.

Proposed Council Directives on the elimination of controls on persons crossing internal frontiers

1.29   A Directive has been proposed on the practical application of the principle of the elimination of controls on persons (Comm Doc 1995 347). It is based on Article 100 of the EC Treaty – requiring the unanimous approval of the Council. The Directive would provide final confirmation that controls at internal borders have indeed been eliminated.

The Directive would take effect only if the flanking measures were themselves in force. These flanking measures are considered essential to maintain a high level of security within the area of internal borders, and the Commission would like them to be implemented as soon as possible. They include the Dublin Convention determining the state responsible for examining applications for asylum lodged in one of the Member States; the draft External Frontiers Convention; the proposal for a Regulation determining the third countries whose nationals must be in possession of a visa when crossing the external borders of the Member States; the Council Regulations laying down a uniform format for visas, and the draft Convention on a European Information System.

A second proposed Directive adapts the secondary legislation on the 1.30 free movement of citizens of the Union (and their families). This proposal is based on Articles 49, 54(2) and 62(2) of the EC Treaty; it would amend the existing secondary legislation to take account of the ending of controls at internal borders required by the Directive. The practical effectiveness of the proposal is therefore dependent on that Directive's entry into force.

Thirdly, a Directive is proposed giving nationals of non-member countries who are lawfully in the territory of one Member State the right to travel for a brief stay in the territory of any other Member State – an entitlement known as the "right to travel". This proposal is based on Article 100 of the EC Treaty. It is the last of the measures accompanying the ending of controls on persons for which a proposal has still to be put forward at Union level. It would also be a considerable step forward in the treatment of non-Union nationals who are lawfully resident in a Member State and who wish to travel in the Community, and of non-Community members of the families of Union nationals.

The proposal would not affect the first entry into the Community of a 1.31 non-Union national or the decision of a Member State to authorise him to remain in its territory for a long stay. Nor would it affect, *a fortiori*, Member States' decisions regarding access to the labour market or to self-employed activity.

Like other flanking measures (*e.g.* the Dublin Convention, for which the ratification process will shortly be completed), this "right to travel" Directive could be applied before controls on persons at internal borders are abolished.

Comments on the Articles

ARTICLE 1   ELIMINATION OF CONTROLS AND FORMALITIES FOR PERSONS CROSSING INTERNAL FRONTIERS

Article 1(1) confirms the commitment which the Member States entered 1.32 into when they inserted Article 7a (formerly Article 8a) into the EC Treaty: they must ensure that the crossing of an internal frontier in the internal market is treated in the same way as the crossing of a boundary between provinces, counties, regions. It follows that:

– the crossing of an internal frontier may not in itself give rise to controls or formalities;
– all persons, whatever their nationality, should normally be able to cross internal frontiers unimpeded;

– internal frontiers may be crossed anywhere and not merely at approved crossing points.

1.33 Only *frontier* controls and formalities are banned (see Art. 3(4)). Article 1(2) thus provides that the obligation to eliminate frontier controls and formalities does not deprive the competent authorities of the law enforcement powers which the legislation of each Member State has conferred on them over the whole of its territory. These powers must be exercised without discrimination between domestic and cross-border traffic; powers to impose controls or penalties which were exercised only on the occasion of, or in connection with, the crossing of an internal frontier would be contrary to Article 7a. Article 1(2) provides that the elimination of controls and formalities for persons crossing internal frontiers does not affect any obligations to possess, carry and produce such documents which are laid down in a Member State's national rules.

ARTICLE 2   TEMPORARY REINSTATEMENT OF CONTROLS.

1.34 This provides that a Member State may reinstate frontier controls where there is a serious threat to public policy or public security. Article 2(3) provides that the period in which a Member State may apply such controls must be limited to what is strictly necessary in order to counter the threat. Article 2(1) stipulates that, in the event of a serious threat, controls may be reinstated initially for not more than thirty days. The period of thirty days is renewable, on one or more occasions, but the other Member States and the Commission must be consulted before each renewal.

ARTICLE 3   THE CONCEPT OF INTERNAL FRONTIER

1.35 The first indent of Article 3(1) makes it clear that the concept of common land frontiers also embraces rail or road terminals for links by bridge or tunnel between Member States, despite the fact that such terminals are not always close to the frontier but may be located some distance inland. Article 3(4) defines the concept of frontier controls or formalities. A frontier control is accordingly first defined as "any control applied in connection with or on the occasion of the crossing of an internal frontier by the public authorities of a Member State". Unless they rely on Article 2, Member States may not apply controls such as those referred to in Articles 5–7 of the draft convention on controls on persons crossing external frontiers. Article 5 lays down the date for implementing the proposed Directive as 31 December 1996.

Forthcoming legislation

1.36 The Commission is committed to the consoldiation, completion and enhancement of the single market, in which goods, persons, services and capital move freely. Accordingly this must be the cornerstone of the

Commission's activity. In regard to the free movement of persons – the freedom to travel – the Commission intends to eliminate border controls by means of the adoption of secondary legislation.

Various proposals have been enacted:

(i)   Council Regulation (EC) No 1683/95, which lays down a uniform format for visas.

(ii)   Council Regulation (EC) No 2317/95, which determines the countries whose nationals must be in possession of visas when crossing the external borders of Member States.

The Commission has proposed a second action plan for tourism, together with a report on the evaluation of the results of the first action plan.

In the transport sector, the Commission is committed to achieving an integrated, safe, efficient, competitive and environmentally friendly transport system. This should take into account the needs of users and workers in this sector. In the long term, this will ensure mobility and cohesion within the European Union and help develop the external dimension.   **1.37**

The Commission hopes to enact legislative proposals in the following areas:

(i)   tighter security on ferry services;

(ii)   introduction of an alternative model for the Community driving licence;

(iii)   measures to protect the rights of airline passengers;

(iv)   a ground handling Directive pertaining to delays in airline travel.

The priorities for the Commission's action in the field of consumer policy will be to step up information and awareness campaigns, to improve consumer representation and to draw up a new action plan for 1996–98.

The Commission hopes to follow up the Green Paper on consumer access to justice and the settlement of consumer disputes in the single market, and to enact the Distance Selling Directive without delay. The creation of an area without internal frontiers has long been an objective – first of the European Community and now of the Union. There are clear benefits for all citizens. Nevertheless, the Union must ensure internal security in a frontier-free area when the controls at internal frontiers have been removed, in order to prevent organised crime from demonstrating both its will and its capacity to exploit weaknesses in the Union's defences.

Title VI of the Treaty on European Union provides the political commitment and the instruments to deal with concerns about immigration and asylum. The Commission will press the council to adopt the draft Internal Borders Convention tabled in December 1993, which is an essential instrument for the free movement of people, and will table an   **1.38** initiative concerning travel rights of nationals of non-member countries. Common rules on conditions of entry by nationals and major principles governing asylum policy, including forms of exchange between Member States will be the major elements of the Commission's contribution. The Commission's approach will be to strike the right balance between ensuring integration and rights of legal immigrants and acting against illegal immigration.

3. Freedom to provide services by tour guides or managers

(i) General

1.39 One of the fundamental principles of the EC Treaty is that a citizen of one Member State must be free to live and work in another Member State as an employee, as a trainee, or as a self-employed person.

The Community adopted the first measures designed to secure freedom of movement for workers as early as 1968 (Council Directive 68/360/EEC (OJ 1968 L257/13)). Several Directives on the right of establishment and the freedom to supply services apply to the tourist industry, cafés, hotels and camping sites, couriers and travel agents.

(ii) Tour guide or tour manager

1.40 Those practising the profession of tour guide or tour manager have encountered particular problems. As far as tour guides are concerned, it is necessary to distinguish between guides wishing to become established in another Member State (covered by Art 57) and guides who accompany tourists to another Member State while remaining based in their country of origin (covered by Art 59 of the Treaty).

In Case C–180/89 *Commission* v *Italian Republic* [1991] ECR I–709 on a preliminary matter discussed by the court, it was pointed out that the activities of a tour guide from one Member State who accompanied tourists on an organised tour from that Member State to another Member State may be subject to two distinct sets of legal rules, one set from each Member State concerned.

A tour company established in another Member State may itself employ guides. In that case it is the tour company that provides the service to tourists through its own guides. Alternatively, a tour company may engage self-employed tour guides established in that other Member State. In that case, the service is provided by the guide to the tour company. In both cases, such services, which are of limited duration, and are not governed by the provisions on the free movement of goods, capital and persons, constitute activities carried on for remuneration within the meaning of Article 60 of the EC Treaty.

(iii)　Article 59

Article 59 provides that: **1.41**

> Within the framework of the provisions set out below, restrictions on freedom to provide services within the Community shall be progressively abolished during the transitional period in respect of nationals of Member States who are established in a State of the Community other than that of the person for whom the services are intended.
>
> The Council may, acting by a qualified majority on a proposal from the Commission, extend the provisions of the Chapter to nationals of a third country who provide services and who are established within the Community.

The provisions of Article 59 must apply in all cases where a person providing services offers those services in a Member State other than that in which he is established, wherever the recipients of those services may be established.

In the case of *Commission* v *Italian Republic*, the Italian Government **1.42** made the provision of services by tour guides accompanying a group of tourists from another Member State, (in relation to guided tours of places other than museums and historical monuments where a specialised guide was required), subject to possession of a licence issued after the acquisition of a specific qualification obtained by success in an examination. The European Court held that the Italian Republic had failed to fulfil its obligations under Article 59 of the EC Treaty. The Court held that Articles 59 and 60 of the Treaty required not only the abolition of any discrimination against a person providing services on account of his nationality, but also the abolition of any restriction on the freedom to provide services, imposed on the ground that the person providing a service was established in a Member State other than the one in which the service is provided. In particular, the Member State cannot make the performance of services in its territory subject to compliance with all the conditions required for establishment; were it to do so the provisions securing freedom to provide services would be deprived of all practical effect.

The European Court had already decided, in joined cases 62/81 and **1.43** 63/81 *Seco* v *EVI* [1982] ECR 223 concerning a salaried tour guide who worked on behalf of a tour operator and accompanied a group of tourists throughout their whole journey, and was travelling abroad with the group and providing commentary on the cultural, historical and artistic features of the country, that the undertaking, acting solely through the intermediary of its Guides, was a provider of services, and this work constituted the provision of services.

19

In Case C–154/89 *Commission* v *French Republic* [1991] ECR I–659, the Court held that the French Republic had failed to fulfil its obligations under Article 59 of the EC Treaty, by requiring persons who provided services as tourist guides accompanying a group of tourists from another Member State, when the service consisted in guiding tourists in places in certain French Departments or communes, (other than museums and historical monuments which may be visited only with a specialised professional guide), to hold a licence which was dependent on the possession of a specific qualification, generally awarded on the passing of an examination.

1.44 The Court again reiterated that the provisions of Article 59 must apply in all cases where a person providing services offers those services in a Member State other than that in which he is established, wherever the recipients of those services may be established. Both Articles 59 and 60 of the Treaty required not only the abolition of any discrimination against a person providing services, on account of his nationality, but also the abolition of any restriction on the freedom to provide services, imposed on the ground that the person providing a service is established in a Member State other than the one in which the service is provided. Further, the provisions of secondary legislation may only enact national measures which are compatible with the requirements of Article 59 of the Treaty.

1.45 The Court in both cases was aware that the impact of a licence requirement would reduce the number of guides who accompanied tourists. A monopoly situation would then arise of tourists being with guides who were not familiar with their language and their interests.

In Case C–198/89 *Commission* v *Hellenic Republic* [1991] ECR I–727, similar facts arose. Under Greek legislation a tourist guide was a person who accompanied foreign or national tourists or visitors to the country, guided them and showed them local points of interest, historic or ancient monuments, works of art of each period, and explained their history and gave general information on classical and present day Greece. In accordance with Greek legislation these activities were restricted to persons with specific training evidenced by a diploma. The Court held that:

> by making the provision of services by tourist guides travelling with a group of tourists from another Member State, where those services consist in guiding such tourists in places other than museums and historical monuments which may be visited only with a specialised professional guide, subject to possession of a licence which requires specific training evidenced by a diploma, the Hellenic Republic had failed to fulfil its obligations under Article 59 of the Treaty.

The provisions of Article 59 must apply in all cases where a person providing services offers those services in a Member State other than that in which he is established; wherever the recipients of those services may be established.

(iv) Article 60

Services shall be considered to be "services" within the meaning of this **1.46**
Treaty where they are normally provided for remuneration, in so far as they
are not governed by the provisions relating to freedom of movement for
goods, capital and persons.

"Services" shall in particular include:
(a) activities of an industrial character;
(b) activities of a commercial character;
(c) activities of craftsman;
(d) activities of the professions.

Without prejudice to the provisions of the Chapter relating to the right of
establishment the person providing a service may, in order to do so, temporarily pursue his activity in the State where the service is provided, under
the same conditions as are imposed by that State on its own nationals.

The Opinion of Advocate-General Lenz in the three Joined Cases
C–198/89 [1991] I–727, C–154/89 [1991] I–659, and *C–180/89 [1991]
I–709,* expressed a summary of the relevant provisions:

(i) That Directive 75/368 (EEC OJ 1975 L167 122) as provided by
Article 2(5) did not apply to tourist guides.

(ii) That the activity of guiding tourists, and providing commentary to
them on objects of all kinds or landscapes, by its nature constituted a
service within the meaning of Article 60(1) of the EC Treaty.

(iii) That the third paragraph of Article 60 must be applied in accordance
with Article 65: as long as restrictions on freedom to provide services
have not been abolished, each Member State shall apply such restrictions without distinction on grounds of nationality or residence to all
persons providing services within the meaning of the first paragraph
of Article 59.

These provisions apply to the provider of services within the meaning of
Article 59.

(v) Free movement of services

The Court of Justice has handed down a series of important judgments **1.47**
concerning the interpretation of the provisions of the EC Treaty on the
free movement of services.

The interpretation of Article 59 by the Court, and the need for transparency of Community rules as required by the Edinburgh European
Council meeting, facilitate a decentralised and correct application of the
Treaty's rules in Member States with a minimum of intervention on the
part of the Community authorities.

In Case *C–288/89 Stitchting Collectieve* v *voor de Media* [1991] ECR
I–4007 the Court summarised the application of Article 59 of the Treaty.

(i) Article 59 of the Treaty entails, in the first place, the abolition of any
discrimination against a person providing services on account of his
nationality or the fact that he is established in a Member State other

than that in which the service is to be provided (see, most recently, the judgments in Case C–244/89 *Commission* v *France* [1991] ECR I–169, paragraph 12, Case C–180/89 *Commission* v *Italy* [1991] ECR I–709, paragraph 15; and Case C–198/89 *Commission* v *Greece* [1991] ECR I–727, paragraph 16).

(ii) National rules which do not apply to services without discrimination as regards their origin, are compatible with Community law only if they can be brought within the scope of an express derogation, such as that contained in Article 56 of the Treaty, (Case 352/85 *Bond van Adverteerders* [1988] ECR 2085, at paragraphs 32 and 33). It also appears from that judgment (paragraph 34) that economic aims cannot constitute grounds of public policy within the meaning of Article 56 of the Treaty.

(iii) In the absence of harmonisation of the rules applicable to services, or even of a system of equivalence, restrictions on the freedom guaranteed by the Treaty in this field may arise as a result of the application of national rules, which affect any person established in the national territory, to persons providing services established in the territory of another Member State, who already have to satisfy the requirements of that other Member State's legislation.

(iv) Such restrictions come within the scope of Article 59 if the application of national legislation to foreign persons providing services is not justified by overriding reasons relating to the public interest, or if the requirements embodied in that legislation are already satisfied by the rules imposed on those persons in the Member State in which they are established, (see, most recently, the judgments in *Commission* v *France* (cited above) paragraph 15; *Commission* v *Italy* (cited above), paragraph 18; and *Commission* v *Greece* (cited above) paragraph 18).

(v) The overriding reasons relating to the public interest which the Court has already recognised include: professional rules intended to protect recipients of the service (Joined Cases 110/78 and 111/78 *Van Wesemael* [1979] ECR 35, paragraph 28); protection of intellectual property (Case 62/79 *Coditel* [1980] ECR 881); the protection of workers (Case 279/80 *Webb* [1981] ECR 3305, paragraph 19; Joined Cases 62/81 and 63/81 *Seco* v *EVI* [1982] ECR 223, paragraph 14; Case C–113/89 *Rush Portuguesa* [1990] ECR I–1417, paragraph 18); consumer protection (Case 220/83 *Commission* v *France* [1986] ECR 3663, paragraph 20; Case 205/84 *Commission* v *Germany* [1986] ECR 3755, paragraph 30; Case 206/84 *Commission* v *Ireland* [1986] ECR 3817, paragraph 20; and *Commission* v *Greece* (cited above) paragraph 21), the conservation of the national historic and artistic heritage (*Commission* v *Italy* (cited above), paragraph 20); turning to account the archaeological, historical and artistic heritage of a country and the widest possible dissemination of knowledge of the artistic and cultural heritage of a country (*Commission* v *France* (cited above) paragraph 17, and *Commission* v *Greece* (cited above) paragraph 21).

(vi) Lastly, the application of national provisions to providers of services established in other Member States must be such as to guarantee the achievement of the intended aim, and must not go beyond that which is necessary in order to achieve that objective. In other words, it must not be possible to obtain the same result by less restrictive rules (see, most recently, Case C–154/89 *Commission* v *France* [1991] I–359).

In Case C–294/89 *Commission* v *France* [1991] ECR I–3591, with regard **1.48** to the issue of the temporary nature of a service, the Court ruled that Articles 59 and 60 of the Treaty cannot be interpreted as meaning that the domestic legislation applicable to nationals of a State, which normally covers a "permanent" activity pursued by persons established in that State, may be applied in its entirety and in the same way to activities of a "temporary" nature pursued by persons established in another State.

In a recent case the Court considered the interpretation of Council Directive 82/489/EEC (OJ 1982 L218/24), on measures to facilitate the effective exercise of the right of establishment and freedom to provide services in hairdressing, ("*Aubertin,*" – The Hairdressers Case – Joined Cases C–29/94, C–30/94, C–31/94, C–32/94, C–33/94, C–34/94 and C–35/94). In this case France required a diploma from its nationals before they were permitted to operate hairdressing salons. No such French diploma was required of nationals from other Member States. A and others operated hairdressing salons in France without holding the relevant diploma and without a qualified manager being present. A contended that the French law was contrary to Articles 52 and 59 of the Treaty because it discriminated against French nationals. The Court held that, as the national court proceedings concerned French nationals who did not claim to have obtained qualifications in any other Member State:

> there is thus no connecting factor between such situations and any of those contemplated by Community law, so that the Treaty rules on freedom of establishment are inapplicable.

(vi) Prohibition on restrictions on the free movement of services

The Court has continually held that Article 59 requires not only the **1.49** abolition of any discrimination against a person providing services on account of his nationality but also

> the abolition of any restriction, even if it applies without distinction to national providers of services and to those of other Member States when it is liable to prohibit or otherwise impede the activities of a provider of services established in another Member State where he lawfully provides similar services. *Commission* v *France* [1991] ECR 1–3591.

The expression "liable to prohibit or otherwise impede" would cover any measure which might hinder trade in services between Member States which affects the ability of the service provider to provide a service. In Case 113/89 *Rush Portuguesa* [1990] ECR I–1417. the Court held:

Articles 59 and 60 of the Treaty therefore preclude a Member State from prohibiting a person providing services established in another Member State from moving freely on its territory with all his staff, and preclude that Member State from making the movement of staff in question subject to restrictions, such as a condition as to engagement *in situ*, or an obligation to obtain a work permit. To impose such a condition on the person providing services established in another Member State discriminates against that person in relation to his competitors established in the host country who are able to use their own staff without restrictions and moreover affect his ability to provide the services.

The Court considered restrictions which increase the cost of the service as being restrictions on the freedom to provide services in Case 205/84, *Commission* v *Germany* [1986] ECR 3755:

the requirements in question in these proceedings, namely that an insurer who is established in another Member State authorised by the supervisory authority of the state and subject to the supervision of that authority must have a permanent establishment within the territory of the state in which the service is provided and that he must obtain a separate authorisation from the supervising authority of that state, constitute restrictions on the freedom to provide services in as much as they increase the cost of such services in the state in which they are provided in particular where the insurer conducts business in that state only occasionally.

In Case C–300/90 *Commission* v *Belgium* [1992] ECR I–305 the Court also dealt with cost implications:

provisions requiring an insurer to be established in a Member State as a condition of the eligibility of insured persons to benefit from certain tax deductions in that State operate to deter those seeking insurance from approaching insurers established in another Member State and thus constitute a restriction of the latter's freedom to provide services.

1.50   It was held in the Joined Cases 286/82 and 26/83 of *Luisi and Carbone* [1984] ECR 377, that the freedom to provide services protects not only those who provide the services, but also the recipients:

. . . the freedom to provide services includes the freedom for the recipients of services to go to another Member State in order to receive a service there, without being obstructed by restrictions, even in relation to payments; and that tourists, persons receiving medical treatment and persons travelling for the purpose of education or business are to be regarded as recipients of services.

By virtue of Article 59 of the Treaty, restrictions on freedom to provide such services are to be abolished in respect of nationals of Member States who are established in a Member State other than that of the person for whom the service is intended. In order to enable services to be provided, the person providing the service may go to the Member State where the person for whom it is provided is established or else the latter may go to the State in which the person providing the service is established.

(vii)   Exceptions and derogations

In Case C–288/89 (above) the Court held that in the light of those   **1.51**
principles

> it should be examined whether a provision such as Article 66(1)b of the
> case, which according to the national court, is not discriminatory, contains
> restrictions on the freedom to provide services, and if so whether those
> restrictions may be justified by overriding reasons relating to the public
> interest.

In Case C–76/90 *Säger* [1991] ECR I–4221 the Court introduced practical criteria for applying these principles, based on the specific situation
of the service provider (who operates from the country in which he is
established); the type of activity concerned; and the protection of the
recipient of the service against the possibility of his suffering loss or damage in the event of non-compliance with the rules of the country in which
the service is provided. All these considerations being subject to Article
66(1)b on the grounds of public interest.

In Case C–76/90, the Court held: **1.52**

> legislation which makes the provision of certain services on the national
> territory by an undertaking established in another Member State subject to
> the issue of an administrative licence for which the possession of certain
> professional qualifications is required, constitutes a restriction on the free-
> dom to provide services within the meaning of Article 59 of the Treaty.

Restrictions are only compatible with Article 59 if it is established that:

> with regard to the activity in question, there are overriding reasons relating
> to the public interest which justify restrictions on the freedom to provide
> services, that the public interest is not already protected by the rules of the
> state of establishment, and that the same result cannot be obtained by less
> restrictive rules (Case C–180/89 *Commission* v *Italy* [1991] ECR I–709).

The Court has always drawn a clear distinction between discriminatory
and non-discriminatory measures.

In Case C–288/89 (above)

> national rules which are not applicable to services without discrimination
> as regards their origin are compatible with Community law only if they can
> be brought within the scope of an express exemption, such as that con-
> tained in Article 56 of the Treaty.

(viii)   Article 56

This Article is aimed at the co-ordination of the constraints within Mem-   **1.53**
ber States on the freedom of establishment due to public policy, public
security or public health:

1. The provisions of this Chapter and measures taken in pursuance
   thereof shall not prejudice the applicability of provisions laid down by

law, regulation or administrative action providing for special treatment for foreign nationals on grounds of public policy, public security or public health.

2. Before the end of the transitional period, the Council shall, acting unanimously on a proposal from the Commission and after consulting the European Parliament, issue directives for the co-ordination of the abovementioned provisions laid down by law, regulation or administrative action. After the end of the second stage, however, the Council shall, acting in accordance with the procedure referred to in Article 189b, issue directives for the co-ordination of such provisions as, in each Member State, are a matter for regulation or administrative action.

1.54 The Court held in the case of C–106/91 *Ramrath* [1992] ECR I–3351 that

in the light of the specific nature of certain professional activities, the imposition of specific requirements for the purpose of applying rules governing these types of activity is not necessarily incompatible with the Treaty.

These requirements are referred to in Article 56 and Article 36 which deal with prohibitions and restrictions on trade and the free movement of goods and services.

Mandatory requirements in respect of other legitimate objectives worthy of protection may also qualify, such as professional rules designed to protect the recipients of services (Joined Cases 110/78 and 111/78 *Van Wesemael* [1979] ECR 35):

Taking into account the particular nature of certain services to be provided, such as the placing of entertainers in employment, specific requirements imposed on persons providing services cannot be considered incompatible with the Treaty where they have as their purpose the application of professional rules, justified by the general good or by the need to ensure the protection of the entertainer, which are binding upon any person established in the said State, in so far as the person providing the service is not subject to similar requirements in the Member State in which he is established.

In Case 352/85 *Bond van Adverteerders* [1988] ECR 2085, the Court held that "economic aims cannot constitute grounds of public policy within the meaning of Article 56''.

(a) Public policy

1.55 Member States have the right and indeed the duty to safeguard the public interest within their territory Case C–294/89 *Commission* v *France* [1991] ECR I–3591). This does *not* mean that

. . . all national legislation applicable to nationals of that state and usually applied to the permanent activities of persons established therein may be similarly applied in their entirety to the temporary activities of persons who are established in other Member States.

Restrictions on the freedom to provide services come within the scope of Article 59 if the application of the national legislation to foreign persons providing services is not justified by overriding reasons relating to the public interest, or if the requirements embodied in that legislation are already satisfied by the rules imposed on these persons in the Member State in which they are established.

In Case C–154/89 *Commission* v *France* [1991] ECR I–659 and in Case C–180/89 *Commission* v *Italy* [1991] ECR I–709, the Court held:

> Accordingly, those requirements can be regarded as compatible with Articles 59 and 60 of the Treaty only if it is established that with regard to the activity in question there are overriding reasons relating to the public interest which justify restrictions on the freedom to provide services, that the public interest is not already protected by the rules of the State of establishment and that the same result cannot be obtained by less restrictive rules.

National restrictions on the free movement of services must not merely be imposed for such a reason, they must furthermore be proportionate and justified *i.e.* be indispensable.   **1.56**

In Case 252/83 *Commission* v *Denmark* [1986] ECR 3713, the Court held that in the insurance sector in general there were imperative reasons relating to the protection of the consumer, both as a policy holder and as an injured person, which might justify restrictions on the freedom to provide services. The Court also recognised that in the present state of Community law, in particular with regard to the lack of co-ordination of the relevant national rules of establishment, as regards the field of direct insurance in general, the requirement of a separate authorisation granted by the authorities of the State in which the service was provided remained justified, subject to certain conditions. On the other hand, the Court considered that the requirement of establishment, which represented the very negation of the freedom to provide services, exceeded what was necessary to attain the objective pursued and that, accordingly that requirement was contrary to Articles 59 and 60 of the Treaty.

In Case 205/84 *Commission* v *Germany* [1986] ECR 3755 the Court considered the necessity of establishment and held: **1.57**

> If the requirement of authorisation constitutes a restriction on the freedom to provide services, the requirement of a permanent establishment is the very negation of that freedom. It has the result of depriving Article 59 of the Treaty of all effectiveness, a provision whose very purpose is to abolish restrictions on the freedom to provide services of persons who are not established in the State in which the service is to be provided. If such a requirement is to be accepted, it must be shown that it constitutes a condition which is indispensable for attaining the objective pursued.

(b) Objectively necessary

The following cases decided that Member States may impose rules which are justified in the general interest and are applied to all persons and undertakings operating in the territory of the state where the service is provided where such requirements are objectively necessary. In Case 205/84 and Case 180/89 referred to above the Court held: **1.58**

... the freedom to provide services, as one of the fundamental principles of the Treaty, may be restricted only by provisions which are justified by the general good and which are applied to all persons or undertakings operating within the territory of the State in which the service is provided, in so far as that interest is not safeguarded by the provisions to which the provider of a service is subject in the Member State of his establishment. In addition, such requirements must be objectively justified by the need to ensure that professional rules of conduct are complied with and that the interests which such rules are designed to safeguard are protected.

The Court has held that a restriction is excessive where the requirements go beyond what is necessary for attaining their legitimate objectives.

A Member State can normally prohibit the provision in its territory of services lawfully provided in another Member State, if the conditions in which it is provided are different to the conditions in the country where the service provider is established.

1.59 As long as the service provided is suitable and statutorily fulfils the legitimate objective pursued by rules relating to public safety or public policy, a Member State cannot justify prohibiting the provision of the service in its territory by claiming that the way that it fulfils the objective is different from the way that is imposed on domestic providers or service providers established in that Member State.

4. Right of establishment by tour guides or managers

1.60 Several Directives cover the area pertaining to the tourist/travel industry.

(i) Directives on the mutual recognition of qualifications

Council Directive 68/367/EEC, of 15 October 1968 (OJ 1968 L260/17), concerns transitional measures in respect of the activities of self-employed persons in the personal services sector.

Council Directive 75/368/EEC, of 16 June 1975 (OJ 1975 L167/22), concerns measures to facilitate the effective exercise of freedom of establishment and the freedom to provide services in respect of various activities (ex ISIC Division 01–85) and in particular, transitional measures in respect of those activities. The preamble to the Directive states as follows:

> Whereas the activities of tourist guides are pursued in certain Member States within fixed territorial limits and are subject to detailed rules. Whereas they should therefore be excluded from this directive with the exception of the activities of couriers and Interpreter Guides.

1.61 Article 2(5) of the Directive provides that it is not to apply to the activities of tour guides, with the exception of the activities of couriers and interpreter guides. This Directive therefore only applies to couriers and interpreter guides. It would seem to suggest that a courier cannot also be a tourist guide for the purposes of this Directive.

Article 3(1) states that a host Member State may require of its own nationals wishing to take up any activity proof of good repute and proof of financial solvency, and accordingly that the state should accept similar evidence from other Member State nationals. Article 3(3) provides that a state can refute such formalities with that of an oath or declaration.

Article 7 provides that as far as general commercial or professional **1.62** knowledge and ability are concerned, the standard is met where the activity in question has been pursued in another Member State for any of the following periods:

(i)   three consecutive years either in an independent or managerial capacity;

(ii) two consecutive years in an independent or managerial capacity for the activity in question, and he has received previous training attested by a certificate recognised by the state or competent professional or trade body;

(iii) two consecutive years in an independent capacity, plus three years in a non-independent capacity.

(iv) three consecutive years in a non-independent capacity, and he has received training by way of examination.

(a)   Mutual recognition of professional training of at least three years

Council Directive 89/48/EEC, of 21 December 1988 (OJ 1989 L19/16), **1.63** concerns a general system for the mutual recognition of third level qualifications involving professional training of at least three years, and entered into force on 4 January 1991.

The Directive is based on the principle that someone who is professionally qualified in one Member State should be able to pursue that profession in other Member States. While the courses concerned are not harmonised, they are considered as being equivalent, taking account of the qualifications obtained and experience acquired in the activity concerned. Article 3 of the Directive provides that:

> Where in a host Member State, the taking or pursuit of a regulated profession is subject to possession of a diploma, the competent authority may not, on the grounds of inadequate qualifications, refuse to authorise a national of a Member State to take up or pursue that profession on the same conditions as apply to its own nationals:
>
> (a) if the applicant holds the diploma required in another Member State for the taking up or pursuit of the profession in question in its territory, such diploma having been awarded in a Member State; or
>
> (b) if the applicant has pursued the profession in question full time for two years during the previous ten years in another Member State which does not regulate that profession, and possesses evidence of one or more formal qualifications.

This Directive will not replace specific Directives already in existence.

1.64   Directive 75/368/EEC on transitional measures, directly regulates the freedom of establishment of tour managers who organise package holidays and/or accompany tourists. Directive 89/48/EEC contains two safeguard provisions to maintain professional standards where the length of education and training which professionals have received in their Member States is shorter than that required in the country they wish to move to. They may be required to produce evidence of up to four years experience in the pursuit of the profession concerned in addition to their professional education and training.

Where the education and training which professionals have received differs substantially from that required in the Member State to which they are going, professionals may be required to undergo an examination (an aptitude test), or they may be required to pursue their profession under supervision for a period not exceeding three years (an adaptation period).

1.65   Usually the individual can choose which method to adopt to gain recognition of qualifications, except for certain specified professions, which require a precise knowledge of national law, where the choice of method is made by the Member State rather than by the applicant.

Those aspects of the tourism profession which entail giving detailed explanations of tourist sites is not covered by the Directive(s).

THE COMMISSION REPORT INTO THE DIRECTIVE

1.66   After the adoption of Directive 89/48/EEC, but before the date set for implementation, the Court of Justice gave judgment in Case C–340/89 1991 ECR I–2357. The Court's judgment confirms that, independently of directives adopted by the Council and the European Parliament on the basis of Article 57 of the Treaty, Article 52 of the Treaty must be interpreted as requiring the national authorities of a Member State, to which an application for admission to a regulated profession is made by a Community national who is already admitted to practise the profession in question in his country of origin, to examine to what extent the knowledge and qualifications obtaining by the person concerned in his country of origin correspond to those required by the rules of the host state; if those diplomas correspond only partially, the national authorities in question are entitled to require the person concerned to prove that he has acquired the knowledge and qualifications which are lacking. In the course of its examination of the migrant's diploma, the host Member State may take into consideration objective differences relating to both the legal framework of the profession in question in the Member State of origin, and to its field of activity.

1.67   The competent authorities must also assess whether knowledge acquired in the host Member State, either during a course of studies or by way of practical experience, is sufficient in order to prove possession of the knowledge missing from the initial education and training.

The examination made to determine whether the knowledge and qualification certified by the foreign diploma and those required by the legislation of the host Member State, must comply with the requirements of Community law concerning the effective protection of fundamental rights. Therefore, any decision taken must be reasoned and open to challenge before a national court or tribunal (Case 222/86 *UNECTEF* v *Heylens* [1987] ECR 4097).

The Commission considers that the Directive must be read in the light of this judgment: in particular when examining a migrant's application for recognition. Competent authorities should take into consideration not only the migrant's "diploma" within the meaning of the Directive, but also any subsequent professional experience and training.

At least 11,000 persons obtained recognition of their diplomas in accordance with Directive 89/48/EEC between 4 January 1991 and 31 December 1994. **1.68**

Article 1(a) contains the definition of a 'diploma' for the purposes of the Directive. It is intended to define the package of qualifications (*e.g.*, University Diploma Post-Graduate Professional Training Course and period of supervised practice) stipulated by national law for entry to a regulated profession.

Article 2 defines the scope of the Directive: the second sub-paragraph of Article 2 excludes from the scope of the Directive professions which are the subject of a separate Directive establishing arrangements for mutual recognition of diplomas, for example 77/452/EEC – Nurses; 78/686 – Dentists.

Article 3 is the crux of the Directive and establishes the general rule that a person who is entitled to exercise a profession in the Member State of origin is entitled to recognition of his or her diploma for the purpose of taking up the same profession in the host Member State. **1.69**

Where a Member State refused recognition of a diploma on the grounds that the profession for which the migrant is qualified is not the "same profession" as that which he/she is seeking to exercise, the question is principally one of fact and can only be determined adequately with the assistance of experts by a national court or tribunal.

In order to obtain recognition, the migrant must, as under Article 3(a), establish that he or she has pursued the same profession in his Member State of origin as the one which he or she now wishes to pursue in the host Member State. The difficulty of identifying the profession arises in this instance because, *ex hypothesi*, the profession is not regulated, within the meaning of the Directive, in the home Member State. A similar problem may arise under Article 3(a), where in the Member State of origin the profession is regulated only by means of a protected title; it then becomes necessary to ascertain whether the activities exercised under this title corresponded to those which are regulated in the host Member State. The question is essentially one of fact (what were the activities effectively exercised by the migrant during the two years in **1.70** question?), and it should be borne in mind that the range of activities which constitute a profession will inevitably vary between Member States (even where the profession is regulated). The Commission has suggested that the following factors may provide assistance in identifying the profession exercised in the Member State of origin:

1.71 – Whether the taking up or pursuit of the profession in the Member State be subject to rules other than the possession of a diploma – such as proof of financial standing, good character etc. In this case, the profession would not be "regulated" within the meaning of the Directive, but the relevant national rules might nevertheless contain a definition of the scope of the professional activities (*cf.*, *e.g.* stockbrokers, financial advisers).

– Membership of a professional organisation, the statutes of which make reference to the activities exercised by their members.

– The existence of regulated education and training which was conceived to meet the needs of a particular profession.

1.72 Some Member States, particularly those who regulate very few professions, argue that the requirement of two years' professional experience works to their disadvantage. Article 3(b) prevents young members of unregulated professions from moving to a Member State which regulates the profession until they have acquired the necessary professional experience. This in turn results in pressure being exerted on national authorities to regulate professions which are currently open to all. Were Member States to cede to this pressure, the Directive would, paradoxically, result in the creation of new obstacles to free movement. A potential solution to this problem would be to transpose to Directive 89/48/EEC, the concept of regulated education and training introduced by Directive 92/51/EEC Article 1(g). Regulated education and training is defined as:

> any education and training which
> – is specifically geared to the pursuit of a given profession and
> – comprises a course or courses complemented, where appropriate, by professional training or probationary or professional practice, the structure and level of which are determined by the laws, regulations or administrative provisions of that Member State or which are monitored or approved by the authority designated for that purpose.

Where a migrant falling under Directive 92/51/EEC comes from a Member State which does not regulate the professional activity but holds a diploma which attests to regulated education and training, he or she is dispensed from the requirements of professional experience.

1.73 In Case C-164/94 *Georgios Aranitis* v *Land Berlin* (Judgment 1 Feb 1996, as yet unreported), the court ruled:

> Article 1(c) in conjunction with Article 1(d) of Council Directive 89/48/EEC of 21 December 1988 on a general system for the recognition and training of at least three years duration must be interpreted as

meaning that a profession cannot be described as regulated when there are in the host Member State no laws, regulations or administrative provisions governing the taking up or pursuit of that profession or of one of its modes of pursuit, even though the only education and training leading to it consists of at least four and a half years of higher-education studies on completion of which a diploma is awarded and, consequently, only persons possessing that higher-education diploma as a rule seek employment in, and pursue, that profession.

The Commission has proposed the possibility of introducing into Directive 89/48/EEC the concept of "regulated education and training", thereby obviating the need for a migrant coming to a Member State which does not regulate the profession in question to demonstrate two years' professional experience. **1.74**

(b)   Mutual recognition of professional training of less than three years

Directive 92/51/EEC (OJ 1992 L209/25), concerns a second general system for the recognition of professional education training, which also aims to facilitate the pursuit of the regulated professions, in respect of those involving courses of less than three years, and was adopted by the Council on 18 June 1992. **1.75**

Article 1(F) of Directive 92/51/EEC provides a definition of regulated professional activities:

(f)   regulated professional activity: a professional activity the taking up or pursuit of which, or one of its modes of pursuit in a Member State, is subject, directly or indirectly, by virtue of laws, regulations or administrative provisions, to the possession of evidence of education and training or an attestation of competence. The following in particular shall constitute a mode of pursuit or a regulated professional activity:
   pursuit of an activity under a professional title, in so far as the use of such a title is reserved to the holders of evidence of education and training or an attestation of competence governed by laws, regulations or administrative provisions;
   pursuit of a professional activity relating to health, in so far as remuneration and/or reimbursement for such an activity is subject, by virtue of national social security arrangements to the possession of evidence of education and training or an attestation of competence.
Where the first sub-paragraph does not apply, a professional activity shall be deemed to be a regulated professional activity if it is pursued by the members of an association or organisation the purpose of which is, in particular, to promote and maintain a high standard in the professional field concerned and which, to achieve that purpose, is recognised in a special form by a Member State and:
   awards evidence of education and training to its members, ensures that its members respect the rules of professional conduct which it prescribes, and confers on them the right to use professional title

or designatory letters, or to benefit from a status corresponding to that education and training.

Whenever a Member State grants the recognition referred to in the second sub-paragraph to an association or organisation which satisfies the conditions of that sub-paragraph, it shall inform the Commission thereof.

1.76 Article 8 of the 1992 Directive provides that, where:

in the host Member State, the taking up or pursuit of a regulated profession is subject to possession of an attestation of competence, the competent authority may not on the grounds of inadequate qualifications refuse to authorise a national of a Member State to take up or pursue the profession on the same conditions as those which apply to its own nationals:
(a) if the applicant holds the attestation of competence required in another Member State;
(b) if the applicant provides proof of qualifications obtained in another Member State and giving guarantees, in particular in the matter of health, safety, environmental protection and consumer protection equivalent to those required by the laws, regulations or administrative provisions of the host Member State. If the applicant does not provide proof of such an attestation or of such qualifications, the laws, regulations or administrative provisions of the host Member State shall apply.

1.77 Article 9 provides that where, in the host Member State, the taking up or pursuit of a regulated profession is subject only to possession of evidence of education attesting to general education at primary and secondary level, the competent authority may not, on the grounds of inadequate qualifications, refuse to authorise a national of a Member State to take up or pursue that profession on the same conditions as those which apply to its own nationals if the applicant possesses formal qualifications of the corresponding level, awarded in another Member State.

This evidence of formal qualifications must have been awarded by a competent authority in that Member State, designated in accordance with its own laws, regulations or administrative provision.

1.78 Article 2 provides that the following Directives will continue to apply; those relevant to this sector (including employed persons), being as follows:

1. 68/367/EEC (OJ 1968 L260/16)
   Council Directive of 15 October 1968, concerning the attainment of freedom of establishment and freedom to provide services in respect of activities of self-employed persons in the personal services sector (ISIC ex Major Group 85):
   1. restaurants, cafés, taverns and other drinking and eating places (ISIC Group 852):
   2. hotels, rooming houses, camps and other lodging places (ISIC Group 853).
2. 68/368/EEC (OJ 1968 L260/19)
   Council Directive of 15 October 1968, laying down detailed pro-

visions concerning transitional measures in respect of activities of self-employed persons in the personal services sector (ISIC ex Major Group 85):

1. restaurants, cafés, taverns and other drinking and eating places (ISIC Group 852):
2. hotels, rooming houses, camps and other lodging places (ISIC Group 853).

3. 82/470/EEC (OJ 1982 L213/01)
    Council Directive of 29 June 1968, on measures to facilitate the effective exercise of freedom of establishment and freedom to provide services in respect of activities of self-employed persons in certain services incidental to transport and travel agencies (ISIC Group 720).

4. 75/368/EEC (OJ 1975 L167/22)
    Council Directive of 16 June 1975, on measures to facilitate the effective exercise of freedom of establishment and freedom to provide services in respect of various activities (ex ISIC Division 01 to 85) and, in particular transitional measures in respect of those activities.

5. 75/369/EEC (OJ 1975 L167/29)
    Council Directive of 16 June 1975, on measures to facilitate the effective exercise of freedom of establishment and freedom to provide services in respect of itinerant activities and, in particular transitional measures in respect of those activities.

Directive 92/51/EEC incorporates the earlier Directives' general features and extends the system of mutual recognition to occupations for which the required level of training is not so high (post secondary school courses of less than three years and levels corresponding to a secondary course). Under these Directives any Community citizen is free to pursue his profession – either by supplying services or by way of establishment – in another Member State, on the basis of the qualifications obtained in his country of origin, together with at least three years professional experience in that country.   **1.79**

The activities of Tourist Guides wishing to become established in another Member State are covered by Article 52 of the EC Treaty (*infra*).

New proposed recognition of qualifications Directives

Community Document Number 96/22 proposes to introduce machinery for the recognition of qualifications relating to professional activities now covered by the existing "general system" directives.   **1.80**

The machinery will permit migrants to apply for the recognition of their qualifications if they do not possess the professional experience required in order to invoke a "transitional measures" Directive.

Those Directives which are based solely on Articles 54(2) and (3) and 63(2) and (3) of the Treaty, whose sole purpose was the abolition of restrictions on grounds of nationality during the transitional period should be repealed. Articles 52 and 59, which have been directly applicable in the Member States since the end of the transitional period, have rendered redundant those Directives which were designed to ensure freedom of establishment and freedom to provide services, since the principle of national treatment has now been given direct effect by the Treaty itself.

1.81   Article 1 of the proposed Directive defines the scope of the machinery by reference to the categories of professional activity listed in Annex A to the proposal.

On recognition of qualifications, Article 3 introduces machinery for the recognition of qualifications, so as to cover the professional activities excluded from the general systems by Article 2 of Directive 92/51/EEC. Recognition of professional experience in Article 4 is unchanged from the "transitional measures" Directives. Article 6 provides for certificates of professional experience – this provision is also common to most of the "transitional measures" Directives. Each Member State must accept, as proof that the requirements laid down by the Directive have been met, certificates issued by the migrant's Member State of origin or by the Member State from which he comes.

Article 7 concerns proof of good repute. Article 12 repeals the Directives on transitional measures and liberalization, the main provisions of which have been included in the proposal. (These include Dir 82/470/EEC, on measures to facilitate the effective exercise of freedom of establishment and freedom to provide services in respect of activities of self-employed persons in certain services incidental to transport and travel agencies.)

(ii)   Articles 126 and 127

1.82   Articles 126 and 127 were introduced into the EC Treaty to facilitate the free movement of professionals. Article 126 places co-operation between Member States on education on a firmer basis, and provides for consultation with the Economic and Social Committee and the Committee of regions. The principle of subsidiarity is firmly enshrined in Article 126(1) respecting the individual responsibility of Member States.

> Article 126
> 1. The Community shall contribute to the development of quality education by encouraging co-operation between Member States and, if necessary, by supporting and supplementing their action, while fully respecting the responsibility of the Member States for the content of teaching and the organization of education systems and their cultural and linguistic diversity.
> 2. Community action shall be aimed at:
>   – developing the European dimension in education, particularly through the teaching and dissemination of the languages of the Member States;
>   – encouraging mobility of students and teachers, *inter alia* by encouraging the academic recognition of diplomas and periods of study;

- promoting co-operation between educational establishments;
- developing exchanges of information and experience on issues common to the education systems of the Member States;
- encouraging the development of youth exchanges and of exchanges of socio-educational instructors;
- encouraging the development of distance education.

3. The Community and the Member States shall foster co-operation with third countries and the competent international organizations in the sphere of education, in particular the Council of Europe.

4. In order to contribute to the achievement of the objectives referred to in this Article, the Council:
   - acting in accordance with the procedure referred to in Article 189b, after consulting the Economic and Social Committee and the Committee of the Regions, shall adopt incentive measures, excluding any harmonization of the laws and regulations of the Member States;
   - acting by a qualified majority on a proposal from the Commission, shall adopt recommendations.

Article 127 is there to supplement vocational training, rather than to **1.83** enforce measures on the Member States. Again the principles of subsidiarity are enshrined in the Article.

Article 127

1. The Community shall implement a vocational training policy which shall support and supplement the action of the Member States, while fully respecting the responsibility of the Member States for the content and organization of vocational training.

2. Community action shall aim to:
   - facilitate adaptation to industrial changes, in particular through vocational training and retraining;
   - improve initial and continuing vocational training in order to facilitate vocational integration and reintegration into the labour market;
   - facilitate access to vocational training and encourage mobility of instructors and trainees and particularly young people;
   - stimulate co-operation on training between educational or training establishments and firms;
   - develop exchanges of information and experience on issues common to the training systems of the Member States.

3. The Community and the Member States shall foster co-operation with third countries and the competent international organizations in the sphere of vocational training.

4. The Council, acting in accordance with the procedure referred to in Article 189c and after consulting the Economic and Social Committee, shall adopt measures to contribute to the achievement of the objectives referred to in this Article, excluding any harmonization of the laws and regulations of the Member States.

(iii) Article 57

1.84 With a view to completing the single market, Article 57 of the EC Treaty provides for the adoption of binding legislation to institute professional recognition and if necessary, to standardise the national training councils.

> Article 57
> 1. In order to make it easier for persons to take up and pursue activities as self-employed persons, the Council shall, acting in accordance with the procedure referred to in Article 189b, issue directives for the mutual recognition of diplomas, certificates and other evidence of formal qualifications.
> 2. For the same purpose, the Council shall, before the end of the transitional period, issue directives for the co-ordination of the provisions laid down by law, regulation or administrative action in Member States concerning the taking-up and pursuit of activities as self-employed persons. The Council, acting unanimously on a proposal from the Commission and after consulting the European Parliament, shall decide on directives the implementation of which involves in at least one Member State amendment of the existing principles laid down by law governing the professions with respect to training and conditions of access for natural persons. In other cases the Council shall act in accordance with the procedure referred to in Article 189b.
> 3. In the case of the medical and allied and pharmaceutical professions, the progressive abolition of restrictions shall be dependent upon co-ordination of the conditions of their exercise in the various Member States.

Article 57 now provides for the new conciliation and veto procedure under Article 189b EC.

(iv) Future initiatives

1.85 The Commission recently published Community document COM(94)596, on mutual recognition of qualifications. The Commission has identified four paths to follow in order to develop the synergies between the different types of recognition of qualifications. These are as follows:

(i)   information;
(ii)   creation of academic and professional networks;
(iii) joint adaptation of courses; and
(iv)   evaluation of quality.

(a) Information

1.86 The Commission advocates that high quality education information sources would contribute to the knowledge of the various educational systems of the Community. Mechanisms to be adopted would comprise national reports covering the content of courses, and the organisation of the professions, together with the access routes to those courses and professions, and the creation of a directory of regulated professions in the Member States.

(b) Academic and professional networks

The establishment of academic and professional networks, would be used for the exchange of information between the Member States concerned, as well as for obtaining a deeper knowledge of the issues of the various forms of recognition.

1.87

(c) Joint adaptation of courses

Those courses already operating under the ERASMUS, COMETT and LINGUA programmes should be reinforced. The Commission wants to encourage initiatives to adapt teaching of those regulated professions which come under the sphere of the general system of professional recognition.

(d) Evaluation

The operation of quality assessment systems in the Member States support the strengthening of mutual trust. By bringing assessment systems into contact with each other, and including members of the professional and business world in those systems, mutual recognition of qualifications will be facilitated.

1.88

The Commission is eager to press ahead with synergies between the areas of recognition. The position at the present time, is that vocational qualifications required in one Member State must, for the purposes of employment in a given profession, be taken into account and be fully or partially recognised in another Member State.

Article 57 of the EC Treaty provides for the adoption of binding legislation to institute professional recognition and, if necessary to standardise national training courses, while Article 126 of the EC Treaty encourages the development of the European dimension in education, including the academic recognition of diplomas and periods of study. However, Article 126 expressly excludes the obligatory harmonisation of the laws and regulations of Member States.

(v)　Article 52

Within the framework of the provisions set out below, restrictions on the freedom of establishment of nationals of a Member State in the territory of another Member State shall be abolished by progressive stages in the course of the transitional period. Such progressive abolition shall also apply to restrictions on the setting-up of agencies, branches or subsidiaries

1.89

by nationals of any Member State established in the territory of any Member State.

Freedom of establishment shall include the right to take up and pursue activities as self-employed persons and to set up and manage undertakings, in particular companies or firms within the meaning of the second paragraph of Article 58, under the conditions laid down for its own nationals by the law of the country where such establishment is effected, subject to the provisions of the Chapter relating to capital.

1.90   However, the profession of tourist guide is regulated in a different manner in different Member States. Some Member States have no regulations. Other Member States reserve the title of tour guide only for those with prescribed qualifications, but tolerate other persons exercising the activity as long as they do not use the protected title. Finally, there are Member States where the activity of tour guide may only be exercised by those having the professional qualifications prescribed and having passed the required examinations. Clearly the mutual recognition of qualifications established by the two Directives mentioned above will be applicable in Member States in which tour guides require professional qualifications.

The different approach to the regulation of certain tourism professions, between northern Member States, where professions such as tour guide tend to be less regulated, and the southern Member States, where tourism is of greater economic importance and such professions tend to be more heavily regulated, does create a wider problem.

1.91   The recent Case C–375/92 *Commission* v *Spain* [1994] ECR 923 highlights this dilemma.

The Court held that the Kingdom of Spain had failed to fulfil its obligations under Articles 5, 48, 52 and 59 of the EC Treaty on the following grounds:

(i)   by making access to the professions of tour guide and guide interpreter subject to the possession of Spanish nationality;

(ii)   by failing to establish a procedure for examining qualifications acquired by a Community national who held a diploma as tour guide or guide interpreter issued in another Member State and comparing them with those required by Spain;

(iii)   by making the provision of services by tour guides travelling with a group of tourists from other Member States (where those services consisted in guiding such tourists in places other than museums or historical monuments which might be visited only with a specialised professional guide), subject to the possession of a licence which required specific training evidenced by a diploma; and

(iv)   by failing to provide to the Commission the information requested concerning the regulations of the Autonomous Communities regarding the activities of tour guide and guide interpreter.

Time alone will tell whether this case has clarified the position of a **1.92**
tour guide wishing to provide his services in another Member State.

The Court has consistently held that a Member State which receives a
request to admit a person to a profession, to which access under national
law depends upon the possession of diplomas, certificates and other evidence of qualifications, and which the person concerned has acquired in
order to exercise the same profession in another Member State, must
consider that request by making a comparison between the specialised
knowledge and abilities certified by those diplomas, and the knowledge
and qualifications required by the national rules. Spain has not yet complied with this judgment.

5. Right of establishment and freedom to provide services by travel agencies

Council Directive 82/470/EEC, of 29 June 1982 (OJ 1982 L213/01), on **1.93**
measures to facilitate the effective exercise of freedom of establishment
and freedom to provide services in respect of activities of self-employed
persons in certain services incidental to transport and travel agencies
(ISIC Group 718) and in storage and warehousing (ISIC Group 720)
concerns the freedom of establishment of travel agencies.

Article 1(2) provides that the Directive will apply to the nationals or
Member States, as provided in Regulation EEC No 1612/68 (OJ 1968
L257/02), who wish to pursue activities as employed persons activities
within Article 2 of this Directive.

Article 2 lists the activities that the Directive applies to, while Article 3 **1.94**
lists the usual titles for such activities, current in the Member States.
Article 2 (Group B) includes the following activities:

(i)   the organising, offering for sale and selling, outright or on commis-
      sion, of single or collective items (transport, board, lodging, excur-
      sions, etc) for a journey or stay, whatever the reason for travelling;
      and
(ii) arranging, negotiating and concluding contracts for the transport
      of immigrants.

In Case C–306/89 *Commission* v *Greece (not yet reported)* the Court held **1.95**
that the Greek Government had failed to transpose Council Directive
82/470/EEC (OJ 1982 L213/01) into effect, and had failed to fulfil its
obligations under the Treaty. Article 8 of the Directive provided that
Member States were to adopt the measures necessary to comply with the
Directive within 18 months of notification. The implementation period
expired on 2 January 1984.

Case 283/86 *Commission* v *Belgium* [1988] ECR 3271 concerned the failure of the Belgian Government to implement Council Directive 82/470/EEC. The Court held that a Member State could not rely on provisions, practices or situations in its internal legal system to justify a failure to observe the obligations and time limits laid down by Directives. The Court held that by failing to adopt within the prescribed period the provisions necessary to comply with Council Directive 82/470/EEC (OJ 1982 L213/01), the Belgian Government had failed to fulfil its obligations under the EC Treaty.

6. Free movement of tourists

1.96 Tourists *per se* are not covered by Articles 48, 52 and 59 of the Treaty, which deal with workers, right of establishment and the right to provide services.

However, in Joined Cases 286/82 and 26/83 *Luisi and Carbone* [1984] ECR 377, the Court held that the movement of a recipient of services (such as a tourist) might not be obstructed to such an extent that the freedom to provide services within the Community is affected. The Court further held that "tourists, persons receiving medical treatment and persons travelling for the purpose of education or business are to be regarded as recipients of services". The freedom to provide services therefore includes the freedom for the recipients of those services to travel to another Member State in order to receive those services there, without being obstructed by any restrictions. Tourists, among others, must be regarded as recipients of services.

1.97 In Case 186/87 *Cowan* v *Tresor Public* [1990] 2 CMLR 613 Ian Cowan, a British citizen who was on a visit in Paris, was the victim of an assault at the exit from a metro station. He was robbed of 150 francs by his assailants, whom it had not been possible to identify. Mr Cowan was seriously injured, suffering from a fracture and crushing of the second lumbar vertebra. Mr Cowan applied for compensation, but the Code of Criminal Procedure only provided for French nationals to claim for compensation. The Court held that the:

> "prohibition on discrimination laid down in particular in Article 7 of the EC Treaty, must be interpreted as meaning that in respect of persons whose freedom to travel to a Member State, in particular as recipients of services, is guaranteed by Community Law, that the state may not make the award of state compensation for harm caused in that state to the victim of an assault resulting in physical injury, subject to the condition that he had a residence permit, or be a national of a country which has entered into a reciprocal agreement with that Member State."

1.98 The Court therefore decided that the French compensation law was discriminatory against non-nationals.

7. "Maastricht 2"

At the time of writing, the Intergovernmental Conference is underway in **1.99**
Turin. There is no clear published agenda. These negotiations are
expected to last for more than a year, yet all 15 states agree on the basic
objective – to reform the EU's institutions and working procedures, so
that the Union can expand in the next dentury to admit as many as 12
new Members. These discussions will stem from the reflection groups'
reports established by the European Council in Corfu in June 1995, the
new members will range from Cyprus, the Czech Republie and Estonia to
Bulgaria, Poland and Slovenia.

Certain areas for discussion were identified at Maastricht in 1992:

(i)   increasing certain legislative powers of the European Parliament;   **1.100**
(ii)   revising provisions of the Treaty in relation to security and
        defence;
(iii)   extending the European Court of Justice's powers;
(iv)   the IGC will also examine the various declarations attached to the
        Maastricht Treaty, including those on civil protection, energy and
        tourism.

As to future developments, the IGC should decide by 1997 on the
insertion of a social title on tourism into the EC Treaty.

These discussions are expected to be lively.

The Package Travel Directive

Chapter 2
The Package Travel Directive

Zahd Yaqub
Barrister

1. Introduction

A Commission paper setting out initial guidelines for a Community pol- **2.1**
icy in tourism was sent to the Council of Ministers on 1 July 1982, which
indicated that, amongst many other things, the Commission would produce proposals for the protection of consumers taking package tours.

The Economic and Social Committee supported the Commission's
intention to produce these proposals in an opinion of 29 October 1983
(OJ 1983 C358/52).

The Committee expressed the view (at 3.12–13)

> that the interests of tourist operators such as hoteliers and travel agents
> must not be neglected, as they frequently have no protection against the
> cancellation of reservations, the bankruptcy of other intermediaries, and
> delays caused by strikes and bad weather . . . the Commission should seem
> to harmonize the conditions for the generation of travel agencies in the
> Member States.

The European Parliament adopted the Committee's opinions on these **2.2**
matters on 16 December 1983 (OJ 1984 C10/281), and agreed with the
Economic and Social Committee in supporting the making of such proposals and recommended (at 3.13) "that the Commission should draw
up a European Statute for travel agencies". The European Parliament
called upon the Commission (at 31a) to prepare Directives "to provide
legal and social consumer protection for tourists by introducing standard
regulations for the journey and the holiday resorts".

The Council of Ministers adopted a resolution on a Community policy
on tourism on 10 April 1984 (OJ 1984 C115/01). The Council invited the
Commission to present proposals to it in the field of tourism, including a
proposal on consumer protection in connection with inclusive holidays.

The Package Travel Directive, 90/314/EEC (OJ 1990 L158/59), was
adopted at the EC Consumer Affairs Minister's Council on 13 June 1990.

2. Article 1: Purpose of the Directive

Article 1 of the Directive sets out the purpose of the Directive: namely the **2.3**
approximation of Member States' laws, regulations and administrative

provisions concerning package travel, including package holidays and package tours.

The Directive aims, by setting minimum acceptable standards, to approximate the laws relating to package holidays and package tours, and to establish common minimum standards of protection.

It is also intended to contribute to the completion of the single market by enabling operators established in one Member State to offer their services in other Member States, and at the same time enable Community consumers to benefit from comparable conditions when buying a package in any Member State.

3.   Article 2: Essential definitions

2.4   Article 2 contains the essential definitions of: Package; Organiser; Retailer; Consumer; and the Contract.

(i)   Package

2.5   The essence of package travel is that what is offered and accepted is a combination of at least two out of three elements. The elements are: transport, accommodation, and other tourist services. The element of travel may be combined with accommodation in a hotel with all meals; with self catering in a chalet or cottage; or with excursions to places of interest or pleasure *from* the holiday destination, the consumer being responsible for providing his own accommodation and meals.

Alternatively, holiday accommodation may be provided where organisers make available sporting equipment and instructions, but no travel, the holiday makers arranging their own travel to and from the holiday place.

The definition of package travel is not confined to package holidays and could cover business and conference travel. The "tourist services" must come as an important part of the package.

Package travel requires at least two out of three of the elements of transport, accommodation and other tourist services, pre-arranged and sold at an inclusive price. A mere rental of holiday accommodation, *e.g.* a cottage or chalet, or a mere flight only, would not be a package, and would not be covered by the Directive.

2.6   In preparing a "package" organisers must ensure that contracts with suppliers provide sufficient information to meet the Directive's requirements. They will need to check brochure information and maintain records of these checks. Furthermore, organisers must monitor the accuracy of brochures throughout their period of validity, or else all inaccuracies in any published brochure will be liable to lead to a breach of the Directive.

(ii) Organiser

> . . ."organizer" means the person who other than occasionally organizes **2.7**
> packages and sells or offers them for sale, whether directly or through a
> "retailer".

The organiser is the individual who constructs the package following market research. He may offer the package from his own resources (*e.g.* sea travel on ships owned by him to chalets owned by him) or partly on the basis of the resources of other persons (*e.g.* a privately owned airline may offer special fare flights to, or near to, a holiday resort).

(iii) Retailer

> retailer means the person who sells or offers for sale the package put **2.8**
> together by the organizer.

The *retailer* advises prospective travellers about the kinds of travel package that are open to them. The retailer will make the reservations and book tickets on request from the traveller. In the majority of package holiday contracts the travel agent is the retailer.

(iv) Consumer

> The "consumer" means the person who takes or agrees to take the package **2.9**
> ("the principal contractor"); or any person on whose behalf the principal
> contractor agrees to purchase the package (the other beneficiaries) or any
> person to whom the principal contractor or any of the other beneficiaries
> transfers the package (the "transferee").

This definition covers an individual or a group of persons taking a package, such as groups of club members or school children.

Article 8 of the Directive provides that whichever of these categories the consumer belongs to, he shall effectively have the benefit of the consumer protection provisions of the Directive.

(v) The Contract

> *The contract* means the agreement linking the consumer to the organizer **2.10**
> and/or the retailer.

The contract may be concluded orally or in writing. Article 4 deals with the contractual aspects of the contract.

4. Article 3: Descriptive matter

1. Any descriptive matter concerning a package and supplied by the **2.11**
    organizer or the retailer to the consumer, the price of the package

and any other conditions applying to the contract must not contain any misleading information.

All descriptive matter published or issued by the organiser or retailer about the package must be legible, comprehensible and accurate.

2.12   Descriptive matter about package travel is usually contained in brochures issued by organisers. It may equally be contained in newspapers or other periodicals, or even in the contract. Wherever it appears it must be stated clearly and comprehensibly. Article 3.2 specifically requires that where a brochure is issued it shall contain adequate information:

> 2.   When a brochure is made available to the consumer, it shall indicate in a legible, comprehensible and accurate manner both the price and adequate information concerning:
>
> (a)   the destination and the means, characteristics and categories of transport used;
>
> (b)   the type of accommodation, its location, category or degree of comfort and its main features, its approval and tourist classification under the rules of the host Member State concerned;
>
> (c)   the meal plan;
>
> (d)   the itinerary;
>
> (e)   general information on passport and visa requirements for nationals of the Member State or States concerned and health formalities required for the journey and the stay;
>
> (f)   either the monetary amount or the percentage of the price which is to be paid on account, and the timetable for payment of the balance;
>
> (g)   whether a minimum number of persons is required for the package to take place and, if so, the deadline for informing the consumer in the event of cancellation.

2.13   The particulars contained in the brochure are binding on the organizer or retailer, unless:

> –   changes in such particulars have been clearly communicated to the consumer before conclusion of the contract, in which case the brochure shall expressly state so;
> –   changes are made later following an agreement between the parties to the contract.

5.   Article 4: Terms of the contract

2.14   This Article requires the consumer to be given a copy of the terms of the contract. Paragraph (1) provides that the contract must contain all the essential terms:

> 1.   (a)   The organizer and/or the retailer shall provide the consumer, in writing or any other appropriate form, before the contract is

concluded, with general information on passport and visa requirements applicable to nationals of the Member State or States concerned and in particular on the periods for obtaining them, as well as with information on the health formalities required for the journey and the stay;

(b) the organizer and/or retailer shall also provide the consumer, in writing or any other appropriate form, with the following information in good time before the start of the journey:

 (i) the times and places of intermediate stops and transport connections as well as details of the place to be occupied by the traveller *e.g.* cabin or berth on ship, sleeper compartment on the train;

 (ii) the name, address and telephone number of the organizer's and/or retailer's local representative or, failing that, of local agencies on whose assistance a consumer in difficulty could call.

  Where no such representatives or agencies exist, the consumer must in any case be provided with an emergency telephone number or any other information that will enable him to contact the organizer and/or the retailer;

 (iii) in the case of journeys or stays abroad by minors, information enabling direct contact to be established with the child or the person responsible at the child's place of stay;

 (iv) information on the optional conclusion of an insurance policy to cover the cost of cancellation by the consumer or the cost of assistance including repatriation, in the event of accident or illness.

(i) Essential information

Paragraph 2 provides that all the terms of the contract must be stated in writing or in such other form as shall be comprehensible and accessible to the consumer. If the contract is concluded in writing, the consumer is to be given a copy of the contract. If concluded in some other way, the consumer is to be given a statement of the contractual terms, which may be set out in one or more documents. The requirements as to signature on the contract have been left to the individual Member States to decide upon. **2.15**

 Member States have to ensure that the package contract contains at least the following important information, listed in the Annex to the Directive:

(a) the travel destination(s) and, where periods of stay are involved, the relevant periods with dates;

(b) the means, characteristics and categories of transport to be used, the dates, times and points of departure and return;

(c) where the package includes accommodation, its location, its tourist category or degree of comfort, its main features, its compliance with the rules of the host Member State concerned and the meal plan;

(d) whether a minimum number of persons is required for the package to take place and, if so, the deadline for informing the consumer in the event of cancellation;

(e) the itinerary;

(f) visits, excursions or other services which are included in the total price agreed for the package;

(g) the name and address of the organizer, the retailer and where appropriate the insurer;

(h) the price of the package, an indication of the possibility of price revisions under Article 4(4) and an indication of any dues, taxes or fees chargeable for certain services (landing, embarkation or disembarkation fees at ports and airports, tourist taxes) where such costs are not included in the package;

(i) the payment schedule and method of payment;

(j) special requirements which the consumer has communicated to the organizer or retailer when making the booking, and which both have accepted;

(k) periods within which the consumer must make any complaint concerning failure to perform or improper performance of the contract.

(ii) Transferability

2.16 Paragraph 3 provides that, where there are serious reasons which prevent the consumer from proceeding with the package, and those reasons are communicated to the organiser or retailer not less than one week before the departure date, the consumer is to be at liberty to transfer his booking to a person:

(i) who is willing to receive it; and

(ii) who satisfies the conditions, if any, applicable to the package and the legal or administrative arrangements for taking part in it.

The transferee will be responsible for paying the balance of the price and for any additional costs arising from such transfer.

(iii) Variation in price

2.17 Paragraph 4 provides that, once the price is agreed, it must not be changed. No variation is to be made in the price unless the contract expressly so allows.

If the contract allows for variations in price, the price may be varied in order to reflect alterations in the following items only:

(i) transportation costs, including the cost of fuel;

(ii) dues, taxes or fees chargeable for certain services such as airport or seaport taxes for landing/entry and departure/exit;

(iii) currency exchange rates.

No other grounds for variation are permitted. The aggregate variation in price may not exceed 2% of the agreed price. Any variation in price, and the reason for it, are to be notified in writing to the consumer without delay.

To ensure that there is a period of total stability of prices paid for the package, once the consumer has paid the price in full he shall then enjoy one of the following benefits, (depending on the national law that governs the contract): either (i) no variation in price during the period of 20 days preceding the date of departure; or (ii) no price variation during the period of three months following the conclusion of the contract.

(iv) Withdrawal from the contract

Paragraph 5 describes the circumstances in which the consumer is to be entitled to withdraw from the contract before departure. The consumer may withdraw if important alterations are made to the terms of the agreed contract, and particularly: **2.18**

(i)   if the price is increased by 10%;
(ii)   if the package is modified significantly; or
(iii) if, for whatever cause, other than the fault of the consumer, departure is unreasonably delayed. The test of reasonableness will be for the courts to decide.

(v) Compensation

Paragraph 6 provides that   **2.19**

> if the consumer withdraws from the contract pursuant to paragraph 5, or if, for whatever cause, other than the fault of the consumer, the organiser cancels the package before the agreed date of departure, the consumer shall be entitled:
> (a) either to take a substitute package of equivalent or higher quality;
> (b) or to be repaid as soon as possible all sums paid by him under the contract.

If the consumer chooses (b), he shall where appropriate, be compensated either by the organiser or by the retailer (it is for the national courts to determine who must pay the compensation) for non-fulfilment of the contract. The duty to compensate does not arise if the cancellation is on the ground that the number of persons who enrolled for the package is less than the minimum number specified by the organiser in the brochure or elsewhere, and the consumer is informed of the cancellation in writing not less than 20 days before the advertised or subsequently agreed date of departure, or if the package is cancelled for reasons of *force majeure* excluding overbooking.

(vi) Failure to provide services

2.20 Pursuant to paragraph 7:

Where, after departure, a significant proportion of the services contracted for is not provided or the organizer perceives that he will be unable to procure a significant proportion of the services to be provided the organizer shall:

(i)   make suitable alternative arrangements if they are capable of being made, so that the consumer is enabled without extra cost to himself, to continue the package unless if such arrangements are impossible to achieve, or the consumer does not agree them;

(ii) provide suitable transport for the consumer to bring him back to the place of departure or to such other return-point as was agreed; and

(iii) compensate the consumer according to the law of the relevant Member State which shall provide for significant inconvenience caused to him, and to the extent that agreed services have not been provided, for non-performance of them.

6. Article 5: Performance of services

2.21 This Article requires Member States to take the necessary measures to ensure that the services for which the consumer has contracted are rendered punctually and efficiently, whether they are performed by the organiser or by a third party. The organiser must construct the package in such a way that the various services which are to be performed for the package taken under the contract, are in fact performed in the manner agreed.

2.22 (Para 1) Member States shall take the necessary steps to ensure that the organiser and/or retailer party to the contract is liable to the consumer for the failure to perform or the improper performance of the contract, unless such failure to perform or improper performance is attributable neither to any fault of the organiser/retailer nor to that of another supplier of the services, on the grounds that (Para 2):

(i)   the failures which occur in the performance of the contract are attributable to the consumer;

(ii) such failures are attributable to a third party unconnected with the provision of the services contracted for, and are unforeseeable or unavoidable;

(iii) such failures are due to *force majeure* such as that defined in Article 4(6), second subparagraph (ii), or to an event which the organiser and/or retailer or the supplier of services, even with all due care, could not foresee or forestall.

(Para 3) In the matter of damages arising from the non-performance or improper performance of the services involved in the package, the Member States may allow compensation to be limited in accordance with the international conventions governing such services.

In the matter of damages other than personal injury resulting from the non-performance or improper performance of the services involved in the package, the Member States may allow compensation to be limited under the contract. Such limitation shall not be unreasonable.

(Para 4) The consumer must communicate any failure in the performance of a contract which he perceives on the spot to the supplier of the services concerned and to the organiser and/or retailer in writing or any other appropriate form at the earliest opportunity.

This obligation must be stated clearly and explicitly in the contract.

The implications of the above rules are far reaching. For example, in selecting and contracting with third persons who are to provide transport, or other services for the benefit of the consumer in connection with the package holiday, the organiser must use proper care and skill, and must make sure that the third persons selected will satisfy the performance requirements of the contract. **2.23**

It is for individual Member States to choose to fix the liability for any deficiency in performance of the services in either the organiser or the retailer. In most States the consumer will have recourse to the organiser.

7. Article 6: Complaints

In cases of complaint, the organiser and/or retailer or his local representative, if there is one, must make prompt efforts to find appropriate solutions.

The consumer is to be informed in writing of the name of the organiser's local representative, if any, at the holiday destination and of the means whereby the consumer may make contact with that person, who must then do his best to put right the consumer's complaints, especially if they are substantial. **2.24**

Member States are to ensure as far as possible that local tourist authorities, whether publicly controlled or private bodies, do actually investigate consumers' complaints concerning their travel packages. If no remedy is forthcoming the local tourist authorities are to provide assistance in the recording of evidence of significant complaints.

This Article contemplates that procedures shall be set up in those Member States which do not already have them, for the rapid, efficient and inexpensive handling of consumer complaints about package travel.

8.   Article 7: Insurance and Guarantee Fund

2.25   This Article provides both for compulsory insurance, and, as a distinct and complementary safeguard, for a guarantee fund, in the event of the organiser's insolvency.

The Commission felt that the public would be better served if organisers in all Member States were under an obligation to take out insurance covering any failure to provide punctually and efficiently the services which the organisers had contracted to supply.

The Commission also advocated the creation in every Member State of a guarantee fund to secure the consumer in the event of the insolvency of the organiser of package travel.

Prior to the Directive, such guarantee funds already existed in Denmark, the Netherlands, Ireland and the United Kingdom.

Article 7 also provides for the security of monies already paid. The organiser or retailer will be required to put in place appropriate arrangements to secure consumers' monies in the event of insolvency for the reparation of the consumer, if applicable in the event of the insolvency; and to monitor the adequacy of the above arrangements.

9.   Article 8: More stringent provisions

2.26   This Article permits Member States to adopt more stringent provisions to protect the consumer in the field covered by the Directive. If Member States already have in their national laws more stringent provisions for that purpose, they are at liberty to keep them.

10.   Article 9: Implementation

2.27   This Article lays down that the Directive should be implemented not later than 31 December 1992.

The Commission has been informed of implementation in all of the Member States.

11.   Omissions of the Directive

2.28   Articles 3 and 4 of the Directive list the information which is required to be provided to the consumer, but fail to require that the consumer be informed as to the rights and obligations connected with the package holiday, and as to the scope of the service offered to them. There still remains an urgent need for the harmonisation of the system of classifying hotels and camp sites, so that consumers have a uniform basis on which to assess the categories of service offered. The Council recommended the introduction of such a system on 22 December 1986 (OJ 1986 L384/54) Council Recommendation 86/665/EEC).

The consumer also needs to be aware of the possible costs arising from the journey or the stay, and the precautions to be taken with regard to health.

The Directive does not define in sufficient clarity the formalities connected with possible provision of health care. The administrative formalities which have to be gone through to obtain reimbursement of health care expenses vary in each Member State. Tourists need to be provided with up to date details of these formalities. Alternatively, further provision enabling tourists to settle medical bills after their return home, rather than in the Member State where the health care is obtained, needs to be made. In the event of problems, both in the host country and in the country of residence, Article 4 of the Directive merely requires the contract to provide details of the passport and visa requirements, and information on health formalities which are required for the journey and stay. Some organisers provide only minimal information.

2.29

Article 4(2) lists the essential information that the contract must contain. The contract needs to be understood by the consumer and the consumer must be made aware of the contents of the contract before signing it. However, the contract does not have to provide for insurance against cancellation, loss of baggage, bad weather etc. This suggests that such insurance remains optional.

12. Overbooking

2.30

The problem of overbooking remains a serious issue in the Community. Discussions have revolved around scheduled flights, and not charters. Tourists are sometimes prevented from travelling or held for other reasons: cancellations for technical reasons, strikes by air traffic control, weather conditions etc. Article 4(2) of the Directive fails to define the circumstances in which travellers are entitled to *compensation* for inconvenience suffered as a result of not being allowed to travel or being delayed. No details are set out concerning compensation for inconvenience caused by loss of baggage for tourists and other consumers.

One of the problems of overbooking suffered by hotels, is where more guests present themselves than the hotel can hold. Overbooking will remain a problem whatever the stringent conditions of the contract.

2.31   A recent written question to the Commission by Luigi Vertemati (PSE) MEP concerned a service referred to as "*pronto soccorso vacanze*" (holiday rescue service), which has been set up by consumer protection groups belonging to the European Bureau of Consumers' Unions. This service was piloted in Italy, with the support of the Commission. It showed that over 5,000 complaints were made by tourists concerning overbooking and other hotel problems. The above complaints have no bearing on the implementation of the package travel Directive.

13.   Recommendations and resolutions

2.32   The European Parliament's Committee on Transport and Tourism Report A3—0155/91 part B has recommended that the European Commission should provide for:

(i)   the publication of a single claim form for each type of service, which should be available to tourists on request;

(ii)   the establishment of a quick, simple and inexpensive procedure for settling disputes related to the provision of services to tourists;

(iii) (a)   the setting up of a Community system for exchange of information on tourist grievances and their treatment, to help identify the sectors where the most problems are encountered by tourists;

(b)   rules need to be laid down to ensure that airlines adhere to the rules concerning compensation procedures for passengers on overbooked flights;

(c)   a harmonised system needs to be set up for the grading of hotels and boarding houses;

(d)   efforts need to be taken to see that all Member States ratify the European Convention on the compensation of victims of violent crime.

2.33   The Committee on Transport and Tourism has also recently passed a resolution on tourism in the approach to the year 2000 (A3—0352/933).

The Committee called on the Commission to give a higher priority to the provision of information and consumer protection. The Commission is recommended to ensure full cover for medical expenses incurred by tourists and standardised costs of treatment in all Member States. The Commission is further recommended to work towards harmonisation of a compensatory damages scheme and a review of safety standards in all tourist accommodation and facilities.

The Committee has called on the Commission to propose a balanced Directive on the overbooking of tourist accommodation and a harmonised European system of classification for tourist accommodation.

The Commission work programme for 1997 on consumer policy will focus on the settlement of disputes involving consumers, and on increasing the clarity of prices and price controls with regard to the consumer.

The Directive fails to provide sufficient information in Article 9 on the minimum measures Member States should incorporate in their legislation.

The average time taken to adopt a Directive is 28 months according to   **2.34**
a recent written question to the then Commission President, Jacques Delors (OJ 1994 C358/46). Could the citizens of a Member State take action for non-implementation if the Commission had not already commenced infringement proceedings against these countries (see Joined Cases C–6/90 and C–9/90 *Francovich* [1991] ECR I–5357)?

14.   Questions for determination by the European Court of Justice

The European Court has been applied to for a preliminary ruling in the   **2.35**
case of *Erich Dillenkofer* v *Federal Republic of Germany and others* (Joined Cases C–178/94, C–179/94, C–189/94, C–188/94 and C–190/94 (OJ 1994 C254/04). Answers to the following 11 questions have been requested from the Court:

   1.   Is Council Directive 90/314/EEC of 13 June 1990 (OJ 1990 L158/59) on package travel, package holidays and package tours, intended to grant individual package travellers, via national transposing provisions, the individual right to security for money paid and repatriation costs in the event of insolvency of the travel organizer (*cf.* paragraph 40 of the judgment of the Court of Justice in Joined Cases C–6/90 and C–9/90 *Francovich*)?

In the case of *Francovich* [1991] ECR I–5357, the Court ruled on the   **2.36**
failure of a Member State to fulfil its obligations under Article 189, and held that:

   The first of those conditions is that the result prescribed by the Directive should entail the grant of rights to individuals. The second condition is that it should be possible to identify the contents of those rights on the basis of the provisions of the Directive.
   Finally the third condition is the existence of a causal link between the breach of the State's obligation and the loss and damage suffered by the injured parties.

The recital to Directive 90/314/EEC provides "community consumers to benefit from comparable conditions when buying a package in any Member State." Further "a consumer should have the benefit of the protection introduced by this Directive irrespective of whether he is a direct contracting party, a transferee or a member of a group on whose behalf another person has concluded in respect of a package."

2.37   Further questions to the Court included:

2.   Is the content of that right sufficiently identified on the basis of that Directive?

3.   What are the minimum requirements for the "necessary measures" to be taken by the Member States within the meaning of Article 9 of the Directive?

Clearly "minimum" measures to comply with the Directive are not spelled out (see Art 189 of the EC Treaty which leaves to the national authorities the choice of form and methods for the implementation of a Directive).

4.   In particular did it satisfy Article 9 of the Directive if the national legislature by 31 December 1992 provided the legislative framework for imposing a legal obligation on the travel organiser and/or retailer to take measures for security within the meaning of Article 7 of the Directive? Or did the necessary change in the law, taking into account the corresponding lead times in the travel, insurance and credit sector, have to come into effect early enough before 31 December 1992 for that security actually to function in the package travel market from 1 January 1993?

5.   Is any protective purpose of the Directive satisfied if the Member State allows the travel organiser to require a deposit towards the travel price of up to 10% of the travel price with a maximum of DM 500 even before the delivery of valuable documents?

6.   To what extent are the Member States obliged under the Directive to act (by legislating) in order to forestall carelessness on the part of the package travellers themselves?

2.38   The Directive provides for consumer rights in Article 4(5). Article 5(2) provides for failures which occur in the performance of the contract which are attributable to the consumer. No other provisions are envisaged in the Directive and this question will impose an interesting clarification for all parties.

7.   (a)   Would it have been possible for the Federal Republic of Germany, in view of the "advance payment judgment" of the *Bundesgerichtshof (BGH)* of 12 March 1987 (BGHZ 100, 157; NJW 86, 1613), to omit altogether to transpose Article 7 of the Directive by means of legislation?

      (b)   Is there no "security" within the meaning of Article 7 of the Directive even if on payment of the travel price travellers were in possession of valuable documents which evidenced in writing a claim to performance against those responsible for providing the individual services (airline companies, hotel operators)?

8.   (a)   Is the mere exceeding of the time limit specified in Article 9 of

the Directive sufficient, as an event giving rise to liability, for the existence of a right to compensation as described in the *Francovich* judgment of the Court of Justice or can the Member State put forward the objection that the period for transposition proved to be too short?

(b) If the objection fails, does that apply even in cases where the individual Member State cannot achieve the protective purpose of the Directive simply by a mere legislative amendment (as for instance with payments in lieu of wages to employees in the event of insolvency), but the co-operation of private third parties (travel organizers, the insurance and credit sector) is necessary?

9. Does the liability on the part of the Member State for an infringement of Community law presuppose an aggravated, that is to say, manifest and serious, breach of obligations?

10. Does liability presuppose that judgment has been given in Treaty infringement proceedings before the event giving rise to damage?

11. May it be concluded from the *Francovich* judgment of the European Court of Justice that, for there to be right to compensation on the grounds of an infringement of Community law, there does not have to be fault generally or at least in the failure, contrary to an obligation, to adopt legislative measures, on the part of the Member State?

The failure of a Member State to transpose the package travel Directive **2.39** by 1 January 1993 would make the State liable for loss and damage as a result of breaches of Community law for which the State can be held responsible.

The question 11 referral to the Court *supra* should be answered as in *Francovich*: "Member States are obliged to make good loss and damage caused to individuals by breaches of Community law for which they can be held responsible".

15. Direct effect/applicability of EC Directives

(i) The EC Treaty

(a) *Article 169*

Article 169 provides that it is for the Commission to commence action, **2.40** and it is matter of discretion for the Commission to decide whether to act.

If the Commission considers that a Member State has failed to fulfil an obligation under this Treaty, it shall deliver a reasoned opinion on the matter after giving the State concerned the opportunity to submit its observations.

If the State concerned does not comply with the opinion within the period laid down by the Commission, the latter may bring the matter before the Court of Justice.

(b)   Article 170

2.41   Under Article 170, a Member State can inform the Commission of another Member State's failure to implement a Directive. However, this is a lengthy process involving the exchange of opinions.

> A Member State which considers that another Member State has failed to fulfil an obligation under this Treaty may bring the matter before the Court of Justice.
>
> Before a Member State brings an action against another Member State for an alleged infringement of an obligation under this Treaty, it shall bring the matter before the Commission.
>
> The Commission shall deliver a reasoned opinion after each of the States concerned has been given the opportunity to submit its own case and its observations on the other party's case both orally and in writing.
>
> If the Commission has not delivered an opinion within three months of the date on which the matter was brought before it, the absence of such opinion shall prevent the matter from being brought before the Court of Justice.

(c)   Article 171

2.42   The time limit for compliance is not clear. If the Court of Justice finds that a Member State concerned has not complied with its judgment it may impose a lump sum or penalty payment on that Member State. No sanction is given for non-payment of any fine.

> 1.   If the Court of Justice finds that a Member State has failed to fulfil an obligation under this Treaty, the State shall be required to take the necessary measures to comply with the judgment of the Court of Justice.
> 2.   If the Commission considers that the Member State concerned has not taken such measures it shall, after giving that State the opportunity to submit its observations, issue a reasoned opinion specifying the points on which the Member State concerned has not complied with the judgment of the Court of Justice.
>
> If the Member State concerned fails to take the necessary measures to comply with the Court's judgment within the time-limit laid down by the Commission, the latter may bring the case before the Court of Justice. In so doing it shall specify the amount of the lump sum or penalty payment to be paid by the Member State concerned which it considers appropriate in the circumstances.
>
> If the Court of Justice finds that the Member State concerned has not complied with its judgment it may impose a lump sum or penalty payment on it.
>
> This procedure shall be without prejudice to Article 170.

(d)   Article 189

2.43   In order to carry out their task and in accordance with the provisions of this Treaty, the European Parliament acting jointly with the Council, the Council and the Commission shall make regulations and issue directives, take decisions, make recommendations or deliver opinions.

A regulation shall have general application. It shall be binding in its entirety and directly applicable in all Member States.

A directive shall be binding, as to the result to be achieved, upon each Member State to which it is addressed, but shall leave to the national authorities the choice of form and methods.

A decision shall be binding in its entirety upon those to whom it is addressed.

Recommendations and opinions shall have no binding force.

(ii)   The *Francovich* case, [1991] ECR I-5357

In the *Francovich* case the Court considered the application of Article   **2.44**
189, and held that:

Community law requires that there should be a right to reparation provided that three conditions are fulfilled.

(i)   The result prescribed by the Directive should entail the grant of rights to individuals.

(ii)   It should be possible to identify the content of those rights on the basis of the provisions of the Directive.

(iii) The existence of a causal link between the breach of the State's obligation and the loss and damage suffered by the injured parties.

When the above principles are not met, the principles of Article 171 will apply.

The *Francovich* case concerned the failure of the Member State to implement Directive 80/987. The Court reaffirmed that a Member State which has not adopted the implementing measures required by a Directive within the prescribed period may not, against individuals, plead its own failure to perform the obligations which the Directive entails. Where a Directive is unconditional and sufficiently precise, those provisions may, in the absence of implementing measures adopted within the prescribed period, be relied upon as against any national provision which is incompatible with the Directive or in so far as the provisions of the Directive define rights which individuals are able to assist against the state (Case 8/81 Becker [1982] ECR 53).

Further, the right of a State to choose among several possible means of   **2.45**
achieving the result required by a Directive, does not preclude the possibility for individuals of enforcing before the national courts rights whose content can be determined sufficiently precisely on the basis of the provisions of the Directive alone.

The Court has affirmed that "full effectiveness of Community rules would be impaired and the protection of the rights which they grant would be weakened if individuals were unable to obtain redress when their rights are infringed by a breach of Community law for which a Member State can be held responsible."

The above covers questions 9, 10 and 11 which were referred to the Court in *Dillenkofer.*

2.46   In Case C–208/90 *Emmott* [1991] ECR I–4269, the Court held that:

> although that provision leaves Member States free to choose the ways and
> means of ensuring that a Directive is implemented, that freedom does not
> affect the obligation imposed on all the Member States to which a Directive
> is addressed to adopt, within the framework of their national legal systems,
> all the measures necessary to ensure that the Directive is fully effective, in
> accordance with the objectives which it pursues. . . .

Member States are required to ensure the full application of Directives
in a sufficiently clear and precise manner so that, where Directives are
intended to create rights for individuals, they can ascertain the full extent
of those rights and, where necessary rely on them before the national
courts (see *Emmott*).

2.47   So long as a Directive has not been properly transposed into national
law, individuals are unable to ascertain the full extent of their rights. The
state of uncertainty for individuals subsists even after the Court has delivered a judgment finding that the Member State in question has not fulfilled it obligations under the Directive, and even if the Court has held
that a particular provision or provisions of the Directive are sufficiently
precise and unconditional to be relied upon before a national court.

Only the proper transposition of the Directive into national law will
bring that state of uncertainty to an end and it is only upon that transposition that legal certainty is created.

It follows that, until such time as a Directive has been properly transposed into national law, a defaulting Member State may not rely on an
individual's delay in initiating proceedings against it in order to protect
the rights conferred upon the agent by the provisions of the Directive
and that any time periods laid down by national law within which proceedings must be initiated cannot begin to run before the time of transposition of the Directive. Any Directive gives a Member State from one to
two years for implementation: at the end of that period an individual may
initiate proceedings.

2.48   The test for direct effect of a Directive was determined in Case 22/87
Commission v *Italian Republic* [1989] ECR 143. The Court held that the test
for direct effect was dependent upon "whether or not the provisions
were unconditional and sufficiently precise." In Case 41/74 *van Duyn* v
Home Office [1974] ECR 1337, the Court held that the Directive must
impose clear and precise obligation on Member States, and it must be
unconditional. If there are conditions, they must be exactly defined. It
must not be subject to further Community legislation or legislation in
Member States, so that Member States have no real discretion (opinion
of Advocate General Mayras).

One of the biggest problems with implementation has been associated
with the creation of guarantee schemes to protect consumers' interests
following the purchase of a package, prior to departure and after departure in the holiday destination. The Commission intends to carry out a

study concerning Article 7 of the Directive and the problems it has given rise to as regards creating guarantee schemes.

On 5 March 1996, the European Court of Justice handed down judg- **2.49** ments in Joined Cases C–46/93 and C–48/93, the *Brasserie du pecheur* case, referred by the Bundesgerichtshof, and the *Factortame III* case referred by the High Court.

In case C–46/93 *Brasserie du pecheur,* a French company based at Schiltigheim (Alsace), claimed it was forced to discontinue exports of beer to Germany in late 1981 because the competent German authorities considered that the beer it produced did not comply with purity requirements.

Case 48/93 *Factortame III* is the latest in a series of legal challenges to the Merchant Shipping Act 1988. The claimants in this case, failing to comply with the conditions on nationality and domicile, were not allowed to fish under the British flag: these conditions were held to be incompatible with Articles 7.52 and 221 of the Treaty (cases C–22/89 and C–246).

The Court considered state liability for acts and omissions of the **2.50** national legislature to be contrary to community law. In the principle cases, Joined Cases C–6/90 and C–9/90 *Francovich and others* [1991] ECR I-5357, the Court held that it is a principle of Community law that Member States are obliged to make good loss and damage caused to individuals by breaches of Community law for which they can be held responsible. The Court stressed that the existence and extent of state liability for damage ensuing as a result of a breach of obligations incumbent on the state by virtue of Community law are questions of Treaty interpretation which fall within the jurisdiction of the Court. Since the Treaty contains no provision expressly and specifically governing the consequences of breaches of Community law by Member States, it is for the Court, in pursuance of the task conferred on it by Article 164 of the Treaty (to ensure that in the interpretation and application of the Treaty the law is observed), to rule on such a question in accordance with generally accepted methods of interpreration – in particular by reference to the fundamental principles of the Community legal system, and, where necessary, general principles common to the legal systems of the Member States.

"It is to the general principles common to the laws of the Member States **2.51** that the second paragraph of Article 215 of the Treaty refers as the basis of the non-contractual liability of the community for damage caused by its institutions or by its servants in the performance of their duties. The Court held in *Francovich and others* that the principle of state liability for loss and damage caused to individuals as a result of breaches of community law for which it can be held responsible is inherent in the system of the Treaty."

The Court held that this principle holds good for any case in which a Member State breaches Community law, whatever organ of the state it was whose act or omission was responsible for the breach.

The second question in case C–46/93 and the first question in case C–48/933 was to consider the conditions under which the state may incur liability for acts and omissions of the national legislature contrary to Community law.

2.52 Although Community law imposes state liability, the conditions under which that liability gives rise to a right to reparation depend on the nature of the breach of Community law which gave rise to the loss and damage. In order to determine those conditions, account should first be taken of the principles inherent in the Community legal order which form the basis for state liability, that is, firstly the full effectiveness of Community rules and the effective protection of the rights which they confer, and secondly, the obligation to co-operate imposed on Member States by Article 5 of the Treaty:

> Community law confers a right to reparation where three conditions are met; the rule of law infringed must be intended to confer rights on individuals; the breach must be sufficiently serious; and there must be a direct causal link between the breach of the obligation resting on the state and the damage sustained by the injured parties.

> . . . as regards both community liability under Article 215 and Member State liability for breaches of community law, the decisive test for finding that a breach of community law is sufficiently serious is whether the Member State or the community institution concerned manifestly and gravely disregarded the limits on its discretion.

Extent of the period covered by reparation

2.53 Were the obligation of the Member State concerned to make reparation to be confined to loss or damage sustained after delivery of a judgment finding the infringement, that would amount to calling in question the right to reparation conferred by the Community legal order.

In addition, to make the reparation of loss or damage conditional upon the requirement that there must have been a prior finding by the Court of an infringement of Community law attributable to a Member State would be contrary to the principle of the effectiveness of Community law – since it would preclude any right to reparation so long as the presumed infringement had not been the subject of an action brought by the Commission under Article 169 of the Treaty, and of a finding of an infringement by the Court. Rights arising for individuals out of Community provisions, having direct effect in the domestic legal systems of the Member States, cannot depend on the Commission's assessment of the expediency of making an action against a Member State pursuant to Article 169 of the Treaty, or on the delivery by the Court of any judgment finding an infringement (*Waterkeyn and others* [1982] ECR 4337).

The Court held in Joined Cases C–46/53 and C–48/93:　　　　　　**2.54**

1. The principle that Member States are obliged to make good damage caused to individuals by breaches of Community law attributable to the State is applicable where the national legislature was responsible for the breach in question.

2. Where a breach of Community law by a Member State is attributable to the national legislature acting in a field in which it has a wide discretion to make legislative choices, individuals suffering loss or injury thereby are entitled to reparation where the rule of Community law breached is intended to confer rights upon them, the breach is sufficiently serious and there is a direct causal link between the breach and the damage sustained by the individuals. Subject to that reservation, the State must make good the consequences of the loss or damage caused by the breach of Community law attributable to it, in accordance with its national law on liability. However, the conditions laid down by the applicable national laws must not be less favourable than those relating to similar domestic claims or framed in such a way as in practice to make it impossible or excessively difficult to obtain reparation.

3. Pursuant to the national legislation which it applies, reparation of loss or damage cannot be made conditional upon fault (intentional or negligent) on the part of the organ of the State responsible for the breach, going beyond that of a sufficiently serious breach of Community law.

4. Reparation by Member States of loss or damage which they have caused to individuals as a result of breaches of Community law must be commensurate with the loss or damage sustained. In the absence of relevant Community provisions, it is for the domestic legal system of each Member State to set the criteria for determining the extent of reparation. However, those criteria must not be less favourable than those applying to similar claims or actions based on domestic law and must not be such as in practice to make it impossible or excessively difficult to obtain reparation. National legislation which generally limits the damage for which reparation may be granted to damage done to certain, specifically protected individual interests not including loss of profit by individuals is not compatible with Community law. Moreover, it must be possible to award specific damages, such as the exemplary damages provided for by English law, pursuant to claims or actions founded on Community law, if such damages may be awarded pursuant to similar claims or actions founded on domestic law.

5. The obligation for Members States to make good loss or damage caused to individuals by breaches of Community law attributable to the State cannot be limited to damage sustained after the delivery of a judgment of the Court finding the infringement in question.

(iii)　The Dillenkofer Judgment

The opinion of Advocate General Tesauro, delivered on 28 November　**2.55**
1995, should be followed by the Court. The question was referred to the

Court by the Landgericht, Bonn. This case should assist towards the implementation of the Package Travel Directive and clarify many issues. The questions submitted to the court were as follows:

2.56
"(1). Is Council Directive of 13 June 1990 on package travel, package holidays and package tours (90/314/EEC) intended to grant individual package travellers, via national transposing provisions, the individual right to security for money paid and repatriation costs in the event of the insolvency of the travel organizer (see paragraph 40 of the judgment of the Court of Justice in Joined Cases C–6/90 and C–9/90 *Francovich*)?

(2) Is the content of that right sufficiently identified on the basis of that directive?

(3) What are the minimum requirements for the 'necessary measures' to be taken by the Member States within the meaning of Article 9 of the directive?

(4) In particular, did it satisfy Article 9 of the directive if the national legislature by 31 December 1992 provided the legislative framework for imposing a legal obligation on the travel organizer and/or retailer to take measures for security within the meaning of Article 7 of the directive? Or did the necessary change in the law, taking into account the corresponding lead times in the travel, insurance and credit sector, have to come into effect early enough before 31 December 1992 for that security actually to function in the package travel market from 1 January 1993?

(5) Is the protective purpose, if any, of the directive satisfied if the Member State allows the travel organizer to require a deposit towards the travel price of up to 10% of the travel price with a maximum of DM 500 even before the delivery of valuable documents?

(6) To what extent are the Member States obliged under the directive to act (by legislating) in order to forestall carelessness on the part of package travellers themselves?

(7) (a) Could the Federal Republic of Germany, in view of the 'advance payment' judgment (*Vorkasse-Urteil*) of the Bundesgerichtshof of 12 March 1987 (BGHZ 100, 157; NJW 86, 1613), have omitted altogether to transpose Article 7 of the directive by means of legislation?

(b) Is there no 'security' within the meaning of Article 7 of the directive even if on payment of the travel price travellers were in possession of valuable documents which evidenced in writing a claim to performance against those responsible for providing the individual services (airline companies, hotel operators)?

2.57
(8) (a) Is the mere exceeding of the time-limit specified in Article 9 of the directive sufficient, as an event giving rise to liability, for the existence of a right to compensation as defined in the *Francovich* judgment of the Court of Justice, or can the Member State put forward the objection that the period for transposition proved to be too short?

(b) If the objection fails, does that apply even in cases where the individual Member State cannot achieve the protective purpose of the directive simply by a mere change in the law (as for instance with payments in respect of wages claims to employees in the event of insolvency), but the cooperation of private third parties (travel organizers, the insurance and credit sector) is necessary?

(9) Does liability on the part of a Member State for an infringement of Community law presuppose an aggravated, that is to say manifest and serious, breach of obligations?

(10) Is it a condition for liability that a judgment establishing a breach of Treaty obligations, delivered before the event giving rise to damage, must have been given?

(11) Does it follow from the *Francovich* judgment of the Court of Justice that for there to be right to compensation on the grounds of an infringement of Community law, there does not have to be fault generally or at any rate wrongful non-adoption of legislative measures by the Member State?

(12) If that conclusion is not correct, could the advance payment judgment of the Bundesgerichtshof have been an acceptable reason justifying or excusing the Federal Republic of Germany for transposing the directive, as defined in the answers of the Court of Justice to Questions 4 and 7, only after expiry of the time-limit specified in Article 9?''

The key section of Mr Tesauro's opinion is given below: **2.58**

''– failure to transpose a directive within the period prescribed thereunder constitutes a manifest and serious breach (Question 9); [*cf.* points 78–84 in Joined Cases C–46/93 and C–48/93]

– a finding of manifest and serious breach does not depend on a prior judgment having been given under Article3 169 against the Member State in breach (Question 10);

– fault, as a subjective component of unlawful conduct, is without relevance for the purposes of establishing liability on the part of the Member State in breach (Question 11);

– the national case-law on advance payments may not be taken into account in order to exclude fault (Question 12).

In the light of the foregoing considerations, Mr Tesauro proposed that the Court reply as follows to the questions referred by the Landgericht Bonn:

(1) Article 7 of Council Directive 90/314/EEC of 13 June 1990 on package travel, package holidays and package tours confers on purchasers of such travel a right to the guaranteed reimbursement of sums already paid over and repatriation costs in the event of the insolvency of the travel organizer and/or retailer; the subject-matter of the content of that right can be identified on the basis of the provisions of the directive itself.

(2) Articles 7 and 9 of Directive 90/314/EEC require the Member States to adopt by 31 December 1992 all measures necessary to guarantee the consumer as of that date the reimbursement of sums deposited or

repatriation in the event of the insolvency of the travel organizer and/or retailer party to the contract.

2.59

(3) Article 7 of Directive 90/314/EEC must be interpreted as meaning that it does not preclude a Member State from authorizing travel organizers to require consumers to make an advance payment of 10% of the total cost of the travel even before documents evidencing claims are issued, provided that in the event of insolvency reimbursement of that advance payment is likewise guaranteed; inasmuch as the national case-law on 'advance payments' leaves consumers to bear both that risk and the risk ensuing from the potential insolvency to which third parties against whom consumers may assert documents evidencing claims are exposed, it does not constitute proper transposition of Article 7 of the directive.

(4) Directive 90/314/EEC does not require Member States to take measures to protect consumers against their own negligence.

(5) Where the other conditions are satisfied, failure to transpose a directive within the period prescribed is of itself sufficient to give rise to an obligation to pay compensation on the part of the State in breach, which may not therefore justify any delay in transposition by claiming either that the period prescribed proved too short or that transposition required interested third parties to be consulted.

(6) Failure to transpose a directive constitutes a manifest and serious breach of the obligations imposed on Member States by Community law; it is not necessary for this purpose that judgment should have been given against the State under Article 169 before the harmful event occurred.

(7) The liability of the Member State in breach and its obligation to pay compensation are not dependent on fault, in the sense of a subjective factor in the unlawful conduct attributable to it; consequently, the national case-law on 'advance payments' cannot justify the delay in transposing Directive 90/314/EEC as far as the obligation to pay compensation is concerned.''

The judgment of the Court is reproduced in Appendix 24. The Court reached a judgment which concurred with Advocate-General G Tesauro's opinion. It held that Article 7 of the Package Travel Directive 90/314/EEC requires the Member States to guarantee that money paid over by purchasers of package travel will be refunded and a guarantee that they will be repatriated in the event of the insolvency of the organiser.

EC Consumer Law Provisions

Chapter 3
EC Consumer Law Provisions

Zahd Yaqub
Barrister

1. Introduction

The completion of a single market has meant the disappearance of   **3.1**
frontier controls and greater competition between services. The consumer has benefited from the ensuing greater choice in purchases available
and choice of forum in which to make those purchases in the Community.
Consumers as tourists have benefited as much as any other sector.

(i) The EC Treaty

The EC Treaty has empowered the Commission to secure a high degree   **3.2**
of consumer protection:

> Article 100a
> 3. The Commission in its proposals . . . concerning health, safety, environ-
>   mental protection and consumer protection, will take as a base a high
>   level of protection.

Such measures are subject to the procedure referred to in Article 189b.

Article 129a
> 1. The Community shall contribute to the attainment of a high level of
>   consumer protection through:
>   (a) measures adopted pursuant to Article 100a in the context of the
>   completion of the internal market;
>   (b) specific action which supports and supplements the policy pursued
>   by the Member States to protect the health, safety and economic
>   interests of consumers and to provide adequate information to
>   consumers.
> 2. The Council, acting in accordance with the procedure referred to in
>   Article 189b and after consulting the Economic and Social Committee,
>   shall adopt the specific action referred to in paragraph 1(b).
> 3. Action adopted pursuant to paragraph 2 shall not prevent any Member
>   State from maintaining or introducing more stringent protective measures.
>   Such measures must be compatible with this Treaty. The Commission
>   shall be notified of them.

Article 3b of the Treaty introduces the principle of subsidiarity which is   **3.3**
applied by Article 129a 3., where it permits Member States to introduce

more stringent measures than laid down in Community legislation, subject to the Commission being notified. Article 3b provides:

> In areas which do not fall within its exclusive competence, the Community shall take action, in accordance with the principle of subsidiarity, only if and in so far as the objectives of the proposed action cannot be sufficiently achieved by the Member States and can therefore, by reason of the scale or effects of the proposed action, be better achieved by the Community.

Article 3 of the Treaty provides that the activities of the Community shall include, *inter alia*: "a contribution to the strengthening of consumer protection."

(ii) Community Action Plans

3.4 The Community action plan to assist tourism has identified the provision of information and greater protection for tourists as a priority measure (Art 4.2 F of the action plan).

In July 1993 the Commission adopted the second action programme for consumer policy (1993–95). This document sets out the priorities for the work of the Commission in the coming years, and focuses on the improvement of four main consumer rights: physical health and safety; consumer information; representation; and the protection of consumers' economic and legal interests in the context of the internal market.

2. Measures to assist tourists

(i) Controls on baggage

3.5 Council regulation (EEC) 3925/91 of 19 December 1991 (OJ 1991 L374/04), pursuant to Article 8A of the Treaty, provides that the internal market shall comprise an area without internal frontiers in which the freedom of movement should result in the elimination of controls on the cabin and hold baggage of persons taking intra-Community flights and the baggage of persons making intra-Community sea crossings. Member States remain free, however, to carry out checks to prevent criminal activities linked in particular to terrorism, drugs and the traffic in works of art.

The above measures only concern Community destinations. Flights from non-Community destinations into a Community state are subject to baggage checks.

Commission Regulation (EEC) 1823/92 of 3 July 1992, which took effect from 1 January 1993, provides for the control of baggage of persons originating in a non-Community airport and transferred in an international Community airport to an aircraft which then continues on to an international airport in the same Member State. Specifically it deals with case of control of baggage of persons originating in an international Community airport and transferred in an airport situated in the same Member State to an aircraft going to a non-Community airport. The regulation provides for baggage checks on flights arriving from non-Community airports. It provides for all checks to be carried out in the first international Community airport of arrival. Where baggage is loaded at a Community airport for transfer at another Community airport, to an aircraft whose destination is a non-Community airport, all controls on cabin baggage shall be carried out in the last international Community airport before departure from the Community. Controls on cabin baggage may be carried out in the airport of departure on intra-Community flights only in exceptional cases, where they prove necessary following controls on hold baggage.

(ii) Controls on means of transport

Council Regulation No 3356/91, adopted on 7 November 1991 (OJ 1991 L318/01), provides that frontier checks and formalities affecting road vehicles and inland waterway vessels, such as inspections of passenger lists on road services, and controls on driving licences and roadworthiness certificates for motor vehicles, have been abolished. **3.6**

(iii) Tax frontiers

From 1 January 1993 private individuals are entitled to make unlimited purchases, tax and duty paid, in other Member States, and will not be liable to pay any additional VAT or excise duty on those purchases when returning to their country of residence. These provisions flow from Directives 91/680/EEC of 16 December 1991 (OJ 1991 L376/01), and 92/12/EEC of 25 February 1992 (OJ 1992 L76/01), which enabled the removal of fiscal controls on internal borders. **3.7**

Excise duty on products acquired by private individuals for their own use and transported by them, must be charged in the country of acquisition.

The Directives provide for a certain period of time to be taken for implementation to allow for the necessary measures to alleviate both the social repercussions in the sectors concerned and particular regional difficulties.

(a) Limits on tax-free purchases

Member States are authorised, for a period ending on 30 June 1999, to exempt certain products from excise duty, when supplied within the limits laid down, by tax-free shops in the context of passenger traffic by air or sea between the Member States. This exemption covers tax-free shopping at airports, and on board aircraft and ferries, and at the two access terminals to the channel tunnel. The limits are set as follows: **3.8**

(i)   200 cigarettes, or 100 cigarettes, or 50 cigars, or 50 grammes of smoking tobacco.

(ii)   1 litre of spirits, or 2 litres of fortified wines and sparkling wines.

(iii)   2 litres of still wine.

(iv)   50 grammes of perfumes, or 1/4 litre of toilet waters?

3.9   Travellers are also permitted to buy not more than 90 ECU worth of other tax-free goods per head per journey.

The vendor has had the responsibility of limiting his sales per traveller and per voyage to the above limits since 1 January 1993. Member States must take the appropriate measures to ensure that travellers are aware of the limits that apply in tax and duty free shops.

The above limits apply equally to travellers entering the EC from third countries. The value limit of tax-free goods per journey has been increased to 175 ECU.

Germany may defer entry into force of the new limits until 31 December 1998 for travellers entering Germany by overland frontiers. Spain may apply, until 31 December 2000, a value allowance of 600 ECU for travellers entering Spain from the Canary Islands, Ceuta and Manila.

(b)   Goods subject to duty

3.10   The Directive only applies to mineral oils, alcohol and alcoholic beverages and manufactured tobacco. The goods transported between Member States must be for the personal and family use of the traveller only. Quantities below the following limits will normally be assumed to be held solely for personal use:

(i)   Tobacco products

cigarettes	800 items
cigarillos (cigars not weighing more than 3 g each)	400 items
cigars	200 items
smoking tobacco	1.0 kg

(ii)   Alcoholic beverages

Spirit drinks	10 litres
Fortified wines (such as port and sherry)	20 litres
Wines (including a max. of 60 of sparkling wines)	90 litres
Beers	110 litres

3.11   Pursuant to Article 9 of the Directive, Ireland is authorised to apply specific guide levels, which may not be less than 45 litres for wine (including a maximum of 30 litres of sparkling wines and 55 litres of beer). Denmark is permitted to maintain those quantitative restrictions on tobacco and spirits which were in force on 31 December 1992.

An individual transporting quantities in excess of the above limits may need to demonstrate, if asked, that the products are for his personal or family use. Provided that this is the case, there will be no additional excise duty chargeable.

In attempting to establish that the products referred to in Article 8 are **3.12** intended for commercial purposes, Member States must take account, *inter alia* of the following:

(i)   the commercial status of the holder of the products and his reason for holding them;
(ii)   the place where the products are located, or, if appropriate, the mode of transport used;
(iii) any document relating to the products;
(iv)   the nature of the products; and
(v)   the quantity of the products.

Where an irregularity or offence has been committed in the course of **3.13** a movement involving the chargeability of excise duty, the duty shall be due in the Member State where the offence or irregularity was committed. Where excise duty is collected in a Member State other than that of departure, the Member State collecting the duty shall inform the competent authorities of the country of departure.

Wherever the irregularity is detected, it shall be deemed to have been committed in the Member State where it was detected.

The Commission shall be assisted by a Committee on Excise Duties, as provided by Article 24.

(iv)   Consumer information programme

In March 1993, the Commission launched a major media information **3.14** programme with a budget of 3 million ECU. The aim was to inform consumer and key groups about existing and proposed European legislation to protect consumer rights.

The first phase dealt comprehensively with European legislation which serves to protect the consumer rights of travellers and tourists.

(a)   Information on hotels

Council Recommendation 86/665/EEC of 22 December 1986 (OJ 1986 L384/54), recommends the development of standardised information provisions for clients in existing hotels, on the basis of a set of easily recognisable symbols, thus permitting consumers across the Member States to assess the range of facilities available in the hotel.

Member States were asked to take steps to ensure that a standard information system was brought into force. This has yet to be realised.

(b)   Fire safety in hotels

Council Recommendation 86/666/EEC of 22 December 1986 (OJ 1986 L384/60), also recommends the provision of a minimum standard of fire safety in hotels across the Community.

3.15   The preamble to the Recommendation provides:

> whereas rules governing fire safety in all hotels do not exist in all the Member States; whereas in many cases where they do exist the relevant provisions are incomplete and contained in several different texts and it is thus difficult to gain a clear picture; whereas they are not always fully observed.

It goes on to recommend measures to be taken to reduce the risk of a fire breaking out, measures for evacuations, fire exits, fire equipment, etc.

The Recommendation provided that Member States had five years to inform the Commission of measures taken to meet the requirements. Only eight of the Member States have notified the Commission of measures taken in this area.

Council Directive 89/106/EEC (OJ 1989 L40/12), on construction products, provides for safety requirements in the event of fire.

(c)   Accident prevention

3.16   Council Decision 3092/94/EEC (OJ 1994 L331/01), adopted on 7 December 1994, set up a four-year Community information system on home and leisure accidents for the purpose of collecting data on home and leisure accidents in order to promote the prevention of such accidents. The establishment of this system is solely intended to achieve a high level of consumer protection, and it does not exceed what is necessary to promote the prevention of such accidents. The system's objective is to collect data on home and leisure accidents with a view to promoting accident prevention, improving the safety of consumer products and informing and educating consumers so that they make better use of products, at both national and Community level.

The Decision does not apply to occupational accidents and illness nor to road, rail, sea or air traffic accidents.

The Annex to the Decision provides that the system shall apply to home and leisure accidents which are followed by medical treatment and which occur in the home or its immediate surroundings, (such as gardens, yards and garages), or during leisure, sports or school activities.

3.17   Proposed Directive COM [93] 646 deals with cableway installations designed to carry passengers, to regulate their design, manufacture, and operation. A very large extent of these cableway installations are mountain lift systems used in high-altitude tourist resorts and consisting of funicular railways, cable cars, gondolas, chair-lifts and drag-lifts.

This proposed Directive deals with steps which must be taken to ensure that users from countries anywhere in the Community, and even beyond, enjoy a satisfactory level of safety. In order to meet this requirement, it is necessary to define procedures and establish examination control and verification mechanisms, and the incorporation of standardised technical provisions.

(v)   Controls on misleading advertising

Council Directive 84/450/EEC (OJ 1984 L250/17), concerning mislead-   **3.18**
ing advertising, provides for minimum objective criteria for determining
whether advertising is misleading. It provides for adequate and effective
means of controlling misleading advertising by taking legal or administrative action.

The definition of "misleading advertising" means any advertising
which in any way, including its presentations, deceives or is likely to
deceive the persons to whom it is addressed, or whom it reaches, and
which, by reason of its deceptive nature, is likely to affect their economic
behaviour. In determining whether the advertising is misleading, account
shall be taken of all its features, and in particular of any information it
contains concerning:

> characteristics of goods or services, their availability, nature, executive,
> composition method and date of manufacture.

The Commission has now proposed an amendment to the Directive,   **3.19**
relating to comparative advertising (OJ 1994 C136/04). The completion
of the internal market will mean an even wider range of choice, given
that consumers could and must make the best possible use of the internal
market. The use of comparative advertising must be authorised under
certain stringent conditions in all the Member States since this will
help demonstrate the merits of the various products within the relevant
range. Under such conditions comparative advertising can stimulate
competition between suppliers of goods and services to the consumers
advantage.

Article 3(a) to Directive 84/450 EEC sets out the following restricting   **3.20**
conditions for comparative advertisements:

(i)   the features to be compared should only be the material ones, *i.e.*
       they must be relevant, essential, important, or significant aspects of
       the goods and services;
(ii)   the comparison should be objectively verifiable, which means that
       any advertiser must be able to provide scientific evidence of the
       claims he makes;
(iii) the elements of the comparison should be chosen fairly, which
       means that they should be comparable and that the information pro-
       vided must be complete.

The Directive provides that the comparisons which are made must not
mislead. The comparison must not cause confusion in the marketplace
between the advertiser and the competitors, nor between the advertiser's
trade mark, trade name, goods or services, and those of its competitors.

An advertisement denigrating a competitor or his trade mark, trade
name, goods or services, must not be allowed. However, the mere fact
that a comparison is unfavourable to a competitor is not in itself to be
considered unfair.

3.21   The provisions in Directive 84/450/EEC on misleading advertising requires the burden of proof to be reversed, so that the advertiser can be called upon to substantiate any claim in his advertisements.

Article 4(1), inserted into the comparative advertising Directive, provides that Member States should ensure that adequate and effective means exist for the control of misleading advertising in the interests of the consumer. Member States must introduce legal provisions for the bringing of legal action to enable consumers to bring such advertising before an administrative authority, which must then decide on complaints or initiate appropriate legal proceedings. The determination of which authorities are to deal with such complaints, is for Member States to decide.

3.22   Enforcement action includes the power to order the cessation of, or to institute the appropriate legal proceedings for an order for the cessation of, the offending advertising. Further measures should also be instituted to prevent its publication on any future occasions.

The Directive permits the voluntary control of advertising by self-regulatory bodies.

Article 7 of Directive 84/450 EEC, allows Member States to retain or adopt provisions with a view to ensuring more extensive protection for consumers. This rule does not apply to comparative advertising, given that the objective of the proposal is to allow such advertising in all Member States under the same conditions.

The Directive provides for Member States to comply with its provisions by 31 December 1995 at the latest.

(vi) Product safety

3.23   Council Directive 92/59/EEC, of 29 June 1992 (OJ 1992 L228/24), concerns general product safety.

This Directive introduces a general obligation on producers, importers and distributors and, in certain circumstances, other companies in the supply chain, to supply safe consumer products.

The Directive also imposes obligations on producers and distributors to monitor the safety of their products, and creates powers and obligations for Member States to ensure compliance of products with safety requirements. A procedure is provided for the notification and exchange of information, in the case of national measures which restrict the placing on the market of products which do not conform with the rules applicable to them, or their withdrawal from the market.

(vii) Statistical information on tourism

3.24   A recent proposal has been put forward for a Council Directive on the collection of statistical information in the field of tourism (OJ 1995 C35/05).

The recitals to the proposal provide that, in order to assess the competitiveness of the Community tourism industry, it is necessary to gain greater knowledge of tourism, the characteristics of the holidays taken, and the profile of tourists and tourist expenditure.

Regular monthly information is required to measure the seasonable influence of demand on tourism accommodation capacity and thereby to assist public authorities and economic operators to develop more suitable strategies and policies for improving the seasonal spread of holidays and the performance of tourism activities.

Article 1 of the proposed Directive provides that, for the purpose of establishing an information system on tourism statistics at Community level, Member States shall carry out the collection, compilation, processing and transmission of harmonised Community statistical information on tourism supply and demand.

3.25 Council Decision 93/464/EEC (OJ 1993 L219/01), on the framework programme for priority actions in the field of statistical information 1993 to 1997, provides for the setting up of an information system on tourism supply and demand statistics.

The collection of statistics will apply to tourist camp sites, and holiday dwellings. It will cover internal tourism, *i.e.* domestic and inbound tourism, and also cover international tourism, *i.e.* domestic and outbound tourism, whereby outbound tourism involves residents travelling in another country (Article 2).

The Annex provides details of the information to be collected, including their periodicity and their territorial breakdown. Information is to be provided on an annual basis on hotels, tourist sites and the arrival and departure of residents.

A breakdown is to be made of information on the number of tourists; the number of trips, domestic and outbound; the duration of a trip; the organisation of the trip; the mode of transport used; and the form of accommodation.

The information is also to be broken down into world geographical zones including EFTA.

3.26 The Directive provides for minimum accuracy requirements to be determined, with particular reference to annual overnight stays at national level (Art 4).

It is envisaged that the Commission will present to the European Parliament, the Council and the Social and Economic Committee, a report on the experience acquired in the work carried out pursuant to this Directive over a period of three years (Art 8).

Article 10 provides for a transitional period, which will end three years after entry into force of the Directive in respect of monthly and annual data, and five years after entry into force of the Directive in respect of quarterly data.

Article 11 provides that precise definitions of the information to be included in the statistical information will be decided after consultation with the statistical programme committee established pursuant to Council Decision 89/382/EEC (OJ 1989 L181/47).

Member States must implement the Directive by 31 December 1995 (Art 13).

3.27   The recitals to the Directive makes it clear that this Directive provides for common actions to be carried out at national level.

From the information derived from these results, the Commission may find areas where action is needed at Community level to assist the tourist and traveller. The Directive will facilitate the Commission in assessing areas requiring action.

3.   Legal measures

(i)   The Unfair Contract Terms Directive 93/13/EEC of 5 April (OJ 1993 L95/29)

3.28   The Directive only deals with contracts for the supply of goods and services. The Directive does not apply to contracts relating to employment, succession rights, rights under family law, or the incorporation and organisation of companies or partnership agreements.

The Directive covers both oral and written contracts.

The Directive defines a consumer as any natural person who is acting for purposes which are outside his trade, business or profession (Art 2B).

The terms of the contract must have been drafted in advance so that the consumer has had no influence on the substance of the terms of the contract, such as a pre-formulated standard contract. Contracts negotiated by the consumer are not covered by the Directive. Where only one specific term has been individually negotiated, this will not exclude the application of the Directive.

The Annex to the Directive provides a list of terms which may be regarded as unfair. Article 3(3) lists 17 terms; from excluding liability in event of death of the consumer, to excluding or hindering the consumer's right to take legal action.

3.29   The Directive provides a requirement to act in good faith. Particular regard shall be had to the strength of the bargaining position of the parties, and whether any inducements were offered to enter the contract. The supplier must deal fairly and equitably with the other party, whose legitimate interest he has taken into account.

The Directive, in accordance with the principle of subsidiarity, provides that Member States may adopt or retain the most stringent provisions compatible with the Treaty to ensure a maximum degree of protection for the consumer.

The Directive came into effect from 1 January 1995.

(ii)   Proposed Directive on liability for physical damage in the supply of services

This proposed Directive is under re-consideration, due to disagreements   **3.30**
within the Council of Ministers. The proposed provisions would cover the
liability of suppliers of services for physical damage to persons or to private goods (OJ 1992 C12/8).

The proposal would not cover damage to business property, or package travel and waste services.

The proposal placed the onus of proof on the injured person to provide proof of damage, and of the causal relationship between the performance of the service and the damage.

Particular difficulties with the proposal would be encountered in the
construction and medical services which are highly litigious areas. The
Directive would be too far-ranging because the proposal is broad, and
it subjects most service providers to a single liability regime. Both
these industries would also potentially see a huge increase in insurance
premiums and would find the proposed measures administratively
burdensome.

(iii)   Air carrier liability in case of accidents

Air carrier liability in case of accidents in international carriage by air is   **3.31**
basically governed by the 1929 Warsaw Convention – to which all
Member States but not the Community are Contracting Parties – and a
number of other instruments which, together with the Convention, is
generally referred to as the Warsaw System. The Warsaw Convention
was established by the worldwide air transport community in order to
provide a worldwide system of standards and rules for the carriage of
passengers by air, and in particular common rules in respect of liability
for passengers and cargo in the event of an accident, loss of baggage
and delay for international air transport while at the same time limiting
costs for air carriers. It included, *inter alia*, the very basic provision that
the airline is presumed to be liable (Art. 17) but that liability is generally
limited to about US $10,000 as a maximum (Art. 22). Nevertheless, the
passenger and the carrier may, by special contract, agree to a higher limit
of liability (Art. 22(1)). The carrier has the right to defend itself against
any claims under the Convention if it proves it took all necessary
measures to avoid the damage, in which case it will not be held liable
(Art. 20(1)). Moreover, the carrier is permitted to reduce its liability
if it can prove the contributory negligence of the injured person (Art.
21). Finally, Article 25 prohibits the carrier from availing itself of any
clauses limiting or excluding liability if it or its agents are guilty of wilful
misconduct.

The Warsaw System has won broad acceptance in so far as it represents   **3.32**
a workable attempt to eliminate, or at least reduce, problems of conflict

of law and jurisdictions by means of a uniform international law. However, it is now generally agreed that the system no longer realises its economic objectives. In short, the limits of liability established by the Warsaw System are too low by today's monetary standards and for today's aviation market.

Attempts have been made over the years to increase these limits within the Warsaw framework. But such attempts have not met with any success due to lack of sufficient number of ratifications for such modifications to the Convention. The Warsaw System indeed suffers from a lack of an automatic adaptation mechanism, which would take account of the impact of inflation and the development of real income.

The only possibility currently available to a victim or next-of-kin for recovering compensation beyond the Warsaw limits is to prove the wilful misconduct of the air carrier. This obligation to prove wilful misconduct in order to break the current limits leads to lengthy and costly litigation for both passenger and carrier, and it is the carrier who generally will have to bear the costs of this complex system. This is detrimental to the interests of air transport policy in general.

3.33   Attempts have also been made outside the Warsaw framework to update the limits. In 1966 the Warsaw Convention was supplemented by a "voluntary" inter-carrier agreement imposed on all carriers flying to, from or with an agreed stop in the United States. This agreement, called the Montreal agreement, raised the applicable limit for passengers in case of death or injury to US $75,000. It also introduced another important element; carriers waived their right of defence under Article 20(1) of the Convention, bringing, therefore, strict liability. By 20 November 1992, Japanese airlines agreed, by special contract incorporated in conditions of carriage and tariffs, that they would waive all restrictions of liability in international transport and would do so under strict liability for claims up to SDR 100,000 (approx. ECU 119,600). The United Kingdom, by adopting the Licensing of Air Carriers Regulations 1992 SI 1992/2992, required that a carrier with a valid operating licence granted by the UK Civil Aviation Authority must make an SDR 100,000 special contract with passengers carried for remuneration or hire. It is worthwhile to note that Italy, by adopting Law 274 of 7 July 1988, compelled all airlines serving a point in Italy to adopt a special contract for SDR 100,000. In recent years most European countries have introduced domestically (and, for their own national carriers also internationally), a higher passenger limit than that prescribed by the Hague Protocol.

Community provisions

3.34   Rules on the nature and limitation of liability for damages of an air carrier in the event of death or injury of air passengers form an essential element of the terms and conditions of carriage in an air transport contract between carrier and passenger. Article 7 of Council Regulation (EC) No 2407/92 introduced with the third package requires air carriers to be insured to cover liability in case of accidents. However, the Regulation does not provide detailed rules as to compliance with this provision. Given, as stated above, that Member States have variously taken steps to increase the Warsaw limit, and even in some cases to modify the nature of liability – leading therefore to different terms and conditions of carriage, and given also that differences subsist between the liability rules for domestic and international transport, it is obvious that the coherence so far achieved in the internal aviation market is at risk of fragmenting.

In addition, one of the most important factors in all modes of transport and thus in aviation is the question of safety and quality of service. The inevitable link between safety and the issue of liability cannot be denied. The original low limit set by the Warsaw Convention was in part a protection for an infant industry whose risk factors were largely unknown and therefore considered to be high. In such a climate the interest was to reduce the financial liability of the carrier as far as possible, even to the detriment of the passenger. Today the situation of the aviation sector is totally different; it is perceived to be one of the safest modes of transport. This image of a safe and high-quality service is at odds with a system whereby the passenger is still treated as taking a risk, justifying a low level of compensation in the event of death or injury. In addition, the fact that, in order to achieve an acceptable level of compensation, the wilful misconduct of the carrier has to be proved leads very often to serious damage to the image of aviation as the safest mode of transport. The aim of the EC air transport policy is to ensure that not only will air transport continue to be the safest way to travel but also that it will be perceived as such. Therefore the issues of liability and compensation should now be legislated for in terms which are consistent with today's aviation industry.

3.35 The objective of the internal aviation market is also to take account of the needs of the air transport user. The low limits currently in place are, as stated above, largely inadequate and unsatisfactory for the passenger victim of an air accident or for his survivors. Moreover, the fact that the passenger has to prove wilful misconduct on the part of the carrier in order to recover compensation above the limits of the Warsaw Convention, makes settlements less predictable, more expensive and time-consuming. Furthermore, due to the complexity of the system – *i.e.* different limits in force and carriers' differing obligations under national law – the passenger is misinformed or not informed at all as to the applicable scheme. It is worth noting that the "Notice" formats of standard tickets make no attempt to inform the passenger of the precise limit that applies to his particular journey. Although the possibility always exists, of course, for passengers to insure themselves on an individual basis, given the confusing situation, it is impossible for the passenger to make an informed decision as to which personal insurance he should take. In a nutshell, not only are the passengers or next-of-kin insufficiently covered by the current low limits, but they have also to face the uncertainty and lack of transparency of remedies when having to seek higher damages than the mandatory limit. Generally speaking it has been recognised, as witnessed by Article 129A of the Treaty, that the Community should contribute to a higher level of consumer protection.

The proposal for a Council regulation on air carrier liability in case of accidents (CD 95/3724) is very much in line with that commitment. The proposal of the Commission has the following main elements:

– a waiving of all limits on liability,
– the introduction of strict liability up to ECU 100,000. This will protect air users even in the case of a terrorist attack that would otherwise leave the innocent passenger without cover. Moreover, by doing so the Community would legalise a practice which has been accepted by airlines for many years and officially formalized in some cases. (In 1966 the MIA introduced increased limits to, from or with an agreed stop in the US to US $75,000 on a strict liability basis. Japanese airlines have, since November 1992, waived liability limits on their flights with a level of strict liability up to SDR 100,000.)

3.36   It would be preferable that all carriers serving a point in the Community adopt the same system. Third-country carriers not subject to Community rules should be requested to inform passengers accordingly, properly and clearly.

Passengers should have the choice of the jurisdiction before which to bring an action. It should include the option to bring an action before the court of the Member State where the passenger has his domicile. This might circumvent the possibilities of confusion that might arise when referring to the law of the domicile.

Priority should later be given to improve the situation in respect of passengers' luggage and cargo, if efforts at international level by carriers and/or governments fail to provide a satisfactory solution.

Such a Community action would have minimal cost implications, because current liability insurance costs for European airlines generally account for about 0.1% to 0.2% of total operating costs. An increase or a removal of the limit will, therefore, only represent a minimal increase in costs of insurance premium – about 0.1% to 0.35% of total operating costs. This will ensure a high level of protection for the air transport user.

(iv) Council Directive in respect of contracts negotiated away from business premises (85/577/EEC) (OJ 1985 L372/31)

3.37   The special feature of contracts concluded away from the business premises of the trader is that as a rule it is the trader who initiates the contract negotiations, for which the consumer is unprepared. This surprise element generally exists only in contracts made at the doorstep, and also in other forms of contract concluded by the trader away from his business premises. In consequence, the consumer is often unable to compare the quality and price of the offer with other offers.

The Directive applies to contracts negotiated away from business premises or during a visit by a trader to the consumer's home or consumer's place of work in circumstances in which a consumer is taken by surprise and signs a contract under some pressure and without time for reflection.

The Directive only applies when the consumer initiates the visit by the trader.

Article 3 provides that the Directive shall apply only to contracts for which the payment to be made by the consumer exceeds a specified amount. This amount may not exceed 60 ECU.

The Directive does not apply to construction contracts, timeshares, **3.38** contracts for the supply of foodstuffs or beverages, or contracts concluded through use of a catalogue which the consumer has a proper opportunity of reading in the absence of the trader's representative.

Article 4 of the Directive requires traders to give consumers written notice of their right of cancellation of contracts covered by the Directive. The form of the notice is not specified in the Directive, but it must include the date, the name and address of a person against whom the right of cancellation may be exercised, the length of the cooling-off period and information enabling the specific contract to be identified.

Article 4 of the Directive leaves it to Member States to lay down appropriate consumer protection measures in cases where the notice of cancellation rights has not been provided as prescribed. It is proposed that the implementing Regulations should provide that failure to give the consumer written notice of cancellation rights in the prescribed form and/or manner should render the contract voidable.

The consumer shall have the right to renounce the effects of his undertaking by sending notice within a period of not less than seven days from the receipt by the consumer.

Article 7 of the Directive leaves it to Member States to provide for **3.39** the legal consequences of the exercise of the consumer's right of cancellation.

Article 8 allows Member States, if they wish, to provide for a higher standard of protection than that set out in the Directive.

(v) Council Directive on the protection of consumers in respect of contracts negotiated at a distance (COM(93)396)

The object of this Directive is to approximate the laws, regulations and **3.40** administrative provisions of the Member States concerning distance contracts between consumers and suppliers. A "distance contract" means any contract concerning goods or services concluded between a supplier and a consumer as a consequence of an organised distance sales or service-provision scheme of the suppliers, where the contract was negotiated and concluded exclusively by means of communication at a distance. (A list of the means of communication covered by this proposal is contained in the annex to this Directive.) For the purposes of this Directive the "consumer" is defined as a natural person, who is acting for purposes which are outside his trade, business or profession. The supplier must be acting in his commercial or professional capacity.

3.41   The Directive does not apply to:

– contracts relating to automatic vending machines;
– contracts concluded at auction;
– contracts concluded with telecommunications operators through the use of public payphones;
– contracts for the supply of foodstuffs and beverages;
– contracts for the provision of services with respect to accommodation, transport, catering or leisure, where the supplier undertakes, when the contract is concluded, to provide these services at a specific date or within a specific period.

3.42   If there is any solicitation of the consumer, he must be provided with the following information:

(a)   the identity of the supplier;
(b)   the main characteristics of the goods or services;
(c)   the price of the goods or services including all types;
(d)   the delivery costs, where appropriate;
(e)   the arrangements for payment, delivery or performance;
(f)   the period for which the offer or the price remains valid;
(g)   the right to withdraw.

3.43   The consumer must receive written confirmation of the information referred to above, in good time during the performance of the contract and at the latest (where goods are concerned) at the time of delivery. For any distance contract, the consumer shall have a period of not less than seven days in which he may withdraw from the contract without penalty, without giving any reason. If no time limit for performance is stipulated, it must not be more than 30 days after the order is forwarded to the supplier.

Member States shall ensure that adequate and effective means exist to enforce compliance with this Directive in the interests of consumers.

Member States have three years to comply with this Directive.

(vi)   Directive on time shares 94/47/EEC

3.44   The purchase of a right to utilise one or several immovable properties on a time share basis is a sector of the tourism industry that is relatively new and growing. In 1992, European time share sales were worth 1 billion ECU, with about 220,000 time share intervals sold in the Community.

The aim of this Directive is to give purchasers a high level of protection for using immovable properties on a time share basis. Contracts for the purchase of the right to use one or more immovable properties on a time share basis must include certain minimal items, including a certified translation of each contract for the purposes of the formalities to be completed in the Member State in which the relevant property is situated. The Directive stipulates minimum obligations with which vendors must comply, and provides for the collection of monies on cancellation.

The Directive defines a "contract" as any contract or group of contracts concluded for at least three years, under which global price or any other rights are established relating to the use of one or more immovable properties for a specified period of the year, which may not be less than one week.

The Directive provides that the vendor is required to provide any per- **3.45** son requesting information on time shares with a document containing a general description of the property or properties. The Annex to the Directive provides a list of items to be included in the contract, including: the identities of all parties; a description of the property; whether the property is under construction, and if so its expected completion date; the services and other facilities the purchaser will have access to (*e.g.* swimming pool); the basis on which the maintenance and repairs of the property will be administered: the price to be paid: a clause prohibiting additional costs; and further information on the right to cancel or withdraw from the contract. The above information is to form an integral part of the contract.

Article 5 provides that the purchaser shall have the right to withdraw from the contract without giving any reason within ten calendar days of both parties signing the contract. If the contract fails to contain all the information required by the Annex to the Directive, a three month period commences and it is only at the end of the three months that the ten-day cancellation period begins.

Member States are required to make provision for the reimbursement of any advance payments in the event of non-completion of the property, or in the case of exercise of the right of withdrawal.

The Directive requires implementation within 30 months from October 1994.

(vii) Cross-border payment facilities

The aim of Directive (EC) No 32/95 on cross-border credit transfers, is **3.46** to improve credit transfer services for individuals as well as business, especially small and medium-sized enterprises, by introducing:

- a minimum standard for the information to be supplied to customers both prior and subsequent to the cross-border credit transfer;
- time limits within which, in the absence of agreement between bank and customer, the institutions of the originator and the beneficiary are required to execute the transfer (five days and one day respectively);
- an obligation to execute the transfer in accordance with the instructions contained in the payment order ("double-charging" ban);
- in the event of non-execution of transfers, without prejudice to any other claim which may be made, an obligation to refund the amount of the transfer up to ECU 10,000 plus interest and charges paid, within 14 banking business days;
- an obligation for Member States to ensure that adequate and effective means exist for the settlement of any disputes between a bank and its customer.

3.47   The Directive forms part of a series of measures aimed at facilitating cross-border payments, of which cross-border credit transfers account for a substantial part, both in terms of volume and of value.

This Directive applies to credit transfers of less than ECU 25,000 for a period of two years after the date of implementation and to transfers of less than ECU 30,000 after this period. In Article II implementation is given to be within 30 months after the date this Directive enters into force.

(viii)   Directive on price indications

3.48   The purpose of Directive 95/276 is to facilitate a comparison of prices, wherever such comparison is relevant (Art. 1). Article 2 contains definitions of relevant terms, for example "selling price" means the price for a given quantity of the product. The unit price and the selling price must be shown for all goods covered by this Directive; Member States may waive the obligation to indicate the unit price of products for which such indication would not be meaningful because of the products' nature or purpose (Art. 6), and products for which such indication would not provide the consumer with adequate information or would be liable to create confusion.

3.49   These prices must otherwise be unambiguous, legible and easily identifiable (Art. 4). Detailed rules for indicating prices shall be laid down by the Member States (Art. 5). Small retail businesses may be subject to certain exemptions until 6 June 2001 (Art. 7). Article 8 deals with penalties which Member States shall lay down and requires Member States to take all necessary measures to ensure that these are enforced. These penalties must be effective, proportionate and dissuasive. The Directive must be brought into force by 6 June 1997 (Art. 10).

Progress in implementing Directives applicable to consumer policy and product safety

Member State	Directive applicable on 31 Dec. 1994	Directive for which measures have been notified	%
Belgium	50	45	90
Denmark	50	46	92
Germany	50	44	88
Greece	50	41	82
Spain	50	41	82
France	50	44	88
Ireland	50	40	80
Italy	50	43	86
Luxembourg	50	43	86
Netherlands	50	45	90
Portugal	50	42	84
United Kingdom	50	46	92

4. Consumer access to justice

(i) Green Paper on consumer access to justice

The transnational nature of tourism means that access to justice by the tourism consumer when a contract has been breached, presents practical problems. The nature of holidays means that, in most cases, the period of time is too short to resolve such problems in the country where the breach took place. The Commission's Green Paper (COM 93/576), considers the issue of what is needed in order to assist the consumer in seeking redress by a method which is swift, effective and inexpensive. The Green Paper fails to define an action programme for the Commission, nor does it suggest any co-ordinated or aligned measures either for individual Member States or for the European Union to take in the future. **3.50**

Access to justice is considered as a fundamental right of citizens of the European Union.

The Economic and Social Committee recently issued its opinion on the Green Paper (OJ 1994 C295/01). The Committee expressed the view that the concept of the consumer needs to be clearly restated. A consumer is presently defined as a natural person who is party to a specific final use relationship on behalf of either himself or his household in the acquisition of goods or services, including public services supplied: **3.51**

(i)   by another person in the exercise of his professional capacity; or

(ii) by a public body in its capacity as provider of public services.

91

The Committee felt that a special system was required to safeguard consumers' rights in or out of court.

The only Member State with a special procedure for resolution of consumer disputes is Ireland. It offers special assistance for consumers in instigating proceedings, and it has a simplified procedure. It requires mandatory attempts at conciliation.

3.52   The Green Paper referred to two French courts which have established such a system, in Dijon and Le Creusot, as part of the Commission-funded pilot project.

Only the United Kingdom has a restrictive practices court to deal with consumer disputes.

The introduction of arbitration procedures in settling consumer disputes as an alternative to court proceedings is gaining interest in the Member States.

The Green Paper also looked at the Portuguese system of arbitration in consumer disputes. The main features are that the procedures are completely free of charge. They are straightforward and speedy. Prior mediation and attempts at conciliation are mandatory. This is carried out by expert jurists who prepare the case for judgment. The arbitrator is required to be a professional judge. The decisions have full legal force. This applies to subsequent enforcement, which is the responsibility of the law courts. The system can readily settle transfrontier consumer disputes arising in Portugal.

The Green Paper does not evaluate the success of these schemes nor suggest conclusions.

(ii)   Tourists as consumers

3.53   Council Decision 92/421/EEC states:

> Community action aims to support initiatives which improve the information of tourists and their protection, in areas such as existing classification systems, sign posting symbols, timeshare arrangements, overbooking and procedures for redress.

To complement the consumer awareness campaign launched by the Commission in March 1993, the Call for Tenders (94/C 122/07) launched by the Commission on 4 May 1994 invited proposals for the preparation of a user-friendly handbook providing relevant consumer information about the member countries of the EEA in order to help tourists protect their rights as consumers when travelling in Europe. Once it is completed, and in order to promote the work, it will be distributed on diskette to a network of 5,000 interested parties.

The problem of overbooking in hotels and the inconvenience caused to consumers gave rise for concern in 1994. The President of the Committee for Transport and Tourism in the European Parliament invited representatives of key organisations to discuss this issue. The Commission was also invited to participate and promised to examine the causes and extent of accommodation overbooking in the EEA.

Moreover, tourists as consumers like to have access to a wide range of **3.54** competitively priced shopping. There is a very close relationship between the tourism and commercial sectors: a village or an area without shops is less attractive for the tourist. This issue was raised at a seminar held in Brussels on 2 December 1994 on the subject of "Services in small villages – the future of retailing in rural areas". Tourists also like lively town centres with retail outlets, promoting local products typical of the area: thus satisfying the tourist consumer also contributes to local development.

(iii) Treaty provisions

The new EC Treaty Article 129A has strengthened the Commission posi- **3.55** tion with regard to protecting the health and safety and the economic interests of consumers. The application of Article 129A will always be subject to the application of the principle of subsidiarity. It will be for the Court of Justice to give a definitive ruling on how it applies in specific cases.

The Treaty on European Union provisions in Article K will strengthen and further improve conditions of access to law and justice for the citizens of Europe in general, and consumers in particular. Article K(1)6 refers to judicial co-operation in civil matters and Article K.3T establishes collaboration with a view to co-ordinating Member States' actions. Article K(3)2 places the initiative upon the Commission in this area to adopt joint jurisdictions or joint actions.

Article 220 of the EC Treaty provides that Member States shall enter into negotiations with a view to securing for the benefit of their nationals:

> the simplification of formalities governing the reciprocal recognition and enforcement of judgments of courts or tribunals and of arbitration awards.

The Council of Ministers, however, is not enthusiastic about seeking harmonisation which would remove the differences and discrepancies between the civil procedural arrangements in the Member States leading to a single judicial area.

The Maastricht Treaty generated hopes for a new impetus in consumer **3.56** policy, due principally to the new Article 129A. This legal basis has not, however, in practice yet been used – constituting a major gap in the development of Community law.

It was hoped that consumer protection legislation, applicable throughout the Union, would specify the highest possible level of protection and safety rather than "a high level", which is a relative and imprecise concept.

The Economic Social Committee suggestions for the review of the Maastricht Treaty in March 1996 include:

3.57 (i) The key position of consumers as serial partners should be reflected in Treaty Article 3(5), by amending it to refer to a promotion of consumer interests rather than consumer protection. Article 129(1) should be amended.

(ii) Further, Article 129A should be revised so as to clarify that the policy and measures to be adopted by the Community in this area fall within its own competence and not that of Member States in accordance with the subsidiarity principle.

(iii) Lastly, the ESC considers that Treaty Article 193 should also be revised so as to provide explicitly for representation of consumers.

3.58 Among the areas where some positive progress has been made to the benefit of the consumer are:

(i) the creation of some cross-border information centres;

(ii) the creation of the new DG XXIV to deal with consumer policy. Its first Director General is Spyros Pappas.

(iii) the preparation of two Green Papers on:
 – access to justice and the settlement of trans-frontier disputes;
 – guarantees for consumer goods and after-sales service;

(iv) the appointment of the first Ombudsman.

3.59 Nevertheless, tangible progress is still needed in certain areas of fundamental importance to consumers, such as:

(i) the delays, mistakes and shortcomings in the transposition of Directives, the differences in the interpretation and application of secondary legislation, and the failure to apply consumer protection legislation;

(ii) the lack of effective information on basic consumer rights and how to exercise them in the internal market;

(iii) the lack of general recognition of the direct horizontal effect of Directives on consumer matters;

(iv) the lack of integrated training programmes for consumers in general and for persons responsible for interpreting and applying consumer law in particular;

(v) the lack of a genuine single market in insurance and financial services in general;

(vi) the lack of a uniform mortgage credit system;

(vii) inequalities in the application of VAT;

(viii) the difficulties in mutual recognition of professional qualifications;

(ix) the lack of concrete results in respect of general consumer safety, safety of services and defective products liability;

(x) the lack of binding rules on unfair advertising;

(xi) the lack of rules for public services in general (postal services, telecommunications, energy, water, etc).

The above problems are highlighted from the Economic and Social Committee Report OJ C39/67.

(iv) Future initiatives

Consumer Committee

The European Commission has always been committed to consulting on **3.60** problems concerning the protection of consumer interests at Community level. The Commission has now set up a Consumer Committee (95/260/EC, OJ L162/272), to be composed of representatives of consumers in all Member States of the European Community, whether they are organised at national, regional or European level. The Committee may be consulted by the Commission on all problems relating to the protection of consumer interests at Community level. The meetings of the Committee are to be chaired by a Commission representative, and the Commission will provide secretarial facilities for the Committee.

Locus standi

Both the Green Paper on consumer access to justice and the European **3.61** Social Committee opinion argue for the removal of the established rules of *locus standi*, so that consumers and consumer associations acting collectively may be guaranteed access to the Court of Justice, by establishing that collective action is admissible within the European Judicial area.

The European Social Committee opinion has invited the Commission to concentrate its efforts on:

(i)   making adequate Community budgetary provision for legal aid in transfrontier proceedings accompanied by the necessary public information;
(ii) a promotion of codes of conduct stipulating the minimum criteria to be enshrined in Commission Recommendations;
(iii) increasing dialogue between all interested groups.

The European Social Committee opinion envisaged the Commission taking legislative action in the following areas:

(i)   compilation of a list of the means available to the public for settling **3.62** consumer disputes in the Member States;
(ii) accompanied by an analysis of incentives for Member States to develop mediation and conciliation services to minimise the number of consumer disputes;
(iii) the establishment of a network of free, or low cost, legal advice offices in all Member States, geared to providing legal information on transfrontier disputes at the pre-proceedings stage;
(iv) the possibility of creating optional legal protection insurance covering all consumer disputes;

(v)   a training programme for all those involved in the application of national law in the Member States from the point of view of Community law;

(vi)   encouraging businesses and professional associations to set up social bodies to follow up consumer complaints.

3.63   The Committee felt an urgent need for an analysis of the legal rights of consumer associations to represent collective interests before the courts in any Member State. The Committee called upon the Member States to focus particular attention at national level on the arrangements for access to the law and justice in general, especially those relating to consumer disputes, and to providing an effective machinery for their settlement. The Committee expects to see the Commission bring more infringement proceedings before the Court of Justice under Article 169.

The Commission will need to find a fine balance between the principles of subsidiarity in Article 3B and the harmonisation and consumer protection provisions of Article 129A and the provisions of Article K.1.6.

Consumer policy priorities 1996–98

3.64   In October 1995, the Commission adopted a Communication on the Priorities for Consumer Policy 1996–1998. The aim of this communication is to indicate the orientation of consumer policy for the next three years.

Ten priorities for action have been identified:

(i)   to improve the education and information for consumers;

(ii)   to complete, revise and update the framework required to ensure that the interests of consumers are fully taken into account in the internal market;

(iii)   to provide safeguards in the financial services available to consumers;

(iv)   to protect the interests of consumers in the supply of essential public utility services;

(v)   to take steps to allow consumers to benefit from the advantages of the information society;

(vi)   to take steps to increase the confidence of consumers in foodstuffs;

(vii)   to encourage the adoption of sustainable consumption behaviour;

(viii) to strengthen and increase the representation of consumers;

(ix)   to assist the countries of Central and Eastern Europe to draw up policies in favour of consumers;

(x)   to reflect on the question of consumer policy.

CONSUMER PARTICIPATION

3.65   Following the Commission's Decision, the functioning and membership of the Consumers' Consultative Council were modified. The European Consumers' Forum was also set up with the aim of bringing together once or twice a year, representatives of those concerned with consumer

affairs, namely producers, consumers, industry, experts and social partners. The first meeting of the Forum took place on 4 October 1994. The
issues discussed were "guarantees and after sales services" and "access of
consumers to justice" – the latter being of special interest to tourists.

CONSUMER INFORMATION AND EDUCATION

In "The European Consumer Guide to the Single Market" which pro- **3.66**
vides useful information about consumer rights within the framework of
European legislation in about 20 different areas, a whole section is
devoted to tourism and travel. It covers the Package Travel Directive and
the Council Regulation on the compensation system for denied boarding
of scheduled flights; car hire across the Member States; the code of conduct relating to central reservation systems, and health cover using the
E111 within the European Union. In view of the growing interest in electronic publications in general and in the internet in particular, the
"European Consumer's Guide to the Single Market" has also been made
available via the World Wide Web.

The "Co-line European Network" represents a pilot project to link a **3.67**
series of databases in Portugal, Spain, France, Luxembourg and Germany
which provide information (references plus a summary) on applicable
consumer legislation at the Community, national and regional level. It
includes issues affecting tourism. The intention is to extend this network
to Ireland, Italy, Greece, Belgium and Austria.

*Proposal for a Council Directive on Injunctions for the Protection of Consumer
Interests*

The first paragraph of Article 100A of the Treaty establishing the Euro- **3.68**
pean Community provides for the:

> Approximation of the provisions laid down by law, regulation or adminis-
> trative action in Member States which have as their object the establish-
> ment and functioning of the internal market.

In principle, it is up to the Member States to implement these mea-
sures on the basis of Article 5 of the Treaty, pursuant to which, as the
Court of Justice recalled in its judgment of 19 November 1991 [cases
C6/90 and C9/90, ECR 1991 p 5357]:

> "Member States are required to take all appropriate measures, whether
> general or particular, to ensure fulfilment of their obligations under Com-
> munity law."

The Court went on to say that "among these is the obligation to nullify **3.69**
the unlawful consequences of a breach of Community law".

The action for an injunction envisaged in this proposal (CD 95/712)
will apply in so far as the substantive law of the Member States has been
harmonised via a Community regulation or Directive. The scope of the
Directive is hence limited to practices coming within the remit of

national laws that have been harmonised under the Directives listed in the Annex to this draft proposal. The draft proposal concerns acts which Community law declares to be unlawful, and hence equivalent provision must exist in all the Member States: the action for an injunction is nothing but a tool to ensure the effective application of the corresponding provision of Community law.

COMMENTARIES ON THE ARTICLES

3.70 The proposal for a Directive is designed to co-ordinate national provisions concerning actions for injunction of practices which are contrary to Community consumer law and which undermine the interests of consumers (Art. 1). Article 1 refers to the list of Directives featured in Annex 1 to the proposal; hence the scope has been limited to infringements of national provisions transgressing the Directives listed in the Annex. The abovementioned Directives were selected because of the impact of their infringement on consumer interests and on the smooth functioning of the single market.

Action for an injunction (Art. 2). The scope having been defined as a list of Community instruments, the first paragraph provides that any infringement of the national provision transgressing these instruments may give rise to an action for an injunction. Actions for an injunction already exist in all Member States, particularly on the basis of Council Directive 84/450/EEC of 10 September 1994 concerning misleading advertising and Council Directive 93/12/EEC of 5 April 1993 concerning unfair terms in consumer contracts.

3.71 Member State experience shows that to be effective, the procedure must allow the Court to:

– take the necessary measures to rectify, where appropriate, the effects of the infringement (*e.g.* Dir. 84/450/EEC on misleading advertising provides for publication of the decision);
– accompany its decision with sanctions provided in national legislation to assure respect for the decision.

Entities qualified to bring an action (Art. 3) in the domain covered, actions for an injunction are "reserved", in most Member States, for certain "qualified" entities.

3.72 In the first group of countries (France, Belgium, Luxembourg) these entities are associations "approved" at national level (which would seem to exclude all associations "approved" in neighbouring countries). In the second group, (the UK, Ireland, Denmark, Sweden and Finland) the action is normally brought by a national authority specifically responsible for protecting consumer interests in the country in question (which means their hands may be tied when an infringement is committed in their country which has consequences only in other countries). In the third group of Member States (notably Germany, the Netherlands and Italy), the action is "open" to all entities which meet certain criteria. This

Article requires Member States to establish, at national level, a list of entities qualified to bring an action as envisaged in Article 2.

Prior notification (Art. 5) allows Member States to maintain (or introduce) a pre-litigation procedure, with a view to allowing the defendant to terminate the infringement "spontaneously", depending on the circumstances. This may take the form of a mandatory or optional "prior" warning issued by the party that intends to bring the action for an injunction.

This proposed Directive will cover the Package Travel Directive, (Art. **3.73** 1(2) of the proposed Directive).

Consumer disputes

The hallmark of a typical consumer dispute is the disproportion between **3.74** the economic sum at stake and the cost of its legal resolution.

Consumer disputes have received particular attention in recent decades, in the context of which the principle of "equality of arms" has been introduced. In consequence certain specific schemes have been implemented: examples include Art. 5 of the Rome Convention on the law applicable to contractual obligations, and 4 of Title II of the Brussels Convention on Jurisdiction and the Enforcement of Judgments in Civil and Commercial Matters. In particular, Articles 13–15 of the Brussels Convention introduce a special scheme governing contracts concluded with consumers stipulating that, under certain conditions, actions brought against consumers may only be brought before the Courts of the country in which the consumer is domiciled.

When the conditions mentioned in Article 13 are satisfied, Article 14 **3.75** provides in addition that actions brought by consumers against the other party to the contract may be heard either before the Courts of the country in which the defendant is domiciled or those of the consumers' country of domicile.

In *Shearson Lehman Hutton,* (judgment of 19 Jan 1993, case C-89/91 [ECR 1-139]), the Court of Justice held that this scheme:

> "derived from a concern to protect the consumer as the party to the contract who was considered to be economically weaker and less experienced in the law than his co-contractor".

5. Appendix

Out-of-court procedures in the Member States

In Denmark, Sweden and Finland, most consumer disputes are handled **3.76** by "consumer complaints commissions" created in the 70s. These commissions are a kind of administrative authority and make their decisions on the basis of a written procedure whose details are regulated by statute.

[They are chaired by a lawyer, and made up of representatives of consumers and professional circles. (In 1993–94, the Swedish commissions received 6,327 complaints.)]

In the Netherlands the "Geschillencommissies" (dispute commissions) play a similar role in what is basically a written procedure. They deliver a binding opinion ("bindend advies") which must be complied with by the parties. The Geschillencommissies are subject to an approval procedure designed to ensure that certain conditions are met and are members of a Foundation set up in 1970. [Consisting of a consumer representative, a representative of the professional organisation of the sector concerned, and an independent chairman. (In 1995 the Geschillencommissies registered 7,167 cases (as opposed to 6,594 in 1993 and 6,027 in 1992 – the annual growth rate is over 8%).] More recently, Geschillencommissies/Commissions des litiges were created in Belgium as well.

In Portugal a free conciliation and arbitration procedure for consumer disputes was established in Lisbon in the context of a pilot project backed by the Commission and the Portuguese authorities, whose very positive results have led to the opening of other similar centres [almost 2,000 cases settled within 40 days].

In Spain a "a sistema arbitral del consumo" was established by Royal Decree of 30 April 1993; in the framework of this system, each arbitration commission consists of a chairman (representing the administration), a consumer representative and a representative of the professionals. [Since their creation the "Juntas arbitrales" have registered over 14,992 complaints.]

3.77   In several countries a mediator (known as "private ombudsman" in the UK and Ireland) has been created in certain economic sectors (most commonly banking and insurance). The task of these mediators is to deal with consumer disputes through mediation, conciliation and (in certain cases) they may deliver a decision which is binding on the professional. The British and Irish Ombudsman Association has recently drawn up minimum criteria binding on its members; in the case of mediators created for certain public services these criteria are normally established by statute.

In other Member States a similar role is played by the Chambers of Commerce (Germany and, more recently, Italy).

National initiatives concerning access to court procedures

3.78   In France a simplified procedure was established by Decree NO 88-209 which facilitates the introduction of claims of up to FF 13,000 before the courts: the "declaration au greffe" (indicating the identity of the parties and the nature of the claim, as well as a summary of the grounds) is standardised in a simplified form which is binding on the defendant when submitted to him by the registrar; likewise, the defendant is provided with a simplified form for setting out his comments.

In England a "simplified summons" may be used for all claims of up to UK £3,000 in the County Courts. This is a simplified form (of exemplary clarity) which is filled in by the complainant and a copy of which is sent by the court to the defendant, together with a reply form (which is just as clear as the first one). If the defendant does not respond within 14 days, the complainant may request the court to issue a payment order; if the defendant contests the grounds the case is referred to a hearing. The "County Court Rules" (1981) specify that the hearing shall be informal and strict rules of evidence shall not be applicable.

In Ireland a similar mechanism was introduced three years ago for small claims by consumers. This procedure, initially introduced for claims of up to 500 punts, now applies to claims of up to 600 punts and it is planned to raise the ceiling to 1,000 punts. The court registrar helps the consumer fill in the form which – after entry in the register – is sent to the defendant; all he has to do is to fill in the special form created for this purpose. If the defendant contests the application, the registrar attempts to reconcile the parties; to this end he may allow them to put their case and/or invite them to negotiate a solution.

In other Member States, such as Germany, equivalent forms exist for certain categories of disputes. In Belgium, forms have been drafted to make it easier to institute proceedings before justices of the peace. **3.79**

In Sweden and Finland, simplified forms have been prepared for bringing complaints to the attention of the "Consumers Complaints Committees".

The forms mentioned above exist only in the national language of the legal codes concerned.

The promotion of out-of-court procedures

At Community level the Commission considers that the initial focus must be on out-of-court procedures, for the following reasons: **3.80**

- markets are evolving far more swiftly than legal codes, and infinitely more swiftly than the negotiations between the 15 Member States;
- the spectacular growth of out-of-court procedures relating to consumer disputes may be interpreted either as a response to sluggishness (and difficulties) in the adaptation of certain legal codes (adopted at a time when disputes were far less numerous and did not cover the typical problems of contemporary society), or as a "filter" to be encouraged so as to overcome the court backlog, or as a challenge to the principle of the unity of the courts; but however one may judge its merits and demerits, this trend applies to most Member States;
- the experience gained by several Member States proves that the "selective" encouragement of out-of-court procedures for settling disputes (providing certain essential criteria are respected) has been

welcomed both by consumers and firms (by reducing the cost and duration of consumer disputes) and is currently supported by all sides concerned.

3.81   In the framework of the internal market, the lessons we can draw from these experiences may be invaluable. Given the proliferation of "out-of-court" bodies of all kinds (mediators, conciliators, arbitrators) and at all levels (sectoral, national, regional and even local) there are two options: either to ignore the phenomenon, fully aware that for most intra-Community consumer disputes the cost of a lawsuit would be disproportionate; or to try to establish "benchmarks" to accommodate the "foreign" consumer, on the same lines practised by the countries who lead the field in this area.

The experience of these countries is that certain out-of-court procedures may play an important role in settling consumer disputes whenever certain minimum criteria have been established to ensure the transparency of the procedure and the independence of the body responsible for dealing with the disputes.

By contrast, the absence of such criteria goes a long way to explaining consumer distrust in certain countries in regard to all forms of out-of-court dispute resolution. The results of the consultation on the Green Paper were revealing in this respect: most of the parties involved would welcome minimum criteria at European level, including the professionals concerned, as well as the European Parliament and the Economic and Social Committee.

3.82   On the basis of the comments and suggestions received, the Commission is urged to define and/or propose a list of minimum criteria, applicable to the treatment of intra-Community consumer disputes in order to facilitate the creation and/or "networking" of out-of-court procedures at internal market level. The establishment of such criteria at European level would make it possible to support and supplement the policies of the Member States that have chosen to promote a "conciliation culture" in the domain of consumer disputes, and should obviously draw inspiration from criteria established at national level.

A draft working outline comprising six minimum criteria is annexed to this Communication (Annex II), three stages are envisaged: in line with the timetable featured in Annex I.

Stage 1:   the working outline is sent to the interested parties for consultation, with an eye to finalising the definition of the proposed criteria.

Stage 2:   the criteria adopted, in their definitive version, are the subject of a Commission Recommendation.

This text should stipulate an observation period (three years) during which the existence of common criteria could facilitate the creation of "approved" bodies in each Member State, on a voluntary basis.

Moreover, the existence of national bodies employing similar criteria **3.83** might make it easier to manage mechanisms for handling intra-Community complaints on a voluntary basis (*e.g.* by creating a single "post office box" to which consumers could direct their complaints, hence obviating potentially arduous research when the professional belongs to a "foreign" system).

Stage 3: At the end of the observation period, the follow-up given to the Recommendation would be the subject of an assessment report accompanied, where relevant, by a proposal designed to ensure compliance with the criteria, in accordance with procedures yet to be determined, and after further consultations.

By way of example, compliance with the criteria could be guaranteed using a scheme similar to the one in force in certain Member States (*e.g.* the UK, Ireland, Sweden, Finland, Denmark or the Netherlands).

The purpose of such a scheme would not be to "regulate" intra-Community disputes but to help the interested parties establish procedures applicable to such disputes, on the same lines as the Office of Fair Trading, for example, in the United Kingdom. (Under the Fair Trading Act, the OFT's task is "to encourage the relevant associations to prepare and to disseminate to their members codes of practice for guidance in safeguarding and promoting the interests of consumers in the United Kingdom"; in this context, a standard procedure has been adopted for handling complaints.)

Simplified access to court procedures

The establishment of out-of-court procedures as recommended in **3.84** Chapter 1 can only be envisaged on a strictly voluntary basis; neither professionals nor consumers can be "obliged" to rely on them.

The situation was aptly summarised by the European Parliament in its Resolution of 22 April 1994 on the Green Paper: "when all amicable procedures have failed, parties must be able to seek legal redress at a cost commensurate with the small sums involved".

To this end, Parliament considers "that it would be appropriate to harmonise to a certain extent the rules governing legal proceedings in the Member States, in order to establish a Community procedure, for claims up to a certain amount, for the rapid settlement of individual transfrontier consumers disputes.

This view is shared by a large number of bodies and organisations that represent users and call for harmonisation of the "ceiling" of jurisdiction for courts of this kind ("justices de paix", County Courts, "Amtsgericht") as well as the global introduction of simplified proceedings (simplified summons, "declaration au greffe") in order to ensure a certain "parity of treatment" of small disputes in all the Member States'. [In most Member States a "simplified" procedure applies to disputes whose value is less than a certain sum; however this sum can vary greatly. *E.g.*, a claim for up to 1,500 Ecus is considered as a "small dispute" (with a view to applying simplified procedures) in France or in Germany, but not in Spain or the UK. The cost and duration of the "treatment" varies as a result, for claims relating to the same amount, depending on the country whose courts have jurisdiction.]

3.85   Given the present state of Community law, the suggestions summarised in the preceding paragraph must be approached with a fair measure of caution. However, a "Community" contribution to solving the problem is conceivable, provided the legal traditions and idiosyncrasies of each Member State are fully respected. Such a contribution could in fact be based on the existing corpus of national rules, while making it possible to improve access to existing national procedures [. . .]

Drawing inspiration from these examples the Member States could adopts a simplified European form for intra-Community disputes with a view to facilitating access to the national courts. [By European "form" is meant a form whose basic structure should be "harmonised" (with an eye to facilitating the translation as well as the handling of the complaint), but there is nothing to prevent Member States from adapting the form to their national traditions and legal codes.] Far from involving harmonisation of procedures, such an initiative would bring them closer to users, namely those justiciable, and provide greater transparency at the very first stage of gaining access to an essential "public service".

Forms have been created (or harmonised) at European level in the context of other problems of everyday life – for example the "E 111" form (to enable citizens to draw sickness insurance benefits in a country other than their country of residence) and other forms adopted in the social security field. Experience shows that these documents, which exist in all Community languages, facilitate access for users and also lighten the workload of the bodies responsible for handling the dossier in question.

From this perspective the idea would not be to harmonise procedures but to provide better access to the procedures that exist in each country as they stand at present – hence encouraging an approximation of the circumstances facing the parties to an intra-Community dispute, currently separated by certain specific barriers.

3.86   The form would be prepared in the 11 Community languages and the "usage instructions" could be defined as follows:

I.   The claimant would fill in the form in one of the Community languages having the status of an official language in the claimant's country of residence; the claim, formulated in this way, would then be transcribed to the equivalent form in an official Community language of the addressee's country and sent to the latter, via the relays indicated by the Member States;

II.   In the section of the form reserved for him, the addressee could either propose a solution as to the substance, or inform the complainant of the existence of an instance which could settle the dispute amicably (mediator, conciliation commission, etc.);

III.   If the addressee did not respond within a given period, or rejected the proposed solution, the form would be forwarded to the competent authority (which would find there the background to the dispute as well as the subject of the complaint and the identity of the parties, in the two languages).

A provisional version of such a form is annexed to this communication; the final version will be established on the basis of wide-ranging consultation with the Member States, the legal professions, and associations representing potential users, on the understanding that recourse to the form by users (consumers and firms) should be optional and not rule out other forms of dispute settlement. In introducing the form, two stages may be envisaged:

–   Stage I: the form is tested in a limited number of border regions.   **3.87**

In order to respect cultural and legal, national and regional particularities, the multipliers are selected on the basis of consultations with the Member States and interested parties. A group of experts representing the Member States supporting the initiative is then responsible for follow-up and drafts recommendations on expiry of an appropriate trial period. The timetable for prior consultations in the context of implementing the initiative is reproduced in Annex I to this Communication.

–   Stage II: the final version of the form is presented by the Commission in the context of a proposal for a regulation which will also define its "usage instructions" on the basis of the results of the trial period.

In this case the "scope" of the form could be the subject of prior consultations with an eye to determining the ceiling for what the Member States consider to be "small claims".

ANNEX I

Indicative timetable concerning measures to be taken to implement the envisaged initiatives   **3.88**

THE PROMOTION OF OUT OF COURT PROCEDURES

–   Consultation of interested parties concerning the working outline featured in Annex II: March–September 1996
–   Adoption of the Recommendation: end 1996
–   Observation period: December 1996–November 1999
–   Preparation and presentation of an assessment report on the operation of the system: December 1999–May 2000.

– Consultation of the interested parties on the draft form featuring in Annex III: March–September 1996 (Member States, Association européenne des magistrats, Council of the Bars and Law Societies of the European Community, representative associations of users: consumers and firms)

– Definition of the working outline concerning the procedures for using the form and selection of the frontier regions in which the form will be tested: October–December 1996 (new round of consultation with the Member States)

– Nomination of the members of the group of experts responsible for following up the initiative: March–April 1997

– Trial period: June 1997–May 2000

– Recommendations of the group of experts on the follow-up to the trial period: June–September 2000

ANNEX II

3.89 Working outline for a recommendation establishing criteria for the creation of out-of-court procedures applicable to consumer disputes

FIRST CRITERION

The impartiality of the body responsible for handling the disputes must be guaranteed by all appropriate means and notably:

– in the case of mediators, by according them adequate guarantees of independence in the performance of their tasks;

– in the case of collegiate bodies, by ensuring joint representation of consumers and professionals in the bodies that handle the disputes, as well as the independence of the third party that chairs the body, whenever provision is made for such a party.

SECOND CRITERION

The effectiveness of the procedure must be ensured by measures guaranteeing:

– the existence of clear and simple forms for submitting claims, available in the eleven Community languages;

– establishment of and compliance with time limits, including preliminary steps which may be imposed on the consumer (example: all remedies internal to the firm have been exhausted);

– attribution of appropriate investigatory powers to the body responsible for taking the decision;

THIRD CRITERION

Adequate publicity must be guaranteed using appropriate means to ensure the transparency of the following elements:

– the existence and scope of the procedure;
– the maximum time limit and possible cost of the procedure for the consumer;
– the criteria governing the "decision" of the body responsible for handling the dispute;
– the legal import of this "decision", spelling out whether it is binding on the professional or whether it is a mere recommendation; in the first case the sanctions for non-compliance must be set out.

These particulars must always be provided in writing to any consumer who has expressed an interest in availing of the procedure.

The decisions, or at least a summary thereof, must be the subject of an annual report accessible to the public.

All decisions must be reasoned and in writing and must be communicated to the parties concerned as soon as possible.

FOURTH CRITERION

When the parties are domiciled in different countries, each party must be informed in writing, and in a language having the status of official Community language in his/her country of residence, of the decision on the dispute, setting out the grounds.

FIFTH CRITERION

Application of the codes of conduct must never result in depriving the consumer of protection afforded to him/her by the mandatory rules of the law of the country in which he/she habitually resides, in conformity with the Rome Convention on the law applicable to contractual obligations.

SIXTH CRITERION

Terms in a contract which have not been individually negotiated may under no circumstances be invoked to prevent consumers from bringing an action before the courts having jurisdiction for the judicial resolution of the dispute.

ANNEX III

3.90

CLAIM

(in certain circumstances this document may replace the letter of formal notice)

SENDER	**ADDRESSEE**
Name:..............................	Name:..............................
First name:..........................	First name:..........................
Address:............................	Address:............................
....	....
....	....

THE BACKGROUND[1]

....
....
....
....
....
....

(1) Specify as precisely as possible:
(a) the dates, places and conditions of purchase, sale or signature of the contract
(b) problems encountered with the product or service

SUBJECT OF THE APPLICATION[2]

....
....
....
....
....

(2) Specify the precise nature of your request (examples: amount of reimbursement, repair or replacement of a product, etc.).

ANNEXES[3]

....
....
....
....
....

(3) Indicate here all details you consider necessary and annex all documents supporting your request

Done at..............,..........
Signature

IMPORTANT:
The Addressee has 15 days to reply from receipt of this document. If no reply is received within this period, the Sender may lodge a copy of the letter of formal notice with the clerk of the court having jurisdiction. This submission will be equivalent to a declaration before the clerk of the court.

Note for the sender:
If the addressee is domiciled abroad, always consult a lawyer or a consumer organisation: they will be able to inform you on the law applicable to the dispute, indicate to you the court having jurisdiction and help you at all stages of the procedure, in accordance with the rules applicable in each country.
If the addressee is domiciled in a Member State of the European Union, your claim may be transcribed to a form equivalent to this one, which exists in all official languages of the Union.

REPLY
(Failure to reply within the ordained time limit may lead to an action being brought before the court having jurisdiction)

I accept your claim and agree to . . . .

within a period of . . . .

I do not accept your claim because . . . .

and, moreover, request as follows . . . .

I certify that I have received your claim and propose the following:

A) record our agreement on the following solution[1]: B) submit the dispute to the body mentioned below[2]:	(1) Example: partial or full reimbursement of the price, repair or replacement of the product. (2) Example: conciliator, arbitration, mediation centre. Specify clearly: – the cost and duration of the procedure, – the legal status of the decision issued by this body (is it binding on the two parties or only on the professional or is it merely a recommendation?)

Done at . . . ., ...
Signature

Sender's reply to the proposals:

concerning proposal A)
. . . .

concerning proposal B)
. . . .

Signature . . . .

Select Bibliography

Books

Beaumont, *European Communities (Amendment) Act 1993* (Sweet & Maxwell, 1994)

Department of Trade and Industry, *European Manual*, Volume 2 (CCH Editions Limited)

Kray, *Tourism and the hotel and catering industries in the EC*

EC materials

Amended proposal for a Council Directive on the protection of consumers in respect of contracts negotiated at a distance (distance selling) COM(93) 396 final (OJ 1993 C308/18)

Community action in the field of tourism (COM (86) 32 final)

Commission Interpretative Communication concerning the free movement of services across frontiers (OJ 1993 C334/03)

Council Decision establishing a consultation and co-ordination procedure in the field of tourism (OJ 1986 C114/11)

Council Decision 92/421/EEC of 13 July 1992 on a Community action plan to assist tourism (OJ 1992 L231/26)

Council Directive 90/314/EEC of 13 June 1990 on package travel, package holidays and package tours (OJ 1990 L158/59)

Council Recommendation 86/666/EEC on fire safety in existing hotels (OJ 1986 L384/60)

Council Recommendation on standardised information in existing hotels (OJ 1986 L384/54)

European Parliament working documents from the Committee on Transport and Tourism:
— Document A2 – 172/86
— Document A3 – 0155/91 Part A
— Document A3 – 0155/91 Part B

Green Paper on access of consumers to justice and the settlement of consumer disputes in the single market of 16 November 1993 (Community Document No 93/576)

Making payments in the internal market (Community Document No 90/447)

Mutual recognition of qualifications (Community Document No 94/596)

Opinion of the Economic and Social Committee on access of consumers to justice and the settlement of consumer disputes in the single market (OJ 1994 C295/01)

Tourism statistics (Community Document No 94/582)

Principles of Travel Law

Chapter 4
Principles of Travel Law
Pim W H de Vos[1]

1. Legal structure of travel and tourism law   4.1

This study is about civil travel and tourism law and does not deal with rules of public law/licensing of travel agents. The purpose of my contribution to this book is to find and if possible to define general rules and principles of travel and tourism.[1]

Travel and tourism law may be defined as that part of the legal system which deals with:

(i)   rules of civil law on travel agencies (tour operators and travel agents);

(ii)   the position of the consumer (traveller, holiday maker) as regards these rules and their application.

The terms "travel agent", "tour operator", "retail agent" may seem to have a more or less clearly defined meaning. As appears from the text, this is however open to question.

(i)   The travel agent

The services of the travel agency are manifold. It is impossible to make an   4.2 exhaustive list of the services provided by travel agents, but some services include: providing tickets for the transportation of people (with their luggage) by aeroplane, railway, ship; reserving seats, making reservations for hotels and apartments; helping to bring about contracts with insurance companies or with other travel agents or tour operators; arranging for the clients to participate in excursions and visits to various events and entertainments; advising clients about destinations, means of transport, and about choosing between tour operators who offer more or less the same product; giving information on passports, visa and health requirements.

---

[1] Pim W. H. de Vos is a senior partner in de Vos & Steinz, Amsterdam. The views expressed in this chapter are his own, and do not reflect the opinions of others in the firm.

[2] Although this is not a quite clear distinction, I will use the expression "travel and tourism" since this is usual in international law. *E.g.* the IBN s Y is called "Travel and Tourism Law"; so is the name of the International Forum of Travel and Tourism Advocates.

4.3   When talking about travel agents it is important to distinguish between actions undertaken as an intermediary, and activities which comprise "his own services as a tour organizer". We could say that the more the travel agent is offering its own services relating to travel – in other words offering his own services or those of his auxiliaries, the more the travel agent is acting as a tour operator. In its original capacity the travel agency is only a booking office: a company which mediates between the traveller and others such as tour operators, carriers and providers of accommodation. This role as an intermediary should be distinguished from the tour operator who offers organised holiday trips, or the carriers, the hotelier, etc.

4.4   As a booking office the travel agent's field of activities comes closest to that of a trade agent. The EC Directive on agency contracts restricts the scope of the EC regulations to the sale of goods, and does not include the mediation of services. In some countries however, the travel agent's activities are regulated by the law of agency. The Netherlands is one of these countries. The travel agent acts as a mediator. Any travel agent who does more than just mediation would do well to remember that he is active in the tour operating field and in doing so should accept the tour operator's responsibility and thus his liability. Law, after all, is not so much concerned with the names given to certain activities, as with the legal qualification of the relationship between parties. Let me give an example.

I ask my travel agent to arrange a four-day trip for me to Florence. He devises a package, consisting of an Alitalia flight, an Avis rental car and four nights in hotel Amore Permanente. Obviously in this situation his responsibility is greater than if I were to use him solely as a reservation office to book an all-in trip offered by tour operator X in a newspaper advertisement or one of the two hundred travel brochures on display in the travel agency. As a booking office the agent is merely a go-between – and has no influence on the product itself. For his mediation the travel agent receives approximately 10% of the package price as a commission. If he composes the package himself, his work is that of a tour operator rather than an agent. In the latter case he is taking the risks and the benefits of the entrepreneur who markets his own inclusive tours (packages).

4.5   Now to the travel agent who does pre-organized tours. It is clear that by presenting himself as a tour operator he exceeds the confines of the booking office and should be willing to bear the consequences. This responsibility is alleviated by the fact that to a certain extent he has influenced the composition of the product by buying the various elements himself. Moreover, his profit margin should exceed the 10% commission he receives as a booking office intermediary.

(ii) The travel contract

4.6   Regardless of whether a travel contract concerns a package tour proper or an individually arranged trip, neither the travel agent nor the tour operator carries out the services concerned. The tour operator basically arranges for others to transport and accommodate his clients. He himself does not execute the travel contract, but just composes the package. To meet market demand he devises certain packages from the enormous variety of transport and accommodation on offer. Because of the large scale of the purchase he can buy at lower prices than the traveller would pay if the he booked with the airline and/or hotel direct.

Setting aside exceptions like the German *Bürgerliches Gesetzbuch* (Civil Code), before the implementation of the Directive on package travel most legal systems did not have specific legislation regarding the travel contract. In view of the qualities described above, the travel contract can be characterised as a *contractus sui generis* – a contract of its own kind or class, which by the very nature of the travel industry is extremely varied. Because the travel contract was not regulated by law, it was necessary to use the general written and unwritten principles of the law of contract as a guide. In so far as transport was concerned, the rules of the law of transport offered a foothold.

The latter mainly grew out of maritime law, which is obvious given the fact that in the nineteenth century carriage by sea was the main mode of travel. With the advent of the train the rules of transport law were extended. When an Englishman rented a "room with a view" in Italy, so beautifully described by Forster, he did so with the landlord directly or through a travel agency. There were no specific rules of law governing the situation. The regulations laid down by the Italian *Codice Civil* about the renting of accommodation were a far cry from the present EC regulations on package tours. Of course direct booking with an Italian hotel or landlord did not hold the guarantee of strong legal protection in the event of complaints or overbooking.

In 1976 I raised for the first time a defence against a complaint filed by a traveller. The case concerned a holiday maker who had rented an apartment in Portugal through a Dutch travel agency. When the water heater in the apartment exploded he was seriously injured, and held the travel agent liable for his injuries. The defence I raised was that the travel agency had acted exclusively as intermediary – though it had also arranged the flight – and the court accepted my view.

To a certain extent the same defence can be used for package tours, as the following example illustrates. As soon as a holiday maker receives his documents and opens his ticket, he is confronted with the carrier's conditions of carriage which form part of the air carriage contract. He himself has not had any contact with the airline – he booked a trip through a travel agent or by telephone, and in many cases does not even know which airline will carry him to his destination. Still, a carriage contract has come about *by the mediation of the tour operator*. No other conclusion is possible.

This applies in the same way to hotels. To the owner of a hotel or apartment the traveller who has booked through a travel agent is his

4.7

4.8

4.9

117

guest, and will in principle be treated in the same way as any other traveller who came to him independently. When checking in, the traveller signs a form which tells him that the general hotel conditions apply. Both the carrier and the hotelier restrict their liability to a great extent in their general terms and conditions which apply to *their* agreement with the traveller.

The same holds true for the fly-drive. The tour operator has arranged for a car to be waiting for the traveller at the airport. Before he is given the keys and papers the traveller must sign a car rental contract to indicate his acceptance of the terms of rental as – unilaterally – drawn up by the rental agency with regard to deductibles, deposit etc. In this case too, the tour operator's role was to mediate as an agent in the conclusion of an agreement.

The essence is that the tour operator has others carry out the contract.

(a) Selbsteintritt

4.10   The concept of *Selbsteintritt* (roughly translated as "self entry") originates from German law. It relates to situations in which the tour operator does not have others carry out the obligations to which he is committed under the travel contract, but does so himself. (For the moment I will disregard the question of whether *Selbsteintritt* still applies if in carrying out his obligations under the contract the tour operator nevertheless uses separate companies. Given the ratio of this tenet it should not make any difference.) The idea is that a tour operator who carries out the services himself is not dependent on others and therefore may not hide behind them. It is *his* plane, *his* hotel, etc – and if something goes wrong he should take the blame. We have already seen that in that case his performance should not be judged by the rules of the travel contract, but by the specific rules for carriers or hotel keepers.

The travel contract between traveller and tour operator is basically established by the oral agreement: it is essentially concluded as soon as the offer of the tour operator is accepted by the traveller. Acceptance can take place either directly (booking by telephone for instance), or via the intermediary service of a booking office. A written contract is not demanded, unless the specific law system would require a written contract instead of the oral agreement. The same goes for the agreement made between a client and a travel agent acting as an intermediary booking office.

4.11   The EC directive obviously derives from the same principle, since in Article 2(5) "contract" is described as "the agreement linking the consumer to the organizer and/or the retailer".

The tour operator's offer in an advertisement or brochure is a public offer which in principle can be accepted by anyone. In accordance with the New Dutch Civil Code of 1992, the general conditions of the Association of Dutch ANVR tour operators contains the following provisions:

- The travel agreement is reached by the traveller's acceptance of the tour operator's offer. Acceptance can take place either directly, or via the intermediary service of a booking office.
- The tour operator's offer is free of obligations and can, if necessary, be withdrawn by him. Withdrawal should take place as swiftly as possible following acceptance – at the very latest within eight office hours after acceptance.
- In order to conclude the agreement and the implementation thereof, the traveller shall provide the booking office with the necessary information about him/herself and possible other traveller(s).
- A person who, in the name of or acting on behalf of another person, concludes a travel agreement, is severally responsible for all obligations ensuing from the agreement. The (other) traveller(s) is/are responsible for his/her/their own share.
- If the agreed tour is included in a publication issued by the tour oper- **4.12** ator, the facts contained therein become part of the agreement. If the tour operator has included general conditions in the general part of the programme which are in conflict with the booking conditions, the most favourable stipulations are applicable to the traveller.

The tour operator is not bound by obvious faults and mistakes in a publication. Deviations from or additions to the tour offered by the tour operator can be requested on medical grounds (medical essentials). The tour operator must make realistic efforts in order to carry out such a request, unless this cannot, in all reasonableness, be demanded of him.

Medical essentials require the explicit written consent of the tour operator. The tour operator has the right, in that case, to charge the following costs:

(i)   for the deviating or additional organisational costs, up to a sum of Dfl. 50 per booking (Dfl. 25 for own means-of-transport tours, if shorter than five days of stay in the Netherlands);
(ii)   communication costs;
(iii) possible extra costs, charged by providers of services involved in the implementation of the tour.

These requests also require the explicit, written consent of the tour operator.

- The tour operator does not bear any responsibility for photographs, folders and other informational material issued under the responsibility of third parties.

In the (scarce) literature about the nature of the travel agent some **4.13** authors make a distinction between, on the one hand, activities of the travel agent acting as "an intermediary", and on the other, activities consisting in "own services". This is not a fine distinction, since the travel agent's actions as an intermediary certainly are his own services for which he should take responsibility – and it might well appear that actions which at first appear to be "own services" are in fact merely (or primarily) those of an intermediary. So to follow this distinction as a starting point for legal qualification is wrong either way.

But what must a travel agent actually do to be distinguished from other activities and business? In my opinion the core of his activity as a travel agent lies in his concern with a) transport and b) accommodation. All other services mentioned are and could be rendered by other lines of business – or are subsidiary to his main concern – that of dealing with transport and accommodation.

4.14   One characteristic of the travel agent does not need further explanation: that is that the travel agent as such is not the actual supplier of transportation and accommodation. Of course it may well be that in a particular case a person or company operating as a travel agent occupies himself with transport or accommodation, but in that case those activities are not legally those of a travel agent but those of a coach company or a hotel keeper – so that essentially the relation with the client is governed by rules of transport and hotel law, so far as it exists. (A very clear example of this occurs under the Warsaw Convention, where the travel agent when chartering an aircraft is considered to be the contractual carrier; this is discussed further below.)

A tentative definition of a travel agent could be: the person who obtains for another (his client) the supply by a third party of transportation and accommodation. The EC Directive on package travel, package holidays and package tours – which others will comment on later in this book – distinguishes between "organiser" and "retailer". The first is the person (or company) who, other than occasionally, organises packages and sells or offers them for sale, whether directly or through a retailer. This, in the sense of the Directive, is the person who sells or offers "for sale" the package put together by the organiser. I will go into this terminology later on, but first I would like to look more closely at the nature of what I would call the "genus travel agent". The type "travel agent" includes two species – first travel agent as retailer/booking office, and second the tour operator – the travel agent who organises tours.

(iii)   The holiday maker

4.15   Less than one hundred years but more than two thousand kilometres per hour separate the first French aeroplane of the second half of the last century, from the Concorde of today.

In the old days the boat crossing to America or the Far East was adventurous, and bound to take a toll. With the increase in motorised traffic and in particular the development of air travel, man's mobility has increased enormously in the twentieth century. Although travelling has become comparatively safe, the traveller does not sleep in his own bed, does not eat the meals cooked by his wife or mother and has to wait and see whether the holiday resort lives up to the pretty picture in the brochure. A traveller to far-away destinations knows little of the culture, customs or standard of living in the place where he will be spending those two or three important weeks; but his expectations are high. He has been looking forward to this holiday for months – often saving up for the entire year. In the period immediately before the holiday he has probably been putting in long and hard hours, and now, finally setting out on his trip, feels exhausted. The children are whining, tired from the long journey; they are plagued by mosquitoes and the heat in paradise.

It was a good deal: $600 per person for seventeen days. The price/quality ratio is not even that bad. The room is all right, but the mattresses are rather hard and there is no air conditioning; when the holiday maker opens his windows, he can hear various groups of elated fellow holiday makers who are either just tipsy or drunk, but at any rate noisy, yelling under his window until the early morning in Icelandic or Swedish, or some other scarcely intelligible language, noisy Dutchmen, loud Italians and finally some Englishmen throwing each other into the pool so conveniently located near the apartment.

The next morning the holiday maker is woken by screaming children who take over the pool. By the time he gets up he is completely worn out. Breakfast is a disappointment – stale rolls, two minute containers of jam and one packet of Spanish butter. Tea does not taste like home and the local coffee is just as undrinkable. On top of that they had to wait five minutes before they were seated, as it is high season. When one of the children develops an inflamed ear the tour representative will definitely have a hard time and hear a never-ending succession of complaints.

(iv) The business traveller

Obviously the business traveller's situation is completely different. He is used to travelling without the burden of a family. He will often travel to a business destination and stay at a hotel which he knows or which forms part of a chain with which he is familiar. He is subject to other risk factors however, such as delays causing him to miss his connecting flight – which in the worst case could mean missing an important appointment and thus a contract.

4.16

(v) The travel industry

Many different parties are involved in the organisation and execution of trips. These parties can be roughly divided into three types of business:

4.17

(a) Travel agents as booking offices

This is the business which mediates between the traveller on the one hand and businesses arranging or executing the trip on the other.

(b)   Suppliers of accommodation, transport and auxiliary services

These suppliers supply the actual product, that is, the transport, hotels, golf courses, rental cars. This category includes the handling agent in so far as he does not act purely as a trade agent.

(c)   The tour operator

The tour operator is the business concerned with the organisation of package tours – usually associated with holiday tours. Organised business trips are just as important, for example a tour operator may organise a business trip for one or several persons, or perhaps an entire company outing.

(vi)   Package tours

4.18   The EC Directive on Package Tours,[3] which will be discussed at length in this book, may give rise to the misunderstanding that every organised holiday tour falls within the scope of this Directive and the statutory regulations based on it in the various Member States of the European Community. Package tours are *trips organised beforehand which are offered ready-made to the public for whom these trips are intended.* This may be a regular holiday trip to a sunny destination, or a specific group tour such as a cultural trip to the treasures of Egypt, a cycling tour through Turkey, mountaineering or white water rafting. Holiday trips may be taken within your own country and include just two overnight stays, or be a four-week tour of Thailand or Indonesia.

In short, there is a large variety of trips which all share one predominant characteristic: the travel agent and tour operator do not carry out the trip themselves. This is done by staff of the carrier, the hotelier or the landlord of the apartment, local guides on the excursion, the pilot of the plane hired in Mexico for a special day trip, the State Opera singers if the trip includes a visit to the opera, etc.

(vii)   Tour operators

4.19   I have stressed that a tour operator himself does not carry out the trip. Apart from a single tour operator who, usually accommodated in a separate company, has a charter company, the tour operator cannot be regarded as an air carrier. Most tour operators do not take their guests to their own hotels and apartments but to accommodation "bought" from third parties. For so-called fly-drives, the tour operator even offers a rental car as part of the package. Whenever possible, he will purchase this car from a reputable car rental agency such as Avis or Hertz, but in many countries he will have to get the cars from a local rental company

---

[3] Council Directive of 13 June 1990 on Package Travel, Package Holidays and Package Tours (90/134/EEC).

which uses outdated vehicles in a bad state of repair. What should he do? His client wants a car, and these are the best he can get.   **4.20**

A tour operator may be expected or required to use a reasonable degree of care and skill in the selection of the third parties that are to provide the services and products contracted for. Tour operators are also required to give their travellers sufficient information so that they know what to expect: first and foremost the brochure describing the trip should present as accurate a picture as possible.

The traveller's expectations should be judged by those of the average traveller. If the tour operator knows, or should know, that there is a chance of disturbing construction work going on next to, or even worse, in the hotel, the client should be told of this in advance.

Preferences

When booking their trip many clients indicate special preferences – such   **4.21** as a room with a sea view or an apartment close to the sea or the pool. Although the tour operator should make every effort to comply with expressed wishes, he will not always be able to guarantee that they will be met. It is therefore important that both the brochure and the person taking the reservation make it clear that it is not certain whether those wishes will be granted. If the preference is so essential that the traveller only wants to enter into the travel contract if it is certain that his preference will be met, it becomes an "essential condition" – which should be distinguished from a mere preference.

2.   The nature of the services of the travel agency

The French author G. Ripert[4] wrote that "agents de transport" (trans-   **4.22** portation agents) basically should be considered as proxies ("mandataines"). However he describes how, under the influence of the modern desire for total security, and the development of what he calls the "civilisation of leisure", the agent's role and responsibilities have been extended. A travel agent often assumes or pretends to assume the function of hotel keeper or carrier – in which case they are subject to the corresponding contractual responsibilities.

Rodiére had already stressed the growing role and corresponding responsibilities of the travel agent in 1960.[5] He answers the question whether the agent is an intermediary or a carrier thus: if the agent uses his own means of transport he is a carrier and responsible as such. But he makes a further refinement. When the agent presents himself to his client *as if* he were accountable for the transportation, he should be held liable for this. Everything depends on the nature of the services promised by the agent!

---

[4]   Ripert, G, *Traité élementaire de Droit Commercial* (Paris, 1970), p. 224 ff.
[5]   Rodière, R, *Droit des Transports III* (Paris, 1960), p. 227 ff.

4.23   A distinction must be made between:

(i)   responsibility for personal conduct;
(ii)   responsibility for third parties.

The agent is responsible for what he does or does not do when he makes reservations for his clients. Of course he can also be held responsible for giving wrong advice, or making misrepresentations, in his own capacity as a travel agent. Where he must also supply services (e.g. means of transportation and accommodation in different places), the travel plan must be in order.

A primary obligation of the agent is to make it completely clear to the client what has been done for him (and accordingly, what he should take care of himself). The traveller is entitled to know what he can expect, in so far as the agent knows or, as a good travel agent, should know. If the agent supplies certain services of transportation or accommodation himself, he is responsible as a carrier or hotel keeper. The same applies when he has presented himself as such to his clients, who may keep him to his word.

4.24   Claims against the travel agent often concern bodily harm or injury suffered as a result of transportation. If the agent was the carrier (which is seldom the case), or had presented himself as such, he is of course responsible for the physical security of his clients – unless force majeure is at issue. However, if he has not engaged himself in that capacity – either by express agreement or by implication through his behaviour – the agent should not be responsible for the conduct of a third-party carrier. The same rules apply according to Rodière, when other incidents occur such as theft or loss of luggage.

The principle that the responsibility of the travel agent depends on the nature of what he promised to his client was used by the German Supreme Court in its decision of 18 October 1973.[6] In this case the travel agency stipulated that it was only a intermediary – and this fact was repeatedly and clearly brought to the notice of the client. The Court considered that the nature of every contract should be looked at individually, and that in that context how the parties understood their mutual relation is centrally relevant. The Court in this case found that a travel agent can present any travel performance as the object of an intermediary travel contract, but it is also free to engage itself on its own responsibility to realise the desired performance. Whether the one or the other is the case depends on the presentation of its services by the agency and the way in which the prospective client may have understood them.

4.25   According to the German jurisprudence the organiser of an inclusive tour (*Pauschal-reise*) enters into direct contractual relations with the traveller. Such a contract is considered to be a contract of undertaking

---

[6] Bundesgerichtshof 18 Oct 1973, VII ZR 241/72. *Fremdenverkehrsrechtlichen Entscheidungen*, Klatt, Band 7, p. 228.

(*Werkvertrag*). This "construction" was defended by some German authors – amongst them Eberle[7] – who construed the organised travel contract as a contract of undertaking. The reasoning and justification these authorities give is that the traveller who enters into a travel contract on the basis of the tour operator's brochure does not want to be confronted with several contractors. He does not know those suppliers of services and cannot judge their reliability. It is for that very reason that he addresses himself to the organising agency: in case of difficulty he wants to deal with one person.

Actions in court in a foreign country (against a foreign company) will be very hard. But what was the justification for this strict liability for services provided by others? (In the foregoing I stressed that the travel agent, as mediator or tour organiser, does not render the services of accommodation and transport himself.) Eberle's answer to this question is amazing: that the aforementioned (supposed) considerations of the travellers should find foundation in the fact that they paid an "inclusive price". Needless to say this is hardly a justification. But still the German courts held the tour operator liable not only for his own defaults, but also for those of his "subcontractors" (*Erfüllingsgehilfe*) that is the suppliers of services such as carriage and accommodation.

3. Damages

If the tour operator fails in his obligation to provide a holiday of the contracted quality, the question arises to what extent the traveller will be entitled to claim damages.   **4.26**

Damages can arise from the non-performance or the improper performance of the services included in the package. Those damages should be distinguished as:

(i)   *material damages:* reimbursement of the travel sum; costs; other damages, such as loss of income

and

(ii)   *non-material damages:* smart-money, compassionate allowance, compensation (or whatever it may be called), because of personal injury.

With regard to non-material damages the question can be asked whether the traveller is entitled to compensation for useless spent holiday time or for loss of enjoyment.

First of all compensation could be allowed for that part of the holiday for which the traveller is supposed not to have had value for money. A

---

[7] Eberle, *Die Haftung des Reiseveranstalters* (Der Betrieb, 1973), Beilage 2, p. 3 ff.

certain, often arbitrary part of the travel sum can be reimbursed. This may be approached in the following way. Suppose that the inclusive price for the holiday was f 1000 and the tour operator paid 10% commission to the travel agent for his mediation. A gross amount of f 900 rests. It was a package consisting of a return flight to Palma de Mallorca and a nine-day stay in hotel Sol y Mar, full board. Everything in the hotel was less than promised in the brochure, but not a disaster. The air transport was all right and cost the tour operator f 450. The hotel cost him f 400 and ancillary services such as transfers from the tour operator's agent in Palma f 20. So the margin for the tour operator was no more than f 30, overheads included.

4.27   Had the client "bought" his own ticket, made his own reservation for Sol Y Mar, and arranged his own transport to and from the hotel, transport and accommodation would probably have cost him at least f 1.400. Now the hotel was not quite right, but he had a bed, a (noisy) room and pretty poor food. What should he get?

We should also consider the fact that the tour operator had made the reservation for an allotment of 20 rooms not less than nine months before in order to have the hotel included in the brochure, and that at that time everything seemed to be perfectly in order: for years before he had only had satisfied clients. Again, what would be a reasonable compensation? I would say that for the traveller any amount is too little, and for the tour operator every amount too much, in view of his pretty low margins.[8] Nevertheless the client will not be satisfied with f 200 compensation. He wants more.

(i)   Uselessly spent holiday time

4.28   A German traveller claimed an amount of DM 1.500 for uselessly spent holiday time, which claim was denied by the lower court on the ground that such damages could be awarded only in so far as the claim was based on contractual liability.

The German Supreme Court however[9] held that if a *Lebensgut* (asset of life) has to a certain extent been commercialised so that it can be "bought" for money, it could be considered as an asset of life with its own economic value. Thus one may say that time is money. The Court added a pretty important consideration to this judgment by stressing that not every minor default in the holiday can give ground for such a claim. It considered that usually such complaints can be made good by partial restitution of the travel sum. Only when the aim of relaxation and enjoyment of the holiday has totally failed should compensation for uselessly spent holiday time be awarded.

---

[8]   The profits of tour operators in the Netherlands are before tax, since I have been working in this branch (1974) not higher than 0.75 – 2% of the turnover. As far as I hear from my collegues in other EU Member States, this is more or less the overall picture.

[9]   Bundesgerichtshof 10 Oct 1979, VII R 231/73. *Fremdenverkehrsrechtliche Entscheidungen*, Klatt, Band 8.

Mere discomfort only gives rise to non-material damages, which according to this Supreme Court should not be compensated. So ruled the *Oberlandesgericht* (Court of Appeal) in Nürnburg in 1976,[10] a case concerning noisy construction work being carried out in the neighbourhood of a hotel in Gran Canaria. The tour operator had warned his clients that the work was going on – "of course only in daytime". The clients forwarded a claim against both the tour operator and the travel agents for damages equal to half of the travel sum.

The Court of Appeal considered that the agreement of an inclusive tour was a contract of undertaking, and came to the conclusion that the tour operator as organiser of the holiday had to ensure the fulfilment of the obligations arising from the travel contract. Accordingly he was liable for damages because of the fact that the purpose of the holiday could not be achieved. But the non-material harm (discomfort) could not be made good by means of compensation, according to Vermans principles of contractual liability. **4.29**

(ii) Reduction of travel sum and damages

In Germany the responsibility of the tour operator has developed into strict liability. The German Supreme Courts demand a lot from the tour operator. **4.30**

In 1979 specific legislation on the travel contract with tour operators came into force, which legislation – the first within the European Union – will no doubt have been influential on the European Commission when it started working on proposals for a Directive on package tours.

The German travel law does not provide a scale for compensation in cases of improper performance by the tour operator's sub-contractors. The Frankfurt Court however, loaded with claims, designed the so-called "Frankfurt Table on Reduction of Travel Prices" – meant to determine the measure of reduction of the travel sum in cases of improper performance. In this scale (table) the different defects in services are related to percentages of the travel sum. For instance: deviation in the distance to the beach – 5–15%; no balcony – 5–10%; defect of water closet – 15%; bad cleaning – 10–20%; noise during the day – 5–25%; noise at night – 10–40%.

There is no need to say that I am not an advocate of this system: the award of accurate compensation depends on looking at the individual circumstances and gravity of the complaints. On the other hand it should be recognised that, especially in cases of minor complaints, a scale would be practical and preventative. Preventative because it would help both traveller and tour operator to determine what compensation could be obtained. In practice, we should see reduction on the price – in effect reimbursement. **4.31**

---

[10] OLG Nürnberg, 27 Apr 1976, MDR 12/1976, p. 1020.

No detailed system of compensation or damages is embodied in the EC Directive on package travel. The European legislator left this issue to the Member States. Certain guidelines however were given (Art 5(2)):

(i)   in the matter of damages other than personal injury, Member States may allow compensation to be limited under the contract;
(ii)   but such limitation shall not be "unreasonable" (whatever that may be);
(iii)   the Member States may allow limitation of the compensation in accordance with the international conventions governing such services, such as the Warsaw Convention (see para 4.38).

4.   The tour operator and air transport

4.32   A substantial share of holiday travel involves travel by air. The 1960s saw the emergence of charter flights, and in some countries – in particular those within the European Community – this type of transport has really taken off. Briefly, charter contracts are air transport contracts in which a tour operator, either alone or with colleagues, "buys" seats in an aeroplane to a specific destination which is very popular during certain periods. This transport is different from scheduled air transport in that it is not carried out according to a published fixed timetable. KLM flies to Tel Aviv and back seven days a week, whereas Transavia, a charter company, flies once or several times a week, chartered by several tour operators.

Charters specialise for example in tours to Israel – or rather to Eilat, a resort on the Red Sea sandwiched between the desert, Jordan and Egypt. It is possible to take a scheduled flight from Amsterdam, then a Transavia charter plane back from Eilat to Amsterdam.

The cheap economy class ticket for the scheduled flight is almost twice as expensive as the charter ticket. The scheduled plane was a lot more comfortable and roomier. The difference in price can of course be explained by the empty leg which the scheduled airline faces. On a chartered flight the occupancy rate is much higher, because the charter company is much more flexible: it only flies on days and during periods in which the tour operators have assembled enough passengers. Be this as it may, the KLM ticket and the Transavia ticket contained the same conditions of transport, which were an indication to me that I had entered into an air transport contract with the company concerned. The heading already makes this clear: *"Conditions of contract"* – that is, in an agreement between airline and passenger.

The wording of Article 8 of the conditions of contract also confirms
4.33   this:

This ticket is good for carriage for one year from date of issue, except as otherwise provided in this ticket, in carrier's tariffs, conditions of carriage, or related regulations. The fare for carriage hereunder is subject to change prior to commencement of carriage. Carrier may refuse transportation if the applicable fare has not been paid.

When a scheduled flight is involved, the tour operator to a certain extent operates as the carrier's agent. He "sells" a ticket like a normal IATA agent does, making a reservation for a flight. After its mediation the agent "disappears" from the relationship: a contract of carriage, embodied in a ticket, is constituted between the carrier and the passenger.

As already mentioned, the ticket establishes and embodies the right of the *passenger* to be transported by the carrier under the conditions laid down. By issuing the ticket the charter airline has undertaken to carry the passenger. By having the ticket paid through the tour operator the carrier takes the risk that the tour operator will not pay him in time, or rather will not in time pay over the money paid by the passenger for his transport. In the foregoing I have argued that to a certain extent the tour operator should be regarded as the representative of the charter airline – who leaves it to the tour operator to decide which passengers will fill the seats reserved on the plane. Another factor is whether the charter airline issues the ticket in the name of the passenger or, as is commonly done, lets the tour operator print the names of the passengers on blank tickets from his stock. The charter airline is in principle not interested in who it is carrying. On flight X the tour operator has booked some 150 seats for his customers. To comply with a number of formalities the charter only requires a passenger list in time for departure.

In 1981 I had the pleasure of defending a test case on behalf of **4.34** the Guarantee Fund of the Dutch Travel Agents and Tour Operators Association (ANVR) on this subject. The case had been filed due to the insolvency of one of the association's members, a tour operator. Eventually the Supreme Court held that in this specific case there was no duty of carriage.

The Dutch Supreme Court found that the charter contract does not create a contractual obligation between the carrier and the passenger, although he was in the possession of a ticket. The airline was allowed to use the same defences against the passenger as the passenger could use against the airline.

What exactly defines the relationship involving a charter is uncertain. The German Supreme Court,[11] unlike the Dutch Supreme Court, held that the carrier had a duty to carry the passengers involved, even though the tour operator had not fulfilled its obligations arising from the charter contract. Just imagine a situation in which the carrier could invoke

---

[11] Please note that this is a contract *sui generis* – a contract with a unique nature, other than a sale of goods.

towards the passenger what he calls "conditions of carriage", have a tour operator issue a ticket to this passenger and then refuse to carry this passenger because the tour operator, his agent, has defaulted.

This scenario gives rise to an important question for our subject: suppose there is no binding contract between a charter airline and its passenger. What then would be the basis for the applicability of the conditions of carriage the airline seeks to invoke? Doesn't referring to these conditions imply that there is a contractual relation between charter airline and passenger? I should say there is no much doubt about this. Does not the heading "Conditions of contract" speak for itself?

(i) Restriction of liability

4.35 Article 9 of the conditions of contract gives rise to some questions. It reads as follows:

> Carrier undertakes to use its best efforts to carry the passenger and baggage with reasonable dispatch. Times shown in timetables or elsewhere are not guaranteed and form no part of this contract. Carrier may without notice substitute alternate carriers of aircraft, and may alter or omit stopping places shown on the ticket in case of necessity. Schedules are subject to change without notice. Carrier assumes no responsibility for making connections.

Does this article contain an unreasonably onerous restriction of liability? The object of the article, and others like it, is to restrict the liability of the carrier pursuant to Article 23 of the Warsaw Convention. The first question which arises is whether such restrictions conflict with Article 19 in conjunction with Article 23 of the Warsaw Convention. The second question is whether this clause should not be considered unreasonably onerous in view of EC Directive 93/13/EC (OJ 1993 L 95, of 5 April 1993) on Unfair Terms in Consumer Contracts.

Article 3 of this Directive reads as follows:

> 1. A contractual term which has not been individually negotiated shall be regarded as unfair if, contrary to the requirement of good faith, it causes a significant imbalance in the parties' rights and obligations rising under the contract, to the detriment of the consumer.
> 2. A term shall always be regarded as not individually negotiated where it has been drafted in advance and the consumer has therefore not been able to influence the substance of the term, particularly in the context of a pre-formulated standard contract.
>   The fact that certain aspects of a term or one specific term have been individually negotiated shall not exclude the application of this Article to the rest of a contract if an overall assessment of the contract indicates that it is nevertheless a pre-formulated standard contract.
>   Where any seller or supplier claims that a standard term has been indi-

vidually negotiated, the burden of proof in this respect shall be incumbent on him.

3. The Annex shall contain an indicative and non-exhaustive list of the terms which may be regarded as unfair.

It seems to me that this clause is in conflict with the provisions contained in B and K of the list of the terms which might be unfair, and by that null and void or annullable by the court.   **4.36**

It could also be in violation of Article 19 of the Warsaw Convention, by which the carrier is liable for damage arising from the delay in the air transport of travellers, luggage or goods. I will not go into the fact that by virtue of Article 20 the carrier may avoid liability if he can prove that he and his subordinates have taken every precaution to avoid the damage, or that they were not in a position to take such precautions.

(ii)   The tour operator

Regardless of the type of air transport the tour operator is naturally always involved as a party. Before the Directive on package travel one could argue that the tour operator only acted as an agent for the airline. He was the one who put the package together, but the carrier was responsible for the carriage, luggage etc.   **4.37**

(a)   The Directive on package tours and the Warsaw Convention

Article 5(2) of the Directive establishes the liability of the organiser of a package tour for damages arising from the non-performance or improper performance of the *services involved in the package*. The Member States *may allow such compensation to be limited in accordance with the international conventions governing such services*. Here the Warsaw Convention comes into the picture.   **4.38**

The first question which arises is whether the respective Member States allow and incorporate this defence in their legislation. The Dutch legislator did so. The others should do so too, in order to exclude unacceptable discrepancies between the liability of the airline on the one hand and the tour operator on the other. It would not be reasonable to charge the tour *organiser* with a liability which the signatories to the Warsaw Convention found to be unreasonable *vis-à-vis* the carrier, taking into account the risks and difficulties of carriage by air.

The next question is what the position of the tour operator would be who operates in a country which has not adopted the Warsaw defences in its legislation. The answer may be surprising. In my opinion the limitations of the Warsaw Convention still apply. Why?

The tour operator is the *contractual carrier*, to be distinguished from the actual carrier, but nevertheless the carrier under the Warsaw Convention. A *charter* is nothing but the lease of an aircraft or a part of it, or the lease of x seats with a crew provided by the owner.   **4.39**

The carrier who performs the service of carriage contracted for between an inclusive tour operator and his clients is the servant or agent or auxiliary of the tour operator.[12]

In the relation with the traveller the tour operator is the contracting carrier. In the meaning of the Convention the carrier is, first of all, the person who has "entered into a contract for carriage in his own name and has undertaken to execute his duties thereunder"! Whether or not the person operates an air transport undertaking is, as far as I can see, irrelevant.

The principal duty of the carrier is to ensure that the carriage is performed at the agreed date and hour, but he is not obliged to perform it himself. He can in fact arrange to have it performed by another person or undertaking ("actual" or substitute carrier), but he remains responsible for its performance.

4.40 The passengers have, as a part of the package, concluded a contract of carriage with the tour operator, so the tour operator is the *contractual* carrier responsible under the provisions of the Warsaw Convention, and can invoke the defences of the Warsaw Convention. That is why I am inclined to conclude that he does not necessarily need his national legislator to implement the EC Directive.

Still it is better for him to be provided with those defences in the national law. The provisions of the Warsaw Convention, except as otherwise provided, are mandatory (Art 32). This means in the first place that clauses in (general) conditions of carriage which infringe the rules of the Convention will be null and void.

In the second place it is a treaty, so it is also mandatory for the national legislator. If for instance the Greek legislator does not implement the Warsaw Convention defence for the tour operator, an interesting matter arises: the battle between, on the one hand the EC Directive, which explicitly allows the Member State *not* to grant the tour operator the application of the Warsaw Convention; and on the other hand the Warsaw Convention, which applies automatically because the tour operator should be considered as an air carrier.

4.41 The liability of air carriers in cases of negligence is basically governed by what is called in the Warsaw Convention "other instruments", including the 1955 Hague Protocol and the 1961 Guadalajara Convention. The Guatamala City Protocol and the four protocols signed in Montreal in 1975 are not yet in force, because an insufficient number of countries have ratified these instruments. In 1996 a "voluntary" agreement between airlines to include certain conditions in a contract of carriage is to be concluded, called "The Montreal Inter-Carrier Agreement" (MIA).

The Warsaw Convention and other instruments are generally referred

---

[12] This is apparently also the standpoint of the EU legislator, since in the EU Directive on package travel the tour operator is charged with what I usually call a "central liability".

to as the "Warsaw System", which provides for limitations on the liability of airlines. The EC Commission has presented a proposal for a Council Regulation on air carrier liability in cases of air accidents. The goal of this regulation is to improve the position of the travellers. This is quite understandable. The original low limit set by the Warsaw Convention was quite reasonable at a time when the commercial aviation industry was in its infancy. The risk factors were unquantified and therefore assessed as rather high. Nowadays the situation is completely different since air travel is considered to be one of the safest modern means of transport. That is why it is more than reasonable to lower the threshold of liability, and it is likely that within five years the liability of air carriers will indeed be enlarged in the favour of travellers.

(b)   The relation between the tour operator and the air carrier

Let us now observe some other aspects of the relation between tour oper-   **4.42**
ators and air carriers. Basically, the same provisions of liability (should) apply for both the tour operator and the carrier: they are both "carriers" in the sense of the Warsaw and Guadalajara Conventions (though the question remains how this will work out in practice).

However, the charter contract and the general conditions of carriage provide a framework in which the carrier lays down a great many provisions – some of which are covered by the Warsaw System, some of which are not.

The principle of freedom of contract allows the parties concerned to do exactly this – and Article 32 of the Warsaw Convention specifically allows the carrier to do so – in so far as his conditions do not infringe the rules laid down in the Treaty.

The internationally applied Charter Agreement, also used by the Dutch charter airlines, contains a standard liability clause, Article 9:

> Unless expressly otherwise agreed in this charter agreement ... (the charter carrier) its officers, employees and agents ... shall never be subject to any other and/or higher liability than provided for in the Convention of Warsaw as amended in ...
>
> Charterer shall indemnify ... (the carrier) its officers ... etc. ... against all consequences if arising from the carriage, ... (carrier) is being charged with any other and for higher liability as mentioned above.

Thus the carrier limits his liability towards the tour operator to his   **4.43**
Warsaw liabilities, not accepting any liability beyond that. This may look reasonable, but in the circumstances, it is not. There is no problem when the tour operator is charged with a claim covered by the Warsaw Treaty. Then the tour operator invokes the limitations. But as far as I can see there are two categories of case in which there will be a discrepancy between his responsibilities, and those of the tour operator as the contracting carrier.

1 WHERE THE WARSAW CONVENTION DOES NOT APPLY

4.44 (i)   The Warsaw Convention does not apply when there is no "international air transport" within the meaning of the Treaty. That is:
– when the transport is not international; or
– when there is no transport (e.g. where boarding is denied due to overbooking).

(ii)   It is held that some sorts of delay cannot be considered to be delay in the meaning of Article 19 (delay in the transportation by air of passengers, baggage and goods). If the delay results in the passenger or baggage remaining on the ground instead of leaving on the agreed flight, this is not a delay but breach of contract or non-performance of the contract, which is not covered by the provisions of the Convention. Consequently the restrictions of liability set out in the Convention *do not apply*.

(iii) Those limits can also be avoided when the carrier cannot invoke the application of the Convention because he did not meet the formal requirements for application, such as:
– the issue of a ticket (Art 3);
– the issue of a proper baggage check (Art 9);

If, for instance, a stewardess takes a piece of hand-luggage into storage during the flight without delivering the baggage check required by Article 4 of the Warsaw Convention, and the contents of the bag get lost, that Article will not be applicable.

2 APPLICATION OF ARTICLE 25

4.45 The second category covers the cases in which in principle the Convention applies, but the limitations cannot be invoked due to the application of Article 25.

This Article prevents the carrier availing himself of the limits of liability specified in Article 2 if it is proved that:

> the damage resulted from an act or omission of the carrier, his servants or agents, done with the intent to cause damage, or recklessly and with knowledge that damage would probably result

Briefly, the plaintiff (passenger) must prove that there has been wilful misconduct or gross negligence: for instance that the pilot was drunk or took unacceptable risks.

To return to our discussion of the tour operator. We have seen that the tour operator can be sued under the provisions of the EC Directive – or more correctly, under provisions of the national law on the travel contract implemented according to the EC Directive. With respect to air transport, the traveller will base his claim on the system of Article 5(2) of the Directive on Package Tours, that is on the "purchase" of a package.

When there is no package but a business trip or simply transport, the **4.46** traveller in most EC countries has no specific protection, but must rely on common contract rules. Still it can be argued that he is entitled to safe transport, performed according to what was promised in the timetable and/or ticket.

The charter carrier will however invoke the limitation of his liability set out in the aforementioned Article 9. His liability is restricted to the Warsaw liability, which means that he cannot be held liable for the over-booking. Thus the tour operator has no recourse – if the limitation of Article 9 is valid, which as I mentioned in para 4.35, I doubt.

In the case of a package tour the tour operator encounters two specific problems. First of all the consumer enjoys the unfair contract law protection. Secondly he is protected by the regime of the EC Directive. The tour operator cannot therefore restrict his liability as far as he would like to – and as far as he should try to, considering his charter contract. He should incorporate in his general travel conditions the same limitations as the carrier has laid down in the charter contract, but that would be null and void, since the national law prohibits him from doing so as a consequence of the Package Travel Directive.

The Unfair Contract law will also apply to the relation between the airline and passenger.

This leads to the following observations. As far as a charter is involved, **4.47** the passenger will receive the ticket (with its provisions) not at the time the contract was concluded, but later – it is usually delivered to the passenger only one or two weeks before the date of travel. Consequently (e.g. according to the German and Dutch law relating to the application of contract terms), the conditions of carriage may not be applicable. They must have been separately agreed upon.

A solution may be to incorporate those conditions in the travel contract. Tour operators will presumably not be eager to do this: why should they help the carriers who in turn rely on such rigid provisions as Article 9? For the tour operators the principal means of protecting themselves is to establish a well-balanced charter contract with the airline.

Besides the conditions of air transport there are a great many general conditions used by other suppliers, which should also be incorporated into the travel contract: hotel conditions, car rental conditions, ferry boat conditions, railway carriage conditions, conditions concerning bus transport by coach etc. etc. The tour operator already has problems incorporating its own proper and valid conditions, and making them acceptable for the clients and/or consumer organisations. This will not be easier when, on the basis of the EC Directive on Unfair Contract Terms, the legislations of all the Member States will provide protective regulations against onerous or unfair contract terms.

Finally, the tour operator who sells through travel agents will need their cooperation regarding the use of general conditions, because the contract will then be concluded through the agent.

(c) Denied boarding

4.48 Reference should be made to the aforementioned EC regulation on denied boarding concerning scheduled flights. Article 5(1) provides that the carrier is obliged to compensate the tour operator in case of a package tour. The regulation provides for a minimum compensation of:
- ECU 150 for flights up to 3500 km;
- ECU 300 for flights of more than 3500 km.

According to Article 3 the carrier must set down the rules which it will follow in the event of overbooking of a flight. Many airlines have as yet failed to do so.

DENIED BOARDING: APPLICATION OF THE FORGOING

4.49 A businessman asks the tour operator to arrange an incentive trip for the whole company. The return flight was scheduled for arrival at 22.30 hours, on Sunday night. No seats were available on that flight due to overbooking.

The businessman and his entire personnel arrive on Monday, at 12.30 hours. He makes a huge claim because of loss of profit.

The tour operator cannot plead the limitations of the Conventions, for we saw that overbooking is not "delay", but a non-performance/breach of contract. The tour operator encounters two more problems. First, under the regime of the EC Directive overbooking is no longer *force majeure*. Moreover, beyond the scope of the Directive, in most EC countries it will be held that the tour operator is responsible for the faults of his auxiliary.

The second problem the tour operator faces is the limitation of the carrier's liability set out in the charter contract and/or conditions of carriage – issued by IATA for instance.

4.50 The tour operator is fully liable for the damages and will seek for recourse from the airline. To do so he needs to have "bought" the seats without the restriction that the airline is only liable as far as the Warsaw Convention charges him.

The same applies when wilful misconduct or gross negligence on the part of the airline is alleged – for instance in the case of the drunken pilot who was the best client of the tax free shop on board. In these cases the Warsaw limitations will not apply (Art 25): the airline will refer to the clause in which it has restricted its liability to what Warsaw prescribes.

5. Package travel

4.51 The liability of the tour operator ("retailer" or "travel agent" if so opted for by the legislature) is defined rather clearly when it comes to "real" package tours within the meaning of the EC Directive on "package" or "inclusive" tours. Following the example of the German Reiseveranstalter who was placed under a statutory liability as early as the 1970s, the introduction of this Directive has put an end to many years of discussion about the degree to which the tour operator is liable for any defects in the execution of the holiday trip. I will not discuss this Directive in detail as it will be explored further in other chapters.

I do, however, wish to highlight two aspects which are closely related to the introduction of the concepts of tour operator and package travel. (Above I pointed out the importance of appraising on a case-to-case basis whether there is a travel contract within the meaning of the Directive and the regulations based thereon in the country in which the trip is offered.)

(i)   Reflexive action

Firstly there is what I should like to call the reflexive action of European   **4.52**
rules and regulations on package travel. The possibility cannot be ruled out that where there are no specific rules on the liability of tour operators for trips not covered by this EC Directive, the courts will resort to analogous application of the Directive. A word of warning: the European rules on liability for package travel have already caused a revolution by imposing major liability on the tour operator for a great number of things which could go wrong with package travel. This liability is very far-reaching and even extends to defects which are absolutely beyond his control and which he could not have prevented. These defects are attributed to the tour operator owing to policy decision made by the European Community. Although this choice is commendable from the viewpoint of consumer protection, the rules should be applied with great care. For example, a tour operator who designs a trip at the request of a customer should not be equated with a tour operator who in advance plans, buys and offers the package to the public.

(ii)   Recourse

The second aspect relates to the other side of the coin. Even when the   **4.53**
first drafts of the Directive concerned were being discussed, various sides pointed to the lack of remedies open to the tour operator in the event of breach of contract, in particular by local carriers and accommodation providers in countries where it is not so easy to seek redress. During the 1980s I repeatedly pointed out the absurdity of the situation in which mostly small tour operators had no possibility of preventing overbooking. Spain in particular was a notorious example. Hotels sold too many beds and it was left to the tour operators to find accommodation for their customers. Travellers who were not put up in the accommodation they had been promised could only pray that equivalent accommodation would be available. If not, complaints and claims would pour in. Even if the overbooking was known about for weeks in advance, it still proved futile to attempt to order the hotelier – by means of summary proceedings or other local legal action – to make the accommodation purchased available. Where hotels in France, England or Germany were concerned, I would succeed with the help of a local counterpart, but in Spain it was a mission impossible. The same phenomenon occurs in air carriage.

In this context the Convention on Jurisdiction and the Enforcement of Judgments in Civil and Commercial Matters (EEX Convention) is of course relevant, but much water will flow under the bridge before the remedies available in Europe will be at a level high enough to be effective. I regret to say that my experience as counsel for the Guarantee Fund and for tour operators has taught me that there is a big difference between the rules and their enforcement by minor courts in the various holiday destinations in Southern Europe, Asia and South America.

6.   Conclusion

4.54 At the beginning of this chapter I referred to the adventurous character of travel and the central factor that so many different parties are involved in a trip. The basic principle is that a traveller has the right to require his trip to proceed according to his expectations. If it does not, he has the right to expect that the person to whom the failure of his trip is to be attributed will be held liable. Basically, the same applies to a travel contract as to any other agreement, such as a contract of sale or a contract for services – to which the travel contract is somewhat similar.

I incline to the conclusion that this construction will frequently lead to inequity, when the bona fides of the parties are taken into consideration or when individual cases are construed according to unfair contract terms law.

The New GATT: Implications for the travel and tourism industry

Chapter 5

The New GATT: Implications for the Travel and Tourism Industry*

Dr Mario A Kakabadse
Counsellor
WTO

1.   Introduction

The General Agreement on Trade in Services (GATS), which was estab-   **5.1**
lished as a result of the Uruguay Round, provides for the first time a set
of multilateral rules for the conduct of services trade and simultaneously
creates a framework for a continuing process of liberalisation. Suppliers
of travel and tourism-related services from all participating countries,
both developed and developing, can expect to benefit directly from the
new services agreement and the trade liberalisation achieved in the
Uruguay Round.

2.   Results of the Uruguay Round: from GATT to WTO

The Marrakesh ministerial meeting which took place in April 1994   **5.2**
marked the conclusion of the world's most comprehensive treaty to liberalise international trade. Ministers from 110 countries and from the
European Union formally brought to an end seven and a half years of
complex trade negotiations – the Uruguay Round – when they put their
names to the Treaty. The Uruguay Round has not just been about lowering trade barriers and opening markets around the world. It has in fact
been about completely overhauling the GATT trading system.

  The Round has extended the rule of law to cover virtually every aspect
of world trade both now and in the future. In addition to improving existing disciplines in goods trade and reinforcing the dispute settlement
mechanism to make it speedier and more efficient, GATT rules will now
apply to the major growth areas of international trade, notably intellectual property and services. Up to now these have been completely outside
the multilateral system, and therefore exposed to arbitrary regulatory

---

* The views expressed in this paper are those of the author and not necessarily of the organisation for which he works.

intervention and as a result, to limits on their growth potential.

5.3 This expanded and strengthened trade system will find permanent institutional expression in the Round's biggest innovation: the creation of the World Trade Organisation. In place of the provisional agreement on which GATT has operated since 1947, the entire world trade system will now function within the institutional structure of a fully-fledged international organisation.

This new institution – which administers a set of comprehensive rules applying to all areas of trade, will provide a forum for continuing negotiations, and act as an effective "fair trade policeman" to settle disputes – is going to play an enhanced role in the international economy by assuring the predictability and stability necessary for the increased levels of growth and investment which will be generated by the successful conclusion of the Uruguay Round.

5.4 In this new policy environment, services – long an afterthought on the trade agenda – move to the front and centre of the trade policy stage. Services means all tradeable services, including telecommunications and data processing, banking and insurance, all types of transport, the broad range of professional and business services, as well as the services produced by the travel and tourism industry.

3. Services in international trade

5.5 If the Uruguay Round had done nothing else at all, to have brought services within the framework of GATT principles, would in itself constitute the most important development in the system since 1948. It is no exaggeration to say that the services agreement could bring trillions of dollars of business under comprehensive multilateral trade rules involving the participation of some 120 member countries, with more to follow.

International trade is increasingly services trade, the United States having the largest share of such trade, followed by France, Germany, Italy, the United Kingdom, and Japan. In 1992 these six countries accounted for 50% of total world trade in commercial services, which currently amounts to one trillion dollars or 20 % of total world trade. The largest category of commerical services consists of international tourism receipts, covering both purchases of services and goods by tourists and passenger fare receipts, and accounts for more than one-third of total services trade. The GATS will apply multilateral rules for the first time to such international service transactions.

5.6 One problem in assessing trade flows in services is that the volume of such trade is seriously underestimated: government statisticians acknowledge gross under-reporting of services exports, in some areas perhaps by as much as 50%. One reason is that official balance-of-payments statistics have had difficulty in keeping pace with developments in communications technology, which have spawned a wide range of tradeable services as well as the means of delivering them.

The GATS also establishes rules for the treatment of foreign service suppliers that operate outside their home countries through the establishment of a local presence in a foreign market. On a worldwide basis it is estimated that such sales could amount to at least another one trillion dollars, but they could be considerably more.

4. The General Agreement on Trade in Services

The Uruguay Round was the first time that trade in services has been addressed in the context of multilateral rules, and the establishment of the General Agreement on Trade and Services was one of the Round's key results. It attempts to create a level playing field, or a common set of rules of the game, for services that will contribute to the growth and expansion of the services industries themselves as well as of the world economy that they serve. **5.7**

But the Uruguay Round negotiations in services achieved a great deal more than the establishment of a framework of rules for the liberalisation of cross-border and investment-based trade. There is not only a framework agreement but also commitments by a large number of countries to liberalise and to guarantee access to foreign service suppliers in virtually all service sectors, including travel and tourism, which is a development that nobody thought remotely possible at the start of the Round in 1986.

(i) The structure of the GATS

The GATS consists of a preamble and 29 Articles, followed by eight Annexes, eight Ministerial Decisions and an "Understanding" on financial services. Appended to the GATS as integral parts of the Agreement, are the individual country schedules of liberalisation commitments, and in many cases national lists of exemptions to the most favoured motion (MFN) or non-discrimination principle. **5.8**

(a) Articles of the Agreement

A   PART 1

Part I (Article I) defines the scope of the GATS. It covers a wide range of possibilities for selling all commercially tradeable services in foreign markets, whether supplied cross-border (through electronic transmission), or at home, to foreign customers (*e.g.* tourism); or by a foreign commercial presence (such as in banking); or through the movement of labour into foreign markets (consultancy services, construction projects). **5.9**

B PART II

5.10 Part II sets out general obligations and disciplines. Article II guarantees most-favoured-nation treatment among all Members, although specific exemptions of a limited duration are provided for. Transparency requirements in Article III include publication of all relevant laws and regulations. Article IV contains provisions to facilitate the increasing participation of developing countries in world services trade through the negotiation of market opening commitments. The provisions covering economic integration in Article V are analogous to those in Article XXIV of GATT, requiring *inter alia*, arrangements to have substantial sectoral coverage.

Since domestic regulations and not border measures, have the most significant influence on services trade, Article VI mainly provides for assuring the fair and objective administration of laws and regulations affecting trade in services. Article VII facilitates market access by providing for the recognition of foreign qualifications and standards and by encouraging the adoption of international standards where feasible. Article VIII states that Members are required to ensure that monopolies and exclusive service providers do not abuse their position and Article IX stipulates that restrictive business practices should be subject to consultations between Members with a view to their elimination.

5.11 Under Article XI Members are obliged, as a general rule, not to restrict transfers and payments for current transactions relating to negotiated commitments. As in the GATT, Article XII permits the imposition of trade restrictions, subject to certain conditions, in the event of balance-of-payments difficulties. The GATS contains both general and security exceptions in Article XIV which permit Members to take measures, *inter alia*, to protect the consumer and prevent fraudulent practices. The Agreement leaves to future negotiations the development of disciplines on emergency safeguards, government procurement and trade-distorting subsidies (Articles X, XIII and XV).

C PART III

5.12 The Part III provisions contained in Articles XVI, XVII and XVIII are the heart of the Agreement. The extent to which service markets will be opened up to foreign competition is determined by the kind of market access and national treatment commitments that countries negotiate and inscribe in their national schedules. The intention of the market access provision is to eliminate progressively a number of mainly quantitative restrictions. The national treatment provision contains the obligation not to discriminate against foreign service suppliers.

D PARTS IV, V AND VI

5.13 Part IV establishes the basis, in Articles XIX and XX, for progressive liberalisation in the services area through successive rounds of negotiations and the development of national schedules of commitments. Article XXI also permits Members to withdraw or modify scheduled commitments after a period of three years on the basis of compensation for affected parties. Part V of the Agreement contains institutional provisions relating to consultation and dispute settlement (Articles XXII and XXIII), the establishment of a Council on services (Article XXIV) and other technical matters (Articles XXV and XXVI). The final provisions in Part VI (Articles XXVII–XXIX) cover denial of benefits, definitions and Annexes.

(b)   Annexes

The GATS comprises eight Annexes, four of which merit particular atten-   **5.14** tion. The Annex on the movement of natural persons requires that people providing services under a specific commitment shall be allowed to provide the service in accordance with the terms of that commitment. The Annex on financial services (largely banking and insurance) provides the right for GATS Members to take prudential measures, including for the protection of investors and deposit holders and for ensuring the integrity and stability of the financial system. The Annex on telecommunications requires that access to, and use of, public telecommunications services and networks should be accorded to another Member on reasonable and non-discriminatory terms, in order to enable the supply of a service included in its schedule. The Annex on air transport services excludes from the agreement's coverage traffic rights and directly related activities. However, it states that the GATS does apply to aircraft repair and maintenance services, marketing, and computer reservation services.

(ii)   How the GATS is designed to work

The GATS is the first multilateral, legally enforceable agreement which   **5.15** covers trade and investment in services. Its basic aim is like that of the GATT for goods: to expand world trade by liberalising markets and to put that liberalisation process on a secure basis. The guiding principles for this are familiar from GATT experience.

(i)   There should be *trade without discrimination,* meaning that all Member countries conduct their trade on a basis of equality and all share in the benefits of any moves towards lower trade barriers.

(ii)   *Protection should be transparent:* the GATT for goods urges that tariffs should only be used where domestic protection is necessary and the GATS requires that barriers to market access and discriminatory restrictions on operation in foreign markets are clearly identified and catalogued.

(iii)   *A stable basis for the progressive liberalisation of trade* is ensured through parties undertaking to respect the reduced levels of protection that have been negotiated: in GATT jargon this is referred to as ''tariff binding" and in the GATS as "binding the level of market access and national treatment". The idea is the same – to make the process of barrier reduction irreversible.

5.16   The keys to achieving effective liberalisation in any service sector are contained in the provisions on market access and national treatment. Reducing and eliminating barriers to market access and national treatment around the world have long been the principal objectives of the travel and tourism industry, and they are now built into the GATS. When fully implemented and respected in practice by the Member countries, the market access and national treatment provisions guarantee that suppliers of all kinds of travel and tourism services will enjoy two kinds of commercial freedom: first, the freedom of access to the markets of other GATS parties, subject only to fair authorisation provisions; and, in addition, the associated freedom necessary to establish the types of business operations appropriate to the services they provide; second, the freedom from discriminatory regulation, and other unfair trade-distorting treatment by government authorities, which will guarantee that suppliers of tourism services will be treated in the same manner as their foreign competition (except in cases where foreign countries have reserved the right to discriminate).

5.17   The liberalisation objective of the GATS applies to regulatory measures (including laws, regulations or rules) of Member countries which restrict the ability of foreign suppliers to gain access and operate without discrimination in a market. The rules of the GATS, together with the specific market-opening negotiations that have taken place under those rules, seek to expand trade between parties to the agreement by liberalising the specific ways of supplying services internationally. The primary concern of the GATS is therefore to open up and then guarantee market opportunities for the different ways of supplying services as follows:

(a)   Cross-border trade

5.18   The idea is to permit service suppliers of one Member country to deliver services from abroad into the territory of another Member country. Tour operators or travel agents typically provide a range of services, such as travel arrangements and booking or travel advice, cross-border by means of a telecommunications network. Specific provisions in the services agreement will facilitate the transborder flow of information by guaranteeing the foreign supplier fair and non-discriminatory access to, and use of, telecommunications networks.

(b)   Consumption abroad

5.19   This mode of supply is concerned with the freedom of a Member's residents to purchase services in the territory of another Member.

(c)   Services supplied through a commercial presence

The GATS gives service suppliers the opportunity to establish and   **5.20**
expand a commercial presence in the territory of another Member country in order to produce and sell services. By covering all legal forms in
which a service supplier may be present in a market, including through a
branch, agency, subsidiary or joint venture arrangement, the agreement
takes into account that there is often a need in services trade for the
establishment of an infrastructure in the importing country. In the
tourism sector some form of commercial presence for say, travel agents
and tour operators, is often essential in order to market services on a
significant scale in the country where the commercial presence is situated. The GATS agreement is designed to identify and then progressively
eliminate obstacles which affect companies providing services to facilitate
travel; some obvious obstacles being limitations on foreign investment/
equity participation, restrictions on the establishment of foreign-owned
entities including local equity requirements, unreasonable difficulties in
obtaining licences, (for example to operate as a travel agent), or discriminatory restrictions on access to reservations systems. Moreover the GATS
will curb government restrictions on the transfer of funds into and out of
the country concerned.

(d)   Movement of personnel

GATS rules not only cover cross-border and investment-based trade but   **5.21**
also possibilities for the entry and temporary stay in foreign markets of
individual service suppliers (or "natural persons" as they are defined
under the Agreement). In common with many other services, the successful provision of tourism services depends to a large extent on the applied
knowledge, expertise and technical skills of company owners and employees. The ability to move key personnel – be they managers of a travel
agency or technical specialists in a hotel – into foreign markets in order
to provide a service is an essential component of business strategy for all
kinds of tourism-related enterprises with international operations. The
reality around the world, however, is that nearly every country has visa,
residence and work permit restrictions which can impede or delay the
movement of professional, managerial, technical and other personnel to
the country locations where they are needed.

The GATS agreement will benefit tourism service businesses by pro-   **5.22**
viding a framework for negotiating the temporary entry and stay of (both
skilled and unskilled) services personnel into the territory of other Member countries for the specific purpose of providing services. In this
respect, it should be emphasised that the GATS does not in any way prevent state authorities from controlling, for security, health or economic
reasons, the admission and stay of foreigners in general and foreign
workers in particular. Liberalisation negotiations under the GATS are

not about the free movement of labour across borders, and so do not require any changes in national immigration laws.

(iii) Benefits of the GATS

5.23 It is clear the services agreement focuses primarily on the reduction and eventual elimination of restrictions which affect the international supply of virtually all commercially tradeable services. In the travel sector it will thus mainly be of benefit to the wide range of entities which supply tourism-related services, be they companies providing services to facilitate travel; those providing transportation; or hotels, resorts, or car hire firms which supply reception facilities.

Beyond its liberalisation provisions, the GATS will reduce uncertainty for service suppliers by guaranteeing that business conditions and the "rules of the game" are made transparent, so that service suppliers have access to relevant government rules, legislation and decrees affecting the industry. Since domestic regulations, not border measures, have the most significant influence on services trade, the GATS provides for the assurance of fair and objective administration of law and regulations affecting trade in services. The agreement also facilitates market access by providing for the recognition of foreign qualifications and standards and by encouraging the adoption of international standards where feasible. The dispute settlement procedures under the World Trade Organisation will for the first time provide an international mechanism for resolving services trade disputes between governments that affect the services sector, including the travel and tourism industry.

5.24 In effect, the GATS establishes non-discrimination as the predominant and enforceable international standard by which regulatory treatment of foreign services and service suppliers is to be judged. Given the Agreement's (soon to be) global coverage in terms of country participation and its application to *all* services sectors, this amounts to an historic trade policy accomplishment. Before the GATS, international trade rules for services had very limited recognition and there was no legal basis for binding sovereign governments to respect and abide by them.

(iv) The GATS and the consumer of tourism services

5.25 Although the GATS is primarily concerned with the supply of services, it also recognises the fact that trade in services takes place when consumers move abroad to purchase services, the best known example being tourism itself. The growth and development of international tourism may be considerably affected by any restrictions on the ability of the individual tourist: (a) to leave his country of origin, complete his visit and return home; and (b) to obtain the means of payment for the tourism services purchased abroad. The GATS Agreement is likely to have only an indirect effect on the liberalisation of such restrictions. This is because restrictions relating to visa and other frontier/customs requirements for entry and exit fall outside the scope of the Agreement, which applies only to measures affecting the supply of a service. Furthermore, under the GATS, foreign exchange restrictions are not negotiable as trade barriers but are subject to the general disciplines of GATS Article XII ("Restrictions to Safeguard Balance of Payments"), which provides for separate procedures for such measures.

However, in terms of the protection of the consumer in the tourism and other services areas, GATS Member governments are not prevented by their GATS obligations from taking the necessary measures (provided that these do not discriminate arbitrarily nor constitute a disguised trade restriction), *inter alia,* to protect public morals and human life or health; ensure consumer safety; and prevent deceptive or fraudulent practices or deal with the effects of defaults on services contracts. 5.26

5. Liberalisation of tourism services in the Uruguay Round: the schedules of commitments

(i) The nature of schedules

The travel and tourism industry in many countries has long supported the idea of a services agreement which is effective in terms of opening up new trade and investment opportunities, eliminating distortive practices that restrict competition, and guaranteeing long-term stability in market access and regulatory fairness. The answer as to how effective the negotiations have been lies in each participating country's schedule of legally binding liberalisation commitments. These schedules are complex documents in which each country identifies the service sectors to which it will apply the market access and national treatment obligations of the GATS, and stipulates any reservations from those obligations that it wishes to maintain. Commitments are entered with respect to each of the four modes of supply which constitute the definition of trade in services in Article I of the GATS (as explained above); these are: cross-border trade, consumption abroad, trade via a commercial presence and movement of personnel. 5.27

When making a commitment, say in the tourism sector, a government binds or "freezes" the specified level of market access and national treatment, and undertakes not to impose any new measures that would restrict entry into or operation in the market. Commitments are therefore a guarantee to economic operators in other countries that market conditions will not be changed to their disadvantage. Commitments can only be withdrawn or modified following agreement of compensatory adjustments with affected countries and no withdrawals or modifications may be made until three years after entry into force of the Agreement. Commitments can, however, be added to or improved at any time. 5.28

(ii) Results in tourism services

5.29   As a result of the Uruguay Round, 95 country schedules of commitments have been submitted, the great majority of them including legally binding commitments in several tourism and travel-related activities. The main sub-sectors covered relate to "core" tourism services provided by hotels and restaurants, travel agencies and tour operators, tourist guides, convention organisers, marina operators, tourism training enterprises, and tourism transport companies (*e.g.* sightseeing buses, car and boat rentals) and suppliers of recreational, entertainment and sporting services.

To the extent that markets are already liberal, these commitments will ensure that they remain liberal. Where discrimination and market access restrictions still exist, they have been identified and catalogued and will be subject to liberalisation in future negotiations. This outcome, whereby the ultimate goal of open markets around the world is to be reached progressively, has been portrayed by some as disappointing. But it is as unrealistic to expect wholesale global liberalisation to be achieved overnight in services trade as it would have been in goods trade when the GATT was founded.

5.30   Liberalisation of air transport, which plays a pivotal role in moving the bulk of international tourists and thereby promoting many travel destinations and travel distribution networks, has been limited because the GATS specifically excludes traffic rights and the supply of services directly related to the exercise of traffic rights. When the GATS enters into force it will apply to only three air transport "business activities": aircraft repair and maintenance services, selling and marketing of air transport services and computer reservation system (CRS) services, a number of countries having undertaken liberalisation commitments in these areas in the Uruguay Round.

6.   Future outlook

5.31   The Uruguay Round package, including the GATS, which was concluded in December 1993, and signed by Ministers in Marrakesh in April 1994, entered into force on 1 January 1995. Out of a potential membership of 152 countries and territories, 76 governments became Members of the WTO on its first day, with some 50 other governments at various stages of completing their domestic ratification procedures, and the others engaged in negotiating their terms of entry.

While liberalisation of services trade was not fully achieved in the Uruguay Round, it is likely that this will come reasonably quickly in the years ahead, as more countries become familiar with what was only recently considered to be an alien subject. Rapid developments in communications will see to that, as will the accelerating growth of trade in services. The Uruguay Round Services Agreement and the initial set of liberalisation commitments constitute a major step down the road of dismantling restrictions which hamper trade in services, and provide a sound basis on which to build future commitments. It should be remembered, however, that underpinning the entire services package – the rules and the market access commitments – is the clearly recognised right of every country to regulate its own national services sectors in order to ensure the quality of the service and the competence of the service provider.

Part II

Travel Law in the Member States

Belgium

Chapter 6

Belgium

Cedric Guyot
Derk, Star Busmann, Hanotiau

1. Regulatory authorities

(i) General

The Belgian Constitution has been substantially modified in order to **6.1**
create a federation of regional communities.[1] Tourism is no longer
regulated at a national level, at least so far as concerns cultural aspects,
the economic consequences and the exploitation and construction
authorisations.

However, matters relating to travel contracts remain under the authority of national legislation.

It has to be admitted that the current situation is not perfectly clear for
tourism professionals and especially for new investors, who have to consult various local, regional or state administrative authorities before being
able to operate.

(ii) Licences

Any person seeking to establish a travel agency has to apply for a licence **6.2**
to the *Commissariat Général au Tourisme* (which is a national administration),
pursuant to the conditions set forth by the Royal Decree of 30 June 1966.[2]

A person who is seeking to open and operate a hotel in the French-speaking
part of Belgium must obtain a licence from the Administration of the
French Community. The construction of a building for such hotel will require
a building permit issued by the Communal or Provincial Administration.

It is therefore advisable for an operator in the tourism sector to first
prepare all administrative steps and relevant documentation before starting an investment.

(iii) Travel organisations

The national representative organisations in Belgium are the ABTO **6.3**
(*Association Belge des Tours Opérateurs*) and the UPAV (*Union Professionnelle*

---

[1] Modification of the Constitution on 8 August 1980, *Official Journal* of 15 August 1980, special
law of 8 August 1988.
[2] Law of 21 April 1965, *Official Journal* of 10 June 1965 and Royal Decree of 30 June 1966,
Official Journal of 27 July 1966.

des Agences de Voyages). Such organisations have established regional branches in order to take account of the current federalisation trend in Belgium.

The main "operators" in the tourism industry are the travel agencies and the tour operators, in view of the fact that they are the source of clients for any other operator, such as hotels, vacation resorts, carriers, rent-a-car companies, or others. This Chapter focuses on the new Belgian legislation governing organised travel contracts and travel agency contracts.[3]

2. Travel contracts

6.4   Belgium was a signatory to an international Treaty on Travel Contracts of 23 April 1970, which was adopted by the Law of 30 March 1973.[4]

However, taking into account the European Directive of 13 June 1990 relating to package travel,[5] the Belgian authorities decided to withdraw from the Treaty on Travel Contracts and to pass new legislation in conformity with the EC Directive. The new legislation was adopted on 16 February 1994[6] and entered into force on 4 October 1994 (hereinafter "the Law").

6.5   The main objective of the Law is to regulate the activities of the tour operators and travel agents in order to:

(i)   prevent claims from tourists;
(ii)   fix the liability of each contractor;
(iii)   offer solutions to the claim, if any; and
(iv)   oversee resolution of the claim out of court, if possible.

The Law makes a clear distinction between organised travel contracts and travel agency contracts. An organised travel contract is: any contract under which a person undertakes in his own name to obtain for another, for a lump sum, at least two of the following three services:

(i)   transport;
(ii)   lodging;

---

[3]   Law of 16 February 1994 governing organised travel contracts and travel agency contracts entered into force on 4 October 1994, published in the *Official Journal* of 1 April 1994.

[4]   Law of 30 March 1973, adopting the international treaty on travel contracts of 23 April 1970, *Official Journal* of 17 May 1973. See, concerning tour operators and travel agencies, (for convenience, the titles have been translated): Van Acht, M, "The liability of tour operators" (RW, 1975) 2305. Libouton, J, "The international treaty of Brussels on Travel contracts of 23 April 1970 (JT, 1973) 121. Wymeersch, E, "The travel contract: a study on a treaty on travel contracts" *Rapport 9° Congrès Académic de Droit Comparé* (1974) 201. André, R, "Liability of Travel Agencies" *Les responsabilités* 466. Verwilghen, M, "The travel contract" *Annales de droit* (1978) 155.

[5]   EEC Directive 90/314 of 13 June 1990 (OJ 1990 L158/59) relating to Package Tour Holidays.

[6]   Law of 16 February 1994 governing organised Travel Contracts and Travel Agency contracts published in the *Official Journal* of 1 April 1994.

(iii)   other tourist services not linked with transport or lodging which are not accessory to the transport and lodging;

in a combination previously organised by the said person and/or by a third party, on condition that the services include an overnight stay or exceed a period of 24 hours.[7]

A travel agency contract is: any contract under which a person under-   **6.6** takes to obtain from another, for payment of a price, either an organised travel contract or one or more isolated services, making it possible to complete any journey or period of stay.

The traveller is defined as any person who benefits from one of the contracts mentioned above, whether the contract has been entered into or the price paid by or for such person.

Three important general issues arise: **6.7**

(i)   The new legislation is applicable to travel agency and organised travel contracts sold or offered for sale in Belgium. This means that, if a travel agent acts as agent for a tour operator or travel organiser which is not established in Belgium, he is considered, *per se*, as the travel organiser in relation to the traveller.[8]

(ii)   Without prejudice to the application of an international treaty for certain services covered by a travel contract, any clause contrary to Belgian law or to the decree on its implementation is invalid, if it limits the rights of the traveller or increases his obligations.

(iii)   Travel agreements are usually multi-party agreements or groups of contracts. The Law creates a presumption of liability on the travel organiser or agency towards the traveller. If problems occur, it is up to the travel organiser or agency to claim against third parties, such as carrier, hotels, etc. Moreover, during the travel itself, the traveller also concludes agreements with various third parties by signing hotel bills, invoices, tickets, etc. The legal issues relating to travel may involve various agreements or legislations, unless the travel is a full package concluded with and paid at once to a travel organiser.

Finally, tourism law is also regulated by various other areas of legisla-   **6.8** tion which have to be taken into account, such as transport law, the Fair Trade and Practice Act, construction law, labour law and the indirect and direct taxation rules.

Furthermore, legislation does exist in Belgium concerning the access to certain commercial activities, by which the applicant has to demonstrate his ability to exercise such activities (certificates, studies, previous experience, etc).

---

[7] The separate invoicing of different parts of a single lump sum does not release the travel organiser or travel agency from the obligations of this law (art 1, 1°, al 2 of the Law).

[8] Art 2, § 2 of the Law.

3. Information and advertising

(i) General

6.9 The Law sets forth various obligations and duties regarding the conditions of travel promotion. The objective of the legislation in this respect is to make sure that the traveller receives fair and objective information and description about the journey or period of stay.

The description of the services offered to the traveller, their price and all other conditions applicable must not contain any misleading information.[9]

(ii) The brochure

6.10 All brochures made available to the traveller, must state clearly, legibly, accurately and unambiguously the price, and details such as:

(i)   the destination and description of the itinerary;

(ii)   the characteristics and categories of transport to be used;

(iii)   the type of lodging (situation, category, level of comfort and features);[10]

(iv)   the type and number of meals included;

(v)   general information regarding passport and visa, as well as the health formalities required for the travel and stay;

(vi)   that, for package holidays, a minimum number of people are required for the journey to take place.[11]

The brochure or other documents also have to mention the general conditions offered by the travel organiser or agent, such as:

(i)   the amount or percentage of the price to be paid as a down payment and the schedule for payment of the balance;

(ii)   the usual information regarding subscription of a cancellation and/or assistance insurance.

6.11 Finally, the travel organiser and the travel agent must specify in their promotional documentation, the type of travel and the public for which it is intended.[12]

The information contained in the travel brochure is considered as binding upon the travel organiser or agent who has drawn up the brochure, unless the changes in this information have been clearly notified in writing to the traveller prior to the conclusion of the contract, or

---

[9] Art 4 of the Law. See also, concerning advertisements, the Fair Trade and Practice Act of 14 July 1991, arts 22 to 30.

[10] Moreover, the traveller's attention must be drawn to the difference between this classification and the current legislation in Belgium. Such obligation is considered as going too far by the travel agencies.

[11] In the case of cancellation, the last date when the traveller will be informed shall be communicated in advance to such traveller (art 5, 7° of the Law).

[12] Art 5, 9° of the Law.

unless any modifications have been made pursuant to a written agreement between the parties. Indeed, case law has always confirmed the principle that the traveller has the right to travel under the conditions that could be reasonably expected pursuant to the description made in the promotional documentation.[13]

Such general information described in the brochure or other promotional documents is addressed to the potential traveller and/or customer. The travel agent is also bound by the Fair Trade and Practice Act, which fixes the rules concerning general acceptable practices and different types of sales such as liquidation sale, joint offer of services, promotion, rebate techniques, sales by mail, advertisement, etc.[14] This Act is applicable to any seller of goods and services having a direct contact with the customers. **6.12**

In Belgium, there is currently an important case pending regarding the promotion of travel made by a tour operator using the direct mail technique. Travel agencies are claiming that such a sale technique is against the principles of fair trade and practice in the tourism sector.[15]

(iii)   Pre-contractual obligations

In the first stage, general promotional documentation is dispatched by the travel agency to the customer. **6.13**

In the second stage, the customer, as a prospective traveller, is looking for more precise information by contacting or visiting such travel agency. The law provides that the travel organiser as well as the travel agency have a specific pre-contractual obligation towards that specific potential traveller.

Prior to the conclusion of the travel contract, the travel organiser or agent must notify the traveller in writing of:

(i)   general information regarding passports and visas, as well as health formalities required for the travel and the stay;
(ii)   the contractual conditions applicable to the contract; and
(iii)   information on the subscription and contents of cancellation and/or assistance insurance.

(iv)   Pre-departure information

At the third stage, when the contract is concluded, the travel organiser and/or travel agent are bound to supply to the traveller in writing, at the latest seven days[16] before the departure date, with the following information: **6.14**

---

[13] Comm Brussels, 11 April 1988, *DCCR*, 1990, 138. Comm Liège, 19 January 1989, *Pas*, 1989, III, 73. Comm Liège, 18 June 1986, *JLMB*, 1987, 876.

[14] Fair Trade and Practice Act of 14 July 1991, *Larcier*, T. I, 474, *Official Journal* 29 August 1991.

[15] *Wagons-Lits Travel* v *Federation of travel agencies L'Echo* 16 February 1995, 5.

[16] The period of seven days is not applicable if the contract is concluded only a few days before the departure.

(i)   timetables, stopovers and changeovers as well as the seat to be occupied by the traveller;[17]

(ii)   the name and address (with telephone and fax) of the local representative of the organiser and/or travel agent;[18]

(iii) when children only are involved, information making it possible to establish direct contact with the child or with the person responsible at the place of its stay.

6.15   However, the travel organiser and/or agent may ask information of the traveller regarding his specific requirements. The traveller must supply the travel organiser and/or agent with all useful information which is specifically asked of him.[19]

4.   The travel organiser contract

(i) Formation of the contract

6.16   When the journey is booked, the travel organiser or its local representative, the travel agent, must issue the traveller with an order form (*Bon de Commande*).[20]

The Law provides that the travel organiser contract comes into force as soon as the traveller receives written confirmation of the booking issued by the travel organiser. If the content of the order is different from the confirmation, or if the confirmation is not issued at the latest within 21 days of the signature of the order form, the traveller may assume that the journey has not been booked. He will be entitled to an immediate reimbursement of all amounts already paid.

Some authors have suggested that the travel organiser contract requires a written document, not only as evidence, but as a condition for its existence.[21] However, it can be maintained that the Law does not specifically derogate from the basic principle of the Civil Code, which provides that a contract is formed as soon as there is an agreement (oral or in writing) on the object and on the price.[22]

6.17   It appears from the preparatory work of the Law that legislation is

---

[17] Art 17, 2°, (a) of the Law: even though the indication of the seat is required by Law, it is well known that in case of travel by air, the allocation of the seat shall only be made at the airport after registration.

[18] Where such representatives and organisations do not exist, the traveller must be given a telephone or fax number which would allow him to make contact as quickly as possible with the travel organiser or agent.

[19] Art 8 of the Law.

[20] The content and legal requirements of such order form are specified in the Fair Trade Practice Act of 14 July 1991, art 39.

[21] Van Bellinghen, The current situation of travel contracts, the new travel law in Belgium, report 28 April 1994, 45.

[22] Art 1341 Civil Code, *Larcier*, T. I, 118.

considering the travel organiser contract as a contract to be concluded in two steps: order form, and confirmation.[23]

Nothing would however prohibit the customer and the travel agent from concluding everything at the same time, if technically possible.

(ii) Terms

The travel contract must state at least the following terms and conditions: **6.18**

(i)   name and address of the organiser and/or travel agent;

(ii)   name and address of the institution which warranties the services of the travel organiser and/or travel agent;

(iii)   the traveller's name and address and, if necessary, the beneficiary third party;

(iv)   the place and date of the beginning of and the end of the travel, and, if these cover different staying periods, the various periods and dates;

(v)   the means, characteristics and categories of transport used, the dates, times and places of departure and return;

(vi)   the total price covering all the services provided for in the contract;

(vii) the information regarding any price revision and the exact method of calculation;

(viii) the schedule and methods of payment of the price;

(ix)   any special requirements of which the traveller has informed the travel organiser or agent when booking the travel;

(x)   conditions of termination of the contract;

(xi)   conditions of cancellation of the contract by the traveller and travel organiser/agent;

(xii) the methods and periods in which the traveller must make any claims for default of incorrect execution of the contract;

(xiii) the conditions of cancellation insurance, assistance insurance or any other insurance, as well as the name and address of the insurance company.

The litigation provision will be dealt with below, taking into account **6.19** that a special arbitration system may be agreed upon by the parties.

If relevant to the travel organiser contract concerned, various other details must be included in the contract:

(i)   specification concerning the lodging;

(ii)   types and number of meals;

(iii) description of the itinerary;

(iv)   visits, excursions or other services included in the total price agreed between the parties; and

(v)   any special requirements made by the traveller.

---

[23] Preparatory work of the Law: Doc Parl Senat Session 1991–92, Doc 488/1/2/3; Doc Parl Chamber Session 1992–93, Doc 146/2 and 3.

6.20   When a package tour is organised for a group of travellers, the travel organiser contract must provide for the minimum number of people required for the travel organiser contract to be executed, and the last date for informing the traveller of any cancellation. This deadline for cancellation must not be more than 15 days prior to the departure.[24]

However, if the information provided for is given in full or in part in a programme, in a travel brochure made available to the traveller, or in the order form, it is acceptable that the travel contract merely contains a simple reference to such documents. The receipt of the programme or brochure by the traveller must be specifically mentioned in the contract.

Even though a travel organiser contract can be considered as *intuiti personae*, which means specific to the person concerned in the travel, the traveller may transfer his reservation to a third party.[25] The contract is only transferable by *the traveller*, not by the travel agent or by the travel organiser.

(iii)   Variation of the agreement

6.21   The Law provides that any variation from the terms of the brochure or promotional document, not mentioned in the contract, has to be agreed upon by the parties in writing.

If, prior to departure, one of the essential elements of the contract cannot be carried out, the travel organiser must inform the traveller as quickly as possible, before his departure. Moreover, he must inform the traveller of the possibility of cancelling the contract without being penalised. The traveller must then notify his decision to the travel organiser/agent as quickly as possible, but, in any case, prior to departure.

If the traveller accepts the proposed variation, the contract should be modified accordingly. If the traveller does not accept the proposed variation, he has three choices:

(i)   either to accept another offer of an equivalent or a higher quality, without having to pay any supplement; or,

(ii)   to request a reduction of price for a replacement offer of a lower quality; or,

(iii)   to request the reimbursement of all sums already paid by him under the contract.

(iv)   Cancellation or breach of contract

6.22   The traveller may not require any compensation for breach of contract if

---

[24] Art 10, § 2, 3° of the Law.
[25] Art 12 of the Law.

the cancellation made by the travel organiser/agent is the consequence of an "Act of God" (*force majeure*).[26]

If it appears during the travel that a major part of the services covered by the contract cannot be carried out, the travel organiser has the obligation to take all necessary steps to offer to the traveller an appropriate substitute, free of charge, in order to continue the journey. In the case of difference between the services provided for and the services actually provided, the travel organiser must compensate the traveller for this difference.[27]

If such agreements are impossible, or, if the traveller does not accept the substitutes for a valid reason, the travel organiser must supply him with an equivalent means of transport which will bring him back to the departure place and, if necessary, compensate the traveller.

The traveller may cancel all or part of the contract at any time. If the reason for cancellation is caused by him, he shall indemnify the travel organiser/agent for the loss undergone as a result of such cancellation. However, the indemnity may not be more than the price of the travel contract.[28] The legislation imposed a limitation on the indemnity in favour of the traveller. The travel agent or organiser must be paid as if the traveller had been present for the entire journey.   **6.23**

5. The travel agent's contract

In order to avoid any doubt as to the obligation of the respective parties, **6.24** the Law provides that "any contract concluded by the travel agent with a travel organiser or with persons supplying individual services, is considered as having been concluded by the traveller."[29] This Article is ambiguous. However, it should be interpreted as: "any contract concluded by the travel agent in favour of a traveller (. . .)." This means that the travel agent is only considered as an intermediary, and not as the organiser, for the application of the Law. However, in addition to the obligation to provide information (which is the same as for the organiser), the travel agent has a general obligation to advise the traveller.

In some circumstances, the travel agent could also be the travel **6.25** organiser, but, most of the time, the travel agent is offering packages or journeys which are organised by third parties.

Any sale by a travel agent of:

(i)   travel;
(ii)   a service linked with travelling;
(iii) a stay; or
(iv)   other services.

---

[26] Act of God is understood as abnormal and unforeseeable circumstances beyond the control of the party which invokes them, the consequence of which could not be avoided in spite of all due actions taken (*e.g.* flood, hurricane, revolutions, strike, etc).
[27] Art 15 of the Law.
[28] Art 19, § 5 of the Law.
[29] Art 21 of the Law.

must be covered by a written contract, unless it relates solely to transport.

6.26   The travel contract concluded between the travel agent and the traveller must include the following terms and conditions:

(i)   the name and address of the travel agent;

(ii)   the name and address of the institution guaranteeing the travel agent's services;

(iii)   the name and address of the traveller, and, if necessary, of the beneficiary third party or parties;

(iv)   the place and date of beginning and end of the travel and stay, and, if these are covering different staying periods, the various periods and dates;

(v)   the means, characteristics and categories of transport used, the date(s), time(s) and place(s) of departure(s) and return(s);

(vi)   the total price covering all the services provided for in the contract, the method of calculation of any price revision, the schedule and means of payment;

(vii)   any special requirements made by the traveller;

(viii) the conditions of termination of the contract;

(ix)   conditions of cancellation of the contract by the traveller and the travel agent;

(x)   methods and periods in which the traveller must make any claim for breach of contract;

(xi)   conditions of cancellation or assistance insurance and references of the insurance company;

(xii)   other information concerning lodging, meals, itinerary, excursions and other services included in the price;

(xiii) in order not to be considered as a travel organiser, the travel agent must also include in the contract the name and address of the travel organiser and confirmation that he is acting as an intermediary for the travel organiser;[30]

(xiv)   the place and date of signature.

6.27   The other rules concerning cancellation of the contract by either the traveller or the agent are the same as those concerning the travel organiser, *supra*.

The main difference between the two contracts is the scope and application of liability towards the traveller.

6.   Liability of the travel organiser and the travel agent

6.28   The travel organiser is responsible for the proper performance of the contract in accordance with the expectations which the traveller may

---

[30] Art 23, § 3 of the Law.

reasonably have, on the basis of the provisions of the travel organiser contract and the obligations arising from it, independently of the fact that these obligations must be fulfilled by him or by other service providers. This obligation is without prejudice to the travel organiser's right to pursue any other service providers if the latter are responsible for any failure of performance.

Moreover, the travel organiser is also responsible for the actions and negligence of his staff and representatives, acting in the execution of their work, as much as for its own acts and omissions.

The travel organiser is responsible for any damage suffered by the **6.29** traveller due to failure to comply with all or part of his obligations. He is not responsible however, in the following cases:

(i)   where the breach of, or the failure in the peaceful execution of, the contract are imputable to the traveller;

(ii)   where unforeseeable or insurmountable breaches of contract are due to a third party, who is external to the services provided for in the contract;

(iii)   the failure to perform is due to an Act of God;

(iv)   the failure is due to an event, not including overbooking which the travel organiser could neither foresee nor avoid, even with the greatest caution.

If any of these failures occur, the travel organiser is also bound by a duty of care which means that he has the obligation to help and assist the traveller in difficulty. There is a possibility, authorised by the Law, to charge for the costs incurred by the travel organiser in the exercise of his duty of care to the traveller.[31]

Any failure or breach of contract should be notified by the traveller as **6.30** soon as possible, in writing or in any other suitable form, to the providers of the local service concerned. The traveller must in any case confirm his claim by registered mail to the organiser and/or the travel agent, at the latest one month after the end of the journey.[32] A second limitation period is provided by the Law for any court action. Court actions based on travel contracts (except in case of death or injury) must be initiated within a time period of one year.[33] Such a one-year period starts on the date on which the travel should have ended, or has ended pursuant to the travel contract.

The travel agent is also responsible for the proper execution of the **6.31** contract in accordance with the reasonable expectations of the traveller on the basis of the provisions of the travel agent's contract. The travel agent is responsible for any mistake or error made in the execution of his obligations. He could not be held responsible if the breach or failure

---

[31] Art 18, § 2 *in fine* of the Law.
[32] Art 20 of the Law.
[33] Art 30, § 2 of the Law.

was caused by the reasons or events listed above in relation to travel organisers.

The travel organiser and/or agent shall also be bound, in the case of failure to comply with any of his obligations, to grant fair compensation for what is defined by law as the "lack of enjoyment of the journey".[34]

6.32 The travel organiser and/or agent may not exclude his liability for non-physical damage arising from his actions or negligence, intent to cause harm or serious default. If he does not himself supply the services included in the travel contract, the travel organiser and/or agent may limit his responsibility with regard to material damage and compensation for lack of enjoyment of the journey, to double the price of the journey.[35]

If a service covered by the travel contract is subject to the application of an international treaty, the travel organiser may exclude or limit his responsibility in accordance with the international treaty governing these services.

The travel organiser and/or agent may not exclude or limit his liability for damages caused by death or injury of the traveller.

Actions to which a travel contract subject to this law may give rise by reason of death, personal injury, or other harm to the physical or mental health of the traveller, cannot be brought into court after a two-year period: the period of two years starts on the final date of the travel contract which gave rise to the dispute.

6.33 In the case of injury or other harm to physical or mental health causing the death of the traveller after the final date of the travel contract concerned, however, the limitation period commences on the date of the death, but may not exceed three years calculated from the final date of the travel contract.[36]

7.   Forms of redress

6.34 In addition to the normal proceedings before the court, the law provides for specific remedies in the case of infringement or dispute in relation to travel contracts.

The remedies provided by the Law of 14 July 1991 on Fair Trade Practices and Consumer Protection may be applied, which means that a stop order or an injunction can be obtained from the President of the Court

---

[34] Art 19, §§ 4 and 5 of the Law.

[35] Art 19, § 5 of the Law.

[36] Travel agents and/or organisers who are parties to a travel contract must demonstrate that they hold sufficient guarantees to ensure compliance with their obligations to the traveller in the case of insolvency. Moreover, the travel organiser and agent must subscribe to an insurance which should cover their professional liability towards the traveller (Arts 36 and 37 of the Law).

of Commerce if a travel organiser or travel agent does not respect the provisions of the Law.

Some provisions, if not respected, can also lead to criminal sanctions.[37]

Some powers are also granted to the Ministry of Economic Affairs, which is competent to seek and record the infringements to the provisions of the Law. The agents appointed by the Ministry may send the offender a warning notice in order to put an end to an unlawful action.[38] If such a warning is not respected, the Ministry may bring an action in court, or communicate the infringement to the Public Prosecutor. The appointed agent may also settle the matter by imposing an administrative fine.

6.35

The Law also provides for the enforcement by Royal Decree of the general conditions for travel contracts. Such general conditions have been adopted after negotiation between representatives of both consumers and travel organisations.[39] This means that the majority of the brochures or travel promotion documentation contain the same general conditions, even though they are not strictly imposed by a Royal Decree.

Finally, the Belgian Consumer's Association created an arbitration tribunal specifically designed for travel and tourism litigation. The costs are very limited. Such an arbitration tribunal has been authorised, in principle, by the Law of 16 February 1994,[40] but was already previously recognised by the Ministry of Economic Affairs in April 1993.

6.36

The arbitration Commission on travel disputes may resolve disputes, not only when a Belgian operator organises a trip, but also when a foreign operator serves customers through a Belgian intermediary. In the latter case, the intermediary may be brought before the Commission. This results in a very strong position for any consumer in the travel industry of Belgium. However, it is a necessary condition for the application of the Law that the contract be constituted in Belgium.[41]

The model general conditions of the Commission[42] imposed by most operators in Belgium, stipulate, in Article 16, that complaints should be made known as soon as possible, before, during or after the trip. After the trip has ended, the consumer has one month to file a complaint with the travel operator (art 16,3). Article 17 deals with complaints which cannot be solved among parties. Such conflicts are to be brought before

6.37

---

[37] Art 33 of the Law, only fines are applicable: BEF 25,000 to BEF 2 million.

[38] The warning is notified to the offender within three weeks of the infringement by registered letter with acknowledgement of receipt. The warning states:
  (i)   the alleged events and the provisions which have been infringed
  (ii) the period within which this must be terminated
  (iii) the legal consequences if the warning is not respected (art 32 of the Law).

[39] Since the summer of 1993, the main professional organisations relating to Tour Operators and Travel Agents have agreed to adopt these general conditions of contracts, which means that most of the brochures and promotional documentation in Belgium shall include such general conditions.

[40] Art 38 of the Law.

[41] Preparatory Work Senat, 1992–1993, 15 July, 1995, 488–2.

[42] Model of "*vzw geschillencommissie reizen*", J.A. De motstraat 24–26, 1040 Brussels.

the arbitration Commission within four months after the conclusion of the trip.

Physical injury is excluded from the Commission's jurisdiction and should be dealt with by a regular court (art 17,2).

6.38   There is no right of appeal (art 17,3).

The procedural rules of the arbitration Commission are laid down in the "*Règlement des litiges*". Consumers and travel operators are equally represented in the arbitration Commission (art 5 of the Rules). The consumer decides whether the case will be handled in the French or in the Dutch language (art 9 of the Rules).

A final decision must be rendered within a month after the last hearing (art 23 of the Rules).

8.   Financial services

6.39   Travellers in Belgium must pay their hotel, restaurant, visit or other bills or invoices in Belgian Francs. Most hotels will exchange main foreign currencies.

(i)   Credit cards

6.40   All major credit cards are accepted in Belgium by way of direct payment.

Unlike financial institutions in other countries, Belgian banks do not automatically give credit facilities to holders of cards like Visa and Eurocard. Therefore, they cannot be qualified as real "credit" cards.

Banks usually demand sufficient provisional funds to cover the monthly payment accreditation of the holder's bank account. Banks do grant credit facilities to individual bank account holders, to the effect that certain cardholders also obtain credit, including by the use of their Visa, Eurocard, etc.[43]

As to the legal consequences of payment by way of credit card, Belgian scholars are divided: some say payment occurs when the receiver is presented with the right card and signature, whereby the card is charged for a specific sum of money. Others see similarities with money transfers, whereby no payment is made until the bank account of the cardholder is debited.

The courts hold the general view that the different parties involved are independent from each other, and that payments by credit card cannot afterwards be revoked.[44]

6.41   In the case of loss or theft, the responsibility for wrongful use by third persons usually weighs on the cardholder. Contractual clauses however

---

[43] Theus, P, and Peeters, I, "*Lexicon van de kredieten en zekerheden*" (Kluwer, Deurne) 131.
[44] Van Ryn, J and Heenen, J, "*Opérations de bourse et de banque*", 1961–69 (*RCJB*, 1972) 353.

may impose responsibility on the financial institution, *e.g.* where the theft or loss is reported immediately. Unlike cheques, access to credit cards can be easily blocked, which makes them a safer instrument not only for the holder, but also the issuer.

An interesting judgment of 18 January 1987 held that the bank was responsible when a client continued to withdraw money by debiting his previously closed account.[45] Courts consider such situations as technically easy to prevent for any modern bank and that such a bank is therefore responsible for the consequences of its own negligence.

(ii)   Traveller's cheques

Traveller's cheques are cheques provided by the issuing institution   **6.42** against payment, in the customer's own currency, of the cheque's net value and a commissioner's fee. They then entitle the holder to obtain the net value in a (foreign) currency.

Although their legal status is still under discussion in Belgium, traveller's cheques are a generally accepted means of payment. All major banks provide cheques in foreign currency and accompanying services. Cashing-in the cheques may be carried out in all offices of major banks.

(iii)   Cheques

Cheques constitute valid payment independently of the relationship   **6.43** between the holder and the receiver. Stolen cheques or cheques found after loss can thus be used by third persons at the expense of the owner. Responsibility basically lies with the owner of the cheque. However, when the financial institution itself is guilty of gross negligence or fraud, or when cheques are forged after valid acceptance, liability may shift away from the original owner.[46]

Precisely because of this liability, banks advise their clients to keep the bank card separate from the cheques themselves. Banks which fail to warn the user of a cheque of these risks, are liable for pre-contractual negligence. There are attempts by banks to prevent the payment of cheques, drawn after theft or loss, by setting up databases containing lists of "bad cheques", identified by way of their serial number. The double signature system for cashing traveller's cheques provides for greater safety for traveller's cheques than other cheques. However, some financial circles are still very apprehensive about the use of cheques in general, and seek ways to replace them as much as possible by more secure means of payment.

---

[45] Buyle, J, Thunis, X, "*Becommentarieerde rechtspraak in Bank-, and en beursrecht*", 1991 (*TBH*, 1992) 951–1016.
[46] Van Tilborgh, C, "Credit cards, Traveller cheques and Eurocheques", Verz W (1983) afl. 241, 41–47. De Vroede, P, "*De cheque, de postcheque en de reischeque*" (Kluwer, Antwerpen, 1981) 192.

9. Health and safety standards

(i) Accommodation

6.44   In order to protect travellers in Belgium, legislation imposes strict rules for health and safety of accommodation, as well as for transport.

No person or body may provide holiday accommodation in Belgium without an official authorisation. Technical committees have established various ground rules for safety and hygiene. These rules are contained in a Royal Decree of 17 July 1964.[47] The main conditions concern minimum standards for rooms, elevators, lighting, telephone lines etc.

(ii) Transport

6.45   Several regulations have been adopted in Belgium regarding Health and Safety Standards for Bus, Rail, Air and Sea Transport. All these different forms of transport are subject to special licences and certificates. Specialised implementation mechanisms ensure the safety of transportation.

Bus services need an authorisation by an executive body or by the Minister of Communication (depending on the frequency of the service). Such authorisation will only be given after an inquiry into the conditions under which the service operates.[48]

In 1947, a compulsory insurance requirement was imposed on operators of buses in favour of passengers, their baggage and third persons.[49] Quality checks of the vehicle ensure that basic technical requirements are met. The drivers themselves are subject to regular medical tests.

Since 1843, the Belgian railway police is in charge of the safety of railway infrastructure. An 1895 regulation introduced measures to improve the safety of transport by rail, and concerns signs and indications, prohibitions on carrying loaded guns on trains, and also prohibitions on entering a train when affected by a contagious disease etc.[50]

Aeroplane operators are subject to very detailed safety provisions and a great number of security checks are imposed by law. Even in 1937, severe prison and even death sentences were imposed on individuals who, on board an aeroplane, intentionally jeopardised passenger safety.[51]

Commercial exploitation of the airways is regulated by a Ministerial Decree and by multilateral treaties.[52]

6.46   The 1944 Chicago Convention standardises services on the ground and establishes procedures for inquiry into airline accidents, and is applicable

---

[47] Flemish Decree of 29 July 1987 and Decree of the French Community of 24 December 1990, see Bruylant, 506.

[48] Royal Decree of 30 December 1946; see Bruylant, 886.

[49] Regent's Decree of 15 June 1947; see Bruylant, II, 890.

[50] Royal Decree of 4 April 1985; see Bruylant, II, 874.

[51] Law of 27 June 1937; see Bruylant, II, 143.

[52] Ministerial Decree of 6 May 1991; see *Official Journal* of 5 June 1991.

in Belgium.[53] The 1971 Montreal Convention deals with external security threats, and is also applicable in Belgium.[54]

Sea transport is regulated by dozens of different statutes and treaties. Travel operators should be aware of at least some of these rules, especially when they concern health and safety.

Important innovations and modernisations were made in 1972, when a **6.47** new law on the safety of ships was passed.[55] Apart from detailed building prescriptions and rules on maintenance, a certificate of seaworthiness has been created. A Maritime Inspection Service has been established to check the implementation of these norms.

A crucial matter of security is the formation of competent crews. Specific legislation gives detailed requirements concerning the personnel on board.[56] Since 1993, a kind of "driver's licence at sea" was introduced, to be obtained only after the passing of exams.[57]

Once at sea, international treaties regulate signalling, frequencies for radio transmissions, rescue and assistance at rescue, lifeboats etc. Belgium is also a signatory to the important London Convention of 20 October 1972.[58]

10. Rights against transport operators

In general, transport operators are liable for damage to the traveller's **6.48** property or person: almost all such damages constitute a breach of contract. The courts accept that *e.g.* loss of property or injury are contractual shortcomings, since travel operators should ensure that "the passenger arrives safe and sound at the place of destination, with all his luggage, at the foreseen day and hour".[59]

Cancellations are usually covered by insurance, subscribed to by the traveller at the time of reservation, and although the operator is liable for most of the damage, limits on liability (called "ceilings") are usually agreed upon in international treaties, to which Belgium is a party.

The Warsaw Convention of 12 October 1929 limits the liability of airline operators for damage inside the aeroplane during take-off, flight or landing, for delays and damage caused in the process of handling the baggage, and for general delays.[60] Operators can however repudiate their liability by proving that all necessary precautions were taken, or could not be taken due to unexpected or unavoidable circumstances. The

---

[53] Chicago Convention on civil aviation of 30 April 1947.
[54] Montreal Convention of 23 September 1971.
[55] Law of 5 June 1972; see Bruylant, II, 598.
[56] *cfr* n 53.
[57] Royal Decree of 2 June 1993; see *Official Journal* of 25 June 1993.
[58] See Bruylant, II, 600.
[59] In French case law: "*Obligation de résultat*" (Cass of 11 November 1991).
[60] See Bruylant, I, 456.

maximum amount for which the operator is liable is BEF 250,000 per person, BEF 250 per kilo of luggage and BEF 5,000 for handluggage.[61]

6.49   The Berne Convention of 9 May 1980 limits the liability of railway operators for loss of baggage to 40 units per kilo of luggage to a maximum of 600 units per piece.[62] Damage to the baggage must be entirely repaid, as long as it is not more than the fixed maximum for loss of baggage. Delays in delivery are regulated in great detail by the Treaty. Cars, damaged or lost, cannot lead to a liability of more than 6,000 units. Total liability is limited to a maximum of 70,000 units.

The Athens Convention of 13 December 1974 limits the liability of sea transport operators to BEF 700,000 in the case of death or injury, to BEF 12,500 in the case of cabin baggage, to BEF 50,000 for cars, and BEF 18,000 for other baggage.[63]

Bus operators may be charged under the liability clauses of Articles 1382 to 1384 of the Belgian Civil Code. There is no limitation on indemnification.

6.50   Pursuant to general legal principles, there is no liability on the operator when the accident or cancellation happened due to an external cause.

11.   Conclusions

6.51   The fields of tourism and related services are increasingly developing themselves into a specific business for which the legal issues are more and more important. The trend in Belgium, as shown in this new legislation is to protect the traveller on a national basis, as far as the internationalisation of travel creates risks and uncertainties as to the rights and possibilities of action for such traveller.

However, tour operators, travel agents and other travel service partners must not be extensively limited by legislation, otherwise they will lose their competitive capacities. Indeed, the tourism sector is quite active in what is known as "self regulatory rules", such as Codes of Conduct. It will be interesting to see how the courts will apply the new legislation within the next months and years.

---

[61] Art 22 of the Warsaw Convention.
[62] Art 6 of the first appendix of the Bern Convention; see Bruylant, I, 469.
[63] Art 9 of the Athens Convention.

Denmark

Chapter 7

Denmark

Ulrik Andersen
Dragsted & Helmer Nielsen

1. Regulatory bodies

In Denmark the Ministry of Justice is responsible for the implementation **7.1**
of the EC Package Travel Directive. The Directive has been implemented
by way of the Package Travel Act[1] which entered into force on 1 October
1993.

The Package Travel Act applies compulsorily to the sale of "packages",
which are defined as follows:

> The prearranged combination of not fewer than 2 of the following when
> sold or offered for sale at an inclusive price and when the service covers a
> period of more than 24 hours or includes overnight accommodation:
> a) transport;
> b) accommodation;
> c) other tourist services not ancillary to transport or accommodation and
>   accounting for a significant proportion of the package.

The Danish Ministry of Industry administers the Travel Guarantee **7.2**
Foundation Act,[2] which provides for the establishment of an independent institution, the Travel Guarantee Foundation, which, in certain
circumstances, may provide financial help or assistance to "stranded"
consumer travellers in the case of the travel agency's or tour operator's
financial difficulties. According to the Travel Guarantee Foundation Act,
every travel agency and tour operator in Denmark must register with the
Travel Guarantee Foundation in order to sell or arrange holidays. In
addition, a guarantee for DKK 200,000 must be established as security for
amounts which the Foundation has to pay to travellers according to the Act.

The "Forbrugerklagenævn" is a Danish complaint body which may be
used by consumer purchasers of goods or services. A complaint may
relate to any part of the contractual relationship between the commercial
seller of the good or service and the consumer.

The *Forbrugerklagenævn* was set up by way of an Act,[3] and falls under the **7.3**
area of responsibility of the Danish Ministry of Industry.

The consumer complaint body may deal for example, with complaints
from private consumers relating to the provision of public transport

---

[1] Act No. 472 of 30 June 1993
[2] Act No. 104 of 28 February 1986, as subsequently amended.
[3] Act No. 305 of 1974, as subsequently amended.

services. Complaints from consumers relating to goods or services from a private seller may only, generally speaking, be dealt with if the consideration payable by the consumer was between DKK 500 and DKK 20,000. The consumer complaint body may not deal with a complaint if the complaint falls within the area of responsibility of another recognised complaint body for a particular industry. In Denmark, there is a recognised consumer complaint body for the travel industry. That body is known as the *Rejseankenævn*.

7.4   The Danish *Rejseankenævn* is a consumer complaint body which deals with complaints in respect of all holiday or travel arrangements organised or sold in Denmark and involving:

(i)   travelling abroad; or
(ii)   domestic travelling with at least one stay overnight.

The travel complaint body's decisions are binding upon its members, unless the member in question within 30 days after the decision informs the body that it does not intend to be bound by the decision. In that case, the traveller will have to pursue the claim before the national courts.

In practice, however, most organisers and agency members accept the rulings of the *Rejseankenævn*.

This travel complaint body is a very useful and appropriate forum for the determination of disputes between a consumer traveller and an organiser or agent of holiday and travel arrangements. In this way, the consumer traveller may relatively quickly and at very little expense get a decision as to whether the traveller is entitled to compensation or

7.5   damages.

Danish travel bureaux have established their own trade association known as the Association of Danish Travel Bureaux or *Danmarks Rejsebureau Forening*. The purpose of the association is to work as a representative and nationwide trade association for travel bureaux in Denmark and to further the interests of its members.

The main areas of activities of the members of the association are:

(i)   the issue of tickets for various means of transport, as agents on behalf of the transport operators;
(ii)   the organisation of holidays, *e.g.* package holidays;
(iii) travel agency business, *e.g.* reservations and bookings of hotels and restaurants; and
(iv)   incoming business, *e.g.* the preparation and organisation of stays and holidays in connection with foreigners' visits to the Nordic countries.

7.6   The *Danmarks Rejsebureau Forening* is a membership association. Application for membership should be sent to the association secretariat.

The association has recently issued for use by its members a set of general terms and conditions for participation in tours and holidays which corresponds with the new Package Travel Act.

Another membership association in the Danish travel industry is the *Foreningen af Rejsearrangører i Danmark*, which is the trade association for Danish charter bureaux. This association has approved a set of general terms and conditions for use by its members which generally corresponds with the new Package Travel Act.

Health and safety standards for the use of different means of transportation in Denmark are administered by several ministerial bodies, depending on the type of transport in question.

The carriage of passengers by sea and inland waterway falls under the **7.7** Ministry of Industry and the Danish Maritime Authority, the *Søfartsstyrelsen*. The Danish Civil Aviation Authority, under the Ministry of Traffic, administers rules and regulations pertaining to the aviation industry. The Ministry of Traffic administers rules and regulations relating to the carriage of passengers by rail. Finally, the carriage of passengers by bus falls under the Ministry of Justice and the Ministry of Traffic.

2. Legal and professional rules

According to section 6 of the Travel Guarantee Foundation Act, every- **7.8** body who organises or sells in Denmark on behalf of travel agents or tour operators, package holidays, must register with the Travel Guarantee Foundation.

Travel agencies or tour operators become liable to payment of fines and/or imprisonment, if they arrange or sell such holidays in Denmark without being registered with the Foundation.

In addition, a travel agency/tour operator must put up a guarantee for DKK 200,000 with a bank or insurance company. Such a guarantee must be in favour of the Foundation, and must cover any amount which the Foundation can claim back from the agency or operator when the Foundation has provided financial support to consumer travellers in accordance with the Act. The Foundation may provide such financial support, if, due to the operator's or agency's financial difficulties, the holiday does not live up to the description of the holiday purchased by the traveller (see *infra*, heading 5).

Amounts thus paid by the Foundation to or for the benefit of the con- **7.9** sumer traveller may be claimed back by the Foundation from the operator or agency in question, which typically means that the Foundation will draw on the guarantee put up by the agency or operator.

In principle, any person can operate as a tour operator or travel agency in Denmark. Danish nationals and nationals from other EU or EFTA countries[4] may freely carry out the business of a tour operator or travel

---

4 Save for individuals from Switzerland. Switzerland did not accede to the European Economic Agreement between the EU and the EFTA countries.

agent in Denmark. Nationals from other countries will, generally speaking, need a visa and a work permit.

A travel agency or tour operator business may be established as any type of legal entity. Individuals may operate through a firm, partnership or a limited liability company. Foreign companies wishing to operate in Denmark may either set up a subsidiary or a branch office in Denmark.

7.10   There is no generally recognised set of professional rules in Denmark applicable to travel agents, tour operators, or the like. The two membership associations, the Association of Danish Travel Bureaux and the Association of Travel Organisers in Denmark, however, set some professional standards in their by-laws for their members.

For instance, a travel bureau will not be admitted as a member of the Association of Danish Travel Bureaux, unless it can provide the association secretariat with documentation that it is registered with the Travel Guarantee Foundation and that it will carry out travel bureau business in a fully responsible way.

If a member cannot satisfy these requirements it may be excluded from the association.

3.   General business organisation

7.11   Travel or tour businesses need not be established in a certain legal form. The travel agency or tour operator business may be run through a firm, partnership, limited partnership[5] or through a limited liability company (A/S or ApS). A foreign limited liability company operator or agency may run its Danish activities through a Danish subsidiary or branch office.

4.   Special legal requirements

7.12   The Danish Companies Act does not contain any special provisions for companies which operate in the travel and tourist industry.

Nor are there any special provisions in Denmark as to ownership of travel agencies or tour operators, except for the general rules on the establishment of a business in Denmark as a foreign citizen. As mentioned under 2, *supra*, every citizen from another EU or EFTA country may work and operate as travel agent or tour operator in Denmark, whereas citizens from other countries are, generally speaking, dependent upon a visa and a work permit.

There are no restrictions as to ownership of Danish companies in the

---

5   The so-called *Kommanditselskab* or K/S.

travel industry. Danish companies may thus freely be owned by foreign interests. However, a Danish company must always have a managing director who resides in Denmark or in one of the other EU or EFTA countries. In addition, at least half of the board of directors of a Danish company must be resident in Denmark or in one of the other EU or EFTA countries.

There is no legal requirement that a travel agency or tour operator **7.13** take out special insurance, such as professional negligence insurance or the like. However, transport operators are required to take out liability insurance pertaining to specific means of transportation, for example protection and indemnity cover for a passenger ferry.

A travel agent or tour operator, however, must put up the guarantee, mentioned under heading 2, *supra*, with a bank or insurance company for DKK 200,000 to cover any outlay by the Travel Guarantee Foundation which may become necessary because of the financial difficulties of the agent or operator.

May travel agencies and tour operators then limit their liability *vis-à-vis* **7.14** the consumer traveller? The answer to that question is multi-fold.

If the activities concerned fall within the scope of the Package Travel Act,[6] the "organiser" and the "retailer", as defined in the Act, may only limit their liability if permitted by the relevant international conventions for certain types of transportation.[7] Otherwise, the organiser and retailer may not limit their liability in order to limit or exclude the rights conferred upon the consumer traveller according to the Act. The rights of the consumer are set out under 5 *infra*.

A tour operator or travel agent carrying out activities falling outside the scope of the Travel Package Act is, generally speaking, entitled to limit his liability for losses suffered by a consumer traveller in connection with a specific travel arrangement. However, the travel agent or tour operator may not contract out of the rights and safeguards of the traveller under the Travel Guarantee Foundation Act (see headings 5 and 6 *infra*).

The general rules in the Danish Bankruptcy Act[8] apply to the bank- **7.15** ruptcy or the winding up of businesses in the travel and tourism sector.

According to the Bankruptcy Act, an undertaking which is not capable of paying its debts and liabilities may notify the probate court that it has suspended its payments. The probate court will immediately appoint a supervising liquidator, whose task it will be to go through the affairs of the undertaking in question in order to establish whether the business should continue or whether it should be wound up. During the suspension of payments, the undertaking may continue its activities, but the supervising liquidator will have to consent to all major transactions.

---

[6] See under heading 1 *supra*.
[7] The Warsaw Convention as far as international carriage by air is concerned and the Athens Convention as far as sea carriage of passengers and their baggage is concerned.
[8] Act No. 298 of 1977, as subsequently amended.

7.16 The probate court will issue a bankruptcy or winding up order in respect of an insolvent undertaking, if so requested by the undertaking itself or by a creditor of the undertaking. The probate court will immediately appoint a trustee, who will act for and on behalf of the bankrupt undertaking.

The Danish Bankruptcy Act provides that a bankrupt undertaking which, prior to the bankruptcy order, has entered into a mutual contractual arrangement with a third party, is still bound by such arrangement and has to perform its obligations according to the arrangement, notwithstanding the bankruptcy. The contracting third party is also bound by the arrangement, but may require of the trustee that he make up his mind within a reasonable period of time as to whether the bankrupt undertaking intends to perform its obligations under the arrangement. If the trustee has not made up his mind after the lapse of a reasonable period of time, or if the trustee informs the contracting party that the undertaking does not intend to perform its obligations, the contracting party may consider it a breach of the arrangement, entitling the contracting party to rescind the arrangement.

7.17 The bankruptcy rules apply to a bankrupt tour operator or travel agent. However, the consumer traveller who is faced with a tour operator's or travel agent's bankruptcy after having booked his holiday usually need not make use of the Bankruptcy Act. The consumer traveller will typically resort to his rights under the Travel Guarantee Foundation Act, according to which the Travel Guarantee Foundation may financially support a traveller who is severely adversely affected by the agent's or operator's financial difficulties. The Travel Guarantee Foundation Act is described under headings 5 and 6 *infra*.

5. Consumer rights and safeguards

7.18 The travel agency and tour operator business is, like any other business carried out in Denmark, subject to the legal safeguards of the Danish Marketing Act.[9] According to the Marketing Act it is not permissible for a business to give false, misleading or misrepresentative information in advertisements, brochures, catalogues, or the like when describing goods or services for sale. In addition, every business must comply with the marketing code of conduct of the Act. The Danish Marketing Act therefore confers upon the consumer a number of legal rights and safeguards.

The Danish Consumer Ombudsman is the supervising authority which ensures that the Marketing Act is complied with. In the case of non-compliance the Consumer Ombudsman may commence court proceedings,

---

[9] Act No. 297 of 1974, as subsequently amended.

with a view to subjecting the non-compliant business to an injunction or a fine, and in some cases even to imprisonment.

Following the implementation of the EC Package Travel Directive, a **7.19** new code of conduct has been established for information to be given in brochures, and other marketing material, in connection with the sale of package holidays covered by the EC Directive (*infra*).

According to Danish contract law a tour operator or travel agency is bound by the holiday booking once the holiday has been agreed with the consumer orally or in writing. The agent or operator will only under very special circumstances be entitled to cancel the holiday, or to charge extra for extra costs, such as increased fuel prices. That is the legal position, if no special agreement has been made to the contrary between the consumer traveller and the agency or operator.

For that reason the Association of Danish Travel Bureaux and the **7.20** Association of Travel Organisers in Denmark have both issued a set of general booking conditions, which are used to a large extent by members of the associations when travel and holiday bookings are made for their customers. The general conditions make special provisions for cancellations, repayment of deposits, price increases, etc and generally accord with the new Package Travel Act.

However, neither of the two sets of general booking conditions contain a provision on "overbooking", which is becoming a more and more frequent problem in the tourist sector. According to Danish contract law, the traveller is generally speaking entitled to compensation, if, due to overbooking on the part of the organiser, the traveller has had to go on another, more expensive holiday or if, for instance, due to overbooking the traveller has had to put up with a holiday stay of a lesser quality.

The use of booking conditions is particularly relevant when the holiday **7.21** or travel arrangement sold is not a "package" as defined by the EC Package Travel Directive. If the Danish Package Travel Act applies to a transaction, the organiser and retailer have to comply with a detailed set of rules and regulations. The provisions of the Act apply compulsorily and may not therefore be contracted out of by the organiser's or retailer's use of general booking conditions.

The Package Travel Act contains detailed provisions about the information to be provided by the organiser or retailer about the package to the consumer. For instance, the price for a particular package must be clearly stated in brochures, advertisements and other marketing material. All information supplied to the consumer must be accurate and not misleading.

The Minister of Justice has, in conjunction with the Consumer Ombudsman, issued a Statutory Instrument[10] setting out the type of information which must be contained in brochures made available to the

---

[10] Statutory Instrument (*bekendtgørelse*) on Package Holidays No. 776 of 21 September 1993.

consumer. The Statutory Instrument basically corresponds to the requirements of the EC Directive, in particular to Article 3 of the Directive, but
the Danish Ministry of Justice seems to have gone into more depth about
the type of information required.

7.22   A brochure made available to the consumer must always indicate in a
legible, comprehensible and accurate manner both the price and adequate information concerning, *inter alia*:

(i)   the destination and the means of transportation used;
(ii)   the type of accommodation, its location, degree of comfort, etc;
(iii)   the meal plan;
(iv)   the itinerary;
(v)   general information on passport and visa requirements;
(vi)   the amount or percentage of the price to be paid on account and
        a timetable for payment of the balance; and
(vii)   whether a minimum number of persons is required for the pack-
        age to take place.

7.23   The traveller may cancel the package, in which case the organiser may
only claim payment of a reasonable amount by the traveller, taking into
account the time of cancellation and the nature of the package. If the
organiser's right of cancellation is limited as against his subcontractors/
tour operators, the organiser may limit the travellers' right of cancellation likewise.

The traveller may also cancel the package if, less than 14 days before
departure a *force majeure* situation, such as an act of war, civil unrest, or
the like, arises at or in the vicinity of the destination. In that case the consumer is entitled to repayment of all amounts paid for the holiday.

The organiser may only increase the price for the package agreed
upon, if such price increase is attributable to changes in:

(i)   transport costs;
(ii)   taxes, dues or fees for particular services, such as airport and port
        dues;
(iii)   exchange rates applicable to the package in question.

Price increases must be introduced by the organiser no later than 20
days before the time of departure.

7.24   If the organiser cannot deliver the package agreed upon and the traveller suffers a loss as a result thereof, the traveller is entitled to be compensated by the organiser, unless:

(i)   the cancellation was due to the fact that the agreed minimum num-
        ber of participants did not enrol for the package in question;
(ii)   the cancellation or the lack of performance was caused by the
        traveller himself; or
(iii)   the cancellation or the lack of performance was caused by a third
        party or *force majeure* circumstances which could not have been fore-
        seen or avoided by the organiser.

If the package turns out to be "defective", the traveller can require that **7.25** the organiser remedy such defect, unless such remedial action is excessively costly or burdensome for the organiser. In the event that the defect is not remedied, the traveller may claim a reduction in the price. The organiser may offer to remedy a defect or problem with the package, in which case the traveller cannot claim a reduction in the price or rescind the agreement, provided the problem is rectified within a reasonable period of time, and without expense or inconvenience for the traveller.

When the package holiday has been purchased through a retailer, the traveller may direct any claims and complaints against the retailer and/or the organiser. The retailer and the organiser are jointly and severally liable for the due performance of all the package obligations.

The Danish Package Travel Act does not regulate the situation where **7.26** the organiser cannot perform his duties due to financial difficulties. However, the Danish Travel Guarantee Foundation Act,[11] which applies to the sale of all holiday and travel arrangements, or package holidays, gives the traveller the right to compensation, if, due to the financial difficulties of the organiser or the retailer, the holiday is cancelled or materially falls short of the standards agreed upon.

An undertaking is in "financial difficulties" when it has suspended its payments, has been subjected to bankruptcy or winding up proceedings, or if other circumstances indicate that the undertaking is not capable of satisfying its financial obligations.

When a travel agent is in such financial difficulties and, as a result thereof, the agent has to cancel the holiday before it has commenced, the traveller may claim that any amounts paid in advance to the agent be repaid by the Foundation. Where the holiday has commenced, but the traveller cannot get transportation home due to the organiser's financial difficulties, the Foundation must arrange for such transportation home within a reasonable period of time.

In the event that the financial difficulties result in a serious breach of **7.27** the holiday arrangements, for instance if the traveller does not get proper accommodation, the Foundation may compensate the traveller.

The traveller must ask for such compensation from the Foundation no later than three months after the holiday in question.

6.   Forms of redress

The consumer traveller has various means of redress, if the holiday or **7.28** tour arrangements are breached by the organiser.

As mentioned under 5, *supra*, the traveller may rescind the holiday agreement in the case of serious breach of the agreement by the

---

[11] Act No. 104 of 1986, as subsequently amended.

organiser, for instance if the organiser cancels the holiday without a legitimate reason. In addition, the traveller will be able to claim damages or compensation for the losses suffered as a result of the breach.

The traveller will also, generally speaking, be entitled to damages or compensation, if the holiday arrangements do not live up to the standards agreed upon with the organiser.

The traveller may commence legal proceedings in order to obtain such compensation or damages. However, a more appropriate forum for determination of such disputes is the travel complaint body known as the *Rejseankenævnet*. The complaint body may award compensation to travellers.

A traveller may complain to the *Rejseankenævn* in respect of all holiday or travel arrangements organised or sold in Denmark involving:

(i)   travelling abroad; or
(ii) domestic travelling with at least one stay overnight.

7.29   The *Rejseankenævn* will not accept a complaint unless the complainant has first, in vain, addressed his complaint to the organiser or agency in question. The traveller must pay a minor fee to the *Rejseankenævn*, but such fee will be repaid if the *Rejseankenævn* makes its decision in favour of the complainant in accordance with the complaint, in whole or in part.

The decisions of the travel complaint body are binding upon its organiser and agency members, unless the member within 30 days after the decision informs the *Rejseankenævn* that the member does not wish to be bound by the decision. In that case, the traveller will have to pursue the claim before the national courts.

7.30   If the travel arrangement purchased does not qualify for a complaint to the *Rejseankenævn*, for example because the arrangement involves domestic travel without accommodation, the consumer traveller may complain to the consumer complaint body known as the *Forbrugerklagenævn*.[12] A consumer may complain to the *Forbrugerklagenævn inter alia* if the complaint relates to a public transport service or if it relates to private services rendered, in respect of which the consideration payable by the consumer was between DKK 500 and DKK 20,000.

Decisions made by the *Forbrugerklagenævn* are not enforceable against the organiser of a holiday, but the decisions are in fact usually complied with by the addressees. If the organiser refuses to follow a decision, the consumer will have to pursue the claim before the national courts.

7.31   When the consumer traveller wishes to claim compensation for cancellation or lack of performance in respect of a holiday arrangement due to the organiser's financial difficulties, it must be claimed in accordance with the Travel Guarantee Foundation Act and the request for compensation must be directed to the Foundation itself.

---

[12] As set up in accordance with Act No. 305 of 1974, as subsequently amended.

The consumer traveller has a legal claim against the Foundation where the arrangement is cancelled before it has commenced and the traveller may claim repayment of any prepaid amounts. The traveller also has a legal claim against the Foundation where he is stranded at the place of destination without any transportation home. Where the traveller's claim for compensation relates to the standard of performance of the holiday, as compared to that agreed upon, the consumer does not have a legal claim as such against the Foundation. Any compensation payable will be determined at the complete discretion of the Foundation.

7. Insurance requirements

There are in Denmark no legal and professional rules as to the requirement for travel agents and businesses to obtain insurance. **7.32**

8. Regulation of insurance

Individual travel insurance and hire car insurance for tourists and travellers in Denmark are governed by the Danish Insurance Contract Act.[13] The Danish Insurance Contract Act endorses to a large extent the principle of freedom of contract. Certain basic rights of the assured, as set out in the Act, must form part of an insurance contract. The contents of an insurance contract are otherwise left to the parties to decide. Insurance contracts will usually be made subject to the insurance company's general terms and conditions for that particular type of insurance. Most Danish insurance companies co-operate on the establishment of identical terms and conditions for standard insurance policies, such as travel insurance and hire car insurance. **7.33**

Many types of individual travel and hire car insurance enable the traveller to obtain compensation or insurance cover during the holiday, so that the traveller himself does not have to lay out monies for repair, or the like, during the holiday. If no special provision is made in the insurance contract for such immediate compensation or cover, the traveller will typically have to lay out the monies himself and claim cover when he returns from holiday.

If a dispute arises with the insurance company, for instance as to the extent of the cover, the assured may complain to the insurance complaint body, the *Forsikringsankenævn*, which may make a ruling on such a dispute. The decisions of the insurance complaint body are binding upon the insurance company members, unless they notify the body in writing within 30 days that they do not intend to follow the decision. The assured will then have to pursue his claim before the national courts. **7.34**

---

[13] Act No. 129 of 1930, as subsequently amended.

As far as car liability insurance is concerned, the EC Directives on liability insurances for vehicles[14] has ensured that a system be established in the Member States, including Denmark, according to which claims for death, personal injury or other damage, covered by car liability insurance, must be paid to the relevant parties as quickly as possible.

9. Health and safety standards

7.35 The Danish Veterinary Directorate supervises health and safety standards in relation to hotels, restaurants, etc in Denmark. The regulations, which are very detailed, are considered quite strict.

Health and safety standard regulations for bus, rail, air and sea transport operators, on the technical side, generally follow the recognised international conventions on safety for the different types of carriage.

Buses and vehicles are subject to the strict regulation of the Traffic Act[15] and to the supervision of the Ministries of Traffic and Justice.

Rail carriage is subject to the Danish Railway Act.[16]

Carriage by air is subject to the Danish Aviation Act[17] and to the supervision of the Danish Civil Aviation Authority.

7.36 Carriage by sea is subject to the Danish Maritime Act[18] and Regulations and to the supervision of the Danish Maritime Authority.

The sea transport operator may limit his liability in accordance with the Athens Convention and the air transport operator in accordance with the Warsaw Convention.

10. Rights against transport operators

7.37 The rights of consumers against transport operators in the case of cancellation, lack of performance, or the like, basically follow general Danish contract law as set out at heading 5, *supra*. A consumer may, generally speaking, in the absence of an agreement to the contrary, sue the transport operator for compensation or damages, if the transport purchased is cancelled and the traveller suffers a loss as result thereof.

However, transport operators are generally permitted to limit or exclude their liability for such losses and most transport operators have, indeed, limited and/or excluded their liability for such losses in their general terms and conditions of transport.

Personal injury, death and loss of or damage to property arising in connection with transport is regulated in detail in the Transport Acts

---

14 Directive 166/72, as amended by Directive 5/85, as amended by Directive 232/90.
15 Act No. 287 of 1976, as subsequently amended.
16 Acts No. 109 of 1969 and No. 117 of 1921, both as subsequently amended.
17 Act No. 109 of 1969, as subsequently amended.
18 Act No. 170 of 1994, as subsequently amended.

mentioned under heading 9, *supra*. Where a traveller sustains personal injury or dies in connection with transport he or his estate will usually be entitled to damages for the losses suffered. The transport operator's liability for such injury or death is strict. The transport operator may also be held liable for damage to or loss of property, such as hand baggage. The transport operator's liability for such losses will usually be presumed.

11. Financial services

The supply and use of credit cards, cash cards, switch cards and other payment systems in Denmark is regulated by the Danish Payment Card Act.[19] Every issuer of such payment cards must be registered with the Consumer Ombudsman, who is responsible for supervision and administration of the Act.

7.38

The issuer of a payment card must comply with the provisions of the Act, to make the payment system as consumer friendly as possible and to provide detailed information, as set out in the Act, to the consumer about the payment system. The Consumer Ombudsman may interfere with and make rulings about the practices of a card issuer, if the Act is not followed. However, the decisions of the Consumer Ombudsman are not binding upon the card issuer. If the issuer does not comply with the decision of the Ombudsman, the Ombudsman has to commence legal proceedings against the issuer before the national courts.

A card issuer may be penalised with fines or imprisonment in case of non-compliance with the Act.

7.39

The supply and use of traveller's cheques in Denmark is regulated by the Danish Cheque Act.[20] The Act, which generally speaking follows the Geneva Conventions, regulates the civil law relationship between the bank, the issuer of the cheque, the drawer and the drawee, etc. Cheques and traveller's cheques may only be supplied in Denmark by banks or other credit institutions which are subject to the Danish Credit Institution Act[21] or similar legislation.

A bureau de change, whose sole business is to purchase and sell different currencies, and which does not maintain deposit accounts, or the like, is not subject to the Credit Institution Act. The establishment and operation of such bureaux de change follow the general rules of establishment and operation of a business in Denmark, see headings 2 and 3, *supra*.

A bureau de change will therefore also have to follow the provisions of the Marketing Act,[22] which means *inter alia* that a bureau will have to advertise its exchange rates and fees to the public, for example in fully legible writing at or outside the bureau.

7.40

---

[19] Act No. 284 of 1984, as subsequently amended.
[20] Act No. 69 of 1932, as subsequently amended.
[21] Act No. 199 of 1974, as subsequently amended.
[22] See heading 5. above.

12. Compensation for victims of crime

7.41   The Danish State provides compensation in respect of any person who sustains death or personal injury as a result of a criminal act commited in Denmark. Compensation may also be claimed for damage to or loss of the victim's personal belongings.

Compensation is payable even if the offender is unidentifiable. The compensation will be reduced to the extent that the victim can claim compensation for the losses from the offender himself, or from insurance companies, or the like.

The Danish state may also pay compensation for criminal acts commited outside Denmark if the victim is a Danish resident or Danish citizen at the time of the crime.

13. Time share regulation

7.42   There is no specific regulation of time share agreements in Danish law. Time share agreements are subject to the general principles of Danish contract law, in particular contract law pertaining to the sale and purchase of land.

The EC Directive on Time Share Agreements[23] will provide the consumer purchaser with some of the legal rights and safeguards which do not exist under Danish law today.

14. Passport and frontier control

7.43   Citizens of any of the Scandinavian countries may freely travel from one Scandinavian country to another without a passport. There is thus no passport control of a Scandinavian citizen tourist entering Denmark from another Scandinavian country.

Danish citizens travelling from Denmark to another country, including an EU or EFTA country, or returning to Denmark from such country, must carry their passports.

Tourists from the EU and EFTA countries visiting Denmark will be subjected to passport control in Denmark.

---

[23] Directive 47/94.

Finland

Chapter 8
Finland

Ahola, Pentzin, Rantasila & Sokka Oy*

1. Introduction

Finland is signatory to the EEA Treaty concerning the European Econ- **8.1**
omic Area, binding on Finland since 1 January 1993. The EEA charter
and its regulations which are consistent with the respective EU Regulations and Directives have been adopted as such in the Finnish law as part
of the Finnish judicial system, with the exception of certain Regulations,
where a period of transition has been granted pursuant to the Treaty. A
statutory provision may not be applied, if it conflicts with a provision of
the main EEA agreement, or a protocol or supplement to the EEA
Treaty, or if it conflicts with any EC Directive referred to in the supplement to the EEA Treaty, provided that such Directive is compelling and
governs the relations between an individual and a public power, or if it
conflicts with any EC regulation referred to in the supplement to the
EEA Treaty. The Finnish legislation has been harmonised with the provisions of the EEA Treaty.

Finland joined the EU on 1 January 1995.

The tourist industry in Finland is considered as a service industry,
and the importance of tourism as an aspect of free movement is widely
recognised.

Inter-Nordic treaties have been instrumental in removing the obstacles **8.2**
to free movement between the Nordic countries. As a result of such
agreements, the movement between the Nordic countries still remains
more liberal today than between Finland and the other EEA countries, or
between Finland and other parts of the world.

2. Regulatory authorities

The Ministry of Trade and Industry is the highest authority supervising **8.3**
the activities of companies and businesses. Subordinated to the Ministry,

---

* Ahola, Pentzin, Rantasila & Sokka Oy was founded in 1993. The firm's areas of practice
include mostly business law in the following fields: corporate and business law, investment and
securities, banking law, shipping law, contracts, international business transactions, commercial law, real estate law, bankruptcy and insolvency, taxation law, arbitration, litigation,
industrial property, copyright law, competition law, marketing law and creditor's rights. The
firm's profile can best be identified in its dedication to the service of its clients, large and
small, in all matters, complicated and simple, all this with 20 years' experience and expertise
resulting in an ability to serve business management in any business law problem it may face
while operating in, from or into Finland.

the National Board of Patents and Registration supervises trade registrations and maintains a Trade Register on commercial companies, foundations and registered commercial names.

8.4 Issues relating to consumer protection belong also to the competence of the Ministry of Trade and Industry, and the National Consumer Administration is the corresponding supervising authority. The office of the Consumer Ombudsman was established to supervise the legality of marketing and contractual terms. The Consumer Ombudsman prepares an annual report on his activities. The law provides that the Consumer Ombudsman shall use his best effort to persuade businesses to voluntarily refrain from improper activities. The Consumer Ombudsman is entitled to issue a temporary prohibitive resolution to prevent an improper activity. Disputes between consumers and businesses are resolved by the Consumer Complaints Board and issued as recommendations.

The Ministry of Trade and Industry supervises the protection of sound and proper business competition. The authorities established for this purpose are the Office of Free Competition, which studies and investigates competitive conditions and restraints of trade, as well as the Competition Board, which handles and settles disputes arising due to restraints of trade.

8.5 The Ministry of the Interior is the competent authority in matters concerning the residence and employment of foreigners.

The Ministry of Social Affairs and Health is the competent supervising authority in questions of health, safety and foodstuffs regulation. As the highest supervising authority, the Ministry of Social Affairs and Health also controls the activities of insurance companies.

The regional authority in each Finnish county is the County Administration, which grants travel agency licences, traffic operating licences, and supervises compliance with health and safety regulations. Each municipality also has a municipal health board which supervises compliance with health regulations. The local police supervises compliance with safety regulations and is the local authority responsible for matters relating to trade licences and traffic operating licences.

The central organisation of travel agencies is the Finnish Travel Agency Association, which safeguards the interests of travel agencies and has, together with the National Consumer Administration, drafted the general terms of package tours. The Finnish Tourist Guides' Association is the professional organisation of travel guides. The Finnish Tourist Board was established to promote tourism in Finland, whereas the Finnish Tourist Agency is responsible for domestic travel, wilderness tours, excursion and camping activities.

8.6 Disputes should in principle be brought to a court of first instance for judgment. The country is divided into judicial circuits, each of them with a circuit court. According to the provisions of the Consumer Protection Act, Securities Markets Act and Savings Banks Act, the Market Court as a special court is the competent authority for handling and resolving matters relating to the regulation of marketing and contractual terms, as well as on matters referred to in the Unfair Trade Practices Act.

The rulings of the Market Court and the courts of first instance can be **8.7** appealed to courts of appeal. The resolutions of the courts of appeal can be appealed to the Supreme Court, subject, however, to the Supreme Court having granted a permission to appeal. The decisions of administrative authorities can be appealed to the county administrative courts and as the last instance to the Supreme Administrative Court. The resolutions of Finnish courts can be appealed as a last remedy to the European Court of Human Rights and under certain circumstances disputes concerning Finnish law may be handled by the administrative bodies of the EC.

3. Legal and professional rules

(i) Freedom of business

Finland adheres to the principle of freedom of business. According to **8.8** this fundamental rule, any natural person domiciled in the territory of the European Economic Area who has full legal capacity over himself and his property, is entitled to operate in Finland in a legal business consistent with good business practice (Act on the Freedom of Business, 1919/122[1]). In addition, the law provides that certain fields of business are subject to special conditions.

Also entitled to operate in business are Finnish corporations and foundations, as well as foreign corporations and foundations with a registered branch in Finland and which are established and have a domicile, central administration or principal place of business in an EEA Member State. Other foreign entities may apply for a trade licence from the Ministry of Trade and Industry.

A business operating in a business location or assisted by persons other **8.9** than family members, requires a notice of registration of the business or trade to the local police district. Businesses subject to a trade licence and foreign businesses must also submit a report of new business to the Trade Register. If the business has no permanent domicile in Finland, it must have a representative domiciled in Finland, vested with the authority to receive summonses and other notices on behalf of the business in question.

In addition to the above, travel agency operations are governed by special statutory regulations (Travel Agency Decree 442/68 with subsequent amendments). The Decree concerns travel agency operations

---

1 This article refers to each regulation by indicating its respective number in the Statute Book of Finland on the year of issue. Subsequent amendments to the Acts or Decrees are not indicated separately. The legislation has been examined up to August 1994.

with the exception of the following: the provisions do not govern tours to Finland sold or marketed in Finland; traffic operators or their agents; leasing of traffic equipment; tours; or guide and information activities. Special legal provisions also govern the use of motor vehicles and other automotive machines, accommodation and catering operations, and aviation activities.

(ii) Foreign business operators

8.10 A foreigner wishing to carry on business in Finland must upon arrival in Finland have a valid passport, and in the case of prolonged stay, a residence permit. A person other than a citizen of an EEA Member State will also require an entry visa granted by a Finnish diplomatic mission, unless otherwise stipulated in international treaties binding on Finland.[2] Any foreigner whose stay exceeds three months requires a residence permit. The residence permit is granted for a fixed period which can be extended, or it can be granted as a permanent residence permit, provided that certain preconditions are fulfilled. A citizen of an EEA Member State and his/her spouse, dependent parents or children under 21 years of age[3] are granted a fixed-period residence permit for five years, and a citizen of any other country in principle for one year. The application must generally be submitted to the Finnish diplomatic mission in the applicant's country of permanent residence. A person who comes to Finland for the purpose of paid employment must have a work permit. A precondition for granting a work permit to a foreigner is that he/she has a valid visa or residence permit (Aliens Act 378/91; Aliens Decree 142/94).

8.11 A foreign business operator must follow the same procedure as Finnish citizens and submit a report of new business and a notice to the Trade Register as described above.

National interests can be safeguarded by restricting the transfer of control to foreigners or foreign corporations and foundations in nationally significant companies (Act on Supervision of Acquisitions by Foreigners 1612/92). Significant national interests may mean, for instance, safeguarding national defence, preventing serious economic, social or environmental consequences, and ensuring public order and the safety and health of citizens. Companies whose workforce exceeds 1,000 persons and whose latest audited turnover exceeds FIM one billion, or whose latest balance sheet total exceeds FIM one billion and which transfer to foreign control, may also be subject to supervision or restrictions.

8.12 If the above conditions are fulfilled, the foreign owner must seek

---

[2] Finland has signed numerous treaties on the abolition of visa obligation.
[3] A Finnish citizen becomes of age upon his/her 18th birthday.

the approval of the Ministry of Trade and Industry for the acquisition, provided that the foreign buyer has received a number of the company's shares conferring a vote equivalent to at least one-third of the total number of votes or one-third of the control in a company significant for national defence. This provision is consistent with the regulations of the EEA Treaty.

4. General business organisation

There are no special regulations governing companies which operate in **8.13** the tourist industry; instead, the general legal provisions applicable to various types of business in general also apply to travel operators. A natural person who has full legal capacity over himself and his property is entitled to operate in the travel business, provided that he has submitted a report of new business and a notice to the Trade Register, and has been granted the trade licence required for operating in travel business. A duly established commercial company may also operate in the travel business, provided that it has obtained the required trade licence.

Businesses may operate either as title-holders to a commercial name or **8.14** in any one of the three legal company forms. If two or more persons operate as business partners under mutual agreement, they form a partnership company or a limited partnership company (Act on Partnership Companies and Limited Partnership Companies 389/88). Any citizen of an EEA Member State who has full legal capacity over himself and his property may be a party to such an agreement. The parties to the agreement, *i.e.* the partners, are liable for the commitments of such a company as for their own debts. If the agreement restricts one or more partners' liability for the commitments of the company, the legal form is a limited partnership company, whereas otherwise the legal form is a general partnership company. A general partnership company and a limited partnership company are independent legal entities which may acquire rights and titles and enter into commitments, and act as interested parties in courts and towards other authorities.

Travel business may also be operated as a limited company, whereby at **8.15** least half of the founding shareholders, being natural or legal persons, must be domiciled in an EEA member state. The Ministry of Trade and Industry may grant an exemption from this regulation. The shareholders are liable for the commitments of a limited company only to the amount of the share capital which they have invested in the company. A limited company is managed and externally represented by a board of directors whose members shall be notified to the Trade Register. The control of a limited company is exercised by its shareholders. Generally all the shares of a limited company confer equal voting rights.

All commercial corporations must be entered in the Trade Register.

5. Special legal requirements

(i) Travel agency licence

8.16 In addition to being subject to the general provisions governing business operations, operation of a travel agency is only allowed on permission of a licence granted by the respective County Administration to entrepreneurs complying with the provisions of the Travel Agency Decree (442/68).

The Travel Agency Decree defines travel agency operation as the organisation, sale and marketing of tours and travel services on a permanent basis and for financial profit. The applicability of the provision does not depend on the duration of the travel. However, the provision does not concern domestic tours and other travel services, *i.e.* tours destined to Finland and sold or marketed in Finland, traffic operations, or travel guide and information activities. A travel agency operator must apply for a licence from the County Administration, which licence, however, is not dependent on market demand.

8.17 After the applicant has been granted a travel agency licence, he must make a report of new business before starting operation and submit the notice required for the chosen legal type of company to the Trade Register. The travel agency must start operation within six months of the date of licence, or else the licence may be terminated.

(ii) Preconditions for granting a licence

8.18 A travel agency licence may be granted to the Finnish State, to an individual, a Finnish registered corporation, or to a foreign corporation or foundation with a registered branch in Finland, provided that the required guarantee has been acquired. An individual who applies for a travel agency licence must be over 25 years of age, have full legal capacity over himself and his property, have a solid financial status, be known as a respectable and dependable person, and have at least three years of practical experience of the business in question based on his previous activities, and possess an adequate professional competence relevant in each case.

If the travel agency operator does not personally act as a full-time manager of the business, the responsible full-time official must be over 25 years of age, have full legal capacity over himself and his property, be known to be a respectable and dependable person, and have at least three years of practical experience of the business in question based on his previous activities, and possesses an adequate professional competence as a travel agency operator.

8.19 For a travel agency licence to be granted to a corporation, it is required that the corporation must be financially stable, and that the corporation's managing director or the like, or the responsible partners must be known to be respectable and dependable persons who have full legal capacity over themselves and their property, and the travel agency business must be managed by a responsible official approved by the National Consumer Administration and who fulfils the above requirements of responsible official.

A travel agency that has branch-offices, must at each branch-office have **8.20** a responsible operator who is over 20 years of age, has full legal capacity over himself and his property, and possesses sufficient practical experience and an adequate professional competence to operate the branch, and who is approved by the National Consumer Administration.

The term "full legal capacity over himself and his property" means that the person must be of age, and not be under guardianship or in bankruptcy. A certificate testifying to a person's full legal capacity may be obtained upon request from the court of first instance in the area of the person's domicile in Finland. In practice, solid financial status means that there are no records of payment irregularities of the applicant in any public files. A person "known to be respectable and dependable" means that the criminal records contain no entries concerning the person. "Sufficient practical experience and professional competence" have not been defined by the legislation. It should be noted that the travel agency operator is required to have three years' experience of travel agency operation, whereas the person responsible for a branch is required to have sufficient practical experience. Nor does the law give a definition of professional competence, and in any case no specific diplomas or degrees are required.

A foreigner must present certificates which contain the relevant infor- **8.21** mation, issued by the authorities of his home country. Citizens of EEA Member States may apply for recognition of their examination certificates or diplomas of their certificates from learning institutions, or they can pass respective qualification examinations in Finland (Decree on Recognition of Examination Certificates of Citizens of EEA Member States, 1622/93; Decree on Recognition of Education and Professional Training of Citizens of EEA Member States, 580/94).

(iii)   Guarantee

A further requirement for granting a licence is that the applicant must **8.22** present a guarantee accepted by the County Administration, whose amount will be determined depending on the type, extent and financial status of the business. The common practice is to arrange a guarantee through an insurance company or a bank. The guarantor must accept liability for the compensation obligations which the travel agency may have towards its clients for the tours or travel services organised, sold or marketed by it, to a sum accepted by the County Administration, if the applicant's own funds are not sufficient to cover them. The sum is meant to safeguard the claims of all parties who have an agreement with the travel business, in the event of bankruptcy or other insolvency situation.

(iv) Special administrative provisions

8.23 The person who manages a travel agency must meet the above requirements. The travel agency may have branches, in addition to which it may have representatives who act as agents for one travel agency only. The representatives act under the responsibility and supervision of the travel agency. A representation agreement must always be executed in writing, and the representative must act in the name of his principal in his business activities and publicity campaigns. The County Administration must be notified of the representation agreement and receive one original copy of the agreement before the representative may start operation. The termination of such a representation relationship must be notified following the same procedure.

8.24 One of the auditors of the travel agency must be a Chartered Public Auditor or an Approved Public Auditor approved by the Chamber of Commerce. Persons who have passed the auditor's examinations organised by the Chamber of Commerce, are entitled to use these respective professional titles. A person who has passed a foreign auditor's examination must pass the examination organised by the Central Chamber of Commerce to be qualified in Finland. The travel agency must submit every year a report on operations to the County Administration including financial statements and all the information necessary for supervision. At the request of the County Administration, the travel agency shall also forward any other information and clarification relating to its operations which the authority may deem necessary.

(v) Termination of business and bankruptcy provisions

8.25 The County Administration must also be notified of the termination of business. The County Administration may cancel a granted travel agency licence, provided that the statutory preconditions for travel agency operation are no longer fulfilled. If an individual business operator or the responsible official of a travel agency fails to comply with the relevant rules and regulations, or if irregularities have been revealed in its operations, the County Administration may issue a warning to the person in question or prohibit the person from operating in the business during a specific period or indefinitely. It is a criminal offence to operate a travel agency without the required licence.

The bankruptcy legislation (Bankruptcy Act 31/1868) concerns all companies and natural persons. Under certain conditions, a company may be petitioned by way of a restructuring instead of bankruptcy (Restructuring Act 47/1993). The overriding principle is that the assets of a bankrupt company must be distributed to the creditors in proportion to their receivables. However, pledgees, creditors entitled to alimony and holders of industrial mortgages are considered as preferential creditors. According to the previously valid law, salary receivables and taxes were also considered as preferential receivables. The old law is still in some respects applicable to bankruptcy proceedings initiated prior to 1 January 1995.

If a travel agency business is petitioned in bankruptcy, or if an individual **8.26** travel agency operator dies, the respective trade licence will also expire. However, the bankrupt's estate or the deceased's estate is entitled to continue the business under the previous licence for a period not exceeding one year. If the business operator or responsible official dies or is petitioned in bankruptcy, a new responsible official must be presented within three months to the National Consumer Administration for approval. The guarantee required from the travel operator will most often safeguard the interests of parties who have an agreement with the travel operator, especially in bankruptcy situations.

6.   Consumer rights and safeguards

(i)   Consumer protection

The most essential law for safeguarding consumers' interests is the Con- **8.27** sumer Protection Act (38/78). The Consumer Protection Act has been amended to harmonise with the regulations of the EEA Treaty.

The Consumer Protection Act governs marketing, contractual terms, and liability relating to the exchange of consumer commodities. Also the offer and sale of travel services belongs in the scope of the Consumer Protection Act. It is not, however, applicable to the sale of insurance policies or services. Compliance with the Consumer Protection Act is supervised by the National Consumer Administration and the National Foodstuffs Administration.

The Consumer Complaints Board under the National Consumer Administration examines disputes between a consumer and a business operator submitted for its resolution by the consumer. The Consumer Complaints Board issues recommendations and publishes a so-called monthly black list, which is a list of businesses which have not followed its recommendations; however, the Board has no judicial authority. The Board is headed by the Consumer Ombudsman.

Generally, it is forbidden to use marketing methods which are inde- **8.28** cent or otherwise improper. It is forbidden to give untrue and misleading information, similarly it is forbidden to claim that a price is reduced more than it actually is, compared to the previously charged price. Tie-in merchandising and promises of random benefits are also illegal practices.

The business operator who has commissioned or carries on an illegal marketing activity may be prohibited from continuing the illegal marketing, and the prohibition may be enforced by imposing a conditional fine. The Consumer Ombudsman can issue a temporary prohibitive resolution, while the final resolution on the matter is given by the Market Court.

8.29   Consumer commodities may not be offered under contractual terms which are unreasonable considering the price of the commodity and other relevant factors. The use of unreasonable terms may be prohibited and the prohibition may be enforced by imposing a conditional fine. The Market Court issues the final prohibition concerning a contractual term, while the Consumer Ombudsman can issue a temporary prohibition.

(ii)   Direct marketing and mail orders

8.30   Direct marketing and mail orders refer to the marketing of consumer commodities to consumers by telephone; or in person, outside the business operator's business location, or based on a brochure, catalogue or advertisement (Consumer Protection Act 38/78, Chapter 6). The business operator must in each case give the consumer a special, duly dated document specifying the operator's name and address, type of the consumer commodity, price and other contractual terms. The consumer is in each case entitled to cancel the agreement within seven days of receipt of the sales document, or if the commodity is received later, on receipt of the first item. The National Consumer Administration may upon application, grant the business operator a licence to carry out home or mail orders, which restrict the consumer's rights, provided that the restriction is deemed necessary to safeguard the interests of consumers, taking into account the local conditions and the special characteristics or the method of manufacture of the consumer commodity.

(iii)   Consumer protection in the tourist industry

8.31   The Consumer Ombudsman and the Finnish Travel Agency Association have jointly negotiated and approved the general terms and conditions applicable to the marketing and sale of package tours. The general terms of package tours bind tour operators professionally but not legally. Detailed regulations governing marketing by travel agencies and the responsibilities of tour operators are included in The General Terms and Conditions of Package Tours, and compliance with these regulations is supervised by the National Consumer Administration and the Consumer Ombudsman. The terms were last amended on 1 February 1990. The definition of tour operator according to the General Terms and Conditions of Package Tours refers to a company or person who organises a package tour. The definition of tour operator in the Travel Agency Decree is consistent with the definition of the Package Travel Directive.

The tour operator's brochure must include the General Terms and Conditions of Package Tours, or mention where these terms may be obtained. A tour operator is permitted to deviate from the general terms only if it is justified by the special nature of the tour, and only if it has been clearly mentioned. The tour operator and the consumer can mutually agree to modify the terms, provided that the agreement is made in writing.

(iv) Travel agreements between tour operator and consumer

The travel agreement must always contain at least the services and arrangements which the tour operator and the passenger have mutually agreed on. The basis for the agreement is the information mentioned in the tour operator's documents, as well as what the passenger may reasonably expect on the basis of all the information supplied. Although, according to the General Terms and Conditions of Package Tours, it is not obligatory to give detailed information in the brochure, the tour operator's liability towards the passenger depends on "what the passenger can reasonably expect from his tour on the basis of all supplied information". According to the General Terms and Conditions of Package Tours, an agreement is established when the passenger pays the advance payment requested by the tour operator.

8.32

(v) Cancellation or interruption of a tour

The passenger's right to cancel a tour without a valid reason has been restricted. If the tour is cancelled 28 or 14 days before the beginning of the tour, the passenger may cancel the tour by paying either the handling costs or the advance payment. If the tour is cancelled 48 hours before the beginning of the tour, the travel agency is entitled to charge 50% of the price of the tour, and if the tour is cancelled later than 48 hours before the beginning of the tour, the entire price of the tour. If the passenger has an urgent reason, according to those mentioned in the General Terms and Conditions of Package Tours, the tour operator is obliged to accept the passenger's cancellation against a so-called no-show fee, included in the price and announced in advance. Similarly, the passenger is entitled to cancel the tour if the tour operator essentially changes the travel arrangements. If the cancellation is due to changes made by the tour operator, or to conditions at the place of destination, the passenger is entitled to claim reimbursement of the entire price of the tour plus compensation for expenses which have become redundant due to the cancellation. The passenger is entitled to interrupt the tour provided that war, natural disaster or another comparable reason at the place of destination imperils the passenger's life or health, or if the tour operator has grossly neglected his obligations. In such circumstances, the tour operator is responsible for assisting in arranging the return trip.

8.33

The tour operator is entitled to cancel the agreement if the passenger has not paid the price of the tour before its beginning. However, the tour operator must allow for a reasonable period of payment and must notify the passenger of his right to cancel the agreement due to a failure of payment, in the written documents delivered to the passenger.

(vi)　Variation of the agreement

8.34　Under certain circumstances, the tour operator is entitled to adjust the agreed price of the tour. The tour operator's right to price adjustments is limited to reasons due to changes in tax rates or public fees, currency exchange rates or fuel prices. If the increase exceeds 10% of the price of the tour, and the listed price of a tour departing on the same day to the same destination and based on the cheapest accommodation alternative, the passenger is entitled to cancel the agreement.

The tour operator is entitled to change the tour programme provided that the agreed programme cannot be implemented due to reasons beyond the tour operator's control. The tour operator may also change the agreed tour plan due to an insufficient number of passengers, provided that the changes do not essentially alter the agreed tour. The tour operator is entitled to cancel the tour if a sufficient number of passengers have not been booked on the tour. However, such cancellations must be notified at the latest 28 days prior to the beginning of the tour.

(vii)　Right to compensation

8.35　The tour is inadequate, if it does not meet the agreed standard or if it deviates from what the passenger is entitled to request. When assessing inadequacy, the marketing information given by the tour operator is taken into consideration. The tour operator is primarily required to remedy the inadequacy on the basis of the passenger's complaint. If the inadequacy is not remedied promptly at the tour operator's expense, the passenger is entitled to a price reduction. If the passenger suffers damage due to the inadequacy of the tour, the tour operator must compensate for the damage. Compensatable damages may include, *inter alia*, direct costs incurred due to the inadequacy of the tour, as well as the costs relating to necessary measures which have become irrelevant, or loss of earnings due to delayed return, or extra costs caused by overnight accommodation arrangements. The tour operator is not liable for indirect damages unless caused by a gross negligence of the tour operator. The passenger also has the obligation in each case to use his best efforts to restrict the extent of damage.

8.36　The tour operator is not liable for compensation for damage caused by the passenger's own negligence. The tour operator is liable for compensating personal and material injuries and damages caused to the passenger due to loss of luggage and inability to use the belongings due to the loss, provided that the damage was due to the error or negligence of the tour operator or his employee. The tour operator is liable for compensation for damage caused by companies and persons contracted by him to fulfil his contractual obligations, unless it can be proved that the tour operator had acted with due care. When assessing the tour operator's compensation liability, the compensation provisions of the Transport Acts are also taken into consideration.

However, the tour operator is released from liability for damage caused **8.37** due to reasons beyond the tour operator's control, and which could not have been anticipated at the time of concluding the agreement. Such reasons include, *inter alia*, wars, natural disasters, contagious diseases or strikes.

(viii) Disputes

The passenger must in each case present a claim to the tour operator or **8.38** the tour operator's representative in a verifiable manner specifying the inadequacies of the tour. Any observations and compensation claims must be presented in writing not later than two months after the end of the tour, unless there are special grounds for extending the period of claims. Compensation liability is governed by the Compensation Act (412/74). Pursuant to the Compensation Act, the party who has caused damage to another party either intentionally or negligently is liable to compensate for the damage. The Act is not applied to contractual compensation liability, *e.g.* to the compensation clause of the General Terms and Conditions of Package Tours.

Disputes between the tour operator and the passenger due to the interpretation of the agreement may be brought by the passenger to the Consumer Complaints Board for handling. The Consumer Complaints Board may issue a recommendation in the matter, but its ruling is not legally binding. If other remedies fail, the disputes must be brought to a court of first instance for judgment.

7. Forms of redress

(i) Damages

The period of limitation of the tour operator's liability towards the con- **8.39** sumer is ten years, pursuant to the Compensation Act (417/74). Liability for compensation is based both on the provisions of the Compensation Act and on the General Terms and Conditions of Package Tours. The tour operator is liable for compensating the consumer for damage caused by the error or negligence of the tour operator or his employee. The tour operator is liable for compensation for damage caused by companies and persons contracted by him to fulfil his contractual obligations, unless it can be proved that the tour operator had acted with due care.

Compensatable damages include personal and material injuries, as well as damages due to the loss of baggage and those caused by the inability to use the lost goods. As regards damages occurred during air and sea transport, the tour operator has limited his maximum liability in the General Terms and Conditions of Package Tours to that of the carrier.

8.40   The tour operator is also liable for compensating the consumer for the inadequacies of the tour. A tour is inadequate if it does not meet the agreed terms or the passenger's reasonable expectations on the basis of the travel agreement. The marketing information given by the tour operator is relevant when assessing the inadequacies. The tour operator must compensate the passenger for the damage caused by the inadequacy of the tour, provided that the damage was due to the intention or negligence of the tour operator or his representative. The tour operator is not liable for indirect damages, unless due to the tour operator's gross negligence. Neither is the tour operator liable for damage which is due to the passenger's own negligence.

In each case, the tour operator has released himself from liability for damages caused due to reasons beyond the tour operator's control and which could not have been anticipated at the time of concluding the agreement, *i.e.* so-called *force majeure* reasons. *Force majeure* reasons include, *inter alia*, wars, natural disasters, contagious diseases, strikes and other similar events. Even in such cases, the tour operator must inform the passenger promptly of the *force majeure* reasons and use his best effort to minimise the extent of damage suffered by the passenger.

(ii)   Price reduction

8.41   The passenger is entitled to request a price reduction because of inadequacies of the tour. The tour operator must in principle be granted an opportunity to remedy the inadequacy on the basis of the passenger's complaint. The passenger may refuse the rectification only if it causes him considerable inconvenience. Minor changes in the tour schedule, insignificant in proportion to the tour as a whole, or delayed arrival at the destination, or delayed return, are not considered as significant inconveniences provided that the change of schedule is due to reasons beyond the tour operator's control and is less than ten hours. However, if the change is due to congested air space, exceptional weather conditions or other similar reasons, a delay not exceeding 24 hours is not considered as such an inconvenience.

(iii)   Claims procedure

8.42   The passenger must present a claim concerning the inadequacy or damage suffered in a verifiable manner at the place of destination to the tour operator's representative, or directly to the tour operator. According to the General Terms and Conditions of Package Tours, complaints and compensation claims must be presented in writing within two months of the end of the tour, unless there are special grounds for extending the period of claims. The passenger may bring the matter to the Consumer Complaints Board, or to the court of first instance in the place of the passenger's domicile for handling.

Notwithstanding the limitations of liability in the General Terms and Conditions of Package Tours, the tour operator's liability is under most circumstances at least as great as that of the carrier or the hotel. However, the period of limitation for the tour operator's liability is in each case ten years, whereas the time limit of the carrier's responsibility has significantly been reduced. It should further be noted that, pursuant to the Consumer Protection Act (38/78), a contractual term may always be conciliated or entirely rejected, if deemed unreasonable. The question of reasonableness is in the last instance determined by the court. **8.43**

8. Insurance requirements

(i) Voluntary insurance

The tour operator's insurance cover must in principle be arranged by means of voluntary insurance arrangements. The Insurance Agreements Act (132/33) determines the minimum requirements of an insurance agreement. It is permitted to deviate from the provisions of the Act unless expressly prohibited or considered as prohibited. The new Insurance Agreements Act (543/94) entered into force on 1 July 1995. Its provisions concerning the protection of the insured, when the insured is a consumer, are compelling. The Act pays special attention to consumer protection in the marketing of insurance policies, in addition to the contents of insurance terms. **8.44**

(ii) Employee's insurance

The employer must provide an accident insurance policy for his employees (Accident Insurance Act 608/48). The insurance must be arranged with an insurance institution authorised to issue employees' accident insurance policies. Employees' accident insurance compensates the employee for an injury or disease caused at work, or in work-related circumstances, for instance when commuting to or from work, or when the employee tries to protect or save the employer's property or human lives in conjunction with his work. Also employment-related diseases may be compensated. **8.45**

(iii)   Traffic insurance

8.46   Every owner or permanent possessor of a motor vehicle is obliged to take a traffic insurance (Traffic Insurance Act 279/59). The Traffic Insurance Act has recently been harmonised with the regulations of the EEA Treaty. The Traffic Insurance Act provides that a traffic accident will be compensated from the traffic insurance of the motor vehicle, even when no one is personally liable for the compensation of damages. The compensation payable under traffic insurance is determined on the basis of the applicable provisions of the Compensation Act.

8.47   Compensation is paid for personal injury and for damage to the motor vehicle or to the clothing and other personal belongings worn or carried by the passenger. If the person injured in the traffic accident has contributed to the damage, the compensation for damages, other than personal injury may be reduced or entirely rejected. The insurance company where the motor vehicle is insured must be indicated in the vehicle's registration book. Compensation is to be claimed from the insurance company and, if necessary, action brought against the insurance company. Claims and legal actions must be initiated within three years from the date when the injured learned of the damage and details of the insurance company liable to pay compensation for the damage. The competent court is the general court of first instance in the municipality where the injury took place, or where the insurance company in question has its domicile in Finland, or, in the case of a foreign insurance company, where it has its Finnish branch, or where the injured party according to the population register is domiciled in Finland.

8.48   The primary liability for compensation in other words belongs to the insurance company. However, if the owner, driver or passenger of the motor vehicle has caused the accident either intentionally or due to gross negligence, or if the damage occurred negligently while driving a motor vehicle which had been obtained as a result of a crime which could not be considered as minor, or if the person had caused the accident by driving the vehicle under the influence of alcohol or other intoxicant, the insurance company is entitled to claim repayment of the compensation paid, from the offending party (Traffic Insurance Act Art 20).

In principle, the driver's or owner's personal injury is not compensated from the traffic insurance of a motor vehicle registered outside Finland.

8.49   Damages and injury caused by a motor vehicle insured in Finland in the EEA territory, where the accident occurred during direct passing from one EEA member state to another member state, are compensated under Finnish insurance, unless the national legislation of the country in question on compensation of traffic accidents requires a better insurance cover. The Finnish Traffic Insurance Act provides the insured remarkably better protection than the minimum standards of The Third Motor Insurance Directive (90/232/EEA).

9.   Regulation of insurance

The consumer's insurance protection is primarily based on voluntary   **8.50**
insurance agreements between the consumer and the insurance company. The Insurance Agreements Act (132/33) stipulates the minimum
requirements of insurance agreements. It is possible to deviate from the
provisions of the Act in the agreements, provided that the deviation is
not expressly prohibited or considered as prohibited. The new Insurance
Agreements Act (543/94) entered into force on 1 July 1995. Its provisions concerning the protection of the insured when the insured is a
consumer, are compelling. The Act pays special attention to consumer protection in the marketing of insurance policies, in addition to insurance
terms. The Insurance Companies Act (1062/79) stipulates the special
requirements for the activities of insurance companies in addition to the
regulations concerning corporate rights. Only a party who has been granted
the required licence is permitted to carry on insurance operations.

The operations of insurance companies are supervised by the Ministry
of Social Affairs and Health (Insurance Companies Act 1062/79). The
law contains detailed provisions on insurance companies' share capital or
guaranteed equity and reserve funds. Only a natural or legal person who
has been granted the required trade licence by the State Council, may
carry on insurance operations, whereby at least half of the founding partners must be domiciled or have a permanent residence in the EEA territory. An exemption can be granted by the Ministry of Social Affairs and
Health. The activities of all insurance companies operating in Finland
are governed by Finnish law (Art 4).

It is customary that consumers will be offered travel insurance policies   **8.51**
in conjunction with package tours, covering personal injury in the case of
accident and death, damage or loss of baggage, and damage caused due
to the interruption of the tour. In addition to voluntary insurance, the
passenger is protected by the traffic insurance legislation.

10.   Health and safety standards

(i)   Transport safety

The safety of vehicles is defined in terms of minimum standards; the ful-   **8.52**
filment of these minimum standards requires that the vehicles must be
inspected. The Vehicle Inspection Decree (1702/92) applies to all vehicles registered in Finland. The vehicles must be inspected in principle
each year to ensure that they fulfil the minimum requirements of the
Decree on Vehicle Structures and Equipment (1256/92). The Central
Motor Vehicle Register of Finland is the authority supervising the inspection of motor vehicles.

8.53   A traffic operation licence is required to carry persons in road traffic. The licence may be a public transport licence, regular route traffic licence, taxi licence or a licence for transportation of patients. The authorities competent to issue such licences are the local police authority, the County Administration and the Ministry of Transport and Communications. The traffic licence generally requires that the applicant has passed the required examination (Act 343/91; Decree 666/94). Citizens of EEA Member States can apply for recognition of their examination certificates of diplomas, or certificates from learning institutions, or they can pass a qualification examination (Decree on Recognition of Examination Certificates of Citizens of EEA Member States, 1622/93; Decree on Recognition of Education and Professional Training of Citizens of EEA Member States, 580/94).

The safety regulations governing air traffic are included in the Aviation Act (595/64). The Act has recently been harmonised with the corresponding regulations of the EEA Treaty. Finland has also adhered to several international aviation conventions and on 22 April 1949 accepted the International Civil Aviation Convention as binding on Finland. Finland has reciprocal air traffic agreements with a number of countries.

8.54   The National Board of Aviation supervises the airworthiness of aircraft. Aircraft deemed fit for air traffic are granted the respective status certificate for a fixed period. Operating as a carrier in regular air traffic or other aviation for the purpose of financial gain requires a licence granted by the National Board of Aviation, unless otherwise required pursuant to an agreement with another country. On 11 June 1971 Finland also adhered to the international convention on prevention of crimes and certain other acts in air traffic; on 17 December 1971 to the Convention on prevention of illegal seizure of aircraft; and on 10 August 1973, to the Convention on prevention of illegal acts against the safety of civil aviation. The law for preventing criminal acts against the safety of air traffic (Act on Measures to Protect Air Traffic in Certain Circumstances, 842/71), complements the provisions of the above international conventions.

The Maritime Act (674/94) contains regulations governing sea traffic and mostly follows the Hamburg rules. The captain of the vessel is primarily responsible for its seaworthiness, although the responsibility extends also to the shipping company and shipowner. The corresponding Decree contains separate provisions on the inspection of vessels. The Ministry of Transport and Communications and the National Board of Navigation are the competent supervising authorities. The safety regulations governing sea traffic are similar to the corresponding international agreements.

8.55   Rail traffic is, in practice, managed by the State Railways, which is a state utility. The operations of the State Railways are managed by the National Board of Railways and the subordinate railway districts (Decree on the Administration of State Railways, 273/87). An individual may also establish a railway, provided that the State Council grants the required licence. The Railway Transport Decree (714/75) governs both the traffic which the State Railways have agreed to execute, and the connecting traffic between the State Railways and other railway operators.

Pursuant to the Decree, the National Board of Railways issues instructions for maintaining order and safety on trains and in railway areas. The Railways Board is in principle responsible for injuries caused by its personnel, or by persons contracted by it for the execution of transport while performing their duties. (Art 8). However, this reponsibility is subject to the restrictions specified in the Decree. The safety provisions issued by the National Board of Railways are consistent with the regulations of the COTIF Convention to which Finland has adhered (ConvA 4 and 5/85).   **8.56**

(ii)   Hotels and restaurants

The primary measures needed to establish a hotel or restaurant are: a report of new business, and the necessary trade licence (Decree on Accommodation and Catering Establishments, 727/91; Business Freedom Act 122/91), as well as a notification to the Trade Register, if the legal form of the company so requires (Trade Register Act 129/79). In addition to the report of new business, a written notice of the business must be made to the local health authority, to the fire and rescue authority and the police in the place of business. Detailed information about the activities of the business as required by the Decree must be delivered to the police. An accommodation or catering establishment must fulfil the structural and technical requirements specified in separate regulations governing fire safety and rescue operations, health care, town planning and building. Compliance is supervised by the County Administration and the police, as well as by the fire and rescue authorities and health authorities. In the case of violation, the police or the County Administration may issue a warning, or limit the opening hours of the establishment, close it for a fixed period, or cancel the licence (Art 14).   **8.57**

The Health Care Act (469/65) contains detailed health regulations. The municipal health inspector supervises, *inter alia*, that hotels and restaurants comply with health regulations. Hotels and restaurants must apply for separate alcohol distribution licences from the State Alcohol Monopoly (Alcohol Act 549/68).   **8.58**

11.   Rights against transport operators

(i)   Transport of persons by road

No special compensation provisions exist for road transport. Generally, the provisions of the Compensation Act (412/74) apply. There are no   **8.59** legal provisions concerning the responsibility of the traffic operator for damage caused by delay. The traffic operator's responsibility may be considered presumed. The carrier is to be responsible for the damage caused by delay, unless he can prove that he is not guilty of an error or negligence. Traffic insurance (whose provisions are described in 7, *supra*) compensates for personal injuries sustained in road traffic.

(ii) Transport of persons by air

8.60   The Air Transport Act (387/86) applies to both domestic and international traffic. The provisions of the Act are mainly compelling in favour of the passenger. As regards liability for personal injuries, the carrier's liability is strict, except for cases where the damage is solely due to the health condition of the passenger (Art 17). As regards damages due to delay or damaged baggage, the air carrier's liability for negligence is presumed (Art 20). In other words, the carrier is liable for the damage caused by him unless he can prove that he is not guilty of an error or neglect. The carrier's liability is restricted. For personal injuries the highest limit of compensation is SDR 100,000[4] per passenger, for damage caused by delay SDR 4,150 per passenger, and for the destruction, loss or other damage to baggage SDR 1,000 per passenger.

8.61   According to the Air Transport Act, any condition releasing the freight carrier from liability, or for lowering the upper limit of liability below the above stated sum, is void. However, in order not to forfeit his right to receive compensation, the passenger must make a written claim immediately: for luggage within seven days, and for goods within 14 days of receipt. The complaint concerning delay must be made within 21 days of the date the luggage became available to the recipient. A compensation claim must be filed in court within two years of the date of the aircraft's arrival at its destination or when it should have arrived (Art 29). The action may be processed in a country which has adhered to the Warsaw Convention on harmonising international air transport regulations, (dated 12 October 1929, with subsequent amendments), or, where the freight carrier has its domicile or principal place of business, or an accredited office, or at the place of destination. An action to claim compensation for personal injury or damage to baggage may also be filed in a court of the country where the freight carrier has an office, provided that the passenger has his domicile or permanent residence in the country in question.

(iii) Transport of persons by sea

8.62   The carrier is liable for damages caused during sea transport (Maritime Act 674/94, Art 3). The carrier's liability is restricted to SDR 175,000 per

---

4 Special Drawing Right refers to a special drawing right as defined by the International Monetary Fund.

person for a passenger's personal injury, and to SDR 4,150 per person for damage caused by delay. The carrier's liability for damaged baggage is restricted to SDR 1,800 per each passenger's hand baggage. The carrier is entitled to deduct SDR 20 from the amount of damages for damaged baggage and SDR 20 for damage caused by delay, as the passenger's excess deduction. If, however, it can be proved that the carrier had caused the damage intentionally or due to gross negligence, the liability will not be restricted. It is not permitted to deviate from the above provisions, provided that the transport takes place in Finnish, Norwegian, Swedish or Danish internal traffic, or in traffic to or from these countries, regardless of other laws which may be applicable to such transport or any other transport generally governed by Finnish law. A compensation claim or a claim due to the death or injury of a passenger, as well as a compensation claim based on damage to baggage, must be filed within two years of the date of arrival. Finnish law requires that the action must be filed in special maritime courts established in conjunction with certain other courts, although it is in principle also possible to designate another court for settling disputes.

(iv) Transport of persons by rail

The Act on Liability for Damages Due to Use of Railways (8/1898) and the Railway Traffic Decree (714/75) stipulate the liability of the Railways. Basically, if a personal injury is caused due to the use of railways, the railway owner is liable to pay compensation. However, the compensation may be conciliated or refused, if the injured party has either intentionally or negligently caused the damage, or if the damage was due to *force majeure*. Pursuant to the Railway Traffic Decree, the railway is liable to compensate for damaged or delayed luggage. However, the railway is not liable to compensate for the damage suffered by the passenger due to the delay. An action to claim compensation from the railways must be filed within three years of the date when the journey ended, if the claim concerns damaged luggage, and within two years of the date of damage, if the compensation is claimed for personal injury. **8.63**

(v) Carrier's or tour operator's liability

The compensation liability of all carriers is limited to cases where the damage is not due to *force majeure*. The amount of payable compensation may be conciliated or refused, if the injured person or the owner of the damaged goods had personally caused the damage either intentionally or negligently. In principle, it is always necessary to make a compensation claim. The amount of the carrier's liability is restricted, and the time limits for bringing action to receive compensation are also relatively short. **8.64**

However, the tour operator's liability also concerns in principle all parties whom the tour operator has contracted to execute the tour. Compensation claims against the tour operator must be made within ten years of the date of damage.

12. Financial services

(i) Banks

8.65 Financial operations may be carried on by banks and credit institutions. The founders of a deposit bank or credit institution must apply for a licence from the Ministry of Finance (Credit Institutions Act 1607/93). Deposit banks and credit institutions are supervised by the Financial Inspection, subordinated to the Bank of Finland (Financial Inspection Act 503/93).

A deposit bank is only allowed to carry on banking operations and related activities, including currency exchange, financing operations and financing facilities. The commercial name of a deposit bank must include the word or element "*pankki*" or "*bank*".

To ensure its solvency, the deposit bank's cash reserves must be equal to at least 10% of its debts. To safeguard the stability of their business and depositors' receivables, deposit banks are required to be members of the Guarantee Fund. The Fund's articles of association and their modifications are approved by the Ministry of Finance.

8.66 The marketing activities of deposit banks are supervised by the Financial Inspection. A deposit bank may not give untrue or misleading information in its marketing nor otherwise engage in practices which from the customer's perspective are inappropriate or improper. Marketing which does not include information necessary for the customer's financial safety shall always be deemed to be inappropriate. The Office of Free Competition supervises compliance with the Trade Competition Act. When assessing the appropriateness of contractual terms, the safeguarding of depositors' interests must be taken into consideration. The Financial Inspection may, under the penalty of a conditional fine, prohibit a deposit bank from using illegal marketing practices or contractual terms. The Market Court is the competent authority in the last instance to resolve the matter.

(ii) Credit institutions

8.67 A credit institution may carry on banking operations and other related activities, but is not permitted to accept deposits from the public. The provisions concerning the solvency of deposit banks as such are applicable also to credit institutions. The stipulations on marketing and unfair trade practices concerning banks are also applicable to credit institutions. A credit institution may establish a foreign branch subject to a licence granted by the Ministry of Finance. A credit institution which has been granted a licence to operate in an EEA Member State may establish a branch or otherwise offer the services referred to in the Credit Institutions Act and covered by its trade licence (Act on Foreign Credit Institutions and Financial Institutions in Finland 1608/93).

Branch office operations are governed by the Deposits Banks Act or the Financial Activities Act. They are supervised according to the Financial Inspection Act.

A foreign credit institution must apply for a trade licence from the **8.68** Ministry of Finance for the establishment of a branch or representation. In addition, the Financial Inspection must receive a corresponding notice of the institution from the supervising authority in the home country. The application must be presented to the Bank of Finland and to the Financial Inspection for statements. A trade licence for establishing a branch may not be refused, if the institution's business is stable and its supervision has been organised in an adequate manner.

(iii) Currency

The Bank of Finland supervises the currency exchange risks associated **8.69** with capital transactions of deposit banks and other credit institutions. If the operations include currency transactions, the bank or institution must, before starting operation, give a clarification of the planned activities and the adequacy of its risk management system to the Bank of Finland. If the bank or credit institution meets the requirements determined by the Bank of Finland, it will be granted a licence to operate in currencies (Resolution of the Bank of Finland for applying the State Council resolution concerning the implementation of the Currency Act 1089/93). A person residing in Finland must inform the Bank of Finland of payments to and from residents of foreign countries, as well as receivables from residents of foreign countries, and foreign debts and receivables to residents of foreign countries. Single currency transactions however need not be notified, and funds on foreign bank accounts need not be reported, provided that their value does not exceed FIM 50,000.

The use of cheques is governed by the Cheque Accounts Act (244/32). On 30 December 1993, Finland also adhered to the Convention for harmonising cheque account legislation, and for regulating certain legal inconsistencies concerning cheque accounts.

13. Compensation for victims of crime

(i) Preconditions for compensation

The party who has suffered damage due to a criminal act is entitled to **8.70** claim compensation from the party who has committed the crime (Compensation Act 412/74). A precondition for compensation is that the injuring party has caused the damage intentionally or negligently. The claim for compensation may be presented in court in conjunction with the criminal prosecution.

Injury caused by a criminal act may also be compensated from government funds (Act on Compensation of Damages Caused by Criminal Act from Government Funds, 935/73). Finland adhered to the European Convention on compensation payable to victims of violent crimes on 8 February 1991. Compensation may in principle only be paid provided that the crime has been reported to the police, or that the compensation claim has been filed in court in the case of criminal prosecution.

(ii) Personal injury

8.71 Compensation for personal injury may be paid from government funds, if the crime was committed in Finland. However, compensation will not be paid without a special reason in the following cases: if the crime has been committed on board a foreign vessel while in Finnish territorial waters; or on board a foreign aircraft while in Finnish air space; or if both the offender and the victim of the crime at the time of the crime were in Finland temporarily and for a short period; or if the legal connection with Finland is otherwise insignificant. From the compensation paid from government funds will be deducted the sums which the applicant has already received or is likely to receive due to the same injury, pursuant to some other law or insurance.

A person who has sustained personal injury will be compensated for healthcare costs, pain and suffering and permanent injury, drop in earnings or alimony, as well as for clothing or other articles damaged in conjunction with personal injury.

(iii) Damage to property

8.72 Damage to property is compensated from government funds only if the offender had been in the custody of an institution *e.g.* due to crime, use of intoxicants, mental illness or other similar reason, and has committed the crime while outside the institution on leave or having escaped from the institution or official custody. Material damage is also compensated when caused by a person in the custody of an institution in Iceland, Norway, Sweden or Denmark for any of the above reasons, while that person was staying in Finland on leave, escape or other similar reason.

No compensation is in principle payable for damage to material property, if the guilty party and the injured party were living in the same household at the time of the criminal act.

(iv) Procedure

The compensation may be conciliated, or its payment can be refused, if **8.73** the injured party has contributed to the damage, or some other factor irrelevant to the act has contributed to the damage. The compensation application must be made to the State Treasury. The applicant's right to claim compensation from the offender is transferred to the State from the date when the State Treasury has decided to pay compensation.

The right to receive compensation is less dependent on the legal provisions relating to the person or nationality of the injured party than on the place of the criminal act and the person who has committed the crime.

14. Time share regulation

(i) Legal structure

Time share properties may in Finland be sold or let within the framework **8.74** of legally acknowledged company forms. Companies may own and possess real property and apartments. The company's articles of association or memorandum of association must indicate the rights and obligations in the company conferred by the shares. Generally the entities engaged in time share operations are limited companies. In limited companies, the shareholders exercise the decision-making authority at shareholders' general meetings and appoint a board of directors for the company. A shareholder is liable for the company's commitments only up to the amount of the share capital invested by him, and can only be obligated to pay the fees and charges specified in the articles of association (Companies Act 734/78; Housing Companies Act 809/91). The shareholder is entitled to sell his share freely on market terms.

(ii) Marketing

The provisions of the Consumer Protection Act (38/78) are applicable to **8.75** the marketing and sale of shares in time sharing properties, provided that the target of marketing or the buyer is a consumer.

15. Passport and frontier control

(i) Passport and visa controls

As a rule, every Finnish citizen may obtain a passport (Passport Act **8.76** 642/86). A Finnish citizen is entitled to exit the country, provided he has a personal passport. The passport is granted for ten years, but can at the request of the applicant be granted for a shorter period. Upon official request, the passport may be granted for less than ten years to the following: a person who has been reported to the police or official prosecutor, suspected on reasonable grounds of a crime which may be punishable by imprisonment of more than one year; who has been sentenced to unconditional imprisonment; who has been sentenced to a fine exceeding a certain number of day-fines and has not served the punishment; who can on reasonable grounds be suspected of abusing his passport to commit a crime; who has been found to be incapable of taking care of himself; or who is a conscript over 17 but under 30 years of age, unless he proves that his military service is not an obstacle for granting a passport.

8.77   The passport is granted upon application to the police of the area of the applicant's domicile. The police are also responsible for considering the obstacles for granting a passport. The decision of the police may be appealed to the County Administrative Court. A minor may be granted a passport provided that his/her guardians give their consent. A person over 18 years of age is considered to be of legal age. Persons under 15 years of age may be entered on their parents' passports.

Finnish citizens can travel without a passport to Iceland, Norway, Sweden and Denmark pursuant to a treaty signed on 12 July 1957. Nordic citizens can also reciprocally travel to Finland without a passport, and the above countries do not inspect the passports of the signatory states.

8.78   It is required in principle that a non-Nordic citizen arriving in Finland must be in possession of a valid passport granted by the authorities of his home country, as well as a visa or residence permit for a prolonged stay granted by a Finnish diplomatic mission. A group travelling together may also have a group passport indicating the names and birth dates of all the members of the group. Each group member must further have an identity document issued by the competent authority of his home country. The visa obligations have been abolished by reciprocal treaties with several states. A person travelling in a group having a previously appointed group leader can be granted a group visa.

8.79   A foreign citizen who intends to stay in Finland for more than three months must obtain a residence permit. A citizen of an EEA member state who stays in Finland seeking work is allowed to stay for a reasonable period thereafter even without a residence permit, provided that he is still looking for work and that he has actual possibilities of finding it. The residence permit is granted for a fixed period, or even permanently, if certain preconditions are fulfilled. A citizen of an EEA Member State, his/her spouse, dependent parents or children under 21 years of age are granted fixed-period residence permits for five years, and citizens of another country in principle for one year. The permit application should generally be submitted to the Finnish diplomatic mission in the country where the applicant has his permanent domicile.

A person is entitled to stay in Finland on an aliens' passport only if endorsed with a valid residence permit.

If a foreigner intends to accept paid work in Finland he must, upon **8.80** arrival, be in possession of a work permit granted by a Finnish diplomatic mission. Work permits can be granted only on special grounds to a foreigner after his arrival in the country. The work permit is granted for a fixed period or until further notice, and may include certain pre-conditions. A precondition for the validity of a work permit is that the foreigner has a valid visa or residence permit. The work permit must be applied for from the Finnish diplomatic mission in the country where the applicant is domiciled, or under certain conditions from the local employment office (Aliens Act 378/1991; Aliens Decree 142/1994).

If a co-operation agreement has been signed between a Nordic country and any other country concerning the inspection of passports, the passport, visa and residence permit of a foreigner transferring from one Nordic country to another must generally be inspected only in one of the signatory states (Treaty between Finland, Iceland, Norway, Sweden and Denmark on the Abolition of Passport Inspection between Nordic borders, 12 July 1957).

(ii) Customs

The Finnish territory, territorial waters and air space constitute a customs **8.81** territory (Customs Act 573/78 with subsequent amendments). Goods imported to or exported from the country must be customs-cleared. A passenger arriving from abroad may, however, bring duty-free the personal belongings needed for his travel, and a separately stipulated quantity of purchases (Customs Tax Act 575/78).

According to the resolution of the National Board of Customs, the value of customs-free purchases may not exceed FIM 1,500, and additionally a passenger may bring along tax free purchases up to 200 cigarettes, or a corresponding amount of another tobacco product, one litre of strong alcoholic beverages, one litre of mild alcoholic beverages, and two litres of beer. If the travel is made by sea and both the departure and destination are in Finland, it is stipulated as a further condition that the duration of the travel must be at least 24 hours. If the travel is of a shorter duration, tax-free purchases are not permitted.

Chapter 9
France
Marc Jobert
Avocat à la Cour

1. Regulatory authorities

In order to understand how and by whom tourism is regulated in France, **9.1**
it is essential to have some idea of the administrative subdivisions that
exist in France.

France is divided into 21 *régions* each composed of two of more *départements*. There are 99 *départements* in all. In turn each *département* is composed of a large number of cities, towns and villages, which are all called
a *commune*. A small village with a few inhabitants is a *commune*, just as is a
large city such as Lyon or Marseille. There are approximately 36,000 *communes* in France. France is by tradition a centralised state, and much is
decided in the various government ministries in Paris. In each *région* and
in each *département* there is a *préfet*, a senior civil servant, who represents
the State, and supervises the local representatives of the various ministries.

Local government is slowly becoming more important, but its regula- **9.2**
tory activity is still weak compared to that of the state. It is however very
active in promoting local resources and in subsidising what it considers to
be local priorities. There are various forms of elected local government at
the level of the *commune, département*, and *région*.

It may come as a shock to those who think of France as the Land of
Descartes and of Napoleon and of rational philosophy, to find out that
tourism is not regulated in France by a single central authority.

There is of course a central administration in charge of Tourism. This
administration has at times been a separate ministry within the government, but very often it is included in the domain of another ministry, for
example Foreign Trade. Over the years it has "travelled" a great deal,
from one ministry to another. It was until recently part of the Ministry for
Transport, Equipment and Tourism and since May 1995 is a Ministry in
its own right.

Officially the central administration is in charge of preparing and im- **9.3**
plementing government policy as regards tourism. It drafts the regulations
applicable to the various professions involved (travel agents, hotels, etc).
It co-ordinates the initiatives of the various local authorities and private
groups and corporations. It supervises the funding distributed throughout
France. It initiates studies and analyses of tourism in France. It promotes
tourism in France abroad, and handles EC and international matters, etc.

However, there are also a dozen or so further ministries which play a part in shaping the French public policy relating to Tourism. For example, the ministries in charge of the Economy, Agriculture, Urban planning, Youth, the Sea, and Culture. The tourism administration is in charge of only one-fifth of the government funding of tourism. The rest of the funding is controlled by other ministries. At the national level, in addition to the the central administration for tourism, there are a number of advisory bodies and agencies including:

(i)   *L'Agence Française de l'Ingénièrie Touristique*, a think tank, whose members include a number of professionals, such as Club Med and the French railways, who offer expertise and financial know-how to the French tourism industry.

(ii) *La Maison de France*, whose members include more than 600 local tourist bureaux, hotel groups, unions of travel agents, professionals like Air France or Pierre et Vacances, etc, promotes tourism in France through a network of more than 40 offices abroad.

(iii) *Le Conseil National du Tourisme*, an advisory board consisting of 200 members representing all the important actors in the tourism industry. It advises the Minister in charge of Tourism on a number of issues. For example, it gives an opinion on the appeal, before the Minister, of sanctions taken against a travel agent by the *Préfet*.

9.4   At the local level, the representatives of the state, the *Préfet de Région*, and the *Préfet du département*, have an important role. They grant the administrative authorisations necessary to a number of bodies which are essential to the tourist trade. They control the day-to-day application of regulatory standards in matters of hygiene, public safety, etc. They co-ordinate the activities of the various local bodies, and supervise the allocation of public funding. For example, the *Préfet* grants the licence which travel agents need to carry on business and gives the approval to local tourist associations which is necessary to receive public finding. The *Préfet* also supervises the civil servants who inspect hotels and restaurants to enforce safety and hygiene regulations.

The mayor of the *commune* has a regulatory function in matters that affect tourism, such as parking regulations, opening hours, beach safety, urban planning and building permits.

9.5   Local government is very active in promoting tourism, either by direct action, by state funding and subsidies, or by participating in various associations, committees and similar bodies. These operate mostly at the level of the *commune*, but also at the level of the *département* and the *région*.

The most well known structure, which the average tourist will certainly have been in contact with at least once, is the local tourist bureau, or tourist information office. These are run by associations or by municipal structures (*offices municipaux du tourisme*). There are more than 3,000 local tourist information offices run by associations.

Communes which are classified as tourist destinations may impose on tourists staying inside the city limits a small tax per night (*taxe de séjour*).

There are in addition very many professional organisations which are **9.6** active in the tourist industry. There are organisations and associations of hotels, restaurants, bars, cafés, night-clubs, camping sites etc with various local, and regional subdivisions. The main travel agents' organisation is the *Syndicat National des Agents de Voyages* (SNAV). This is a professional union organised under the French Labour Code and specifically authorised to represent the profession of travel agents before government bodies and in collective labour agreements. About two-thirds of the profession are members of SNAV. The SNAV has various regional, local, and categorial subdivisions. The *Association Professionnelle de Solidarité des Agents de Voyages* (APSAV) was created by the SNAV to provide its members with a financial guarantee. Under French Law this guarantee is required of all travel agents.

2. Legal and professional rules

(i) Regulatory requirements

Under French Law, access to the profession of travel agent or tour operator **9.7** is regulated. It is not possible to just "set up shop". There are certain minimum requirements and a licence must be obtained. Criminal sanctions may be imposed on those who operate without a licence and the business may be closed by order of the criminal court.

There are, however, no special requirements concerning the legal form in which travel agents operate, which may be a limited liability company, partnership, sole trader, or any other form acceptable for businesses. There are no special rules concerning the winding up of travel agents other than the obligation to have a financial guarantee.

The profession was first regulated by law in 1937. The current applicable legislation is the law of 13 July 1992 and decree no. 94–490 of 15 June 1994, enacted as a result of the European Directive of 13 June 1990. This legislation replaces the law of 11 July 1975 and the decree of 28 March 1977. It regulates the activities of those who sell "products" made by other professionals, and those whose put together package tours and other similar products, and it distinguishes between two categories: professionals operating for profit, and non-profit associations and similar bodies.

The definition of a package tour (*forfait touristique*), inspired by the **9.8** Directive, is:

(i)   the combination of at least two operations concerning transport, and lodging, or other tourist services not accessory to the transport or lodging, and representing a significant proportion of the package;

(ii) a duration of at least 24 hours, or one night; and

(iii) an all-inclusive price.

The definition does not apply, however, to individual hotels, restaurants, passenger carriers, and guides.

(ii) Licence requirements

9.9 To be allowed to establish themselves as travel agents or tour operators operating for profit, professionals must request a licence to be issued by the local *Préfet*. The *Préfet* verifies, after consulting a local commission made up of tourism professionals and civil servants, whether the application satisfies the conditions set out by Law.

9.10 The conditions are:

(i)   Morality; the applicant must not have a criminal record and must not be prevented from running a business by any administrative, criminal, or judicial sanction.

(ii) Professional aptitude; the applicant must be an experienced professional. Minimum requirements are three years experience in tourism at managerial level, or a university degree in tourism and two years experience in tourism; or five years experience in another branch.

In the case of an applicant coming from another EC country, the minimum requirements are six years experience at managerial level, or three years experience at managerial level and five years at a lower level. If the applicant has a university degree in tourism, the requirement is at least three years at managerial level or five years at a lower level. If the applicant has studied tourism for only two years then the work experience requirements are of four and six years respectively.

If the agent runs more than one office, then a salaried employee, with the professional aptitude described above, must be hired.

(iii) Financial guarantee; the applicant must have a financial guarantee from a bank, insurance company, or a collective guarantor, with its main office inside the European Community, in order to guarantee the obligations of the travel agent to his customers, to bring them back to their point of departure and to be able to refund the monies held on their behalf. The minimum guarantee is 5% of the agent's turnover, or 350,000FF. The *Préfet* determines the exact amount that must be posted by each travel agent within his jurisdiction.

Most travel agents are guaranteed by APSAV (*Association Professionnelle de Solidarité des Agences de Voyages*) which was created by the main union of travel agents (see above). APS will stand in place of travel agents who fail to honour their commitments, and provide their customers with an equivalent product.

(iv) Insurance; the applicant must take out insurance cover for their worldwide liability to customers, other professionals, and third parties, for substantial and nominal damages, caused by the agent, his employees or correspondents acting in his name. The agent must indicate in his brochures and commercial documents the nature and extent of the insurance coverage taken out.

(v) Office space; the applicant must have a proper office, with an independent entrance for his customers, two rooms, and at least 35 m² of office space.

9.11 Even after it is granted, the licence to operate may be taken away if one or more of the five required conditions are no longer complied with, or if the travel agent has committed repeated and serious breaches of his obligations as a travel agent.

The agent is regulated not only in the establishment of his main office but also in the setting up of correspondent and branch offices. Agents who have a licence, may set up branch offices and sales counters without any prior approvals, but they must report the opening of such offices to the authorities, and file the relevant documents. These offices must have a local manager who possesses the qualifications necessary to obtain a licence.

9.12 If agents allow other professionals to sell their products as correspondents (agents acting for the travel agent in his name, under his liability), then they must have the contracts made with these correspondents approved by the authorities. The contracts must contain a number of standard clauses and a number of supporting documents must be filed with the *Préfet*.

Other professionals, besides travel agents, can also sell holiday packages. Professionals such as real estate agents, organisers of holiday accommodation or leisure activities and passenger carriers can apply for permission to sell holiday products, as long as this is not their main activity. The holiday package must not represent more than 50% of what they normally sell (for example, bus with hotel, or flat rental with meals). The *Préfet* decides if permission can be granted and may revoke such permission in the same way as for regular travel agents. A financial guarantee and insurance coverage is also required.

9.13 A licence system also exists for non profit-making organisations. It resembles the system previously described for commercial travel agents. The purpose of the system is to protect the public against fraud and incompetence, but also to prevent commercial enterprises from deceiving the public by posing as non profit-making organisations. Non profit-making organisations can only sell to members of their associations. They can only promote their products among their members and are not allowed to advertise to the general public. In many cases, however, it is very easy to become a member of an association for a nominal sum, allowing direct competition with travel agents.

The licence requirement concerns organisations who regularly engage in the sale of travel products, but not those who only do so on a one-off basis. For example, an association of lawyers who organise an annual congress would not be obliged to apply for a licence.

9.14　The profit and the non-profit licence application procedures have been somewhat harmonised by the law of 1992, which is more demanding for non profit-making organisations than the previous law (1975). If they do not have to have office space like commercial agents, non profit-making organisations still have to satisfy similar requirements concerning morality, insurance and professional aptitude. The financial guarantee obligation is adapted to the status of a non profit-making organisation with a lower minimum guarantee and the possibility of obtaining a guarantee by being a part of a group of tourist associations.

Travel agents established in other EC countries and wishing to provide services to customers in France, also require a licence. They must provide the minister in charge of tourism with a statement from their national government stating that they are authorised to operate as a travel agent and that they have an adequate financial guarantee.

(iii)　Guides

9.15　The subject of tour guides and the rules which apply to their profession may appear to be a relatively minor aspect of tourism law, but it has resulted in some important cases before the European Court of Justice.

A decree of 13 October 1983[1] created a rather strict system by punishing by a fine those who work as guides without a professional identity card, as well as those who employ such guides. It is not possible to work as a guide without first obtaining such a card, which is in effect an administrative authorisation. The card is granted to those who have certain diplomas or who pass an exam set by the ministry in charge of tourism. In addition, a certain number of persons are not obliged to obtain a card, because of their high level of qualification: for example university professors, museum officials, etc.

The monopoly granted to professional guides by this system did not cover all of France, but only certain cities or areas considered to be worthy of protection on account of the monuments and other tourist attractions that they contained.

9.16　However the monopoly ran into difficulties when faced with foreign tour operators, who preferred to employ their own national guides, rather than local guides.

The EC Commission considered this monopoly, and similar monopolies in Greece and Italy, to be contrary to the principle of freedom of services within the EC, and the EC Court of Justice was asked to decide the issue.

The Court decided, in the case of France, that the monopoly was contrary to Article 59 of the EC Treaty. The Court did not say, however, that any national legislation on this matter was contrary to the Treaty, but

---

[1] Decree No 83–912, JO 15 October 1983.

only that any limitation should be imposed only where required by the general interest, and only because the country where the tour operator was established did not provide for rules which effectively protected this general interest. The Court considered that French Law (as well as that of Greece and Italy) went beyond what was necessary to promote historical treasures and to communicate in the best possible way the cultural and artistic heritage of those countries.

As a result, France has changed its legislation. The law of 13 July 1992 **9.17** limits the obligation, imposed on tour operators and the like, to employ qualified guides (*i.e.* card holders) to visits to museums and historical monuments, instead of to certain geographical areas and cities as previously. It is still necessary to possess a professional card, which may be obtained by foreign guides under certain conditions.

3. Consumer rights and safeguards

(i) Statement of general conditions of sale

Under French law, travel agents must give their customers a written docu- **9.18** ment stating the obligations of each party and containing the general conditions of sale of the travel agent. The *arrêté* of 14 June 1982 set out the minimum requirements for the conditions of sale. Its provisions were an important source of inspiration for the EC Package Travel Directive,[2] which in turn led to the law of 13 July 1992.[3]

The regulations concerning the sale of holiday products are applicable to all travel and holiday products except for international air, rail and sea transport and furnished holiday flats, which have their own specific regulations.

(ii) Travel agreement between tour operator and consumer

The sale of a package tour must be accompanied by the signing of two **9.19** copies of a written contract, signed by both parties and bearing the name and address of the travel agent, of the insurance company, of the guarantor and of the organiser.

Before a contract is signed, the travel agent must provide the consumer with the following information in writing:

(i)   the place of destination, description of the means of transportation;
(ii)   the category and class of accommodation;
(iii)   the meals included;
(iv)   the itinerary in the case of a tour;

---

[2] Directive 90/314 (OJ 1990 L158/9).
[3] Title V; JO 14 July 1993, p9459.

(v)   the administrative and medical formalities necessary to cross borders during the trip;

(vi)   the visits, excursions included or cost thereof if optional;

(vii)   the minimum or maximum size of the group, and cancellation date if minimum size is not reached (date must be at least 21 days prior to departure);

(viii) the amount of down payment and payment schedule;

(ix)   the conditions of possible modification of contract;

(x)   the cancellation terms;

(xi)   the insurance included in contract; and

(xii)   the optional personal insurance.

9.20   This information is contractual, unless the travel agent reserves the right to modify it, and clearly states how and on what basis it may be modified.

The contract itself must include similar information to that contained in the above list, including:

(i)   the price of the package, including information on airport and local tourist taxes;

(ii)   specific clauses requested by the customer and accepted by the agent;

(iii)   the means by which the customer can complain to the travel agent about the quality of the holiday package;

(iv)   the particulars of the insurance contract taken out by the customer;

(v)   the date by which the customer must advise the travel agent of a transfer to someone else of the contract;

(vi)   the undertaking by the travel agent to give the customer, in writing, information on the local representative of the agent on site, or the necessary emergency telephone numbers; and

(vii)   in the case of a minor, a telephone number enabling the parents to contact their child.

9.21   The contract must also contain the following terms:

(i)   The last payment may not be of less than 30% of the purchase price and should be made in exchange for the necessary travel documents (aeroplane tickets etc).

(ii)   The contract may be transfered by the buyer to another person than the original customer, provided that the agent is informed by registered mail, at least seven days before the start of the trip. This is to enable the customer who changes his mind to minimise his loss by finding someone to replace him. The original customer and his replacement are jointly liable for the payment of the holiday package.

(iii)   The price of the package may not be increased, unless a specific clause is included in the contract. Even with such a clause, an increase in price is not possible less than 30 days before the start of the trip. It can only be increased as a result of an increase in the cost of transportation, of taxes and airport fees, or of the rate of foreign exchange.

(iv)   The travel agent is entitled to modify an essential element of the contract only if he can not perform his obligations because of an exterior element beyond his control (*force majeure*). In that case the customer must be informed immediately by registered mail, and has the option of terminating the contract, without penalty, or of accepting the modified contract.

(v)   The customer is entitled to a reduction in price if the quality of the package is diminished. The customer may also sue for damages and ask to be compensated.

(vi)   In the case of cancellation by the agent without the customer being at fault, a full refund must be made and, in addition, the customer is to be paid an indemnity equivalent at least to the financial penalty he would have had to pay if he had cancelled.

(vii) If the contract is modified after the start of the holiday, the travel agent must offer an equivalent product (similar hotel, for example, if the one chosen by the customer is not available). Even if the replacement product is more expensive, there should be no extra charge for the customer, and if it is less expensive the customer is entitled to a refund. If the travel agent can not provide the customer with an equivalent product, or if the customer has due cause to refuse the replacement solution, then the agent must provide the customer with transportation to the point of departure.

(iii)   Liability of travel agents

Travel agents are fully liable. Under article 23 of the law of 13 July 1992, **9.22** they are responsible for the proper execution of their contractual obligations, whether these obligations were to be carried out by themselves or by subcontractors or sub-agents.

To avoid liability the agent must prove that the faulty or imperfect execution of the contract was due to:

(i)   the negligence of the customer; or
(ii)   the action of a third party not involved in the holiday package, which is unforeseeable and which could not be remedied at the time; or
(iii) *force majeure*.

This is close to "strict liability", and it should facilitate action by injured **9.23** or dissatisfied customers.

The law only came into force in December 1994, so there are no published court decisions on this point so far. However, reference can be made to cases under the law of 1975. The courts had already extended the limits of the travel agents' liability quite considerably. One of the most famous cases is that of the Rio taxi:[4]

A couple who were on holiday in Rio took a taxi, hired by the local representative of their travel agent, to see one of the more famous tourist sites. The taxi had an accident and both passengers were killed. The travel agent was found negligent in not hiring a taxi with full insurance coverage.

9.24 Even before the law of 13 July 1992, the French courts had already gone far beyond holding that mistakes made by travel agents themselves were negligent (wrong hotel, wrong dates, misleading descriptions, etc), and had considered that the agents were also liable for the negligence of the professionals that they hired to carry out part of the holiday package (hotel, bus, ship, etc). The courts considered that negligence could include: a poor choice of means of transport; not investigating safety conditions prior to the customer's trip; etc. Travel agents were therefore already liable for negligence of other professionals.

9.25 Some examples will give the reader an idea of how far the courts had gone. Travel agents had been found negligent for:

(i)   not being careful in the selection of a means of transportation,[5] or

(ii)   in the choice of a bus driver;[5]

(iii)   in not investigating the safety of an optional boat trip which was to be paid directly by the customer to the boat's owners;[6]

(iv)   a fire in a hotel;[7]

(v)   the interruption of a trip due to a strike which should have been known to the travel agent;[8]

(vi)   for lack of a contigency plan in the case of an accident;[9]

(vii)   taking tourists into a dangerous area;[10]

(viii)   a bus accident caused by the negligence of a bus driver hired by a transport company working for a tour organiser;[11] and

(ix)   not informing parents that the holiday village they had chosen was crossed by train tracks, even though the brochure said that there was private access to the beach. A child was killed by a train while going to the beach.[12]

9.26 The travel agent has a duty to provide the customer with a "proper functioning holiday package, in conformity with the contract and with the description contained in the tour operator's brochure".

---

[4] Cass. Civ., 5 January 1961, *Compagnie Internationale des Wagons-lits et des grands express européens*, JCP 1961. II. 11979.

[5] Cass. Civ., 15 October 1974, JCP 1975. 18071 bis; Paris, 30 March 1989, D. 1989, IR, P.141.

[6] Cass. Civ., 29 January 1991, Bull. Cass. I No 40.

[7] Paris, 11 March 1993, Gaz. Pal. 1993. 1 somm. 164.

[8] Cass. Civ., 3 November 1983, JCP 1984. II. 20147.

[9] Cass. Civ., 10 November 1971, D.1972,593, JCP 1971. IV. 289.

[10] Cass. Civ., 15 December 1969, D.1970.326.

[11] Cass. Civ., 3 May 1977, JCP-CI 1977, 6177, Bull. Civ. 1ère, 195.

[12] Cass. Civ., 29 June 1976, JCP 1978, 18995.

The travel agent must also provide for the safety of his customers. That **9.27** safety obligation has been construed as including five main points:

(i)   a duty to inform customers;
(ii)   a duty to help customers;
(iii) caution in organising outings and tours;
(iv)   caution in choosing local services; and
(v)   a duty to supervise local services.[13]

The new law will make it even more difficult for the travel agent to avoid liability.

(iv)   Consumer protection

In addition to the protection afforded to consumers by the law of 13 July **9.28** 1992, tourists may invoke general consumer protection laws. There are a number of statutes which apply to the sale of goods and services to consumers and which can be useful to tourists.

For example the law of 10 January 1978[14] provides that abusive clauses in consumer goods and services contracts are void. The courts have affirmed their authority to strike out such clauses from contracts.

Tourism consumers can also invoke the consumer laws on:

(i)   door to door sales;
(ii)   consumer credit; and
(iii) misleading advertising.

European Directives also exist in these areas:
Misleading Advertising Directive[15]
Contracts negotiated away from Business Premises Directive.[16]

(v)   Liability of hotels

In the nineteenth century, the hotelier or innkeeper was considered to **9.29** be a master in his own home and therefore entitled to select his customers as he pleased. He could refuse to rent a room without having to give any specific reason for his refusal. French law now treats the renting of a hotel room as a standard service contract, and this is no longer the case. Current free competition legislation[17] obliges retailers to sell their goods or services to all customers who are willing to pay for them. Hotels must therefore have a valid reason to turn away a customer, such as abusive or drunken behaviour, for example. They can also evict a

---

[13] Pierre Py, *Droit de Tourisme*, Dalloz, 1994, p328.
[14] No 78–23, JO 11 January 1978.
[15] 84/450/EEC, OJ 1991 L180/14.
[16] 85/577/EEC, OJ 1992 L107/7.
[17] Ordonnance No 86–1243 of 1 December 1986.

customer for improper behaviour. Criminal sanctions for racism[18] may apply to hotel directors who turn away prospective customers because of their race or nationality.

9.30 Hotels are also prohibited from linking the rental of a room to the purchase of other goods and services, such as meals, for example.[19]

Hotels must honour bookings made by customers. They are liable for damages if they fail to do so. Customers are also liable for cancellations, but in practice it is rare for a court to award damages to a hotel unless the customer is a professional (travel agent) booking a large number of rooms.

9.31 If a sum of money has been paid by the customer to confirm his reservation, the courts usually consider that it is a down payment and that a contract exists. Under this interpretation it is not possible for the hotel to cancel the contract. However under article 1590 of the Civil Code such a payment may be considered to be an *arrhes*. If so, the customer may cancel the contract by forfeiting the amount of the payment and the hotel may do likewise by reimbursing the customer twice the amount paid. The courts usually consider that article 1590 does not apply unless the parties have clearly stated that they wish it to apply to their contract.[20] Therefore, in most cases, hotels who cancel reservations are in breach of contract and are fully liable to their customers.

The limitation period applicable to hotel bills is six months. Hotels have a special lien on the baggage and personal belongings of their customers in order to recover outstanding hotel bills. They can also ask for criminal prosecution of customers who do not pay their bills, under article 313–5 of the Criminal Code. Customers risk a six day to six month prison term, and a 500 to 1,500 franc fine, provided their stay in the hotel did not exceed ten days. No criminal sanctions are applicable if the customer had been staying in the hotel for more than ten days.

9.32 The liability of hotels is traditionaly divided into two different categories: "means" and "results". In some areas, such as personal injury to customers, the hotel has an obligation of means, in others, such as theft, it has an obligation of results. In the first category, the hotel must only prove that it has used the proper means to achieve the desired results (a safe stay in the hotel, for example); in the second it must prove that the desired results were in fact achieved (safety of baggage).

4. Health and safety standards – hotels

9.33 Hotels have a duty to provide their customers with safe premises and a safe and secure room.

---

18 Law No 72–546 of 1 July 1972.
19 Ordonnance No 86–1243 of 1 December 1986.
20 Cass. Com., 3 May 1965, Bull. Civ. III. No 280, p253.

(i) Personal injury

A customer who is injured while in the hotel can not invoke automatic **9.34**
liability on the part of the hotel, but must prove that the hotel was negligent.[21] There are numerous examples of this type of liability. Some classic
examples of injuries for which the hotel will be held liable, are:

(i)   staircase in poor condition;[22]
(ii)   defective gas heating;[23]
(iii)   glass doors without security handles;[24]
(iv)   electric shock from a faulty lamp;[25]
(v)   fighting between customers, which the hotel manager did nothing
        to stop.[26]

The hotel was not held liable where a cupboard fell on a customer.[27]

The hotel shared the liability with the customer in the case of a fall on
a staircase between a dimly lit room and a brightly lit room.[28]

(ii) Damage to property

The liability of hotels for stolen baggage is more extensive than that for **9.35**
personal injury.

Under articles 1952–1954 hotels are automatically liable for baggage,
clothes, and other personal belongings stolen from the hotel, including
objects stolen from the hotel car park.

Hotels can only escape from liability if they can prove *force majeure* or
customer negligence.

The hotel was considered not liable in the case of a customer who left
his room key in the lock;[29] and in the case of a theft by an employee of
the victim.[30]

The hotel shared liability with a customer who: left his window open[31]
and did not inform the hotel of the value of the objects contained in his
bags.[32]

Contractual limitation of liability concerning hotels is void under **9.36**
French Law. The hotel is liable without monetary limits if the customer's
belongings were stolen while in the custody of the hotel (hotel safe,

---

21 Cass. Civ. 6 May 1946. JCP. 1946. II. 3226 (note Rodière).
22 Cour d'Appel, Paris, 14 October 1954, D. 1955. somm 176.
23 Poitiers, 8 February 1966, JCP 1966. IV. 131.
24 Cass. Civ., 25 November 1969, JCP 1970. IV. 8.
25 Nîmes, 14 May 1986, Rey c. Taisse.
26 Cass. Civ., 2, 24 February, 1965, Perrin c. Avy, Bull. 1965, 2, 189.
27 Cass. Civ., 15 July 1964, JCP 1964. II. 3828.
28 Cass. Civ., 1ère, 14 February 1966, D.1966, 433.
29 Cass. Civ., 1ère, 10 May 1954, Gaz. Pal. 1955. I. 45.
30 Cass. req., 5 February 1894, S: 1895. I. 417, Pau, 8 April 1930, DH 1930 373.
31 Aix, 20 May 1946, JCP 1946, éd. G. II. 3345.
32 Amiens, 21 May 1975, JCP 1976, éd. G. IV. 175.

reception, etc), or if the hotel staff were negligent. If the belongings were stolen from the customer's room or elsewhere in the hotel without being in the custody of the hotel, there is by law a limit on the amount of compensation that can be awarded. This limit is 100 times the price of one night in the hotel and 50 times the price if the theft took place in the hotel car park.

9.37   The most difficult task for the customer who claims damages for theft in the hotel will be to establish the value of his or her loss.[33] In most cases there is little evidence of what was stolen and of its value. French courts tend to take into consideration the category of the hotel and the personal wealth of the customer in order to calculate the value of the stolen goods. For example, a famous opera singer in a five star hotel will be awarded a larger amount than a student staying in a one star hotel. Obviously this method is not very scientific, and customers will be well advised to deposit any valuables in the hotel safe and to ask for a detailed receipt.

5.   Forms of redress

9.38 The same forms of redress are available to tourism consumers as to other consumers.

They can bring proceedings before the local courts: "the Tribunal d'Instance" for small claims, and the "Tribunal de Grande Instance" for more substantial cases. They also have the option of going before the "Tribunal de Commerce" which is staffed by elected non-professional judges whose main activity is working in commerce or industry. Arbitration clauses in consumer contracts are illegal.

Consumers may also complain to the following:

(i)   the public prosecutor, if a criminal violation has taken place;
(ii)   the *Direction de la Repression des Fraudes*, which handles consumer complaints;
(iii) the SNAV, a professional union; or
(iv)   the guarantor of the travel agent, who may reimburse the customer if the travel agent fails to do so.

6.   Rights against transport operators

9.39 A number of international conventions regulate travel by sea, rail, road and air. Tourists travelling to a holiday destination will in many cases be using a means of transport which is in whole or in part regulated by an international convention. Carriage from one country to another, as

---

[33] Cass. Civ., 1ère, 4 November 1986, *Société Innova Hotel c/ Dugova*.

opposed to domestic transport, is regulated by these conventions, but in some instances domestic transport can be regulated by legislation which refers to or is inspired by an international convention.

The French courts consider that the carrier and the passenger are in a **9.40** contractual situation and that the liability of the carrier for injuries or other damage suffered by the passenger is a contractual one. The carrier has a contractual obligation to bring the passenger "safe and sound" to the point of destination.[34] The French Supreme Court has extended this principle to all forms of transport (metro, taxi, ship etc).

The passenger must arrive at his or her destination, free from injury, with his or her baggage, and on time. If this is not the case, the carrier is liable, unless it can prove that the accident, delay, or loss of baggage was due to an external cause beyond its control. This principle can be explained by the fact that, for the courts, the passenger is a passive person in a vehicle or ship which he or she does not command, while the carrier is a professional who undertakes to provide a safe journey. *Force majeure* can be used as a defence by the carrier, but the French courts place the burden of proof on the carrier. For example, criminal sabotage of a railway during a strike is not considered to be a case of *force majeure*.[35]

The obligation of safety extends not only to the use of a vehicle, train or vessel, but also, to a lesser degree, to the time during which the **9.41** passenger is in the railway station, bus stop, harbour etc.[36] The carrier must ensure that all precautions are taken so that the passenger is safe while waiting to embark on the journey.

(i) Transport of persons by air

French Law[37] provides that French air carriers are subject to the same **9.42** regulations as international air carriers.

The Warsaw Convention (12 October 1929), as amended by the Hague Protocol (28 September 1955) and the Guadalajara Convention (18 September 1961) is applicable to all flights leaving or arriving in France.

The Montreal Convention (4 May 1976) provides for more favourable financial compensation for passengers who are the victims of injuries, if the flight originated from the United States, or had the United States as a destination or stop.

The vast majority of air carriers are members of IATA, which obliges them to adopt standard conditions in their contracts with passengers.

Under the Warsaw Convention each passenger must be provided with **9.43** a ticket containing information such as the points of departure and destination, the name and address of the carrier, and a statement on the

---

[34] Cass. Civ., 21 November 1911, D.1913, 1.249.
[35] Cass. Civ., 1ère, 30 June 1953, D.1953, 642.
[36] Cass. Civ., 1ère, 1 July 1969, JCP 1969, 16091; 12 July 1970, JCP 1970, 16488.
[37] The law of 2 March 1957.

possible application of the rules of liability contained in the Convention. If no ticket is issued or the ticket is incomplete, then the limitations of liability contained in the Warsaw Convention are not enforceable.

The carrier is liable in damages for the death or injury of a passenger by accident on board the aircraft or in embarking or disembarking. It is further liable for loss or injury to registered baggage, if sustained during the journey. It is also liable for any delay in the carriage of passengers and their baggage.

9.44   EC regulations[38] provide that air carriers must have specific rules in case of overbooking of a flight. These rules must organise a volunteer system and define priorities (unaccompanied minors, disabled persons, etc).

If the carrier cannot provide a passenger with a seat, the passenger must be offered a choice between reimbursement, a seat on the next flight, or a seat on another flight at a later date. The passenger is in any case entitled to financial compensation of 150 ECUs if the flight is less than 3,500 km, and of 300 ECUS if it is of more than 3,500 km. This compensation may be reduced by 50% if a seat is found on another flight leaving within two hours. The carrier must also provide, if need be, the following services, free of charge: a telephone call; meals; and hotel accommodation.

These various forms of compensation are without prejudice to the rights of the passenger to resort to legal action if he or she feels that additional compensation is necessary.

9.45   Liability of the air carrier under the Warsaw Convention is almost automatic if the passenger has suffered an injury. The French courts have adopted an extensive interpretation of liability under the Warsaw Convention.

Liability may be avoided if the carrier can prove that itself, its agents or servants took all necessary measures (due diligence) to avoid the damage or that it was impossible to take such measures, or that it was a case of *force majeure*. This is usually very difficult to prove. If, for example, there is no known cause of the accident, then the courts tend to consider that the carrier is liable.[39]

Another example of a wide interpretation by the French courts is found in the definition of embarking and disembarking. The courts have found this to mean much more than simply entering and leaving the plane, and to include all forms of airport transport.[40] The French courts (contrary to other foreign courts) have also found that it is possible to interrupt the two year period of the Warsaw limitation period.[41]

9.46   Any limitation of liability by contract is void under the Warsaw Convention, which sets its own limits. These limits are set out in terms of how

---

[38] Council Regulation of 4 February 1991.
[39] Cass. Civ., 1ère, 11 July 1966, Rev. Fr Dr. Aérien., 1966, 454.
[40] Cass. Civ., 1ère, 18 January 1966. Rev. Gén. Air., 1966, 32 (note du Pontavice).
[41] Cass. Civ., Ass. Pl., D.S. 1977, 89.

much financial compensation may be awarded by the Courts. The most important limits are:

(i)   250,000 gold francs for death or injury; and
(ii)   250 gold francs per kilo for registered baggage.

The limit in France for domestic flights, is 500,000 FF.[42]

The Warsaw Convention limits are not applicable if the victim can prove that the injury was the result of intentional or reckless negligence of the carrier or its agents.

(ii)   Transport of persons by rail

The first international Convention relating to the transport of persons by rail was signed on 23 October 1924, in Berne. The current applicable Convention is that of 9 May 1980.[43]   **9.47**

Under the Convention the railway is liable for all injuries suffered by passengers, unless it can prove that:

(i)   the accident was caused by exterior factors to the operation of the railway, that could not be avoided despite the efforts of the railway; or
(ii)   that the negligence of the passenger caused the accident; or
(iii)   that the accident was caused by a third party, and the railway did all that was necessary to try to prevent the accident.

The amount that a passenger can receive as damages for injuries or death is limited to 70,000 DTS (unit of currency of the International Monetary Fund). However this rule does not apply to countries which have no limits in their national law, which is the case of France.   **9.48**

Clauses that otherwise limit liability are prohibited.

The railway is liable for loss of baggage, unless it can prove that the loss of baggage was due to passenger negligence; the poor condition of the baggage; or to circumstances that the railway could not prevent and whose consequences could not be avoided. The maximum limit on damages is calculated according to the weight of the baggage

The railway is also liable, according to the French courts, for delay and late arrival, but such liability may be limited by contract.

The limitation period for bringing claims against the railways is three years.

(iii)   Transport of persons by sea

The Conventions relating to the transport of persons by sea are those of Brussels (29 April 1961) and London (19 November 1976).[44] The   **9.49**

---

[42] Law No 82–375 of 6 May 1982.
[43] Decree of 25 August 1987, JO 3 September 1987.
[44] JO 1 January 1987, decree No 86–1371 of 23 December 1986.

Convention of Athens of 13 December 1974 is not yet applicable in France.

The applicable national law is that of 18 June 1966 on maritime transport and cruises.[45]

(a) Cruises

9.50 Cruises are subject to stricter regulations than ordinary holiday packages. The organiser of a cruise is liable for any damage or injuries suffered by passengers and their baggage. The passenger can act directly against the organiser even if the damage is due to another professional involved in the cruise (for example the boat driver).

If the damage is due to the maritime transport itself (for example in the case of shipwreck) then the limitations of liability provided by international treaty are applicable (see *infra*). The passenger can receive no more than a set maximum amount for loss of life, injury or loss of baggage.

9.51 Each passenger must be provided with a ticket including the following information:

(i)   name and type of vessel;
(ii)   name and address of the organiser;
(iii) class, and number of cabin, and price of cruise;
(iv)   port of destination and departure, date of departure and arrival;
(v)   ports of call during the cruise; and
(vi)   ancillary services.

(b) Ordinary maritime transport

9.52 The liability of an operator of a ship is not as extensive as that of the operator of a bus or train.

In many cases the burden of proof of liability rests on the passenger. The operator of the ship must be shown to have been negligent (ship not seaworthy, navigation error, etc).

However, in the case of a "collective" accident, such as shipwreck, fire, explosion, or a major accident, the operator is liable for all deaths and injuries, **unless** the operator can prove that the accident is not due to any negligence on the part of the ship's crew or operator.

The operator is liable for any delay due to negligence in the commercial operation and maintenance of the ship.

The amount of money that can be awarded to passengers for injury or loss of baggage is set out by Article 7 of the London Convention on Maritime Liability (19 November 1976). These limits can be removed if the passenger can prove that the injuries or losses were due to criminal or inexcusable negligence.

9.53 The total liability of the operator of the ship for personal injury and

---

[45] Law No 66–420 of 18 June 1966 and decree No 66–1078 of 31 December 1966.

loss of life is limited to an amount equal to the number of passengers that the ship is authorised to transport, multiplied by 46,666 DTS (unit of currency of the International Monetary Fund). This limit only applies if the contract does not have a higher limit.

Liability for loss of or damage to baggage differs according to the nature of the baggage: **9.54**

(i)   *Hand baggage*: the passenger must prove that the loss was due to negligence. The maximum indemnity is 3,000 FF.

(ii) *Registered baggage*: the carrier must prove that the loss was not due to his negligence. The maximum indemnity is 7,500 for cabin baggage, 10,000 for stowed in the hull baggage and 30,000 FF for tourist vehicles.

(iii) *Valuables in safe*: the carrier is automatically liable. There is no limit to the amount of the indemnity.

The limitation period is two years for personal injury, and one year for baggage.

If a passenger fails to embark before the departure of the vessel, by reason of *force majeure*, or death of the passenger, the contract is cancelled. The passenger and his family are entitled to a refund of three-quarters of the price of the ticket, provided the operator was notified before the vessel's departure. No refund is possible after the ship's departure. **9.55**

Where the trip is cancelled, the passenger is entitled to a full refund and to an indemnity of half of the price of the ticket, unless the operator can prove that the cancellation was due to an event beyond his control.

Where the trip is interrupted, the passenger is entitled to a full refund, and to damages, unless the operator can prove that the interruption was due to an event beyond his control.

If the operator is not diligent in the operation of the ship, and substantial modifications are made in the ship's schedule or itinerary, the passenger may cancel and ask for damages.

(iv)   Transport of persons by road

The relevant international convention,[46] is not yet applicable to France. **9.56**

The only applicable convention is the Rome Convention on choice of Law,[47] which may be used to determine which country's law should be applied to a claim made by a passenger. Under Article 5.2 of the Rome Convention, the choice of applicable law can not deprive the consumer of the right to claim the protection afforded by the consumer protection laws of his country of residence.

Where French law is applicable, the passenger carrier (*i.e.* the bus operator etc) is liable for any injuries suffered by the passenger during

---

[46] Geneva, 1 March 1974, modified by that of 6 July 1978.
[47] 19 June 1980, Decree 28 February 1991, JO 3 March 1991.

the trip, unless the carrier can prove that the accident was due to *force majeure*, to a third party, or to the negligence of the passenger.

9.57   Tour buses in France are subject to a classification system, somewhat similar to that of hotels. They are rated according to quality, comfort and maintenance. Each bus must have a sign indicating its rating. If not, a fine of up to 10,000 FF can be imposed on the owner of the bus.[48]

7.   Financial services

(i)   Traveller's cheques

9.58   France has no specific legislation on traveller's cheques. It is therefore mostly up to the issuers of such cheques to set out the rules governing the issue, the form and the cashing of the cheques. Each bank or group of banks has its own regulations.

A traveller's cheque is payable at each branch office of the bank and various correspondent offices. A tourist who bought cheques in a foreign country in dollars, and had them stolen in Paris, is entitled to have them refunded in francs at the issuer's correspondent office in Paris.[49] A traveller's cheque can be freely endorsed under French law and transferred to third parties, such as stores, or hotels, for example.

Some contracts try to prevent the issuer from being liable if the cheques are stolen or lost without the bearer reporting the loss. Under French law such a clause is not valid in the case of gross negligence of the issuer, for example if the bank did not verify the identity of the bearer of a stolen checque.

(ii)   Credit cards

9.59   Credit cards were first introduced in France around 1955. After a slow start because of competition between various banks, each with its own card which was incompatible with the others, the number of credit cards in use is rapidly expanding. There are now more than 20 million cards in use. The unification of the major French banks under the name of *Carte bleue* affiliated with Visa, now enables the consumer to have access to more than a half-million stores, hotels and restaurants in France. Cards bearing the Visa logo are by far the most widely used in France, followed by Eurocard-Mastercard, Diners Club and American Express.

Most cards issued in France have incorporated an electronic chip with a personal identification number. This number is required not only to withdraw cash from automatic machines, but also in order to pay in many shops, hotels and restaurants.

---

[48] Art 81 of the decree of 15 June 1994.
[49] Trib. com. Paris, réf., 24 July 1985: Gaz. Pal. 1986. 1 somm. 19.

Credit cards are defined by a law of 30 December 1991[50] which dis-   **9.60**
tinguishes between cards that enable the bearer to pay for goods and
services and those which enable the withdrawal of cash. Most credit cards
now permit the bearer to carry out both operations.

On the European level, there are two recommendations of the Council:

(i)   8 December 1987, on the European Code of Conduct for
       electronic money; and
(ii)   17 November 1988, on the relations between the bearer and issuer
       of credit cards.

The courts have accepted the validity of electronic signature (by a code
number) of purchases made by credit card.[51]

The courts appear to consider that the use of a card with its code
number is sufficient, even in case of theft, to oblige the bearer to pay.[52]
There is a presumption that the bearer was negligent, even if in fact the
bearer was not careless.

Once the card has been used for a purchase, the bearer can not refuse   **9.61**
payment by giving instructions to his bank, except in three cases:

(i)   theft;
(ii)   loss of card; or
(iii) bankruptcy of the bearer.

The use of a credit card without sufficent funds in one's bank account
is not a criminal offence under French law, however using an expired or
cancelled card is.[53]

(iii) Holiday cheques

Holiday cheques are vouchers issued by corporations for their employees.   **9.62**
The system is optional and designed to help low-income employees to go
on holidays.[54] It was inspired by the Reka cheque created by Switzerland
in 1939.

The cheques are paid for by the employee with a subsidy from the
employer and from the state. They can be used to pay for hotel accommodation, transport, meals and various other holiday expenses.

(iv) Bureaux de change

In the early 1980s, foreign exchange was tightly controlled in France and   **9.63**
it was quite difficult to open a bureau de change, except for those within
banks.

---

[50] Law No 91–1382.
[51] Cass. Civ., 1ère, D.1990, jurispr. 369.
[52] Paris, 29 March 1985; Paris, 17 October 1986: D.1981, jurispr. (note Galvada).
[53] Cass. Civ., Crim., 24 November 1983, D.1984, jurispr. 465. Trib. gr. inst. Créteil, Ch. corr. 15
     January 1985, Inf. rapp. 344.
[54] Ord. No 82–283, 26 March 1982.

Since that time, legislation has been considerably liberalised. No governmental authorisation is now required, a simple declaration to the Bank of France and to the French Customs Administration is all that is necessary.

A bureau de change must post outside its place of business the rates charged to customers, so that potential customers can compare prices. There are few other rules specifically applicable to this activity.

8. Compensation for victims of crime

9.64   The European Convention for the compensation of victims of violent crime[55] provides that compensation is granted, if not available by other means, by the State to such victims.

Compensation is granted to victims who are citizens of one of the countries party to the Convention, and to those who are citizens of one of the member countries of the Council of Europe, and to permanent residents of the State where the crime was committed. France considers that for the purpose of the Convention all EC nationals are to be treated as French citizens.

Articles 706–3 to 706–14 of the Code of Criminal Procedure set out detailed rules as to how and under what conditions compensation may be awarded to victims of crime. The victim must be an EC national or a permanent resident of France.

9.65   The crime committed must not relate to a car or hunting accident. Injuries for which compensation may be made, are: death; permanent injury; temporary incapacity of more than one month; and rape.

Compensation may be reduced or refused if the victim contributed to the crime or was in any way responsible for the injuries suffered.

The victim receives financial compensation calculated in the same manner as before the French criminal courts, and thus can receive awards for pain and suffering, loss of income, medical bills, and physical disability.

The application for compensation is heard by a commission composed of two professional judges and one lay person who has shown interest in the problems of victims of crime.

The application must be filed within a time limit of three years after the crime, or one year after the final judgment in the criminal proceedings introduced against the person accused of the crime.

9.66   It is also possible to be compensated for theft, fraud and embezzlement, but only if the crime has left the victim in a difficult financial situation and if the victim has very little income. In addition, compensation is limited to a relatively small sum.

---

[55] 24 November 1983, published in France by decree No 90–447 of 29 May 1990, D; and A.L.D. 1990. 249.

9. Passport and frontier control

Traditionally, foreigners wishing to visit France must have a valid passport **9.67** and a visa issued by the French Consulate of their country of residence.

In the 1970s and early 1980s, this rule was relaxed for a number of countries. After a number of terrorist actions carried out on French soil in 1986, visa requirement were reinstated for all foreigners (except EC nationals). Many countries protested against this restriction on travel. In more recent times the obligation to have a visa has been cancelled for a number of countries. Approximately three-quarters of all foreign tourists can now enter France without a visa, including tourists from the EC, USA, Canada, Japan, and from the countries that are members of the Council of Europe.

Tourists from third world countries have found it increasingly difficult to come to France. Not only do they have to obtain a visa, but in many cases they have to prove that they have sufficient means to pay for their stay in France and their return journey. Citizens from many African or Arab countries have to produce a *certificat d'herbergement*, which is a statement from the person with whom they plan to stay. This document is verified by the mayor. In many cases obtaining such a document can prove quite difficult, some mayors being very suspicious of the real reason behind the trip to France.

The decision to grant a tourist visa is discretionary and no effective **9.68** legal remedy is available if the application for a visa is turned down.

It is outside the scope of this book to deal with French Immigration Law in depth. Further information is found in the Ordonnance of 2 November 1945. This Law has been modified no less than eight times in the past 14 years.

Strict procedures are applicable to tourists upon arrival in France. It is not unusual for tourists to find themselves refused admittance at the French border or at the airport on arrival for various reasons, such as improper travel documents, no visa, or security reasons. This can be very upsetting, especially if the person is travelling on a package tour with a group.

Article 5 of the Ordonnance of 2 November 1945 offers the tourist who **9.69** should find him or herself in such a predicament a few guarantees:

(i)   the decision not to admit must be in writing and must give the reasons why it was taken;

(ii)   the tourist must be informed of his rights, by way of an interpreter if necessary;

(iii) he or she can make a phone call to the person with whom he or she expected to stay (friend, family, hotel etc), to his consulate, and to a lawyer;

(iv)   the tourist can not be deported against his will for 24 hours. After that time he or she may be deported without further notice; and

(v)   after four days, if he or she is still held in custody, he or she must be brought before a judge who decides whether it is necessary to further detain him or her. The tourist has the right to counsel, and can have one appointed by the court if need be.

9.70   For EC nationals, however, border controls have been greatly reduced. Passports are no longer necessary, identity cards are sufficent. In many cases, EC nationals are waved through by the border police, or even cross the border without even seeing a police officer.

In addition, on 14 June 1985, France signed the so-called "Schengen Agreement" (modified on 19 June 1990). The purpose of this agreement, signed by nine EC countries, is to do away with national border controls and replace them with a single EC-wide border. Tourists who are admitted to one EC country would be able to travel freely to the other "Schengen" countries without any immigration controls at the various national borders.

10.   Time share regulation

9.71   Time sharing was invented by a French engineer, Louis-Emile Poumiers, in 1967. It became very fashionable in the 1970s, under the name of *multipropriété*. Time share agreements staged a comeback in France in the early 1990s under the English name of "time sharing", the essential difference being that under its former name it was marketed as a real estate investment, whereas under its new name it is sold as a holiday opportunity. Whatever the name, time share agreements have a bad reputation. The upkeep of the flat is usually expensive, resale extremely difficult and exchanges complicated.

The law of 6 January 1986 offers the buyer some protection. It is only applicable to contracts signed in France or with French companies.

The law regulates the operations of corporations that own time share properties. These corporations can be created in any form existing under French law for ordinary companies. They can even be co-operatives. They are normally created by property professionals, who then progressively sell the shares to individual buyers.

9.72   The law also regulates construction contracts, so that the buyer has the guarantee that the property will be built.

The law also regulates advertising, and prohibits the use of the word property owner: i.e. *propriétaire*. Only the term "shareholder" is allowed, so that potential buyers will not be misled into thinking that they are actually buying property.

An additional protection is afforded to shareholders by a special provision of the law that limits the liability of shareholders to their initial investment.

Some protection can also be found in various consumer protection **9.73** laws. For example, if the shares were sold at the buyers' home or in a hotel, under the law of 22 December 1972 the buyer may cancel the sale up to seven days after having signed the contract.

However, it is generally felt that this protection is insufficient, especially in view of the fact that there is a great deal of crossborder selling.

The EC proposal for a Directive on Time Share Agreements[56] should lead to a new law in France. Improvements would include:

(i) an information document in the buyer's native tongue;
(ii) 14 days for the buyer to cancel the contract (28 days if the holiday flat is not in his country of residence); and
(iii) protection even if the sale is concluded outside the EC.

---

[56] COM 93/587 SYN.

Germany

Chapter 10
Germany

Dr Christoph Hasche[1]
Wessing, Berenberg-Gossler, Zimmermann, Lange

1.　Introduction

Even in times of depression and economical difficulties, tourism is a boom- **10.1**
ing market. It appears that an interesting trip to a holiday resort is something which people, even if their income has decreased, are not willing to
give up. People would rather save money spent on clothes, cars or amuse-
ment rather than spend their holidays without travelling. Even if a substantial majority of German tourists travel abroad, spending money in other
countries, the internal economical impact of tourism is still remarkable.
The German tourism industry has a turnover above DM 20 billion. The
money spent by Germans reflects a 25% share of the European tourism
market. The average German employee has 29 working days off per year as
holiday. Twenty-five per cent of all travels are made on package tours.

　The growing national and international tourism market made it necessary to create laws complying with the needs of the industry and its customers. In Germany, the first steps were made in 1979, when the German
Civil Code (*Bürgerliches Gesetzbuch* – BGB) was substantially amended. The
amendment implemented 11 articles regulating the legal relations
between the package tour operator and its customer. The legal questions
connected with these 11 articles are considered to be "the travel law".
This travel law has been changed recently as a consequence of the EC
Directive on package tours (*infra*).

　Whereas the travel law specifically regulates the contractual relations **10.2**
between a tour operator and its customer, administrative law deals with
the questions regulating the tourism industry by the state, municipal
authorities and other regulatory bodies. In the area of administrative law
there are no codes specially tailored for the tourism industry, so that only
the general rules and regulations are to be observed.

2.　Regulatory authorities

(i)　Tour operators and travel agencies

In Germany, there is no regulatory body or public agency especially in **10.3**
charge of tour operators and travel agencies. The German economy is

---

[1] Dr Christoph Hasche is a partner of the law firm Wessing, Berenberg-Gossler, Zimmermann,
Lange, with offices in Hamburg, Munich, Frankfurt, Düsseldorf, Berlin, Leipzig and Brussels.
He specialises in transport and travel law. He has published articles on travel law, and the
book *"The Claim for Compensation of a Tour Operator under para 651 i BGB"*. He was a lecturer
on travel law at the University of Lüneburg.

based on the principle that everybody is entitled to do lawful business as he likes, unless the law requires a permission to do so. There is no legal requirement to obtain a permission to open and maintain a travel agency, or to work as a tour operator. No public licence is required and, in principle, no public control is used to monitor what the industry is doing.

10.4   The only code which has to be observed in this connection is the General Industrial Code (*Gewerbeordnung – GewO*). This Code merely requires that any person who wishes to establish a new business – whether in the tourism industry or any other industry – has to inform the competent municipal authority. No special qualification, licence, or certificate has to be submitted. The municipal authority will inform the tax authority as well as the Chamber of Commerce.

In accordance with paragraph 38 of the GewO most of the German States have issued decrees regulating the duties of travel agencies. According to these Travel Agency Decrees (*Reisebüroverordnungen*) each entrepreneur has to keep records of each contract entered into, including the name of the tour operator, the customer, the customer's address and date of birth, the agreed services, the price and the payments received. The travel agency must have a proper book-keeping system. The travel agent must keep copies of all advertisements and must answer all questions connected with the above issues which may be raised by the municipal authorities.

10.5   The competent authorities are located in each state where the entrepreneur has its place of business. The Federal Government in Bonn and Berlin does not deal with single companies. The Federal Department of Economics is only involved if it comes to general questions and the overall promotion of the entire industry. The Federal Department of Justice was responsible for the implementation of the European Package Travel Directive.

(ii)   Air carriers

10.6   Operation of an air carrier is heavily regulated. In addition to the International Conventions which Germany has adopted, the following German codes exist:

(i)   The Air Carriage Code (*Luftverkehrsgesetz*): This code stipulates the permissions and approvals to be obtained for operating an air carrier company.

(ii)   The Air Carrier Admission Code (*Lufverkehrszulassungsordnung*): This code explains the technical and organisational details which have to be complied with in order to get the necessary permissions.

(iii)   The Code on the Title of Aircrafts (*Gesetz über Rechte an Luftfahrzeugen*): This code contains provisions applicable for financing and emcumbrances regarding aircraft.

The Federal Department of Traffic is responsible for all matters relating to air traffic in Germany.

(iii) Bus tourism

The operation of bus tours is also highly restricted. Not only the technical safety of buses, but also the reliability of the bus tour operator is thoroughly observed. The relevant legislation is the Code of Transportation of Persons (*Personenbeförderungsgesetz*) which stipulates the conditions under which a person may operate a bus tour.

10.7

The Code of Transportation of Persons contains 61 articles, and stipulates that any person who wishes to operate a bus tour needs permission to do so. The permission is only granted for certain tours. The permission may only be granted if the safety and the ability of the tour operator is guaranteed (para. 13(1)1); if there are no facts which suggest the unreliability of the applicant (para. 13(1)2); and if the applicant can prove that he has experience in the business (para. 13(1)3). The Code also applies to tours crossing the German border.

A more detailed list of duties and obligations are set out in the Decree regarding the Operation of Automobile Enterprises carrying Persons (*Verordnung über den Betrieb von Kraftfahrunternehmen im Personenverkehr –* BOKraft) and in the Decree regarding Access to the Profession as an Entrepreneur Transporting Persons (*Verordnung über den Zugang zum Beruf des Straßenpersonenverkehrsunternehmers –* Berufszugangs–Verordnung PBefG).

10.8

European Directives also have to be observed, in particular Directive 684/92 Regarding Common Regulation of Border Crossing Passenger Traffic with Buses, which has been implemented into German law.

(iv) Travel at sea

For maritime carriers the most important safety regulations are those contained in the international Conventions which are signed by Germany. The shipping industry tries to maintain international standards for safety on board vessels.

10.9

The Athens Convention dated 13 December 1974 has been incorporated into German law by the Second Code of Amendments to the Maritime Law (*Zweites Seerechtsänderungsgesetz*). Although Germany did not ratify the Convention, it has amended para 664 of the German Commercial Code (*Handelsgesetzbuch* – HGB). This amendment contains the most important regulations of the Athens Convention, but increases the limits of liability.

(v) Overall liability

Independently of the laws and regulations specially directed at tour operators, travel agencies, air carriers, bus operators or vessel owners and

10.10

operators, German law also has various regulations which are applicable to all of them, in as far as they are selling more than one tourism service. In such a case the company is considered to be a tour operator. For all tour operators the travel law contained in the German Civil Code is applicable. This, however, contains only contractual duties and no administrative law.

3. Legal and professional rules

10.11 The legal and professional rules guaranteeing the freedom of persons to establish themselves as travel agents or tour operators and to operate in the travel industry derives from the German constitution, the Basic Code (*Grundgesetz* – GG). Article 12 of the GG guarantees that all Germans have the right to choose their profession, place of work and place of education freely. Only the operation of certain Codes, (*supra*), may restrict the way the business is done.

4. General business organisation

10.12 Every entrepreneur is free to organise its business as it likes. There are no rules requiring a certain form of establishment of travel or tour businesses. The form of the business is at the discretion of the entrepreneur.

For tax and liability reasons most companies are operated in the form of a limited liability company (*Gesellschaft mit beschränkter Haftung* – GmbH).

5. Special legal requirements

10.13 The German company law does not have any provision expressly mentioning the travel and tourism industry. The travel and tourism industry only has to observe the general rules which are set out in the German company law.

Insurance is not required, although it is to be recommended. Insurance cover is widely taken, but not mandatory. The German bankruptcy law does not contain any provision especially tailored for the travel and tourism sector. Only in as far as the insolvency of a tour operator affects the performance of a special tour, the European Package Tour Directive has made it necessary to amend the German law, (see 6, *infra*).

A travel agency or tour operator may limit its liability. One method is to enter specific agreements with the customer containing provisions regarding limited liability (see 6(i), *infra*). The second and more general method is to work under the shelter of a company with limited liability. For a GmbH a share capital of DM 50,000 is required. The possibility of piercing the corporate veil of a GmbH and establishing the liability of the shareholder or managers is small. The limitation of liability can only be broken under rare circumstances.

6. Consumer rights and safeguards

(i) The travel law

The travel law itself, paras. 651 a–651 il BGB, contains provisions to guar- **10.14**
antee a minimum standard in favour of the customer. It applies only to the relation between a customer and a tour operator. A travel agency is also considered to be a tour operator if it appears that the agency accepts responsibility for the performance of the service provided (*i.e.* hotel company, air carrier, restaurant, car rental company etc). In other words, a company cannot escape from its liability as a tour operator by claiming to be a mere agent or broker. The travel law will look behind these words to see whether the company appears to be the responsible party.

The travel contract may be concluded orally, but must be confirmed in writing.

The customer is entitled to claim a remedy for any discrepancy **10.15**
between the contract and the factual situation at the place of destination of the travel. He may only claim damages if he has duly requested such remedies. If the tour operator does not comply with these requests, the customer may reduce the price for the travel. In extreme cases he may also cancel the contract and arrange for a premature return trip back home. These rights may be claimed even if the tour operator cannot be held responsible for the defects of the tour. If, however, the tour operator can be proven to be at fault, the customer can also claim damages. The customer may claim remuneration for the disappointment of not being able to spend his holiday as planned (para. 651 f BGB). The tour operator is entitled to restrict his liability, by agreement with the customer, to a maximum of three times the price for the tour. Such an agreement can be made by putting a corresponding clause into the General Terms and Conditions of the tour operator. The limitation is not valid if the tour operator acted with gross negligence, or intentionally, causing damage to the customer.

(ii) Standard business conditions

The German law governing Standard Business Conditions (*Gesetz zur* **10.16**
Regelung des Rechts der Allgemeinen Geschäftsbedingungen – AGBG) also contains important provisions for the protection of consumers. As the

terms of the travel contract are widely stipulated in the General Business Conditions, the law applies in almost every case. Paragraph 9 (1) of this law reads as follows:

> Provisions in Standard Business Conditions are invalid if they unreasonably discriminate against the contractual party to the advantage of the presenter in contravention of the principle of good faith. In case of doubt, unreasonable disadvantage is to be assumed if a provision (i) is not in accordance with the essential principles of the statutory provision from which it deviates; or (ii) limits essential rights or duties arising from the nature of the contract to such an extent that achieving the purpose of the contract is jeopardised.

The Code further explains in which particular cases the travel contract is invalid.

(iii)   Unfair competition

10.17   The German law on unfair competition also protects the interests of the consumer. Misleading or untrue advertisements are not permitted; hidden surcharges or rebates of more than 3% must not be promised or granted; and price agreements among tour operators are unlawful. The German law on unfair competition is greatly influenced by EC legislation. Various Directives have been implemented.

In order to draft general business conditions for a tour operator or for travel agencies, the AGBG must be observed. Moreover, a very extensive number of precedents have to be observed. It is in any case advisable to consider the recommendations of the German Tour Operator Association (*Deutscher Reisebüroverband* – DRV) which issued a model for the General Business Terms of Tour Operator.

7.   Forms of redress

10.18   The main forms of redress available to the consumer are: the right of fulfilment of the contract by performance by the tour operator; the right to reduce the travel price; the right to cancel the contract; and the right to receive compensation. The amount of compensation depends on the extent of the defects and the damage caused. Arbitration is rarely agreed upon, so the consumer has to go to the ordinary courts at the principal place of business of the tour operator in order to obtain the redress. He must do so within six months after the end of the trip.

There are no special tribunals or regulatory authorities who decide on tourism actions. If the customer claims payment of more than DM 10,000.00, he must obtain the assistance of a lawyer in order to go to court. Otherwise he may act in person. The consumer often seeks support and advice from the consumer associations; private associations which also fight for fair treatment of consumers in the tourism industry.

8. Insurance requirements

Travel agencies do not have to obtain insurance. For tour operators the **10.19** situation is slightly different, as the EC Directive on package tours 90/314 has been implemented into German law. It is now a requirement that the customer has sufficient security for the performance of the tour operator, even in cases where the tour operator goes bankrupt. For this purpose the customer is entitled to insurance cover which is arranged by the tour operator. Alternatively, the tour operator must produce a bank guarantee for a customer.

There is no other requirement for insurance in the tourism business.

9. Regulation of insurance

The individual tourist may buy insurance cover to any extent he likes. **10.20** Health insurance, insurance against theft and burglary of luggage as well as accident insurance are very common. Moreover, customers may insure the risk of being liable for fees after cancelling the travel contract. This insurance only applies if the customer had a good reason for its cancellation.

General liability insurance for hiring a car is mandatory. Collision damage insurance and third party insurance are also available.

10. Health and safety standards

The legal rules governing health and safety standards are set out in a vari- **10.21** ety of laws. The laws cover all aspects of health and safety, including the possibility of closing down unhygenic kitchens in restaurants; setting the standards of building houses and hotels; standards for building and importing cars; and regulations covering fire or emergency exits for buses, trains, aircraft or vessels, to mention only a few.

Municipal authorities, sometimes assisted by the police, closely monitor whether the various rules, regulations and standards regarding health and safety are observed. Technical Supervision Associations (*Technische Überwachungsvereine* – TÜV) have the expertise for the technical side of safety rules.

11. Rights against transport operators

The rights of consumers in the event of cancellation, damage or loss of **10.22** property, injury and death, depend on which form of transportation was used. Germany has signed the Warsaw Convention and its amendments; it has also implemented the Athens Convention into German law. These Conventions apply in the event of damage, injury and death suffered in aircraft or ships. Generally speaking, remote damages are not recoverable and compensation for pain and suffering is limited to small amounts.

12. Financial services

10.23 Credit cards are widely used in Germany. The use of credit cards is not restricted by law. Only the contract between the consumer and the company who issues the credit card contains limits for the consumers. These contracts, which are mainly drafted by the banks, contain various conditions which specify the limits which the customer has to observe when using the credit cards. The same applies to traveller's cheques.

A company wishing to issue its own credit cards for its customers, must check whether it will then be operating in the banking business. In this case, various laws and restrictions have to be observed, in particular the Code of Credit Business (*Kreditwesengesetz* – KWG).

This law also applies if one opens and operates a bureau de change. To open such a bureau, permission must be obtained from the Federal Agency for Credit Business, Berlin. Only if reliability and financial soundness is proven in an extensive examination may the applicant expect to get the necessary permission.

13. Compensation for victims of crime

10.24 In the case of criminal injuries, it is the offender who is liable on a tortious basis. Direct loss and damage must be compensated. Remuneration for pain and suffering is limited to small amounts in German courts. If the offender is unknown or unable to pay the compensation, the victim may apply for social aid, which is granted under certain circumstances.

14. Time share regulation

10.25 There are no laws or regulations particularly directed at time share agreements in Germany. Time share agreements are checked by the court under the application of the German Civil Code (BGB) as well as the Code of General Business Conditions (AGBG).

There are no plans for implementing new rules into German law as to time share agreements. Only in so far as the EC proposal for a Directive on time share agreements comes into force, will German legislators be obliged to implement the Directive into German law.

15. Passport and frontier control

Controls at the German border have changed greatly since the Treaty on European Union and the Schengen Agreement, in force since 26 March 1995. In accordance with this Treaty tourists from EC countries are no longer controlled, although if certain suspicions arise the controls may be exercised more frequently. It is more a political than a legal question how often and under which preconditions controls are carried out. As Germany sees more and more people coming from East European countries seeking asylum, entry to Germany is likely to be controlled more strictly and frequently.

10.26

Greece

Chapter 11
Greece

Takis G Kommatas*
Takis G Kommatas Law Offices

1.   Regulatory authorities sector

(i)   The Ministry of Tourism

The Ministry of Tourism is the highest regulatory body in the tourism **11.1**
sector.

The Ministry was founded by Law No 1835/1989 with the exclusive
object of planning national tourist policy and supervising all the other
regulatory bodies of the sector. Then, by Presidential Decree No
417/1991, the Ministry was abolished and all its powers and authorities
were transferred to the Ministry of National Economy. Finally, with the
Presidential Decree No 459/1993, the Ministry of Tourism was re-
established with the following authorities:

(i)   supervising the Hellenic Tourism Organisation (the EOT);
(ii)   supervising the School of Tourism Professions;
(iii)   supervising the Hotel Chamber;
(iv)   supervising the Companies controlled by the EOT.

The Ministry also has responsibility for planning and fulfilment of the **11.2**
policy on tourism, and is also competent to propose to all governmental
bodies and ministries the adoption of measures relating to the above.

Finally, the Ministry of Tourism also supervises the Casinos Committee,
established by Laws 2129/1993 and 2160/1993.

(ii)   The Hellenic Tourism Organisation (EOT)

(a)   Historical notes

The first steps towards a civil authority dedicated to dealing with tourism **11.3**
affairs were made after the end of the First World War, when, in 1919,

---

* Takis G Kommatas graduated from the Law Faculty of Athens University in 1969 and has
attended postgraduate seminars abroad in EC law, English and American law. He entered
practice in 1971 and he has been a lawyer at the Supreme Court of Athens since 1978. He is
senior partner in the firm Takis G Kommatas Law Offices, which represents a wide variety
of clients including major Greek and international corporations. He specialises in corporate,
civil and business law, foreign investments and acquisitions. He has published a number of
papers on various legal matters.

the "Foreigners' and Expositions Bureau" was founded, renamed in 1922 the "Foreigners' and Exposition Service".

The Hellenic Tourism Organisation (EOT) was founded in 1929 under the form of a public law legal entity having as its object the development and reinforcement of tourism.

It was after the end of the Second World War that, first as the General Secretariat of Tourism, and then (Law 1624/1951) as the Hellenic Tourism Organisation (EOT), this institution obtained the legal form it has today.

11.4   This last law was subsequently amended by Law 2160/1993 as amended by Law 2206/1994, which introduced several changes to the statutes of the EOT and in general changed the whole aspect of tourism in Greece.

The EOT is considered by the above mentioned Law as a legal entity having the same privileges as the state.

(b)   Functions and authorities

11.5   The EOT is a legal entity of public law, sited in Athens, under the supervision of the Minister of Tourism.

The main object of the EOT is to organise, develop and promote tourism in Greece. For the fulfilment of this object the EOT:

(i)   submits to the government proposals for the determination of policy on tourism;

(ii)   implements the tourist policy which the government has determined;

(iii)   co-ordinates the actions of the competent bodies for the service of tourism;

(iv)   studies, completes and supervises the works of development of tourism, and elaborates the relevant plans;

(v)   elaborates and implements the programmes for promotion of tourism in Greece and abroad.

(vi)   undertakes all other activities or actions that contribute to the organisation, development and promotion of tourism;

(vii)   constructs and exploits all tourist installations;

(viii) takes responsibility for tourist education;

(ix)   supervises tourist installations and activities of every kind;

(x)   finances the public services, local self-administered organisations (OTA), persons or corporate bodies whose activities contribute to the promotion of the purposes of EOT;

(xi)   organises tours, festivities and shows for the promotion of tourism.

A   THE BOARD OF DIRECTORS

11.6   The Board of Directors of the EOT consists of nine members: the President, seven directors, and the Secretary General of the EOT. All members are appointed by the Minister of Tourism for a term of three years.

The Board of Directors has the following duties:

(i)   to propose the policy on tourism;
(ii)   to resolve on the annual budget of the EOT, the budget for invest-
       ments, the account of the management and the balance sheet of
       the EOT;
(iii) to decide on the plan of works and activities for the carrying-out of
       tourist policy;
(iv)   to approve expenses on programmes of tourist promotion and
       advertising;
(v)   to approve all actions regarding the property of the EOT;
(vi)   To approve commissions and idemnities in excess of Drs
       5,000,000; and
(vii) to approve all money transactions of the Secretary General of the
       EOT exceeding Drs 120,000,000.

B   THE SECRETARY GENERAL OF THE EOT

The Secretary General of the EOT has full administrative authority. He is   **11.7**
in charge of personnel of the EOT and is responsible for the proper
function of the organisation. He also has the following duties:

(i)   to take care of the implementation of the approved programme
       on tourism;
(ii)   to propose the annual budget of the EOT;
(iii) to manage the estate and the income of the EOT;
(iv)   to represent the EOT in the formation of contracts, in all relations
       with third parties, in courts and in front of any authority;
(v)   to approve all money transactions up to Drs 120,000,000 ; and
(vi)   to decide on taking legal measures.

C   THE PRESIDENT OF THE EOT

The President of the Board of Directors of the EOT has, in general, the   **11.8**
following duties:

(i)   to convoke the Board and preside at meetings;
(ii)   to supervise the activities of the EOT in general as to their confor-
       mity with the decisions of the Board; and
(iii) to represent the EOT in the conclusion of contracts with similar
       foreign organisations and institutions.

(iii) Committees for the promotion of tourism

A committee for promotion of tourism is established in every Prefecture   **11.9**
(*Nomarchia*) in accordance with the provisions of Law 2160/1993 (art 1
para 13). The object of the committee is the planning of promotion of
tourism in the region.
    The committee for promotion of tourism is established by a decision of

the Prefect (*Nomarch*) and consists of representatives of the public administration and the local self-administered organisations.

2.   Legal and professional rules

(i)   Legal requirements for establishment as a travel agent

(a)   Definition

11.10   The Greek Tourism Law (art 1 para 1 of Law 393/76, as amended),
defines travel agencies as:

> Legal enterprises, organised on a permanent basis dedicated to the trans-
> portation, movement and lodgment (stay) of persons or groups of persons,
> inside the country and abroad with the use of means and services of the
> enterprise.

The general definition of a travel agency is further defined in paragraph 2 of the same article, where the operations of travel agencies are
described.

(b)   Services permitted to travel agencies

11.11   In accordance with article 1 paragraph 2 of Law 393/76, travel agencies can:

(i)   prepare and organise tours or excursions;
(ii)   mediate between the tourist and the state or third parties in order
        to cover the needs of the tourist; and
(iii)   perform services relative to the sector of tourism in general.

The above services include: booking of hotel rooms or tickets, issuing of
transport tickets, providing services such as visas, passports, preparation
of conventions, organising parties, renting cars etc.

(c)   Categories of travel agencies

11.12   According to the provisions of article 1 paragraph 3 of Law 393/76, travel
agencies are divided into two categories: travel agencies of general
tourism, and travel agencies of domestic tourism.
   Both kinds of agencies are entitled to perform the permitted services,
but agencies of domestic tourism cannot organise trips, tours or excursions abroad and are exclusively oriented to offer services inside the territory of Greece. The criteria of distinction between the types of agencies is
their "competence in lieu".
   Furthermore, travel agencies of domestic tourism, can organise tours
inside Greece, in which foreign tourists may participate only if they are
resident at the place of business of the agency, and only if those tourists
participate individually and not in groups.

(ii) Licence requirements

(a) Entitled persons

According to the provisions of Presidential Decree 288/1991, citizens of **11.13**
any Member State of the European Union have the right to obtain the
licence for a travel agency under the same terms and conditions as a
citizen of Greece. The law gives both physical persons and legal entities
the right to obtain a licence.

The provisions of the law consider a "European" legal entity to be a
legal entity founded legally in accordance with the conditions and the
terms of the legislation of the Member State of its origin, and also having
its place of registration and its central administration or its main establishment (installation) inside the Community (EU).

Persons or legal entities, citizens of a third country, are also entitled to **11.14**
obtain a licence from the EOT, in accordance with the provisions of the
Presidential Decree, provided that:

(i)   the country of their origin maintains a status of reciprocity for
        Greek citizens; and
(ii)   they appoint a special proxy in Greece.

(b) Terms and conditions

A   PERSONAL CONDITIONS

A person is entitled to obtain the licence to operate as a travel agent pro- **11.15**
vided that "*intuitu personna*" the following requirements are satisfied:

(i)   The applicant has legal capacity.
(ii)   The applicant has not been condemned to a sentence of imprison-
        ment longer than three months, for the crime of theft, extortion,
        fraud, forgery, pilfering, smuggling, use and trade of drugs, sexual
        and moral offences and/or violation of legislation regarding the
        protection of national currency. The above are proved by a copy of
        the criminal record of the applicant.
(iii) The applicant has graduated from a Lyceum or sixth grade Gym-
        nasium, proved by the relevant certificate, (for the Greeks), or has
        graduated from an equivalent, recognised, foreign school. If this
        requirement is not met, the certificate may be substituted by a
        certificate from the competent authority of the Member State of
        origin, which must certify that the applicant has the relevant edu-
        cation or experience. The Presidential Decree adopts various crite-
        ria in order to consider whether the applicant is sufficiently
        qualified or experienced for the position of a travel agent. Rele-
        vant criteria are: six years of experience as administrator or man-
        ager of a relevant enterprise; or a combination of three years'
        experience and three years' education in a tourist school; or six
        years' experience as an employee of a tourist enterprise, in combi-

nation with two years of education; etc. Since the law does not make any strict reference to citizens of a State outside the European Union, the above conditions apply, *mutatis mutandis,* to those citizens as well.

(iv)   Sufficient knowledge of the Greek language, and at least one of the other official languages of the European Union. The ability of foreigners to speak Greek, and of Greek nationals to speak one of the other EC languages, will be examined and confirmed by a public officer of the EOT.

(v)   The applicant must not have been declared bankrupt. This requirement has to be proved by a relevant certificate of the clerk of the Court of First Instance. This certificate, as for the certificate of Criminal record (above (ii)), should be renewed every five years.

If one of the above requirements is not met, the applicant may appoint another person to be responsible for the Agency.

B   OBJECTIVE CONDITIONS

11.16   The applicant, in the case of a licence for a travel agency of general tourism, should have an independent installation (office) with an area of 20 m² minimum. For a travel agency of domestic tourism an area of 12 m² minimum is required. This is verified by a relevant certificate of the competent police station.

The same person or legal entity is entitled to hold more than one licence, subject to the condition of having different offices, and payment in respect of each one of them of the relevant guarantee.

The travel agency offices must be independent. It is strictly prohibited to operate a travel agency under the same roof as another enterprise, with the exception of hotel, car rental agency, etc.

These conditions are also applicable in the case of a legal entity. It is understood that the "personal conditions" should apply to the legal representative(s) of the legal entity.

C   FINANCIAL CONDITIONS

Deposit of a guarantee

11.17   The applicant for a licence for operation of a travel agency must deposit with the EOT:

(i)   an invoice from a Public Treasury for payment of stamp duties;

(ii)   an amount of Drs 3,000 in favour of the EOT and an amount of Drs 1,000 for the Fund of Social Insurance of Officers in Radio and Tourism; and

(iii)   a guarantee amounting to:

(a) Drs 300,000 if the application concerns a travel agency of general tourism;

(b) Drs 100,000 in respect of a travel agency of domestic tourism. This guarantee must be renewed every five years.

Forfeiture of the guarantee

The guarantee may be called in in favour of the EOT in order to cover: **11.18**

(i)   the insurance contributions of the agency regarding social security of the tour operators;
(ii)   pecuniary penalties or sanctions imposed on the agency; and
(iii) claims of third parties deriving from debts and transactions of a tourist character.

Before the EOT decides to forfeit the guarantee, the travel agency will be called in to arrange its obligations in a time period of not less than a month.

If the notice period lapses without any action on the part of the agency, without further notice, the EOT may decide on forfeiture. If the claims of third parties exceed the amount of the guarantee, then the EOT will be satisfied by priority, and the balance (if any) will be distributed to the rest of the creditors.

After the calling-in of the guarantee, the travel agency will be called on   **11.19** to replace the amount of the guarantee within a period of 15 days, if not its licence will be suspended. If after a period of three months the agency has not replaced the guaranteed amount, its licence will be definitively cancelled. If the travel agency wishes to obtain its licence once again, a deposit of double the guarantee amount will be required.

(iii)   The future status of travel agencies

The recently issued Law 2160/1993 in article 6 paragraphs 9 and 10 pro-   **11.20** vides that

> By a Presidential Decree issued following the proposal of the Minister of National Economy [its authority on the matter is already transferred to the Minister of Tourism according to the provisions of art 5 para 1 *et seq* of Presidential Decree No 459/1993], the terms and conditions of operation of tourist agencies, the guarantee as well as any other relevant provision of the existing legislation (which will be respectively amended), will be regulated.

To date the relevant Presidential Decree has not been issued.

Nevertheless, the law has adopted a new system of control of enterprises operating in the tourist sector, according to which the licence requirement is replaced by a special operation mark, provided by the EOT (art 3).

With regard to the details regarding this special mark, the law autho-   **11.21** rises the Secretary General of the EOT to issue an administrative decision in which all the required elements and conditions for obtaining the mark will be regulated.

The law provides, *inter alia*, that the above administrative decision should include provisions and details regarding the content of an obligatory statement which must be submitted to the EOT before the operation of the agency (or other enterprise), in which all the technical conditions and the personal VAT identification number of the enterprise should be mentioned. This statement will have the character of the solemn statement of article 8 of Law 1599/1986.

11.22 According to the provisions of the same article even existing tourist enterprises will have, in a time period of nine months from the date of issue of the relevant administrative decision, to obtain this special operation mark. By a decision of the Ministry of Tourism, all businesses operating in the sector of tourism must file the relevant application in a period of eight months.[1]

(iv) Sanctions

11.23 Article 4 paragraph 3 of Law No 2160/1993 provides the following sanctions:

(i) Anyone who is exerting undue pressure on a person or groups of persons in order to persuade them to accept or to reject travel or transport services, restaurant or entertainment services or touristic lodgings etc, may be punished according to the provisions of article 458 of the Penal Code (imprisonment of up to six months).

(ii) Anyone dealing with persons or groups of persons without the relevant licence to exercise this profession, or any person negotiating or mediating in order to provide clientele to enterprises or services referred to in the above paragraph, may also be punished according to the provisions of article 458.

(iii) According to the provisions of article 4 paragraph 4 of Law No 2160/1993, a fine of Drs 1,000,000 is imposed on travel agencies of general or domestic tourism, or on the representatives of foreign enterprises, as well as on any person contracting with article 2 enterprises who are operating without the special operation mark, or providing clientele to enterprises and lodgings operating without the mark.

(iv) Furthermore, an independent fine of Drs 100,000 is imposed on businesses (including travel agents) for every infringement as a result of which a tourist was deprived of hotel services (accommodation etc) due to the fact that reservations exceeded the number of the available beds of the enterprise.

(v) According to the provisions of article 4 paragraph 5b subpara-

---

[1] Newspaper "Kathimerini" of 2 April 1994.

graph 3 of Law 2160/1993, a travel agent who is not offering to its clientele the services, comforts and/or goods promised or advertised in writing, or whose provided services, or goods are obviously of inferior rate or quality, will be punished with a fine of Drs 200,000.

(vi)   In addition, a pecuniary penalty of up to Drs 5,000,000 will be imposed on travel agents advertising tourist installations different to the ones described in the relevant contracts (art 4 para 9 of Law 2160/1993).

(v)   Legal forms of business

According to Greek legislation a travel agency need not necessarily have   **11.24**
a particular legal form. Persons and legal entities are entitled to operate as travel agents no matter what legal form they have.

Greek company law does not have any special provisions for companies which operate in the travel and tourism industry.

Likewise, there are no special provisions as to ownership and management of travel agencies or tour operators. Nor are there any specific provisions for the obligatory insurance of travel agencies or tour operators.[2]

There are no limits to business liability and therefore the rules and the provisions of the Civil Code apply (for example art 330 or 914 of the Civil Code regarding the compensation of the contracting party in the case of failure of performance of the contract, or in the case of damage due to acts of the agent). According to the general clause of the Greek Civil Code on "contractual liberty", a travel agent may, in the relevant contract, limit its liability with a specific clause. This limitation is not binding on the other contracting party.

(vi)   Insolvency or winding-up

According to the provisions of the Royal Decree of 2–14 May 1835 (Com-   **11.25**
mercial Law) every agent is considered to be a merchant.

Consequently, a travel agent can be declared bankrupt according to the provisions of commercial law. Greek bankruptcy law has no special provisions for travel agencies, and so the general rules regarding bankruptcy proceedings are implemented.[3]

According to the general bankruptcy provisions, if a travel agent is declared bankrupt, the consumer-tourist who had entered into a travel or other tourist contract, and had prepaid the price of it, will be protected. The consumer will be one of the general creditors and may be satisfied totally or in part, subject to the existence of assets of the bankrupt.

---

[2] Levantis, E, *Company Law* Vols I–V (Athens, 1989); Rokas, N, *Commercial Companies Law* (Athens, 1984).
[3] Rokas, K, *Bankruptcy Law* (Athens, 1978), 34–43.

(vii) Tourist guides

(a) Legal terms

11.26   Under Greek legislation, a tourist guide is a person who accompanies foreign or local tourists or visitors to the country, guides them and shows them local points of interest, historic or ancient monuments, works of art of each period, and explains their significance, their purpose and their history, and gives general information on classical and contemporary Greece (art 1 para 1 of Law 710/1977).

These activities are restricted to persons with specific training, evidenced by a diploma.

The profession of tourist guide may be exercised only if the individual has a relevant licence issued by the EOT.

(b) Conditions

11.27   The tourist guide licence is granted to Greeks or citizens of other Member States, who have graduated from the Tourist Guide School of the EOT provided that:

(i)   they have accomplished their military service, or they are legally exempted from it; and

(ii)   they have not been condemned to a sentence of imprisonment longer than three months, for the crimes of theft, extortion, fraud, forgery, pilfering, smuggling, use and trade of drugs, sexual and moral offences, violation of the legislation regarding the protection of national currency, perjury, false denunciation and defamation.

11.28   According to the provisions of Presidential Decree No 273/1993, a tourist guide-citizen of another Member State is free to provide his services in Greece when accompanying a group of tourists coming from another Member State of the European Union, during an organised excursion under a certain schedule, with the exception of visits to museums or other historical monuments.

The foreign tourist guide must have:

(i)   either the relevant professional licence, issued according to the legislation of the Member State of his origin; or

(ii)   a certificate issued and confirmed by the competent authority of the Member State of his origin, by which it is certified that the applicant has exercised the profession of tourist guide for at least two years, during the period of the last ten years, and also that the tourist guide has graduated from a school of the second or third degree of education and possesses the relevant Diploma which certifies that the tourist guide is educated upon matters of Greek civilisation.

11.29   The Presidential Decree No 273/1993 was issued in order to harmonise Greek legislation with the provisions of Article 59 of the EEC Treaty. This regulation has followed the decision of 26 February 1991 –

Case C–198/1989 *Commission of the European Communities* v *Hellenic Republic*[4] in which the court ruled that: the "Hellenic Republic had failed to fulfil its obligation under Article 59 of the EEC Treaty. . . ."

3.   Consumer rights and safeguards

(i)   Definitions

The Greek legislation for the protection of the consumer consists of Law   **11.30**
No 2251/1994, which governs the legal status of the consumers when entering any kind of agreement, and of several other special laws, among which are laws regarding matters of tourism such as Law No 2190/1991 (*supra*).

According to the terminology of Law 2251/1994, a consumer is defined as:

> A physical person or legal entity, to whom the products or services offered in the market are addressed or the person making use of such products or services, provided that he is their final receiver. The receiver of an advertising message is also considered as consumer.

and a seller or supplier as:

> any physical or legal entity supplying goods or performing services to consumers, and acting for purposes related to his trade, business or profession. The advertised person is also considered as a supplier. The supplier is also considered the producer as far as his liability for defective products is concerned.

These definitions are derived from EC Directives 84/450 EEC on "mis-   **11.31**
leading advertising", 85/577 EEC on "protection of the consumer in respect of contracts negotiated away from business premises"; and also are harmonised with the relevant terms of Council Directives 90/314 "on package travel, package holidays etc" and 93/13 "unfair terms in consumer contracts"; and finally with the proposal for a Council Directive (COM(93) 396 SYN 411) "long distance selling". The definition of "consumer", as described in Greek Law, is wider than the one in the Directives, because it considers as "consumers", legal entities and groups of persons.

According to the definitions, a tourist is considered to be a consumer, for the purposes of Law 2251/1994, and the travel agent, tour operator, hotel owner etc as a seller or supplier, and so the provisions of those Laws are applicable to travel or holiday agreements.

The provisions of Laws 2251/1994 are considered as obligatory, with the result that clauses under which the consumer renounces his right to benefits under those Laws are null and void.[5]

---

[4] Case C–198/1989 *Commission of the European Communities* v *Hellenic Republic* [ECR] I–727–744.
[5] Liakopoulos Th, in Liakopoulos, Christianos, Michalopoulos, *Consumer's Protection Law* (Athens, 1993) 27.

(ii)   Misleading advertising

(a)   General provisions

11.32   Law 2251/1994, regulates the matter of advertising and the rights of the consumer (art 9).

According to these provisions: "advertising" means:

> Any announcement made in the context of trade, business, craft or professional activity in order to promote the supply of goods or services.

"Misleading advertising" means:

> any advertising, the context and form of which in any way deceives or is likely to deceive the persons to whom it is addressed or whom it reaches and which, by reason of its deceptive nature is likely to affect their economic behaviour.

The definitions of advertising and misleading advertising are in accordance with those of Council Directive 84/450.

11.33   Law 2251/1994 sets the criteria for determination whether an advertisment is misleading or not, specifically:

(i)   the characteristics of goods or services, such as their availability, nature, execution, composition method and date of manufacture or provision, fitness for purpose, uses, quantity, specification, geographical or commercial origin or the results to be expected from their use, or the results and material features of checks carried out on goods or services,or persons who have not given their written approval for the use of their statement for the advertising;

(ii)   the appreciation of the advertising is based on the idea that the technology or the scientific achievements of a certain country, different to those of the country of origin, are directly or indirectly proving the quality of the goods;

(iii) the price or the manner in which the price is calculated and the conditions under which the goods are supplied or the services provided; and

(iv)   the nature, attributes and rights of the advertiser, such as his identity and assets, his qualifications, and ownership of industrial, commercial or intellectual property rights, or his awards and distinctions.

11.34   Furthermore, Law 2251/1994 determines "misleading advertising" to occur where:

(i)   the appreciation of the advertising is based on statements made by persons who appear as scientists, specialists or authorities on a matter, without actually being so;

(ii)   the advertising is presented as the result of journalistic research, comment or scientific announcement without it being clearly or expressly stated that it is an advertisement; or

(iii)   the advertising includes scientific terms or idioms, or results of researches, or parts of text of a scientific or technical character, in order to represent the advertising announcement as based on a scientific basis, which it is not.

The provisions of Law 2251/1994 also regulate the matter of so-called **11.35** "illicit advertising", which is considered to be advertising which offends against morality. "Illicit" advertising is described as advertising which:

(i)   aims to or is likely to provoke anger, fear or annoyance or to exploit those sentiments and the superstitions of the consumer;
(ii)   is discriminating and offends social groups, races, religions, sexes, age, nationality, origin, beliefs and physical or spiritual differences;
(iii)   creates the image of an extremely tempting offer, especially to children, youngsters and to the most vulnerable groups of the population;
(iv)   directs the advertising message directly to the subconscious, without allowing its receiver the opportunity to judge it;
(v)   promotes indirectly goods which are different from the ones which are the apparent context of the advertising message, without this promotion being the intellectually main or indispensable part of the message;
(vi)   exploits the tendencies of the public towards gambling and easy profits;
(vii)   aims to, or has as a result, the denigration of a competitor, its reputation or that of its product, by using false or slanderous statements;
(viii)   represents attributes of the products in comparison to others when those attributes are not essential or comparable; and
(ix)   provokes confusion in the market between the advertiser and his competitor, or the products or services of the advertiser and his competitor(s).

The Law 2251/1994 (art 9 para 7) provides that TV and radio special reg-   **11.36** ulation on the matter of the definition of illicit advertising for the protection of children and other vulnerable groups of the population may define as illicit more forms of advertising.

Both misleading and illicit advertising, as described above, are prohibited (art 9 paras 2 and 5).

The Law 2251/1994 also includes some provisions on the matter of advertising which indicates directly or indirectly the identity of a certain competitor or some products or services offered by said competitor (comparative advertising), which is allowed only if the advertising:

(i)   is comparing objectively the main, similar and objectively chosen, characteristics of the competitive goods and services;
(ii)   is not misleading;
(iii)   does not provoke confusion in the market between the advertiser

and his competitor(s) or their trade names or other distinctive features or the products or services of the advertiser and his competitor or competitors;

(iv) does not diminish or slander a competitor or his trademarks or other distinctive features, products, services or his activities, and

(v) does not aim to exploit the reputation of the trademark or of other distinctive features of the competitor.

11.37 Furthermore in Article 9 para 10–13 of Law 2251/1994, certain dispositions are adopted which relate to the protection of the consumer's private life and provide more specifically that all kinds of direct advertising should not offend the private life of the consumer and that the advertiser should not use information or elements of the consumer's private life, known to the advertiser from former transactions or other generally obtainable sources, such as business catalogues etc, unless the consumer allows the above use. The consumer has the right to ask the supplier to erase all personal information of the consumer and to cease all relevant advertising.

In paragraph 9 of the above Article 9 of Law 2251/1994 it is provided that the reproduction or mention in an advertising message of the results of comparative tests of goods or services made by third persons, is allowed only after the written consent of the person responsible for the test is given. In that case the advertiser is responsible for this test as if it had been made under his supervision or by himself.

11.38 This Law has restricted the special forms of redress granted to the consumer by the former Law 1961/1991 (in art 21 para 1), but has granted greater "power" to the consumer's unions (*infra*). The consumer who is offended or harmed by an illicit or misleading advertisement has the power (in cases where he can prove "legitimate interest") to proceed to the courts with the "general" forms of redress provided by the Law.

Finally in Article 14 of Law 2251/1994 (para 3) it is provided that the Ministry of Commerce has the right to impose a sanction (fine) of Drs 500.000 up to Drs 20.000.000 to the violators of the provisions of this Law. In case of repetition of the violation the Ministry has the right to double the above sanction (fine) and if the violation is further repeated the Ministry of Commerce has the right to order the cessation of the violating business in whole or in part for a period up to one year.

(b) Special provisions

11.39 Law 2160/1993 provides for several administrative sanctions to be imposed on suppliers who are advertising services falsely. The provisions of Law 2160/1993 regarding advertising regulate for the most part false advertising, and not "misleading" or "illicit" advertising.

The sanctions imposed on a travel agent who does not offer his clients the advertised services, facilities etc or who offers services inferior to the ones advertised are dealt with at heading 2, *supra*. The sanction of Drs

200,000 may be imposed on all persons operating in the tourism industry, if the services provided are not as advertised. Likewise, a penalty of up to Drs 5,000,000 is imposed on the travel agent who advertises tourist installations different to the ones referred to in the relevant contract.

(iii)   Contracts negotiated away from business premises (art 3 of Law 2251/1994)

Greek legislation has included into the system of "the consumer's protection", matters relating to contracts negotiated away from business
premises, by harmonising Greek Law with Council Directive 85/577.   **11.40**

The *ratio legis* of those articles is to provide efficient protection to the
weaker party of a contract, when this party is "isolated" from the "market".
The consumer, or purchaser of such contracts, has to be protected
because he is not in a position to evaluate all the attributes of the product
or the services of the contract, for the reason that the contract is not
agreed in the "natural environment" of the market, and so the consumer
can not check if his interests are protected and/or compare this contract
to others of competitors of the supplier. Finally the aim of the (Greek as
well as the European) legislation is to avoid surprising the consumer, a
common phenomenon in "door to door" selling.[6]

According to the provisions of Article 3 paragraph 1 of Law 2251/1994
contracts negotiated away from business premises are considered the
contracts for the supply of goods or services made following the supplier's initiative without the express request of the consumer or after the
visit of the trader to the consumer's residence, domicile or place of work
or to a place chosen by the supplier away from its business premises.

The provisions of article 3 of Law 2251/1994 apply also to: **11.41**

(i)   contracts for the supply of goods or services other than those for
        which the consumer requested the visit of the trader, unless when
        the consumer requested the visit, he knew, or could reasonably
        have known, that the supply of those other goods or services
        formed part of the trader's commercial or professional activities,
        or if the products or services are directly connected to the ones for
        which the request was made;

(ii)   contracts in respect of which an offer was made by the consumer
        under conditions similar to those described in paragraph 1 of Arti-
        cle 3 of Law 2251/1994, even if the consumer is not bound by that
        offer before its acceptance by the supplier.

The above provisions do not apply to: **11.42**

(i)   contracts made between the consumer and roundsman without
        permanent business premises (registered offices);

---

[6] Christianos, B, *op. cit.* 44.

(ii)   contracts for the construction, sale and rental of immovable property, or contracts concerning other rights relating to immovable property. However, contracts for the supply of goods and for their incorporation in immovable property, or contracts for repair to immovable property do fall within the scope of this Law;

(iii)   contracts for the supply of food or beverages or other goods intended for current consumption in the household and supplied by regular roundsmen;

(iv)   contracts for the supply of goods or services provided that all three of the following conditions are met:

    (a)   the contract is concluded on the basis of a seller's catalogue which the consumer has the proper opportunity of reading in the absence of the seller's representative,

    (b)   that an intention for continuity of the contract between the seller's representative and the consumer, in relation to that or any subsequent transaction, exists,

    (c)   both the catalogue and the contract clearly inform the consumer of his right to return goods to the supplier within a period of not less than seven days from delivery, or otherwise to cancel the contract within that period without any kind of obligation other than to take reasonable care of the goods;

(v)   insurance contracts; and

(vi)   contracts for securities.

11.43   The home of the consumer, according to the provisions of Article 3 of Law 2251/1994, is also considered to be the consumer's hotel room.[7]

The contracts concerned must be in writing (if not in written form, then the contract is null and void – Article 3 paragraph 1 of Law 2251/1994), and a copy of the contract must be given to the consumer. The following must be included in the text of the contract, otherwise the contract is invalid:

(i)   the name or the trade-name and the full address of the supplier, or of the person contracting in the supplier's name and behalf. It is not sufficient that just the post office box is mentioned;

(ii)   the exact date and place (with all details) of the conclusion of the contract;

(iii)   a detailed description of the nature and characteristics of the goods or services to be provided;

(iv)   the terms and conditions of performance, and specifically the time of delivery of the goods or the services concerned; and

(v)   the price and the conditions of payment, and, in the case of payment by instalments, the interest rate and the maximum legitimate interest rate.

---

[7]   Christianos, B, *op. cit.* 68.

The supplier must also include written notice in the contract of the consumer's right to cancellation, provided by article 3 paragraph 1, passage vi and paragraph 4 of Law 2251/1994. **11.44**

In article 3 paragraph 1, passage vi of Law 2251/1994 it is also provided that a draft document of withdrawal must be attached to the text of the contract.

Under article 3 paragraph 4 of Law 2251/1994 a cooling-off period of ten working days from the date of signature of the contract, is adopted, during which the obligation of the consumer to pay the price is suspended, and during which the consumer has the right to withdraw from the contract. This period offers the consumer (who has often been surprised by the supplier, *e.g.* by door to door sales), the required time to reconsider the signed contract, and to be informed about the existing terms in the "relevant" market.

During the period of ten working days the consumer is free to withdraw from the signed contract without any further obligation on his part. It is sufficient that the notice from the consumer is posted by registered post before the end of that period. The right of the consumer to withdraw may be exercised by using the draft document attached to the contract or otherwise. **11.45**

The consumer, during the ten day period, is *free* to withdraw from the contract, meaning that no special justification for his decision is required. This right is reserved only to the consumer, so the supplier cannot withdraw from a contract without a legitimate basis (article 382 *et seq* of the Civil Code). In both cases the right of withdrawal should be exercised in good faith and in an appropriate manner.

It should be mentioned that the consumer can not resign from his right to withdraw and that during the above period the collection of any amount even as advance payment or guarantee, or issue of checque or bank notes and drafts is prohibited and that the consumer is not obliged to keep or carefully maintain or return the product or the sample sent by the supplier, unless the product or sample was requested by the consumer or otherwise agreed.

(iv) Long distance contracts

Greek legislation has adopted provisions for the protection of the consumer in respect of long distance contracts. **11.46**

A "long distance contract" is defined in Law 2251/1994, article 4 as a special form of a contract, without the presence of parties, by the use of technical communication for the transmission of the offer for conclusion of the agreement and the acceptance.

According to the provisions of article 4 of Law 2251/1994 the relevant contracts are null and void if the consumer has not been informed through the means of technical communication especially about the following:

(i)   the supplier's identity;

(ii)   the characteristics of the goods or services;

(iii)   the price, the quantity and the cost of transportation and the VAT (if VAT is not included in the price);

(iv)   the method of payment, the delivery and the performance of the contract;

(v)   the duration of the validity of the proposal for the conclusion of the contract, and

(vi)   the right of the consumer to withdraw.

11.47   As far as this last right is concerned, the regulations of article 3 (*supra*) apply also, meaning that the supplier is obliged to provide to the consumer information regarding his right to withdraw and also to include in the relevant documents a draft document of withdrawal.

The consumer has the right to withdraw from the contract within a minimum period of ten days, if a longer period is not agreed. The consumer is obliged to return the good to the supplier, but it is prohibited to charge the consumer with expenses other than the cost of the transportation.

Law 2251/1994 has ratified the majority of the dispositions included in the EC Commission proposal for a directive regarding long-distance contracts (COM (93) 396 SYN 411).

11.48   Article 4 paragraphs 3–5 deals with the matters of (a) the payment of expenses for the transmission of the consumer's acceptance or for the performance of the contract, which should not be paid by the consumer (unless otherwise agreed); (b) the delivery of goods to the consumer without prior order on his part (when the consumer would have to pay their price in order to acquire them or when the consumer would have to return them). In that case the consumer has the right to deal with the good or service freely, without being obliged to pay its price, unless the above delivery was obviously due to a mistake, in which case the consumer should, for a reasonable time period, keep it for the supplier's disposal. The lack of answer to the above proposal, can not be treated as a consent on the part of the consumer. Finally (c), the non-application of the above dispositions (under b) in cases where the supplier is not able to deliver the ordered good or to perform the ordered service, and instead delivers a similar good or performs a similar service of the same quality and price, provided that the supplier informs the consumer in writing about his right to return the good if this last does not satisfy him. The above dispositions (under b) do not apply to cases of delivery of samples or advertising gifts.

11.49   Furthermore, paragraph 11 of article 4 of Law 2251/1994 defines that the above dispositions do not apply to:

(i)   automatic sale machines;

(ii)   places of automatic sales;

(iii)   contracts for the supply of food, beverages or other goods intended for current consumption in a household, supplied and delivered by regular roundsmen.

(iv) contracts for performance of services with pre-booking services having as their object transport, hotel reservations, entertainment and nutrition.

Finally article 4 paragraph 8 of Law 2251/1994 provides that in cases **11.50** where the proposal for the conclusion does not include any disposition regarding the time of the performance of the contract, this should be performed within 30 days from the receipt of the consumer's order, and also that the use of the means of technical communications for long-distance contracts, should not offend the consumer's private life.

(v) Unfair contract terms

Article 2 of Law 2251/1994 deals with the regulation of the so-called **11.51** "General Clauses of Transactions", defining as such "the terms formed by the supplier for an indefinite number of contracts between him and the consumers".

The general clauses do not bind the consumer if he or she ignored them without intention at the time the agreement was concluded, and the supplier has not informed him or her about their existence, or has deprived him or her of the possibility to have full and real knowledge of their content.

According to the Law, those terms must be clearly and simply expressed, in order that their meaning is understood by the average consumer. Contracts negotiated in Greece and performed in Greece must be drafted in Greek. This is contrary to the provisions of Council Directive 93/13, according to which those terms should be drafted "in plain, and legible language" (Art 5). The Law excludes the general terms of international transactions.

The "standard" terms (if printed) must be printed in a clear and legible way and in an obvious part of the document.

In the interpretation of "standard" terms, the rule is that "where there is doubt about the meaning of a term, the interpretation most favourable to the consumer prevails" applies.

Terms agreed by the parties after special negotiations (special terms) **11.52** prevail over the relevant general clauses.

In article 2 paragraph 6 of Law 2251/1994 Greek legislation has adopted the system of an indicative description of what is considered to be an unfair term.

In article 2 paragraph 6 an unfair term is defined as:

general clauses having as a result the disturbance of the balance of the rights and obligations of the contracting parties at the expense of the consumer.

The Law considers that those general clauses are null and void.

The unfair character of a general clause incorporated in a contract is defined after considering the nature of goods or services that the contract is related to, the total of the special conditions and all the other clauses of the contract or of another contract on which the first contract is depending.

11.53   Consequently, Greek legislation defines as unfair the terms which:

(i)   provide the seller or supplier, without reason, with an extremely long period for the acceptance of the consumer's proposal regarding the conclusion of an agreement;

(ii)   exclude or limit the contractual obligations and liabilities of the supplier;

(iii)   determine that the termination of the contract by the consumer has to take place in an unreasonably short period, and by the supplier during an unreasonably long period;

(iv)   automatically extend or renew a contract for an unreasonably long period, if the consumer does not terminate the contract within a certain period;

(v)   permit the supplier to dissolve or alter the terms of a contract on a discretionary basis, without a certain special and important reason;

(vi)   permit the supplier to terminate a contract of indefinite duration without a reasonable period;

(vii)   give the supplier the right to determine whether his performance is in conformity with the contract;

(viii)   give the supplier the indefinite right to determine the time of performance of his obligation;

(ix)   determine that the goods or services supplied by the supplier is not obliged to fulfil the substantial conditions of the consumer, or be in conformity with the sample, or with the pre-agreed and determined special use by the consumer or otherwise be in conformity with their common use;

(x)   permit the supplier not to perform his obligations without special reason;

(xi)   without an important reason does not determine the price of the contract and does not permit its definition by criteria specially defined and reasonable for the consumer criteria;

(xii)   limit the liability of the supplier for hidden defaults of the product;

(xiii)   exclude or limit unreasonably the supplier's liability;

(xiv)   transfer the liability of the seller or importer exclusively to the manufacturer of the product or to a third person;

(xv)   limit the obligation of the supplier to fulfil the obligations of the supplier's duties or make the performance of his obligation depend on a special procedure;

(xvi)   permit the supplier to terminate the contract on a discretionary basis, if this is not also permitted to the consumer, or to keep all the advance payments made for the performance of the obligations not yet performed, in case the contract is terminated by the supplier;

(xvii) having as result the exclusion of the consumer from his rights in case of non-performance or inadequate performance of the contract by the supplier, even if the above are provoked by the supplier's fault;

(xviii) exclude the right of the consumer to withdraw in the case of increase in the price, which is, according to the contract terms unreasonable for the consumer;

(xix) exclude or limit the consumer's legal right not to perform the contract;

(xx) exclude the right of the consumer to proceed to retention when the supplier does not execute his obligations;

(xxi) oblige the consumer credited with the price of the goods or services to issue a post-dated bank cheque;

(xxii) exclude the right of the consumer to object to third parties succeeding the supplier;

(xxiii) exclude the consumer's right to propose a compromise to the supplier;

(xxiv) clauses by which the consumer is presumed to be informed about the terms and conditions of the contract or the quality of the provided goods or services, when in fact he is ignorant of them;

(xxv) bind the consumer to pay in advance an extremely large part of the price even before the start of performance by the supplier, although the supplier did not undertake the obligation to perform the consumer's order on a basis of certain conditions nor does the supplier's performance concern services with a reservation (hotels etc);

(xxvi) permit the supplier to demand unreasonably large warranties from the consumer;

(xxvii) impose on the consumer a burden of proof which, according to the applicable law, should be with another party to the contract, or limit the consumer's means of proof;

(xxviii) determine an unreasonably short period during which the consumer may complain to the supplier or exercise legal remedies, otherwise his rights are excluded;

(xxix) provide that the supplier has the exclusive right to supply the consumer with the required spare parts and accessories, and to perform the service or repairs of the product;

(xxx) require any consumer who fails to fulfil his obligations to pay a disproportionately large amount in compensation;

(xxxi) exclude or hinder the jurisdiction of the competent court upon the matters of the contract, and require the consumer to take any dispute exclusively to arbitration or exclusive foreign jurisdiction.

Finally, Law 2251/1994 provides (a) that (art 2 para 8) the supplier can not rely on the invalidity of the whole of the contract on the excuse that it contains one or more unfair terms, and (b) that (art 2 para 9) the above dispositions apply to all contracts having Greece as the place of conclusion or performance even if the contract's competent law is different from the Greek.

(vi) Booking conditions and cancellations

(a) Hotels

11.54 The rights of the consumer when entering a holiday agreement, in so far as it concerns his relations with the hotel owner, are regulated by the administrative decision of the Secretary General of the EOT No 503007/1976, ratified by Law 1652/1986 (art 8).

According to the provisions of this Decision, the hotel owner is obliged to let all his vacant rooms to the requesting consumer-tourist and also to supply him with all the comforts and accommodations advertised (Art 1 of the Decision). The hotel owner cannot refuse to let to any person unless the person is ill, drunk or unclean.

If the consumer wishes to book a hotel room by means of a letter, telephone call, telegram or fax, the hotel owner is obliged to inform the consumer of acceptance within a period of three days in writing or by telegram or fax. The hotel owner has the right to demand a payment in advance of 25% of the total price of the accommodation. The contract for the accommodation and the booking, is completed when the above acceptance is received by the consumer, or when he pays the required percentage as advance payment.

The consumer has the right to cancel his reservation by notice to the hotel owner at least 21 days before the booked date of his arrival. If the consumer does not inform the hotel owner within the above time-limit and if the consumer does not use the room for the initially-agreed period of the reservation, he is obliged to pay to the hotel owner half of the total amount owed to him for the period during which the consumer will not be using the booked room (art 3 of the EOT's Decision 503007/76).

11.55 The booking of the room is considered to have the duration of one day, if not otherwise agreed. It is also considered to be mutually extended for the next day, if the hotel owner does not inform the consumer of the termination of the contract and if, in turn, the consumer has not informed the hotel owner.

The calculation of the price due to the hotel for the booking of a room includes the date of the arrival of the client but not the date of his departure. If the consumer does not leave before midday, the rent of half a day is due. Furthermore, if the consumer keeps the room after 18.00 hours, he is obliged to pay the whole rent for that day.

If the hotel owner does not fulfil the reservation obligations and is not in a position to provide the consumer with the booked room or rooms, he is obliged to ensure the consumer has accommodation in another hotel of the same quality, under the same conditions and comforts. In that case the hotel owner is obliged to cover the expenses of transportation of the consumer to this other hotel, and the potential difference between the prices of the two hotels. If the hotel owner is not able to fulfil these legal obligations, he is obliged to indemnify the consumer by paying him the total amount for the agreed period of reservation. It is irrelevant if the consumer has agreed the reservation directly with the hotel, or is the bearer of a voucher.

11.56 Law No 2160/1993 imposes on all enterprises in the sector of tourism, a separate administrative fine of Drs 100,000 for every infringement depriving the tourist of hotel services (accommodation, comforts etc) due to the fact that reservations exceeded the number of available beds of the hotel.

Furthermore, the provisions of the Civil Code regarding non-performance, or inadequate performance of contracts are also applicable, as well as the provisions of Law No 1961/1991. For these last, their obligatory character may exclude and prevail over the application of the provisions of the EOT's Decision if the rights provided to the consumer by Law No 1961/1991 are more favourable to the consumer.

Finally, the consumer, whose reservation is cancelled without justification by the hotel owner, has the right to demand compensation for all further damages or losses caused him by such action.

(b) Allotments

11.57 Articles 11–13 of Decision 503007/1976 of the Secretary General of the EOT, regulate the system of allotments, meaning the reservation contracts between hotels and travel agencies and/or tour operators.

These contracts must include the following information:

(i)   the type of the rooms to be booked (single, double, with bath etc);
(ii)   the exact duration of the stay;
(iii) the maximum and the minimum number of days of the agreed stay;
(iv)   the price for the stay, and whether with breakfast, half board, full board, etc.

The hotel owner has the right to demand from the travel agency the payment in advance of 25% of the total price of the allotment. If the hotel owner does not perform the allotment contract, he is obliged to return the advance payment, and also to indemnify the travel agency for all further damage or losses.

11.58 The agency or tour operator has the right to cancel the whole or a part of the reservations made, provided that this cancellation will take place at least 21 days before the agreed arrival of the consumers-tourists. In that case the payment of indemnity is not required. Likewise, the hotel owner in the release period has the right to cancel the reservations of beds not confirmed by a voucher or rooming list.

(c) Loss of property

11.59 The consumer has, according to the provisions of the Greek Civil Code, the rights set out below against the hotel owner in respect of damage or loss of property.

The hotel owner is liable for all kinds of loss or damage or theft of property brought by the consumer into the hotel, unless the damage or the loss of the object was due to the nature of the object, to the consumer himself, or to *force majeure*. The liability of the hotel owner is excluded when the consumer, unreasonably, does not inform the hotel owner about the loss, provided that the consumer knew about it.

Finally, the hotel owner has a legal pledge over the belongings of the consumer for his demands against the consumer, for the stay or other services.

4. Forms of redress

(i) General

11.60 Article 20 of the Hellenic Constitution provides that "Every person shall be entitled to receive legal protection by the courts and may plead before them his views concerning his rights or interests, as specified by the law". This constitutional right is granted, without any discrimination, to all persons, Greeks and foreigners, and also to legal entities or unions provided that the Greek courts are competent. The regulations of the Rome European Convention on "Human Rights" are also applicable.

(ii) Jurisdiction of the Greek civil courts

11.61 Article 3 of the Civil Procedure Code (CPC) provides that the Greek courts have jurisdiction over Greeks and foreigners only if a venue may be established in Greece. The Court has the obligation to examine whether its jurisdication is established, without any demand being made by the litigant parties, even if the defendant is absent.

According to the provisions of article 23 of the Civil Procedure Code, all actions must be filed before the court of the area where the defendant has his domicile, so if the defendant (*i.e.* a travel agent or a hotel owner) is domiciled in Greece, the Greek courts are competent (*e.g.* in Crete the relevant courts of Crete are competent). If the defendant has no domicile in Greece or abroad, then the court of his residence will be competent. If the court of residence is unknown, then the court of his last domicile or residence in Greece is competent to judge the case (art 23 of the CPC). A legal entity or corporation is deemed to have a "domicile" or residence in the area where its head office is located (art 25 para 2 of the CPC). These are the clauses (conditions) of "general" jurisdiction of the Greek courts.

However, in the Civil Procedure Code, exceptions are adopted, among which are the jurisdictions involving real property (*i.e.* actions relating to Time Share Agreements), and contracts. According to the provisions of article 29 of the Civil Procedure Code, actions relevant to matters of real property must be judged by the court which is located in the area of the real property. In the case of contracts, the venue is alternatively determined by the place where the contract was executed or performed, signed, or scheduled to be executed (art 33 of the CPC). **11.62**

Finally, an alternative basis of jurisdiction of Greek Law is provided in article 40 of the Civil Procedure Code. According to this article, persons not domiciled or not residing in Greece, may be judged, and the relevant proceedings against them may be brought, in the court where property of the defendant exists. The regulations of the European Convention of Brussels (1982) are also applicable.

(iii)   Forms of civil redress

Civil cases in Greece are judged either by the First Instance Courts or by the Magistrates Courts. The Civil Courts are composed of regular "professional" judges, with no participation by a jury, or laymen. The competence of the court depends on the value of the object of each case. Magistrates Courts are competent for values up to Drs 600,000. The One-Member First Instance Courts are competent for values between Drs 600,000 and Drs 3,000,000. If the value of the case exceeds the sum of Drs 3,000,000, the First Instance Court will consist of three Members. Appeals against the decisions of a Magistrates Court are brought in front of the Three-Members First Instance Court (art 18 para 2 of CPC), while the appeals against the decisions of the First Instance Courts are brought in front of the Court of Appeal. The decisions of the Court of Appeal, and also decisions issued by all other courts, may be brought, on special grounds, in front of the Supreme Court (*Areios Pagos*). **11.63**

Greek legislation recognises (in general) two ways of judicial protection in front of Courts of First Instance, (i) the action (lawsuit) and (ii) the application for temporary (security) measures.

An action is filed in front of a Court of First Instance and should be served on the other litigant party (in principle) 30 days before the hearing if the defendant is domiciled or resident in Greece, or 60 days before the hearing if the defendant is domiciled abroad. **11.64**

An application regarding the adoption of temporary (security) measures, in cases of danger to the interests of the applicant, safeguarding or related to matters of an urgent nature, is filed before the One-Member Court of First Instance, and the relevant procedure is characterised by its speed, simplicity of the evidence, the lack of the right to appeal against the relevant decision, and the freedom of the judge some time in the future to suspend the implementation of the decision issued and of the measure ordered.

11.65 The Greek Code of Civil Procedure recognises two kinds of "Procedures", the "Regular – or General – Procedure" and a variety of "Special Procedures" (*i.e.* labour disputes arts 663–676 of the CPC, and cases at the hearing of which the rules of the labour disputes are applicable; disputes arising from motor-vehicle accidents; and disputes on leases) (arts 647–662 of the CPC). The special procedure of the "Disputes on Leases" is relevant on the basis that, according to the provisions of Law 1652/1986, time share agreements are considered to be lease agreements.

Finally, the winning party of a dispute has the right to execute the decision, provided that the decision is final, which means that either the court that issued it has deprived the litigant parties of any further jurisdiction on the issue, or that no appeal or opposition has been filed within the time limit provided by the law, or that the appeal filed is rejected by the competent Court of Appeal. Certain judgments are not subject to appeal. A decision becomes irrevocable if it cannot be assailed by any means of appeal, or if appeals have been rejected. First instance decisions issued in the presence of both litigant parties become irrevocable, if an appeal has not been filed three years after their date of issue, or 30 days (60 days for the party residing abroad) from the service of the decision. Decisions by default become irrevocable if an appeal has not been filed, three years after their date of issue, or 45 days from service. Decisions of the Court of Appeal become irrevocable if an appeal at the Supreme Court is not filed 30 days after their service or three years after their issue.

11.66 In principle a final and irrevocable decision may be executed within three days of service. A decision declared "provisionally or temporarily executable" may be executed within the same period regardless of whether it is being appealed or not (arts 907–908 of the CPC). All executable decisions are to be effected by a competent court bailiff (retained and paid by the winner of the dispute). The court bailiff has the following means at its disposal in order to execute the decisions:

(i)   Decision ordering the delivery or requisition of a movable asset: The bailiff detaches it and delivers it to the claimant.

(ii) Decision ordering the acquisition or requisition of immovable property: The bailiff expels the debtor (*i.e.* the lessee staying longer than the agreed period) from the property, and installs the claimant there.

(iii) Decision ordering the debtor to act or to refrain from acting: (*i.e.* the hotel owner is not recognising his obligation to cede the use of the booked room, or the travel agent is not fulfilling his obligation). A monetary fine and/or personal arrest is imposed on him.

(iv)   Decisions awarding sums of money to the claimant may be enforced by the following means: seizure of the debtor's movable or immovable property and/or personal arrest).

The debtor has a variety of means of legal redress against the execution of judgments, such as opposition to the procedure followed, or errors of the entitled persons (bailiff, notary public etc, arts 930–933 *et seq* of the CPC).

(iv)   Redress against administrative decisions and state measures

(a)   General

An administrative decision (*e.g.* of the Ministry of Tourism) harming or illegally affecting the interests of a person or legal entity (Greek or foreign) gives the right to file either an "application for annulment" of the decision in front of the "Council of State", or a redress in front of the "Regular Administrative Courts".

11.67

(b)   Application for annulment

The basic condition for the admissibility of the "application for annulment" is the "legitimate interest" of the applicant. This condition is wider than the condition of recognised legal right which is required for the admissibility of an application in front of the Regular Administrative Courts.[8]

11.68

The harmful administrative decision must be challenged by means of the "application for annulment" in front of the "Council of State" (*Symvoulio Epikrateias* – SE) within a period of 60 days (90 days if the applicant is domiciled abroad) starting from the publication (in the Government Gazette) or the notification of the decision to the applicant, or from the knowledge of the content of the decision/action of the Authority.

The application for annulment is legally filed only if the applicant has previously exercised a recourse in front of the competent authority (if required to do so). The application is brought against the result of this recourse or against the absence of any result on this recourse.[9]

Finally, in order to proceed to the hearing of the relevant application, the court (SE) requires that no other redress or recourse is pending in front of an administrative authority or another court (of Civil, Administrative or Criminal Justice).[10]

The application is substantiated if the following grounds exist:

11.69

(i)   the authority which issued the administrative decision was not competent (incompetency of the authority);

(ii)   the action or decision has not followed the normal procedure;

---

[8] Speliotopoulos, E, *Manual of Administrative Law* Vol 2 (Athens, 1986) para 451, 425–426.
[9] Speliotopoulos, E, *op. cit.* paras 468–469, 440–441.
[10] Speliotopoulos, E, *op. cit.* para 484, 455–456.

(iii)   the decision or action is illegal, meaning that is not in conformity with certain provisions of the Law; and

(iv)   was issued by an abuse of authority (art 48 of the Legislative Decree 170/1973).[11]

11.70   Because the Council of State is the Supreme Court of Administrative Justice, its decisions on the matter are not subject to any legal review or objection.

The consequence of a judgment of the Council of State (if it accepts the application) is to annul the administrative decision concerned, and to order the Administration to comply with the decision (consequently in case of an application issued on the "absence" of an administrative action or decision, the Council of State orders the Administrative Authority to proceed to such an act). The judgment has effect only as between the parties.

(c)   Application in front of the Regular Administrative Courts

11.71   An administrative dispute is judged by the so-called Regular Administrative Courts. The First Instance Administrative Court, which is the main administrative court and is composed of either one or three members, (its composition depending on the value of the object of the case), covers disputes on taxation, monetary claims against the State, and public corporations. Appeals against decisions of the One-Member First Instance Administrative Court are brought before the Multi-Member First Instance Administrative Court. The decisions of this Multi-Member First Instance Administrative Court are subject to a right of appeal to the Three-Member Court of Appeal, or to the Five-Member Administrative Court of Appeal, its composition depending on the value of the object of the case. At the head of all the regular administrative courts is the Council of State, before which decisions of the Court of Appeal, or all other Courts on special grounds, may be challenged.

Greek law recognises two kinds of legal redress in front of the Regular Administrative Courts, being: (i) the means of "redress" by which the applicant demands the annulment of a harmful "individual" administrative decision; and (ii) the means of a "plea", regarding monetary claims against the state or other public authorities. Both have to be filed within a period of 60 days (90 days if the applicant resides abroad) from the date of publication, notification (service), or knowledge of the decision, otherwise the claim is proscribed. Disputes on taxation have to be filed within a period of 20 days from the date of the service of the decision concerned.

11.72   The judgments of the Administrative Courts of First Instance must be challenged within a period of 30 days from the service of the judgment

[11] Speliotopoulos, E, *op. cit.* para 491, 461.

concerned. Finally, the judgment of the Court of Appeal may be legally challenged before the Council of State within a period of 60 days (90 days for the party residing abroad) starting on the date of the service of the judgment concerned.

(v) Arbitration

Arbitration is not unknown to Greek Law. On the contrary, arbitration   **11.73** decisions may be effected and enforced as the judgments of the "Regular" Courts. In addition, Greece has ratified by Law the International Convention of New York on arbitration.

Moreover, Greek legislation, accepting the concept of arbitration, has recognised (in civil cases only) the freedom of persons and potential litigant parties to appoint arbitrators instead of approaching the competent courts. The freedom to establish arbitrators in cases where a civil court would be competent, is contractual, and so the normal jurisdiction of the civil courts is not excluded. Finally, in Greek Law an *ex lege* arbitration does not exist. In addition, a "general" or "standard" clause of a holiday contract or agreement, by which disputes deriving from the contract are exclusively taken to arbitration, and by which the jurisdiction of the "regular" courts is excluded, is null and void (art 25 para za of Law 1961/1991).

(vi) Other forms of redress

The only not *stricto sensu* judicial form of redress, granted to the con-   **11.74** sumer in general, and also when entering into a holiday agreement, is the one recognised by Article 11 of Law 2251/1994.

According to the provisions of this article, in every Prefecture (*Nomarchia*), a Bureau is established to deal with the extra-judicial friendly resolution of disputes on the consumer's rights between suppliers and consumers, relating to the performance of services or supply of goods. The relevant application must be filed by either the consumer, the supplier or the union of consumers.

The hearing of the application must take place within 15 days from the filing of the application in front of a Three-Member Committee consisting of a lawyer member of the Local Bar (as president); a representative of the Local Chamber of Commerce; and a representative of the Local Union of Consumers, as members. The committee should decide on the dispute within seven days from the date of the hearing. The decisions of this Committee are deprived of any substantial effect, but are estimated and considered as judicial presumptions in front of the competent courts.

Finally, the EOT supervises all enterprises operating in the tourism   **11.75** industry, so that a consumer has the right to report all infringements of the relevant legislation to this regulatory body.

(vii) Associations and consumer unions

11.76 Article 10 of Law 2251/1994 defines the matters of the foundation, organisation and function of the consumers' unions. According to the above provisions the unions of the consumers are founded and operate under the regulations of the above Law and Articles 26–29 of Law 2000/1991, in combination with the regulations of the Civil Code. For the foundation of a consumers' union at least 100 persons are needed (in cities of population less than 3,000 inhabitants, the union may be founded by just 20 persons). A consumer has the right to be member in only one consumers' union.

The unions have as their exclusive task the protection of the interests of the consumers. They can represent the consumers in front of the courts and all competent authorities, inform and advise the consumers; finally they can file the "collective lawsuits" (a form of the Roman *actio popularis*). This constitutes a new form of redress introduced by the above Law. This lawsuit, which aims to protect the general interests of the consumers, can be filed only by consumers' unions having at least 500 members and registered to the relevant record of unions at least two years before the filing of the lawsuit. Furthermore, all consumers' unions have a legitimate right to file lawsuits, applications for security measures, applications for annulment, or pleas in front of the regular administrative courts and also to intervene in pending cases of their members in order to support their rights as consumers.

11.77 More specifically, by filing the above "collective lawsuits" the unions may demand:

a) The omission of the supplier's illegal action especially when this attitude consists in the formulation of unfair terms, illegal sales outside business premises or distance sales, or in violation of the dispositions regarding the service after the sale and in the production, import and distribution of defective products, dangerous to the safety and the health of the public, or by misleading, illicit, comparative or direct advertising. The unions may also demand the seizure or destruction of defective and dangerous products or the restitution of the misleading or comparative advertising by all necessary means among which is also a revision of the advertising at the expense of the advertised person.

b) Pecuniary indemnity for moral damage. This last is defined by the court after taking into consideration the stress caused by the violation, the size of the defendant supplier and especially his annual turnover, as well as the need for general and special protection, and

c) The adoption of security measures in order to ensure the demands for omission or pecuniar idemnity pending issue of an executable decision. If the case is production, distribution etc of defective products, dangerous to public health and safety, the appropriate measure may be the seizure of the products.

The competent court in front of which the above lawsuit should be **11.78** filed is the Three-Members Court of First Instance of the residence or domicile of the defendant or one of the registered offices of the radio or TV station, if the lawsuit refers to a TV or radio commercial (advertising). The court judges the lawsuits at the soonest date of hearing (in cases which refer to a) and b) above) and hearing takes place in accordance with the rules of the special "voluntary" procedure (εκουσία). The court also has the right to order the temporary execution of the decision and this judgment has lawful results *erga omnes* even if they were not litigant parties.

Finally, according to the provisions of Article 10 paragraph 10 of the Law 2251/1994 the "collective lawsuit" may also be filed by the Industrial, Commercial or Professional Chambers of Commerce.

5. Insurance requirements

(i) Individual travel insurance

According to the provisions of Presidential Decree No 103/1990, which **11.79** amended Legislative Decree No 400/1970, travel insurance is brought into Greek insurance legislation, defined by the law as "tourist assistance".

"Tourist assistance" includes the assistance provided to persons who are in a difficult situation during movement or absence from the place of their domicile or their permanent residence.

This assistance includes the undertaking of an obligation to provide immediate assistance to an entitled insured person in a difficult situation due to an accidental factor, under the conditions or terms of the relevant insurance policy, provided that the required insurance premium has been paid. Tourist assistance may be offered in money or *in specie*. The assistance *in specie* may take the form of services offered by the personnel of the insurance company. The activities and assistance provided by a specialised Greek legal entity of non-profitable character, where the accident has occurred in Greece, are excluded from the provisions of the law when those activities are limited only to:

(i) the immediate repair of a vehicle, for which the assisting party **11.80** uses, usually, its own personnel or its own materials;

(ii) the transfer of the vehicle to the nearest or most appropriate place for the repair and the potential transportation of the driver and passengers of the vehicle to the nearest place from where they will be able to continue their trip;

(iii) the transfer of the vehicle from a place outside Greek territory and the possible transportation of the driver and passengers to their domicile or to the place of start of the trip, or to their destination in Greece.

(ii) Automobile insurance

11.81 According to the provisions of Law 489/1976 as so far in force, the owner, possessor (if other than the owner) and driver of a motor vehicle, are all objectively liable for all damages and personal injury caused to a third party (or to his property or car) due to the movement of a motor vehicle. This civil liability must be covered by a relevant "Automobile Civil Liability Insurance Policy". Consequently, according to the provisions of Law 489/1976, all automobiles (and in general all motor-vehicles) travelling inside Greek territory must be insured by a policy covering the "Civil Liability" of the car. Foreign cars entering into Greece are subject to this obligation, and so cars from non-Member States, not having a "Green Card" (certificate of International Insurance), are usually not permitted to enter the territory of Greece. These cars must be insured at the border by so-called "Border Insurance", which is agreed between the car-owner and the Greek department of the International Bureau of Insurance. The Bureau is entitled to settle all damages or injury caused to third parties by a foreign car within Greek territory, and is obliged to indemnify the injured if the foreign car was supplied with the relevant Certificate of International Insurance (Green Card) by a foreign Bureau.

11.82 Cars hired by a tourist or traveller are not excluded from the regulations of Law 489/1976. According to the provisions of Ministerial Decision 532253/1976, governing the terms and conditions of establishment and operation of car rental enterprises, all automobiles owned by car rental enterprises must be insured for "civil liability" by an insurance company operating in Greece.

Furthermore, according to the provisions of Law 489/1976, the injured party has a so-called, "direct claim" against the insurance company of the insured party. The insurance company cannot produce against the injured person objections deriving from the insurance policy and objections related to the agreement between insurer and the insured, such as the non-payment of the premium.[12] Nevertheless, the insurance company has the right to claim from the insured person all the amounts paid as indemnity to the injured person if the accident was due to the fault of the insured, and this fault is an infringement of the insurance policy (*e.g.* the insured driver was drunk).

The limits on insurance are fixed by Law at the amount of Drs 7,000,000 for damage to property and at Drs 35,000,000 for personal injury, but the parties (insurance company – insured) have the right to agree higher amounts of liability than the amounts fixed by the Law.

11.83 If the offending car was not insured, the injured person is entitled to an indemnity from a legal entity established by law, known as the "Subsidiary Fund for Insurance of Automobiles' Civil Liability" which

---

[12] Rokas, J, *Introduction to Private Insurance Law* (Athens, 1992) para 167, 100.

is responsible and obliged to cover all damage and injuries caused to a person by an uninsured automobile. All insurance companies operating in Greece, covering car civil liability must participate in this "Fund".

In addition, the injured person may satisfy his claims regarding the indemnity for damage of property or personal injury, by bringing a relevant action against the insured and the insurance company in front of the competent court (the Single-Member Court of First Instance) of the place of the accident, according to the provisions of the Civil Procedure Code, which will be judged following the special Procedure of the "Disputes arising from motor vehicle accidents". The applicable law will be the law of the state in the territory of which the accident occurred.

The Third Council Directive 90/232/EEC regarding the approxima-   **11.84** tion of Member States' legislation relating to insurance against civil liability in respect of the use of motor vehicles, which provides that the insurance policy covers the entire territory of the Community.

Finally, Greek law permits the consumer to cover, not only the civil liability of the car (which is obligatory), but also all damage caused to his own automobile, by an insurance policy covering the risks of fire, theft, mechanical damage and/or accident. The insurance company covering these damages will have to indemnify the insured for all damage (according to the terms and the limits of the insurance policy and the law), and it will then "substitute" the insured in all his claims against the responsible owner/possessor/driver and/or the insurance company of the offending car.

6.   Health and safety standards

(i)   Accommodation health standards

(a)   Hotels

Every hotel owner is under an obligation to ensure the regular main-   **11.85** tenance of the hotel building, the mechanical equipment, furniture and linen and, generally to immediately restore all relevant damage; and the hotel owner is obliged to make all improvements required by legislation and imposed by the competent authorities.

For hotels ranked class C and above, the continuous supply of hot water is obligatory to all bathrooms and showers. Likewise the continuous heating of the building during the winter period up until April is compulsory.

The cleaning of the rooms and all premises of the hotel must be perfect and absolute. The hotel must be disinfected twice a year. Special attention must be given to thorough and regular cleaning and order of the restaurants, offices, and kitchens, and the function of the drainage system must be in perfect condition. The cleanliness and the appearance of the linen and utensils must also be faultless.

11.86   All towels must be replaced with clean ones every day, and bed-linen must be replaced at least:

(i)   once a day for hotels ranked class A;
(ii)   three times a week for hotels ranked class B and C;
(iii)   two times a week for hotels ranked class D and E; and
(iv)   once a week for inns.

In any event new bed-linen must be used for a new customer no matter how short his predecessor's stay at the hotel room.

(b)   Apartments/rooms to let/traditional villas/hostels

11.87   The health requirements must also be fulfilled by all kinds of tourist lodgings, relative to their function and nature. For example, a traditional villa must have appropriate furniture.

(c)   Camping

11.88   Special provisions are included in tourist law regarding the installation, functioning and health conditions of a camp site.

A   SURFACE AREA

11.89   In order to obtain the relevant licence from the EOT, a camp site must have a minimum surface area of 8,000 m² (for camp sites ranked class C), 15,000 m² for camp sites ranked class B, and above 20,000 m² for camp sites of high quality (class A).

The camp site must also be sited 250 m away from a hotel, in a healthy area, with natural beauty of surroundings. A camp site can not be sited near schools, hospitals, factories or graveyards.

B   FACILITIES

11.90   Camp sites must have telephones and electricity and the necessary installations for water supply, and in particular a supply of 150 litres of water per person per day.

All camp sites must have, *inter alia*, an internal system of roads and WCs, showers, laundries, cooking places and car parking.

A camp site is ranked as class A if it includes: a reception room; a parking place; a management bureau; a telephone cabin: separate toilet facilities for each sex, with a lavatory isolated from the rest of the installations at the front of the camp site; a first aid room; a letter box and safety deposit box; a bar with a surface area of 80 m²; self-catering cooking places; a food store supermarket; laundry installations; one W.C. for every 15 persons; one shower for every 15 persons (half of these should supply hot water); a children's lavatory for every 30 persons; all bathrooms must have hot and cold water.

There are a few differences between the three classes of camp sites, relating to their surface area and facilities.

(ii) Accommodation safety standards

Greek legislation has special provisions regarding the fire protection of hotel accommodation.   **11.91**

Every tourist installation must have fire escapes leading to safe places. At least two fire exits must exist for each floor of the building, at different sides of the building. These fire escapes are not permitted to pass through other rooms, and must end in open places, such as yards, which must be safe for the public. The route to the safe gathering place must be protected by an automatic "sprinkler" system. This escape route must also be isolated from the rest of the installation with fire resistant material. All doors should open to the direction of the gathering place. No mirrors or other reflecting objects that might in case of panic misdirect persons, should be placed near these doors or fire exits.

All vertical openings, at stairs etc, must be blocked by hermetically sealed fire-resistant doors with directions to a fire escape, in order to avoid the transmission of the fire from floor to floor.

All of the route to the fire escape must be indicated with lighted signs with the inscription "EXIT" and an arrow pointing the direction. Those signs must be brightly lit. The fire escape corridor must also be well lit.   **11.92**

In every lodging, besides the special fire alarm system, a tannoy system should also exist, by which the public and personnel may be directed to a safe place.

All lodgings must also have a fire hydrant system, automatic sprinkler system, necessary instruments and tools (*e.g.* axes), two fire extinguishers of dry powder placed in every hall or corridor, and two other fire extinguishers for the central boiler.

The personnel of the hotel must also receive instructions on dealing with fire and panic, and on matters of fire protection. A fire protection team, specially trained to face those accidents, must be formed from among the personnel.

Finally, for reasons of fire protection, the following are prohibited: **11.93**

(i)   the construction of the building and especially of the stairs and fire escapes in non fire-resistant materials;

(ii)   the placing of furniture, or other kind of objects which might block public circulation near or in front of stairs, doors and fire escapes;

(iii) the installation of projectors with strong thermal radiation that might cause fire;

(iv)   the decoration and covering of the walls and floors with flammable materials;

(v)   the storage of flammable liquids, fuel and other hydro-carbonated materials in lodgings or other places reached by the public; and

(vi)   smoking in high risk locations.

(iii) Tourist buses

11.94   Tourist buses circulating in Greece must fulfil the following requirements:

(i)   a bus must be withdrawn from circulation at the latest 18 years after the date of manufacture;

(ii)   all tourist buses more than three years after construction must be checked annually:

    (a) regarding technical safety standards, by the competent authorities of the Ministry of Transportation and the local Prefecture (*Nomarchia*);

    (b) regarding their appearance, by the competent authorities of the EOT.

The authorities will issue the relevant document or certificate of control, in which all the repairs required and the time limits for repair will be stated. The documents must be notified within a period of ten days from the date of control to the Central Services of the EOT. Before the expiry of the time limit, the buses must be checked again, and if they have not been repaired, an administrative sanction or fine will be imposed on the owner of the bus. If a tourist bus is not presented for this second control, the relevant circulation licence will be suspended;

(iii)   all tourist buses must be covered by an insurance policy, covering damage to the vehicle as well as damage to the passengers of the bus;

(iv)   the daily distance covered by a bus must not exceed 630 km. It is also compulsory that the bus must stop at least twice a day for at least half an hour;

(v)   in all tourist buses operating trips or excursions abroad, the presence of a tourist guide and a second driver is compulsory;

(vi)   buses operating excursions inside Greece must be accompanied by a licensed tourist guide if the excursion programme includes visits to archaeological or historical sites;

(vii)   in the case of excursions or travel abroad, the tourist bus must have a detailed programme of the itinerary and the stops of the bus. This written programme must be announced/notified to the passengers and signed by them;

(viii)   all excursion programmes must be detailed;

(ix)   all drivers, guides etc, must behave politely and respect the wishes of the tourists on matters of music (volume, quality) and smoking;

(x)   smoking is prohibited on tourist buses during excursions inside
      Greece or abroad, as follows:
      (a) in the first five seats in buses with more than 20 places;
      (b) in the first two seats in all other buses.

7.   Rights against transport operators

(i)   Transport of persons by air

(a)   General

The air transport of persons and goods is regulated in Greece for inter-   **11.95**
national flights by the provisions of Obligatory Law 596/1937, by which
the "Warsaw Convention" for the "unification of regulations relating to
the international air transportation", as amended by several Protocols,
was adopted by Greek legislation; and for domestic flights by the provisions of Law 1815/1986 the "Code of Aerial Law".

(b)   Cancellation

A   DOMESTIC FLIGHTS

There are no specific provisions regulating the rights and obligations of   **11.96**
the contracting parties in the case of cancellation, therefore it could be
argued that the relevant provisions applicable in the case of delay also
apply to this case. The carrier (airline) is obliged to perform the contract
of air transport properly, and is liable to indemnify the passenger for
non-performance or inadequate performance, unless it proves that it had
taken all measures to avoid the cancellation.

According to the above, an unreasonable cancellation of the passenger
reservation by the carrier is an infringement of the obligation of the
carrier to perform the transport contract. Consequently, the consumer
has the right to compensation and reimbursement of the amount paid.

If the provisions relating to delay do not apply in case of cancellation,
then the provisions of the Civil Code regarding contractual obligations
apply, so that the passenger has the right to withdraw from the contract,
or to demand further compensation for all damage or losses, or to withdraw from the contract and at the same time demand compensation (art
387 of the Civil Code).

B   INTERNATIONAL FLIGHTS

The "Warsaw Convention" does not have any specific provisions regulat-   **11.97**
ing the liability of the air carrier in the event of cancellation, and consequently the provisions of Chapter III of the Convention, regulating the
liability of the carrier for damage or loss caused by the delay of transport
of passengers could be applicable. If these provisions are applicable, the

liability of the carrier is considered as "objective" or "*ex lege*",[13] meaning that the carrier is released from any obligation for compensation if it had taken all measures to avoid the incident, and the accident has occurred as a consequence of a factor outside the authority of the carrier, such as acts of God or war etc considered as *force majeure.*

(c) Damage to or loss of property

A DOMESTIC FLIGHTS

11.98 According to Chapters 14 and 15 of the Code of Aerial Law (Law 1815/1986), the carrier is responsible and liable for all damage to or loss of the passenger's property (baggage, luggage) occurring during the flight (including the period, during which the luggage is under the care of the carrier (*e.g.* embarkation or disembarkation of the passengers)). The carrier's responsibility is considered as objective,[14] and the carrier is released from any responsibility to indemnify the passenger if it is in a position to prove that it had taken all measures and precautions to avoid this loss or damage.

Article 110 of Law 1815/1986 provides for a pecuniary limitation of the liability of the carrier. In the case of damage or loss of baggage, the liability of the carrier is limited to the amount of Drs 4,000 per kilo. The luggage of the passenger must be weighed before delivery to the carrier. This limit of liability is not applicable if the damage is due to intention (*dolus*) of the carrier or its staff. Likewise, the limitation is not applicable in the case of an express declaration of the real value of the baggage and its contents by the passenger before delivery to the carrier, and payment of an extra fee by the passenger.

For baggage carried by the passenger inside the aeroplane, the liability of the carrier is limited to the amount of Drs 30,000 in total.

B INTERNATIONAL FLIGHTS

11.99 The liability of the carrier in the event of loss or damage of baggage of the passenger is "objective", according to the provisions of the Warsaw Convention. The carrier is released from any obligation if it proves that it had taken all measures and precautions to avoid this loss or damage, or that the damage was caused by the passenger. The carrier's liability to compensation is unlimited if the damage to or loss of property is due to intention (*dolus*) or negligence.

The limit of the carrier's liability in the event of damage to or loss of property, amounts to 250 golden francs per kilo, unless the passenger had declared in writing to the carrier the real value of the contents of his baggage before delivery to the carrier and had paid an extra fee. As far

---

[13] Georgakopoulos, L, *Manual of Commercial Law* Vol 2 "Commercial actions – Contracts" (Athens, 1991) 335–336.

[14] Georgakopoulos, L, *op. cit.* 322–324.

as baggage carried by the passenger inside the aeroplane is concerned, the liability of the carrier is limited to the amount of 5,000 francs in total. The passenger's right to be indemnified for damage or loss of baggage is prescribed, if no written protest is filed within seven days from the receipt of the baggage or, in the event of loss or delay, within 21 days as from the day that the baggage should have been delivered. The relevant action must be filed in court within two years from the arrival of the aeroplane or the day the aeroplane should have arrived. The passenger cannot renounce those rights, and all relevant agreements are considered null and void.

(d)   Personal injury or death

A   DOMESTIC FLIGHTS

According to the provisions of Law 1815/1986, the carrier is liable to indemnify the injured passenger or the heirs of the passenger in the event of death, and in general all persons entitled to compensation, according to the provisions of the Civil Code, if the injury or death has taken place during the flight (including taking off and landing, boarding and disembarkation). The liability of the carrier is objective (meaning that the passenger is not obliged to prove intention (*dolus*) or negligence of the carrier, who bears the burden of proof). The carrier is released only if the injury or death was due to a pre-existing health condition of the passenger. The liability of the carrier in the event of death cannot exceed the amount of Drs 4,000,000 (even if there is more than one entitled person), but in the case of intention (*dolus*) by the carrier or its staff, liability is unlimited.   **11.100**

B   INTERNATIONAL FLIGHTS

According to the provisions of the Warsaw Convention, the liability of the carrier in the event of death or injury is regulated in the same manner as in the provisions of the "Code of Aerial Law". The difference is that in the case of international flights the limit of the carrier's liability is 250,000 golden francs per person. Liability is unlimited in the case of intention (*dolus*) or negligence of the carrier or its staff. The relevant claims for indemnity should be brought in front of the competent courts within two years from the day the aircraft finally arrived at its destination, or the day it should have arrived at its destination.   **11.101**

(ii)   Transport of persons by sea

(a)   Cancellation

The seventh chapter of the sixth title of the Code of Private Maritime Law regulates all matters deriving from contracts of transport of persons by sea.   **11.102**

Article 179 of the Code provides that the relevant contract is dissolved if the trip was cancelled due to an unexpected event. *Ex argumentum ad contrario*, it is thought that this law, in combination with the provisions of the Civil Code, grants the passenger the right to claim compensation in the case of a cancellation due to an event which is not accidental, but provoked by the sea transporter. This is justified by the provisions of the same Code, according to which the passenger is obliged to pay at least half the price of the sea passage in the case of withdrawal, or not being on board by the time of the departure of the ship.

The liability of the sea transporter is objective. The transporter is released if he proves that he had taken all measures to avoid the incident (art 134 of Code of Private Maritime Law).

(b) Damage to or loss of property

11.103   The provisions regulating the common freighting of goods are also applicable on matters of liability of the transporter in the event of damage to or loss of property of the passenger.

According to those provisions, the transporter's liability is objective, and he is responsible for all damage and losses due to defects of the ship and actions of the captain or the crew.

Article 141 of the Code of Private Maritime Law provides that, by a Presidential Decree, the liability of the transporter will be limited, and a maximum amount due to the injured passenger per unit or per item will be fixed. This Decree has not yet been issued, so that the transporter is to date liable for unlimited compensation.

(c) Delay

11.104   Article 180 of the Code of Private Maritime Law provides that, in the case of delay of the trip, the passenger has the right to stay on board and also has the right to food, according to the provisions of article 176. In the case of prolongation of the delay, the passenger has the right to withdraw from the contract and is therefore released from the obligation of payment of the price of the transportation (freight), while maintaining the right to compensation.

(d) Personal injury or death

11.105   No special provisions regarding the responsibility of the transporter in the event of injury or death of the passenger are adopted by the Code of Private Maritime Law, so that the provisions of the Civil Code are applicable. Thus, according to the provisions of articles 914–922 of the Civil Code, the injured person (or his heir(s) in the case of death), has the right to demand compensation, including compensation for mental injury.

(iii)   Transport of persons by rail

(a)   Introduction

11.106   The Organisation of Railroads of Greece (OSE) has the monopoly of all rail transport in Greece. The OSE also has the monopoly of all international rail transport for trips starting or ending in Greek territory (art 3 Law 674/70). The contract of rail transport in Greek law, is characterised by the lack of any special provisions as to the obligation for indemnity of the passenger on the part of OSE in the event of delay or cancellation, therefore the provisions of the Civil Code apply.[15]

(b)   Damage to or loss of property

According to the provisions of art 87 of Ministerial Decision of the Ministry of Transport A/200098/3079/1968, the responsibility of the railroad company is regulated by the provisions of the Civil Code, in the event of loss or damage of luggage carried by the passenger.   **11.107**

In respect of recorded luggage (delivered to the transporter) article 88 of the Ministerial Decision provides that the responsibility of the transporter is "objective", and therefore the railroad transporter is released from any obligation to indemnify the passenger in case of events considered as *force majeure* or if the damage or loss was caused by the passenger or was due to the quality or the nature of the baggage. The transporter has the burden of proof regarding the factors excluding its responsibility. The responsibility of the transporter is unlimited in case of intention (*dolus*) or negligence on the part of the transporter or its staff.

The article also provides that baggage is considered lost if not delivered within 14 days from the date of the relevant claim of the passenger.   **11.108**

The liability of the railroad transporter is limited to the amount of Drs 400 per kilo in the case of total loss of baggage, provided that the passenger proves the amount of the damage or the loss, otherwise the limit is Drs 200 per kilo. In addition, the cost of freight is reimbursed to the passenger. In the case of damage, the railroad company (OSE) is obliged to indemnify the passenger for the value of the damaged property.

(c)   Personal injury or death

According to the provisions of article 87 of the Ministerial Decision, the compensation due by the transporter to the passenger in the event of death or injury is regulated by the relevant clauses (914 *et seq*) of the Civil Code. Consequently those provisions (see (ii)(d) *supra*) apply.   **11.109**

(iv)   Transport of persons by road (bus)

(a)   Domestic itineraries

A   IN THE EVENT OF CANCELLATION

Greek Law has no special provisions regarding the liability of the bus carrier in the event of cancellation, and so the relevant provisions of the Civil Code regarding non-performance or inadequate performance of contractual obligations are applicable.   **11.110**

---

[15] Georgakopoulos, L, *op. cit.* 305.

B DAMAGE TO OR LOSS OF PROPERTY AND PERSONAL INJURY
OR DEATH

11.111 The bus carrier (owner and/or driver) is objectively liable for all damage or losses occurring on board, as well as death or injury caused by the bus to the passenger or his luggage. Liability is excluded in the case of damage due to the fault of the passenger or to an inevitable fact (*force majeure*). Consequently, the liability of the bus carrier (owner and driver) towards passengers (and all third parties) is obligatorily covered by an in-surance policy (art 6 Law 489/76). The regulations of Greek law on prescription of the claim vary in respect of the harmful event, and in particular:

(i) if the damage or loss was due to intention (*dolus*) or negligence of the transporter or the driver, the prescription period is 20 years (art 249 of the Civil Code) starting from the end of the year during which the damage occurred;

(ii) damage due to delay is prescribed within a period of six months starting from the delivery date (art 693 of the Civil Code);

(iii) damage or loss of property due to simple negligence of the carrier is prescribed within a period of six months starting – in the case of complete loss or damage of the property – from the time of the agreed delivery, and – in the case of partial damage – from the date of receipt of the luggage (art 107 of Commercial Law).

(b) International itineraries

11.112 Greece has adopted the regulations of the International Treaty of Geneva of 1954 (Law 3588/1956), known as CMR Treaty of Geneva 1956 (Law 559/1977).

An insurance policy covering the bus and the liability of the transporter against third parties (passengers included) to be issued for all international itineraries, is obligatory.

8. Financial services

(i) Traveller's cheques

11.113 Traveller's cheques are known in Greece, but legislation has not yet adopted any special provisions on the matter. Greek legal theory considers the so-called "traveller's cheque" to be a "commercial" mandate or debenture or bond (acknowledgment of a debt),[16] and not a means of payment, namely the "common" cheque. Likewise Greek academic authorities considers the traveller's cheque as a safety measure, helping

---

[16] Georgakopoulos, L, *Manual of Commercial Law* Vol 2 "Commercial actions – Bonds" (Athens, 1985) para IX, 111.

the bearer (client of the bank) to avoid a dangerous transfer of cash abroad.[17]

In the proposed Commercial Code, which was submitted to the Hellenic Parliament in 1989, but has not yet been voted on and accepted, a whole Chapter (the fifth of the 4th Book, art 266–272) is dedicated to the regulation of traveller's cheques. By its provisions, a statute on traveller's cheques will be introduced into Greek legislation in an efficient and comprehensive manner.[18]

(ii) Bureaux de change

The statute on "Bureaux de change" was recently introduced by Decision No 492/1992 of the Monetary Committee of the Bank of Greece.   **11.114**

(a) Legal conditions of establishment

The Decision No 492/1992 (*supra*) requires that the applicant has a certain legal form in order to obtain the relevant licence for such transactions (art A.1 of Decision 492/92). More specifically a "bureau de change" may be established and operate in Greece only if the applicant is a limited company (it is not necessary for it to be a bank or other credit institution), and the following requirements are fulfilled: **11.115**

(i)   to have as its exclusive object the operation of such bureaux de change;

(ii)   to deposit, in cash, a capital sum of at least Drs 80,000,000;

(iii)   in the relevant application the exact number of bureaux de change that the applicant wishes to operate and establish and their location must be exactly defined;

(iv)   to have the required organisation and the necessary financial and technical infrastructure; and finally

(v)   to appoint two persons of credibility and professional education dedicated to the management of the bureaux.

The licence may also be granted to a limited company under formation, provided that within a period of two months the required procedure for its foundation will be completed according to the provisions of Greek company law.

(b) Operations of bureaux de change

Article 2 of the Decision, provides that the relevant licence concerns the following operations: **11.116**

(i)   purchase of foreign currency, traveller's cheques and Eurocheques; and

---

[17] Rokas, N, "Bonds" (Athens, 1992) 150–151; Alexandridou, G, *Traveller's cheques* [1975] *Commercial Law Review* 527.

[18] Schinas, J, *Project of Commercial Code 1989* (Athens, 1991) 218–220.

(ii)   advance payment in drachmae to the bearers of credit cards issued abroad.

11.117   The amounts of foreign currency collected by those bureaux must be transferred, within the next three working days, to banks authorised to proceed in transactions on foreign currency. If the purchased amount of foreign currency exceeds the amount of 20,000 ECUs the bureau is obliged to deposit it at the competent bank within the next working day (art 4 of Decision No 492/1992 of the Monetary Committee as amended by Decision No 504/92 of the Committee).

The bureau must have in a visible place the list of currency rates applied by the bureau and also the amounts of percentages of the bureau's commission (art 6 of Decision 492/92 as amended by Decision 504/92).

The regulatory authorities supervising bureaux de change are: the Committee of Currency (of the Bank of Greece) which is authorised to decide on the relevant applications regarding the establishment of bureaux; and also the Direction of Control of the Application of Currency Rules of the Bank of Greece, which is authorised, in general, to supervise matters of the legitimate operations of the bureaux concerned.

(iii) Credit cards

11.118   Greece, by means of Ministerial Decision F1–983/1991 of the Ministries of Commerce, National Economy and Justice, has harmonised Greek legislation with the Council Directive 90/88 of 22 February 1990, which amended Council Directive 87/102 of 22 December 1986.

The provisions of this Ministerial Decision are applicable only to credit cards (and other credit contracts) supplied in Greece, and regulate the minimum obligatory content of the relevant contract.

It is provided that, unless otherwise defined in the contract:

(i)   the maximum amount of credit is Drs 200,000;
(ii)   the maximum duration of the credit is one year.

According to the provisions of article 7 of the Ministerial Decision, the implementation of its rules is excluded on matters regarding contracts of credit:

(i)   for the purchase of rights on an immovable property;
(ii)   for credit which is ensured by a mortgage;
(iii)   for lease agreements;
(iv)   for credit which is not subject to any interest or other burdens;
(v)   for credit which provides that the payment will be made in one instalment; and

(vi) for credit concluded by a bank or other similar credit institution, under the form of advance payments in a credit and debit account.

According to the provisions of article 9 of the Ministerial Decision: **11.119**

(i) all contracts for credit cards have to be in writing and a copy of the contract must be given to the consumer;
(ii) in the contract the following must be mentioned:
1) The Annual Real Compound Interest (EPE).
2) The conditions according to which the Annual Real Compound Interest may be modified.
3) A strict description of the amount, the number and the dates or the frequency of the instalments to be paid by the consumer in order to settle the credit. Likewise in the contract the amount, number and frequency of the payment of the interest and other expenses must be defined, as well as the total amount of the instalments (if that is possible), or else the method of calculation of the above figures, if they are not known at the time of signature of the contract.
4) The method of calculation of the Annual Real Compound Interest and all relevant information on the matter, and also a special reference to those figures or expenses or burdens which are included and taken into consideration for the calculation (such as expenses owed by the consumer in case of non-performance of his contractual obligations).

The credit card contracts must also include special reference to: **11.120**

(i) the maximum amount of credit;
(ii) the conditions of payment/settlement; and
(iii) a period of withdrawal on the part of the consumer, whenever a right of withdrawal is provided.

In the case of credit contracts granted for the purpose of the purchase of goods, if the consumer defers the performance of his obligation regarding the payment of instalments, the provisions of the Civil Code on the rights of the supplier (of the goods) or the credit institution apply. In the case of withdrawal by the card holder, the item must be returned and the amount paid will be reimbursed.

Likewise, it is provided that if the card holder pays his debt before its **11.121** expiry date, he is entitled to a deduction of the total cost of the credit. This deduction is equal to the difference between the rest of the amount due at the date of the settlement, and the present value of the above amount at the date of the payment/settlement, calculated with compound interest.

Finally, it is provided that all other consumer rights granted by the provisions of other Laws are not affected by the regulations of the Ministerial Decision.

9. Compensation for victims of crime

11.122 Greek legislation does not provide for any special compensation to a person suffering injury as a result of violent crime, with the exception of the "Anti-terrorist Law", by which public officers, victims, and persons suffering damage to property from a terrorist act are compensated by the state.

The victims of a crime (violent or not) may either be litigant parties in the criminal case tried in front of the Criminal Courts, or may choose to exercise their rights for indemnity and compensation by bringing a claim in the competent Civil Courts.

10. Time share regulation

(i) Introduction

11.123 Greece introduced in its legislation the Statute on Time sharing later than other European countries. Law 1652/1986, in combination with the Ministerial Decision A 9953/DIONOSE/1789/11 December 1987 of the Vice-Minister of National Economy, governs the subjects and terms of time sharing agreements.

The *ratio legis* of its provisions is more or less the same as that which obliged the other Member States of the EU to introduce and establish statutes on time sharing, namely the development of tourism in order to increase the number of foreign tourists visiting Greece.

(ii) Terms

11.124 Contrary to other European legislations, Greek Law 1652/1986 characterises the right of a consumer to a time sharing holiday as a contractual right, and the time sharing agreement as an obligation. Furthermore, the time sharing agreement in Greece is a mixture of a lease contract, and a contract for the performance of services.

According to the provisions of article 1 of Law 1652/1986, a time sharing lease is the contract according to which the lessor (proprietor, landlord) undertakes the obligation to concede to his tenant every year, and for a time period provided in the contract, the right to use a tourist lodging or hotel room and to provide him with the relevant services. On the other hand, the tenant is obliged to pay the agreed rent. The duration of the contract can be from five up to 60 years.

The law may be applied to hotel units and general tourist installations functioning under a licence of the EOT.

This contract must have the form of a notarial deed, and must be transcribed at the Mortgage Registry. After this registration, the contractual right of time sharing can be raised against all third parties, so that this right obtains the character of a quasi-real property right.

(iii) Justification

The reason that led Greek legislation to adopt the regulations of Law 1652/86 regarding the system of a time sharing lease, is the restriction of the Greek Civil Code regarding real property rights, (such as ownership), which prohibit property rights shared in time.[19] If legislation adopted the system of time shared property, instead of time shared leases, it would be necessary to modify or amend the relative provisions of the Civil Code, so that hotels or other tourist units would no longer be single entities, but shared, and so separate properties, shared in time, would be formed. Such an amendment would overturn the whole real property law of the Civil Code.

11.125

(iv) Law 1652/1986

(a) The contents of time share contracts

A   THE SUBJECTS OF THE LEASE

According to the provisions of article 3 paragraph 1 of Law 1652/1986, and of article 3 paragraph 1a of Ministerial Decision 1789/1987, contracting parties of a time sharing lease may be physical persons or legal entities.

11.126

Furthermore, it is not necessary that the lessor must also be the owner of the lodging (art 2 para 1 of Ministerial Decision 1789/1987).

B   OBJECTS

The obligation to provide the use of the lodging

In order that a tourist installation is subject to the provisions of Law 1652/1986, it must be in one of the following functional forms: classic-type hotels; apartments; tourist villages; or villas; and be ranked as at least class B under a licence of the EOT.

11.127

Furthermore, and for the protection of the consumer-tenant, the Greek legislator only permits partial subjection to the system of time sharing leases of the tourist units.[20] Thus, the owner is obliged to keep and maintain the classical character of its unit as a hotel, and to continue the performance of relevant services. Only 49% of the total beds of an existing hotel unit may be offered on the time share system. For new units this percentage is 70%.

Finally, a hotel may only apply the time sharing system, if the lodgings or rooms leased are functionally and organically united in one installation.

---

[19] Toussis, A, *Real Property Law* (Athens, 1988) para 64, 284.
[20] Themeli, Chris, *Timesharing Lease according to the Greek Law* (Salonica, 1992) 54.

Performance of "related" services

11.128   The consumers or tenants of the time sharing lease contract must have the same or equal treatment as the other clients of the hotel unit or installation.

C   THE RENT

General

11.129   The obligation of the tenant in a time sharing agreement is the payment of rent for the lodging, in exchange for the offer of the use of the lodging and services performed (art 1 para 1 al. of Law 1652/1986).

   The rent for those leases must be agreed in money. It may be agreed that it will be paid in foreign currency. With regard to the method of payment, art 5 para 1 of Ministerial Decision 1789/1987 rules that payment may be made once or by instalments. In whatever method the total amount of the agreed rent has to be paid within the first 18 months of the contract.

Rent payable in foreign currency

11.130   The rent due for the lodging of a time sharing lease may be agreed as payable in foreign currency. If the tenant is permanently resident or has its head office in a foreign country, the rent *must* be agreed to be paid in foreign currency, and the owner-lessor is obliged to transfer it to the Bank of Greece within one month as from its receipt (art 1 para 3 Law 1652/1986). This will apply also in case of a sublease of the lodging to a foreigner (art 6 para 7 of the abovementioned Ministerial Decision) but in that case the transfer must be made by the prior tenant and not by the lessor.

D   DURATION OF THE CONTRACT

11.131   In the time sharing agreement (besides the agreement for the duration of the lease), the parties must agree about the exact calendar period during which the owner-lessor must offer the use of the lodging and the relative services.

   The minimum and maximum duration of the contract are fixed in Law 1652/1986 (art 1 para 1 al. b), according to which the duration of a time sharing lease may be from five to 60 years. This regulation, in combination with the notarial deed of the time sharing contract, protects the interests of the tenant. Taking also into consideration that all time sharing contracts must be notified to the EOT, and that the EOT is entitled to control and supervise the interpretation and the performance of those contracts, it is clear that the legislation has provided for the protection of the tenant, who is the weaker party of the contract.

E OTHER PROVISIONS WHICH MUST BE INCLUDED IN THE TIME
SHARING CONTRACT (ART 3 PARA 1 OF MINISTERIAL DECISION
1789/1987)

The other provisions which must be included are: **11.132**

(i)   the exact definition and description of the lodging/room and its
       movable equipment. All the articles of the lodging must be de-
       scribed in the contract for the time sharing lease, and in the case of
       damage or destruction, they must be replaced by the lessor-owner;
(ii)   the detailed method of calculation and payment of the functional ex-
       penses (maintenance costs) that proportionally burden the tenant;
(iii) clauses for the conditions and possible cost of the use of sport,
       recreation installations, or other extra services offered to the
       tenant. Installations of this nature include swimming pools, car
       parks, clubs, TV rooms, bars, pubs, discotheques, tennis courts, golf
       courses etc;
(iv)   the application of Greek Law and jurisdiction of the Greek courts;
(v)   clauses referring to the possibility of a sub-lease or offer of the use
       of the lodging/room from the tenant to a third person;
(vi)   the "Regulation" applicable to the relations between the owner-
       lessor and the tenant which are an obligatory supplement of the
       contract.

According to the provisions of article 2 paragraph 1 of Ministerial Deci-   **11.133**
sion 1789/1987, this Regulation, in which all the obligations and rights of
the parties are set out in detail, is an essential condition, and it must be
filed, together with the application of the owner to the EOT for the
licence for time sharing.

This Regulation must include provisions regarding:

(i)   the maintenance of the lodgings and, in general, of the whole
       installation in perfect condition;
(ii)   the immediate repair of all damage and the regular renewal of the
       equipment;
(iii) the continuous occupation of the required personnel for the full
       function of the unit and the payment of wages, expenses etc of
       personnel;
(iv)   the payment of all kind of taxes, rights etc due to the State, Muni-
       cipalities or third persons and the payment of all other
       obligations deriving from the operation of the unit;
(v)   the definition of the rights, competence and the method of convo-
       cation, decision, and general regulation of the functions of the
       general assembly of tenants, which is the main body for protection
       of the tenants' rights.

All of these points must be included in the Regulation, otherwise the
whole contract is invalid.

The Regulation is subject to the approval of the EOT.

(v) The general assembly of tenants

11.134 According to the provisions of article 7 paragraph 1 of the Ministerial Decision 1789/1987, the main object of the general assembly of tenants is to control and supervise the implementation of the clauses of the time sharing agreement and its Regulation.

The legal form of this assembly is that of an association of persons, without legal personality, and the provisions of the Civil Code regarding associations are applicable. The members of this assembly are the tenants.

The general assembly also has the right to be a litigant party, and is represented in front of the courts by its administrator. The administrator is elected by the general assembly, and is entitled to supervise the performance of the Regulation and to secure the proper and continuous function and administration of the whole hotel unit or installation.

The lessor-owner has the right to participate in this general assembly only for the time period during which the lodgings/rooms are not leased. The Ministerial Decision does not define the basis of calculation of the votes of the lessor-owner, and when the lodgings are considered not to be leased. Also, no reference is made to the rights of sub-tenants.

(vi) Control by the EOT

11.135 Law 1652/1986 and Ministerial Decision 1789/1987, in order to secure the protection of the consumer, entrust the control of time sharing contracts and their Regulations to the EOT.

The control of the relevant contracts is limited to their conformity with the provisions of the legislation (*supra*).

If the Regulation is not in accordance with the provisions of Law 1652/1986 and Ministerial Decision 1789/1987, the EOT has the right to reject the application of the owner regarding the licence required for the units to be submitted to the system of time sharing.

(vii) Sanctions

11.136 According to the provisions of article 4 paragraph 2 of Ministerial Decision 1789/1987, the EOT has the right to impose sanctions on the lessor in the case of irregularities or violations of contractual obligations by the lessor, or in the case of infringements of the Tourism Law in general.

Thus, if the violation is a serious breach of a contractual obligation, the EOT may impose on the lessor the penalty of a temporary or definitive suspension of the decision, under which the lessor obtained the licence, to submit his hotel unit to the status of time sharing lease.

(viii) Further protection of the consumer

11.137 The provisions of the Civil Code regarding the "common" lease are also applicable in the contracts of the time sharing lease.

In the case of infringements or violations of some of the contractual obligations of the lessor, the consumer-tenant has the following rights:

(i)   the right given to the creditor of a contract if the debtor has not performed or is not properly performing the contract (arts 374–383 of the Civil Code in combination with arts 584–585 of the Civil Code);

(ii)   the right to suspend or decrease the payment of the rent, in the case of real or legal defects, or even omission of the agreed capacity of the lodging, or general performance of the contract (arts 576, 583 of the Civil Code);

(iii)   the right to compensation (arts 577, 578, 583 of the Civil Code);

(iv)   the right to demand the lessor to correct the real defect or the missing agreed capacity and also to cover the relevant expenses of the tenant if the lessor delays in complying with its obligations after the due term;

(v)   the right to terminate the lease in case of: hindrance of the use of the lodging; removal of use of the lodging by the lessor (art 585 of the Civil Code); the use may harm the health of the tenant or his family (art 588 of the Civil Code). Furthermore, the tenant may also demand the return of prepaid rent;

(vi)   the right to notify those infringements or violations of the contractual obligations of the lessor to the EOT, so that the EOT may impose sanctions.

(ix)   Removal of mortgages and security for debts

According to the provisions of article 3 paragraph 1 of Law 1652/1986, **11.138** all mortgages, prenotations of mortgage and seizures for the security of debts to the state, municipalities, banks etc burdening the building, hotel units etc which are leased according to article 1 of the Law, must be erased and removed, if a letter of credit from a Greek or foreign bank for the total amount of the debt is provided to the creditor. According to paragraph 2 of the same article, in order to erase or remove these burdens, the rents of the relevant leases may be conceded to the creditor or to the guarantor bank.

With this regulation, Law 1652/1986 introduces a new statute for securing debts against banks or other loan organisations in place of the classical way of securing creditors. Through this provision, the legislation is attempting to give the consumer a feeling of security regarding his rights.

(x)   Substitution of successors of the contracting parties

Article 2, paragraph 1 al. a, regulates the substitution of the successors of **11.139** the contracting parties to the lease, in order to protect the consumer's position, by securing the continuation of the contract.

According to the above, both contracting parties have the right to transfer all their rights and obligations, so that the application of article 610 of the Civil Code, according to which, in the case of a lease longer than 30 years, both parties may freely terminate the contract, is excluded.

According to the provisions of article 2 paragraph 1 al. b, the heirs of the tenant have the right to terminate the contract of the time sharing lease, in accordance with the provisions of article 612 of the Civil Code. This termination of the contract of the time sharing lease has effect *ex nunc*. Furthermore, it is provided that the heirs of the tenant do not have the right to demand the partially or totally prepaid rent. On the other hand, the death of the lessor does not entitle his heirs to terminate the contract of the time sharing lease.

11.140   On transfer of the contract to a new owner the buyer of the tourist installation or of the lodging leased enters into the time sharing lease according to the provisions of article 614 of the Civil Code. Thus, the existing lease is not interrupted, but transferred with the real property. This means that the new lessor has no right to demand the rent prepaid to the predecessor, and the tenant, if he had partially or totally prepaid the rent for the lodging, is released as against the new owner (art 2 para 3 of Law 1652/1986).

(xi)   Legal status of time share agreements [according to the rules and provisions of Law 1652/1986 and how this will be affected by the EC proposal for a Directive on Time Sharing Agreements (COM (93) 487 SYN 415)]

(a)   Introduction to the amended Proposal COM (93) 487

11.141   The *ratio legis* of the Proposal on "The protection of purchasers/tenants in contracts relating to the purchase of a right to utilise one or several immovable properties on a time sharing basis" is described in its Explanatory Memorandum, and is:

> The creation of a status of common rules able to ensure the legal and economic security of the consumer in a domain in which he is the weaker party (purchase of the right of time sharing agreements),

for the reason that time sharing contracts have a transfrontier nature, (exercised in Member States other than the one of the residence of the consumer), and also because of the divergences in national legislation of the four Member States regarding time sharing agreements (which is characterised by the Memorandum as incomplete).

The main object of the proposal, as described in the Memorandum (*i.e.* the protection of the consumer) will be effected by:

> laying down minimum information which the consumer must have prior to signature, and a time limit, after signature, during which the consumer may withdraw from the contract.

(b) Amendments that might affect the provisions of Law 1652/1986

A TERMINOLOGY

The amended proposal has changed the title of the Directive from ". . . **11.142** Directive concerning the protection of purchasers in contracts relating to the utilisation of immovable property on a time sharing basis" to "the protection of purchasers in contracts relating to the purchase *of a right to utilise* one or several immovable properties on a time sharing basis" and as described in the Memorandum, was made in order to . . . "cover more exhaustively the characteristics of certain time sharing arrangements which are widely used in certain Member States".

According to the spirit of the amended proposal it seems that the aim of the Directive is not to introduce a definite legal form regarding the contracts to "the purchase of a right to utilise . . ." so that the legal form of the lease in Greek Law will not be affected.

The legal form of the time sharing agreement as a lease (as referred to **11.143** in Greek Law) is also recognised by the amended provisions of article 2 of the Proposal, according to which a "contract relating to the purchase of a right to utilise one or several immovable properties on a time sharing basis", means any contract by which a vendor (lessor) transfers or undertakes to transfer to a purchaser (tenant), on payment of a certain price, a right, having [either] the characteristics of an obligation . . . to utilise one or several immovable properties during a determinable time of the year.

The amended proposal also adopts a wider meaning regarding "immovable property", according to which a building or part of a building to be built, is also considered as immovable property. This amendment does not affect the provisions for time sharing agreements in Greece, which provide that a hotel or a tourist unit still to be built can also be subject to the system of time sharing.

B THE PROTECTIVE STRUCTURE OF THE PROPOSAL

Vendor's liability for delay, defective performance etc of the services which burden the vendor (Art 3(b) of the Proposal).

The purchaser (tenant) has several rights in the case of non-performance **11.144** or defective performance of the contract of the lease, based upon the general clauses of the Civil Code regarding the "common" lease (see (viii) *supra*). The variety of measures to be taken according to these provisions ensures completely and exhaustively the right of the consumer (lessee) in the case of defective performance on the part of the vendor (lessor), so that it will not be necessary for Greek legislation to adopt special provisions in order to ensure the liability of the vendor. The only special regulation relating to non-performance on the part of the vendor (lessor), adopted by Greek legislation, is the regulation of the administrative sanction of suspension of the licence by the EOT.

The right of the consumer to "do as he wishes with the properties or shares concerned" (Art 3(c) of the Amended Proposal)

11.145 According to the provisions of Law 1652/1986 and the relevant "common lease" provisions of the Civil Code, the purchaser (tenant) has all the rights of a "common tenant", *i.e.* the rights to use the leased property in an appropriate manner for the contractual use.

It is believed that the above regulations of Greek Law will not be affected by the provisions of the amended Directive Proposal, for the reason that the whole spirit of Article 3(c) of the Proposal is to ensure that the only obligation on the purchaser (tenant) is to pay the stipulated price. On the other hand, the European legislation did not wish to ensure the absolute freedom of the purchaser (tenant), taking into consideration the limited duration of his residence in a certain apartment, hotel room etc, since if a system is adopted according to which one party (the tenant) has the right "to do as he wishes" as against all other parties, (the owner and the future tenants), it will harm the whole protective structure of the statute, and also may raise disputes between the parties.

For these reasons it is believed that Article 3(c) of the Amended Directive Proposal, interpreted *stricto sensu*, will not affect the provisions of Greek Law according to which the freedom of the consumer to "do as he wishes" is limited by the general clause of good faith.

The involvement of the purchaser (tenant), in an appropriate manner, in the process of making decisions about the properties concerned (Art 3(d) of the Amended Directive Proposal)

11.146 The Regulation (required by Law 1652/1986 as the obligatory supplement to the time sharing lease contract (see (iv) E *supra*)) must, *inter alia*, define the rights, competence and general regulation of function of the general assembly of tenants. If this Regulation (which is submitted to the EOT together with the application of the owner for the time sharing licence), does not include provisions regarding the general assembly, and more specifically about the participation of the tenants, the whole contract is null and void.

Article 3(d) of the Amended Directive Proposal, requires Member States to make provision in their national legislation to ensure the right of the purchaser (tenant) to be involved in the process of decision-making concerning the management and maintenance of the property concerned. It is also required that this right must be effected in an appropriate manner, which may affect the provisions of Greek Law. In particular, this Regulation, and its provisions concerning the function of the General Assembly are drafted by the owner, who, *a priori*, is not concerned to ensure the rights of the consumer. In that case it is probable that the right of the consumer to be involved in the process of decision-making regarding the management and maintenance of the shares concerned will not be effected in the most satisfactory way.

Thus, Greek legislation is obliged to amend the relevant provisions regarding the function of the general assembly of tenants, by defining the matters of participation of the owner, and the other terms and conditions, which until now had been left to the goodwill of the owner.

Information to the consumer, relevant documents, advertising of a time share agreement (Art 5 of the Amended Directive Proposal).

The provisions of Article 5 of the Amended Directive Proposal constitute a new regulation for Greek Law, and will affect positively the existing legal status of the time sharing agreement in Greece, with the exception of the general clauses of Law 2160/1993 (see (iv) B and E *supra*), (and also the provisions of Law 2251/1994 applicable to the matter). The obligation to inform the consumer properly about the contents and the structure of the agreement, described in Article 5 of the Proposal, must be adopted by Greek legislation as it stands, since it is not contrary to any of the provisions of Law 1652/1986. **11.147**

The Contract and its Content (Article 6 in Combination with Annex I)

The provisions of Article 6 of the Amended Directive Proposal, in combination with those of Annex I of the Proposal, are in general the same as the provisions of Law 1652/1986 and Ministerial Decree 1789/1987, concerning the content of the time sharing agreement. **11.148**

Only three points have not yet been adopted by Greek Law: (i) the language of the document, which must be one that the purchaser (tenant) states he knows (art 6 para 2); (ii) the possibility of reselling the right (Annex I item i); and (iii) a means of withdrawal from the contract (Annex I, item k). It is believed that those points will easily be included in the status of time sharing agreements without any further difficulty, for the reason that they are in accordance with the spirit of Law 1652/1986.

When a contract becomes definite. The right to withdraw – advance payments – loans concerning the payment of the price of the contract (arts 7 and 8 of Amended Directive Proposal).

Article 7(1) and (2) provide that, for a period of 28 days, a contract concerning the use of an immovable property on a time sharing basis is not definitive, and also that during that time the consumer (tenant) has the right to withdraw from the contract. The reason for those regulations, as stated in the Commission's Explanatory Memorandum, was to provide the purchaser with "a single cooling-off period" during which to evaluate and think more easily about the advantages or disadvantages of the contract, before it comes in to force. **11.149**

This security, provided to the purchaser, has not yet been adopted by Greek Law. Greek legislation will therefore have to adopt the "cooling-off" period of 28 days.

These remarks are also applicable to the provisions of Article 7(2) and **11.150**

(3) of the Amended Directive Proposal, taking into consideration that the notice of withdrawal from the contract, and the obligation of the vendor to reimburse all payments made by the purchaser, are in accordance with the existing protective structure of Greek Law.

Finally, the amended Article 8 of the Proposal, according to which, in the case of exercise of the right of withdrawal from the time sharing contract (as stated in Article 7) on the part of the consumer, he also has the right to cancel any loan, with which the price of the contract for the use of immovable property on a time sharing basis was entirely or partly covered, is in accordance with the aim of Greek legislation to protect the weaker party to a contract, and so Greek Law can be amended accordingly (*c.f.* the Regulation of Law 1652/1986 regarding the removal of real burdens etc from the immovable properties concerned).

(xii) Conclusions

11.151 It is believed that the provisions of Law 1652/1986, in their present form, and equally in the form that they will obtain after the adoption of the Amended Proposal for a Council Directive, provide satisfactory protection of the consumer (tenant).

11. Passport and frontier control

(i) EU citizens

11.152 All citizens of the 15 Member States of the European Union have the right to visit Greece and enter into Greek territory by the simple demonstration of the European Passport of their country of origin, or National Identity Card, according to the provisions of article 3 Presidential Decree 499/1987. No further confirmation, visa or other requirement is necessary. Likewise, the citizens of any EC Member State may leave Greece without any special requirement, and on the simple presentation of the passport or presentation of the national identity card.

(ii) EFTA citizens

11.153 According to the provisions of Law 2155/1993, which confirmed the Treaty of 2 May 1992 regarding the European Economic Area, citizens of EFTA countries have the same rights regarding passport and frontier control as the citizens of a Member State of the EU, save for Switzerland, which has not signed the Treaty.

Bibliography

1   Levantis, E, *Company Law* Vols I–V (Athens, 1989–1992).   **11.154**
2   Georgiadis, A, Stathopoulos, M, *Civil Code* Vols I–VII (Athens, 1975–1992).
3   Rokas, N, *Commercial Company Law* (Athens, 1984).
4   Liakopoulos, Christianos, Michalopoulos, *Consumer's Protection Law* (Athens, 1993).
5   Speliotopoulos, E, *Manual of Administrative Law* Vol 1, 2 (Athens, 1986).
6   Georgakopoulos, L, *Manual of Commercial Law* Vol 2 "Commercial Actions – Law of Bonds" (Athens, 1985).
7   Georgakopoulos, L, *Manual of Commercial Law* Vol 2 "Commercial Actions – Contracts" (Athens, 1991).
8   Rokas J, *Introduction to Private Insurance Law* (Athens, 1992).
9   Georgiadis, A, *Real Property Law* (Athens, 1991).
10 Themeli, Ch, *Timesharing Lease according to the Greek Law* (Salonica, 1992).
11 Iatrou, Ath, *An Outline of the Greek Civil Law* (Athens, 1986).
12 Efthymiatou-Poulakou, Ant, *Elements of Tourism Legislation* (Athens, 1987).
13 Maniatopoulos, P, *Aerial Law Code* (Athens, 1989).

Ireland

Chapter 12
Ireland
Walter Beatty*

1. Regulatory authorities

The first direct government intervention in tourism dates back as far as **12.1**
1925, when the Minister for Industry and Commerce set up the Irish
Tourist Association. A statutory framework for the promotion and development of tourism in Ireland was first established in 1931 with the
Tourist Traffic Development Act. This legislation has been updated
periodically since then, with the result that there is now in place a multi-
faceted administrative framework. The role of successive governments
has largely been in policy formulation and strategy development, with
more specific responsibilities for tourism divided among state and semi-
state bodies. As the economic importance of the industry developed, so
too did a number of government initiatives and bodies to facilitate the
development of the industry.

(i) The Department of Tourism and Trade and The Department of Transport, Energy and Communications

In 1993, the Department of Tourism was merged with the Department of **12.2**
Trade to form the Department of Tourism and Trade. The Department
of Tourism and Trade determines national policy and development
priorities and monitors implementation of government policy. The state-
sponsored bodies are charged with the implementation of these policies.
The three paramount objectives of Irish tourism policy are:

(i)   to create more jobs in the tourism industry;
(ii)   to generate additional foreign exchange earnings from tourism;
        and
(iii)   to attract additional numbers of foreign visitors to Ireland.

In 1993, the Department of Energy was merged with the Department **12.3**
of Transport and Communications to form the Department of Transport,

---

* Walter Beatty BA LLM ACI ARB is a partner in the firm of Vincent & Beatty, Soliciters, 67/68
  Fitzwilliam Square, Dublin 2. Vincent & Beatty is one of Dublin's leading law firms, which
  practices in all areas of commercial law.

Energy and Communications. This department is responsible for formulating national policies connected with aviation, rail and road transport, the supply and use of energy, and exploration and postal, telecommunication and broadcasting matters. The state-sponsored bodies and executive offices under the auspices of the Department include:

(i) Coras Iompair Eireann and its three subsidiaries: Iarnrod Eireann responsible for rail travel; Bus Atha Cliath, responsible for bus transport in Dublin; and Bus Eireann, responsible for road and rail transport in Ireland;

(ii) Aer Lingus – responsible for domestic and international air transport; and

(iii) Aer Rianta – responsible for airport management.

(ii) Bord Failte

12.4 Bord Failte Eireann was established in 1955 as a result of the amalgamation of two tourism bodies, namely: Fogra Failte, which had responsibility for information and publicity, and An Bord Failte which carried out all other duties. The Bord is the executive agency responsible for promoting and developing tourist traffic in and to Ireland, through the implementation of government policy. It is a statutory body and its powers and functions are set out in the Tourist Traffic Acts 1939–87. It also has specific responsibilities for regulating standards and is from time to time engaged in the administration of various grant schemes for the development of accommodation and amenities, using exchequer and, more recently, EU funding. The government provides over 80% of the Bord's funding, with the remainder generated by the Bord's commercial activities. The Bord's main activities are:

(i) the overseas marketing, guidance and support for the tourism industry;

(ii) the co-ordination of tourist industry activities;

(iii) the monitoring of quality and standards in tourist accommodation;

(iv) the market research in the tourism industry; and

(v) the identification of tourist market opportunities and associated development requirements.

12.5 It is run by a board of directors, comprising representatives of the government and the tourist industry, and it reports to the Department of Tourism and Trade. It has had an immeasurable impact on the development of the tourist industry in Ireland. One of its more recent activities is a joint venture between the Northern Ireland Tourist Board and Bord Failte, which has developed a system known as "Gulliver" which, funded by both Tourist Boards and by the International Fund for Ireland, is a revolutionary information and reservation system for the tourist industry throughout Ireland. It provides up to date information on a wide range of services, ranging from accommodation and transport, to events and activities. Visitors to Ireland can now get answers to specific questions quickly and efficiently without having to consult brochures or guides, and instant reservations can be made for a range of services. Gulliver is available at most tourist information offices, and at various hotels and guesthouses, and will soon be available at Bord Failte offices and overseas centres.

(iii)   The Irish Travel Agents Association (ITAA)

12.6 The ITAA was founded in 1970 to create and maintain standards among its members for the betterment of the consumer and the industry. Those seeking membership have to meet stringent requirements in terms of financial stability and staff expertise, and members are bound by the constitution of the ITAA. The person, firm or corporation carrying on the business of a tour operator or a travel agent must have been carrying on business for a period of at least 12 consecutive months before they can apply for membership. A member who is engaged in the business of both retail travel agent and tour operator and whose gross annual turnover in the tour operating business exceeds IR£200,000, may apply for membership of the ITAA as a tour operator. Otherwise he may qualify as a travel agent.

The ITAA has various codes of conduct, namely: conduct between tour operators and retail agents; between retail agents and members of the public; between retail agents and principals who are not members of ITAA; and between retail agents themselves.

12.7 The ITAA has a disciplinary committee. If a contravention of the rules of the ITAA has been established this committee has the power to:

(i)   caution the member;
(ii)   reprimand the member;
(iii)   impose a fine not exceeding £5,000;
(iv)   suspend the member from membership; or,
(v)   expel the member from membership.

From this it can be seen that the ITAA carries considerable weight in the regulation of a tour operator or a travel agent's business. A copy of the terms of membership of the Association can be obtained from their registered office at 32/34 South William Street, Dublin 2.

(iv)   Regional Tourism Organisations (RTOs)

12.8 Bord Failte has regional companies which it partly funds, along with the local authorities and the private sector tourist interests in the various regions. The regional companies are responsible at local level for tourist development and promotion, for visitor services, and for the initial assessment of any investment projects applying to Bord Failte for grant support.

12.9 The regions were initially chosen on the criteria of compatibility, but a further restructuring which occurred in 1989, redefined RTOs to correspond with the EU Regional Planning Areas. Each regional organisation was set up as a public company limited by guarantee and its board is made up of local authority members, local industry representatives, and members of the public. Funding has been mainly provided by Bord Failte, with the remainder made up by local authorities, commercial activities and subscription fees.

(v) Shannon Free Airport Development Company (SFADCo)

12.10 The government designated SFADCo as the regional development authority for the Mid-Western region of the country. SFADCo is responsible for overseeing tourism and development in that particular region, and for carrying out functions performed by the RTOs in all other sub-regions. Since it was established in 1959 the company has greatly improved both Shannon Airport and the Shannon region in a number of ways. The world's first duty-free airport shop was established there, together with the first airport tax-free zone, which quickly attracted overseas industry to operate in its customs-free environment.

(vi) County Enterprise Partnership Boards (CEPBs)

12.11 In March 1993, the government announced details of the tourism functions of the proposed County Enterprise Partnership Boards. They will have a significant role in tourism development in each county. The CEPBs are involved in the "hands-on" developmental work at county level, while the RTOs will have responsibility for tourism development at regional level.

The CEPBs are responsible for stimulating, assisting and co-ordinating community and rural-based enterprise projects in the tourism sector in order to maximise job creation. They will assist in the development of county action plans for tourism which will feed into an agreed regional plan.

(vii) Council for Education, Recruitment and Training (CERT)

12.12 There is a separate state agency known as CERT, responsible for the recruitment, education and training of staff at all levels of the hotel, catering and tourism industry. Its object is to ensure high operational standards in the industry and to develop a skilled, professional workforce.

(viii) An Taisce

12.13 An Taisce is widely recognised as being the most influential conservation body in Ireland and plays an important role in preserving the natural

326

beauty of Ireland, which is one of the main attractions for foreign visitors. It contributes significantly to issues and debates surrounding conservation matters and has had a significant effect on changes in legislation. It was founded in 1948 and is an independent voluntary body, which has no state support, but relies on donations and subscriptions to survive. It currently has a membership of over 7,000 people in 31 local associations throughout the country.

(ix) The Irish Tourism Industry Confederation (ITIC)

The ITIC is highly developed and plays an active role in developing the tourist industry and influencing policy decisions. The ITIC is an umbrella organisation representative of the industry as a whole, *i.e.*, the carriers, hotels, other accommodation sectors, and tour operators etc. In addition, the individual sectors have representative bodies which are active on issues of concern to their respective sectors.

12.14

(x) The Irish Hotels Federation (IHF)

The IHF was founded in 1937 to represent the hotel and guesthouse industry. It provides a wide range of services, including economic and legal advice to its members, which include over 70% of all registered hotels and guesthouses in Ireland.

12.15

Members include:

(i)   the Irish Caravan Council; representing caravan parks.
(ii)   the Restaurant Association of Ireland; the representative body for gourmet, visitor, family and fast food restaurants.
(iii)   the Failte Tuaithe; represents some operators of farmhouses.
(iv)   the Irish Cottage and Holiday Homes Association; which represents operators of cottages and holiday homes.
(v)   the Irish Budget Hostels; an independent hostels group representing budget-price hostels.
(vi)   Irish Farm Holidays; responsible for publicising farm holidays at home and abroad, with respective guides.
(vii)   the Town and Country Homes Association; which promotes its specific sector and members as a group.

2.   Legal and professional rules

(i) Licensing

The Transport (Tour Operators and Travel Agents) Act, 1982 ("the 1982 Act") has the following long title:

12.16

> An Act for the Regulation of the Travel Trade and for the protection of customers of Tour Operators and Travel Agents, and for those purposes it enables the Minister for Transport to issue Licences to Tour Operators and

327

Travel Agents, and to require Tour Operators and Travel Agents to enter into and to maintain Bonds, to provide for the establishment of a Fund to be known as The Travellers Protection Fund and for the payment of contributions by Tour Operators towards the resources of that Fund; and to provide for other matters connected with the foregoing.

12.17   It is the main statutory provision regulating the business of travel agents and tour operators. The Act defines a "Tour Operator" as a person other than a carrier who arranges for the purpose of selling or offering for sale to the public, accommodation and travel by air, sea or land transport to destinations outside Ireland. A "Travel Agent" is defined as "a person other than a carrier who, as agent, sells or offers to sell to, or purchases or offers to purchase on behalf of the public, accommodation and air, sea or land transport to destinations outside Ireland".

A tour operator is one who buys in bulk the components of the travel trade, for example, airline seats or accommodation, and packages them for retail sale by travel agencies or in some cases direct to the public. By buying in bulk they pay less for these services than the public, so that they can be compared to wholesalers in any trade, buying in bulk and distributing the product by way of retail sale. The small tour operator can be differentiated from the travel agent because its packages are available through other travel agents. Travel agents are, as the definition says, agents and are acting as such for tour operators and for carriers, and they earn commission on what they sell.

12.18   A travel agent is a necessary link in promoting particular tours, especially if the tour operator does not also operate a retail travel agency. A travel agent keeps stocks of the tour operators' brochures and is familiar with available package tours, so that he may recommend particular tours to meet the clients' needs. The general rules of agency apply. The consumer dealing with a travel agent is often unaware of the existence of the tour operator.

Under the 1982 Act a person shall not carry on business as a tour operator (s4) or as a travel agent (s5) or hold himself out, by advertisement or otherwise as carrying on such business, unless he is the holder of a licence under the 1982 Act, authorising the carrying on of such business.

(a)   The travel agents' or tour operators' licence

12.19 An application for a travel agents' or a tour operators' licence is made to the Secretary of State of the Department of Tourism, Energy and Communications. It is made on a specific form available from the Department, and is accompanied by the applicant's latest accounts, duly audited and certified by an accountant who is qualified to audit accounts, covering a 12 month accounting period ending on a date not earlier than 12 months before the date of the application.

The amount of the annual fee payable to the Department on an application for a travel agents' licence is £243. A similar annual licence fee is payable by a tour operator if its licensable turnover is less than £500,000.

If it is more than £500,000, the fee increases gradually, depending on the level of turnover. A Schedule of Fees for the tour operators' licence is contained in the Tour Operators Regulations, 1993 (SI 1993/182). In addition, fees for a late application for a licence are prescribed in both cases. There is no late application fee if the delay is due to circumstances outside the control of the applicant.

An applicant's attention should be drawn to the heavy penalty provisions relating to false or misleading statements for the purpose of obtaining a licence, which are set out in section 20(3) of the 1982 Act. This section provides that: **12.20**

> any person who, for the purpose of obtaining for himself or for any other person, a Licence under this Act, makes a statement which he knows to be false, or who recklessly makes a statement which is false in a material fact shall be guilty of an offence and shall be liable on conviction on indictment to a fine not exceeding £5,000 or, at the discretion of the Court, to imprisonment for a term not exceeding two years, or to both such fine and imprisonment.

In the case of a tour operator only, the operator's licence, together with any conditions attached thereto, must be displayed for the information of the public in a prominent position on all premises owned or occupied by the licensee, and the operator must also publish, in a prominent position, all brochures and publicity material issued in connection with the operator's business. There is authority for the view that if the licensee is negligent or careless in doing this the licence may be revoked by the Minister. **12.21**

The applicant for a tour operators' licence or a travel agents' licence may be a sole trader, a partnership, an unincorporated body or a company incorporated under the Companies Acts 1963–90.

If the applicant is an unincorporated body, it must furnish the full name, private address and nationality of the principle officers (chairman, secretary and treasurer) and trustees of the body.

If the applicant is a company incorporated under the Companies Acts 1963–90, it must furnish the full name, private address and nationality of every member of the board of directors, the company secretary and senior management personnel, and the persons or entities in real or effective ownership or control of the company. It must also state whether the company has a shadow director within the meaning of section 27 of the Companies Act 1990 (defined as "a person in accordance with whose directions or instructions the directors of a company are accustomed to act"), and if so, the full name and private address of the person concerned. It must state whether the company is a subsidiary of another company within the meaning of section 155 of the Companies Act 1963, or whether it is a holding company of any other company or companies within the meaning of Section 155 of the Companies Act 1963. A copy of the company's memorandum and articles of association, Certificate of **12.22**

Incorporation and Certificate of Registration of any trading or business names must be furnished, along with confirmation from the company's auditor that the annual return has been forwarded to the Registrar of Companies in accordance with section 127 of the Companies Act 1963, as amended by Section 15 of the Companies Act 1982. Applicants for a travel agent's or tour operator's licence must give full details of any shareholding of more than 10% held by the applicant or by any director, shareholder or partner of the applicant in any other company, including shareholdings held in the name of a spouse, nominee or agent of the applicant or a director shareholder or partner of the applicant (para 3 of Appendix to SI 1993/182 – "the Appendix").

12.23 Under the heading of borrowings, credit arrangements, etc, details of any overdraft facility, security given for an overdraft, details of mortgages, liens, charges or other encumbrances must also be furnished to the minister. The amount and nature of the directors' loans invested in the company must also be disclosed (para 4 of the Appendix). A description of the title under which premises in which the travel agent or tour operator trades are held is also a requirement.

The applicant must provide details of companies, enterprises or business ventures with which the applicant or any director, shadow director, shareholder or partner was previously associated in a proprietorial role, or as a director or shareholder. The applicant must disclose any involvement with any bankruptcy or winding-up proceedings in relation to these, and must furnish details of any prosecutions against the applicant or any director, shadow director, shareholder or partner for fraud, embezzlement, larceny or other offences involving dishonesty, or under the Consumer Information Act 1978 or under the Sale of Goods and Supply of Services Act 1980, and the outcome of such prosecution.

12.24 Other information that the applicant must disclose on his application includes: membership of trade associations (s7); previous years' and projected turnover levels where not included in the audited accounts (s8); details as to the nature of the contracts the business will enter into (s9); premises and staffing (s10); bonding details (s12); and details of the applicant's legal representatives, bankers and accountants.

In any case where a person whom the minister has reason to believe is engaged in the business of a tour operator, purports to be trading as an agent, the minister may require such person to provide sufficient written evidence from that person's principals to establish the existence of such agency (s3(b)).

(b) New entrants to the travel trade

12.25 New entrants to the travel trade, whether as a travel agent or as a tour operator, who do not have the required audited accounts available, are required under the Regulations (Sched 1 of the Appendix) to furnish the following:

(i) an audited opening balance sheet;

(ii)   a projected monthly cash flow statement and trading and profit and loss account for the first year of trading;

(iii)   a projected balance sheet at the end of the first year of trading;

(iv)   a breakdown of projected turnover under the following headings and the rate of commission expected under each heading:

    (a) IATA (International Air Transport Association) scheduled airline tickets;

    (b) other scheduled airline tickets;

    (c) package holidays; and

    (d) boat and rail tickets;

(v)   confirmation from the applicant's auditor that the auditor is satisfied that the projections and calculations made in (ii), (iii) and (iv) above, insofar as the accounting policies and calculations are concerned, are properly compiled on the basis of any accompanying assumptions made by the applicant, and are presented on a basis consistent with the accounting policies normally adopted by the applicant.

(c) *The tour operator's/travel agent's obligations*

12.26 Under the Regulations (SI 1993/183 – Travel Agents and SI 1993/182 – Tour Operators) governing the licensing of tour operators and travel agents respectively, strict control of the tour operator/travel agent is ensured by provision for meticulous maintenance of the books, accounts, and records of the agent/operator. In this regard the agent must keep at his place of business:

(i)   annual accounts duly audited and certified in accordance with Regulation 7 (which provides for the production of such accounts upon an application for a licence);

(ii)   a record, which may be in ledger, computer or other form, of all daily receipts and expenditures, including all monies placed on deposit;

(iii)   a full record of all bank lodgments and a regular and proper bank reconciliation; and

(iv)   copies of all contracts entered into by the licensee relevant to the business of the licensee and valid for the period of the licence.

Proper maintenance of items (i) to (iv) above is regulated by the power conferred on the minister that they be produced to the minister, or to a person duly authorised, upon request.

(d) *Refusal of a licence*

12.27 Once an application has been made for a licence as a tour operator or travel agent, the Minister for Transport, Energy and Communications has the power to refuse to grant a licence (s6 of the 1982 Act). A licence will be refused to a person if the minister is not satisfied that the financial, business and organisational resources of such person, and any financial arrangements made or to be made by such person, are adequate for discharging such person's actual and potential obligations. These obligations are in respect of the activities in which such person is engaged or in which such person proposes to engage if the licence is granted. The minister will also refuse a licence if, having regard to the past activities of the applicant or of any person employed by the applicant, or if such person is a body corporate, having regard to the past activities of any director, secretary, shareholder, officer or servant of the body corporate, the minister does not believe that such person is a fit and proper person to carry on business as a tour operator or travel agent, as the case may be. The decision is at the minister's discretion.

12.28   In addition, the minister has the power to revoke or vary any term or condition of a licence where the holder of the licence is in breach of, or fails, neglects or refuses to comply with any term or condition of a licence under the Act (s8 of the 1982 Act).

(e)   Appeal process

12.29   The minister is obliged to notify the holder of a licence of the minister's proposal to revoke or vary a condition thereof and of the reasons for such proposal. The minister must consider any representations made to him in writing by the holder within seven days of the minister's notification. After the minister has heard these representations the minister shall notify the licence holder if the minister still wishes to refuse, revoke or alter the licence and the holder of the licence may within a further seven days appeal to the High Court against such refusal, revocation or alteration of the licence (s9 of the 1982 Act). An appeal shall not lie against a decision of the minister where, owing to the failure or inability of the tour operator or travel agent to meet financial or contractual obligations, payment has not been made pursuant to the bond or from the fund (see (ii) below) to a customer and the licence has been revoked on this ground.

(f)   Power of entry and inspection

12.30   Under Section 11 of the 1982 Act, a person authorised by the minister may at any time enter into any premises in which the minister has reason to believe a person is carrying on business as a tour operator or travel agent, and inspect and examine books, accounts, or records required to be maintained under a licence.

(g)   Offences and penalties

12.31   A person who carries on business, or holds himself out as carrying on business as a tour operator or as a travel agent without a licence is guilty of an offence and liable, on conviction on indictment, to a fine not exceeding £100,000 or, at the discretion of the court, to imprisonment for a term not exceeding five years, or to both a fine and imprisonment.

Where an offence under the Act is committed by a body corporate and the offence is proved to have been committed with the consent or connivance of, or to be attributable to any neglect on the part of, any director, manager, secretary or other similar officer of such body or any person who is purporting to act in such capacity, such person, as well as the body, shall be guilty of an offence and shall be liable to be proceeded against and punished accordingly (s22.1 of the 1982 Act).

(ii) Security

One of the conditions that must be complied with under the 1982 Act before a licence will be granted, is that the tour operator and travel agent enter into some kind of satisfactory arrangement with the minister for the protection of the consumers who enter into contracts with tour operators or travel agents. The satisfactory arrangements in the form of a bond can be used for various purposes, for example, the provision of travel facilities for customers trying to get home, or the reimbursement to customers of expenses incurred by them due to the agent's or operator's failure.

12.32

A Travellers' Protection Fund has been provided for under the 1982 Act. The purpose of this fund is to make payment in respect of losses or liabilities incurred by an agent or operator who either has held a licence at one time and no longer does so, or whose licence has just been revoked. This protection fund is called into play when all the moneys payable under the bond mentioned above have been paid out. It is therefore a type of back-up fund raised by contributions from organisers.

Therefore prior to the grant of a licence a tour operator is required to furnish a bond equivalent to 10% of the operator's annual licensable turnover, and an agent is required to furnish a bond equivalent to 4% of the agent's annual licensable turnover. The Travellers' Protection Fund established by the 1982 Act is available to meet any shortfall which may arise if the amount of a bond is inadequate.

The Package Holidays and Travel Trade Act 1995 ("the 1995 Act") introduced new provisions for security requirements. Section 22 of the 1995 Act states that a package provider shall have sufficient evidence of security for the refund of money paid over and for the repatriation of the consumer in the event of insolvency. The section goes on to provide that if the package is one in respect of which the provider is required to hold a licence under the 1982 Act, and is covered by arrangements entered into for the purposes of the 1982 Act, the operator shall be deemed to have satisfied this requirement.

12.33

However, the 1982 Act applies to the tour operator and travel agent who engages in the arrangement of holidays to destinations outside Ireland. This creates a vacuum for the operator or agent who organises packages within the state in addition to outside the state. The security arrangement which they had entered into under the 1982 Act only covers them for packages which involve travelling outside the state. It is now the case that these tour operators and travel agents will have to enter into further security arrangements to cover packages within the state.

In relation to new entrants to the industry as tour operators or travel agents they will firstly have to be licenced under the 1982 Act. They can then choose to enter into a security arrangement under the 1982 Act in respect of packages outside the state and enter into a security arrangement under the 1995 Act in respect of packages within the state. Alternatively, they can enter into a security arrangement under the 1995 Act in respect of all packages both within the state and outside the state.

12.34   As a package provider under the 1995 Act can include a carrier such as a ferry company or airline, those carriers who do provide packages now fall within the definition of "organiser" as set out in section 3 of the 1995 Act, and accordingly are required to comply with the security requirements under the 1995 Act. Carriers were exempt under the 1982 Act from having to obtain a licence. However the 1995 Act amended the definition of a carrier contained in the 1982 Act to exclude carriers providing packages outside the state. Accordingly carriers who provide packages to destinations outside the state will have to be licenced under the 1982 Act. Carriers who provide packages regardless of whet her the packages are within the state or outside the state will still have to enter into a security arrangement under the 1995 Act (or under the 1982 Act where appropriate).

12.35   If the package provider does not hold a licence under the 1982 Act and is not required to hold such a licence, or if he does hold the licence but provides packages to destinations within the state only, he will be deemed to have satisfied this requirement of section 22 of the 1995 Act if he makes one or more of the arrangements set out in sections 23 to 25 of the 1995 Act. A package provider who does not make the necessary arrangements for security shall be guilty of an offence (s22(3).)

Sections 23 and 24 set out details of security by way of bonding. In each section the bond must be of an amount to cover the insolvency of the package provider and must be capable of:

(i)   refunding all moneys paid over by consumers under or in contemplation of contracts for packages which have not been fully performed or repaid; and

(ii)   the repatriation of consumers where appropriate; and

(iii)   any reasonable expenses necessarily incurred by the approved body.

There are two "approved bodies" so far and these are the Irish Travel Agents' Association and the National Youth Council. The amount of the fee payable on application to be an approved body for the purposes of sections 23 or 24 of the 1995 Act is £250 as provided for the Approved Bodies (Fees) Regulations 1995 (SI 1995/236).

12.36   The difference between bonding under sections 23 and 24 is that under section 23 the "approved body" is one which has a reserve fund or insurance whereas under section 24 the "approved body" does not. The effect that this difference has on the package provider is that if the approved body with which it enters into a bond has a reserve fund or insurance then the amount of the bond it needs to enter into is 10% of its annual licensable turnover, whereas if there is no such reserve fund or insurance the bond figure is 15% of its annual licensable turnover (SI 1995/270).

The third and last alternative for security arrangements under the 1995 Act is contained in section 25 which covers the situation where a package provider takes out an "appropriate policy" of insurance in the event of the insolvency of the package provider. The insurance policy must cover the loss of money paid over to it under or in contemplation of contracts for relevant packages and the costs of repatriation of consumers based on administrative arrangements as established by the insurer.

An "appropriate policy" means one which does not contain a condition providing that no liability shall arise in the event of some specified thing being done or omitted to being done after the happening of the insured event. There cannot be a condition that liability shall not arise in the event of the failure of the policy-holder to make payments to the insurer in connection with that policy or with other policies, nor can it provide that no liability shall arise unless the policy-holder keeps specified records.

(iii) Conclusions

To implement the provisions of Article 7 of the Directive it will be necess-   **12.37**
ary to amend section 2 of the 1982 Act. In that section the definition of a tour operator and the definition of a travel agent both exclude carriers who are defined in the 1982 Act as "persons whose principle business is the provision of transport by land, sea or air on aircraft, vessels, or other modes of transport owned and operated by such person". The exclusion of carriers from the 1982 Act will be removed and carriers who are package organisers/retailers, where the package includes overseas transport, will need to be licensed and bonded in the same way. The definitions of tour operator and travel agent will be amended to provide for greater clarity in this respect.

3   Consumer rights and safeguards

(i) Liability

Introduction

When examining the liability of tour operators and travel agents to the   **12.38**
consumer it is vital to understand the complex relationship that exists between the tour operator, the travel agent and the consumer. The 1995 Act refers to the common tour operator as being "the organiser", and to

335

the travel agent as being "the retailer". Accordingly in the discussion that follows the tour operator and travel agent are referred to as "the organiser" and "the retailer" respectively.

The consumer is often under the impression that when they book a holiday they are entering into a contract with the retailer. This is not the case. The consumer in fact enters into a contract with the organiser. The retailer merely acts as an agent for the organiser and although the retailer plays a large role in the process of the negotiations and the conclusion of the contract, the organiser is the party responsible for providing the services contained in and abiding by the terms of the holiday contract. In this regard the 1995 Act defines the contract as an agreement linking the consumer to the organiser (whether directly with the consumer or through a retailer (s2(1)).

In addition to referring to the organiser and the retailer, the 1995 Act also refers to the "package provider". The package provider is the organiser or, where the retailer is also party to the contract, both the organiser and the retailer. The 1995 Act goes on to state that if the organiser is established outside the state and the retailer inside the state, where the transport components of the package commence outside the state, then the retailer is the package provider.

COMMON LAW

The law of tort

(a) Negligence

12.39 The term negligence generally suggests inadvertence or inattention on the part of the organiser or retailer. An action for negligence is based on the breach of a duty to exercise reasonable care where damage results. Duty and negligence are co-related. Over the past century four main conceptual elements of the tort of negligence have developed. They are:

(i)   duty of care, i.e. the existence of a legally recognised obligation placed on a person to conform to a certain standard of behaviour for the protection of others against unreasonable risks;

(ii)   a failure to conform to the required standard;

(iii)   actual loss or damage is sustained by the person suing;

(iv)   a sufficiently close causal connection between the conduct and resulting injury/loss to the person suing.

If the consumer can prove that there was a failure on the part of the organiser/retailer to conform to the required standard, and that he suffered actual loss or damage as a result, then he will more than likely be able to rely on the tort of negligence. The requirements of (i) above is satisfied if there is a relationship between the organiser/retailer and the consumer and obviously (iv) above will be satisfied when the injury-loss suffered by the consumer happens while on holiday where it was within the control of the organiser/retailer to avoid the injury/loss. As regards what is the "required standard" under the tort of negligence the courts have tended to ask whether the defendant acted as "the reasonable man" would have done. In the context of the organiser/retailer of a holiday the facts of each case will have to be taken into account. For example – the provision of substandard accommodation by the organiser to the consumer when the organiser had received many complaints about the accommodation in the past from other consumers yet persisted in selling it, would amount to negligence.

There are two primary defences to a negligence action. Firstly, the **12.40** defence of contributory negligence arises where although the organiser/retailer is guilty of negligence the consumer has also been at fault in failing to take due care of himself or his property. To take the above example, if the consumer was well aware that the accommodation was substandard but accepted it because it was being provided at an extremely cheap rate then he could not claim the organiser was wholly negligent in providing substandard accommodation.

The second defence is that of voluntary assumption of risk. If the organiser/retailer can show that the consumer before the act complained of agreed to waive his legal rights in respect of it, the consumer's action must be dismissed. The idea of agreement here involves "some intercourse or communication" between the plaintiff (or consumer) and the defendant (or organiser/retailer) from which it may reasonably be inferred that the plaintiff (or consumer) assured the defendant (or organiser/retailer) that he waived any right of action he may have in respect of the latter's negligence (*O'Hanlon* v *ESB* (1969) IR 75 at 92). However the organiser/retailer should have in mind the impact of the EC (Unfair Terms in Consumer Contracts) Regulations 1995 which is discussed below.

(b) Negligent misstatement

The renowned 1963 House of Lords decision of *Hedley Byrne & Co Ltd* v **12.41** *Heller & Partners Ltd*, [1964] AC 465 which made its way into Irish law in the High Court decision of *Securities Trust Ltd* v *Hugh Moore & Alexander Ltd* [1964] IR 417, held that a duty of care in making statements existed whenever there was a special relationship and there had not been a disclaimer in responsibility. Therefore if an organiser/retailer makes a false statement about a resort, for example, and a third party relies on it and suffers loss, then tortious liability will be imposed on the organiser/retailer.

The organiser and the retailer are clearly in this special relationship with the purchaser of a holiday if for no other reason that by virtue of the fact that they are parties to a contract. However there is a defence to negligent misstatement if the consumer was specifically told that the organiser/retailer was not making any promises and the consumer should not rely on what was being said as it was merely a statement of opinion – i.e. a disclaimer of responsibility. Again the organiser/retailer should be familiar with the impact of the EC (Unfair Terms in Consumer Contracts) Regulations 1995.

(c) Deceit

12.42   The tort of deceit is the wrong of deceiving the consumer so that "harm was caused" to the consumer because the consumer acted on the misrepresentation. It involves the organiser or retailer wilfully making false statements with the intent that the purchaser of a holiday will buy that particular holiday in reliance on what was promised and with the result that he does so act and suffers harm in consequence. There are four main elements to this tort:

(i)   There must be a false representation of fact – the organiser/ retailer must have made a positive false statement – a mere passive non-disclosure of the truth, however deceptive, will not amount to deceit in law (*Arkwright* v *Newbold* [1881] 17 Ch D 301).

(ii)   The representation must be made with the knowledge of its falsity.

(iii) It must be made with the intention that it be acted upon by the purchaser of the holiday – making a false statement in a brochure would prima facie suggest that the organiser/retailer intended the consumer to act upon it.

(iv)   It must be proved that the consumer has acted upon the false statement and has sustained damage by doing so. The holiday-goer will have to prove that any statement falsely made was materially detrimental to his holiday.

Obviously if any of the four elements of the tort of deceit are absent an action in deceit will fail. The main defence pleaded in an action for deceit is that there was a genuine belief by the person making the statement that it was true.

The law of contract

(a) General

12.43   If an organiser/retailer enters into a written or oral contract with a consumer then both parties are bound by the terms of that contract. There are two primary remedies to any breach of contract (the breach usually arising out of misrepresentation, fundamental breach, etc) available to the consumer, namely, specific performance and damages. In relation to the organiser, by the nature of the subject matter being contracted for, i.e. a holiday, the more common form of redress for a consumer is that of damages by means of monetary compensation.

The purpose behind an award of compensation was explained in *Robinson* v *Harman* (1848) Ex 850 at 855 as being designed to put the plaintiff "so far as money can do it . . . in the same situation . . . as if the contract had been performed".

(b)   Terms and conditions of the contract

The enforceability of the terms and conditions of the travel contract are   **12.44**
worth mentioning because most if not all organisers require that a travel
booking made by a customer be on a standard booking form. The reason
for this (apart from the obvious administration advantages) is that it will
incorporate the terms and conditions that are usually contained in the
brochure into the contract between the organiser/retailer and its customer. In theory, the consumer is entitled to negotiate terms and conditions, but in practice it will be a standard form travel contract and
negotiations are rare. At common law the rules on standard form contracts in Ireland have been the subject of much caselaw. The guiding
principle can be deduced from *Parker* v *Southeastern Railway* [1877] LR2
CP 416, where the deciding factor was that reasonable notice of the terms
of the contract had to be given for the terms to be enforceable. In Ireland the contractual requirement of the reasonable fitness of services was
pronounced upon in *Brown* v *Norton* [1954] IR 34. The Irish courts adopt
the "contra proferentum" rule – the doctrine that the construction least
favourable to the person putting forward the standard form contract
should be adopted against him, provided that this causes no injustice (*In
Re Sweeney Kennedy Arbitration* [1950] IR 85).

The obvious defence for the organiser/retailer is to claim that reasonable notice of the terms of the contract has been given to the consumer.
In practice only uncommon terms would have to be specifically drawn to
the attention of the customer.

STATUTE

With regard to the pre-contractual relationship, section 45(1) of the Sale   **12.45**
of Goods and Supply of Services Act 1980 ("the 1980 Act") provides that:

> "Where a person has entered into a contract after a misrepresentation has
> been made to him by another party thereto and as a result thereof he has
> suffered loss, then, if the person making the misrepresentation would be
> liable to damages in respect thereof had the misrepresentation been made
> fraudulently, that person shall be so liable not withstanding that the mis-
> representation was not made fraudulently . . ."

However a person shall not be liable if he proves that he had reasonable grounds to believe and did believe up to the time the contract was
made that the facts represented were true.

(a)   The Consumer Information Act 1978

Section 6(1) of the Consumer Information Act 1978 ("the 1978 Act")   **12.46**
provides that a person who makes false or misleading statements as to a
service shall be guilty of an offence.

Section 8(1) of the 1978 Act makes it an offence to publish misleading
advertisements. A person guilty of an offence under the Act may be liable
on summary conviction to a fine not exceeding £500.00 or imprisonment
for a term not exceeding six months or to both a fine and imprisonment.

The relevant provisions of the 1978 Act are part of the criminal law, imposing penalties on the organiser or retailer who is in breach.

The 1978 Act provides for defences of genuine mistake; accident; innocent publication of a misdescription; or reliance on information supplied by a third party.

(b)   The Sale of Goods and Supply of Services Act 1980

12.47   Until 1995 statutory intervention in relation to contractual terms had been much more limited than intervention by the courts.

Part IV (s39) of the 1980 Act introduced an implied term as to the skill, care and diligence of the supplier of services, in the course of a business (which obviously covers the organiser). Section 40 of the 1980 Act allows for the variation or exclusion of terms by agreement or usage of terms only if it is fair and reasonable to allow this exclusion or variation. Exclusion of liability in respect of pre-contractual representations is permitted by Part V of the 1980 Act if the exclusion is fair and reasonable in the circumstances. The Schedule to the 1980 Act furnishes us with criteria for the test of fairness and reasonableness. The Schedule states that for a term to be fair and reasonable, the test is that it shall be fair and reasonable having regard to the circumstances which were, or ought reasonably to have been, known to, or in the contemplation of the parties when the contract was made.

In relation to the organiser therefore, the 1980 Act provides that terms may be excluded by express agreement, by a course of dealing between the parties, or by usage. If the recipient of the service is a consumer then it is necessary for the supplier to show that the exclusion clause is "fair and reasonable" in accordance with the criteria laid down in the Schedule to the 1980 Act. The supplier of the service must also have specifically brought the consumer's attention to the exclusion clause.

Any exclusion of liability by the organiser is permissible if it is fair and reasonable. The 1980 Act Schedule provides that in determining the fairness or reasonableness of a contractual term regard should be had to:

(i)   the strength of the bargaining positions of the parties;
(ii)   whether or not there was an inducement to the consumer to agree the term;
(iii)   whether the customer knew the term existed;
(iv)   if the liability was excluded as a result of non-compliance with another term, whether that compliance was reasonable.

12.48   Therefore it is a defence to a claim under the 1980 Act that the consumer's attention was specifically drawn to the term excluding liability and the possible consequences of accepting such a term were outlined to the consumer (e.g. explaining to the consumer that the retailer or organiser does not guarantee that the heated swimming pool will have heated water in it because the hotel management may be replacing the swimming pool heating system at that time).

Section 40(5) of the 1980 Act provides that the requirement in section 40(1), namely that the exclusion term be fair and reasonable and be brought to the attention of the consumer, does not apply to:

> "A term of an agreement where the international carriage of passengers or goods by land, sea or air, including an agreement between parties whose places of business or residences are situated in the State".

Therefore an organiser can exclude the implied skill and care warranty in relation to the international carriage of passengers. If such an express term exists in the contract then the organiser could rely on this as a defence.

Section 40(6) of the 1980 Act goes further and deals with the carriage of passengers within the state. It states that section 39 (which implies skill and care warranties into the contract), shall not apply to a contract for the carriage of passengers or goods by land, sea, air or inland waterway from one place to another within the state until such date as the minister thinks proper. The minister has not fixed such a date and therefore in relation to the carriage element of package within the state being provided by the organisers, section 39 cannot be relied upon by the consumer.

Many of the carriage exclusions of the 1980 Act are overridden by the Package Holidays and Travel Trade Act 1995 however. The EC (Unfair Terms in Consumer Contracts) Regulations 1995, discussed below, also have an impact on whether or not any exclusion of liability is permitted.

(c)   The Package Holiday and Travel Trade Act 1995

INTRODUCTION

The Package Holidays and Travel Trade Act 1995 ("the 1995 Act") imple-   **12.49** mented The Package Holiday Directive (90/314/EEC) ("the 1990 Directive") on 17 July 1995 and has been effective from 1 October 1995.

Only consumers buying a package will be able to rely on the protection of the 1995 Act. Section 2 of the Act states that a package means the pre-arranged combination of not fewer than two of the following when sold or offered to sale at an inclusive price and when the service covers a period of more than 24 hours or includes overnight accommodation:

(a)   transport;

(b)   accommodation; and

(c)   some other tourist service(s) not ancillary to transport or accommodation and accounting for a significant proportion of the package.

The separate billing of various components of the same package will not absolve the organiser or retailer of liability (s2(1)). This will mean that a range of packages based around a holiday activity such as golf, fishing, hunting etc could come within the definition of "other tourist services" if they are not simply available as a facility.

Under Article 5 of the 1990 Directive Member States have to designate either the retailer or the organiser or both as having responsibility for adhering to the new law in relation to the 1990 Directive. Section 3 of the 1995 Act provides that an organiser can be any person organising packages, and for this reason can cover either the travel agent or the tour operator, though in practice it will usually be the tour operator. It is still important for the consumer to find out who is designated as the party responsible within the country of purchase, if any, as that person is strictly liable in the event of any failure to deliver on the package.

There are certain classes of persons who are considered for the purposes of s 3 of the 1995 Act as "occasional organisers" and as such do not come under the auspices of the Act. The classes include professional, medical, scientific and cultural trade associations or societies which organise a package for the purpose of holding a conference, convention, meeting or seminar. The package should have been arranged in pursuance of the aims or objectives of the body concerned. Other package holiday organisers who are considered to be occasional organisers are community, social, sporting and voluntary organisations, religious or denominational groups and charitable or benevolent institutions. In each of these cases the package holiday must be related to the body's normal line of work or activity. Finally, a firm which organises a package for its employees is considered to be an occasional organiser for the purposes of the Act.

The 1995 Act assists consumers in clarifying exactly what their rights are and in ensuring that they are placed in the position to obtain them. The 1995 Act ensures that detailed and comprehensive information on the holiday must be supplied before departure, so that the consumer will not be stranded in the event of bankruptcy and that the consumer will be entitled to compensation, in certain circumstances, if the holiday does not match the promises made. In this respect the 1995 Act covers some of the ground already covered by the existing consumer protection legislation.

(b) Extent and financial limits of liability

12.50 Section 20 of the 1995 Act places strict liability on the organiser as regards the proper performance of the obligations under the contract to the consumer. The section provides that the organiser is liable to the consumer for the proper performance of obligations under the contract, irrespective of whether those obligations are performed by the organiser, the retailer or other suppliers. The organiser is also liable to the consumer for any damage caused by the failure to perform the contract or the improper performance of the consumer. The liability of the organiser however does not affect any remedy or right of action which the organiser may have against the retailer or those other suppliers of services.

If the failure to perform the contract or the improper performance of the contract are attributable to the consumer, the organiser will not be liable. Likewise no liability arises on the part of the organiser where damage was caused by the failure to perform the contract or the improper performance of the contract where those failures are attributable to a third party unconnected with the provision of services contracted for and which are unforeseeable or unavoidable.

Where damage was caused by the failure to perform the contract or the improper performance of the contract if such failures are due to force majeure (e.g. air traffic control delays, staff strikes, national disasters etc), or are due to an event which the organiser/retailer or the supplier of services could not, even with all due care, foresee or forestall, the organiser is not liable.

In the case of damages arising from the non-performance or improper **12.51** performance of the services involved in the package the contract may include a term limiting the amount of compensation payable to the consumer.

The organiser may not limit liability to less than an amount equal to double the inclusive price of the package in the case of an adult and, in the case of a minor, an amount equal to the inclusive price of the package to the minor concerned.

However no limitation of liability is permissible in the event of death or personal injury or damage caused by the wilful misconduct or gross negligence of the organiser. The contract may provide for compensation to be limited in accordance with international conventions in force governing such services in the place where they are performed or due to be performed (e.g. the Berne Conventions, the Athens Convention or the Warsaw Convention.)

The liability of the organiser contained in section 20 as outlined above cannot be excluded by any contractual term. The question then arises as to where the organiser stands in relation to the limitation of liability vis-a-vis the European Communities (Unfair Terms in Consumer Contracts) Regulations 1995 ("the 1995 Regulations"). It is conceivable that a situation could arise where a consumer suffers loss greatly exceeding twice the price of the package (e.g. all the consumer's baggage lost in transit and the loss is not covered under a separate insurance policy). In that event the consumer could conceivably mount an argument that the limitation of liability is an unfair clause within the meaning of the 1995 Regulations (discussed below) and as such, unenforceable by the organiser.

(c)   The brochure and the 1995 Act

The most popular way in which consumers decide on a particular holiday **12.52** is through a brochure which is generally supplied by a retailer or an organiser and for this reason the brochure plays a vital role in the travel contract. The customer generally cannot see what he is buying so he relies on the description in the brochure. Under the 1995 Act, once the brochure has been published, the consumer is entitled to assume that the information contained in it is accurate and legally binding and no changes can take place unless provision is made for this in the brochure – and the changes notified to the consumer before signing the contract. The 1995 Act provides that if a consumer purchases a package holiday on the basis of information contained in a brochure, whether or not such information is required by the 1995 Act to be included in the brochure, then the particulars in the brochure which were relied on should constitute warranties in the travel contract as to the matters to which they relate.

12.53   Specified information now has to be contained in the brochure under section 10 of the 1995 Act. This obligatory information requires the disclosure of:

(i)   detailed information about the type of transport used to reach the holiday destination;

(ii)   full details of accommodation, including location, category or degree of comfort and main features (swimming pool, restaurant etc). Accommodation approval and tourist classification under the rules of the host Member State must also be included;

(iii)   the meals to be provided;

(iv)   the itinerary;

(v)   passport and visa requirements;

(vi)   health formalities for both the journey and the stay;

(vii)   the advance deposit required and the date when the final balance is due;

(viii) the minimum number of people required for the package to take place, and the deadlines for cancellations on both sides if the package is conditional upon a minimum number of participants;

(ix)   any tax or compulsory charge;

(x)   an address of a nominated agent who will accept service of proceedings in the state should the need arise where the package is offered by an organiser with an address outside the state;

(xi)   the arrangements for security for money paid over and (where applicable) for the repatriation of the consumer in the event of the insolvency of the organiser.

Section 11 of the 1995 Act states that any descriptive matter concerning a package and supplied by the organiser or the retailer to the consumer must not contain any misleading information. In any proceedings against a retailer, as opposed to the organiser, it shall be a defence to show that the retailer did not know and had no reason to suspect that the brochure or other descriptive matter concerned, contained information which was false or misleading.

(d)   The travel contract and the 1995 Act

12.54   The consumer, when booking a holiday through a organiser or retailer, has entered into a contract. Even if a brochure hasn't been supplied the consumer is entitled to his rights under the contract. Consumers should in this respect read the contract and ensure that they understand its terms and conditions prior to entering into it. Consumers will also be entitled to their rights under common law and existing legislation. The 1995 Act sets out a complete "set of rules" for the provision of information before entering the travel contract, before going on holiday, the necessary terms and the form of the contract, price changes, provisions regarding the alteration, cancellation and transfer of the booking and the non provision of services while on the holiday. These rules are discussed in the following paragraphs.

Information which must be provided before the conclusion of the travel contract

An organiser and a retailer who makes available a brochure to a possible **12.55** consumer that does not contain the information listed above is guilty of an offence. A retailer shall not supply to a possible consumer a brochure which he knows or has reasonable cause to believe does not comply with the requirements of the 1995 Act. If the retailer has reasonable cause to believe the requirements are complied with then this shall be a defence. The 1995 Act provides that particulars contained in the brochure shall not constitute warranties as to the matters to which they relate where the organiser's brochure contains a clear and legible statement that changes may be made to the particulars contained in the organisers brochure before the contract is concluded, and provided that those changes are communicated clearly to the consumer and that the consumer has accepted those changes before the contract for the holiday is concluded. A further defence to not supplying the requisite information is where the consumer and the organiser both agree either at the time the contract was made, or after the contract was made, that the particulars, or some of the particulars outlined in the organisers brochure, should not form part of the travel contract.

Organisers and/or the retailer must provide the traveller with advance details, in writing, of visa and passport requirements (and in particular how long they may take to obtain), health formalities, insurance details and arrangements for security in the event of insolvency.

Section 12(3) of the 1995 Act provides that the above requirements are satisfied if the retailer has referred the intending consumer to such information contained in a brochure supplied to the intending consumer. If the organiser or retailer therefore refers the brochure to the consumer and informs him that this is the information that they are required to be given before the conclusion of the contract then the organiser/retailer shall have complied with the relevant section of the 1995 Act (i.e. s12).

Information which must be provided before start of package

Section 13 of the 1995 Act provides for information that must be pro- **12.56** vided by the organiser to the consumer before the start of the package holiday. This information is:

(i)   times and details of intermediate stops and transport connections;

(ii)   details of any cabins or berths on a ship, or sleeper compartments on a train;

(iii)   the name, address and telephone number of the local representative or agency in the resort. If there is not an agency or representative, then an emergency telephone number or other information must be provided that will enable consumers to obtain assistance in the event of any problems;

(iv)   detailed information to assist minors travelling abroad, including emergency telephone numbers enabling direct contact with the child or the person with whom he/she is staying.

Section 13(3)(a) provides that an organiser who does not supply the above-mentioned information before the start of the package shall be guilty of an offence. However if the contravention is due to the failure of the retailer to pass on to the consumer the information supplied to the retailer by the organisers this gives a limited defence to the organiser if he can prove that the retailer did not pass on the information which the organiser supplied through its brochure or other written form. A retailer who fails to provide the consumer with the information as set out will also be guilty of an offence.

As with the information provided before the conclusion of the contract the organiser and retailer can fulfil their obligations under section 13 of the Act by referring the consumer to the information contained in the brochure previously supplied to the consumer, provided that the brochure complied with section 10 of the 1995 Act.

Essential terms of the contract

12.57   Section 14 of the 1995 Act provides that essential terms must be contained in the contract. They include details to be given about:

(i)   destinations and periods of stay;

(ii)   means, characteristics, categories and times of transport;

(iii)   details about the standard of accommodation;

(iv)   meal plans;

(v)   the itinerary;

(vi)   the length of notice that has to be given to the consumer if a minimum number of people are required for the package to go ahead and the minimum number is not reached;

(vii)   visits and excursions included in the package price;

(viii) the retailer, the organiser and the insurer;

(ix)   the price of the package, details of price revisions (if any), the payment schedule and method of payment;

(x)   special requirements of the consumer that have been individually negotiated;

(xi)   the period within which the consumer has a right of complaint (which must not be less than 28 days after the package).

In all cases the information stated above must be contained in the contract.

Form of the contract

Under section 15 of the 1995 Act the contract must be in writing and a **12.58** copy supplied to the consumer. If any term of a contract was negotiated less than 14 days before the holiday then this will be a defence to the organiser not having the term/terms in writing. If an organiser fails to supply the consumer with a copy of the written booking conditions he shall be guilty of a criminal offence under section 15(3) of the Act unless the failure is attributable to the retailer.

Price changes

Once the price of the package holiday has been agreed it cannot be **12.59** changed unless the contract expressly provides for this. Where the contract does so provide for price changes, the method of calculation of the price changes must be stated and the following rules apply regardless:

(i) prices can only be revised due to fluctuation in transport costs (including fuel, landing taxes and fees levied at ports and airports), or exchange rates;

(ii) under no circumstances can prices be changed later than 20 days before departure;

(iii) if there is a price change, the consumer must be informed as quickly as possible, and will then be at liberty to withdraw from the contract, without penalty, or to accept the new terms;

(iv) the method of calculation of the price revision and the circumstances in which a revision may occur must be described in the contract.

If price increases are unacceptable, the consumer is entitled: **12.60**

(i) to be offered a substitute package of the equivalent or higher quality, or if of a lower quality to have the price difference refunded;

(ii) to repayment in full of any money already paid;

(iii) to compensation unless the package is cancelled for reasons already stipulated in the contract (these may include insufficient people booking the package, if specified as a condition of the package, or unusual and unforeseeable circumstances beyond the control of the operator).

If a price increase arises as a result of circumstances other than those contained in section 17, then it would seem that the organiser would have to be responsible for such an increase. The 1995 EC Unfair Contract Terms Regulations would arguably be successfully relied upon by a consumer where a price revision, though in compliance with the 1995 Act, bore no reasonable proportion to the actual changes.

12.61   Transfer of the booking

Under section 16 of the 1995 Act, the consumer who cannot travel under a package which he has reserved has a legal right to assign the package to another suitable person of his choice. This is conditional on the consumer informing the organiser or the retailer within a reasonable time before the day of departure. Both customers are then jointly and severally liable for any remaining balance of the price and any additional costs involved.

If the consumer does not give reasonable notice to the organiser that they wish to transfer the booking then this may allow the organiser/retailer to refuse such a transfer. Alternatively if there is a waiting list then the organiser/retailer may restrict the transfer of the booking to a person of the consumer's choice.

Alteration and cancellation by organiser

12.62 Section 18 deals with the alteration or cancellation of the contract by the organiser. The essence of this section is that if the organiser changes an essential term of the contract, such as price, the consumer must be notified as soon as possible so that they can take appropriate decisions – in particular to withdraw from the contract without penalty or alternatively to accept that variation to the contract specifying the alterations made and their impact on the price. The important thing is that the consumer can withdraw from the contract without penalty. The consumer must tell the organiser or retailer of the consumer's decision as soon as possible. Where the consumer withdraws from the contract, or where the organiser, for any reason other than the fault of the consumer, cancels the package before the date when it is due to start, the consumer is entitled to take a replacement package of equivalent or superior quality, to take a replacement package of lower quality and recover from the organiser the difference in price between the original package and the replacement package, or to have repaid all monies on the contract as soon as possible.

There are two exceptions to the consumer being entitled to be compensated by the organiser for non-performance of the contract. Firstly, where the package is cancelled because the number of people who agreed to take it is less than the minimum number required and the consumer is informed of the cancellation in writing. Secondly, the package is cancelled by *force majeure*, in other words by reason of unusual and unforeseeable circumstances beyond the control of the organiser, the retailer or other supplier of services, the consequences of which could not have been avoided even if all due care had been exercised.

The replacement of the package, the repayment of money and the entitlement of the consumer to compensation are implied terms in every contract. Overbooking will not be regarded as an unusual and unforeseeable circumstance. The consumer is therefore entitled to be compensated irrespective of whether overbooking is the organiser's fault or the fault of the airline or hotelier for instance.

This section does not deprive the consumer of his existing rights under the common law or existing legislation to insist upon performance of his original contract.

Non-provision of services

The basic premise of the 1995 Act is that when consumers set off on holi- **12.63** day they should be secure in the knowledge that the holiday will match the promises and representations made to them. The contract terms should have been agreed in a clear and understandable fashion, the holiday-maker should know that he will not be stranded in the event of bankruptcy of the organiser, and he should know where to go if any problems arise. If for any reason, the holiday does not match pre-holiday promises, the consumer should immediately contact the main representative for the package.

If a significant proportion of services are not provided, for example, if the type of hotel stipulated in the package is not up to standard, the representative with the organiser must make suitable alternative arrangements at no extra cost to the consumer. The consumer is entitled to transport either home or to another agreed location at no extra cost, if the alternatives are unacceptable to him. Where applicable, compensation must also be paid.

If the consumer makes a complaint to the retailer/organiser while on holiday the operator/agent should take immediate steps to deal with the complaint and if he/she does so this can form part of a defence to any proceedings against them.

Conclusion

In conclusion the 1995 Act assists consumers in clarifying exactly what **12.64** their rights are and in ensuring that they are placed in the position to obtain them. The 1995 Act ensures that detailed and comprehensive information on the holiday must be supplied before departure, so that the consumer will not be stranded in the event of bankruptcy and that the consumer will be entitled to compensation, in certain circumstances, if the holiday does not match the promises made.

The law applies to packages sold within the Community regardless of whether the destination is within the Community itself, or beyond its borders. Additional benefits which consumers can expect as a result of this law being implemented are:

- a far higher degree of certainty about what they are buying;
- protection through contract, whether they have bought the holiday direct, have had the holiday transferred to them by a third party or are members of a group booking;
- the ability to make greater choices and comparisons;
- the confidence to make cross border purchases, i.e., buy a package in

another Member State secure in the knowledge that the laws are applicable in every Member State;
- the right to complain, in the knowledge that the supplier must find a solution;
- compensation should the agreed services not be supplied or fail in any way.

(e) European Communities (Unfair Terms in Consumer Contracts) Regulations 1995

12.65 The European Communities (Unfair Terms in Consumer Contracts) Regulations (SI 1995/27) ("the 1995 Regulations") affect all contracts made with consumers from 31 December 1994. The 1995 Regulations implement Council Directive 93/13/EEC on unfair terms in consumer contracts.

The definition of what is "unfair" is embodied in Regulation 3(2) of the Regulations which provides that a contractual term which has not been individually negotiated should be regarded as unfair if, contrary to the requirement of good faith, it causes a significant imbalance to the parties' rights and obligations arising under the contract, taking into account the nature of the goods or services for which the contract was concluded and all circumstances surrounding the conclusion of the contract and all other terms of the contract or any collateral contract.

12.66 Schedule 3 of the 1995 Regulations gives a number of examples of what may be described as unfair terms. They are terms which have the object or effect of:

(a) excluding or limiting the legal liability of a seller or supplier in the event of the death of a consumer or personal injury to the latter resulting from an act or omission of that seller or supplier;

(b) inappropriately excluding or limiting the legal rights of the consumer vis-a-vis the seller or supplier or another party in the event of total or partial non-performance or inadequate performance by the seller or supplier of any of the contractual obligations, including the option of offsetting a debt owed to the seller or supplier against any claim which the consumer may have against him;

(c) making an agreement binding on the consumer whereas provision of services by the seller or supplier is subject to a condition whose realisation depends on his own will alone;

(d) permitting the seller or supplier to retain sums paid by the consumer where the latter decides not to conclude or perform the contract, without providing for the consumer to receive compensation of an equivalent amount from the seller or supplier where the latter is the party cancelling the contract;

(e) requiring any consumer who fails to fulfil his obligation to pay a disproportionately high sum in compensation;

(f) authorising the seller or supplier to dissolve the contract on a discretionary basis where the same facility is not granted to the consumer, or permitting the seller or supplier to retain the sums paid for services not yet supplied by him where it is the seller or supplier himself who dissolves the contract;

(g) enabling the seller or supplier to terminate a contract of indeterminate duration without reasonable notice except where there are serious grounds for doing so;

(h) automatically extending a contract of fixed duration where the consumer does not indicate otherwise, when the deadline fixed for the consumer to express this desire not to extend the contract is unreasonably early;

(i) irrevocably binding the consumer to terms with which he had no real opportunity of becoming acquainted before the conclusion of the contract;

(j) enabling the seller or supplier to alter the terms of the contract unilaterally without a valid reason which is specified in the contract;

(k) enabling the seller or supplier to alter unilaterally without a valid reason any characteristics of the product or service to be provided;

(l) providing for the price of goods to be determined at the time of delivery or allowing a seller of goods or supplier of services to increase their price without in both cases giving the consumer the corresponding right to cancel the contract if the final price is too high in relation to the price agreed when the contract was concluded;

(m) giving the seller or supplier the right to determine whether the goods or services supplied are in conformity with the contract, or giving him the exclusive right to interpret any term of the contract;

(n) limiting the seller's or supplier's obligation to respect commitments undertaken by his agents, or making his commitments subject to compliance with a particular formality;

(o) obliging the consumer to fulfil all his obligations where the seller or supplier does not perform his;

(p) giving the seller or supplier the possibility of transferring his rights and obligations under the contract, where this may serve to reduce the guarantees for the consumer, without the latter's agreement;

(q) excluding or hindering the consumer's right to take legal action or exercise any other legal remedy, particularly by requiring the consumer to take disputes exclusively to arbitration not covered by legal provisions, unduly restricting the evidence available to him or imposing on him a burden of proof which, according to the applicable law, should be with another party to the contract.

The Regulations give the Director of Consumer Affairs the right to **12.67** take action in the courts in order to establish whether standard terms contained in a contract are unfair, and if so to seek an order from the court to remove them from the contract.

The Regulations are geared towards the protection of the consumer. Regulation 5(2) provides that where there is a doubt about the meaning of a term, the interpretation most favourable to the consumer shall prevail. This is somewhat similar to the common law *contra proferentem* rule discussed earlier. The Regulations will only apply to contracts between a seller or supplier and consumer. A consumer is defined as a natural person who is acting for purposes which were outside his trade, business or profession and a seller or supplier is defined as a natural or legal person who is acting for purposes relating to his trade, business or profession whether publicly or privately owned.

The implications for sellers and suppliers of goods and services in the light of the Regulations is that they will clearly have to review their standard conditions for the purpose of eliminating unfair terms. They should examine Schedule 3 to the Regulations and see if any of the examples cited therein are a part of their contract. In the context of package travel, unless the consumer individually negotiates the terms of his contract the Regulations will apply to the standard package travel contract.

The Regulations say that an unfair term in a contract concluded with the consumer by a seller or supplier shall not be binding on the consumer. However, the contract shall continue to bind the parties if it is capable of continuing in existence without the unfair term.

In many ways the 1995 Regulations may be used to compliment the provisions of the Package Holidays and Travel Trade Act, 1995. A number of examples of this are set out below.

12.68 Section 14(1) of the Package Holiday and Travel Trade Act 1995 provides that every package travel contract must contain an essential term providing details of the period within which the consumer must make a complaint about the failure to perform or the inadequate performance of the travel contract provided that such periods shall not be less than 28 days from the date of completion of the package. It could be argued that the 28-day limit could be construed as an unfair term for the purposes of the 1995 Regulations as in certain instances a longer time must be allowed for.

Section 17 provides that a package travel contract shall contain terms and conditions relating to price revision. Section 17(s)(b) sets out three conditions to which any such price revision terms are subject and these have been outlined above. The 1995 Regulations would arguably be relied upon by a consumer to set aside any price revision which while in compliance with the conditions in section 17(2)(b) of the 1995 Act bore no reasonable proportion to the changes in the cost to the organiser.

As mentioned already the Unfair Contract Terms Regulations could affect package travel contacts in relation to the exceptions to the consumer's right to be entitled to compensation in the event of cancellation. Section 18 of the 1995 Act provides that the consumer is entitled to be compensated by the organiser for breach of contract except where the package is cancelled because the number of persons who agreed to take it is less than the number required and the consumer is informed of the cancellation in writing within the period prescribed in the contract for him to be so informed. The Package Holidays and Travel Trade Act 1995 does not provide what period of time may be prescribed in the contract but if this were unusually long after the organiser realised that numbers were short then this could contravene the 1995 Regulations.

12.69 The limitation of liability of the organiser pursuant to section 20 of the 1995 Act could also cause problems vis-a-vis the 1995 Regulations. An organiser cannot limit his liability to less than an amount equal to double the inclusive price of the package in the case of an adult, and in the case of a minor an amount equal to the inclusive price of the package to the minor concerned. It is very possible that a situation could arise where a consumer suffered loss exceeding twice the price of the package (take the example cited earlier where the consumer's luggage is lost in transit and is not covered under a separate insurance policy), and in such a case it could be argued that the limitation clause clearly could not be enforceable.

A prime example of where the 1995 Regulations might affect package travel contracts is when there is a term in the contract relating to cancellation. The typical booking conditions at present provide for the following cancellation charges to be paid by the consumer:

"More than six weeks before departure date any deposit paid shall be forfeited.
Within six to four weeks of departure 30% of the cost of the Holiday is forfeited.
Within four to two weeks of departure 45% of the cost of the Holiday is forfeited.
Within two weeks to 72 hours of departure 60% of the cost of the Holiday is forfeited.
Within 72 hours of departure 100% of the cost of the Holiday is forfeited."

On the other hand however, standard booking forms at present provide that the organiser pays significantly lower compensation if he alters the contract (*e.g.* only £50 within two weeks). This discrepancy would clearly appear to amount to an imbalance between the rights and obligations of the parties to the detriment of the consumer, in contravention of the 1995 Regulations.

(The question of the standard arbitration clause contained in most booking conditions and how it may fall foul of the 1995 Regulations is discussed below under the general discussion on arbitration as a form of dispute resolution.)

(ii) Liability for personal injury

(i) COMMON LAW

12.70 Is the supplier liable for resulting injury sustained by the negligence of the carriers employed by him and, if so, to what extent? Two cases provide some indication of the answer to this question.

The first case is the UK decision in *Wall* v *Silverwing Surface Arrangements Ltd* (unreported). Here a fire exit in an apartment block in which the plaintiff was staying had been blocked by the management of the building in order to avoid access by burglars. As a result the plaintiff, being unable to exit the building, suffered serious personal injury. The injury would not have occurred had the fire exist been in normal working order, which it had been when the organisers' representative had visited the building. Hodgson J stated in holding against the plaintiff:

> "I would find it wholly unreasonable to saddle an organiser with an obligation to ensure the safety of all of the components of the package over none of which he had any control at all."

12.71 In a Canadian case, *Craven* v *Strand Holidays (Canada) Ltd* ([1982] 4 OR 2D 186), the Ontario Court of Appeal considered the situation where the plaintiffs were claiming damages for injuries received when the bus they were travelling in overturned. The bus company had been chosen by the organiser. The Court of Appeal in this case again decided in favour of the defendant organiser because the Court believed it had exercised due care in the selection of the bus company. The Court of Appeal stated:

> "If a person agrees to perform some work or services he cannot escape contractual liability by delegating the performance to another. It is his contract. But if the contract is only to . . . arrange for the performance of services then he has fulfilled his contract if he has exercised due care in the selection of a competent contractor. He is not responsible if that contractor is negligent in the performance of the actual work or service, for the performance is not part of his contract.
>
> A person is not liable for the negligence of an independent contractor unless he has a primary obligation to carry out a non delegable duty imposed upon him by law or by contract. It is clear in the evidence that Strand never undertook to perform the bus transfer but merely to arrange for this to be done by a third party."

Therefore although the organiser is under a duty to exercise skill and care in making suitable arrangements with carriers for accommodation and other parts of the package it is clear that the operator would not be liable for negligence if the operator can prove the exercise of sufficient care in the selection of the arrangements and the instruction of the carriers. An organiser cannot be held liable to accidents that are completely out of his control.

In the event that the injury is as a result of something under the organiser's control then the usual defences of contributory negligence, entire fault of the consumer, voluntary assumption of risk (if applicable), etc will apply.

(ii) THE PACKAGE HOLIDAYS AND TRAVEL TRADE ACT 1995

It now remains to be seen what impact the 1995 Act will have on the legal position in relation to section 20 of the 1995 Act, which provides that the organiser shall be liable to the consumer for the proper performance of the obligations under the contract, irrespective of whether such obligations are to be performed by the organiser, retailer, or other suppliers of services, but they shall not affect any remedy or right of action which the organiser may have against the retailer or those other suppliers of services.   **12.72**

Section 20 suggests that strict liability is imposed on the organiser or retailer with regard to defects in the package. Section 20(2), however, provides that the following defences can be pleaded by the operator/retailer:

(i)   the failures which occurred in the performance of the contract were attributable to the consumer;

(ii)   such failures are attributable to a third party unconnected with the provision of the services contracted for and were unforeseeable or unavoidable;

(iii)   such failures were due to *force majeure* or to an event which the organiser and/or retailer or the supplier of the services, even with all due care, could not have foreseen.

In this regard the 1995 Act appears to be in line with the common law position. Should an accident befall a holiday-maker when abroad an action for damages will not lie against the organiser or retailer in circumstances outside of their control, but the burden of proof that the organiser/retailer is not liable will lie with the organiser/retailer.

(iii) Procedure in the event of disputes

(i) THE ARBITRATION CLAUSE IN THE HOLIDAY CONTRACT

Most travel contracts will contain an arbitration clause which will decide that in the event of a dispute arising between the organiser and the consumer it will be resolved by way of arbitration as opposed to through the courts. Arbitration clauses are generally upheld and supported by the Irish courts provided that the wording of the clause does not have the effect of ousting the jurisdiction of the courts. However the power of the parties to a contract to make arbitration a condition precedent to an action in the courts is lessened in the light of the decision in *McCarthy* v   **12.73**

Joe Walsh Tours Ltd ([1991] ILRM 813). This case decided that a consumer who is a party to a contract for a holiday cannot be compelled to submit a claim for damages for breach of such contract to arbitration where the damages recoverable in such arbitration are limited under the provisions of the arbitration clause unless:

(i)   the consumer's attention was specifically drawn to the arbitration term prior to the contract; and

(ii)   the arbitration term is fair and reasonable.

In this case the clause provided for an Irish Retailers' Association arbitration scheme which limited liability to £5,000.00 for any claim and excluded personal injuries. The court held that it was a provision restricting the liability of the supplier for a breach of an implied term under the statute, and that the provision restricting the liability was not contained in the general conditions of the contract. The court accepted the evidence of the plaintiff that the purported restriction was not brought to his attention. The arbitrator could not apply the scheme as drawn up and the court went on to hold that the scheme was inoperative and incapable of being performed and dismissed the appeal by the defendant.

12.74   Section 5 of the Arbitration Act 1980 enables a court to retrain proceedings brought in the courts by way of a stay when it is established that an arbitration clause has not been observed. However in certain circumstances the court can at its discretion refuse to stay proceedings if it is of the opinion that arbitration is not the most desirable method of resolving the dispute between the parties (*Administratia Assigurarilor de Stat, Winterthur Swiss Insurance Co & Others* v *Insurance Corporation of Ireland Plc (Under Administration)* [1990] 2 IR 247).

Often one will see the consumer bringing the arbitration proceedings against the retailer who is not generally party to the contract or the arbitration clause. The retailer should then claim that the arbitration clause is not binding on him as he is only the agent of the organiser and in fact the organiser is the person properly to be named in the proceedings. The retailer can escape arbitration in this way. For the same reason the organiser cannot join the retailer in any arbitration proceedings instituted against the operator but must pursue him through the courts. However, one will often find in practice that the retailer will assist the organiser in defending any claims.

It is noteworthy that the 1995 Regulations (on unfair terms) outlaw terms which hinder the consumers' right to take legal action which could be interpreted (although it would be a very broad interpretation) as including an exclusive arbitration clause. Most booking conditions forms contain an arbitration clause in the following terms:

"Any dispute or difference of any kind whatsoever which arises or occurs between any of the Parties hereto in relation to any thing or matter arising under, out of or in connection with this contract shall be referred to arbitration under the Arbitration Rules of the Chartered Institute of Arbitrators – Irish Branch."

Organisers generally prefer to have complaints with consumers resolved by arbitration. Arbitration is a quick and cost-efficient way of resolving disputes. **12.75**

Schedule 3 of the 1995 Regulations at paragraph 1(q), refers to terms which have the object or effect of:

> "excluding or hindering the consumer's right to take legal action or exercise any other legal remedy, particularly by requiring the consumer to take disputes exclusively to arbitration not covered by legal provisions, unduly restricting the evidence available to him or imposing on him a burden of proof which, according to the applicable law of commerce should lie with another party to the contract."

The phrase "not covered by legal provisions" implies that it is possible to have exclusive arbitration clauses in consumer contracts. The 1995 Regulations require that there must be a fair system of arbitration. The arbitration clause must not cause "significant imbalance in the parties' rights and obligations". It is essential that the option to choose between arbitration and court must be available in respect of both parties to the dispute. In addition the provisions of the Arbitration Acts 1954–80 must apply to the arbitration. If full judicial supervision is provided for and guaranteed in relation to the application of the principles of justice in the arbitration clause then the clause itself will remain valid with regard to the 1995 Regulations. On the other hand if the arbitration clause is not "covered by legal provisions' then the consumer can successfully argue that it is an unfair contractual term because it creates an imbalance between the parties.

(ii)   SMALL CLAIMS PROCEDURE

The small claims procedure is a relatively new procedure which relates to claims for faulty goods and services not supplied, and bad workmanship which does not exceed in the value the sum of £500.00. The new scheme is a means for the consumer of enforcing claims quickly, inexpensively, and with the minimum of fuss. **12.76**

"Small claim" is defined as "any civil proceeding instituted by any consumer against the Vendor in relation to any goods or services purchased in which the amount of the claim does not exceed the sum of £500.00". Personal injury actions are not available through the small claims procedure and neither are actions for debts. Subject to this, the procedure provides a claimant who intends to issue proceedings in the district court with the alternative of making application to the Small Claims Registrar to have the claim processed through the small claims procedure. This means that for claims which come within the definition of "small claim" the applicant may, instead of issuing an ordinary civil process or a civil process for a debt or liquidated amount, use the small claims procedure which is technically simpler and has a nominal fee of £5.00. An application shall be in writing in the appropriate form, which is called Form SC1, and shall be lodged with the appropriate Small Claims Registrar.

The registrar "shall" consider the application and "may take such steps as he considers necessary whether by way of interviewing the claimant or otherwise, to record the full facts of the claim". He may feel obliged to go beyond the information given by the applicant and seek further information or clarification from others. Where he considers the claim to be inappropriate to the small claims procedure, he shall so inform the claimant and refund the fee of £5.00 paid.

12.77   After the registrar has considered the application and has used his best endeavours to settle the dispute, if neither party agrees then the failure to reach agreement will inevitably mean the matter going before the District Justice.

The claimant and the respondent are liable for their own legal costs and witnesses expenses (if any) incurred under this procedure. Either party may engage a solicitor and call witnesses (including expert witnesses) to accompany them to the meeting with the registrar and, of course, in the district court if the issue goes to a hearing. All expenses must be met by the party incurring them.

Where the terms of a settlement, including an agreement to pay by instalments, are not complied with the registrar may, if requested to do so by the claimant proceed to judgment against the other party.

Obviously the small claims procedure cannot be utilised if the contract between the parties contains an enforceable arbitration agreement.

4.   Health and safety standards

(i)   Fire safety in tourist accommodation

12.78   The EU Council has issued recommendations on fire safety in existing hotels. The Council Recommendation (OJ 1986 L384/54) is intended to reduce the risk of fire breaking out, to prevent the spread of flames and smoke, to ensure that all occupants can be safely evacuated, and to enable the emergency services to take action. To meet these objectives, which are persuasive, precautions must be taken within the establishment so that:

(i)   safe escape routes are available, are clearly indicated and remain accessible and unobstructed;

(ii)   the building's structural stability in the event of fire is guaranteed, at least for as long as it is needed for the occupants to evacuate the building;

(iii)   the presence or use of highly inflammable materials in the wall, ceiling or floor coverings and interior decorations is carefully limited;

(iv)   all technical equipment and appliances operate safely;

(v)   appropriate systems are installed and maintained in proper working order for alerting occupants;

(vi)   safety instructions and a plan of the premises with an indication of the escape routes are displayed in each room normally occupied by guests or staff;

(vii)   emergency fire fighting equipment such as extinguishers are provided and maintained in proper working order; and

(viii)   the staff is given instruction and training.

When applying these principles to existing commercially-run establishments, Member States must take into account a number of technical guidelines set out in a detailed Annex to the Recommendation. There are guidelines on escape routes, guidelines on construction features, guidelines dealing with electric lighting, heating and ventilation systems, fire fighting, alarm and alerting equipment, and guidelines also cover other safety instructions, such as prominently posted and precise instructions in each bedroom indicating the action to be taken in the event of fire.   **12.79**

Member States may use different or more stringent measures than those specified in the guidelines, but they must achieve an equivalent standard of fire safety.

(ii)   The Irish position

The primary legislation governing fire safety in Ireland is the Fire Services Act 1981. The Department of Environment has also issued a number of codes of practice and guides for fire safety in places of assembly, hotels, guest houses and similar premises. The recommendations in those codes and guides are advisory, and compliance with them does not confer immunity from legal obligations under the Fire Services Act 1981 or regulations which may be made under that Act, or any other legal instrument, or under common law.   **12.80**

(a)   The Fire Services Act 1981

There are a number of provisions in the Fire Services Act 1981 ("the 1981 Act") applicable to hotels, guest houses and similar premises: **12.81**

A   LEGAL RESPONSIBILITIES

Section 18(2) of the 1981 Act imposes a duty on persons having control over premises providing sleeping accommodation for guests to:

> take all reasonable measures to guard against the outbreak of fire on such premises and to ensure as far as is reasonably practicable the safety of persons on the premises in the event of an outbreak of fire.

Section 18(3) of the 1981 Act imposes a duty on any person responsible for such accommodation:

> to conduct himself in such a way so as to ensure that as far as is reasonably practicable any person on the premises is not exposed to danger from fire as a consequence of any act or omission of his.

12.82   The Act provides for substantial penalties, with fines of up to £10,000 and/or two years imprisonment for persons convicted on indictment, and for a fine not exceeding £500 on summary convictions.

B   FIRE SAFETY NOTICES

12.83   Under section 20 of the 1981 Act, a fire authority may serve a Fire Safety Notice on the owner or occupier of a "potentially dangerous building", which is defined as a building which constitutes a serious danger to life in the event of a fire occurring therein. Such a notice may prohibit the use of a building (or part of it) and may require the owner or occupier to carry out specified fire precautions to that building. There is provision in section 21 of the 1981 Act for a person on whom a Fire Safety Notice is served, to appeal to the District Court within 14 days from the date of service. In a situation of extreme and urgent concern about fire safety, a fire authority may apply under section 23 of the 1981 Act to the High Court for an order to restrict or prohibit use of a building immediately.

It is an offence under the 1981 Act to fail to comply with the terms of a Fire Safety Notice and penalties similar to those outlined above may be imposed on a person convicted of such an offence.

C   POWERS OF INSPECTION

12.84   Section 22 of the 1981 Act gives powers to any authorised person from a fire authority to inspect premises. It is an offence under section 22(6) to:

(i)   refuse entry to an authorised person;
(ii)   obstruct or impede an authorised person;
(iii)   fail or refuse to give information which a fire authority or an authorised person is entitled to require; or
(iv)   provide false or misleading information to a fire authority or an authorised person.

(b)   Codes of Practice and Guidance Notes issued by the Department of the Environment

A   CODE OF PRACTICE FOR FIRE SAFETY OF FURNISHINGS AND FITTINGS IN PLACES OF ASSEMBLY

12.85   This code of practice gives guidance, in respect of furnishings and fittings, to persons in control of places of assembly, to assist them in discharging their statutory duty with regard to the safety of persons on the premises. The code sets out standards and, where required, the tests necessary to establish compliance with these standards. In particular it recommends that foam and other filling material for use in seating should comply with tests similar to those prescribed for foam, fillings etc, for use in domestic furniture.

The items covered by the code include seating, curtains and blinds, floor coverings, stage curtains, stage scenery, cinema screens, and miscellaneous fittings and decorations.

Persons in control should satisfy themselves that furnishings and fittings which they are having installed in places of assembly have passed the required tests and that they comply with the standards recommended in the Code. They should ensure that they are supplied with certificates of the type indicated in the Code, which will give formal confirmation that the standards recommended have been complied with. These certificates should be retained by the persons in control and should be available for inspection, if required, by an authorised officer of the fire authority.

Compliance with the code does not absolve management of their **12.86** responsibility to comply with any separate measure which a fire authority may require in specific cases.

Where new or replacement furnishings and fittings are being provided, they should comply fully with the standards specified in the Code. As regards existing furnishings and fittings which may not fully comply with the recommendations, these should be replaced by furnishings and fittings which meet the recommendations as quickly as possible. In the meantime, during the phasing-in period of these new items, special care should be taken by persons in control of places of assembly to ensure that any shortcomings arising from deficiencies in the fire safety standards of the furnishings and fittings presently in place are compensated for by greater diligence being exercised in relation to the management of fire safety in the premises.

B   CODE OF PRACTICE FOR THE MANAGEMENT OF FIRE SAFETY IN PLACES OF ASSEMBLY

This Code stresses the importance of undertaking an appropriate fire **12.87** safety programme, and the need to appoint a responsible person to take charge of it. Day-to-day fire prevention measures are a key element in the fire safety management of premises and the Code recommends a number of appropriate precautions including the establishment of good housekeeping practices, periodic inspections, the identification and elimination of potential fire hazards both inside and outside the premises, and the application of safety rules.

Management and staff should undertake fire and evacuation drills so that they will be familiar with what should be done in the event of a fire occurring. In addition it is extremely important that members of the public in places of assembly should be fully aware of the fire safety precautions in the premises. This is achieved by the display of notices specifying the action to be taken in event of a fire or an alarm being given and also by announcements before the commencement of entertainment etc, and at regular intervals while the public are present.

12.88 The Fire Safety In Places Of Assembly (Ease of Escape) Regulations 1985 provide that certain fire safety precautions relating to escape routes and exit doors should be taken by every person having control over a place of assembly, and that a person in a place of assembly should not prevent or obstruct the person in control from complying with the regulations. The regulations are repeated in this Code, as ease of escape is an integral part of fire safety in places of assembly. Additional management guidance is given as to the precautions necessary to ensure the effectiveness of escape routes.

12.89 There is a duty on the person in control of the premises to take all reasonable measures to guard against the outbreak of fire on the premises and to ensure as far as is reasonably practicable the safety of persons on the premises in the event of a fire. This requires the provision of fire protection systems and equipment. The recommended measures for inspecting and maintaining this equipment are set out in the Code.

C   GUIDE TO FIRE PRECAUTIONS IN EXISTING HOTELS, GUEST HOUSES AND SIMILAR PREMISES

12.90 This guide is intended to apply to buildings of varying size and guest capacity. The guide sets out general principles of safety, which should be applied to the individual circumstances of each premises, rather than a set of rules. The approach outlined is intended to minimise the problem of trying to apply prescriptive, model-code design type requirements intended for new buildings to the lay-out and structure of existing premises. The approach proposed for dealing with individual premises requires analysis of the risk of fire occurring and the danger this poses to life and safety, the fire protection provided in a premises, and implementation of a programme of fire precautions to minimise the risk to life and safety. Maximum benefit will only be obtained when the recommendations of the guide as a whole are applied as part of a comprehensive approach to fire and safety.

12.91 Persons in control of existing hotels, guest houses etc are urged by the guide to review the fire safety of their premises by reference to the recommendations in the guide. The recommendations cover most aspects of fire and safety including the building itself, means of escape, the training of management and staff, fire safety management, the safety of furnishings and fittings and so on. In many cases, persons in control will have already in place many of the requirements and in such cases little or no action may be necessary as a result of the guide.

The provisions of the guide should, if correctly and carefully applied, minimise the number of fires and result in reduced potential for fatalities and injuries, as well as limiting property and consequential losses.

(iii)   Hygiene regulations

The operation of most catering establishments is subject to a statutory **12.92** registration procedure which is intended to protect public health against food illness. This statutory registration procedure can be found in Part V of The Health Act 1947 and also in section 38 of The Health Act 1953. Section 38 provides that regulations can provide for the licensing or registration of food premises and section 5 of the 1947 Act confers the power to make regulations on the Minister for Health. In this regard, the minister has created a registration scheme for certain food premises which is to be administered by the health authorities. The scheme can be mainly found in Part IV of The Food Hygiene Regulations 1950, as amended. Part IV of the 1950 Regulations (SI 1950/205) has been amended by the Food Hygiene (Amendment) Regulations (SI 1971/322 and SI 1989/62). The Irish scheme is not unlike the model scheme recommended by the World Health Organisation (see *Food Hygiene in Catering Establishments: Legislation and Regulations* (WHO, Geneva, 1977).

It is not provided in the Regulations who is to be subject to the registra- **12.93** tion procedure. But according to regulation 35, the Minister for Health will provide for the obligation to register food premises as he thinks fit. He has done so in regulation 3 of the Food Hygiene Regulations 1950. The Article includes hotels, holiday camps and restaurants. These types of premises must register with the appropriate health authority before engaging in a food business and failure to do so is a criminal offence.

For the purposes of the above registration, the following definitions apply:

(i)   Regulation 2 of the Food Hygiene Regulations (commencement of Part IV) Order 1951 defines a hotel in the following terms:

'Hotel' means a premises (a) which is registered in the Register of Hotels kept under Part III of the Tourist Traffic Act, 1939 . . . and (b) in which there is accommodation for six or more guests.

(ii)   The same Regulation defines a restaurant in the following terms:

'Restaurant' means a premises in which is carried on the business of selling meals to the public.

The health authority, in considering an application for the registration **12.94** of food premises, is empowered to make one of three decisions.

(i)   If it considers that all of the necessary hygiene standards have been met, it must register the premises and inform the applicant accordingly – section 42(2)(a).

(ii)   If it considers that one or more of the necessary standards are not being met and it does not consider it "expedient" to permit the food business to be carried on in the premises, it must refuse to register the premises and must inform the applicant of the refusal and of the ground for same – section 42(2)(c).

(iii)   If the health authority considers that one or more of the necessary standards are not being met, but it believes that it is "expedient" to allow the food business to be carried on subject to the necessary provisions being complied with, then it can grant a provisional registration of the premises for any period up to six months – section 42(2)(b).

12.95   A detailed discussion of the Hygiene Regulations 1950–71 in a work of the present length would not prove practicable, because of their number and length. However, to give an idea of what is generally expected in the area of food hygiene, the Irish Hotels Federation are presently drawing up a draft document entitled "Irish Standard for Hygiene in the Catering Sector". Although it is accepted that this document will have no statutory basis, it is important to see what would be regarded as the acceptable professional conduct in this area. Briefly, the general principles of the proposed standards are as follows:

12.96   (i)   Hygiene policy – management leadership should ensure a positive attitude and commitment of staff to hygiene.

(ii)   Food safety – great care must be taken when purchasing, storing, handling, preparing and cooking food and in the identification and analysis of risks and the establishment of controls to prevent these risks.

(iii)   Personal hygiene – with regard to the legal responsibility to behave in a manner which will safeguard public health, it is the responsibility of management to develop good personal hygiene practices in their staff.

(iv)   Cleaning – cleaning is an important operation for which staff must be adequately trained. They should be taught the principle of "cleaning as you go".

(v)   Pest control – the breeding and harbourage of pests is facilitated when the premises are not properly constructed and maintained in a clean condition at all times.

(vi)   Storage and transport – food on delivery should be inspected and immediately transferred to suitable stores, and precautions must be taken to ensure that the food is not contaminated during transportation.

(vii)   Zoning – the cooking of foods in different ways should be carried out in separate defined areas to prevent harmful micro-organisms which can be present in raw food being transferred on to ready-to-eat food.

(viii)   Services – proper ventilation, lighting, drainage and waste disposal services must be in place.

(ix)   Premises and structures – to protect public health, the premises, grounds, yards, forecourt and outhouses must be maintained in a hygienic condition.

(x)   Plant and equipment – plant and equipment should be properly installed, safe to use, suitable for the purpose for which it is used, and accessible for cleaning.

(xi)   Training – proper training in hygiene is essential for all food handlers, not just those with the professional qualifications.

(xii) Management training – management are responsible for complying with the requirements of the Irish Standard and to meet with this responsibility, they must be aware of those requirements.

5.   Time share regulation

While time share homes tend to conjure up images of Spanish villas and Portuguese apartments, the time share market in Ireland is in fact doing well, with non-Irish nationals buying homes here, and with an enthusiastic response from Irish people as well, who are keen to secure a holiday home in the country. However, the time share property industry as a whole has a dubious reputation, as many Irish people each year are misled by seductive advertising and persuasive selling by rough time share property dealers. It is not unusual that they have also been denied adequate time to read the small print on contracts. For example, last year, executives of a Gibraltar Company called CR Properties, accused by a British Government agency of operating a "time share scam" and of "misleading the public", set up offices in Dublin. The Office of Fair Trading, the British body which acts as a watchdog for consumers, alerted the Irish authorities, but a lacuna was exposed in consumer legislation. The Office of Fair Trading in London has difficulty in enforcing British consumer legislation overseas and the Director of Consumer Affairs of Ireland can only act if it receives complaints from an Irish resident. **12.97**

Ireland has no case law or statute law on time share arrangements, and for this reason the only action that can be taken in situations such as that mentioned above, is to inform the public and to keep a watch on the time share property company to see that no national legislation is breached by it. **12.98**

Ireland is backing EU action to stamp out abuses relating to time share properties, which have been the subject of increasing complaints in Ireland. Irish time share ownership is the third highest in Europe, coming next only to Britain and Denmark. EU present action is in the form of a Directive concerning the protection of purchasers in contracts relating to the utilisation of immovable property on a time share basis (47/1994 OJ L280).

The Irish Government has not yet enacted legislation in this area, and one would still be advised to exercise caution in dealing with property **12.99** transactions on a time share basis. Any person entering into this type of contract should take note of the following:

(i) the grounds and common areas will have to be maintained in good repair. As well as keeping the apartment or villa itself insured, one should enquire as to how precisely the charge for these matters is calculated, the role of the time share developer in determining the service charge, and the regulation for their collection;

(ii) obtain reputable legal and accounting advice before signing any documentation or parting with any monies. Legal ownership abroad is often quite different from the Irish system. Some time share owners have apparently found they have no legal title to the property when the lenders foreclosed on the development itself or when the promoting company went into liquidation;

(iii) obtain a clear translation of all documents and, while the services of a local lawyer will prove necessary, the purchaser should also ask his national lawyer and accountant for their views on the documentation;

(iv) finally, a purchaser should remember the underlying principle of the time share property transaction, as evidenced in the past, "caveat emptor", let the buyer beware. A purchaser should ensure that the proposed property has been inspected and approved by his architect and/or engineer.

6.   Passport and frontier control

(i)   Goods

(a)   Customs, baggage allowances and entitlements

12.100   If a journey to Ireland commenced in another EU country then, provided the flight or sea voyage did not originate outside the EC, a declaration to customs on arrival is no longer required.

If arrival is by air, exit may be made by the blue channel if it is in operation at the airport of arrival. If arrival is by sea, no red or green channels will be in operation, and exit may be made directly from the port of arrival without going through customs.

Customs will still carry out selective checks and quesitoning on intra-EU travellers to combat smuggling of certain prohibited goods such as drugs, pornographic material etc. A full list of prohibited goods is contained in the Customs and Excise Tariff.

(b)   Goods bought duty-paid/VAT-paid in other EC countries

12.101   There are still some essential differences in VAT rates between the Member States. A two-rate system has however been agreed in principle, with minor transitional arrangements for special cases. On 24 June 1991, the Council agreed in principle that, from 1 January 1993, the Member States would be subject to a standard rate of VAT, which would not be below 15%. In addition to this standard rate, the Member States would be allowed to apply one or two reduced rates, which would not be below 5%, but concerning which no maximum would be fixed. The standard rate of VAT in Ireland is 21%. A list of goods and services to which these reduced rates may apply has been compiled by the EU Commission. The list comprises essential products, as well as goods and services which correspond to social or cultural policy objectives (provided there is no risk to the distortion of competition). As far as the tourist industry is concerned, the list includes passenger transport, tourist accommodation (hotels, guest houses, etc), hire of camping sites, use of sporting facilities, and admission to theatres, cinemas, museums etc. Restaurant services are not included in the standard rate list, and therefore the rate of 12.5% will apply.

At present, provided that they are for personal use, there is no further duty or VAT to be paid on goods one has purchased duty-paid and VAT-paid in other EU countries. Excise products bought duty-paid/VAT-paid in other EU countries will normally be regarded as being for personal use if they fall within the following guide limits laid down by EU law: **12.102**

Cigarettes	800
Cigarillos	400
Cigars	200
Smoking tobacco	1 kg
Spirits	10 litres
Intermediate products (Port, Sherry etc.)	20 litres
Wine (of which only 30 litres can be sparkling)	45 litres
Beer	55 litres

The above are duty-paid/VAT-paid guide limits. If one's purchase of these goods exceed the guide limits, one must, if challenged by Customs, be able to show that they are for personal use, otherwise one will incur a duty liability. Because of derogation in the case of Ireland, the guide limits for wine and beer are lower in Ireland than in other EC countries. **12.103**

(c) Goods bought in duty-free shops

Under EU requirements, sales of duty-free and VAT-free goods to individual travellers are restricted by duty-free shop operators in all EU countries to the quantities below: **12.104**

Tobacco products:

Cigarettes	200 or
Cigarillos	100 or
Cigars	50 or
Grams of tobacco	250

Alcoholic drinks (excluding beer):

Alcoholic drinks exceeding 22% vol (*e.g.* whiskey, gin, vodka)	1 litre or
Alcoholic drinks (other than still wine) not exceeding 22% vol (*e.g.* sparkling or fortified wine, some liqueurs)	2 litres
Still wine	2 litres
Perfume	50 grams (60 mls)
Toilet water	0.25 litre (25 mls)

Other goods (including beer):
IR£142.00 per adult
IR£73.00 for under fifteen year olds.

12.105   Under seventeen year-olds are not entitled to any allowance for tobacco products or alcoholic drinks (including wine and beer). The "other goods" allowance applies only to individual items within the value limits specified.

Duty-free shopping as a concept is seen as contrary to the aims of the single market. However, there is a widely held belief that should such a concept be eliminated, the Transport Industry would lose an indispensable source of revenue. For this reason, the Council agreed on 11 November 1991, that the duty-free regime for sales to intra-Community passengers will be extended until 1 July 1999.

In line with the principles enunciated under the Treaty of Rome, namely the free movement of goods and removal of tax frontiers, the continuation of duty-free sales must operate without custom checks at frontiers. However, there must be a system of control and the Commission is drafting broad guidelines for an alternative system of control. It will be up to the Member States to work out the details and implement the system. The principle of any new system is that the control will be exercised by the shops authorised to sell goods duty-free, and not on individuals crossing frontiers. The authorised shops will not be allowed to sell more than a certain amount of dutiable goods per head per journey.

(d)   Intra-EU Travellers on non-EU flights

12.106   Travellers arriving at an EU airport on board a flight which originated outside the EU, regardless of nationality or country of residence, must clear Customs by going through the Red or Green Channel as appropriate.

(e)   Prohibited/restricted goods

12.107   Certain goods may not be imported, or if imported at all, must only be imported under licence. The principal items are firearms, ammunition, explosives, dangerous substances, indecent or obscene books etc, plants or bulbs, live or dead animals, poultry or birds, hay or straw or articles packed with these materials, meat or meat products. A full list of prohibited and restricted items is contained in the Customs and Excise Tariff of Ireland.

(ii) Persons

(a) General

We are all familiar with the EU principle of the free movement of persons within the territories of the Member States. But what does that principle mean for the tourist? The EU aims to abolish obstacles to the freedom of movement of persons, services and capital. Articles 48, 52 and 59 of the Treaty of Rome 1957 which deal with workers, the right of establishment and the right to provide services, do not provide for persons travelling abroad on holidays.

12.108

Therefore tourists, *prima facie*, would not appear to be covered under the Treaty of Rome.

However, the European Court has held, in Joined Cases 26/83 *Luisi* v *Ministero Del Tesoro* and 286/82 *Carbone* v *Ministero Del Tesoro* [1984] ECR 377, that persons travelling for the purpose of tourism, business, education and health are receiving services. The Court found that money spent by the tourists in the territory of another Member State was payment for services and decided that freedom to provide services included the freedom for recipients of services to go to another Member State in order to receive a service there. In the Court's view therefore, tourists must be considered as recipients of services, and payments concerning the receipt of such services abroad are not to be restricted under Article 106(1). In other words, tourists clearly come within the principle of the free movement of persons in the EU.

When a National of another EU Member State travels to Ireland, he cannot be refused entry, subject to the restrictions laid down in SI 1993/109, discussed *infra*. However, unless the tourist is from Northern Ireland or the United Kingdom, he is only permitted to stay in the country for three months. After this time he must visit the Aliens Section of the Garda Siochana Head Quarters, Harcourt Street, Dublin 2, to apply for an extension of time. The person will be required to fill out a Department of Justice application form for an Irish Residence Permit. However, if the Aliens Section Personnel are satisfied that the tourist is bona fide staying in the country for recreational activities and is not going to take up employment here, then they may grant an extension of time for which the tourist is allowed stay.

12.109

(b) SI 1993/109 – The Right of an EU National to land in Ireland

Any national of a Member State of the EC, in accordance with this Statutory Instrument, cannot be refused leave to land in Ireland unless:

12.110

(i)   such person is suffering from a disease or disability specified in the Second Schedule of the Statutory Instrument. A list of the diseases is contained under two headings.

(1) diseases which might endanger public health which include:
diseases subject to the International Health Regulations for the time being adopted by the World Health Assembly of the World Health Organisation;
tuberculosis of the respiratory system in an active state or showing a tendency to develop;
syphilis;
other infectious or contagious parasitic diseases in respect of which special provisions are in operation to prevent the spread of such diseases from abroad.
(2) diseases and disabilities which might justify decisions on grounds of public policy or which endanger public security, which include:
drug addiction;
profound mental disturbance;
manifest conditions of psychotic disturbance with agitation, delirium, hallucinations or confusion;

(ii)   such person's conduct has been such that it would be contrary to public policy or would endanger public security if such person was granted permission to land;

(iii)   such person cannot provide appropriate evidence that such person has sufficient resources to support himself or herself, their spouse and any accompanying dependants;

(iv)   such person is not able to provide appropriate evidence of full medical insurance in respect of himself or herself, their spouse and any accompanying dependants or;

(v)   such person is not able to provide appropriate evidence that such person is a national of a Member State of the EC.

12.111   Under the Package Holidays and Travel Trade Act 1995, travel companies must provide in their brochures details as to the visa and passport requirements involved in the holiday they are selling.

7.   Insurance requirements

(i)   General

12.112   Formerly, most tour operators insisted that package holiday clients take out mandatory insurance cover, which would be arranged by the tour operator. Both tour operators and travel agents who were selling these holidays earned a commission on this business and clients were captive to their insurer. People who already had insurance cover, for example those who booked their holiday by credit card (which included holiday insurance), might still be required to take out insurance with the tour operator's or travel agent's nominated insurer.

However, from 1993, people travelling abroad on package holidays are no longer obliged to take compulsory insurance from tour operators, following a decision by the Irish Competition Authority. The Authority decided that the policy adopted by the tour operator Falcon Holidays, to make insurance compulsory for customers without giving them a choice of insurer was not in the customer's best interest with respect to EU Competition law.   **12.113**

A travel agent however, may insist that any alternative insurance policy must ensure cover comparable to that offered by the travel agent. Under EC law, travel insurance is not mandatory. However section 12(c) of the 1995 Act, accept that package organisers may provide for mandatory insurance, but that this should not be interpreted as indicating that the regulations authorise a package organiser to restrict the consumer to one insurance policy selected by the package organiser.

The Competition Authority's ruling is given weight by the fact that a number of third parties made submissions to the Authority, including: the Irish Travel Agents Association; The Irish Brokers Association; The Irish Insurance Federation; The Department of Enterprise and Employment; The Consumers Association of Ireland; and The Director of Consumer Affairs. The majority of the submissions were critical of the "one policy" arrangement on travel insurance.   **12.114**

It has not been written in stone therefore that a travel agent restricting a customer to one insurance policy, is in breach of EU competition rules. EU competition law was given effect in Ireland by the Competition Act of 1991. The present emphasis under the Competition Act is on enforcement through private litigation in the courts. The primary role of the Competition Authority which was established under the 1991 Act is to review agreements which are notified to the Authority. Furthermore, it is not obligatory for parties to notify any agreement to the Competition Authority, as notification is a discretionary matter for the parties involved. However, there are proposals which will soon come before the Irish legislature which would give the Competition Authority power of enforcement under the Act. For this reason a Competition Authority ruling is not to be taken lightly.

In general holiday-makers taking out travel insurance are well advised to read the small print carefully, and to ensure that the policy includes: **12.115**

(i)   illness and accident cover that will meet the cost of medical or hospital expenses, emergency flights home (even by air ambulance), extra accommodation costs, travel expenses for a friend or family member, and the cost of returning one's remains in the event of death;

(ii) cancellation cover in order to reimburse the cost of flights and other expenses should one have to cancel one's trip due to illness, injury or a death;

(iii) personal accident cover, which also includes compensation for loss of a limb, eye, permanent disability and death. Many people already carry existing critical illness or permanent disability insurance; and

(iv) cover for loss of baggage and personal effects;

(v) cover in the event that the carrier, whether aeroplane, ferry, or bus company, goes into liquidation, because not all policies automatically insure against this. (However see section above on "Security".)

(ii) The E.111 form scheme

12.116 The E.111 form (in its long form, the "Certificate of Entitlement to Benefits in Kind During a Stay in a Member State") ensures that, at present, citizens of the Member States can enjoy benefits under the National Medical Insurance of other Member States as long as they have the E.111 Form that has been issued by their own health authority. Each country has a different procedure that tourists must follow in order to gain this complementary insurance. It is the Commission's objective to improve the Form E.111 scheme. A more effective system should be introduced containing an internationally recognised document which would enable the tourist to obtain on-the-spot treatment without having to make any initial payment, even if some payment becomes due at a later stage via administrative channels. (See ESC opinion on Tourism, Brussels, February 1984, 21, and ISEC/B5/90, 5.)

A Model for a European Emergency Health Card containing medical information required for the safety of high risk travellers, such as diabetics and people with heart conditions, has been drawn up by the Council of Ministers (see European File 9/87, 7: OJ 1984 C, Page 7 and ESC Opinion on Draft Council Recommendation on the adoption of a European Emergency Health Card: OJ 1984 C 206/11). Such sufferers from serious or chronic illnesses may need urgent medical attention in the event of accident or illness, and often cannot supply their medical history or detailed information with regard to their condition. This creates obvious problems when the tourist seeks medical attention in a foreign country and often through a foreign language. A specimen copy of a European Emergency Health Card is contained in the Annex to the Council Resolution regarding the same. (See OJ 1986 C 184/5.)

12.117 It is worth noting that EU citizens staying temporarily in another European country are entitled to urgent medical treatment on the same basis as residents of the country in which they are staying. It is essential, except in the case of visits to Britain (where the only requirement to qualify for an Irish person is the production of an Irish Passport), to have an E.111 Form to avail of these benefits.

The Form E.111 is available on request from the local health board. The details to be filled out on the E.111 Form (which is called in its long form, the "Certificate of Entitlement to benefits in kind during a stay in a Member State"), are the person's name, date of birth and RSI number. There is a section wherein details as to the names and dates of birth of one's family are to be inserted and a section where the person is to mark in the countries which the person intends visiting. The E.111 Form enables the person who fills out the form and the members of the person's family to obtain benefits in kind from health insurance bodies in the country they are visiting, in the case of sickness or maternity, and/or, provisionally, in the case of an accident at work or occupational disease.

When one of the persons concerned has to seek benefits, including hospitalisation, he should submit the form to the insurance body in the country in which he is staying. The relevant body in Ireland is the health board in whose area the benefit is claimed. The address of the relevant health board can be obtained from the Department of Health, which has its Administrative Head Quarters in Hawkins Street, Dublin 2. **12.118**

(iii) Car hire insurance

Each car hire operator has to provide for the purchase of insurance cover for himself and for his customers, in the light of all the material factors affecting the underwriting assessment of his particular risk. **12.119**

Some car hire operators display copies of their motoring insurance policies in their offices, and draw their customers' attention to these. Others display summaries of cover in a form authorised by their trade association. Some however, do very little to explain to the hirer what insurance cover is provided and what his non-insured contractual obligations will be in the event of trouble. One will find that the car hire operator will draw the hirer's attention to the policy, and that it will then be provided in the hire contract that the hirer is deemed to have full knowledge of the conditions of the insurance policy, and is bound by it as if it were incorporated in the rental agreement itself.

Hiring a car may involve two separate contracts, one with the car hire operator, and another with the insurers. As a potential hirer, one may be asked to complete and sign one document covering both aspects, or two separate documents. Either way one will have to give details of one's age, occupation, length of driving experience, details of one's driving accidents, motoring convictions and prosecutions pending, health defects and other details, and to produce one's current valid driving licence. **12.120**

The hirer will often have to warrant that the hirer and any other person who may be authorised to drive the vehicle is capable and competent to drive the vehicle, and often that they have driven such vehicles for a period of not less than, normally, two years. One may quickly find, because of the rules insurers have established for a car hire operator, that one is ineligible for one or more reasons – for example that one is too young or lacks the necessary driving experience. If so the only thing one can do is to see if another operator has easier insurance acceptance terms, because it is often these terms that control the operators' ability to do business.

12.121   Both the hire contract and insurance documents which are issued, normally make it clear that driving is permitted only by the hirer and by any other person whose full and satisfactory motoring particulars have been provided at the outset. Unless the hirer arranges insurance (which often can only be done with the prior approval of the hire operator), then the car hire company will provide insurance cover for persons using the vehicle only with the permission of the company. Once one has hired a car one cannot, even in an emergency, allow an unauthorised person to drive. One would be in breach of one's contract with the car hire operator and there would be no insurance in operation for that driver's protection, unless one could rely on one's personal insurance cover. In the circumstances, both the hirer and the unauthorised driver run the risk of prosecution.

In the event of an accident, the hirer will be required to immediately report the accident to the Police, and likewise to report the accident to the car hire operator. Whether it is so provided in the contract or not, the hirer should under no circumstances admit or acknowledge liability for an accident.

12.122   The extent of insurance cover which the car hire operator has, in addition to the statutory minimum, is widely variable. The larger operators are more likely not to preclude insurance against accidental damage, fire or theft risks. This does not mean that such operator will inevitably make the operator's hirers responsible for the cost of repair or replacement in the event of damage, fire or theft. Often if the car hire operator is satisfied that the loss or damage to the vehicle during the rental period was not attributable in whole or in part to the act, neglect or default of the hirer or any person for whom the hirer was responsible, then the operator may not require the hirer to pay the full amount. It is essential to look at the clauses of the hiring contract to see if such penalty is imposed in any particular circumstances. If the hirer has his own motor policy and wishes to have peace of mind, it is of course possible to ask for his insurers to add the damage/repair risk on the hired car to his own policy for the term of the hire – but the hirer will of course have to pay an extra premium for this. As a hirer there is only one certainty – that the cover that the operator has in force is substantially less than the normal comprehensive cover that most Irish motorists buy. The car hire company will often not incur any liability or be responsible for loss or inconvenience to the hirer, or any other person whomsoever resulting from delivery delays, break-downs or any causes whatever beyond the car hire operator's control. The company will not generally be responsible for the hirer being unable to use the vehicle during the rental period due to adverse weather conditions, petrol or fuel shortages or due to any other reason whatsoever outside the car hire operator's control.

(iv) The Motor Insurers Bureau of Ireland

Should the driver of a vehicle, whether on hire or owned by the driver, and whether driven by a resident of Ireland or by a non-national, be involved in an accident where a third party is responsible and that third party has deficient insurance cover, then any personal injury claim of the former can be addressed to the Motor Insurers Bureau of Ireland (MIB). The MIB is based on the principle that, if damages are awarded in a court for death or personal injury arising out of the negligent use of a motor vehicle in a public place, and such damages or a part of them remain unpaid after 28 days from the date when the judgment becomes enforceable, then the MIB will pay the amount unrecovered, including taxed costs, provided the claim falls within the terms of the MIB agreement with the government.   **12.123**

(v) Compensation for criminal injury

The Irish Government has in operation a scheme of compensation, for out-of-pocket expenses only, arising from personal injuries criminally inflicted upon a person. This would include compensation for payments such as medical fees, travelling expenses, prescription costs, etc. The scheme is administered by the Criminal Injuries Compensation Tribunal, (CICT) the members of which are appointed by the Minister for Justice and are either practising barristers or solicitors. Compensation is payable out of monies provided by the state. The Tribunal has an address at 13, Lower Hatch Street, Dublin 2.   **12.124**

The CICT may pay *ex gratia* compensation, which is in the form of a lump sum and is in accordance with the scheme in respect of expenses, where the injury is directly attributable to a crime of violence or circumstances arising from the action of the victim in assisting or attempting to assist the prevention of a crime, or the saving of human life. The injury must have been sustained within the state or aboard an Irish ship or aircraft. The word "injury" as used in the scheme includes a fatal injury.

Applications should be made as soon as possible but, except in circumstances determined by the Tribunal to justify exceptional treatment, not later than three months after the event giving rise to the injury. To qualify for compensation, the claimant must be able to show to the Tribunal that the offence that caused the injury has been the subject of criminal proceedings, or that it was reported to the Garda Siochana without delay,   **12.125** or that all reasonable efforts were made to notify the Gardai of the offence and to co-operate with them.

An applicant may be accompanied by his legal adviser or another person, but the Tribunal will not pay the costs of legal representation. Claims are submitted by completing the Tribunal application form which is obtainable from the secretary to the Tribunal at the aforementioned address.

12.126   The European Court of Justice has ruled on the point whether tourists are entitled to claim state compensation in assault cases. In Case C186/87 *Cowan* v *Le Tresor Public* [1990] CMLR 613, Mr Cowan was a British citizen on a visit to his son who was staying in Paris. Mr Cowan was assaulted when exiting from a Metro Station and he successfully relied on Article 7 of the Treaty of Rome. The Court held that in the case of persons to whom EU law guaranteed the freedom to travel to another Member State, the principle of non-discrimination laid down in Article 7 of the Treaty of Rome prevented that state from making the grant of state compensation for physical injury caused to the victim of an assault in that state subject to the condition, either that he held a residence permit, or that he was a national of a country which had a reciprocal agreement with that Member State. The Court referred to the fact that although criminal legislation and criminal procedural rules fell within the province and within the competence of Member States, it was well established that EU Law defined the limits to that competence. Tourists travelling to Ireland are therefore, entitled to claim under the CICT Scheme.

8.   Financial services

(i)   General

12.127   A single market in which goods, services, and persons circulate freely can only be an effective market if the related capital movements also circulate freely. This equally applies to money spent on tourist services by tourists. For the internal market to be complete, the restrictions placed on capital transfers had to be eliminated. If a tourist is to pay for services which he receives in another Member State he will obviously have to export cash, cheques, or some other means of payment. The European Court of Justice has held in the Joined Cases *Luisi* v *Ministero Del Tesoro* and *Carbone* v *Ministero Del Tesoro* [1984] ECR 377, that persons travelling for the purpose of tourism, business, education and health, are receiving services. Accordingly, they could not be made subject to restrictions with regard to payments. Member States are allowed to maintain controls only for the purpose of checking the nature of transactions, for example, checking that a payment is really a currency transfer for the purposes of tourism. *Luisi* and *Carbone* were criminally prosecuted in Italy for breach of currency regulations. They had been accused of taking out of the country foreign currency in excess of the maximum allowed by Italian law. They claimed that the money had been taken out for the purpose of tourism and medical treatment. The Court had to decide whether the payment for these services constituted movements of capital or were merely payments for the provision of services. It found that the money was in fact payment for services and ruled that freedom to provide services included the freedom for recipients of services to go to another Member State to receive a service there.

The European Commission is of the opinion that exchange controls **12.128** considered necessary by certain Member States must not become obstacles to tourism. It is envisaged that in future the ECU will be the common denominational currency and will be used widely as a form of currency, and this would benefit the tourist in particular. At present ECU travellers' cheques are available in all Member States and there is even a credit card in ECU.

(ii) Credit cards

(a) General

The legal rules governing the use of credit cards relate to the implied **12.129** contract between the card issuer and the user. Copies of the terms and conditions are available from the card issuers and they do not vary to any great extent from one credit card company to another. The tourist should pay attention to the following common conditions of use.

The amount of all card transactions, whether originated by the principal card-holder or by an authorised user, will be debited to the credit card user's account. The principal card-holder shall be liable to pay all amounts so debited whether or not a sale or cash advance voucher is signed by the card-holder. Should the card-holder wish to query or dispute any card transaction, he should do so within the number of days provided in the conditions from the date of the transaction being charged to his account.

The credit card company may, from time to time, re-issue a credit card. **12.130** The credit card company may terminate the card facility at any time without notice, or refuse to re-issue, renew or replace the card without affecting the principal card-holder's liability in respect of all prior card transactions. The credit card shall be returned by the principal card-holder on demand by or on behalf of the credit card company. In addition, the credit card company may for reasonable cause, request a merchant to retain and cancel the card (usually by cutting it into two pieces) and to return it to the credit card company.

The card-holder may at any time terminate the agreement with- **12.131** out affecting his liability in respect of all card transactions, fees, charges, interest and costs, by giving notice in writing to the credit card company and returning his card cancelled again, usually by cutting it in two pieces.

If a card is lost or stolen, or if the personal identification number

(PIN) becomes available to any other person, the card-holder must immediately notify the credit card company. Until the credit card company receive effective notification of the loss or theft of the card and/or disclosure of the PIN, the card-holder may remain liable in respect of any unauthorised use of a card. The card-holder shall remain liable, without limitation, in the event that the unauthorised use of the card has been caused or contributed to by the breach by a card-holder of the agreement between himself and the credit card company.

A card-holder whose card is lost or stolen must give the credit card company all information relevant to such loss or theft and must give all reasonable assistance to lead to the recovery of the card. If the card previously reported lost or stolen is recovered, the credit card company usually insists that it be immediately cut into two pieces and returned to them. The card-holder is responsible for taking all reasonable steps to ensure the safety of the card.

Credit card companies disclaim liability if the card is not accepted by third parties for reasons beyond the control of the credit card company.

The amount of any card transaction in a currency other than Irish pounds will be converted at a rate of exchange determined by the credit card company on the date that the card transaction is charged to the company.

Some credit card companies may provide insurance, where for example a trip has been paid for with the card, although all companies stress that this should not be regarded in any way as an alternative to full travel insurance.

(b) Consumer Credit Act 1995

12.132   The Consumer Credit Act 1995 (the "Act of 1995") is designed to give the consumer the maximum amount of information possible in relation to the full costs of borrowing money. The Act covers overdrafts, hire-purchase, credit sales, cheques, credit cards and budget accounts.

Under the Act of 1995, all credit agreements will have to be in writing and signed by the consumer and by or on behalf of all other parties to the agreement. The consumer must be given a copy of the agreement within ten days of signing the document. The consumer then has a so-called "cooling off period" of ten days from the date of receipt of the agreement to withdraw. The agreement must contain: the annual percentage rate of charge (APR); a description of the goods or services covered; a cash price and the credit price; the amount of interest paid; the total amount repayable; and the intervals at which interest is calculated, and, in the case of a credit card, the credit limit and the terms of repayment.

The Consumer Credit Act 1995 will have the effect of ensuring that advertisements for credit are both informative and meaningful.

The Minister for Commerce, Science and Technology intends to bring forward separate regulations which shall lay down clear and composite rules on the advertising of various forms of credit. Section 21 of the Act outlaws the use of any rate of interest, other than the APR, in advertisements for credit. The present practice whereby the nominal rate of interest and the APR are shown together tends to confuse rather than enlighten the consumer. At present, consumers are faced with a barrage of advertising relating to the grant of credit associated with the sale of goods, particularly cars and household items, or the supply of services. In future these advertisements must specify:

- the cash price of the goods or service;
- the total cost of credit;
- the number and amount of instalments;
- the duration of the intervals between instalment payments;
- the number of any instalments which have to be paid before delivery of the goods; and
- details of any deposit payable.

The provisions of the Consumer Credit Act 1995, relating to the form **12.133** and content of credit agreements, combined with the force of the EC (Unfair Terms in Consumer Contracts) Regulations 1995, which render all unfair terms illegal, add up to a powerful protection for consumers.

The minister also proposes to bring forward regulations which shall provide for total transparency of all costs, commissions, expenses associated with housing loans and the related insurance policies.

The justification for banks and financial institutions imposing transaction charges is understandably resented by most consumers and businesses. In this respect one of the most welcome provisions in the Act is the transfer of responsibility for bank charges from the Central Bank to the Director of Consumer Affairs. This will ensure a much more rigorous and effective system of control.

(c) European banking industry – Code of Best Practice

There is in place a Code of Best Practice of the European banking industry **12.134** on card-based payment systems. This document constitutes the European Credit Sector Association's (ECSA's: that is, the Association of Co-Operative Banks of the EU, the Banking Federation of the EC and the European Savings Banks Group), response to the European Commission's "Recommendation concerning payment systems and in particular the relationship between card-holder and card issuer" 88/590/EEC of 17 November 1988 (OJ L317 1988). It has been compiled by the three ECSAs after consultation with consumer organisations and the Commission of the European Communities.

The Code takes into account the Commission's objective to ensure consumer protection throughout the Community on one hand, and the need to maintain competition between service providers as well as a choice of cards with different features to the benefit of the customer on the other hand. Since the main concern lies with the provision of payment facilities to the individual consumer, the Code of Best Practice covers bank payment (credit and debit) cards used by private individuals for their own purposes. It excludes the guarantee function of payment made by cheque.

12.135   It is intended that the Code should be implemented according to the provisions of national law. There is no specific legislation governing the relationship between credit card issuer and credit card user in place in Ireland. The terms and conditions are regulated by the Central Bank. It acts as a general watchdog over issues such as rates of interest charged, terms of repayment and the general relationship between the parties.

The Code of Best Practice provides that the card issuer must make available to the card-holder, in writing, a set of contractual terms and conditions governing the issuing and use of the card. These terms seek to maintain a fair balance between the interests of the parties concerned and must be expressed clearly and be available in the official language of the Member State in which the card is offered.

The terms must specify the basis of any charges, but not necessarily the amount of charges at any point in time. In addition they should specify the period in which the card-holder's account would normally be debited or credited, or within which the card-holder would normally be invoiced. The terms may be altered, but sufficient notice of the alteration must be given to the card-holder, to enable him to withdraw if he so chooses (however any change to an interest rate shall not be subject to the foregoing).

12.136   In relation to the personal identification number (PIN) the card-holder is placed under the obligation to take all reasonable steps to keep safe the card, and the card-holder is under the obligation not to record the PIN or other code, if any, in a form that would be intelligible or otherwise accessible to a third party.

12.137   The card-holder must be provided within a reasonable time, with a written record of a transaction after he has completed it, in a form such as the customary bank or credit card company statement. In addition the card-holder must be provided with a written record immediately after the transaction is completed.

The issuer is to bear the loss of the amount arising from an unauthorised transaction made with the card after the card-holder has notified the issuer in accordance with the relevant terms, of the loss, theft or copying of the card. However, if the card-holder has acted fraudulently, knowingly, or with gross negligence, the card-holder will bear the full loss of the unauthorised transactions made after notification, notwithstanding the issuer's obligation to take all action open to it to stop any further use of the card. The card-holder will bear loss sustained up to the time of notification to the issuer of any loss, theft or copying of the card, but subject to a limit which is to be regarded as reasonable in relation to the type of card in question. However, if the card-holder had been acting fraudulently, knowingly, or with gross negligence, he will be liable to the full amount of loss.

Finally, if the card-holder denies that his card or his PIN have been used to make a transaction, or alleges that such a transaction has been incorrectly executed, the issuer must show, by providing an abstract of its own internal records that the operation was accurately recorded and entered into accounts and was not affected by technical breakdown or other deficiency. The correct recording of previous and subsequent similar transactions shall constitute *prima facie* evidence that the system was functioning properly. In any event should a problem arise in this regard, a complaint may be made by the card-holder to the Irish Ombudsman for Credit Institutions (*infra*). **12.138**

Such a problem was the subject of a decision of the Ombudsman detailed in the 1993 Annual Report of the Ombudsman. A customer discovered that sums of money were withdrawn from his account by the ATM system at different locations and he was certain that he had not made these withdrawals. The Ombudsman sought and was given copies of printed records of the disputed withdrawals and the copy of the branch reports, and ATM debit list, which listed all transactions for the relevant dates. These records showed that there were no irregularities with the workings of the ATMs in question. The Ombudsman concluded that the disputed withdrawals were made by a person who had used the customer's card and knew his PIN, and therefore held for the card issuer.

(d) The Ombudsman for credit institutions

The Ombudsman for credit institutions is an independent and impartial arbitrator of unresolved complaints between a customer and a bank or building society. Under the scheme, the Ombudsman receives and considers certain types of unresolved complaints from individuals in relation to the provision of customer services by participating credit institutions in order to facilitate the satisfaction, settlement or withdrawal of such complaints. All the major banks and building societies in Ireland are participating members of the scheme. The Ombudsman's decision is binding on the credit institutions but not on the complainant. **12.139**

The Ombudsman cannot deal with complaints which concern matters which came to light before 1 October 1990 unless it was reasonable for the complainant not to have known about it before that date. He cannot deal with the matter where the amount in dispute is greater than £25,000.

(iii) Traveller's cheques

In Ireland, traveller's cheques are considered to be cheques, within the meaning of the Bills of Exchange Act 1882 ("the 1882 Act"). In this regard, the normal rules relating to cheques, their status, condition, negotiability or transfer, equally apply to traveller's cheques. Users of traveller's cheques should note the factors set out below. **12.140**

(a) Lost cheque

12.141 In the case where a completed cheque is lost while it is believed to be still in the possession of the drawer, that is before he has issued it, the drawer should inform the banker on whom the cheque is drawn of its loss, and request that a stop be put against its payment in case it should be presented for payment. The Banker can, and most often will, insist that any such request or instruction should be in writing. Very often it is discovered that items which are reported lost have only been temporarily mislaid. The banker, in this situation, must protect himself against the eventuality of the cheque being found and put in circulation by the drawer without notifying the banker of that fact and without cancelling the earlier stop payment instruction.

(b) Replacement of lost cheque by drawer

12.142 The 1882 Act makes provision for the replacement of a lost cheque by means of the issue of a duplicate. Section 69 provides that when a cheque is lost, the holder may compel the drawer to give him another cheque in identical terms, provided the drawer is indemnified against any claim which may be made against him in the event that the lost cheque is found and presented for payment.

(c) Stolen cheques

12.143 Where a cheque is believed to have been stolen, its disappearance should be notified immediately to the banker on whom the cheque was drawn and to the Police. If the cheque is stolen, or believed to have been stolen, while in the possession of the payee or indorsee, the drawer should be notified and requested to place a stop with his banker against payment. The banker is unlikely to accept stop instructions from anyone other than the drawer – his customer. This could apply equally to a cheque reported to have been stolen from the payee or indorsee.

(d) Forged cheques

12.144 Section 24 of the 1882 Act deals with forged signatures on Bills of Exchange. The section states:

> "Subject to the provisions of the Act, where a signature on a bill is forged or placed thereon without the authority of the person whose signature it purports to be, the forged or unauthorised signature is wholly inoperative, and no right to retain the bill or give a discharge therefor or to enforce payment thereof against any party thereto can be acquired through or under that signature, unless the party against whom it is sought to retain or enforce payment of the bill is precluded from setting up the forgery for want of authority.

Italy

Chapter 13
Italy

Stefano Dindo*

Studio Legale Dindo

1. Regulatory authorities

(i) State and region

The organisation of the tourist trade in Italy and the role of the various **13.1**
boards and offices concerned can be better understood if the latter are
briefly placed in context by a review of the territorial divisions established
in the Italian constitution. The relevant constitutional provision in this
respect is the division of the nation into *Regioni* (regions), each comprising
a number of *Province* (provinces) which are in turn divided into *Comuni*
(local authorities).

Each *Regione*, or region, can issue laws pertaining to legislative sectors
listed in the Constitution or, in the case of certain regions, in their
special statute. The Italian system differs in this respect from a federal
organisation, in which the legislative sectors which must be specifically
listed are those under centralised jurisdiction and all those not specified
are automatically decentralised. In Italy, only specified sectors fall within
the scope of regional legislation, all others being the concern of the
central state.

The tourist and hotel trades are among the areas of activity for which **13.2**
legislation in Italy is created by the regions. This provision is, however,
subject to the consistency of regional laws with the "fundamental principles"
laid down by state law. In this respect, Article 117 of the Constitution
specifies that the issuing of regional legislation cannot be opposed to the
interests of the nation or of other regions.

The "fundamental principles" are laid down in national laws known as
leggi quadro (*i.e.* "laws providing a framework"). These formulate the principles to be observed in regional legislation, and administration, ensuring
consistency and uniformity. In many cases, the *leggi quadro* contain not
only a broad statement of intent, but also more specific requirements.

Constitutional jurisprudence specifies that foreign policy is the responsibility only of the state. The regions are thus not empowered to draw
up agreements involving the responsibility or liability of the state towards
other nations. They are, however, allowed to pursue promotional activities

---

* Stefano Dindo has practised as a lawyer in Verona since 1977, as part of the Studio Legale
  Dindo. This legal firm has existed since 1919 and currently comprises seven lawyers, dealing
  mostly with commercial, banking and bankruptcy law.

abroad, subject to the agreement and overall co-ordination of the government.

13.3 An important, controversial issue for the tourist trade is the implementation of European Community regulations. In this respect, the regions are empowered to apply such regulations and to implement the Directives of the European Community "once the first Community law following notification of the Directive has taken effect" (Art 9, Law 86/1989); in practical terms, this means once the Italian Parliament has enacted the annual law by which it is required to update national legislation in fulfilment of Community Directives.

The state law which implements Community Directives for any sector in which the regions have jurisdiction (including tourism) will indicate which basic principles cannot be waived by regional law. The state law also specifies that, in the absence of regional law, it will be wholly applicable, even in those areas for which the region could provide different legislation subject to the Community Directive.

Against this background, the tourist trade involves separate legislative roles of the state and the regions.

13.4 The legislative authority of the state is exercised, in compliance with the Constitution, by the national Parliament. Regional legislative authority is exercised through the *consigli regionali* (regional councils), as specified in the statutes of the regions.

The administrative functions of state and region work in the following way:

(ii) State administration

13.5 Until 1993, the administrative role of the state for matters pertaining to tourism was fulfilled by the Ministero del Turismo (Ministry of Tourism). With the implementation of a regional legislative and administrative system, the creation of the regions was thought to preclude any need for the continuing existence of the Ministero del Turismo. It was therefore abolished as the result of a national referendum held in April 1993.

The new organisational structure of the state administration has been recently redefined with the new statute No 203 of 30 May 1995. This new law, on the one hand, expressly transferred to the regions all the competency and administrative functions – so doing away with the Ministry of Tourism – and has also given the President of the Council of Ministers the general co-ordinating functions:

(i)   the conduct of international relations and Italian participation in the preparation of Community policies;

(ii)   the preparation of Acts and the pursuit of general activities necessary for the enactment of rulings passed by Community institutions, including the Court of Justice;

(iii)   the overall co-ordination and direction of the regions, to ensure, among other objectives, the uniform promotion of the image of

Italy abroad, development of the national tourist market and promotion of group tourism.

The state bodies operating within the tourist sector include the *Ente* **13.6** *Nazionale Italiano per il Turismo* (State Tourist Board), commonly abbreviated to ENIT, which is responsible for the international promotion of tourism within Italy. To this end, the Board can set up offices in other countries. Its functions include the co-ordination of international tourist promotion by other national organisations and bodies.

(iii) Regional administration

Regional laws are executed and regional administrative functions fulfilled **13.7** by a *giunta regionale* (regional executive committee), elected by the *consiglio regionale*. This *giunta* comprises a chairman and a number of *assessori* or regional officers, each with responsibility for a specific sector. The *giunta* includes an *assessore al turismo*, or officer in charge of tourism.

Each region thus has an *assessorato al turismo* (tourism department), which prepares and implements the resolutions of the provincial executive committees. The officer in charge of tourism may also be delegated to perform given administrative functions, which in this case will be carried out directly by his department rather than by the executive committee collectively.

Promotion of local tourist attractions, supervised by the region, is carried out by local bodies called *aziende di promozione turistica* (local tourist offices). Subject to regional authorisation, these also set up public information offices. Generally, the regions delegate part of their competency to the *Province* (provinces) or they can delegate their powers to the *Comuni* (the local authorities).

Matters delegated to provincial and local authorities vary from region **13.8** to region. In many regions, for example, the provincial executive committee is responsible for issuing authorisations to open an *agenzia di viaggio e turismo* (travel agency) and ensuring that regulations concerning travel agencies are enforced. It may also examine applications for authorisations to work in tourism-related activities (guide, language assistant, ski instructor, mountain guide, etc).

In many regions, local authorities are delegated to apply regulations concerning the classification, surveillance and control of tourist accommodation (hotels, residences, camping sites, etc).

In conclusion, the region fulfils its administrative role either directly (through the *giunta regionale* or *assessorato al turismo*), or by delegation. In the latter case, the regional offices in question ensure that administrative duties are carried out by the relevant bodies at provincial level (*giunta provinciale, assessorato al turismo*), or by local authority councils and the departments specifically concerned. The exact nature of the responsibilities given to the provinces varies from region to region, but they are generally quite extensive. Applications are thus, in practice, filed with the province for many of the authorisations required within the tourist trade.

13.9 The review of the organisation of the tourist trade in Italy would not be complete without a brief reference to the many trade associations involved. For example, travel agents and tour operators have three such associations, with offices throughout the country. The same is true of hoteliers.

13.10 These associations are subject to private law and their activities create binding obligations only for their members. One important exception in this respect is the associations' role in negotiating collective employment contracts with their employees' trade unions, since the minimum salary conditions specified in these contracts are applicable to all persons employed in the sector concerned, irrespective of whether they belong to an association.

2. Legal and professional rules

(i) General

13.11 Regulations pertaining to travel agencies and tour operators are set out in the national *legge quadro* (No 217 of 17 May 1983), and in regional laws consistent with the fundamental principles of state legislation.

Some regions have not as yet made regional laws: in these circumstances the applicable law is still that of the old law of 1937 which was modified in 1955 (No 630/1955).

Article 9 of the *legge quadro* defines travel agencies and tour operators as companies which create and organise travel and holidays; equally, they may act as intermediaries for such services. Their activities may include provision of assistance and accommodation for tourists.

Travel agents and tour operators in Italy are thus subject to the same legal regime, in that authorisation for the two activities is subject to the same requirements, and both can be undertaken by the same company.

(ii) Authorisation

13.12 The Italian term *agenzia di viaggio e turismo* (literally, "travel and tourism agency") refers to a company which can perform the services of both travel intermediary and travel organiser. These activities are subject to regional authorisation, issued to applicants satisfying the following requirements:

(i)   knowledge of the administration and organisation of travel agencies;

(ii)   technical, legislative and geographical knowledge of tourism-related matters; and

(iii) knowledge of at least two foreign languages.

Authorisation is subject to payment of a bond (which in some regions may be waived in favour of a bank guarantee). This is held as a guarantee that the obligations of the travel agent/tour operator are correctly fulfilled.

13.13 If the owner of a company authorised to trade as a travel agency/tour operator does not work full-time within this company, the relevant professional requirements must be fulfilled by the person in day-to-day charge of the agency. There is a regional list of persons recognised as fulfilling the requirements for the role of technical director within a travel agency. This list is updated annually, on the basis of an examination organised by the regional authorities. Successful candidates can ask to be included in the list.

13.14 Authorisation to run a travel agency is subject to prior clearance of the application by the Police. This can be denied if the applicant has been sentenced to at least three years' imprisonment without rehabilitation for a deliberate offence, has been on probation or has been declared a persistent offender.

Foreign individuals or companies can obtain regional authorisation subject to a declaration of suitability by the state authority with jurisdiction in such matters (at the time of writing, the Prime Minister). No such restriction applies to citizens of the European Community, who are treated in the same way as Italian citizens. In this respect, Italy has implemented EC Directive 82/470 of 29 June 1982, incorporated into Italian law as Law No 428/29 December 1990 and citizens of the EC can prove the absence of moral and financial impediment by producing an extract from their "judicial record" or, failing this, an equivalent document issued by the Italian authorities or those of the relevant country of origin. Other forms of proof, as specified in Article 3 of the EC Directive, are provided for in Article 3 of the Legislative Decree. The applicant can demonstrate fulfilment of the relevant professional requirements by producing a certificate issued by the foreign state concerned. This document will certify professional experience as owner-manager, or as person in charge/manager of at least a department within an agency, for the minimum duration required by the law implementing the Directive.

13.15 In many regions (not in Liguria and Tuscany) the granting of regional authorisation is also subject to the numerical restrictions of a "regional plan" which specifies the number and distribution of *agenzie di viaggio e turismo* within the region concerned. The purpose of this "plan" is to ensure a uniform spread of agencies throughout the region. It is based on consideration of the numbers of visitors, hotel capacity, population and the economic status of the area.

This system "caps" the number of travel agencies and tour operators within a region. If all authorisations in the plan have been exhausted, new companies cannot be authorised. This means that the only way to commence trading (subject to the requirement listed above) is to buy an existing agency as a going concern.

13.16   It is important to note that the *Autorità Garante della concorrenza del Mercato* (fair trading authority) produced a formal report on 30 June 1995 that a predetermination on an administrative level of the maximum number of travel and tourism agencies could hinder new initiatives, confine those existing, and presumably reduce the total amount of activity by determining the position of monopolistic revenue which is a disadvantage to the consumer. Consequently, the *Authorità Garante* has "reported" the need for modification of those regional legislations which provide for a limitation in the number of authorisations.

The significance, in practice, is that the problem has been raised and the direction indicated by the *Autorità Garante* is to eliminate numerical restrictions; in fact, in these situations one could ask for more time.

Finally, we observe that the national *legge quadro* does not oblige the travel and tourism agencies to provide insurance policies guaranteeing the fulfilment of its obligations towards the client. This requirement is generally specified in individual regional laws, though the minimum sum to be insured remains discretionary.

13.17   Moreover, Article 20 of the Legislative Decree of 17 March 1995 No 111, which implements the EC Directive on Package Travel (90/314) states that the parties to the contract, the travel organiser and the retailer have to be covered by an insurer for civil liability towards the consumer for damages which derive from the default or inaccurate execution of the services which form the basis of the package tour.

(iii) Liability

13.18   The liability of the travel organiser and the travel intermediary will be analysed in the following section regarding the consumer's rights and safeguards.

In this section, we note that the travel organiser or the travel intermediary cannot limit their liability to less than the minimum set out by the international conventions which Italy and the European Union have ratified. In particular, the limits set forth in the Warsaw Convention of 12 October 1929 (concerning international air travel), in the Bern Convention of 25 February 1961 (concerning train travel), and in the Brussels Convention of 23 April 1970 (known as the International Convention on Travel Contracts, hereafter, "CCV"). This is true for the contracts subject to the conditions of the CCV and for those subject to the conditions of the legislative decree of 17 March 1995 No 111, which implemented EC Directive No 90/314 on package travel, package holidays and package tours.

13.19   In these latest conventions it is clear that if these limitations on liability for damages are different to those applying to the person included in the general terms of the contract set forth by the travel intermediary or organiser, there is a special procedure according to which the terms must be specifically approved in writing by the client. As a result of this requirement, the client's approval must be attested to by two signatures – one for acceptance of the general terms of the contract and the other for specific acceptance of the clause regarding limited liability. This is consistent with a general provision of Italian law (Art 1341 of the Civil Code), applicable to all contracts, in which the general terms are laid down by one party including items considered unfair towards the other party.

In conclusion, note that there are travel contracts which are not subject to CCV, nor to the Lesiglative Decree No 111 of 1995 on package holidays. Further, it is theoretically possible for travel agencies to limit their liability without restriction.

13.20 Nevertheless, if the limitation is included in the general terms of the contract set forth by the travel intermediary or organiser, the terms must be specifically approved in writing by the client, as described above. In any case, agreements excluding or limiting liability for fraud or gross negligence are null and void.

The activity of travel intermediary or travel organiser in Italy can be carried out by an individual or a company. Apart from the regulations indicated above, there are no special rules applicable to the travel and tourism agencies as a whole, or for companies operating within the tourist sector; the general rules applicable to any other commercial activity will thus be applicable.

Travel intermediaries and organisers are clearly classed as "traders"/ "businesses" and as such, are subject to bankruptcy law. If the intermediary or organiser can no longer meet his obligations, the court within whose territorial jurisdiction his activity is based can declare a state of bankrupcty. In this case, an administrator will be appointed to recover all the assets of the business and distribute them to creditors subject to *par condicio creditorum.*

13.21 Bankrupcty law is complex and, for reasons of space, cannot be fully dealt with here. It should, however, be appreciated that Italian law gives priority to certain "privileged" creditors such as employees and tax authorities. The client of a travel intermediary or travel organiser is not "privileged" in this way, and in most cases does not receive even a percentage of the credit due in the event of bankrupcty. It should also be noted that, to obtain recognition of a credit in bankrupcty proceedings, it is not sufficient that the credit concerned should be demonstrated by the accounts of the bankrupt concerned. Each creditor must make a specific application, complete with supporting documentation, to the judge designated by the competent court for examination of credit eligibility.

In conclusion, it is important to note that the recent Legislative Decree of 17 March 1995 No 111, implemented the EC directive on package travel, package holidays and package tours (90/314). This new legislation has introduced Article 21, which consists of a guaranteed fund for the purpose of allowing, in the case of insolvency or bankruptcy of the seller or travel organiser, the reimbursement of the price of the tour, or repatriation of the consumer in the case of travel abroad; further, in emergency situations, to provide immediate monetary aid where there has been forced repatriation of tourists from countries which are not members of the EC.

13.22   In fact, the fund is not yet in operaton; it will be operational when the formality of its management and financing has been determined by the Council of Ministers.

3.   Consumer rights and safeguards

(i)   General

13.23   Italy is a signatory of the CCV, drawn up in Brussels on 23 April 1970. This convention was ratified in Italy by Law No 1084 of 27 December 1977.

Article 40 of the agreement leaves participating states the power to decide the extent of its application. Accordingly, Italy has limited its implementation "solely to international travel contracts to be wholly or partly performed in a different state from that in which the contract was drawn up or from which the journey was started". Moreover, with the Legislative Decree of 17 March 1995 No 111, Italy has implemented the EC Directive No 90/314 on package travel, package holidays and package tours. The subject of the travel contract is not the same in all situations: it is therefore necessary to distinguish on the basis of the applicable law in every travel contract.

13.24   There are three possibilities:

A   Contracts subject to Legislative Decree No 111 of 1995.
This legislation in fact governs the vast majority of these contracts, and is applicable under the following conditions:

(i)   the contract must deal with a package tour which has as its objective travel, holidays and package tours, resulting from the pre-arranged combination of not fewer than two of the following when sold or offered for sale at an inclusive price, and when the service covers a period of more than a 24-hour period or includes overnight accommodation:
(a) transport
(b) accommodation
(c) other tourist services not ancillary to transport or accommodation and accounting for a significant proportion of the package;

(ii)   the package tour must be sold or offered for sale in Italy by a travel organiser or by a retailer, authorised by law;

(iii)   the law is still applicable even if the package tours are negotiated outside the commercial areas of the tour organiser and the retailer.

Therefore, some contracts are excluded from the applicable law per-   **13.25**
taining to the package tours; some examples are as follows:

(i)   package tours with a duration of less than 24 hours or, in any case,
       that do not comprise overnight accommodation;
(ii)   travel contracts that have different purposes than recreation which
       are distinct from tourist contracts (*eg* travel in order to participate
       in a course of study, symposiums, etc).

B   Contracts Subject to CCV
If the law on package tours is inapplicable then the CCV applies to
any travel contract concluded by a travel organiser or intermediary
where his principal place of business is one of the countries which apply
the convention. "Travel contract" means either an organised travel
contract or an intermediary travel contract; "organised travel contract"
means any contract whereby a person undertakes in his own name to
provide for another, for an inclusive price, a combination of services
comprising transportation or any other service relating thereto. "Intermediary travel contract" means any contract whereby a person undertakes to provide for another, for a price, either an organised travel
contract or one or more separate services rendering possible a journey
or sojourn.

C   Contracts that are not subject to CCV nor to the legislation pertaining to package tours
An example of this is a package tour with a duration of less than 24 hours
which is purchased and carried out only in Italy, or, even, any contract
where there is not a combination of at least two elements indicated by
the CCV or from the law on package tours.

This type of contract is derived from the laws contained in the Civil   **13.26**
Code, which does not contemplate a specific rule for travel contracts; it
applies by analogy the laws expected for a contract having the same legal
nature.

Nevertheless, while one can say that the legal nature of an intermediary travel contract is that of an agency contract (with the same consequences that would apply – *eg* the general rule pertaining to agency),
the legal nature of the contract finalised by the travel organiser is far
more controversial. There have been different proposals concerning the
travel contract in this respect, such as, a transport, mediation, agency or
sale contract – or as a completely separate entity. The most common view
is that it is most appropriately characterised as an independent contract
(*contratto d'appalto*).

In the description of the laws applicable to the travel contract that
follow, reference will be made first to the rules of the CCV, and then a
demonstration of the difference in the rules in the law on package tours
and the Civil Code.

(ii)   Liability of the travel intermediary

13.27   Article 22 of the CCV specifically deals with the liability of the travel intermediary, stating that:

> the travel intermediary shall be liable for wrongful acts or default he commits in performing his obligations, wrongful acts or default being assessed having regard to the duties of a diligent travel intermediary.

The same article also states that: "The travel intermediary shall not be liable for non-performance, in whole or in part, of journeys, stays or other services governed by the contract".

Liability of the travel intermediary is limited to 10,000 gold francs (*ie* as specified by Art 24 of the Convention).

Concerning contracts subject to the law on package tours, Article 14 of Legislative Decree No 111 of 1995 anticipates that:

> In the case of missing or inaccurate non-fulfilment of the duties assumed by the sale of the package tour, the travel organizer and the seller are held liable for the damages, according to their respective liability in the matter, if it is not proven that the missing or inaccurate performance of their duties was caused by the impossibility of the performance. The organizer or the seller who avails himself of third party services must in any case compensate for the damages sustained by the consumer, save the right of the travel organizer to receive indemnification from those third parties.

13.28   Finally, concerning contracts that are not subject either to the CCV, or to the law on package tours, the applicable discipline, by analogy, is that of an agency contract for which the agent (being the travel intermediary) is bound to execute the order with the diligence of the pater familias (Art 1710 para I of the Codice Civile), and inform the party on whose behalf the order is to be carried out (being the client) of the occurrence of circumstances which might determine its revocation or modification (Art 1710 para II of the Civil Code).

In application of these principles, it has been ruled, for instance, that a travel intermediary charged with the finalisation of a travel contract was liable for not having informed a client of the formalities required for entry into a foreign state (in this case, a client refused entry into Egypt because he was not previusly informed of the need for a visa).

(iii)   Liability of the travel organiser

13.29   For contracts subject to the CCV the liability of the travel organiser is specifically subject to Articles 13, 14 and 15 of the Convention. Such liability clearly applies also to non-fulfilment of obligations by third parties from whom the travel organiser commissions services, albeit subject to the limitations explained below.

For contracts subject to the CCV, any clauses describing the travel organiser as a simple intermediary between the client and individual providers of services (hotels, transport companies, etc) will thus be null and void.

The CCV gives scope for four different views of the travel organiser's liability. According to Article 13:

the travel organiser shall be liable for any loss or damage caused to the traveller as a result of non-performance, in whole or in part, of his obligations to organise as resulting from the contract or this Convention, unless he proves that he acted as a diligent travel organiser.

The non-performance of obligations described here occurs when the travel organiser:

omits to organise (or to organise adequately or to organise in time) any of the necessary conditions for the traveller to be able to enjoy all the services specified in the contract, with the result that the traveller either cannot enjoy them or cannot enjoy them in the terms in which they had been promised.

This is the case, for instance, if a hotel is of a lower class and quality **13.30** than promised, or if an excursion specified in the contract cannot take place because the organiser has not made the necessary arrangements. In such cases, the organiser is not liable if he can prove that he acted as a diligent travel organiser.

Article 13 thus applies to non-performance of obligations in terms of travel organisation. Article 14, on the other hand, concerns cases in which the services described in the contract are provided directly by the travel organiser. In such cases, the organiser is liable "for any loss or damage caused to the traveller in accordance with the rules governing such services".

In other words, if, for example, the travel organiser is directly involved in transport arrangements, and the transport service in question is not satisfactorily performed, the organiser will be deemed liable on the basis of the legislation pertaining to transport. If the unsatisfactory service concerns hotel accommodation, the legislation pertaining to hotel services will apply, and so on.

Article 15 paragraph I, specifies a third possible form of liability, in so far as:

where the travel organiser entrusts to a third party the provision of transportation, accommodation or other services connected with the performance of his journey or stay, he shall be liable for any loss or damage caused to the traveller as a result of total or partial failure to perform such services, in accordance with the rules governing such services.

In such cases,

The travel organiser shall be liable in accordance with the same rules for any loss or damage caused to the traveller during the performance of the services, unless the travel organiser proves that he has acted as a diligent travel organiser in the choice of the person or persons performing the service.

13.31   This provision is neither easy to interpret nor readily distinguishable from that in Article 15 paragraph I. The difference is that paragraph I makes provision for "total or partial failure to perform such services", while paragraph II specifies "loss or damage caused to the traveller during the performance of the services". In the first case, the client's enjoyment of the service is wholly or partly precluded, while the second instance applies to situations in which the client enjoys the service but, in so doing, suffers loss or damage (*e.g.*, loss of possessions left in the safe-keeping of the hotel, or personal injury as a result of non-compliance with safety regulations).

The situations specified in these two paragraphs differ considerably in terms of liability. In the second case, the travel organiser is not liable in accordance with the rules governing the services involved, but solely in terms of *culpa in eligendo* – *i.e.*, only in so far as he is unable to prove that he has acted as a diligent travel organiser in choosing the third party to whom provision of the service has been entrusted.

The liability has an upper limit for each passenger of 50,000 francs for personal injury, 2,000 francs for damage to property and 5,000 francs for any other damage.

13.32   When the travel organiser is liable in accordance with the rules governing individual services, his liability is subject to the limitations specified in relation to those services. Where no limits are specified, those listed in CCV Article 13 paragraph II, will apply.

If the actual damage incurred exceeds the limits set out in Article 13, the traveller can seek reimbursement of the difference by applying directly to the provider of the service, in accordance with Article 15 n 4 of the CCV.

The travel organiser who has compensated the traveller can, in turn, apply for indemnity to the third party responsible for the damage.

The CCV clarified the specific liability of the travel organiser for actions attributable to the third parties whom he enlists for the fulfilment of orders; nevertheless, such laws have been criticised due to their limitations on liability. Now, the new law on package tours (115/1995) has improved the consumer protection rights. In particular, Article 14 of the Decree Law on package tours, No 111 of 1995, which establishes without exception that if the travel organiser avails himself of third party services, compensation must be given for damages that derive from the non-fulfilment of the contract by them. Therefore, the new limitation supersedes the limitations in Article 15 of the CCV, which entailed a limitation of the liability of travel organisers in the *culpa in eligendo*. Concerning the limits on liability in the law on package tours, it is necessary to distinguish between the liability for damages to the person and other forms of liability.

13.33   Article 15 of the Legislative Decree No 115/1995 anticipates that damages to the person will be compensated to the limits of the international conventions to which the European Union and Italy are parties. In particular, the limitations anticipated by the convention of Warsaw which concerned international air transport, the convention of Bern concerning rail transport, and the CCV.

Regarding damages other than those to the person, Article 16 of Legislative Decree No 115/1995, anticipates that, if the amount of compensation is not specifically stated in the travel contract, the amount of damages will be determined by Article 14 of the CCV, which we have already examined (for each traveller 50,000 francs for personal injury; 2,000 francs for damage to property; 5,000 francs for any other damage).

The contract could anticipate a different subject, but, in any case, the amount of compensation for damages will not be less than that which was established by Article 13 of the CCV.

One can see that while Article 15 expressly states that the limits anticipated by the international conventions will apply for the amount of damages payable in respect of personal injury, only the limits anticipated by Article 13 of the CCV will apply in respect of other damages. These limits could be much higher than those anticipated by the international conventions, and that is why there seems to be an apparent contradition in the new legislation on package tours which must be clarified during its application.

Lastly, we must examine the liability of the contracts which are not **13.34** subject either to the CCV, or to the legislation on package tours. We have already mentioned that the answer on this point depended upon the legal nature of the travel contract and that this argument is still the subject of discussion.

Assuming, *arguendo*, that the legal nature of the travel contract is the same as that of an independent contract, (*contratto d'appalto*), the travel organiser will also be liable for defective performance of services by third parties such as hoteliers or transport companies (according to Art 1228 of the Civil Code).

Unless the parties agree otherwise, the debtor who in fulfilling his obligation has recourse to the services of third parties is also answerable for wrongful acts or default by the latter. The liability of the travel organiser is, in any event, excluded when the missing part or inaccurate execution of the contract is attributable to the consumer or is dependent upon an event which was unforeseeable or unavoidable or due to *force majeure* (provided by Art 17, Legislative Decree No 115 of 1995). This is also a general principle applicable to all contracts.

Finally, it is important to note that in contracts subject to the Legisla- **13.35** tive Decree on package tours there is a statute of limitations for actions arising from the travel contract; this is three years for personal damages and one year for damages to the person in relation to transport services comprised within the package tour (eighteen months if the transport began outside Europe) and one year for any other damages (Arts 15 and 16). In contracts subject to the CCV (Art 16) the statute of limitations is two years in cases concerning death, wounding or other bodily or mental injuries, and one year for all other actions; in contracts that are not subject to either the CCV, or to the decree of law on package tours the statute of limitation is ten years – the period generally applicable to all contracts. Where damages derive from transport services, the statute of limitation is one year, rather than eighteen months if the transport began or terminated outside Europe (Art 2951 of the Civil Code).

(iv) Travel agreements

13.36   In addition to regulating the liability of the travel organiser, the CCV makes provision for other aspects of the travel contract having particular importance for the client. When the travel contract is drawn up, for example, the client must be given a travel document bearing the agent's signature or stamp. The attached programme must also be given to the client. The document or programme must detail the terms of the travel contract, including the names of the parties, dates and places of beginning and end of the journey as well as of any stops, all necessary specifications concerning transport, accommodation, the minimum number of travellers required, price, circumstances and conditions under which the traveller may cancel the contract, and any clause providing for arbitration.

A breach by the travel organiser of the obligation to provide the above document does not affect the existence or validity of the contract, which is binding even if not in written form. The travel organiser is, in any case, liable for loss or damage resulting from any breach of this obligation.

13.37   The new law on package tours has made consumer protection more effective, due to a series of provisions which have the purpose of guaranteeing that the consumer receives all necessary information about the trip, that there is a correlation between what is published in the brochure and the substance of the actual travel contract, and that variations, if any, of the conditions will be communicated to the consumer in advance, so that he can decide what to do.

In particular:

Article 9 of the new legislation on package tours anticipates that when a brochure is made available to the consumer, it shall indicate in a clear and accurate manner both the price and information on:

(i)   the destination and the means, characteristics and categories of transport used;

(ii)   the type of accommodation, its location, category or degree of comfort and its main features, its approval and tourist classification under the rules of the host Member State concerned;

(iii)   the meal plan;

(iv)   the itinerary;

(v)   general information on passports and visa requirements for nationals of the Member States concerned and health formalities required for the journey and the stay;

(vi)   either the monetary amount or the percentage of the price which
         is to be paid on account, and the timetable for payment of the
         balance;
(vii)   whether a minimum number of persons is required for the
         package to take place and, if so, the deadline for informing the
         consumer in the event of cancellation;
(viii)   the terms and the method by which the consumer can exercise his
         right to withdraw from the contract in cases where the contract is
         negotiated outside the commercial areas.

The information contained within the travel brochure binds the travel
organiser and the retailer, in relation to their respective liabilities. Modification of conditions to the contract must either be communicated in
writing prior to the signing of the contract or can be communciated
subsequent to the signing as long as it is in writing.

13.38

Article 8 of the new law on package tours stipulates that during the
course of negotiation, but prior to conclusion of the travel contract, the
travel organiser or the retailer must supply to the consumer information
on the applicable laws pertaining to the passport. In addition, prior to
the beginning of the trip the travel organiser must provide information
dealing with schedules, telephones numbers, information on the
optional inclusion of an insurance policy to cover the cost of cancellation
by the consumer or the cost of assistance, including repatriation, in the
event of accident or illness.

Article 7 of the new law on package tours stipulates that the travel contract must contain at least the elements listed in the Article: in particular,
all the elements which were specified by the EC Directive on Package
Tours as follows:

(i)   The amount that has to be paid for the reservation, with the clarifi-   **13.39**
         cation that any amount cannot exceed 25% of the total price and
         that the said amount is *a caparra*, which means, *inter alia*, in the
         application of Article 1385 of the Civil Code, that if the party who
         tenders *caparra* (the consumer) is in non-fulfilment, the other
         party could withdraw from the contract and retain the *caparra*; if,
         instead, the non-fulfilment is on the part of the travel organiser,
         the consumer could withdraw from the contract and demand twice
         the amount of the *caparra* in damages. This rule is not applicable,
         however, if the termination of the contract is dependent upon new
         circumstances for which the travel organiser is not liable.
(ii)   The limits of the insurance coverage and further insurance
         policies agreed on by the traveller.
(iii)   The possible expenses placed upon the consumer for the transfer
         of a contract to a third party.

(iv)   The period within which the consumer must communicate his choice, where there have been intervening modifications to the conditions of the contract.

(v)   The conditions and manner of intervention in the Guarantee Fund in the case of insolvency of the seller or of the travel organiser.

(v)   Modifications of the contractual conditions, cancellations and substitutions

13.40   Article 10 of the CCV provides scope for cancellation of the contract by the travel organiser; specifying that such cancellation is possible:

> if before the contract or during its performance, circumstances of an exceptional character manifest themselves of which he could not have known at the time of conclusion of the contract, and which, had they been known to him at that time, would have given him valid reason not to conclude the contract.
>
> The travel organiser may also, without indemnity, cancel the contract if the minimum number of travellers stipulated in the travel document has not been reached, provided the traveller has been informed thereof at least fifteen days before the date on which the journey or stay was due to begin.

13.41   The client may also cancel the contract at any time, in whole or in part, provided he compensates the organising travel agent in accordance with domestic law or the provisions of the contract. Failing contractual provision, the travel agent must be compensated in accordance with the general principles pertaining to payment of damages, calculated according to the expenses incurred by the travel agent, the work undertaken and any loss of earnings.

The traveller may substitute another person

> for the purpose of carrying out the contract, provided that such person satisfies the specific requirements relating to the journey or stay, and that the traveller compensates the travel organiser for any expenditure caused by such substitution, including non-reimbursable sums payable to third parties.

The new law on package tours takes the substance of the EC Directive as it applies to modification of the contractual conditions, cancellations and substitution.

13.42   Article 11 of this new law anticipates that the revision of the selling price cannot be more than 10%, and can only be done if the possibility of revision was expressly stated in the contract – along with a defined method of calculation in consequence of variation in the cost of transportation, fuel, landing taxes, embarkation and disbarkation in ports, and applicable taxes on exchange. If the increase in price is more than 10% the consumer may withdraw from the contract and obtain reimbursement; in any case, the price cannot increase within the twenty days prior to departure.

If withdrawal by the consumer is determined by the variation in price or by the modification of the contractual conditions in the terms described above, or if the package tour is cancelled for any reason, unless by the fault of the consumer, Article 13 of the law on package tours allows the consumer:

- to receive another package tour equivalent or superior to the original, with no added expense, or a travel package which is qualitatively inferior, but with restitution of the difference in price;
- to obtain reimbursement within seven business days following the moment of discovery of the rescission or cancellation;
- to demand compensation for any further damages dependent upon the non-execution of the contract, save that the cancellation was not due to a *force majeure* or because the minimum number of participants needed for the package was not complete, and the consumer is notified in writing at least twenty days prior to the date of departure.

Article 10 of the law on package tours deals with, in conclusion, the **13.43** transfer of the contract agreed upon, if the consumer declares that he finds it impossible to make use of the package tour – provided that such communciation also contains the identity of the transferee and is effected in writing at least four days prior to departure.

The transferor and the transferee are, in any event, both bound for payment to the travel organiser or retailer.

(vi)   Misleading advertising

This account of consumer protection regulations would not be complete **13.44** without reference to national legislation on misleading advertising (Decree No 74/25 January 1992), contracts negotiated away from business premises (Legislative Decree No 50/15 January 1992) and on unfair terms in consumer contracts (Legislative Decree No 52/6 February 1996), which execute Community Directives 84/450/EEC and 85/577/EEC and 93/131, respectively.

The Italian regulations faithfully incorporate the definitions and criteria of evaluation specified in Articles 2 and 3 of the Community Directive on misleading advertising. In particular, Article 2 of Decree No 74/1992 implements Article 2 of the EC Directive:

> "misleading advertising" means any advertising which in any way, including its presentation, deceives or is likely to deceive the persons to whom it is addressed and which, by reason of its deceptive nature, is likely to affect their economic behaviour or which, for those reasons, injures or is likely to injure a competitor or anyone else.

Article 4(4) of the law on package tours specifically prohibits the **13.45** supply of misleading information on the method of the offered service, on the price and on the elements of the contract – by whatever means the aforementioned information is communicated to the consumer.

(vii) Contracts negotiated away from business premises

13.46 The general provisions of Decree No 50/15 January 1992 regarding contracts negotiated away from business premises also apply as far as the travel contract is concerned. These provisions apply to contracts negotiated when the trader visits the home of the consumer or of another consumer, or the place of work of the consumer, or premises on which the consumer is temporarily present for reasons of work, study or treatment, or during an organised excursion, or by signing an order, or by correspondence, or by ordering from a catalogue which the consumer has been able to consult without the trader. In such cases, the trader is obliged to inform the consumer in writing that he has the right to rescind the agreement, indicating the time limit to be respected and the procedure to be followed for this purpose. The right of cancellation is subject to written notice by registered letter, enclosing a prepaid acknowledgement slip, within seven days of the consumer being informed by the trader of such right. Failing any such information to the consumer, the time limit within which the consumer can avail himself of the right to cancel is 60 days from the date on which the contract is signed. It is sufficient that the letter is posted within the required time limit. It is not necessary that the trader must receive it before the expiry of this limit.

13.47 Notice of cancellation may also be sent by telegram, telex or fax, subject to confirmation by registered letter within 48 hours of such notice.

Within 30 days of cancellation, the trader must reimburse any monies received.

(viii) Unfair terms in consumer contracts

13.48 Italy has implemented the EC Directive 93/13 on unfaur terms in consumer contracts in the Legislative Decree No 52/6 of February 1996.

The method adopted by the Italian legislature is to add to the Civil Code five articles in the section of the code which governs general disposition on contracts.

In the application of the new law, in contracts concluded between the consumer and the *professionista* (defined as any natural or legal person, acting for purposes relating to his trade, business or profession) terms which have the object or effect of:

(i)   excluding or limiting the legal liability of a seller or supplier in the event of the death of a consumer or personal injury to the latter resulting from an act or omission of the seller or supplier;

(ii)   excluding or limiting the legal rights of the consumer *vis-à-vis* the seller or supplier or another party in the event of total or partial non-performance or inadequate performance by the seller or supplier of any of the contractual obligations;

(iii)   irrevocably binding the consumer to terms with which he had no real opportunity of becoming acquainted before the conclusion of the contract;

are ineffective (Act 1469 5th of the Civil Code).

Article 1469 2nd of the Civil Code lists a series of clauses which are **13.49** ineffective unless these terms have been subject to specific negotiation with the individual consumer.

Where the contract is concluded by means of a predetermined form prepared by the *professionista*, then he bears the burden of proof that the unfair clause was the subject of specific negotiation with the consumer.

The list of the unfair terms stems from those supplied in the EC Directive which we have previously referred to (see Art 3 of the Directive and Annex). With regard to package tour contracts, we must note that consumer protection against unfair terms is in any case assured through the specific rules examined in the previous section.

4.   Forms of redress

Decisions of the courts regarding travel contracts are few and far **13.50** between, despite the enormous numbers of such contracts throughout the country. It has been stated that this is not so much because no issues arise as:

> because it is risky for a client to address them, given that compensation is difficult to quantify and in any case limited; the law offers no definite solutions; and tour operators are sufficiently rich to sustain protracted legal proceedings. (G. Minervini, *Il Contratto Turistico*, Riv Dir Comm 1974, p. 278)

If the consumer intends to sue the travel organiser or travel intermediary for non-fulfilment of obligations undertaken as a result of the travel contract and file a claim for damages, he must take legal action. This means engaging legal assistance in accordance with the normal practice for actions in the civil courts. The expense involved can be considerable, even though in the Italian system the party who loses the action must pay both his own legal expenses and those of the other party.

There are no particular procedures or controlling bodies which can, if they deem fit, undertake legal action on behalf of the consumer. The travel contract may, however, contain a clause conferring jurisdiction on an arbitration tribunal. In this event, the case will be decided by the arbitrators, appointed in accordance with the specific provisions of the clause concerned.

It should also be noted that some regional laws provide scope for the **13.51** consumer to file a complaint with the relevant regional authority (Chairman of the Provincial Authorities), reporting the travel or tourist agency for not complying with the law or fulfilling its obligations.

The Chairman of the Provincial Authorities can fine the agency if certain laws are not complied with. An example would be the regulations concerning the preparation and distribution of travel programmes.

5. Rights against transport operators

(i) General

13.52 The transport contract obliges one party (the carrier) to transfer persons and things from one place to another, for a fee.

Two distinct forms of transport are concerned: of persons, and of things. For the latter, the carrier must ensure their safe-keeping during transport. This obligation is not expressly stated where transport of persons is concerned, since nothing is specifically entrusted to the safe-keeping of the carrier; his obligation in this case is to transport the person, and to ensure the traveller's safety and the integrity of his baggage during the journey. It is the traveller's responsibility to co-operate in avoiding damage to his person and the baggage which remains in his keeping, other than in the event of its being explicitly entrusted (as in air transport) to the carrier's safe-keeping.

The general principle in terms of the carrier's liability is established by Article 1681 of the *Codice Civile*, which states that:

> other than liability for any delay or failure in terms of providing transport, the carrier answers for any damage to the traveller's person during travel and for loss of or damage to such effects as the traveller carries with him, unless the carrier can prove that he has implemented all appropriate precautions to avoid damage.

13.53 The burden of proof for the traveller amounts only to demonstrating the existence of the travel contract, the extent of damage sustained and the connection between this and the transport. The traveller is not bound to demonstrate the fault of the carrier: the carrier is exempt from liability only if he can prove, not only that the damage is attributable to a coincidence or to actions by a third party or by the traveller, but also that he took all appropriate precautions to avoid such damage.

This general rule applies to road and rail transport, as well as to air and water transport. The only waivers are those specified in the navigation code and in special laws which differ according to the type of transport involved. Since these special laws create distinct regulations according to the form of transport involved, these should be treated as separate items.

(ii) Transport of persons by road

Bus transport is subject to the relevant general regulations of the transport contract.   **13.54**
Accordingly:

(i)   the general principle to be applied is that set out in Article 1681 *Codice Civile* (*supra*), specifying that the carrier is liable if he cannot prove that all appropriate measures to avoid the damage concerned were taken;
(ii) there being no limit to the carrier's responsibility to compensate for the damage, full compensation must be provided;
(iii) in the case of cancellation, the carrier must compensate for any damage incurred.

(iii) Transport of persons by rail

Rail transport of persons is subject to the regulations covering the terms   **13.55** and tariffs of the state, specified in Law No 911 of 11 October 1935 and subsequent amendments up to and including Law No 754 of 7 October 1977.

In terms of cancellation or delay of the scheduled services, failure to provide a connection, or forced discontinuation of travel, the only obligation of the rail company is to offer the journey or completion of the journey free of charge on another line or train, if possible. If this is not possible or the traveller does not intend to use the replacement service, he can claim a refund of the fare paid if the delay exceeds one hour; if no connecting service is available; or if there is no room for him to board. In this case, the traveller must claim the refund on the same day on which the ticket is purchased or the journey is discontinued. No damages are payable.

In the event of injury arising from a rail accident, the traveller (or, in the event of death, his heirs) has a right to compensation, unless the rail company proves that the accident occurred for reasons for which it cannot be held responsible.

The rail company is liable for any delay in returning baggage to its   **13.56** owner, as well as any damage related to total or partial loss or deterioration thereof, unless it proves that the delay or damage occurred for reasons for which it cannot be held responsible. There are strict compensation limits, differentiated for delay, loss and damage of baggage.

Compensatory action must be taken within one year of the ticket's expiry date, and should be pursued in the ordinary magistrates' courts. Before starting legal action, application for a refund must be made to the railway authorities (except in cases of personal injury), by which it may be accepted or rejected.

If no reply to the application is received within the specified period of

120 days (90 for luggage), the applicant can file a complaint directly with the courts.

(iv) Transport of persons by sea

13.57 Transport of persons by sea is subject to the national "navigation code" and to international agreements.

The relevant legislation in relation to ship transport is Articles 396–418 of the navigation code. Articles 408 and 409 restate the general principles specified in the *Codice Civile* (*supra*), specifying the liability of the carrier for damage incurred by the passenger as a result of delay or cancellation of the service, other than in the event of the carrier proving that the cause of the event cannot be attributed to him (Art 408). Article 409 of the navigation code specifies the carrier's responsibility for personal injury to the passenger as a result of events occurring "from the time of boarding to the time of disembarking", again with the exception of cases in which the carrier can prove that the cause of the event is not attributable to him.

The interpretation which most favours the carrier is that he will be exempt from liability if he can demonstrate that all required protective measures and precautions were taken with due diligence. However, it seems preferable to adopt the stricter view that the carrier must in any case identify the cause of the damaging event and prove that this event "is attributable to fortuitous circumstances or *force majeure*, in other words an unforeseeable element which could not be avoided by his or his employees' actions".

13.58 In terms of international agreements, Italy has not yet ratified the Athens Convention of 13 December 1974, amended by the London Protocols of 19 November 1976 and 30 March 1990. This Convention is far less favourable to the passenger than the relevant Italian regulations, specifying that the burden of proof is to be borne by the damaged party (other than in the event of shipwreck, collision, explosion or defects of the vessel) and that a limit of 700,000 gold francs for each instance of transport is applicable (increased to 175,000 special compensation rights by the 1990 London Protocols).

The reason for which Italy has not ratified the Convention is that the limitation of the carrier's liability is not consistent with a ruling of the Italian Constitutional Court (*sentenza* No 132/1985, also relevant to air transport – *infra*), which allows limitation of the carrier's liability for death or personal injury only if the limitation is appropriate and the law guarantees the passenger compensation. These conditions do not appear to be fulfilled by the Athens Convention.

13.59 The navigation code also covers cancellation or delay of the scheduled service. Where the cancellation is not the fault of the carrier, the passenger may choose either to consider the contract no longer binding, or to make the journey, where possible, on another ship, with a right to compensation of up to double the price of the ticket. This limit on compensation only applies if the cancellation occurred for justified reasons, in the absence of which the damage incurred must be fully covered.

In the event of delay, the passenger has a right to compensation for the damage incurred, as well as board and lodging at the carrier's expense, if these were due to be provided during the journey.

(v) Transport of persons by air

International air transport of persons and things is subject to the conventions collectively referred to as the Warsaw system. This comprises the Warsaw Convention of 12 October 1929 (ratified and implemented in Italy by Law No 841 of 19 May 1932), modified by the Hague Convention of 28 September 1955 (ratified and implemented in Italy by Law No 1832 of 30 December 1962) and the Guadalajara Convention of 18 September 1961 (ratified and implemented in Italy by Law No 459 of 11 June 1967).   **13.60**

Italy has also implemented the further modifications of the Convention specified in the Guatemala Protocol of 8 March 1971 (incorporated into Italian legislation as Law No 43 of 6 February 1981), as well as authorising ratification of the four Montreal Protocols of 25 September 1975. When these protocols are implemented internationally, they will automatically become effective in Italy.

The points set out below on uniform international regulations should be briefly highlighted.   **13.61**

According to the Warsaw Convention, the carrier is exempt from liability if he proves that he took all necessary measures to avoid the damage incurred or that it was impossible for him to take such measures (Art 20). The Guatemala Protocol (ratified by Italy, but not yet internationally implemented) exempts the carrier only when death or personal injury occur as a result of the passenger's state of health (Art 4) or when the passenger caused or contributed to the damage incurred (Art 7).

The Convention limits the carrier's liability for each passenger and item of luggage. In this respect, it is worth noting the important ruling of the Italian Constitutional Court (No 132 of 6 May 1985), allowing limited liability only subject to a sufficient guarantee of sure and appropriate compensation. Failing this condition, the Court considers that the limited liability provided for in the Convention is contrary to the inviolable personal rights safeguarded in Article 2 of the Italian Constitutional Court. Accordingly, the principle of limited liability specified in Law No 84/26 March 1983 has been declared unconstitutional.

Subsequently, Law No 274/1988 ruled that, for flights subject to the Warsaw Convention and those scheduled via Italian airports, the carrier can avail himself of limited liability as provided for in the Convention,   **13.62**

407

subject to the contract specifying a compensation limit of 100,000 special compensation rights, and an equivalent maximum limit for the carrier's civil liability.

13.63   The carrier cannot avail himself of limited liability when:

(i)   he did not issue the ticket or issued it without notice of limited liability;

(ii) the passenger proves that the damage is attributable to an act or omission of the carrier or those acting for him, with wilful intent to damage, or awareness of the likelihood of damage (Art 25).

For international transport, the Warsaw Convention makes no direct provision for liability in respect of unregistered baggage, although the specified compensation limit of 5,000 gold francs per item of baggage (Art 22 n3), subsequently changed to 332 special compensation rights by Law No 84/26 March 1983, presupposes such a provision. For registered baggage, the Convention makes the same provision as for goods, albeit with different transport documents and time limits for claims (seven days for loss or damage and 21 days for delayed delivery – see Art 26 n2).

13.64   Transport not subject to the Warsaw system is covered by Articles 941 *et seq* of the navigation code, which provide substantially the same terms as the Convention. For the purposes of this survey, the important points are:

(i)   scope for the carrier to be exempt from liability if he can demonstrate that all necessary and possible measures were taken to avoid the damage, with all due diligence (subject to the obligation, generally specified in current jurisprudence, that the carrier identify the cause of the damage and indicate the concrete measures implemented to avoid the damage);

(ii) limitation of the liability for death or personal injury (currently L195 million), with no such limitation for wilful damage or severe negligence (navigation code, Art 943);

(iii) the obligation to insure passengers against injury;

(iv) limitation of liability for loss of luggage to L33,000 per kilo.

13.65   The navigation code makes provision for failure of the carrier to fulfil his obligation to provide transport, the relevant item in this respect being Article 942:

> (*Liability of the carrier in transport of persons*). – The carrier is liable for damage resulting from delay and non-performance of transport, as well as accidents to the person of the traveller, from the commencement of embarkation to the completion of disembarkation, unless he proves that he and his employees and operatives took all necessary and possible precautions with due care and attention to avoid damage.

Finally, deliberate overbooking is specifically covered by ruling No 295/4 February 1991 of the EC Council, which states that the carrier must provide compensation for the passengers involved.

6. Accommodation

(i) Classification

The national law on tourism (*legge quadro* No 217/17 May 1983) subdivides tourist accommodation into hotels, motels, holiday villages, tourist residences, camp sites, holiday houses and flats, holiday homes, youth hostels and mountain refuges.

Article 6 of this law briefly defines each of these categories. Article 7 states that individual regional laws must establish criteria for the classification of accommodation, taking into account size, facilities, services and quality of staff.

Stars are allocated from one to five stars for hotels, two to four for residences, one to four for camp sites and two to four for tourist villages. Five star hotels may also be termed "luxury" hotels subject to fulfilling the typical international standards.

Since it is the responsibility of the regions to classify accommodation by a specific law, there are no uniform nationwide standards of classification. There may be considerable differences in this respect from one region to another. There is a national law (DPR 30 December 1970, No 1437) setting minimum space requirements for hotel rooms (eight m² for single rooms, 14 m² for double rooms, and a minimum cubic capacity of 24 m³).

The regional classification however, does not usually set minimum space requirements. It is thus possible, in theory, for a hotel to enjoy a high classification irrespective of room size, provided that the above minimum requirements are met.

Accommodation is classified by the local *Azienda di Promozione Turistica* (see section on regional administration, above), to which any complaints may be addressed.

(ii) Fire safety

The law on fire safety in tourist accommodation has recently been reviewed in the *Decreto Ministeriale* of 9 April 1994 (*Gazzetta Ufficiale* 26 April 1994), which takes into consideration the recommendations issued by the Council of the European Community on 22 December 1986.

Before this *Decreto*, provisional legislation on the subject was introduced in Law No 818/7 December 1984.

The *Decreto* contains detailed technical requirements regarding individual buildings used for tourist accommodation, as well as their facilities and equipment.

Although specific requirements are outside the scope of this account, the following considerations should be borne in mind:

(i) each place of accommodation must have a fire safety inspection certificate issued by the head of the local authority fire brigade, who reports to the Ministry of the Interior, and not to the region;

(ii)   the person in charge of the hotel must train staff in fire procedures such as use of extinguishers, use of the alarm etc. He must also arrange for records to be kept of periodic inspections of facilities, including the electrical and light systems and safety devices; in addition, he must arrange for training meetings and evacuation drill. The register must be available for inspection by the provincial fire authorities;

(iii) detailed instructions explaining what to do in the event of fire must be placed on display, as specified in Article 17 of the *Decreto*, in the entrance hall, on each floor and in each room.

13.69   The *Decreto* specifies different requirements for old and new facilities, those with over 50% of floors replaced, being considered new. Existing accommodation will have to comply with the new requirements gradually, over a period of two to eight years, as stated in Article 21.2 of the *Decreto*.

Each hotel must also provide the local fire authorities with details of scheduled works, by the end of April 1995.

(iii)   Hygiene regulations

13.70   Law No 283/30 April 1962 and DPR No 327/26 March 1980 specify regulations to be respected with regard to the production and sale of food, the use of kitchen and table utensils, premises, equipment and staff. These regulations also establish that such activities are subject to supervision by the health authorities. At local council level, this means the mayor, who exercises this supervision by conducting inspections through the *Unità Sanitaria Locale* (local health authority). Inspections are carried out not only by the *Unità Sanitaria Locale* inspectors, but also by the *nucleo antisofisticazione* of the *Carabinieri* police (NAS).

The opening of trading premises, including accommodation facilities, also requires a health authorisation. This is issued by the *Unità Sanitaria Locale*, subject to prior ascertainment that the required health standards are fulfilled. The inspection will include the building used by the trader itself.

(iv)   Liability for possessions

13.71   The liability of the hotelier for possessions left on the hotel premises was reviewed in Law No 316/10 June 1978, implementing the Convention of the Council of Europe of 17 December 1962.

Decisions of the courts also apply the new legislation to restaurants (Cass. Civ. No 8268/87), but only concerning items which the client removes from his person for the better enjoyment of the meal (overcoat, umbrella etc). Items which the client habitually wears are thus not included, except in so far as deposited in the cloakroom.

Article 1783 of the *Codice Civile* (as modified by the new law) specifies **13.72** that the hotelier is liable for the deterioration, destruction or loss of possessions brought by the client on to the hotel premises. Liability is limited to the value of the possessions concerned, up to the equivalent of 100 times the price of renting a room per day.

Liability is unlimited when the items concerned are deposited at reception or when the hotelier refuses to take into safe keeping items which he is obliged to accept (credit cards, cash, valuables). It is also unlimited when the hotelier is at fault (Article 1785 (ii) of the *Codice Civile*). There is no liability if the theft or deterioration is due to *force majeure*, or is the client's fault.

The law on the subject cannot be waived, and any prior agreement limiting the hotelier's liability is automatically invalidated (Article 1785(iv) of the *Codice Civile*).

7. Financial services

(i) Credit cards

The use of credit cards is not subject to any special legislation in Italy, **13.73** and is thus regulated by the general principles of the law and by the contract between the issuer, the consumer and the trader. The contract generally makes provision for theft or loss of the card, stating that the holder of the card must report its loss or theft to the issuer within a short time limit and specifying who is liable for the risk of unauthorised use.

If the contract does not cover theft and loss, the general provisions of Italian legislation apply and responsibility for damage resulting from theft and loss must be accepted by the card-holder. This does not, of course, preclude the possibility of proceedings against the trader for not correctly following the procedure regarding identification of the card user.

(ii) Traveller's cheques

In Italy, traveller's cheques are considered as cheques within the mean- **13.74** ing established by *Regio Decreto* 21 December 1933 No 1736, concerning cheques and banker's orders. Article 44 of this *Decreto* states that encashment of a cheque can be subject to its being signed twice by the payee, as is the case with traveller's cheques.

In addition, a 1964 circular of the Italian Banking Association (*Associazione Bancaria Italiana, circolare* No 14/18 June 1964) introduced traveller's cheques into national banking practice. This circular was based on resolutions of the 1963 International Banking Conference in Stockholm.

13.75   The characteristics of the traveller's cheque are as follows:

(i)   the cheque is drawn directly by the client and issued by the drawee bank; the bank to which the client applies for the cheque buys it from the drawee and sells it to the client;

(ii)   the client's first signature is placed on the cheque at the time of purchase;

(iii)   the cheque must be presented for encashment within 12 months of the date of issue;

(iv)   to encash the cheque, the client signs it a second time in the cashier's presence.

13.76   Once the cheque has been signed twice by the client, it operates like a normal cheque.

Before paying, the bank must ascertain that the two signatures match. This implies due care and attention, but not specialist or electronic inspection. In other words, any discrepancy in the signatures should be identifiable by close scrutiny, but not require an expert opinion based upon technical considerations.

Loss, theft or destruction of the cheque must be reported immediately to the bank (and Police). Once the period of validity has expired, the bank will refund the face value of the cheque.

In the event of the cheque's being used after its loss or theft has been reported, but before its expiry, the issuer cannot refuse payment, subject to its having been encashed in accordance with the rules (two matching signatures). Theft or loss of the cheque thus does not automatically imply that its value will be refunded by law to the client.

13.77   The regulations are thus limited to stating that there may be a particular kind of cheque for which encashment is subject to its bearing two identical signatures. This is the only guarantee applicable by law to traveller's cheques.

In practice, however, the procedure for refund in the event of loss or theft is set out in the contract signed at the time of purchase, which is therefore the source to be examined with a view to ascertaining the conditions subject to which the client has a right to be refunded.

Almost all traveller's cheques purchased from Italian banks are issued by large international companies, either directly or through their branches or associates, and the face value is not expressed in Italian lire. The reason for this practice is that traveller's cheques are a convenient means of payment if they are readily accepted abroad and the issuing company has a large number of offices in different countries. Only in this way can their loss or theft be reported and refunded.

13.78   Although the terms of refund are specified in the contract, as stated above, there are certain standard conditions to which refund is generally subject, and which are usually included in the contract.

Before the cheque is lost or stolen, the client must (a) have signed it once, but not twice; and (b) have taken the same care with regard to the cheque's safe keeping as would have been the case with an identical sum in cash (this condition requires particular attention).

After the loss or theft of the cheque, the client must (a) report the fact to the issuer, stating the circumstances, the cheque number and the place and date of purchase; and (b) apply to the issuer or his representative for a refund, a valid personal document being required with the application.

8.   Insurance requirements

(i)   General

The insurance contract is generally subject to Articles 1882–1927 of the **13.79** *Codice Civile*, as well as to the specific provisions of the policy concerned.

The various insurance companies have long offered travel insurance policies, covering such risks as:

(i)   cancellation of travel;
(ii)   loss of luggage;
(iii)   difficulties related to illness or accident during travel;
(iv)   breakdown or accident involving the insured party's vehicle and preventing continuation of the journey; and
(v)   accidents to air travellers.

Terms to be examined before signing the contract include, in addition **13.80** to the items covered, the franchise clause and the maximum sum insured. The insured party's contractual rights must be exercised within one year (Art 2952 of the *Codice Civile*).

Almost all tour operators automatically provide insurance at the time when payment is made or the travel package is purchased. Such insurance covers the risks stated in the travel contract, waiving any need for a separate insurance policy.

In some cases the tour operator states that insurance is automatic and compulsory for certain risks, and offers the possibility of stipulating separate optional cover for others. The law does not, however, require compulsory insurance of the client by the tour operator. The travel contract proposed by the tour operator must therefore be examined to ascertain whether insurance against certain risks is provided.

Finally, the consumer *cannot* ask for any automatic insurance provided by the contract to be waived, with a view to obtaining a discount.

(ii)   Car hire insurance

Italy implemented the European Convention of Strasbourg of 20 April **13.81** 1959 as Law No 990/24 December 1969. EC Directives 72/166/EEC (OJ 1972 C103/1), 84/5/EEC (OJ 1984 L8/17) and 90/232/EEC (OJ 1990

L129/33) have also been implemented, and Law No 990/1969 has consequently been amended.

13.82   These laws state that motor vehicles cannot be used unless insured for at least the minimum legal requirements. All hired vehicles must thus meet the legal requirements for third party accident cover.

Law No 990/1969 includes, *inter alia*, the following provisions:

(i)   Article 4, stating that the driver's spouse, kin and cohabitants or dependants have a right to compensation for personal injury only and not for material damage;

(ii)   Article 6, recognising as valid in Italy the insurance of foreign vehicles registered in an EC state providing third party cover for motoring risks;

(iii)   Article 6, stating that, in the event of damage caused by a vehicle registered in an EC state (or another member country of the so-called Green Card system), the legal representative of the participating insurance companies and provider of compensation for the damage shall be the Milan-based Italian Central Office (*Ufficio Centrale Italiano*, or UCI), at which the insured party, insurer and liable party (even if different from the insured party) are legally domiciled;

(iv)   Article 7, requiring that the existence of the insurance policy be proven by a certificate issued by the insurer, stating the period of insurance cover for which the premium has been paid, and that this be displayed on the windscreen so as to be readily visible from outside;

(v)   Article 19, setting up at the *Istituto Nazionale delle Assicurazioni*, a guarantee fund for road accident victims, to provide compensation (through a specifically designated insurance company) in the event of damage caused by uninsured vehicles or those insured by companies which have become bankrupt; this compensation being subject to the limitations specified in Articles 19 and 20, notice of the start of legal action must be served to the UCI, not the domicile of the insured party or insurer, in the event of damage caused by a vehicle registered in the EC.

13.83   With specific reference to provision of insurance cover by the car hire company, the standard contracts offered by all the major companies are similar. In addition to compulsory third party cover, provision is generally made for damage caused by the driver and for theft; such cover is for sums in excess of the specified franchise, generally with rather high maximum limits. Optional terms can also be stipulated to eliminate the franchise clause for damage to the vehicle by the driver or theft.

With regard to theft, the general principle is that the driver is not liable, subject to having behaved with due care and attention. Car hire contracts however, generally specify that the driver is liable. This point should be ascertained when signing the contract, so that complementary theft insurance can be stipulated if preferred.

Finally, the car hire contract generally specifies that the driver cannot allow other persons, even family members, to drive the hired vehicle. It is important that this be ascertained, since non-compliance could invalidate the insurance cover.

(iii) Disputes

In the event of dispute with an insurance company in attempting to obtain the services stated in the insurance contract, or to receive compensation for damage caused by a road accident in which a third party was at fault, the matter must be resolved in the competent court with legal assistance. There are no particular procedures or bodies to settle disputes before the start of the hearing. **13.84**

With specific reference to damage caused by road accidents in which a third party was at fa··ˡ it should be remembered that:

(i) legˀˡ   ᴐe taken only once 60 days have elapsed from the time at which the damaged party applies to the insurer for compensation by registered letter with a receipt coupon (Art 22 Law No 990/1969);

(ii) action can be taken against the driver and owner of the vehicle, as well as directly against the insurance company by which the vehicle at fault is insured (Art 18 Law No 990/1969);

(iii) the definition of the dispute is facilitated by the use of the "friendly report form", required by Article 5 of Law No 39/26 February 1977. This form is issued free by the insurance company. Its completion and return oblige the insurance company to pay the sum considered due within a short time, in the event of there being material damage only.

(iv) Sickness insurance

EC Regulations 1408/71 and 574/92 state that every citizen of an EC Member State, temporarily staying in another Member State, has the right to national medical insurance cover as provided by the host country. **13.85**

To obtain this service, the citizen must have an attestation stating his eligibility for medical cover, issued by the authorities of his home country. This attestation is commonly known as Form E.111. In Italy, it is issued by the local health authority (*Unità Sanitaria Locale*), with which every citizen is registered. A simple application form has to be completed.

The citizen of an EC country who wishes to enjoy national medical insurance in Italy must:

(i) obtain Form E.111 from the health authority of his country;

(ii) present the form to any Italian *Unità Sanitaria Locale*, the address of which can be found in the telephone directory;

(iii) obtain from the *Unità Sanitaria Locale* a "health coupon book", containing coupons for the various health services. These will then be presented whenever a particular service is required.

9. Compensation for victims of crime

13.86   In the event of damage caused by criminal injuries, the damaged party can obviously sue for compensation and mental damages from the person who committed the crime, or who is civilly liable to meet such claims (*e.g.*, employers for damage created by employees).

However, Italian legislation differs from other EC States in not creating a specific state fund for the payment of such compensation. Criminal injuries caused by an unknown or insolvent party can therefore not be compensated at present. The only exception is the Guarantee Fund for Road Accident Compensation related to injuries caused by uninsured or unidentifiable vehicles (*supra* 8(ii) – Car hire insurance).

10. Time share regulation

13.87   Time share agreements are common in Italy, but there is no specific legislation to date. Dealings between buyer and seller, and relations between time share owners are therefore subject to general laws, or to laws involving similar legal considerations.

The most important time share arrangements are those concerning immovable property. In practice, these involve the sale of a second house or other form of accommodation to a number of buyers; the latter become sole and complete owners thereof, but only for predetermined periods of time. Each owner must therefore exercise his rights of ownership on the basis of a rotation system involving the other time share owners, with the result that the accommodation unit concerned is subject to the rights of a number of parties.

Dealings between buyer and seller are, in practice, subject to an *ad hoc* agreement drawn up by the latter and attached to the deeds of sale. Relations between the different time share owners involved are also subject to this agreement.

13.88   There are also "condominium regulations", which state the rights and obligations of time share purchasers regarding common property within the complex where the accommodation unit is situated, and relevant infrastructures.

The legal form generally applied to these agreements is *"communion,"* complemented by specific articles and by the time share regulations.

The legal status of time share agreements is still an ongoing question, and there is no established precedent in terms of decisions of the courts. However, the idea of time share ownership as a *communion* has been confirmed in practice by rulings on a number of cases and in some of the related doctrine.

Pending the introduction of specific legislation, the buyer-seller rela-   **13.89** tionship in the time share agreement is subject at present to the general regulations regarding purchase agreements and the specific terms of the contract (which must therefore be examined very carefully). Relations between time share owners, as well as between owners and the administration of the property complex involved, are subject to the regulations attached to the purchase contract and, according to the rulings of some courts, the regulations of the condominium.

This means, for example, that regulations concerning the appointment of condominium administrators apply, with provision for their revocation at any time by a quorate assembly.

In this respect, any clause in a time share agreement which does not pro-   **13.90** vide for the removal from office of the property administrator with regard to management of common parts, will be considered null and void.

There are no specific laws in this area to safeguard the consumer's rights, and there is no differentiated or extra protection for time share purchases by comparison with normal purchase agreements. However, the law regarding contracts negotiated away from business premises is applicable, meaning that the consumer can withdraw from the agreement within seven days of having signed it. The law concerning unfair terms in consumer contracts will also be applicable once Italy has implemented the European Directive on the subject.

The EC Directive on time share agreements means that Italy will have to   **13.91** draw up national laws, for which there is no specific precedent, on the protection of the consumer's rights. This will imply the following obligations:

(i)   to provide the purchaser, and whoever else may request it, with a prospectus to be included in the contract as an integral part thereof, with details of the property concerned, its condition and any restrictions incumbent thereon;

(ii)   recognition of a right to participate in decisions regarding the administration and upkeep of the property, as well as a detailed system of guarantees to be provided by the seller to the purchaser;

(iii)   inclusion in the contract of a minimum number of items including the precise nature of the right which is the subject of the time share contract, a description of the property and its location, specific information if the immovable property is under construction, periods and dates of use, the overall cost to the purchaser, the annual expenses to be charged to him, any possibility of participating in an exchange project and/or resale of the right; and

(iv)   the right for the buyer to withdraw from the contract within a time limit of at least 28 days after signing the contract.

11. Passport and frontier control

13.92 The law applicable to visitors from EC States to Italy can be found in the EC Treaty regarding the inception of the Common Market. It was integrated into national legislation by Law No 1203/14 October 1957 and subsequently amended by the Treaty of Luxemburg (January 1986), in turn ratified in Italy by Law No 909/23 December 1986.

Articles 52 *et seq* of this Treaty, in terms of the free circulation of persons within the EC, seek to establish equality between nationals of the various EC states. There are thus no particular restrictions regarding tourism in Italy by citizens of other EC states – and no visa requirements.

Where the reason for remaining in Italy is work, the foreign citizen must obtain an authorisation to remain in Italy (*permesso di soggiorno*). This document is required for certain purposes, such as applying to local authorities for registration of residence, or for enrolment at the Employment Office, Chamber of Commerce and similar organisations. The *permesso* cannot, however, be refused to an EC citizen.

13.93 EFTA nationals are subject to the provisions of Law No 300/28 July 1993, ratifying and implementing the Oporto Agreement of 2 May 1992, and the amendments thereto contained in the Brussels Protocol of 7 March 1993, as well as Law No 388/3 September 1993, ratifying and implementing Italian acceptance of the Schengen Agreement of 14 June 1985.

Previously, tourists from EFTA states were subject to the same restrictions as other non-EC citizens in terms of travel to and stay in Italy (Law No 39/1990). They are now subject to the same regime as EC citizens with regard to the waiving of visa and *permesso di soggiorno* requirements, the latter applying only in so far as applicable to EC citizens.

The Oporto-Brussels Agreement rules that citizens of states belonging to the EC and EFTA are free to settle in any other Member State (Art 31). This Article also states that citizens settling in another Member State are free to work on a self-employed basis or set up and run companies, subject to the law of the state in which they settle as applicable to nationals of that state.

Luxembourg

Chapter 14
Luxembourg
Guy Harles
Arendt & Medernach

1. Regulatory authorities

The "Ministère des Classes Moyennes et du Tourisme" is responsible for **14.1**
the implementation of the Package Travel Directive.[1] The business
licence office of this Ministry is responsible for granting business licences
to exercise the activities of travel agent or tour operator.

There are two professional associations of travel agents in Luxembourg. The first is the *Groupement des Agences de Voyages*, and the second
the *Syndicat des Agences de Voyages*.

2. Legal and professional rules

This matter is governed by the law of 28 December 1988[2] (the "Law of **14.2**
1988"), regulating access to the professions of craftsman, trader and manufacturer, and by a number of grand-ducal regulations. Article 1 of the
Law of 1988 provides that nobody may exercise the activities of trader
without having obtained a business licence.

The business licence is granted after an inquiry by the authorities. The
applicant will have to furnish proof of his professional qualifications and
his honourable character. If the applicant is a company, this proof must
be given in respect of the person in charge of the daily management of
the company.

No specific conditions of nationality are required by the Luxembourg
authorities.

3. General business organisation

The Law of 14 June 1994[3] (the "Law of 1994") determines the constitu- **14.3**
tion of the business of travel agent or tour operator.

---

1 Council Directive 90/314/EEC of 13 June 1990 on package travel, package holidays and package tours, OJ 1990 L158/59.
2 Law of 28 December 1988, Memorial A 1988, 1494.
3 Law of 14 June 1994, Memorial A 1994, 1092.

14.4   Article 1 of the law defines the persons to which the provisions of the Law of 1994 are applicable. The provisions are applicable to all physical persons or corporate bodies who carry on business which consists in the organisation or sale of:

(i)   individual or collective travel or stays;

(ii)   services rendered during the travel or stay, principally the issue of tickets of transport, reservation of rooms in hotels or tourist lodging establishments, the issue of tickets of lodging or of catering;

(iii)   services relating to tourist reception, principally picking up the client, the organisation of visits, conferences or other similar manifestations; and

(iv)   package travel, package holidays and package tours.

14.5   The Law of 1994 reproduces the wording of the Package Travel Directive to define the term "package". Article 2 of the Law of 1994 provides that package means the pre-arranged combination of not fewer than two components concerning transport, accommodation and other tourist services not ancillary to transport or accommodation and accounting for a significant proportion of the package, when sold or offered for sale at an inclusive price, and when the service covers a period of more than 24 hours or includes overnight accommodation, even if the different components are billed separately.

There are no specific conditions relating to the legal form of organisation of the travel agent or tour operator.

A travel agent who wants to establish in Luxembourg must have an *établissement stable* (permanent establishment).

4.   Special legal requirements

14.6 Special provisions relating to travel agents and tour operators are contained in the Law of 1994.

Article 3 of the Law of 1994 provides that the travel agent must provide evidence of sufficient financial guarantee (according to the programme of activities in the matter of package travel, package holidays and package tours), to ensure the reimbursement to the client of monies received for the services enumerated in Article 1 of the Law of 1994 (see 3), in the case of bankruptcy or insolvency.

The financial guarantee must include repatriation expenses. The financial guarantee must be incurred with a collective guarantee organisation, a credit institution or by a bank and guarantee insurance.

The Law of 1994 also provides for mandatory insurance for travel agents.

5. Consumer rights and safeguards

The matter of consumer protection is governed by a law of 25 August **14.7**
1983[4] (the "Law of 1983") regarding consumer protection, and a law of
15 May 1987[5] (the "Law of 1987") amending and supplementing various
provisions of the Civil Code, and completing the law of 25 August 1983.
The Law of 1987 is of general application, *i.e.* applies to everybody,
except where it amends the Law of 1983. The provisions of the Law of
1983 only apply to the relationship between a consumer and a trader or
professional supplier of services.

Article 1 of the Law of 1983 provides that a contractual imbalance at
the expense of the consumer, is an abuse and therefore, null and void.
Article 2 describes 20 examples of so-called abusive clauses. All of these
clauses have a common characteristic: they unilaterally advantage the
professional party to the prejudice of the consumer.

The Law of 1987 introduces several articles into the Civil Code to **14.8**
protect the consumer. Article 1135–1 of the Civil Code modifies the
general conditions of trade and provides that:

> The general conditions of an agreement prepared by one of the parties to
> the agreement can be invoked against the other party only if this party has
> had knowledge of them when the agreement was signed and if it is consid-
> ered that this party has accepted these general conditions.

Article 1135–1 specifies that clauses that provide for limited liability in
favour of the author of the general conditions cannot be invoked against
the other contracting party, unless they have been specially accepted in
writing. These two laws are applicable to contracts between consumers
and travel agents.

The Law of 1994 introduces special protection for the clients of travel **14.9**
agents. The content of the protection generally reproduces the Package
Travel Directive. The law provides that when a brochure is made available to the consumer by the travel agent, it must indicate comprehensive
and adequate information relating to the content of the services of transport and accommodation, the monetary amount and the means of payment, the conditions of cancellation of the contract and any passport and
visa requirements. The contract must contain all indications relating to
the name and address of the organiser, of the retailer, of the guarantor
and of the insurer, the determination of the services offered, of the
prices and the means of payment, and the rights and obligations of each
party in the case of modification of the price, or cancellation or assignment of the contract.

Contracts which do not respect these conditions are void.

---

[4] Law of 25 August 1983, Memorial A 1983, 1494.
[5] Law of 15 May 1987, Memorial A 1987, 570.

6. Forms of redress

14.10 Under Article 1 of the Law of 1983, an abusive clause is null and void. The consumer has the opportunity, when he brings an action against the supplier, to invoke the nullity of a clause of the contract or of the entire contract. The judge will examine the clause or the contract and will pronounce, if necessary, the nullity of the clause or of the contract.

The Law of 1983 also permits the President of the District Court to declare the abusive character of a clause or several clauses provided for by a contract, when a complaint is lodged by any person, any professional group or any consumers' association which is represented at the Commission of Prices.

The action is brought and judged by way of summary proceedings (*référé*). When a clause, or several clauses of the contract, has been declared null and void, the supplier may not, in the future, invoke this clause against another consumer. If the judgment is not respected by the supplier, he will be liable to a fine between 3,000 and 100,000 Luxembourg francs, which will be pronounced by the Criminal Court.

Any interested person, professional group or consumers' association may bring a civil action against the supplier and claim damages from him.

7. Insurance requirements

14.11 A grand-ducal regulation is in preparation. It will determine all the conditions relating to the insurance obligations of travel agents.

8. Regulation of insurance

14.12 The law of 6 December 1991[6] as amended,[7] on the insurance sector, describes in article 87 the possibility for persons to contract insurance, on payment of a premium, for assistance in the cases specified in the contract. There are no supplementary legal provisions relating to this kind of contract.

There are no specific provisions regarding hire car insurance.

9. Health and safety standards

(i) Holiday accommodation

14.13 The law of 17 July 1960,[8] as amended, provides that hotels, motels, residential hotels and restaurants must be in possession of equipment which

---

[6] Law of 6 December 1991, Memorial A 1991, 1762.
[7] Law of 18 December 1993, Memorial A 1993, 2150.
[8] Law of 17 July 1960, Memorial A 1960, 1187.

respects the security, health and comfort of clients. This law established the conditions for the security, health and comfort of clients, which are required to be satisfied in order to obtain the authorisation to open this kind of establishment.

A grand-ducal regulation describes the conditions of security, health and salubrity of camp sites.

(ii) Transport

There are no specific conditions under Luxembourg law relating to **14.14** health and safety standards for transport operators. The sole conditions required by law concern the technical conditions for security of buses, trains, ships and planes.

10. Rights against transport operators

(i) General

When a consumer has a contract with a tour operator, under Article 19 **14.15** of the Law of 1994, the tour operator is liable to the consumer for the correct execution of the obligations which result from the contract with the consumer, even if these obligations must be performed by other suppliers.

Article 19 also provides that, without prejudice to the provisions of article 1 of the Law of 25 August 1983 relating to the legal protection of the consumer, the tour operator and the consumer must provide in the contract that in the case of non-performance of obligations (except in the case of fraud or gross negligence), the indemnification for damages other than for personal injury, is limited.

When the non-performance of obligations concerns a supply of services which is governed by an international convention concerning indemnification, the provisions of the international convention are applicable notwithstanding the provisions of Article 19.

(ii) Rail transport

The provisions of the Convention relating to International Rail Trans- **14.16** port and its Protocol and Regulations, signed in Bern on 9 May 1980, are applicable to the matter of damages or loss of property and personal injury or death.[9]

---

9 Convention approved by the law of 4 May 1983, Memorial A 1983, 774.

(iii) Air transport

14.17 A Law dated 19 June 1967[10] on the liability for damages or loss of property, injury or death in the case of air transport, provides that the liability of the carrier is governed by the provisions of the Warsaw Convention of 12 October 1929, of the Protocol which amends this Convention signed in the Hague on 28 September 1955, and of the complementary Convention to the Warsaw Convention signed in Guadalajara on 18 September 1961, even if this transport is not international transport in the meaning of these Conventions.

11. Financial services

14.18 No legal rules govern the supply and use of credit cards and traveller's cheques.

The establishment of bureaux de change is governed by the law of 5 April 1993[11] as modified,[12] relating to the financial sector. In chapter 2, the law submits the activities of bureaux de change to the requirement of obtaining authorisation. The authorisation is granted by the Institut Monétaire Luxembourgeois (IML).

The law provides that the central administration of the company must be located in Luxembourg. When the applicant is a company, the names of the shareholders must be communicated to the IML. The applicant must prove his professional qualifications and honourable character.

12. Compensation for victims of crime

14.19 The Law of 12 March 1984[13], as modified[14], relates to the compensation of certain victims suffering personal injury which results from a criminal offence. This law provides that voluntary acts which present the material character of a crime and which have caused personal injury, and which have as a consequence the death, permanent incapacity or total incapacity for work for more than one month, entitle the victim or heirs of the victim to indemnification.

The victim can obtain indemnification from the state only if the victim cannot otherwise obtain an effective and sufficient indemnification, *i.e.* if the author of the crime is known and solvent, the victim cannot request an indemnification from the state.

---

[10] Law of 19 June 1967, Memorial A 1967, 680.
[11] Law of 5 April 1993, Memorial A 1993, 462.
[12] Law of 3 May 1994, Memorial A 1994, 702.
[13] Law of 12 March 1984, Memorial A 1984, 336.
[14] Law of 14 April 1992, Memorial A 1992, 846.

Luxembourg has also ratified the European Convention relating to the Indemnification of the Victims of Violent Crime, signed in Strasbourg on 24 November 1984.[15]

13. Time share regulation

There is no legislation in Luxembourg protecting the rights of con- **14.20** sumers in respect of time share agreements. The general legislation on consumer protection is applicable.

14. Passport and frontier control

The provisions of the EC Treaty as modified, and the Schengen Conven- **14.21** tion,[16] are applicable to citizens of Member States of the Community.

Under the provisions of the Conventions with each EFTA country, and the Convention on the European Economic Area, there are no border controls for citizens of an EFTA country.

---

[15] Law of 27 February 1985, Memorial A 1985, 207.
[16] Approved by a law of 3 July 1992, Memorial A 1992, 1574.

The Netherlands

Chapter 15

The Netherlands

Marinus Vromans and
Caroline Bleeker
Barents & Krans

1. Regulatory authorities

(i) Introduction: the ANVR (the Netherlands' Federation of Travel Agencies)

The *Algemeen Nederlands Verbond van Reisondernemingen* (ANVR) is the pro- **15.1**
fessional body in the tourism sector which comprises almost all of the
tour operators and travel agents in the Netherlands.

The ANVR was established as an association under Dutch law (*Vereniging*)
in 1966, and as an important self-regulatory body in the tourism sector it
has played a key role in the development of standard trade practices,
codes of conduct, general travel conditions, the setting up of schemes for
consumer complaints, and recently, the conclusion of a Collective
Labour Agreement in the tourism sector with the Trade Unions.

Since 1988 the ANVR has operated as a federation, of which each of **15.2**
the following associations are members:

(i)   *Vereniging van ANVR-Reisorganisatoren* (Association of ANVR Tour
        Operators) (VRO);
(ii)   *Vereniging van ANVR-Reisorganisatoren Inkomend Toerisme* (Associa-
        tion of ANVR Tour Operators in Incoming Tourism) (VRI);
(iii)   *Vereniging van ANVR-Reisagenten* (Association of ANVR Travel
        Agents) (VRA); and
(iv)   *Vereniging van ANVR-Luchtvaartagenten en Zakenreisburo's* (Associa-
        tion of ANVR Air Travel Agents and Business Travel Agents)
        (VLZ).

The structure and organisation of the ANVR Federation is reflected in **15.3**
the diagram shown overleaf.

The ANVR Federation has its office in Hoofddorp (near Schiphol
Airport).

Apart from the member associations mentioned above (VRO, VRI,
VRA and VLZ), the individual members of these four associations are
each also a member of the ANVR Federation. As at October 1995 the
ANVR Federation had 1,752 individual members. If membership of one
of the member associations ceases, individual membership of the ANVR
Federation also ends.

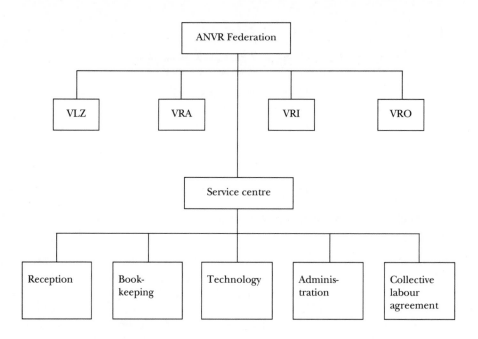

15.4   The activities of the ANVR Federation are financed by its individual members (entry fees and yearly contributions). The ANVR Federation membership fees for 1995 were as follows:

Basic membership fee:	NLG 965
Additional contribution for each vote	
(one vote represents NLG 5,000,000 = turnover):	NLG 425
Technology contribution:	NLG 400

15.5   Members of the board of the ANVR Federation are elected by the members of the ANVR Federation upon a binding proposition of the boards of the four member associations, which each propose a candidate from their respective boards. This binding proposition may be over-ruled by a two-thirds majority vote of the members, provided there is a quorum of two-thirds of the total votes present at the meeting. The remaining members of the board, amongst whom are its president, are elected by the members upon a proposition from the board of the ANVR Federation.

Each member association has one vote. The individual members have a number of votes depending on their turnover. The number of votes ranges from one vote (turnover less than NLG 5,000,000, to five votes (turnover between NLG 20–25,000,000). Above NLG 25,000,000, each additional NLG 6,000,000 turnover or part thereof, gives the right to one more vote. In order to determine the number of votes to which the members are entitled within the Federation, the members have to present the

Federation with a statement concerning their turnover within six months after the end of their accounting year.

The ANVR Federation has laid down a set of internal regulations **15.6** (*Huishoudelijk Reglement*).

Travel business members must keep the ANVR Federation informed of any major changes in relation to their business activities (change of legal structure, change of address, etc).

(ii) Bonding scheme (Federal Resolution Guarantees: Federaal Besluit Zekerheidstelling)

The members of the ANVR Federation are obliged to provide a guarantee **15.7** for the performance of their obligations towards the public, the ANVR Federation itself, its member-associations, and its individual members (travel businesses).

The obligations towards the public to be secured are those which are not secured under the scheme of the Travel Fare Guarantee Fund Foundation (*Stichting Garantiefonds Reisgelden.* (See under Section (iv) *infra.*)

The security to be provided to the ANVR Federation shall take the form of a bank guarantee, or a bond of a major financial institution which is able to provide a security equivalent to a bank guarantee.

The security must be presented when joining the ANVR Federation. It **15.8** amounts to:

(i)   NLG 5,000 for travel agents;
(ii)   NLG 10,000 for tour operators;
(iii) an amount to be fixed by the board of the ANVR Federation for those members which do not participate in the scheme of the Travel Fare Guarantee Fund Foundation.

(iii) Code of conduct

The ANVR Federation has adopted a set of Rules of Conduct which apply **15.9** to its individual members. Most of the obligations laid down in these rules are now part of the Dutch Act on Travel Contracts (effective as from 1 January 1993) and the ANVR General Terms and Conditions. The Act and the ANVR General Terms and Conditions are dealt with in detail under heading 5.

Under the Rules of Conduct the members of the ANVR Federation are entitled to use the logo of the ANVR on all stationery, travel brochures, and all other publications, subject always to mentioning the specific ANVR association of which they are a member.

Members are permitted to offer organised travel only under the appli- **15.10** cation of the ANVR General Terms and Conditions.

In all publications, and at the time of booking, members must always indicate in a clear manner who is the responsible tour operator and must avoid anything which could be misleading. Article 12 of the Code of Conduct of the ANVR Federation refers to the Travel Disputes Committee (*Geschillencommissie Reizen*), which will be dealt with under heading 6 *infra*. This article makes the members of the ANVR Federation subject to this Disputes Committee and its decisions.

Should a member fail to respect a decision of the Travel Disputes Committee, as a result whereof it is ordered to pay a certain amount of compensation to a consumer, the ANVR Federation shall or will be entitled to pay this compensation directly to the consumer under the guarantee given by the Federation to the Foundation of Disputes Committees for Consumer Affairs (*Stichting Geschillencommissies voor Consumentenzaken*). Naturally the Federation has a right of redress against the deficient Federation member and, after payment to the consumer, will be automatically subrogated in the individual member's rights towards the consumer.

15.11 For each decision of the Travel Disputes Committee, as a result whereof a consumer's complaint has been totally or partly upheld, the Federation member must make a contribution towards the amount which the ANVR Federation pays yearly to the Foundation of Disputes Committees for Consumer Affairs, in order to operate the Committee.

The Federation is entitled to use the guarantee, referred to under heading 1.(ii), for settling any debts of its members towards the consumers or towards the Federation.

Under the Rules of Conduct, the Board of the ANVR Federation has powers to impose sanctions on its members ranging from a simple warning, to a maximum fine of NLG 10,000, or suspension of membership for six months.

15.12 If infringement of the Rules of Conduct has resulted in damage to another member of the Federation, the Federation Board may order the infringing member to repair the damage. A decision of the Federation Board, whereby sanctions are imposed on its members, may be appealed before the Committee of Appeal as referred to in the articles of association of the Federation.

The decisions of the Federation Board and of the Committee of Appeal are binding (*bindende adviezen*) under Dutch law, which means that they have the force of contract between the Federation and the members concerned. However, they can only be enforced in law after confirmation by a judgment rendered in the ordinary courts.

(iv) Federal Committee of Good Services (Federale Commissie van Goede Diensten)

15.13 This committee, the members of which are appointed by the ANVR Federation Board, decides disputes between members of the Federation in relation to the operation of a travel business, unless dispute settlement by another body of the Federation is provided for. A third party, not being a member of the ANVR Federation, may request the Committee to deal with a dispute which it has with a Federation member, provided that this third party confirms in writing that it will respect the Committee's decision.

The decision of the Federal Committee has the force of binding advice (*bindend advies*) under Dutch law (*supra*).

(v) Association of ANVR tour operators: Vereniging van ANVR-Reisorganisatoren (VRO)

The VRO is one of the association members of the ANVR Federation   **15.14** and was incorporated in 1988. At the moment it has approximately 145 members.

The minimum membership fee amounts to NLG 2,600 per year. Membership of the VRO automatically results in individual membership of the ANVR Federation. Membership of the ANVR Federation requires payment of additional membership contributions (see (i) *supra*).

The conditions of VRO membership are as follows:

(i)   application for membership of ANVR Federation;
(ii)   the operation of a travel business in the Netherlands in accordance with the applicable legal rules (laws on establishment, see under 2);
(iii)   the selling of arrangements covering more than one day, on a seasonal or yearly basis, in relation to which a sufficient turnover can be realised (at least NLG 1,000,000 per year);
(iv)   registration in the Commercial Register of the Chamber of Commerce;
(v)   a good reputation;
(vi)   sufficient solvency, as evidenced by a statement from its own certified accountant, or investigation by a certified accountant appointed by the VRO Board, and as evidenced by annual accounts and other relevant official data;
(vii)   operation of the travel business without direct or indirect interference from outside (government subsidies or similar support);
(viii) absence of arrangements which distort free competition;
(ix)   commitment to abide with all resolutions of the VRO; and
(x)   availability of sufficient financial security for fulfilment of the financial obligations towards the public, as evidenced by membership of the Travel Fare Guarantee Fund Foundation (*Stichting Garantiefonds Reisgelden*) or an equivalent security.

A rejection of an application for membership may be appealed before   **15.15** the general meeting of members of the VRO. Membership may be granted for a limited period of time.

The VRO may also admit companies which carry out activities closely connected with the travel business as associate members.

If a company carries out several types of activities, of which the travel business represents less than 5% of its total activities, it is not considered to be carrying out travel business, and should register as an associate member.

(vi) Association of ANVR Tour Operators in Incoming Tourism: Vereniging van ANVR-Reisorganisatoren Inkomend Toerisme (VRI)

15.16 This Association was also incorporated in 1988. At the moment, it has approximately 23 members. The Association is very similar to the VRO, but its only members are tour operators dealing with incoming tourism.

(vii) Association of ANVR Travel Agents: Vereniging van ANVR-Reisagenten (VRA)

15.17 This Association was also incorporated in 1988. At this moment, it has approximately 1,420 members. Travel agents are intermediary parties in the conclusion of travel contracts between tour operators, airline companies, suppliers of accommodation etc, on the one hand, and consumers on the other hand. Travel agents do not engage in contractual obligations in their own name, but act on behalf of, in the name of, and for the account of, their principals.

The membership fee of the VRA (apart from the membership fee due to the ANVR Federation) amounts to:

entry fee:	NLG 2,500
minimum yearly membership fee:	NLG 625
additional fee for each branch:	NLG 130

15.18 In the general meetings of the VRA, members have a number of votes in relation to the amount of membership fee which they have paid. Each NLG 100 of membership fee represents one vote.

The internal rules of the VRA lay down the following criteria for membership:

(i) the operation of a travel business as a travel agent and registration as such in the Commercial Register of the Chamber of Commerce;

(ii) having operated the business of travel agent for at least one year before the date of application for membership;

(iii) compliance with the requirements under the Decree on the Establishment of Travel Businesses 1978 (*Vestigingsbesluit Reisbureaubedrijf 1978*) (see under heading 2);

(iv) a good reputation;

(v) sufficient solvency, as evidenced by a statement from its own certified accountant, or an investigation by a certified accountant appointed by the VRA Board, and as evidenced by annual accounts and other relevant official data;

(vi)   operation of the travel business without direct or indirect inter-ference from outside (government subsidies or similar support);

(vii)   absence of arrangements which distort free competition;

(viii) operation of a travel agency in conformity with the objectives and rules of the association and the realisation of sufficient turnover; and

(ix)   availability of sufficient financial security for the fulfilment of financial obligations towards the public, as evidenced by admission to the scheme operated by the Travel Fare Guarantee Fund Foundation or an equivalent security;

(x)   commitment to abide by all resolutions of the VRA.

The VRA Board may appoint a certified accountant for the duration of membership. **15.19**

The Association has organised the Netherlands into various regions, for which the member-travel agents may elect a regional board. The VRA board may be assisted by a regional board or by an ANVR regional council, whenever this is appropriate. Associate membership is also available.

(viii) Association of ANVR air travel agents and business travel agents: Vereniging van ANVR Luchtvaartagenten en Zakenreisburo's (VLZ)

The association was incorporated in 1988 and has the following categories of members: **15.20**

(i)   members who have been appointed by The International Air Transport Association (IATA) as an "approved agent" for the IATA air carriers (the "A-members");

(ii)   members who are non-IATA approved agents, but who are carrying out the business of air transport passage (the "C-members").

C-membership status is limited to two years, within which period A-membership should be acquired. The conditions for membership and the obligations for members are very similar to those required for membership of the VRO or VRA. **15.21**

Many airline companies, hotel chains, central reservation systems and car rental companies are associate members.

The voting power of an A-member is related to the amount of its turnover, and ranges from two votes for less than NLG 2,000,000 turnover, to nine votes for more than NLG 100,000,000 turnover. **15.22**

Apart from the fees due to the ANVR-Federation, admission and membership fees for the VLZ are as follows:

Admission fee:	NLG 2,000
Minimum annual fee:	NLG 500
Each additional vote:	NLG 750
Associated Membership:	NLG 500
No entry fee	

VLZ created the IATA-agents' Guarantee Foundation (*Stichting Garanti-estelling IATA-agenten*), replacing the bank guarantee to be submitted by some IATA-agents to IATA (sometimes up to six weeks IATA turnover) by insurance cover, thereby considerably improving the cash position of its members.

15.23 VLZ closely monitors the automatisation developments, such as computerised reservation systems (Galileo, Worldspan, Sabre and Amadeus), automated ticket and boarding pass systems, and similar projects, and keeps its members informed of these developments.

VLZ also provides its members with management information and a model "business travel policy" on which basis members may set up their own business plan.

VLZ highly values education and training. In 1994, VLZ organized the Business Travel Fair (BTF) for the third time.

A worldwide Hotel Corporate Rate Programme is available to VLZ. The IATA/UFTAA/IHA – voucher was introduced on the Dutch market in 1993. In 1994 VLZ opened its own ticket office at Schiphol Airport.

VLZ is also a member of GEBTA ("the Guild of European Business Travel Agents").

2. Legal and professional rules

15.24 The Decree on the Establishment of Travel Businesses (*Vestigingsbesluit Reisbureaubedrifg 1978*), which had been in force in the Netherlands since May 1978, provided the Netherlands with a set of rules governing the activities of travel businesses. The Decree stated that a licence is required in order to operate a travel business. To be eligible for a licence, certain criteria on commercial knowledge and on professional knowledge had to be satisfied. The Decree on the Establishment of Businesses (*Vestigings-besluit Bedrijven*),[1] which came into force on 1 January 1996, caused the repeal of the Decree of the Establishment of Travel Businesses of 1978. The new Decree applies to various business sectors and contains the main rules of the modernised and simplified establishment legislation. On the basis of this Decree a licence (of the Chamber of Commerce) is still required to operate a travel busienss. As from 1 January 1996 the applicant for a licence to operate a travel business only has to satisfy criteria on commercial knowledge consisting in general entrepreneurial skills (*algemene ondernemersvaardigheden*) and no longer on professional competence. As criteria concerning general entrepreneurial skills, the Decree refers to:

(i) knowledge of market structures and of instruments which are important for the determination of a market strategy;

---

[1] Act of 6 Dec 1995, *Official Journal*, 609.

(ii)   insight in the manner in which a business, from a logistic and organisational viewpoint, is functionally controlled;

(iii)   insight in the manner in which a business, from a financial viewpoint, is functionally controlled and the ability to apply relevant general principles of business economics;

(iv)   insight in the relevant aspects regarding the execution of financial administration;

(v)   knowledge of the relevant aspects in relation to personnel and organisation;

(vi)   knowledge of the legal provisions with regard to the requirements mentioned under (i)–(iii) and (v);

(vii)   the ability to make a business plan, taking into account the requirements mentioned under (i) to (vi).

15.25   General entrepreneurial skills have to be proved by a certificate of general entrepreneurial skills, which can be obtained from the National Economic Development Council (NEDC).

The Dutch Minister of Economic Affairs has issued a regulation[2] which indicates which diplomas comply with the criteria on general entrepreneurial skills.

The rules governing the establishment of travel businesses relate solely to outward travel. Tourism to and within the Netherlands is therefore not covered by these rules.

On 29 June 1982 the European Council adopted the Directive on measures to facilitate the effective exercise of freedom of establishment and freedom to provide services in respect of the activities of self-employed persons in certain services incidental to transport and travel agencies (ISIC Group 718), and in storage and warehousing (ISIC Group 720).[3]

15.26   Article 1 of the Directive stipulates that the Member States of the European Community must adopt the measures set out in the Directive in respect of establishment or provision of services in their territories by natural persons and companies or businesses ("beneficiaries" under the Directive) in the sector of activities including, *inter alia*, travel agencies and tour operators.

Article 6 paragraph 3, in conjunction with article 7 paragraph 3, of the Directive, stipulates that if in a Member State the taking up or pursuit of activities in the travel business is dependent on the possession of general, commercial, or professional knowledge and ability, that Member State shall accept as sufficient evidence and proof of such knowledge and ability a certificate issued by the competent authority in the Member State of origin, certifying that the beneficiary has pursued the activity in that Member State (of origin) for any of the periods and in the capacity as stipulated in Article 6, paragraph 3 (a), (b), (c) or (d) of the Directive.

---

[2] Decree of minister of Economic Affairs, Regeling aanwijsing bewijsstukken van algemene condernamaravaardigheden Vestigingsbesluit bedrijvan, *Officla Gazette* 1995, 247.

[3] Directive 82/470/EEC, OJ 1982 L213/1.

15.27 Article 7, paragraph 4 of the Directive obliges the Member States to designate an authority or body competent to issue the certificates, which a national of a Member State shall submit in support of the application for authorisation to pursue activities in other Member States. The Netherlands has met this requirement by designating the Chamber of Commerce of the territory in which the activities are pursued by the Dutch applicant for establishment and provision of services in other Member States to issue the certificate to Dutch nationals.[4]

The Netherlands has complied with the obligation under the Directive to admit beneficiaries of other Member States who are in the possession of a certificate, as mentioned in the Directive, to establish themselves and provide services in the travel business, by exempting these beneficiaries from the requirement under Dutch law to obtain a licence to operate as a travel business. The request for exemption has to be presented to the Chamber of Commerce in the Netherlands within the territory where the activities will be pursued.

3. General business organisation

15.28 A tour operator or travel agent may chose any legal form which is available under Dutch law for setting up a business.

The business may be set up in the form of a sole trader, which results in personal and unlimited liability. However, it is usually set up as a private company with limited liability (*Besloten Vennootschap* (BV)). The minimum share capital, to be issued and paid up for a BV is NLG 40,000.

4. Travel fare guarantee fund foundation and insolvency law

(i) Introduction

15.29 Dutch company law does not provide for special rules governing the operation of travel agencies and tour operators. Furthermore, there are no specific rules with regard to the ownership and management of travel agencies and tour operators.

There are no statutory rules obliging tour operators or travel agents to insure themselves. However, consumer security in the event of insolvency of tour operators and travel agents, is provided for by the means set out below.

---

[4] Decree of the Ministry of Economic Affairs of 4 October 1983, *Aanwijzing instanties afgifte verklaringen ten behoeve van vestiging in de andere EEG-landen (Designation of competent authorities to issue certificates for establishment in the other EC Member States)*, *Official Gazette* 1983, 195.

(ii) The Travel Fare Guarantee Fund Foundation

(a) General

In the 1970s and 1980s, substantial financial losses were caused by the **15.30** insolvency of a considerable number of tour operators in the Netherlands. Consumer organisations brought political pressure to bear, and the Ministry of Economic Affairs announced its intention to introduce legislation, unless the trade itself worked out a satisfactory voluntary scheme. As a result, The Travel Fare Guarantee Fund Foundation (the *Stichting Garantiefonds Reisgelden*) was created, and has been active since 1 April 1983.

According to the Explanatory Memorandum to the Dutch Act on Travel Contracts (which as part of book 7 of the New Dutch Civil Code, entered into force on 1 January 1993), the Dutch Fare Guarantee Fund (SGR) meets the requirements of article 7 of the EC Directive of 13 June 1990 on package travel, including package holidays and package tours, which reads as follows:

> The organiser and/or retailer party to the contract shall provide sufficient evidence of security for the refund of money paid over and for the repatriation of the consumer in the event of insolvency.

The object of the SGR is to refund consumers should they suffer finan- **15.31** cial loss, or to repatriate them in cases where the tour operator, travel agent, carrier or supplier of accommodation fails to perform owing to financial incapacity. With a few exceptions, consumers receive a certificate of SGR coverage in return for a payment of 15 Dutch guilders. A consumer who books through an agent which is admitted to the SGR scheme, is obliged to pay the SGR contribution. Currently, approximately 1.5 million certificates are issued per annum.

(b) Admission to the SGR scheme

At present, the SGR covers approximately 95% of all tour operators and **15.32** travel agents in the Netherlands. Air carriers do not as yet participate in the SGR scheme. It is not necessary to be a member of ANVR (The Netherlands' Federation of Travel Agencies) to join SGR. There are marketing and financial conditions for admission but, in general, anyone in the tourist industry in the broadest sense, may participate in the fund provided they are marketing their products on the Dutch market. It is not essential for participants to be located in the Netherlands, but a travel contract must be concluded with a consumer resident in the Netherlands, in order to be eligible for coverage under the scheme.

However under article 4A of the Regulations of the SGR, participating **15.33** companies domiciled abroad and their branch offices in the Netherlands are not entitled to provide to consumers the SGR guarantee. These companies are obliged to offer the products, which they aim to sell on the Dutch market, through the intermediary of participating travel agents, which are domiciled in the Netherlands. At the same time, the SGR under article 2 para 3 of the SGR-Regulations created the possibility for Dutch tour operators (*i.e.* domiciled in the Netherlands) to "export" the SGR guarantee together with their products abroad.

Article 2 para 3 reads as follows:

> The foundation also has as its objective to pay compensation to or in the interest of consumers in relation to travel agreements as referred to in article 7:500 Civil Code, of which the travel arrangements were originally destined for the Dutch market, but which were offered in other Member States of the EU by a participating tour operator, domiciled in The Netherlands, either directly or through the intermediary of a travel agent domiciled in that particular EU member state, if these consumers suffer financial losses as a result of non-performance, because of financial insolvency by a particular tour operator, and provided that this tour-operator at the moment of conclusion of the travel agreement was entitled to provide the guarantee.

(c)   Requirements regarding solvency and liquidity

15.34   The participant must meet the following requirements regarding solvency and liquidity.

In connection with solvency:

(i)   equity must in no case be less than 40,000 Dutch guilders;
(ii)   equity must be at least 20% of the total capital;
(iii) when the amount of equity is calculated under (i) and (ii), no account is to be taken of intangible assets; and
(iv)   when the amount of equity is calculated under (ii), the total amount of all bank guarantees to be given by the participant to the Foundation, or guarantees considered equivalent thereto by the board of the Foundation, shall be counted as equity.

In connection with liquidity:

(i)   liquidity must always be enough to cover fixed charges during at least one month;
(ii)   for the purpose of calculating the amount of liquidity, debts to third parties in current account are only taken into consideration if the continuity of the business of the applicant or participant is under threat.

15.35   Bank guarantees may be counted as part of the equity referred to above. Deferred debts are considered to be capital. Participants are also required to provide a bond for 1.5% of the risk-bearing sales as determined by the SGR Board, which percentage is subject to annual increase or decrease by the board.

The board may in certain circumstances require the submission of additional bank guarantees.

The arrangement with the SGR may be terminated by the participant or by the SGR Board, which has wide powers of search and entry under the participation rules. Recourse to a committee of appeal is available in the event of dispute.

(d) Nature of the SGR guarantee

The SGR will guarantee repayment of travel fares paid in advance by the **15.36** consumer. Consumers also have a right to repatriation in the event of a participant's insolvency. The SGR will normally arrange another holiday for those who leave early, however, there is no obligation on them to do so.

For cover under the SGR it is a *conditio sine qua non* that the relevant booking agent must be a participant in the SGR. Should a non-participating tour operator, carrier, or supplier of accommodation become insolvent, the SGR will provide cover under the scheme, provided that the travel is booked through a company which is a participant in the SGR scheme. In that case the travel agent himself, through whom the holiday has been booked, will be ultimately liable for the damage.

Only when the travel agent is declared insolvent will the SGR assume ultimate liability. As a result, travel agents are naturally reluctant to represent non-participating companies, because of the risk of being ultimately liable for claims from the Foundation. Therefore non-participating companies will encounter difficulties in having their products marketed through travel agents in the Netherlands. An exception to this rule is the case of the airline carriers, which do not yet participate in the SGR scheme.

The potential liability of travel agents in the event of insolvency of an **15.37** airline company will therefore be considerable. Proposals have recently been presented by the SGR, in conjunction with ANVR, to have the airline companies join the scheme, which will result in increased exposure of the SGR. As a result the SGR proposes to require an additional contribution from the consumer for SGR cover in the event of the insolvency of an airline company. For their part, tour operators fulfil the responsibility placed on them under the Directive, by providing consumer protection by selling through participating travel agents.

(e) Stichting Garantiefonds ANVR v Martinair-Holland NV (Judgment of 6 June 1989 of the Dutch Supreme Court)

Having made a payment under the SGR scheme, the SGR is subrogated **15.38** in the rights of the consumer. This subrogation of the SGR led to litigation between the old style ANVR Guarantee Fund and Martinair-Holland NV. The facts are set out below.

KMC Travel International Tour Operators BV ("KMC") had concluded charter agreements with Martinair for air transport of its clients. These clients had paid for their tickets to KMC, and KMC, who had Martinair blank tickets at its disposal, had issued these tickets to its clients. However, KMC had not paid Martinair for these tickets. Shortly before the scheduled date of departure KMC went bankrupt. As a result the receiver in the bankruptcy of KMC terminated the charter agreements with Martinair with immediate effect. Martinair refused to provide air transport for the clients of KMC. The ANVR Guarantee Fund paid Martinair for the tickets, so that KMC's clients could be transported. Thereafter the Guarantee Fund, subrogated in the rights of KMC's clients, submitted a claim against Martinair to the Dutch Court for the recovery of the monies paid by the Fund to Martinair under the scheme.

15.39   The Guarantee Fund presented the following grounds for its claim against Martinair:

(i)   an air ticket is a bearer document which gives the holder title to transport;

(ii)   KMC had concluded the agreement with Martinair as agent and representative of its clients, so that a direct contractual relation was created between Martinair and KMC's clients;

(iii)   Martinair had created, by its own behaviour, the impression that KMC was its agent, for example by issuing blank tickets to KMC, so that payment by KMC's clients to KMC discharged KMC's clients of their obligation to pay Martinair for the tickets;

(iv)   KMC had stipulated a right to transport against Martinair in the interest of KMC's clients, so that KMC's clients could enforce their right to transport directly in relation to Martinair. (This argument was only used in the courts of lower instance and not before the Supreme Court.)

15.40   The Dutch courts rejected the Guarantee Fund's grounds of claim against Martinair. The Supreme Court ruled that KMC had concluded the agreement in its own name, and for its own risk and account, charter agreements with Martinair, which provided for transport by Martinair of KMC's clients. KMC's clients could only require performance from KMC, and not directly from Martinair. It remains unclear whether argument (iv) by the Guarantee Fund would have been more successful had it been also used before the Supreme Court.

The German Supreme Court ("Bundesverfassungsgericht") in a similar case has accepted the establishment of a direct contractual link between the consumer and the airline company on the basis of the "third party right" doctrine. Under the Dutch Civil Code, as appplicable since 1 January 1992, the position will be in line with German law.

(f)   Conclusions

15.41 On balance the SGR is a success: public perception is excellent and there is governmental support. Since the start of operation of the scheme in

1983, there have been 40 bankruptcies, resulting in payments amounting to 13 million Dutch guilders paid by the SGR under the guarantee scheme. The largest single outlay was three million Dutch guilders. However, there remains a long term risk. If the largest Dutch tour operator were to go bankrupt, the SGR would follow suit. Consumer contributions are being increased to build up capital reserves. The outcome of a Supreme Court case in relation to tax issues on accumulated funds will be decisive for the pace at which these further reserves can be built up.

(iii)   Insolvency law

There are no Dutch statutory rules that specifically govern the insolvency **15.42** or winding-up of businesses in the travel and tourism sector. The normal rules apply. The Dutch Bankruptcy Act of 1893, as amended, (*Wet van de 30ste september 1893, Stb.140, op het faillissement en de surséance van betaling*),[5] includes two different insolvency regimes, which generally apply to all legal and natural persons.

The two basic regimes are bankruptcy (*faillissement*) and moratorium or suspension of payment (*surséance van betaling*). While bankruptcy aims at the liquidation and distribution of the debtors' assets, the purpose of suspension of payment is to give the debtor a chance to reorganise its debts and to continue its business for the benefit of both itself and its creditors.

5.   Consumer rights and safeguards

(i)   Introduction

(a)   General

When discussing consumer rights under travel contracts, one must realise **15.43** that, in fact, the process of entering into a travel contract may be divided in two steps.

(i)   In the first place there is the information stage. This stage deals with how the travel package is offered and presented. Problems may arise when that information is presented in a misleading way (misleading advertising); or in a way that puts too much pressure on the decision-making process (door-to-door selling and telemarketing). These issues will be discussed under (iii), (iv) and (v) *infra*.

(ii)   In the second stage the travel contract is concluded, which results in certain obligations for both parties. These obligations are laid down in the travel contract itself and in the travel conditions

---

[5]   Act of 30 September 1893, Official Journal 140.

(general conditions, which for the most part determine the contents of the travel contract). The travel contract and travel conditions and the incorporation of the EC Directive on package travel of 1990 into Dutch legislation will be discussed under (i) and (ii) *infra*.

(b)   Legislation and regulations: before and after 1992

15.44   Before 1992 there were no special regulations governing the travel contract. Only general rules of contract law applied, and for the most part, travel contracts were determined by general travel conditions drafted by the ANVR (the Netherlands Federation of Travel Agencies). There were no special regulations regarding general conditions either. Legal text books and the Supreme Court alone had set some standards by which individual conditions were judged.

After 1992 some important events took place.

(i)   On 1 January 1992, Books 3, 5, and 6 of the (New) Dutch Civil Code came into effect, causing major changes in the relationships between parties concluding a contract.

(ii)   On 1 January 1992 the Act on General Conditions (*Wet Algemene Voorwaarden*) also came into effect, incorporating a totally new Section 3 on General Conditions into Chapter 5, Contracts in General (*Overeenkomsten in het algemeen*), of Book 6 (Contract Law), of the Civil Code.[6] This Act gives the consumer many safeguards by having included, among other things, a "black" and "grey" list of stipulations respectively considered or assumed to be unreasonably onerous, and for that reason being subject to nullification by the courts, if used in a contract. Because of the existence of this Act, most of the EC Directive of 5 April 1993 on onerous stipulations in consumer contracts,[7] which had to be incorporated into Member States' legislation by the end of 1994, had already been incorporated, and therefore only minor changes will have to be made.

The (ANVR) travel conditions are general conditions and are therefore also governed by the new Section 3, Chapter 5, Book 6 of the Civil Code.

(iii)   On 1 January 1993 the Act on Travel Contracts (*Wet op de Reisovereenkomst*) came into effect, incorporating the EC Directive of 13 June 1990 on package travel, including package holidays and package tours.[8] With this Act, Chapter 7A on the Travel Contract was added to Book 7 of the Civil Code, Special Contracts (*Bijzondere overeenkomsten*)[9] which, for the most part, sticks closely to the text of the Directive.

---

6   Arts 6:231–6:247.
7   93/13/EEC (OJ 1993 L95/29).
8   90/314/EC (OJ 1990 L158/159).
9   Arts 7:500–7:513.

(iv)   Because of the Act on General Conditions and the EC Directive on package travel, the ANVR felt obliged to adjust its Travel Conditions (*Algemene Reisvoorwaarden*), which it did during 1992, in co-operation with the consumer organisations *Consumentenbond* and *Konsumentenkontakt*, anticipating and sticking closely to the Act on Travel Contracts, which in 1992 was still in draft stage. In June 1995 the ANVR Travel Conditions were slightly amended. (For a translation of the ANVR Travel Conditions see Appendix 1 to this Chapter.)

It may be clear, that after 1 January 1993 the rights and obligations of parties concluding a travel contract have considerably changed. **15.45**

First, the special rules on the travel contract, as laid down in Chapter 7A of Book 7 of the Civil Code, will determine the consumer's and tour operator's rights and obligations. Where no special regulation is given, the general rules of Dutch contract law apply. Furthermore, the ANVR Travel Conditions will considerably determine the travel contract's contents. These conditions are governed by the special rules on general conditions laid down in Chapter 5, section 3, of Book 6 of the Civil Code.

(ii)   The travel contract

(a)   General

Chapter 7A of Book 7 of the Civil Code was incorporated as a result of the EC Directive of 13 June 1990 on package travel, including package holidays and package tours. The objective of the Directive is to counter unfair competition and to bring consumer protection more onto the same level within the European Community, by harmonising the legislations of the individual Member States. Total harmonisation is not attempted: Article 8 of the Directive offers Member States the possibility of drawing up more stringent rules to protect the consumer.[10] **15.46**

In conformity with the Directive, Dutch law introduces almost strict (no fault) liability for the tour operator in relation to the execution of the package travel it has sold. Both the Directive and Dutch law specifically deal with package travel.[11]

It is possible that at a later stage, the Act on Travel Contracts will also cover contracts not exactly covered by the definition of the Directive, for example, self-drive holidays which provide only for accommodation.[12] (The ANVR Travel Conditions already do so, since they also apply to car and bus holidays.)

---

[10] Explanatory Notes, TK 22506, No. 3, 1.
[11] Explanatory Notes, TK 22506, No. 3, 2.
[12] Explanatory Notes, TK 22506, No. 3, 4.

(b)   Definitions (article 7 : 500 Civil Code)

15.47   Article 500 reads as follows:

1.   In this chapter and in the regulations based on it, is considered as:
     (a)   **tour operator**: the person who, during the course of business, offers pre-arranged holidays, in his own name to the public or a group of persons;
     (b)   **travel contract**: the contract whereby the tour operator obliges himself towards his contracting party to provide a pre-arranged holiday offered by himself, which includes an overnight stay or a period of 24 hours and also at least two of the following services:
          1   transport;
          2   accommodation;
          3   another tourist service, not related to transport or accommodation, which forms a significant part of the holiday;
     (c)   **traveller**:
          1   the tour operator's contracting party,
          2   the person to the benefit of whom the holiday has been stipulated and who has accepted that stipulation, or
          3   the person to whom, in accordance with article 506, the legal relationship with the tour operator has been transferred.
2.   The person who, during the course of business, acts as an agent for a tour operator not residing in the Netherlands, will be considered towards his contracting party to be a tour operator.

15.48   Paragraph 1 of this article, in conformity with the Directive, gives definitions of the tour operator, the travel contract, and the traveller.

The Directive makes it mandatory upon the national legislation to apply the regulation to the tour operator and/or retailer who sells in his own name a package put together by somebody else. Dutch legislation however, only gives a definition of the tour operator.

Only the person to whom the definition of tour operator applies may conclude a travel contract, and will then be responsible for the proper execution of the travel contract. Since the legislation has imposed such a stringent liability on the tour operator (see under article 7:507), this definition is very important.

Usually, a travel agent only sells package travel as an intermediary in the name of a tour operator, in which case only the general rules on intermediaries will apply, as laid down in the Civil Code.

However, the travel agent may sell in its own name, in which case the definition of tour operator will apply. This means that the travel contract concluded in that capacity will be governed by chapter 7A on Travel Contracts.

15.49   Of major importance is paragraph 2, which states that a travel agent who sells package travel for a foreign tour operator is considered to be a tour operator himself. This means that chapter 7A on Travel Contracts will apply to the travel agent as well as the foreign tour operator, even if he is acting as a travel agent.

The definition of the travel contract also includes the definition of package travel, as laid down in article 2 of the Directive. While there are many pros and cons of that definition, it is clear that many interpretations will be possible, and that in the end it will be up to the courts to decide whether the disputing parties have concluded a travel contract or not.

In Article 1 of the ANVR Travel Conditions, the same definitions are **15.50** used. However, in article 1.2 the ANVR has also made applicable the definition of a travel contract to those contracts in regard to car and bus holidays, which otherwise may not have been covered by the definition. Furthermore, in deviation from the Act on Travel Contracts a definition of a travel agent is given in paragraph (d), probably because in other articles of the Travel Conditions references are made to the travel agent in particular. There is no mention of a travel agent being considered as a tour operator, where he is acting for a foreign tour operator. However, since this situation is regulated in Article 7:500 of the Civil Code, that rule will already be part of the travel contract.

(c)   Information to be given before and after concluding the travel contract (articles 7:501–502)

These articles incorporate article 3 paragraph 2, and article 4 paragraphs **15.51** 1 and 2, of the Directive, which give detailed instructions about exactly what information travel brochures must contain, and what other kind of information the traveller must receive before and after concluding the travel contract.

Both articles 7:501 and 502 refer to secondary legislation which will further define this information. This has become the Package Travel Decree (*Reisbesluit*).[13] Article 7:501 speaks about information which should be given to the traveller before concluding the travel contract. This article is further defined in articles 1 and 2 of the Package Travel Decree.

According to article 1, the travel brochure must contain the following **15.52** information:

(i)   name, address and telephone number of the tour operator;
(ii)   the amount or percentage of the travel fare, which has to be paid in advance, and the period of time in which the balance has to be paid;
(iii)   information about the necessary travel documents;
(iv)   information about the possibility of cancellation insurance; and
(v)   the period of time in which the traveller should inform the tour operator that the holiday does not meet his expectations.

---

[13] Package Travel Decree of 15 January 1993, Statute-book 1993, 43.

15.53   Article 2 states that, if relevant, the brochure should also contain:

(i)   with regard to transport:
   (a)   an indication of means of transport to be used, its features and possibly its category;
   (b)   an indication of the places of departure and arrival and hours of departure and arrival, as specifically as possible;

(ii)   with regard to accommodation:
   (a)   an indication of the place or places of the accommodation, if possible with travel directions;
   (b)   an indication of the accommodation, with possibly its features and category;
   (c)   the period of stay;
   (d)   mention of the number and kind of meals included;

(iii)   the tourist services which form a significant part of the holiday;

(iv)   that a minimum number of persons is required, and that number will be incorporated in the contract, as well as the final date by which the traveller will be informed about cancellation of the holiday, in case that number of persons cannot be met.

15.54   According to Article 3, the following information should be given to the traveller before starting his holiday:

(i)   the name, address and telephone number of the local representative of the tour operator or, when there is no representative, of the local authorities who can assist the traveller; and

(ii)   information about the possibility of a travel insurance.

Article 4 states that, if relevant, the tour operator should also provide the following information before the start of the holiday:

(i)   timetables of public transportation, stops and connections;

(ii)   the (seat)location assigned to the traveller, as in a cabin on a ship or a sleeping-car in a train; and

(iii)   how contact can be made with a minor, travelling abroad on his own, or with the person, who is locally responsible for his stay.

15.55   The ANVR has incorporated these articles in its Travel Conditions in articles 3 (payment); 4 (tour cost); 5 (information); and 6 (travel documents). Article 17 gives extensive information about how claims should be submitted. (See Appendix 1 to this chapter and heading 6.)

Since the information laid down in these articles is considered to be part of the general conditions of the contract, articles 231 etc of Book 6 of the Civil Code are also applicable. Based on article 6:234, the tour operator is obliged to give the brochure to the consumer before the conclusion of the travel contract.

(d)   Cancellation by the traveller (Article 7:503)

15.56   Article 7:503, paragraph 1, gives the traveller the possibility of cancelling the holiday at any time. This is a deviation from article 4 paragraph 5 of the Directive in favour of the consumer.

Article 7:503, paragraph 2, states that if the traveller cancels because of a reason for which he can be held liable, he must pay the damages sustained by the tour operator. These damages however, cannot be more than the travel fare. The traveller has the possibility to insure himself against this risk with cancellation insurance, and there is also the possibility of substitution (see 7 (ii)).

Article 503, paragraph 3, states that if the traveller cancels the holiday for a reason for which he cannot be held liable, he must receive a refund or remittance of the travel fare, or part of it if he had already started the holiday.

The ANVR Travel Conditions in article 9 give a detailed regulation of the amount of damages to be paid in case of cancellation by the traveller. However, there is no mention of whether the traveller is liable or not. Since article 7:513 forbids deviation from chapter 7A of Book 7 of the Civil Code to the disadvantage of the traveller, article 9 of the Travel Conditions should only be applied in the case of liability of the traveller. Otherwise, it would be possible for the traveller to pay damages even when he was not liable for the cancellation. **15.57**

A distinction is made between own transport tours and other holidays. The amount of damages to be paid is dependent on how many days in advance the holiday is cancelled. However, the amount of damages cannot be more than the travel fare. There is a special regulation in case a member of a travel group cancels.

By stipulating certain percentages of the travel fare to be paid in advance, in case the traveller cancels, the tour operator does not have to prove that the damages to be paid are indeed a reasonable compensation for losses incurred. This elaborate scheme on damages could be considered onerous, according to article 6:237(i) (general conditions), which states that any stipulation that obliges a party, who cancels for another reason than breach of contract, to pay a fixed money amount, will be assumed unreasonably onerous, unless that amount is a reasonable compensation for losses incurred or for lack of profit. **15.58**

However, paragraph 3 of article 9 of the Travel Conditions gives the traveller the opportunity of proving that the losses actually incurred by the tour operator because of the cancellation are less than the amounts mentioned in paragraph 1. If that is the case, the traveller only has to pay the lesser amount.

(e)   Cancellation by the tour operator (article 7:504)

According to this article, the tour operator, unlike the traveller, may only cancel the travel contract because of important circumstances (para 1). This is a deviation, in favour of the consumer, from article 4 paragraph 6 of the Directive, which gives the tour operator the opportunity of cancelling the contract in any circumstances. **15.59**

If the tour operator cancels because of a circumstance for which he cannot hold the traveller liable, he must offer the traveller another holiday of the same or better quality. If the traveller does not accept this offer, the tour operator must give a refund or remittance of the travel fare, or part of it, if the holiday had been partly enjoyed already (paragraph 2).

15.60   If the traveller sustains damage or has been deprived of travel enjoyment because of the cancellation, the tour operator must compensate him for that, unless:

(i)   the contract is cancelled because the minimum number of persons required for the holiday to take place has not been met, and the traveller has been notified of that fact within the time stipulated in the contract (see also under sub-section 2.c);

(ii)   the cancellation is a result of *force majeure* (which does not include over-booking). The same definition for *force majeure* as given in article 4 paragraph 6 of the Directive has been used.

For the possibility of limiting the amount of damages to be paid, see under sub-section 2.j, and for a more detailed definition of deprivation of travel enjoyment, sub-section 2.1.

The ANVR Travel Conditions provide the same regulation in articles 10 and 11. Paragraph 3 of article 11 also gives guidelines determining whether or not the offered alternative holiday is of the same or better quality. Circumstances, which may influence that decision are also listed.

(f)   Change by the tour operator (article 7:505)

15.61   According to paragraphs 1 to 3 of this article, the tour operator may stipulate that he can make the following changes in the travel contract:

(i)   an essential change because of important circumstances;
(ii)   a minor change because of important circumstances;
(iii)   an increase of the travel fare until 20 days before the beginning of the holiday, because of changes in the costs of transport, including fuel costs, taxes or exchange rates, provided the tour operator explains how the increase is calculated.

The traveller has the following choices:

(i)   in the case of (i) and (iii), he can refuse the change;
(ii)   in the case of (ii), he may only refuse the change if it is really to his disadvantage.

15.62   Paragraph 4 gives the tour operator the right to cancel the travel contract if the traveller refuses the changes. The tour operator has to refund or remit the travel fare, or, if the holiday had already begun, part of the travel fare. In the case of (i) and (ii) he also has to compensate for losses incurred and for deprivation of travel enjoyment, for which reference is made to article 7:504 paragraph 3. These articles incorporate article 4, paragraphs 4 and 5 of the Directive.

Article 7:505 paragraphs 1 and 3, only give the traveller the right to refuse the proposed change, not to cancel the contract. Only the tour operator may do this, after the traveller has refused the proposed change.

The ANVR Travel Conditions have incorporated the rules regarding **15.63** changes to the contract by the tour operator in article 11. This article obliges the tour operator to submit an alternative offer to the traveller, who can reject the alteration. The alternative offer shall be at least equivalent to the original offer.

In the case of changes during the course of the holiday, the tour operator must take such measures, that the holiday may be continued, and if that is impossible, he must provide return transport home (para 8).

(g) Substitution of the traveller (article 7:506)

This article incorporating article 4 paragraph 3 of the Directive, gives the **15.64** traveller the right to transfer his legal relationship with the tour operator to a third party who meets the requirements of the travel contract. He can do this up until seven days before the beginning of the holiday. In deviation from the Directive, article 7:506 does not require that the traveller must be *unable* to enjoy the holiday himself.

The transfer will take place by agreement with the third party and notification thereof to the tour operator. Both the transferring traveller and the third party will be jointly and severally liable for the travel fare and the costs involving this transfer.

The ANVR Travel Conditions have incorporated the right of substitution in article 8, the text being almost identical to article 7:506.

(h) Liability of the tour operator (article 7:507)

This is probably the most important article of chapter 7A on Travel Con- **15.65** tracts. It incorporates article 5 of the Directive.

Article 7:507 reads as follows:

1. The tour operator is obliged to execute the travel contract in accordance with the expectations which the traveller reasonably could have, based on the travel contract.
2. If the holiday does not proceed according to the expectations which the traveller reasonably could have, based on the travel contract, the tour operator is obliged to compensate the damages sustained, unless the tour operator or the third parties whose assistance it uses in executing the contract cannot be held liable for the shortcomings in the execution, because:
   (a) the traveller can be held liable for the shortcomings in the execution;
   (b) a third party, who is not involved in the delivery of services included in the holiday, can be held liable for the shortcomings in the execution of the travel contract, while these shortcomings were unforeseeable and impossible to correct; or

    (c)   the shortcomings in the execution of the contract are a result of *force majeure* as meant in article 7:504 paragraph 3(b), or a result of an event, which the tour operator or the third party whose assistance he uses in the execution of the travel contract could not foresee or correct with due regard to all possible carefulness.

    3.   The tour operator is, depending on the circumstances, obliged to give help and assistance to the traveller, if the holiday does not proceed in accordance with the expectations the traveller reasonably could have, based on the travel contract. If its cause can be blamed upon the traveller, the tour operator is only obliged to give help and assistance if that can be reasonably asked of him. In that case the expenses incurred will be charged to the traveller. The expenses incurred will be charged to the tour operator if he or the third party whose assistance he uses in the execution of the contract can be held liable for the shortcomings in the execution according to paragraph 2.

15.66   According to this article, the tour operator commits a breach of contract if he does not fulfil his obligation to provide the holiday offered, as defined in the article. This may have the following consequences:

(i)   the traveller will be entitled to cancel the contract (article 6:265 Civil Code);

(ii)   the traveller will be entitled to ask compensation for damages, including compensation for being deprived of travel enjoyment (paragraph 2, and articles 7:510 and 511);

(iii)   the tour operator may be obliged to give help and assistance (paragraph 3).

15.67   Liability is almost strict, as in principle the tour operator will be held liable as soon as the holiday does not proceed according to the traveller's expectations, while the cause of the change barely matters. Furthermore, the tour operator is also liable for shortcomings caused by third parties he has used in the execution of the travel contract.

There are only three exceptions:

(i)   the tour operator or the third party he uses cannot be held liable for the shortcomings because of *force majeure,* or another unforeseeable and uncorrectable event;

(ii)   the shortcomings, which were unforeseeable and unavoidable, may be blamed on a third party, who has nothing to do with the execution of the contract;

(iii)   the traveller may be liable for the shortcomings.

15.68   Under the ANVR Travel Conditions, liability is regulated by article 12.

(i) Limitation of liability (articles 7:508 and 7:509)

15.69   Article 508 of Book 7 of the Civil Code does not allow a tour operator to exclude or limit his liability for death or personal injury of a traveller.

However, if the contract of travel contains a service to which an international convention applies, the tour operator may limit his liability in the case of damage for personal injury in accordance with the limitation of liability allowed by the international conventions governing the relevant service. This issue will be discussed under heading 10.

As a result of article 509 of Book 7 of the Civil Code, a tour operator is not allowed to exclude or limit his liability in the case of acts or omissions done with intent to cause damage, or recklessly and with the knowledge that damage would probably result.

With regard to liability for damage other than that caused by death or injury, the Civil Code permits the tour operator to limit its liability to a maximum amount of three times the travel fare. With regard to immaterial damages suffered by the consumer, the tour operator may limit its liability to the amount of the travel fare.

The same limitations are used in article 14 of the ANVR Travel Conditions. Liability is also excluded where travel or cancellation insurance covers the damages sustained.

(j)   Immaterial damages (articles 7:510 and 7:511)

Article 7:510 states that the tour operator, when he can be held liable for **15.70** shortcomings in the execution of the travel contract, may be obliged to compensate for immaterial losses, provided the shortcomings have resulted in deprivation of travel enjoyment.

Article 7:511 limits the amount of this compensation to a maximum of three times the travel fare.

(k)   Protection against financial incapacity of the tour operator (article 7:512)

See heading 4, on Travel Fare Guarantee Fund Foundation and Insol- **15.71** vency Law.

(l)   Mandatory law (article 7:513)

This article states that no deviations from chapter 7A may be made, to **15.72** the disadvantage of the traveller.

(iii)   Misleading advertising

The stipulation about misleading advertisement (*misleidende reclame*) has **15.73** been part of Dutch contract law since 1980, and only a few changes have been made since then. It is contained in Book 6, chapter 3, section 4 of the Civil Code in articles 194 to 196, and therefore applies to all contracts in general, and equally to the travel contract in particular.

Article 6:194 reads as follows: **15.74**

A person who makes public or causes to be made public information regarding goods or services which he, or the person for whom he acts, offers in the course of a profession or business, acts unlawfully if this information is misleading in one or more respects, such as with regard to:

(a) the nature, composition, quantity, quality, characteristics or possibilities for use;

(b) the origin, the manner and time of production;

(c) the volume of supply;

(d) the price or its method of calculation;

(e) the reason or purpose of the special offer;

(f) the prizes awarded, the testimonials or other opinions or declarations which third persons have given, or the scientific or professional terms used, the technical results or statistical data;

(g) the conditions under which goods are supplied, services are rendered or payment is made;

(h) the extent, content or duration of the warranty;

(i) the identity, qualities, skill or competence of the person by whom, or under whose guidance or supervision, or with whose cooperation the goods are or have been produced or the services are rendered;

(j) comparison with other goods or services.

15.75   This article lists several conditions under which information-giving can be unlawful. Since this list is not exhaustive other conditions may be added as well, although it will be ultimately up to the courts to decide if those conditions are unlawful or not.

Article 6:195 lays it upon the person against whom an action is brought, pursuant to article 6:194, to prove that he did not act unlawfully. It is also up to him to prove, where he did act unlawfully, that he is not liable for his actions. This provision makes it easier for the person who sustains damage because of these actions to bring suit against the liable person.

15.76   Article 6:196 paragraph 1 reads as follows:

> If a person has caused damage to another or is likely to do so by making information described in article 194 public or by causing it to be made public, the judge, upon the demand of that other person, may not only forbid the former person from making such information public, but he may also require him to publish a rectification of that information or to have it published, in the manner indicated by the judge.

This paragraph speaks for itself. It gives the injured party an effective tool to stop the person causing the damage and to make him publicly apologise for the damage. Paragraph 2 gives the same right to legal entities.

Since the principles of the EC Directive of 10 September 1984 on misleading advertising were already part of Dutch legislation, no special amendment of Dutch law was required as a result of this Directive.

(iv) Contracts made away from the place of business

On 7 September 1973 the Act on Door-to-door selling (*Colportage-wet*)[14] **15.77**
came into effect. This Act protects the consumer against door-to-door
salesmen and other suppliers of services who, away from the office
premises, try to pressure a consumer into entering an agreement he may
not have entered into at all, if he had been given more time to consider
the offer.

The EC Directive regarding the protection of the consumer in relation
to contracts concluded away from the office premises of 20 December
1985[15] had to be incorporated in Dutch legislation, which was done on 3
July 1989 by way of an Act amending the Act on Door-to-door selling.

One of the changes which was made, was in paragraph 3 of article 1,
which gives several definitions. Paragraph 3 now states that a personal
visit by a salesman which has been initiated by the consumer, does not
count as door-to-door selling, unless it regards the delivery of other
goods or performance of other services than the goods or services in relation to which the consumer had invited the salesman to visit. This exclusion is on the condition that the consumer did not or reasonably could
not know that these goods or services were part of the salesman's commercial or business activities. This change was made as a direct result of
article 2 of the Directive.

Article 24 of the Act on Door-to-door selling has been amended in **15.78**
such a way that it now incorporates the stipulation, laid down in article 4
of the Directive, that the deed which is drawn up when the contract is
concluded, must contain information as to the means and the period of
time during which the contract may be dissolved, as well as the name and
address of the person against whom this right can be activated. The seven
day period, in which the contract may be dissolved was already part of
Dutch legislation.

Article 5 of the Directive states that the legislation of the individual
Member States should determine how and on what conditions the
contract may be dissolved. Article 7 of the Directive states that the legal
consequences of dissolving the contract are to be determined by the
individual Member States. How and on what conditions the contract
may be dissolved, is regulated in Dutch Law in article 25 of the Act
on Door-to-door selling. However, the consequences are not regulated
in this Act, but may be found in the general rules of Dutch contract
law.

The other principles of the EC Directive were already part of the Act **15.79**
on Door-to-door selling, as a result of which no further changes had to be
made.

---

[14] Act of 7 September 1973, *Official Journal* 71.
[15] 85/577/EC (OJ 1985 L372/31).

(v) Long distance contracts

15.80 There is also the problem of offers made by way of direct mail, telemarketing, television sales, fax, etc. The draft EC Directive of 21 May 1992[16] speaks of agreements entered into from a distance. In Article 2 the Directive gives a definition:

> every contract regarding a good or service, which is concluded without the simultaneous, physical presence of the supplier and the consumer and by using a telecommunication-technique for making the offer and the order.

In Appendix I, the Directive gives a non-exhaustive list of these telecommunication techniques: non-addressed printed mail; addressed printed mail; standard letter; telephone with human intervention, telephone without human intervention (radio, electronic mail, telefax, television, etc, etc).

15.81 Dutch legislation does not provide for any special rules on this subject as yet, except for article 7 of Chapter 1 (purchase and change) of Book 7 (special contracts) of the Civil Code. This article, like article 8 of the draft Directive, deals with deliveries not asked for, and reads as follows:

1. The person to whom a thing has been sent and who may reasonably assume that this has been done in order to induce him to buy is, irrespective of any communication by the sender to a different effect, entitled, in his relationship with the sender, to keep the thing by gratuitous title, unless it can be imputed to the recipient that the sending has taken place.
2. If the recipient sends the thing back, the costs thereof are borne by the sender.

15.82 For the rest, the draft Directive gives several rules on how to limit certain communication techniques, presentation, contents of the offer to conclude the contract, television offers, etc, which are subjects not dealt with by Dutch legislation.

However, several organisations in the field of direct mail, sales promotion, mail order etc, have set up their own Codes of Conduct for their members, according to which the members must act, and which, more or less, safeguard the consumer's rights. They often also contain regulations about complaint procedures for prospective customers. One of those institutions, for example, is the DMIN, the Netherlands Direct Marketing Institute. It is the umbrella organisation for the Dutch direct-marketing world. It links different groups: consultancy firms, individual consultants, suppliers of specific direct-marketing products and services, and the users thereof. It positions itself as an interest group for marketing communication by mail, telephone, and other media.

15.83 It has drawn up several codes:

(i)   Mailbox advertising and door-to-door sampling Code;

---

[16] 92/C 156/05, 14.

(ii)   Listbrokering Code;
(iii)   Telephone marketing Code; and the
(iv)   Code of Conduct regarding the Act on Personal Identification.

Most of the principles laid down in the draft Directive, can, more or less, be located in those codes. Although they are not yet part of Dutch legislation, they are part of commercial practice.

At this moment there is no Act yet being drafted on this subject, and it remains to be seen if Dutch legislation will anticipate the draft Directive by trying to do so, or will wait until the draft Directive has been approved.

6.   Forms of redress

On the basis of article 17 ("Complaints") of the ANVR terms and conditions, **15.84** which apply to most travel contracts, a consumer who has complaints about a package holiday may take his case to either the Travel Disputes Committee or to the civil courts. In principle, he is free to choose. However, in personal injury cases the consumer must institute proceedings in the courts, as the Disputes Committee is not competent to hear such cases.

Disputes regarding the implementation of package holidays are often brought before the Disputes Committee. The Committee has acquired a certain status in the Netherlands. It is easily accessible to consumers, the procedure is not subject to a great many formalities and, above all, consumers may present their case easily themselves without the assistance of a lawyer. The proceedings are informal and no appeal lies against the rulings of the Disputes Committee.

If consumers wish to have the opportunity to appeal, they should bring their case before the civil courts. However, a decision of the Disputes Committee may be referred to the civil courts for review on the basis of the reasonableness of the decision. There is no real need for an appeal procedure since the majority of the disputes relate to package holidays in which, not only the total travel fare, but also the claim does not exceed the sum of NLG 2,500.

Under section 38 of the Judicial Organisation Act (*Wet op de Rechterlijke* **15.85** *Organisatie*) there is equally no right of appeal against the judgment of the magistrates' court in cases involving claims under this amount. It is wrong therefore, to believe that consumers are not entitled to apply to the courts if they so wish.

Generally, the Disputes Committee does not specify the legal grounds on which it holds the tour operator liable for non-performance by the suppliers of services. Nor is it clear what criteria it applies in determining the award of compensation. As far as providing criteria for the size of the compensation is concerned, the Disputes Committee models its awards on the practice of the civil courts, which use virtually the same criteria (*i.e.* reasonableness and fairness).

15.86   The following observations can be made with respect to the competence of the Disputes Committee to deal with disputes:

(i)   The Committee is empowered to take account of disputes regarding a holiday provided by a tour operator which operates the ANVR conditions. These conditions include an article on the handling of complaints, in which the Disputes Committee is designated as the authority entitled to issue a binding recommendation.

(ii)   The Committee is also empowered to hear a dispute if it has been designated as the authority entitled to issue a binding recommendation by a tour operator other than an ANVR member. However, the Committee always applies the ANVR conditions, as this is a requirement of its own constitution. (In such cases the tour operator must pay higher costs to the Committee than would otherwise be charged.)

(iii)   The Committee is not empowered to hear disputes concerning transport contracts. These are subject to separate conditions, often laid down in international conventions. With regard to air transport, the Committee has no power over the transport contract which comes into being between the passenger and the carrier: passengers receive a ticket issued in their own names (*i.e.* personally) as proof that a transport contract has been concluded. The same applies in principle to coach transport, but here the tour operator quite often also doubles as the carrier. In that case, the Committee considers the travel conditions to be applicable and therefore holds that it is competent.

(iv)   If a complaint against booking offices is referred to the Committee, these offices are entitled to argue that the Committee is not competent. This is because the conditions which apply between the tour operator and the traveller and in which the Disputes Committee is designated as the authority entitled to issue a binding recommendation, do not apply to the relationship between the traveller and the booking office. In practice, ANVR booking offices are always willing to be called as a party in a dispute and accept any ruling ordering them to pay compensation. Even non-ANVR members, such as banks which sell holidays, have not hitherto disputed the competence of the Committee and have as a matter of course abided by any binding recommendations.

15.87   Under article 6 of the Regulation of the Disputes Committee, a dispute may be dealt with by the Committee only if the consumers have submitted their complaint to the travel company in accordance with the provisions of the ANVR conditions. Under these conditions, the travel company must be notified in writing within one month of the end of the holiday or, if the holiday is cancelled, within one month of the original date of departure. If the complaint is not dealt with by the travel company to the satisfaction of the consumer, either party may, within a period of a maximum of three months from the notification to the travel company, refer the dispute to the Committee in writing and request a ruling.

Under article 15 of the Regulation of the Disputes Committee, the **15.88** Committee has the following powers if it considers all or part of the consumer's complaint to be justified:

(i)   it may require the travel company and the consumer to perform the contract;

(ii) it may set aside the contract; or

(iii) it may order the travel company to pay a specified sum in damages, and may give any other ruling which it considers fair and reasonable in order to end the dispute.

When determining damages, the Committee is required under its Regulation to take account of both material and immaterial damage (inconvenience and distress) suffered by the consumer. The Committee may also encourage the parties to reach an amicable settlement.

In 1992 the Committee gave rulings in 1,052 cases. The average sum **15.89** awarded in damages for the 741 complaints held by the Committee to be well-founded, was NLG 920. In 91 of the 295 cases which were dismissed, the tour operators had made an offer to the consumer before proceedings were instituted. In such cases the Committee held that the offer was reasonable in relation to the seriousness of the complaints, and that the offer had been wrongly refused by the consumer. It then proceeded to make an order binding the travel company to pay the damages referred to in the offer. In all 204 complaints were rejected by the Committee without any compensation.

The complaints submitted in 1992 related mostly to the quality of the accommodation provided. A number of disputes also related to the general surroundings of the accommodation. The consumers also complained in a number of cases that they had been put in different accommodation from that for which they had booked.[17]

7.   Insurance requirements

Dutch law does not set any requirements for travel agents or travel busi- **15.90** nesses generally, to obtain insurance.

8.   Regulation of insurance

(i)   Travel insurance

Dutch law does not provide for any special rules governing travel insur- **15.91** ance. Only general rules of contract law (Books 3, 5 and 6 of the Civil Code) and insurance law (arts 246–286 of the Code of Commerce) apply.

---

[17] Annual report 1992 of the ANVR Travel Disputes Committee.

Article 3 paragraph (b) of the Package Travel Decree provides that a traveller must receive information about the possibility of travel insurance before starting his holiday (see heading 5, *supra*). However, there is no obligation on the tour operator or the traveller respectively to provide or obtain such insurance. If the traveller does decide to obtain travel insurance, he is free to conclude this travel insurance agreement with the insurer of his own choice. He is not required to arrange for such travel insurance through his travel agent or tour operator.

There are no special legal rules governing the contents of travel insurance. The insurer can decide what and how much cover he wants to offer, and the traveller can decide whether to accept this offer or not. The insurer usually offers several packages, differing in maximum coverage and premium amount.

15.92   Exactly what is covered and under what conditions, is described in the travel insurance policy conditions. These are general conditions, and are therefore subject to the chapter on General Conditions of Book 6 of the Civil Code. As discussed under heading 5, this chapter is a result of the Act on General Conditions which came into effect on 1 January 1992. In this chapter, two articles are of special importance, article 6:236 ("the black list") and article 6:237 ("the grey list"). These two articles list stipulations that will or may be considered by a judge, when appealed to, as unreasonably onerous.

If the travel insurance policy conditions contain such an onerous stipulation, the judge may annul them in the event of a dispute between the insurer and the traveller. In the case of other disputes between the insurer and the traveller, the normal rules of legal proceedings apply.

(ii)   Hire car insurance

15.93   Hire car insurance is, like regular car insurance, governed by the Act on Liability Insurance of Motor vehicles (*Wet Aansprakelijkheidsverzekering Motorrijtuigen*).[18] This Act makes it compulsory that a motor vehicle be insured against civil law liability which it may cause in traffic. Article 3 obliges the possessor, holder or long-term user of the car to insure the motor vehicle against this risk.

The explanatory notes to the Act state explicitly that hiring a car for a relatively short period of time does not make it mandatory for the lessee to insure the motor vehicle. This duty rests on the car rental agency.

15.94   According to article 22 of this Act, the minimum amount for which the insurance will have to be effected is regulated by a separate Decree. Article 6 of the Act, provides that the injured party can recover damages from the liable party (the insured), and that he also has an individual right against the insurer. Articles 23–27 describe the Motor-traffic Guar-

---

[18] Act of 30 May 1963, OJ 228, as amended by Act of 15 April 1992, OJ 203

antee Fund, from which the injured party has the right to claim damages if:

(i)   it can not be determined who is the liable party;
(ii)   if the motor vehicle was not insured;
(iii)   if the motor vehicle was stolen;
(iv)   if the insurer is unable to pay damages; or
(v)   if the motor vehicle was excluded from being insured.

Articles 30–37 make non-compliance with insurance obligations a **15.95** criminal offence. Besides being fined, penalties are: to be taken into custody, or to have the driver's licence suspended and to be forced to pay a certain amount into the Motor-traffic Guarantee Fund.

Several EC Directives on this subject have been incorporated into national law in the meantime. The third EC Directive of 14 May 1990 has been incorporated in the Act since 1 January 1993.

According to article 1 of the third Directive, it is mandatory that the insurance must cover the liability for bodily injury of all passengers except the driver. Therefore article 4 of the Act had to be redrafted, resulting in the possibility for the driver only to be not insured against the risk of bodily injury caused by his own car.

Article 2 of the third Directive requires that payment of a single premium should provide cover for the whole European Community. For this reason article 3 of the Act had to be adjusted.

Article 3 of the third Directive makes it mandatory upon the Member **15.96** States, that the Guarantee Fund does not make its payment of damages dependent upon whether the injured party can prove that the liable party cannot or will not pay. Article 26 of the Act, in which payment by the Fund was dependent on this proof, had therefore to be slightly adjusted.

Article 4 of the third Directive states that in the event of a dispute between an insurer and the Guarantee Fund about who should pay the injured party, Member States should take measures to ensure the injured party is paid at once by one of these two. The insurer and the Fund may then determine afterwards, between themselves who should bear the loss. To incorporate this article, a new paragraph 4 of article 25 of the Act had to be included.

Finally, article 5 of the third Directive determines that parties to an accident must have easy access to the identity of the insurers of the motor vehicles involved. This principle was already regulated by article 13 of the Act. The Motor vehicle Department in Veendam keeps a register of insurers.

The requirement of article 6 of the Directive: incorporation by the end **15.97** of 1992, has been fulfilled.

When hiring a car from a car rental agency, the lessee automatically pays the insurance premiums for the liability insurance the rental agency is required to obtain for the rental car. The lessee has only a few choices left: he can pay for additional collision damage waiver, and he may obtain some additional insurance for cargo, etc.

For the rest, as for travel insurance, it is up to the car rental agency what other conditions it stipulates when renting out a car. Again, care should be taken that these conditions are not in conflict with the Act on General Conditions.

9. Rights against transport operators

(i) Introduction

15.98   It is not always clear to consumers who their contracting partner is. The contracting partner of a consumer/traveller may be, *inter alia*, a travel agent, a tour operator, or a (passenger) transport company.

If a consumer not only books carriage, but a combination of travel services, the consumer has concluded a contract for a package holiday with the tour operator. With regard to package holiday contracts the Directive of the European Council of 13 June 1990 on package travel, including package holidays and package tours[19], applies. The Dutch Act on Travel Contracts of 24 December 1992 implemented the EC Directive on Package Holidays (see heading 5, *supra*).

On the basis of the EC Directive and the articles in Book 7 of the Dutch Civil Code with regard to the travel contract, the tour operator is liable for the proper performance of the services which he has undertaken to provide. It does not matter for this purpose whether he performs the obligations himself, or arranges for them to be performed by a third party. If a tour operator is liable, its liability for the damage that is a result of its shortcoming is, in principle, unlimited. In the case of damage for personal injury, a tour operator may limit its liability only in accordance with an international convention governing the relevant service. For the Netherlands two international conventions governing transport have entered into force: the Warsaw Convention of 1929 on International Carriage by Air, and the Bern Convention of 1980 on International Carriage by Rail.

15.99   With regard to all the travel services available, a consumer might want to book the service of carriage only. In this respect, a consumer could book an air journey with an air carrier, a tour operator, or through a travel agent: a contract of carriage will be concluded between the (air) carrier and the consumer.

Under Dutch law, contracts of carriage are subject to international conventions, the rules of Book 8 ("Transport") of the Dutch Civil Code (if these rules are not contrary to the rules of an applicable international

---

[19] Directive 90/314/EEC (OJ 1990 L158/59).

convention and/or other rules of mandatory law), and applicable conditions of carriage.[20]

(ii) Contracts for the carriage of passengers

(a) Carriage by air

The Convention for the Unification of Certain Rules relating to International Transport by air, signed at Warsaw, 12 October 1929, as amended by The Hague Protocol, 1955 and supplemented by the Convention of Guadalajara, 1961, contains rules that are applicable to international carriage by air of passengers and their baggage.

15.100

The Warsaw Convention and all its further amendments constitute "the Warsaw system". The following components of the Warsaw system have entered into force in the Netherlands.[21]

(i) The Warsaw Convention of 12 October 1929; The Warsaw Convention was ratified on 1 July 1933.[22] The two main objectives of the Warsaw Convention were to create uniformity of the law and to protect the young and financially weak airline industry.

(ii) The Hague Protocol of 1955; The Hague Protocol was ratified on 21 September 1960. It did not change the principle of passenger liability, but doubled the original passenger liability limit.

(iii) The Guadalajara Convention of 1961; The Guadalajara Convention was ratified on 25 February 1964. The sole purpose of this Convention is to extend the application of the Warsaw Convention to the "actual carrier", which is not a party to the contract of carriage, but which performs the actual carriage by virtue of the authority of the "contractual carrier". This Convention became a Supplementary Convention that deals with chartering.

(iv) The CAB 18900 Inter-Carrier Agreement of 1966 (the Montreal Interim Agreement); this agreement is not an international agreement, but a private agreement between the carriers operating international services to, from or via US territory on the one hand and the United States Civil Aeronautics Board on the other hand. This agreement, which is based on article 22, paragraph 1 of the Warsaw Convention permitting special contracts, raised the limit for passenger liability to US$75,000 (including legal fees) or US$58,000 (without fees). All (Dutch) airlines flying to the United States are party to this agreement.

---

[20] Rinkes, JGJ and Verstappen, JMP, *Algemene voorwaarden in het lucht-vervoer van personen (General conditions concerning the aircarriage of persons)* (Dutch Magazine for Consumer Law, 1994, No 2, 61).

[21] Cleton, R, *Hoofdlijnen van het vervoersrecht (Headlines of the law of carriage)*, W.E.J. Tjeenk Willink (Zwolle, 1994), 217.

[22] Decree of 12 July 1933, *Official Journal* 365.

(v) The Malta agreements of 1974 and 1980; these agreements are not formal agreements, but undertakings by the Malta Group of Western European government lawyers to raise the liability limit of article 22, paragraph 1 of the Warsaw Convention for death or personal injury suffered by a passenger. In London, in 1974, the Malta Group informally agreed to raise the limitation amount per passenger to US$58,000. Similarly, six years later in Lisbon, an informal agreement was reached to increase the limitation amount to 80,000 Special Drawing Rights (SDR), (equivalent to approximately US$100,000). These increased limitation amounts may be introduced either by way of a special contract on the part of the air carrier, as permitted by article 22, paragraph 1 of the Warsaw Convention, or by national legislation.

15.101   The following components of the Warsaw system have not yet entered into force: the Guatemala Protocol of 1971, and the Montreal Protocols of 1975.

The Dutch Act on Air Transportation of 10 September 1936 (*Wet Luchtvervoer*)[23] implements the Convention and extends the rules of the Convention to carriage which is not "international carriage" as defined by the Convention.

Furthermore, the contracts of passenger carriage by air may be ruled by applicable general conditions of carriage (for instance, the General Conditions of Carriage (Passenger and Baggage) of the Royal Dutch Airline, KLM, or the General Conditions of Carriage for Passengers and Baggage of Martinair). These general conditions of carriage contain, *inter alia*, articles and provisions as provided for in the Warsaw Convention and the Dutch Act on Air Transportation.

(b) Carriage by road

15.102   There are no international rules or conventions in force for the Netherlands with regard to international carriage by road. Both international and national passenger carriage by road are regulated by articles 1140–1166 of Book 8 of the Dutch Civil Code. Articles 80–92 of Book 8 of the Dutch Civil Code are the general articles concerning national and international passenger carriage. These rules are applicable to all types of transport.

Furthermore, contracts of passenger carriage by road may be governed by the applicable general conditions of carriage.

(c) Carriage by rail

15.103   The Netherlands ratified the Convention on International Carriage by Rail of 9 May 1980 (COTIF) on 1 May 1986. Appendix A to the Treaty

---

[23] Act of 10 September 1936, *Official Journal* 523.

contains uniform rules concerning international rail carriage of passengers and their baggage (CIV).

The Dutch rules that apply to national and international carriage by rail are codified in articles 100–116 of Book 8 of the Dutch Civil Code.

Furthermore, there may be general conditions of passenger carriage by rail that are applicable to the contract of carriage. In this respect the Dutch Railways Company, NS, uses general conditions for the carriage of passengers and their luggage.

(d)   Carriage by sea

The Netherlands is not a party to the Athens Convention of 1974 relating   **15.104** to the Carriage of Passengers and their Baggage by Sea. However, the Convention has served as a guide for the provisions of Book 8 of the Dutch Civil Code.

International passenger carriage by sea and inland waterways are governed by articles 500–528 (sea) and 970–986 (inland waterways) of Book 8 of the Dutch Civil Code.

(iii)   Liability of the carrier for death or personal injury

(a)   Carriage by air

Article 17 of the Warsaw Convention and article 24 of the Act on Air   **15.105** Transportation stipulate:

> The carrier shall be liable for damage sustained in the event of the death or wounding of a passenger or any other bodily injury suffered by a passenger, if the accident which caused the damage so sustained took place on board the aircraft or in the course of any of the operations of embarking or disembarking.

Article 20 of the Warsaw Convention and article 29 of the Act on Air Transportation stipulate:

> The carrier shall not be liable if he proves that he and his agents have taken all necessary measures to avoid the damage or that it was impossible for him or them to take such measures.

The principle of liability is based on the concept of presumed fault, which means that the carrier is liable for death or injury sustained in an accident on board the aircraft, unless it proves that all necessary measures had been taken to avoid the damage, or that it was not possible to take such measures. In this respect the liability of the air carrier is rather rigorous.

(b)   Carriage by rail and road

Article 26 of the COTIF-CIV regulates the liability of the carrier by rail.   **15.106** Articles 1147, 1148 and 1155 of Book 8 of the Dutch Civil Code apply to the liability of the carrier by road, and articles 105 paragraphs 1 and 2, and 109, to the liability of the carrier by rail.

15.107 On the basis of these articles of Book 8, a passenger who wishes to hold a carrier responsible for damage suffered resulting from bodily injury or death will have to prove that:

(i) there was an accident;
(ii) the accident took place in connection with or during the carriage;
(iii) the passenger was wounded or died as a result of that accident; or
(iv) the passenger or his rightful claimant has suffered damage as a result thereof.

The carrier by rail or road is not liable in the case of *force majeure* or if the carrier proves that the damage is attributable to the passenger.

(c) Carriage by sea

15.108 Articles 504 (carriage by sea) and 974 (carriage by inland waterways) of Book 8 of the Dutch Civil Code, stipulate that the carrier is liable for damage sustained in the event of death or personal injury of the passenger, if the accident which caused the damage took place during the carriage, and in as far as the accident was caused by circumstances that could have been avoided by a careful carrier or, the consequences of which could have been prevented by the carrier.

(d) The liability of the carrier for baggage

15.109 The Convention of Warsaw, the COTIF-CIV and Book 8 of the Dutch Civil Code, also contain articles with regard to the liability of the carrier towards the passenger in the case of loss or damage with regard to the following types of baggage: unchecked baggage; checked baggage; and cars that are taken on board a ship.

(iv) Limitation of liability

(a) Carriage by air

15.110 Article 22 of the Warsaw Convention, as amended by the Hague Protocol, stipulates:

> In the transportation of passengers the liability of the carrier for each passenger shall be limited to the sum of 250,000 francs (16,600 SDR, which is approximately NLG 44,500). If, in accordance with the law of the Court to which the case is submitted, damages may be awarded in the form of periodical payments, the equivalent capital value of the said payments shall not exceed 250,000 francs.

Nevertheless, by special contract, the carrier and the passenger may agree to a higher limit of liability.

Article 30 of the Dutch Act on Air Transportation is in conformity with article 22.

15.111 The general conditions of carriage (passenger and baggage) of the

468

Royal Dutch Airlines, KLM, contain an article stipulating that, in the case of international carriage, the limitation of liability of the KLM with respect to each passenger for death, wounding or other personal injury *has* been increased by special contract, as mentioned in article 22 paragraph 1 of the Convention, to the sum of 100,000 Special Drawing Rights (which is approximately NLG 276,000).

Martinair, another Dutch Airline, has, in its general conditions, limited liability for death or for bodily injury to passengers to the sum of US$58,000.

The general conditions of carriage of both KLM and Martinair contain an article stipulating that, in accordance with article 22 paragraph 1 of the Convention, they have agreed that, as to all international carriage by KLM and Martinair to which the Convention applies and which, according to the contract of carriage, include a point in the United States of America as a point of origin, a point of destination or agreed stopping place, the limit of liability for each passenger for death, wounding or other bodily injury shall be the sum of US$75,000 inclusive of legal fees and costs except that, in case of a claim brought in a state where provision is made for the separate award of legal fees and costs, the limit shall be the sum of US$58,000 exclusive of legal fees and costs.

On the basis of article 22 paragraph 2 of the Warsaw Convention, and article 30 paragraph 2 of the Act on Air Transportation, the liability of the carrier with regard to checked baggage is limited to an amount of 250 francs per kilogram (which is approximately NLG 44.40). **15.112**

With regard to unchecked baggage, paragraph 3 of article 22 of the Convention stipulates that the liability of the carrier for damage and/or loss is limited to an amount of 5,000 francs per passenger (which is approximately NLG 890).

(b)   Carriage by road, rail and sea

The Decrees executing articles 85, 110 (rail), 518 (sea), 983 (inland waterways) and 1105 (road) of Book 8 of the Dutch Civil Code, determine that the liability of the carrier (by rail, road or sea) for death or personal injury, is limited to an amount of NLG 300,000 per passenger. With regard to baggage, the liability of the carrier is limited to an amount of NLG 2,200, but with regard to a vehicle or a ship that has been accepted to be transported, to an amount of NLG 20,000. **15.113**

(v)   Time limitation of actions

As a result of article 29 of the Convention of Warsaw, any right to damages shall be extinguished, if no legal action has been brought within two years after the occurrence of the events giving rise to the claim. **15.114**

The COTIF-CIV stipulates that claims with regard to death or injury have a limitation period of three years and that all other claims have a limitation period of one year.

With regard to contracts of carriage which are regulated by the rules of Book 8 of the Dutch Civil Code, and claims resulting out of these contracts, a limitation period of one year exists. However, with regard to death and personal injury, a longer limitation period of three years exists.

10. Financial services

(i) The Consumer Credit Act

15.115 Under Dutch law the supply of credit facilities by professional institutions, including the supply of credit cards, is governed by the Consumer Credit Act (*Wet op het Consumentenkrediet* (WCK).[24] The main provisions of the Act are discussed below.

(a) General

15.116 The WCK gives a legal framework for the supply of credit facilities by professional organisations to non-professional users of credit facilities. The Act governs nearly all of the professional supply of credit facilities up to a limit of NLG 50,000. Credit facilities exceeding this amount are not governed by the WCK.

The WCK applies only to credit transactions in which the supplier of the credit facility ("the supplier") participates during the course of business, and in which the other party, ("the consumer"), is a non-professional, natural person. Consequently, the supply of business credit facilities is excluded from the working of the WCK.

Article 1 of the WCK defines a credit transaction as an agreement under which one party (the supplier) makes available to the other party (the consumer) a certain amount of money, obliging the consumer to make one or more payments to the supplier, where at least one of the payments by the consumer takes place at least three months after the supply of the facility.

(b) Licence

15.117 According to article 9 of the WCK, it is prohibited to supply credit facilities to consumers without a prior licence granted by the Ministry of Economic Affairs (*Ministerie van Economische Zaken*).

The applicant must provide in writing, together with the application, relevant information about its business, such as:

(i) an excerpt from the Commercial Trade Register of the Chamber of Commerce;

(ii) financial data of the applicant (annual report);

---

[24] Act of 4 July 1990, *Official Journal* 395.

(iii)   the articles of association of the applicant;
(iv)   a draft of the credit facility agreement;
(v)   the criteria for granting or refusing an application for a credit facility;
(vi)   information regarding the collection of outstanding payments; and
(vii)   a draft of the prospectus to be used by the applicant, which must meet certain specific regulations.

Within three months from the date of the application, the Secretary of **15.118** Economic Affairs must decide on the application (art 11 of the WCK).
The licence will be granted, unless there are reasons to believe that:

(i)   the information provided with the application, does not match the actual circumstances; or
(ii)   the applicant supplying credit facilities does not act in accordance with the regulations provided in the WCK; or
(iii)   the applicant will not act for its own risk and account.

Furthermore, the Secretary of Economic Affairs may grant the licence subject to certain restrictions and/or conditions.
After the licence is granted, the licensee will be registered in a special register.

(c)   Recruitment and treatment of credit facility applications

The supplier of credit facilities is obliged to provide its clients with a free **15.119** prospectus in which the conditions applicable to the credit transaction, are set out. The Ministry of Economic Affairs provides rules regarding the contents of this prospectus.
The supplier is not permitted to supply a credit facility exceeding NLG 2,000, without obtaining written data regarding the financial credibility of the client.

(d)   The credit transaction

The supply of a credit facility is effected by a written agreement. The **15.120** agreement must meet certain legal standards. Article 30 of the WCK stipulates elements that the agreement must contain (such as the names and addresses of both parties, the amount of the facility both in numbers and in writing, the amount of the periodical payments, the payment schedule, possible guarantees, the client's authority to refund prematurely), whereas article 33 of the WCK stipulates certain provisions that are considered null and void (such as a provision that entitles the supplier to increase compensation due under the facility, or a provision that obliges the consumer to assign part of his salary to the supplier by way of guarantee).
Where the facility does not exceed NLG 2,000 a written confirmation of the transaction by the supplier is sufficient.

(e)   Supervision by the Ministry of Economic Affairs

15.121   A licensee is obliged to manage the administration of its business in such a way that it enables the officials of the Ministry of Economic Affairs to verify whether the obligations under the WCK are properly met by the licensee.

In this regard the licensee is obliged to provide the Ministry with a yearly statement of the number of credit transactions entered into, as well as with the amount of the credit facilities supplied. Moreover, the licensee is obliged to submit to have its books controlled on a yearly basis by an independent accountant, and to provide the Ministry with the resultant report.

Specially appointed officials of the Ministry of Economic Affairs have far reaching authority to verify whether the licensee has met its obligations under the WCK.

The Secretary of Economic Affairs may grant a discharge of certain obligations under the WCK.

(ii)   Identification of credit card-holders

15.122   On 1 February 1994, the Identification of Financial Services Act (*Wet Identificatie Financiele Dienstverlening*) came into effect.

This Act extends the identification obligations on the financial service industries. Before this Act came into effect only banks were obliged to identify their clients.

The Act does not specifically mention credit card companies. However, the Decree of 29 July 1994 concerning the designation of financial institutions and financial services with respect to the Identification of Financial Services Act expressly states that the Act does cover the financial transactions of credit card companies.

As a result of the application of the Act to credit card companies, they will have to establish and register the identity of the card-holders. Should the card-holder already be known to the company, identification is not requested. According to the Act, all clients who have opened accounts before 1989 are considered to have been identified pursuant to the Act.

In certain situations the financial service institutions may rely on earlier identification by another financial service institution.

(a)   How identification takes place

15.123   The Act distinguishes between the identification of natural persons and legal entities.

Natural persons may be identified by:

(i)   a valid passport;
(ii)   a valid Dutch driver's licence;
(iii)   a valid residence permit; or
(iv)   a municipal identity card.

Companies established under the laws of the Netherlands may be identified by: **15.124**

(i)   a certified excerpt from the Commercial Trade Register; or
(ii)   a deed drafted by a Dutch Civil Law Notary.

Companies registered within the European Community may be identified by:

(i)   a deed drafted by a Civil Law Notary enlisted in the country of registration of the company.

Companies registered outside the European Community may be identified by:

(i)   a deed drafted by a Dutch Civil Law Notary.

In establishing the identity of the client, the following data must be **15.125** registered by the financial service industries:

(i)   the name, address, and place of registration of the company, as well as its representatives;
(ii)   the type, date, and place of issue of the document used for identification;
(iii)   the type of the financial service; and
(iv)   if the financial service regards the issue of a credit card, the credit card number and corresponding account number.

Furthermore, the Act prescribes that the data must be registered and kept by the financial service institution for at least five years after termination of the facility, during which time, the financial service institution may be obliged to issue the registered data to certain authorised institutions.

(iii)   Traveller's cheques

Under Dutch law no legal requirements exist with regard to the supply of **15.126** traveller's cheques. The Consumer Credit Act is not applicable, as the supply of traveller's cheques is not considered a credit facility. Therefore, the supply of traveller's cheques is governed by the general terms and conditions of the institutions that supply traveller's cheques.

(iv)   Bureaux de change

The Act on Financial Relations with Foreign Countries (*Wet Financiele* **15.127** *Betrekkingen Buitenland 1994*)[25] prescribes that bureaux de change are obliged to report to the Dutch Central Bank ("De Nederlandsche Bank"). De Nederlandsche Bank is the supervising banking institution in the Netherlands.

---

[25] Act of 28 May 1980, *Official Journal* 321.

15.128   Bureaux de change are obliged to report to the Nederlandsche Bank the following data:

(i)   the name and address of the bureau de change;

(ii)   the clientele at which the bureau de change aims its activities;

(iii)   an indication of the annual turnover;

(iv)   the name and address of the financial institution (bank) to which the bureau de change sells its surplus currencies and from which it buys its currencies.

The Act of 15 December 1994 concerning Bureaux de Change regulates the establishment of Bureaux de Change in the Netherlands. The scope of this Act is comparable to WCK. Under the Act registration of Bureaux de Change is obligatory. The Dutch National Bank handles the registration and supervises the Bureaux de Change in the Netherlands.

11.   Compensation for victims of crime

15.129   An entity in the Netherlands, comparable to the UK Criminal Injuries and Compensation Board, is the Dutch Damages Fund for victims of Violent Crimes (*Schadefonds Geweldsmisdrijven*), hereinafter referred to as the "Damages Fund". The Dutch Act of 26 June 1975 (*Wet voorlopige regeling schadefonds geweldsmisdrijven*)[26] provided for the implementation of a Damages Fund for the victims of violent crimes. On the basis of this Act, payments may be made to anyone who has suffered physical injury caused by a violent crime committed in the Netherlands. The violent crime must have been committed maliciously, and must have caused serious injury to the victim. The Act allows material damages payments up to a maximum amount of NLG 25,000, and immaterial damages payments up to a maximum of NLG 10,000. The request for payments must be directed to the Commission Damages Fund for victims of Violent Crimes, at the Palace of Justice in The Hague.

15.130   In 1986, payments were made in the Netherlands by the Damages Fund for a total amount of NLG 1,490,857. In 1989, the Damages Fund paid a total amount of NLG 2,095,290 to victims of violent crimes.[27] In 1985, an amount in excess of 35 million pounds sterling was paid by the UK Criminal Injuries Compensation Board to claimants.[28] One may conclude that the Damages Fund in the Netherlands is of much lesser importance than its counterpart in the United Kingdom.

15.131   Victims who have suffered injury caused by a violent crime in the

---

[26] Act of 26 June 1975, *Official Journal* 382.

[27] Hazewinkel-Suringa/Remmelink, *Inleiding tot de studie van het Nederlandse strafrecht (Introduction to the study of Dutch criminal law)* (1991) 757.

[28] Dias, RWM and Markesinis, BS, *Tort law* (Clarendon Press, Oxford, 1989) 35.

Netherlands normally have to look for compensation either through their own health/social security insurance, and/or through the general statutory rules with regard to compensation for injuries caused by an unlawful act, *i.e.* on the basis of article 162 of Book 6 of the Dutch Civil Code, in conjunction with article 95 of Book 6 and following of the Dutch Civil Code.

Article 162 stipulates:

1 A person who commits an unlawful act towards another which can be imputed to him, must repair the damage which the other person suffers as a consequence thereof.

2 Except where there is a ground of justification, the following acts are deemed to be unlawful: the violation of a right, an act or omission violating a statutory duty, or a rule of unwritten law pertaining to proper social conduct.

3 An unlawful act can be imputed to its author if it results from his fault or from a cause for which he is answerable according to law or common opinion.

Article 95 stipulates:

The damage which must be repaired pursuant to a legal obligation to make reparation consists of material damage and other harm, the latter to the extent that the law grants a right to reparation thereof.

Damages may only be obtained by suing the author of the crime/unlawful act, which implies that the latter's identity must be known to an injured person. The injured person may then proceed with civil litigation against him. In order to be entitled to damages paid by the author of the crime/unlawful act, the injured person must prove that he has suffered damage, caused by an unlawful act, which may be imputed to the author thereof. The injured person may claim damages by way of compensation for the costs of recovery, and further compensation for all other harm caused by the injury, both material and immaterial.   **15.132**

12.   Time share regulation[29]

(i)   Introduction

The Netherlands have yet not introduced any legislation specifically deal-   **15.133**
ing with time share agreements. In this section we will see whether the phenomenon of time sharing can be fitted into already existing legal concepts under Dutch law.

Time sharing (in Dutch also called periodical property or a periodical lease) is an institution, whereby a unit, *e.g.* an apartment, located in a holi-

---

[29] Source: Arduin, RJA, "*Timesharing van onroerend goed vergeleken*" (Kluwer, Deventer 1993).

day resort or villa estate, either through the transfer of title of property, or through the transfer of "economic property", is transferred to a number of private persons jointly, who each, during a limited, usually accurately described, periodically recurring period of time, are entitled to make use of this unit. During their stay, they are also entitled to use further facilities of the resort.

The right to a time share is a patrimonial right (*vermogensrecht*) under Dutch law.

15.134   A patrimonial right may be valued in money, which can be concluded from the fact that it can be economically exploited, especially when it can be transferred.

Patrimonial rights may be divided in two main categories:

(i)   personal rights, which give the holder of such rights a claim against other persons;

(ii)   real rights, which give the holder a right to enjoy a good (including the right to enjoy the proceeds thereof), as well as the right to dispose of the good.

Parties may not in principle establish real rights other than those explicitly created by statutory law (Dutch Civil Code). (This is called the "closed system" of real rights.)

The real right of property is the most complete real right. Property is considered as a whole and of unlimited duration. Property limited in time is not recognised under Dutch law. However the owner of a right of property may vest a limited (real) right (*e.g.* servitudes, long lease, building and planting rights) on his property. Also a right of co-ownership is recognised under Dutch law. However property limited in time is not recognized in Dutch law.

(ii)   Time sharing as community or co-ownership

15.135   It is doubtful whether time sharing can be construed as co-ownership under Dutch law, since, under Book 3, article 178 para 1 of the Civil Code, each of the co-owners as well as the holder of the limited (real) rights is entitled to a division of the common property. It is not clear whether or not the holder of a time share right is entitled to request division of the community or co-ownership. It is therefore unclear whether or not community or co-ownership is suitable as a legal instrument under Dutch law for time sharing.

(iii)   Time sharing as a right to an apartment ("appartementsrecht")

15.136   The *Appartementsrecht* is specifically regulated in the Dutch Civil Code. It has a dualistic character, since it grants the holder of such right a real right, consisting of two components:

(i)   a share in the property of the real estate; and

(ii)   the exclusive right to use specific parts of the building and its grounds.

The *Appartementsrecht* may be considered as an independent real right, which may be registered as such in the public property registers of property. A community exists between the holders of an *Appartementsrecht*. However a holder of an *Appartementsrecht* does not have the right to claim division of the community.

The Civil Code stipulates that the relation between the holders of   **15.137**
Appartementsrechten should be regulated in a *Reglement,* in conformity with the minimum requirements laid down in the Civil Code.

The right of *Appartement* can in its turn be divided into more individual (sub) rights of *Appartement.* Since the right of *Appartement* gives its holder an exclusive right to a share of the real estate, it is not suitable as such for time sharing.

However, because of the possibility of dividing the right of *Appartement* into two or more (sub) rights of *Appartement,* the system of *Appartementsrechten* may be used as a basis for the introduction of new specific legislation, which will construe the right of time sharing as a limited real right under Dutch law. The possibility of a division of the right of *Appartement* according to periods of time should be introduced as a variety of the already existing right to divide the right of *Appartement* into (sub) rights of *Appartement.*

(iv)   Time sharing as "erfpacht"

Erfpacht is a real right, which gives the holder thereof the right to hold   **15.138**
another person's real property and to use and enjoy it. The rights and obligations between the owner and the holder of the right of *Erfpacht* follow the transfer of the property as well as of the right of *Erfpacht.*

It is possible to use the institute of *Erfpacht* for the construction of time sharing rights, since the parties are free in the determination of the duration of the right of *Erfpacht.* However, specific arrangements should be made for the administration of the joint interests of the buyers. As a possibility, it has been suggested that the joint holders of time sharing rights constitute an association or a co-operative association, which acquires the right of *Erfpacht* on the property.

(v)   Time sharing and usufruct

The right of usufruct is linked to the lifetime of its holder and is there-   **15.139**
fore not suitable for the construction of time sharing rights.

Since none of the real rights mentioned above is completely suitable for time sharing, the solution must be sought in a combination of existing, or possibly new, real rights, together with personal rights (under contractual basis).

(vi) The owner of the property

15.140 The holders of the time share rights will be the shareholders of a public limited company or a private limited company. However the shareholders will not have sufficient protection against the powers of the directors of this company, who may sell or encumber the real estate without authorisation from the shareholders. Any limitation on the powers of the directors to do so, will not have any external effect. Moreover the private limited company only has named shares, the transfer of which is subject to restrictions laid down by company law, which makes the acquisition of time sharing rights by a private limited company not practical.

An alternative is the issuing of certificates on real estate by a limited company which formally owns the real estate, thereby creating a division between legal ownership and economic ownership, a situation which may be compared with a situation under common law. Although the structure can be used for time sharing, it is considered that the interests of the holder of economic rights/holders of certificates are not sufficiently protected, for instance in the event of bankruptcy.

(vii) Time sharing as a contractual right (under a lease agreement)

15.141 The specific conditions of a particular time share agreement, determine whether it can be considered as a lease agreement under Dutch law. One of the conditions of lease agreements, the granting of a right to enjoy the property throughout a certain duration, may create particular problems in the construction of a time share agreement as a lease agreement. The fact that the "lessor" of time sharing rights is often obliged to supply other services, may also disqualify the time share agreement as a lease agreement under Dutch law.

If the time share agreement can be construed as a lease agreement under Dutch law, a transfer of title of property of the leased property does not affect the rights of the lessee/holder of the time share rights. It depends whether the time share rights are considered as a right to enjoyment of the property for a very limited period of time (in which case it is not a lease agreement under Dutch law), or as a right to enjoy the property for a longer, although interrupted, period of time (in which case the time share agreement *may* be considered as a lease agreement under Dutch law).

15.142 Experts consider that, for the protection of the purchaser, it is necessary to introduce a system combining both a real right to the property, and a system of contractual rights, specifically dealing with time sharing.

With respect to the contractual aspects, the Netherlands will have to introduce new legislation as a result of the EC Directive on time sharing.

(viii)   Directive on time sharing

On 26 October 1994 the EC Council of Ministers adopted the Directive on the Protection of Purchasers in Contracts Relating to the Purchase of a Right to Utilise One or Several Immovable Properties on a Timeshare Basis (OJ L 280 of 29.10.94, p 83).

15.143

The Directive does not deal with the property aspects of the matter, but deals with the contractual aspects of timesharing. This is not surprising, since the law applicable to immovable property is exclusively the domain of the lex rei sitae – the place where the immovable property is situated.

The EC Directive on timesharing obliges the Member States to bring their national law in line with the minimum requirements laid down in the Directive, before 1 May 1997.

As a result of the adoption of the EC Directive on timeshare contracts, the Netherlands, which has no specific provisions concerning this type of agreement, will have to introduce a set of statutory provisions regulating timeshare contracts, which will grant at least the same protection to the consumer as that given under the EC Directive.

The Netherlands will probably introduce a new section in title 7 (special agreements of the Civil Code), which title also includes a section on travel agreements.

13.   Passport and frontier control

Dutch rules governing passport and frontier control of tourists from the EC and EFTA countries are codified in the Dutch Foreigner Act of 13 January 1965 (*Vreemdelingenwet*).[30] This Act contains rules regarding admittance and expulsion of foreigners; supervision with regard to foreigners residing in the Netherlands; and the guarding of the frontier.

15.144

The Foreigner Decree of 19 September 1966 (*Vreemdelingenbesluit*)[31] implements the Foreigner Act.

The Regulation of 22 September 1966 (*Vreemdelingenvoorschrift*)[32] executes the Foreigner Act and the Foreigner Decree.

As a result of the EC Council Directive of 21 May 1973 on the abolition of restrictions on movement and residence within the Community for nationals of Member States with regard to the establishment and provision of services,[33] two articles of the Foreigner Decree and one article of the Foreigner Regulation were amended in order to comply with the provisions of the Directive.

---

[30] Act of 13 January 1965, *Official Journal* 40.
[31] Decree of 19 September 1966, *Official Journal* 387.
[32] Regulation of 22 September 1966, *Official Journal* 188.
[33] Directive 73/148/EEC (OJ 1973 L172/14).

15.145   Article 49 of the Foreigner Act stipulates that, with regard to the implementation of a Treaty or a mandatory decision under international law, the Foreigner Act may be deviated from by administrative measures (*Algemene Maatregelen van Bestuur*) in favour of foreigners in general, or certain categories of foreigners in particular.

Chapter VI (articles 91–102) of the Foreigner Decree implements the Benelux Treaty, the EC Treaty (Treaty of Rome of 1957), the Treaty on European Union (Maastricht Treaty), and the European Economic Area Treaty. The heading of Chapter VI reads "Deviations from the Act in favour of foreigners by virtue of international obligations: Benelux, EC and EEA".

On the basis of article 91 of the Foreigner Decree, a foreigner who is a national of a State that has ratified the EC Treaty, the Treaty on European Union, or the European Economic Area Treaty, and who complies with the obligations of being in possession of a document for crossing the frontier, must be admitted to the Netherlands, unless:

(i)   he constitutes an actual threat to civil order or national safety; or

(ii)   suffers from one of the diseases or ailments stipulated in the Appendix to the Decree (this does not apply to nationals from Belgium or Luxembourg); or

(iii) he becomes a public charge upon the state of the Netherlands or another public authority.

15.146   The document for crossing the frontier with regard to nationals of States that are Members of the EC Treaty, the Treaty on European Union or the European Economic Area Treaty, is a valid national passport or a valid identity card. These nationals entering the Netherlands with a valid document have the right to remain in the Netherlands for three months without a residence permit.

However, on the basis of article 19 of the Foreigner Act, the officials in charge of guarding the frontier or supervising foreigners, are authorised to stop persons who can be presumed to be foreigners, in order to determine their identity.

Customs Officials and officials of the Royal Military Police are responsible for guarding the frontier. The officials of the Municipal Police are the frontier guards at the Rotterdam harbour.

As a result of the Benelux Treaty, frontier control is only administered at the outer frontiers of the Benelux countries.[34] Therefore no control is exercised at the frontier between Belgium and the Netherlands.

15.147   With the entry into force of the Implementation Agreement to the Treaty of Schengen[35] on 26 March 1995, no control is exercised by Dutch

---

[34] The Benelux Treaty of 11 April 1960 was ratified by the Netherlands by Act of 23 June 1960, *Official Journal* 239.

[35] Member States of the Treaty of Schengen are: The Netherlands, Belgium, Luxembourg, Germany, France, Spain, Portugal, Italy and Greece

authorities on people as they cross frontiers of the Netherlands with Belgium and Germany or on people arriving in the Netherlands travelling directly from a harbour situated in another state that is a party to the Treaty of Schengen. As a result of the entry into force of the Implementation Agreement no control should be exercised on people travelling directly from an airport situated in another state that is party to the Treaty of Schengen either. However, this aim has not yet been realised in the case of passengers travelling to or from Schengen states by air. A pier, which separates passengers travelling from outside the Schengen states from passengers travelling from one Schengen state to another is being constructed. Meanwhile a magnetic card system was introduced at Schiphol Airport to separate the "Schengen" passengers from the "non-Schengen" passengers, which turned out not to be error-proof. Due to the experienced practical difficulties in physically separating passengers, passport control is again being exercised since 1 May 1995 on all air passengers. Expectations are that Schiphol Airport will have overcome the logistic difficulties in December 1995 and that no more passport control will be exercised on air passengers as from 10 December 1995.

15.148 Article 94 of the Foreigner Decree stipulates that persons authorised to stay in the Netherlands are foreigners who have a right to stay on the basis of the EC Directives and the EC Regulation mentioned in article 94.

One of these Directives is the Council Directive of 21 May 1973, on the abolition of restrictions on movement and residence within the Community for nationals of Member States, with regard to establishment and the provision of services. This Directive concerns foreigners who are nationals of a Member State of the European Community or the European Economic Area, who move to another Member State wishing to establish themselves to pursue activities as self-employed persons, or to provide services in that State, or who go to another Member State as recipients of services.

Foreigners who belong to one of the categories of persons authorised to stay in the Netherlands on the basis of the EC Directives mentioned in article 94 of the Foreigner Decree, may obtain a residence permit for the Netherlands for five years. There are some exceptions to this rule. Article 96, paragraph 2 of the Foreigner Decree, stipulates that the period of a residence permit for persons receiving services shall only be of equal duration with the period during which the services are provided.

15.149 In the past, different views were held on the legal position of the tourist under the EC Treaty. The European Court of Justice, in the case between the Italian Public Prosecutor and Luisi and Carbone has expressed its opinion on the position of the tourist under Community law.[36] Mrs Luisi and Mr Carbone were fined by the Italian authorities for infringing the Italian Act on the export of capital (exchange control

---

[36] Decision of 31 January 1984, Joined Cases 286/82 and 26/83, *Luisi* and *Carbone* [1984], ECR 377.

regulations). Italian citizens were not permitted to export more than 500,000 lire per year for tourist purposes. The Italian Criminal Court, before which the case was brought, asked for a preliminary ruling under article 177 of the EC Treaty from the Luxembourg-based EC Court of Justice.

The Luxembourg Court had to decide whether tourism services supplied in one Member State *i.e.* Germany, to residents from another Member State *i.e.* Italy, were governed by the principle of free movement of services. The question being: Could tourism services be considered as "services" under the Treaty?

15.150   The EC Treaty refers to the supplier of services who moves from one Member State to the other in order to provide his services in that other Member State. In the sector of tourism it is mostly the receiver of the services who moves to the Member State of the supplier.

15.151   The Court ruled that the Treaty required the free movement of services, irrespective of the fact that the supplier of services moves to the receiver of the services, or that the receiver moves to the Member State of the supplier, even if the services themselves as such are moved from one Member State to another Member State (for instance post, telephone, cable and other communications systems). The Court considered a tourist to be a receiver of services under the Treaty. A special relation between supplier and receiver (for instance by contract) is not necessary. On the basis of this decision, the freedom of movement of tourists has been confirmed by the European Court of Justice.

Appendix

Booking Conditions for the Association of ANVR Tour Operators

15.152 These Booking Conditions pertaining to the Association of ANVR Tour Operators were drawn up in June 1995, in consultation with the Consumers' Organisation and in the framework of the Commission for Consumer Affairs (CCA) of the National Economic Development Council (NEDC).

Article 1
Introductory stipulation

Article 1, part 1

15.153 These Booking Conditions cover the following definitions:
- (a) **Tour operator**: he who, in the practice of his company, offers, in his own name, already-organised tours to the public or to a group of persons.
- (b) **Travel agreement**: the agreement through which a tour operator commits himself, to the opposite party, to the provision of the already-organised travel which he is offering and which consists of one overnight stay or a period of more than 24 hours, as well as at least two of the following services:
  - (1) transport;
  - (2) accommodation;
  - (3) some other tourist service, not related to transport or accommodation, but which constitutes a significant part of the tour.
- (c) **Traveller**:
  - (A) the opposite party to the tour operator; or
  - (B) the person whose needs are answered by the stipulated tour and who has accepted the stipulation, or
  - (C) the person to whom, in accordance with Article 8 of these booking conditions, the legal relationship to the tour operator has been transferred.
- (d) **Booking office**: the company which acts as intermediary between the traveller and the tour operator, in reaching the travel agreement.
- (e) **Working days:** Monday up to and including Saturday, except for recognised holidays.
- (f) **Office hours:** Monday up to and including Friday, 09.00–17.30 hrs; Saturday, 10.00–16.00 hrs, except for recognised holidays.
- (g) **Communication costs:** telefax, telephone, telegram and telex costs.

Article 1, part 2

The booking conditions are applicable to all travel agreements as well as to agreements related to tours using own means of transport and commuter journeys by bus. The tour operator can stipulate that these booking conditions are also applicable to agreements related to other tours, on the condition that these are stated in the publication..

Article 1, part 3

The sums stated in these conditions include VAT, wherever applicable.

Article 1, part 4

Regarding river and sea cruises, different conditions may be applicable, for which the relevance shall be stipulated in the offers in question.

Article 2

Reaching and contents of a travel agreement

Article 2, part 1

15.154   The travel agreement is reached by the traveller's acceptance of the tour operator's offer. Acceptance can take place either directly, or via the intermediary service of a booking office.

Article 2, part 2

The tour operator's offer is free of obligations and can, if necessary, be withdrawn by him. Withdrawal should take place as swiftly as possible following acceptance, at the very latest within eight office hours after acceptance.

Article 2, part 3

In order to conclude the agreement and the implementation thereof, the traveller shall provide the booking office with the necessary information about him/herself and possible other traveller(s).

Article 2, part 4

A person who, in the name of or acting on behalf of another person, concludes a travel agreement, is severally responsible for all obligations ensuing from the agreement. The (other) traveller(s) is/are responsible for his/their own share.

Article 2, part 5

If the agreed tour is included in a publication issued by the tour operator, the facts contained therein become part of the agreement. If the tour operator has included general conditions in the general part of the programme and these should be in conflict with the booking conditions, the most favourable stipulations are applicable to the traveller.

The tour operator is not bound by obvious faults and mistakes in a publication.

Deviations from or additions to the tour offered by the tour operator can be requested on medical grounds (medical essentials). The tour operator shall make realistic efforts in order to carry out such a request, unless this can, in all reasonableness, not be demanded of him.

Medical essentials require the explicit written consent of the tour operator.

The tour operator has the right, in that case, to charge the following costs:

(a) for the deviating or additional organisational costs, up to a sum of Dfl. 50 per booking (Dfl 25 for own-means-of-transport tours, if shorter than five days or stay in the Netherlands);

(b) communication costs;

(c) possible extra costs, charged by providers of service involved in the implementation of the tour.

If the tour operator is prepared to process requests for alterations on grounds other than medical grounds (other essentials), he is entitled to charge the following costs:

(a) organisational costs connected to the request, at Dfl. 60 per booking (Dfl. 30 for own-means-of-transport tours, if shorter than five days or stay in the Netherlands);

(b) communication costs;

(c) possible extra costs, charged by providers of service involved in the implementation of the tour.

These requests also require the explicit, written consent of the tour operator.

Article 2, part 6

Regarding tours in which transport is included, if the length of tour is stated in days, then the days of departure and arrival are calculated as whole days, regardless of the departure and arrival time. Departure and arrival times, regarding the transport components of the tour, shall be mentioned in the travel documents. These times are definite. The tour operator can only deviate from these times on the grounds of legitimate reasons and within reasonable limits. In such cases, Articles 11 and 12 are not applicable.

Article 2, part 7

The tour operator does not bear any responsibility for photographs, folders and other informational material issued under the responsibility of third parties.

Article 3
Payment

Article 3, part 1

15.155 When reaching a travel agreement, a sum (down payment) shall be paid, equal to 10% of the total agreed tour cost. It shall be at least Dfl. 100 per traveller, unless otherwise stated in the publication in question.

In the case of own-transport tours, the down payment, when reaching an agreement on hotel accommodation, is a percentage equal to the above. The down payment for all other forms of accommodation, such as bungalows, apartments, motor boats, (sailing) yachts, permanent caravans and camping site lots, shall be 30% of the tour cost.

Article 3, part 2

The remainder of the cost must be in the possession of the booking office at least six weeks before the day of departure (for own-transport tours, before the arrival date at the first booked accommodation).

A traveller who does not pay on time is in default. He will be notified in writing by, or in the name of, the tour operator, after which he still has the possibility to pay the amount owing within seven working days. If the payment is then still missing, the agreement is considered as being cancelled on the default day. The tour operator is entitled to charge the cancellation costs owed. This being the case, the stipulations of Article 9 become applicable and the previously paid monies shall be

taken into account when determining the cancellation charge.

Article 3, part 3

Should the travel agreement be reached during the six weeks period before the date of departure, then the whole cost of the tour must be paid immediately.

Article 4
Tour cost

Article 4, part 1

The published fare is applicable per **15.156** person, unless otherwise stated. Included in this are the services and arrangements stated in the publication.

Article 4, part 2

The published fare is based on the prices, exchange rates, levies and taxes, such as were known to the tour operator at the time of going to press of the publication.

Article 4, part 3

In the case that the entire fare has been paid on time, the tour operator shall not change the fare during the time period of six weeks before the day of departure (for own-transport tours, before the arrival date at the first-booked accommodation). It is only in the case of an extreme increase in the fuel costs that the tour operator can, up until 20 days before the day of departure, deviate from this stipulation. The Association of ANVR Tours Operators and the Consumers' Organisation shall together decide whether or not such a situation is applicable. If no agreement can be reached, an independent party shall, in mutual consultation, be requested to pass a binding verdict.

The tour operator shall inform the traveller as to the way in which the increase has been calculated.

Article 4, part 4

If the whole fare has not been paid on time, the tour operator is entitled – up until 20 days before the commencement of the tour – to increase the fare in conjunction with changes in the transport costs (including fuel costs), the taxes owing and the applicable exchange rate. The tour operator shall, in that case, inform the traveller(s) as to the way in which the increase has been calculated. The changes in question can also give rise to a decrease in the fare unless this, bearing in mind the related costs, cannot in all reasonableness be demanded of the tour operator.

Article 4, part 5

The traveller is entitled to reject an increase in the fare, as stated in Article 4, part 3 and Article 4, part 4, above.

He is bound – under threat of default – to make use of this right within three working days after receiving the announcement about the increase.

If the traveller rejects the fare increase, the tour operator is entitled to cancel the agreement. He is bound – under threat of default – to make use of this right within seven days of the traveller's receiving the announcement about the increase. In that case, the traveller is entitled to exoneration or immediate reimbursement of already-paid monies. Articles 11 and 12 are not applicable.

Article 5
Information

Article 5, part 1

15.157 On departure and during the tour, the traveller shall be in possession of the necessary documents, such as a valid passport or, where permitted, a tourist card and the possibly stipulated visa, proof of injections and vaccinations, driving licence and green card.

Article 5, part 2

If the traveller should not be able to make (complete) use of the tour. due to lack of any (valid) document, then he shall bear all the consequences entailed, unless the tour operator has undertaken to take care of that document and the lack of it can be attributed to him or the tour operator has failed in his duty to provide information, as specified in the hereinafter following part.

Article 5, part 3

General information regarding passports, visas and possible formalities regarding health regulations shall be provided by the tour operator, or on behalf of the tour operator, at the latest on the reaching of the travel agreement. The traveller shall himself obtain the necessary complementary information from the relevant authorities and shall verify – in good time before departure – whether or not the information received earlier has been changed.

Article 5, part 4

The traveller shall be provided with information, by or on behalf of the tour operator, as to the opportunity for taking out insurance against cancellation costs, as well as travel insurance.

Article 6
Travel documents

The necessary travel documents shall be placed in the possession of the traveller at least 10 days before the day of departure (for own-transport tours, 10 days before the arrival date at the first-booked accommodation), unless this period has, for justifiable reasons, to be exceeded.

Article 7
Alterations made by the traveller

Article 7, part 1

The traveller can, after reaching the travel agreement, request alterations. Up until 28 days before departure (for own-transport tours, before the arrival date at the first-booked accommodation), these alterations will as far

15.158

486

as possible be implemented, in which case they will be confirmed in writing by the tour operator. Applicable here is the condition that the traveller pays the altered fare according to the ruling of Article 3, with the deduction of the already-paid monies. Furthermore, he is obliged to pay the alteration costs of Dfl. 60 per booking (for own-transport tours, Dfl. 30 if shorter than 5 days or stay in the Netherlands), as well as to pay possible communication costs.

Article 7, part 2

The decision on a request for alteration shall be made as speedily as possible. Any refusal shall be accompanied by the reasons thereto. The traveller can either retain or cancel the original agreement. In the latter case, Article 9 becomes applicable. If a traveller does not react to the refusal of his request, the original agreement shall be executed.

Article 7, part 3

Alterations are, in general, not possible later than 28 days before the day of departure (for own-transport tours, 28 days before the arrival date at the first-booked accommodation).

Article 8
Substitution of traveller

Article 8, part 1

15.159 The traveller can, in good time before the commencement of the tour, allow him/herself to be replaced by another person. The applicable conditions are:
  (a) the other person conforms to all the conditions contained in the travel agreement; and
  (b) the request is submitted at the latest 7 days before departure, or sufficiently early that the necessary arrangements and formalities can be implemented; and
  (c) the conditions stipulated by the service providers involved in the implementation are not in opposition to this substitution.

Article 8, part 2

The notifier, the traveller and the person who replaces him/her are severally responsible towards the tour operator for the payment of the still-owing part of the fare, as well as the alteration and communication costs and the possible extra costs resulting from the substitution, as indicated in Article 7, part 1.

Article 9
Cancellation by the traveller

Article 9, part 1

If a travel agreement is cancelled, each **15.160** traveller is – apart from possible reservation costs owing – answerable for cancellation costs.

See the stipulations in Section 1.2, regarding cancellation of agreements related to own-transport tours. The general stipulations under Section 1.1 are applicable to cancellations of all other agreements to which these conditions apply.

If a tour consists of different parts, to which different cancellation regulations apply, then these specific, different regulations become applicable.

1.1. General:

  (a) on cancellation up until 56 days before the day of departure: Dfl 75 per person, up to a maximum of 25% of the fare;
  (b) on cancellation as from (and including) the 56th day up until the 28th day before the day of departure: the down payment, up to a maximum of 25% of the fare;
  (c) on cancellation as from (and including) the 28th day up until the 14th day before the day of departure: 50% of the fare;
  (d) on cancellation as from (and including) the 14th day up until the day of departure: 75% of the fare;
  (e) on cancellation on the day of departure or later: the entire fare.

1.2. For own transport tours:

1. In the case of hotel accommodation:
(a) on cancellation up until 42 days before the day of arrival: 10% of the tour cost;
(b) on cancellation as from (and including) the 42nd day up until the 28th day before the day of arrival: 30% of the tour cost;
(c) on cancellation as from (and including) the 28th day up until the 7th day before the day of arrival: 60% of the tour cost;
(d) on cancellation as from (and including) the 7th day up until the day of arrival: 75% of the tour cost;
(e) on cancellation on the day of arrival or later: the total tour cost.

2. In the case of offers per accommodation unit:
(a) on cancellation up until 42 days before the day of arrival: 30% of the tour cost;
(b) on cancellation as from (and including) the 42nd day up until the 28th day before the day of arrival: 60% of the tour cost;
(c) on cancellation as from (and including) the 28th day up until the day of arrival: 90% of the tour cost;
(d) on cancellation on the day of arrival or later: the total tour cost.

Article 9, part 2

The cancellation costs indicated in this article shall not exceed the fare/tour cost..

Article 9, part 3

If the traveller demonstrates that the damage suffered by the tour operator is less than the sum indicated in the first article, then he will be charged the lower costs.

Article 9, part 4

In the case that there is no cancellation, but that the traveller chooses for substitution, Article 8 becomes applicable.

Article 9, part 5

Deviating cancellation regulations can be applicable to some tours or parts of tours – such as cruises, scheduled-service tours and circular tours; however they are only applicable if this has, ahead of time, been clearly stated in the related publication.

Article 9, part 6

(A) The cancellation of an agreement by one or more travellers who have jointly booked accommodation in a hotel room, apartment, holiday flat or other accommodation, serves as the cancellation of all agreements, so that the sums paid by all travellers, stipulated in the parts above, have to be paid.
(B) If the remaining travellers so wish, and if the size of their groups falls in the price column for this accommodation, the respective agreements remain intact. Sub-heading C then becomes applicable.
(C) The travellers mentioned in sub-heading B shall pay the fare as indicated in the price column for the remaining number of travellers.
(D) If the remaining travellers wish to enter a new agreement for the same period and same accommodation, the cancellation charge received for the left-over traveller(s) will be deducted from the new fare(s). Furthermore, the total sum of the cancellation fee and increased fare(s) shall never exceed the fares for the original travellers.

Article 9, part 2

A cancellation by the traveller will only be processed on working days and during office hours. Cancellations outside these office hours shall be processed on the next ensuing working day.

Article 10
Cancellation by the tour operator

The tour operator is entitled to cancel the agreement with immediate effect, **15.160** if the number of applications is less than the required minimum total, as stated in the publication. The cancellation shall take place in writing and within the time period stated in the publication. Articles 11 and 12 are not applicable.

Article 11
Alterations, possibly followed by cancellation by the tour operator

Article 11, part 1

15.162 The tour operator is entitled to alter the agreed upon provision of service on one or more essential points, due to grave circumstances.

'Grave circumstances' is considered as being circumstances of such a nature that no further commitment by the tour operator to the agreement can reasonably be demanded.

If the reason for the alteration can be attributed to the traveller, any ensuing damages shall be borne by the traveller.

If the tour operator has saved money through the alteration, the traveller is entitled to his/her share of the amount saved.

Article 11, part 2

The tour operator must, within 48 hours (2 working days) of the commencing of the grave circumstances, submit a proposal of alteration to the traveller in the form of an alternative offer. This obligation lapses, if the reason for the alteration can be ascribed to the traveller. The traveller can reject the alteration(s).

Article 11, part 3

The alternative offer shall be at least equivalent (to the original offer). The equivalence of alternative accommodation shall be judged according to objective criteria and should be determined according to the following circumstances, which shall be apparent from the alternative offer:

(1) the location of the accommodation in the destination;
(2) the type and class of the accommodation;
(3) other facilities offered by the accommodation.

In the above-mentioned judgement, the following should be taken into account:

(1) the composition of the tour group;
(2) the particular characteristics of the traveller(s) in question, as known to the tour operator and confirmed in writing by him;
(3) the traveller's desired deviations from the programme or additions thereto, such as confirmed in writing by the tour operator;
(4) the documented personal circumstances made known upon application by the traveller(s) as being of essential importance to him/her/them.

Article 11, part 4

If the offer by the tour operator mentioned in part 2 is rejected by the traveller or if a similar offer is not made, then Article 6 becomes applicable.

Article 11, part 5

The tour operator is permitted to alter the agreement on a non-essential point, due to grave circumstances which are immediately communicated to the traveller.

In such a case, the traveller can only reject the alteration if it places him/her at a disadvantage of more than limited magnitude.

Article 11, part 6

The traveller who makes use of his/her right to reject the alteration or the alternative offer as mentioned above shall make this known within three working days after receiving the notification of the alteration. In that case, the tour operator is entitled to cancel the agreement with immediate effect.

He is bound – under threat of default – to make use of this right within seven working days after receiving the traveller's statement about the alteration. The traveller is, in that case, entitled to exoneration or reimbursement of the fare (or, if the tour has already been partly used, reimbursement of a proportional part thereof) within two weeks, without prejudice to his possible right to compensation for damages as mentioned in part y of this article.

Article 11, part 7

In the case of cancellation as specified in the previous part, the tour operator reimburses the traveller for damage suffered, unless the cancellation is the result of *force majeure* as mentioned in Article 12, part 4, in which over-booking is not included.

Article 11, part 8

(A) If, after the traveller(s) has/have left, a significant part of the services, as related to the agreement, should not be provided or if the tour operator realises that he will not be able to provide a significant part of the services, then the tour operator shall make suitable, alternative arrangements, bearing in mind the continuation of the tour.

(B) If such rearranging should prove impossible, or if due to sound reasons is not accepted by the traveller(s), the tour operator shall provide the traveller(s) with an equivalent means of transport, to bring him/her/them back to the location of departure or to another location for return, in mutual agreement with the traveller(s).

(C) Damage to the traveller issuing from this alteration shall be borne by the tour operator, if the default in the implementation of the agreement can be ascribed to him in accordance with the stipulation in Article 12.

Article 11, part 9

The tour operator, without prejudice to the stipulation in Article 15, part 1, is under an obligation to inform the traveller as to any alteration, implemented by him/the tour operator, in the departure time.

This obligation does not apply to the return journey for travellers who have exclusively booked transport and/or for whom the accommodation address is not known.

Article 12
Liability and *force majeure*

Article 12, part 1

Without prejudice to the stipulation in Articles 10, 11, 13, 14 and 15, the tour operator is under an obligation to execute the agreement in accordance with the expectations which the traveller may, in all reasonableness, have on the grounds of the agreement. **15.163**

Article 12, part 2

If the tour should not turn out according to the expectations stipulated in part 1, the traveller is under an obligation to communicate this as soon as possible to the parties concerned as stipulated in Article 17, part 1.

Article 12, part 3

If the tour should not turn out in accordance with the expectations stipulated in part 1, the tour operator is under an obligation to reimburse possible damage, unless the default in the compliance cannot be ascribed to him or to the person whose assistance he uses in the execution of the agreement, because:

(a) the default in the execution of the agreement can be ascribed to the traveller; or

(b) the default in the execution of the agreement can be ascribed to a third party not included in the provision of services which are part of the tour; or

(c) the default in the execution of the agreement can be ascribed to an occurrence which the tour operator or the party whose assistance he uses in the execution of the agreement, taking into account all possible care, could not be envisaged or avoided; or

(d) the default in the execution of the agreement can be ascribed to *force majeure*, as stipulated in part 4 of this article.

Article 12, part 4

Force majeure is interpreted as abnormal and unforeseen circumstances, independent from the will of the party who pleads it and of which the consequences could not have been avoided, in spite of all precautionary measures.

Article 13
Help and support

The tour operator, according to the dictate of circumstances, is under an obligation to help and support the traveller, if the tour does not turn out according to the expectations which the latter may, in all fairness, have on the grounds of the agreement. The costs ensuing therefrom shall be borne by the tour operator, if the default in the execution of the agreement can be ascribed to him, according to the third part of Article 12.

If the cause can be ascribed to the traveller, the tour operator is under an obligation to provide help and support to a degree which, in all fairness, can be required of him. The costs are, in that case, to be borne by the traveller.

Article 14
Exclusion and restriction of the tour operator's liability

Article 14, part 1

15.164 If the tour operator, on the grounds of Article 12, is held responsible for damage suffered by the traveller, his liability shall be limited or ruled out in accordance with the applicable international treaties. Nor does he accept liability for damage for which a claim for compensation consists of the bulk of a tour and/or cancellation costs insurance.

Article 14, part 2

If the tour operator is liable to the traveller for the loss of travelling pleasure, the compensation amounts, at the most, to the equivalent of the tour fare.

Article 14, part 3

Without prejudice to the stipulations in the above parts of this article, the liability of the tour operator for damage other than caused by the death of or injury to the traveller is restricted to, at the most, three times the fare, unless there is a question of intention or flagrant guilt on the part of the tour operator. In that case, his liability is unlimited.

Article 14, part 4

The rulings out and/or limitations of the liability of the tour operator, as included in this article, are also applicable on behalf of the employees of the tour operator, the booking office and providers of service, as well as their personnel, unless this is ruled out by treaty or law.

Article 15
Obligations of the traveller

Article 15, part 1

The traveller(s) is/are under the   **15.165** obligation to conform to all instructions by the tour operator in the promotion of a satisfactory execution of the tour and is/are liable for damage caused by his/her/their improper behaviour, as judged according to the criteria for the correct behaviour of a traveller.

It is up to each traveller, at the latest 24 hours before the announced time of departure of the return journey, to verify the exact time of departure through contact with the tour leader or the tour operator's local agent.

Article 15, part 2

The traveller who causes or who threatens to cause hindrance or nuisance, so that a satisfactory execution of a tour is thereby considerably impeded or can be impeded, can be excluded from the (continuation of the) tour by the tour operator, if it cannot reasonably be demanded (of the traveller) that he/she complies with the agreement.

All resulting costs shall be borne by the traveller, if and in so far as the consequences of hindrance or nuisance can be ascribed to him/her. If and in so far as the cause of the exclusion cannot be ascribed to the traveller, he/she will be reimbursed with the fare or a part thereof.

Article 16
Interest and debt-collecting costs

15.166 The traveller who has not, on time, fulfilled a financial obligation to the tour operator, is – apart from the still-owing amount – under the obligation to pay interest of 1% for each delayed month or part thereof. Furthermore, he/she is obliged to reimburse extrajudicial debt-collecting costs equal to 15% of the amount owing, with a minimum of Dfl. 100, unless this amount, taking into consideration the debt-collecting activities, is unreasonable.

Article 17
Complaints

Article 17, part 1

15.167 An established fault in the execution of the agreement as stipulated in Article 12, part 2, shall be reported as speedily as possible to the provider of service in question, so that the latter can implement a suitable solution. If the fault cannot be resolved within a reasonable period and if it causes a deviation from the quality of the tour, this must be immediately reported to the tour leader.

If the tour leader is not present or cannot be contacted, then the traveller should immediately make contact with the tour operator in the manner prescribed by the latter. The communication costs will be reimbursed by the tour operator, unless it is apparent that, in all fairness, it was not necessary to make this contact.

Article 17, part 2

If the fault is not satisfactorily resolved and gives cause for a complaint, the traveller should report this in writing as soon as possible to the tour leader or, if this is not feasible, to the tour operator.

If a complaint cannot be satisfactorily resolved, it must, at the latest within one month of return to the Netherlands, be reported in writing accompanied by reasons, and submitted to the booking office.

If the complaint does not apply to the execution but to the realisation of an agreement, this should, within one month of recognition by the traveller of the facts related to the complaint, be reported to the booking office.

Article 17, part 3

If a complaint is not satisfactorily resolved on time or if no satisfaction has been achieved, the traveller – if so desired – can, within a period of maximum three months after the completion of the tour (or after the original date of departure) submit the complaint in writing to the Travel Arbitration Board, Surinamestraat 24, 2585 GJ The Hague. The Arbitration Board will issue a verdict according to the conditions stipulated in the relevant code. The verdict of the Arbitration Board is executed by means of a ruling which is binding to both parties. A fee shall be paid for the processing of a complaint.

Article 17, part 4

The traveller who does not wish to avail him/herself of the procedure of binding advice as stipulated in the aforegoing part, is entitled to turn to an appointed judge. This right to judgment expires one year after the conclusion of the tour (or, in the case that the tour was not executed, one year after the original date of departure).

Article 17, part 5

The ANVR shall take on the obligations of a member towards a traveller, and the binding advice imposed on him by the Arbitration Board, if the member has not fulfilled the obligations within the period stipulated in the binding advice; unless the member has, within two months of the date of the binding advice submitted it to the judge for review.

The traveller is required to submit a written appeal to the ANVR, in order that this guarantee shall be applicable.

Portugal

Chapter 16
Portugal

Henrique dos Santos Pereira
M P Barrocas & Associados

1. Regulatory authorities

(i) General Board of Tourism

The main regulatory body is the General Board of Tourism (*Direcção-* **16.1**
Geral do Turismo), whose activity is ruled by Decree Law No 328/86, dated
30 September 1986. The *Direcção-Geral do Turismo*, acting under the supervision of the government, is responsible for:

(i)   promoting and orientating the utilisation and preservation of Por-
        tugal's tourist resources;
(ii)   orientating, disciplining, superintending and supporting the hotel
        and catering trades, including tourist complexes, cultural and
        sports amenities, and places of entertainment of tourist interest;
(iii)   rendering technical support to town councils and to the regional
        tourist boards within the scope of the responsibilities hereby
        allocated to them.

The *Direcção-Geral do Turismo* is entitled to call meetings with any other
bodies who may have to be consulted, in order to comply with the legal
requirements, whenever there are matters pending which require their
views and/or joint decisions and/or comments or advice about cases in
hand.

Within the scope of (i) above, the Presidency of the Council of Minis- **16.2**
ters, through the *Direcção-Geral do Turismo*, is responsible for: advising on
regional planning, municipal plans and/or development plans whenever
the approval and/or ratification thereof lies with the government; and
proposing areas considered to be worth developing or exploiting for
tourist purposes.

Within the scope of (ii) above, the Presidency of the Council of Ministers,
through the *Direcção-Geral do Turismo*, is responsible for the following:

(i)   approving, without prejudice to any responsibilities allocated to
        other bodies by the laws in force, the location and plans of hotel
        establishments and of all or any other establishments mentioned
        in the following sub-paragraphs;
(ii)   declaring other types of accommodation to be of value for
        tourism;

(iii)   assigning "tourist complex" status to tourist developments;

(iv)   certifying places of entertainment and cultural and sports amenities as being of tourist interest;

(v)   grading hotel establishments and other types of accommodation, and altering their grades;

(vi)   issuing permits to open the establishments referred to in the preceding paragraphs;

(vii)   authorising obligatory minimum charges in certain establishments;

(viii)   superintending the establishments referred to in this law, particularly as regards the state of the premises and the quality of the service rendered;

(ix)   ordering the correction of faults detected in establishments covered by this law, particularly as regards the state of their premises and/or services;

(x)   following up complaints about services and/or premises;

(xi)   punishing infringement of the provisions of this law and its statutory regulations; and

(xii)   ordering the closure of establishments covered by this law whenever any of the cases expressly referred to herein occur.

16.3   The regional tourist boards are also responsible for superintending establishments, as envisaged in (viii) above.

The local town council and the relevant regional tourist board must be informed of decisions to close down any establishments. In accordance with the provisions of Decree-Law No 328/86 and its statutory regulations, town councils are responsible for the following:

(a)   reporting on the location and plans of the those establishments referred to in (i) and (ii) *supra*, in conjunction with all other relevant departments;

(b)   approving the location and plans of catering and similar establishments excepting those incorporated in any of the undertakings referred to in (a) *supra*, but without prejudice to the competence of any other bodies to intervene in this matter in accordance with the laws in force;

(c)   grading catering and similar establishments and changing the grades thereof;

(d)   issuing permits to open those establishments referred to in (iii) *supra*;

(e)   inspecting the premises of such establishments and ordering any necessary improvements; and

(f)   penalising those establishments covered by (b) *supra* for infringement of the provisions of this law and its statutory regulations.

16.4   The provisions of paragraphs (c) and (d) are implemented by the executive committees of the regional tourist boards, whenever they exist, provided they have the necessary resources to do so.

Competence is transferred to those Committees by means of a government memorandum issued at the request of the chairman. The executive committee may delegate all or any of the powers to its chairman. **16.5**

All or any of the powers referred to in (i) to (xii) *supra* may be delegated to the town councils or to the local mayors at their request, provided they have the necessary resources to implement such powers. Some of the powers referred to in (i) to (xii) *supra* may also be delegated to the regional tourist boards, provided they have the resources required to implement them.

Whenever such powers have been transferred, the opinion of the *Direcção-Geral do Turismo* should be sought beforehand, either directly or through the local town council, on the following matters: **16.6**

(i) feasibility of the project and the highest grade for which it is eligible;
(ii) tourist value of places of entertainment and of cultural and sports amenities; and
(iii) any prerequisites to have the undertaking classified as a tourist complex (*conjunto turístico*) or as tourist accommodation (*alojamento turístico*). This opinion will be appended to the relevant application for approval of the project.

(ii) Conselho Nacional de Turismo

The *Conselho Nacional de Turismo* was created by Decree Law 234/87, dated 12 June 1987. It is a consultation body that works with the Minister of Commerce and Tourism and is presided over by him. The *Conselho Nacional de Turismo* has the competence to assert that every subject concerning the tourist sector is subject to deliberation by its president. **16.7**

(iii) ENATUR – Empresa Nacional de Turismo

The *ENATUR – Empresa Nacional de Turismo* (EP) was created by Decree Law 662/76, dated 4 August 1976. The state is the sole owner of all the capital in the company. Its main duties are: **16.8**

(i) to manage the assets, facilities and financial holdings that belong to it, or that it holds by virtue of any contract;
(ii) to co-operate in the restoration and utilisation for tourist purposes of monuments and other buildings of historic/cultural value.

(iv) Instituto Nacional de Formação Turística

The *Instituto Nacional de Formação Turística* was created by Decree Law 333/79, dated 24 August 1979. Its main purpose is to create, maintain **16.9** and develop the necessary structures and means for professional tourist education, namely schools, hotels, and courses and to monitor education.

(v)   Instituto de Promoção Turistica

16.10   The *Instituto de Promoção Turistica* was created by Decree Law 402/86, dated 3 December 1986. Its main purpose is the promotion and defence of the image of Portugal as a tourist destination as well as the representation of Portuguese tourism abroad.

(vi)   Fundo de Turismo

16.11   The *Fundo de Turismo* was created by Law No 2082, dated 4 June 1956. It is designed to assure the patronage of tourism in the country and in particular, to help and stimulate the development of the hotel industry and other activities closely related to tourism, namely, by granting loans at low interest rates .

2.   Legal and professional rules

16.12   The access to and exercise of the activity of travel and tourism agencies are regulated by Decree Law No 198/93, dated 27 May 1993, which transfers to the internal legal system European Council Directive 90/314/EEC, dated 13 June 1990. Decree Law No 198/93 is regulated by Regulation No 24/93, dated 19 July 1993.

These legal instruments determine the purpose and regulate the exercise of the activity of travel and tourism agencies, as well as the licensing of agencies; relations between agencies; guarantees of responsibility to clients; and the inspection of the agencies' activity.

3.   General business organisation

16.13   In the Companies' Code there are no specific rules regarding business organisation in the travel industry or tourism sector. Consequently, such businesses do not have to be established in a certain form and can be formed, as a rule, as one of the following legal entities:

(i)   a partnership;
(ii)   a private company; or
(iii)   a public company.

Partnerships may take the form of *sociedade em nome colectivo* or *sociedade em comandita.* This type of organisation is not commonly used, due to the joint and unlimited liability of the partners.

The usual form of business organisation is by way of private companies **16.14** or public companies, which are respectively called *sociedade por quotas* (private limited company) and *sociedade anónima* (public limited company). The *sociedade por quotas* and the *sociedade anónima* are very similar in general terms, as both are companies with limited liability, which means that the shareholders are only liable up to the extent of their contributions to the share capital. Thus, creditors of the company are not permitted to call upon them personally for payment of debts.

The steps to establishing a *sociedade por quotas* or a *sociedade anónima* **16.15** are:

(i)   To request a certificate of acceptability of the intended name, preferably indicating one or two alternative names;

(ii)   the preparation of the articles of association of the company, including, the company registered office, the objects of the company, the share capital (minimum of PEsc 400,000 in *sociedades por quotas* and PEsc 5,000,000 in *sociedades anónimas*), the rules on management, transfer of shares and distribution of profits;

(iii)   opening a bank account in the name of the company. The capital paid-up by the shareholders must be deposited in this bank account before the signature of the notarial deed of incorporation;

(iv)   signature of the notarial deed of incorporation of the company;

(v)   after the execution of the notarial deed of incorporation, the corporate bodies of the company may withdraw the deposited amount;

(vi)   notification to the tax office of the commencement of business;

(vii)   registration of the company with the Mercantile Registrar.

4.   Special legal requirements

As previously mentioned, the ordinary regulations applied to commercial **16.16** companies do not include any specific rules concerning travel agencies.

However, Decree Law No 198/93 establishes certain requirements for the activity of the travel and tourism agency. Thus, such agencies may only have the following activities for objectives:

(i)   the organisation and sale of organised trips;

(ii)   the reservation of services in tourist facilities;

(iii)   the sale of tickets and reservation of places on any means of transport;

(iv)   the intermediation in the sale of services of similar agencies, national or foreign; and

(v)   the reception, transfer and assistance of tourists.

These activities can only be carried out by companies licensed as travel and tourism agencies, such a licence being granted by the *Direcção-Geral do Turismo.*

16.17   Travel and tourism agencies must carry out their activities in autonomous facilities which are exclusively designated for the agencies' activities. Finally, travel and tourism agencies are bound to post a bond and to draw up civil liability insurance as a guarantee to their clients.

5.   Consumer rights and safeguards

(i)   The travel contract

16.18   Travel and tourism agencies are responsible to their clients for the total execution of obligations arising from the sale of organised trips, even if these obligations are carried out by a third party, without loss of the right by the agency to claim back from that third party any expenses and/or compensation so paid.

Agencies that advertise organised trips must have programmes for the trips, which must state clearly and accurately the following elements: the price of the organised trip; terms and conditions under which alterations are legally permitted; taxes and dues related to the trip that are not included in the price; the amount and terms of the deposit; the origin, itinerary and destination of the trip, periods and dates, times and places of departure/arrival; the qualification and rating of the accommodation.

16.19   The agency is liable for the total accomplishment of this programme, and must immediately notify the client when, due to events beyond its control, the agency cannot accomplish the obligations arising from this contract. If the non-performance concerns any essential obligation, the client may eventually cancel the contract without any penalty, or accept in writting an alteration to the contract and an eventual price change.

The agency may only change the price of the trip if both of the following are satisfied:

(i)   the contract expressly provides for this change and determines the precise rules of calculation of the change;

(ii)   the change derives only from a variation of the costs of transport, fuel, or chargeable taxes and dues or exchange fluctuations.

The agency may not, in any event, increase the price during the 20 days preceding departure. An illegal change in price confers on the client the right to cancel the contract.

(ii)   Cancellation

16.20   If the client cancels the contract in the above conditions or if, by reason of an event not imputable to the client, the agency has cancelled the organised trip before the departure date, the client has the right, without prejudice to the civil liability of the agency, to:

(i)   be immediately reimbursed for all amounts paid; or

(ii) to choose another organised trip, in which case any eventual differ-
      ence in price must either be reimbursed to the client or paid by
      him.

There is no civil liability on the agency when: **16.21**

(i)   the cancellation is due to the number of participants in the organ-
      ised trip being lower than the minimum required, and the client is
      informed in writing in due time about the cancellation;

(ii) the cancellation is not due to overbooking, but is due to unpre-
      dictable and irregular circumstances whose consequences could
      not have been avoided in spite of due diligence on the part of the
      agency.

The client may always cancel the contract at any time and the agency
must reimburse him for any previously paid amounts, deducting the
charges that justifiably arise from the beginning of the fulfilment of the
contract and its cancellation, and a percentage of the service price, of no
more than 15%.

(iii)   Insurance bond

Travel and tourism agencies are bound to post a bond and to obtain civil   **16.22**
liability insurance. It is obligatory to insure:

(i)   the reimbursement of the amount received from clients;

(ii) the reimbursement of extra expenses incurred by the clients due to
      services that were not provided, or were provided deficiently;

(iii) the recovery of damages caused to clients or to third parties, by
      actions or defaults by the agency or its representatives; and

(iv) repatriation and assistance to clients.

The bond must assure at least the fulfilment of the duties provided in
subparagraphs (i) and (ii). The amount guaranteed by the bond must
be 5% of the annual turnover of the agency, but it cannot be less than
PTE 5,000,000 nor higher than PTE 50,000,000.

Interested clients can make demand directly of the guarantor, when   **16.23**
exercising any right covered by the bond.

Compulsory civil liability insurance must include the risks arising from
the travel and tourism agencies' activity, assuring the fulfilment of the
obligation provided in (i) *supra*, and in all cases, as an accessory risk, the
obligations provided in (iv). The minimum amount included in the
insurance is PTE 15,000,000. The text of the uniform policy of civil
liability was approved by the Administrative Regulation No 936/91, dated
16 September 1991.

(iv) Breach of contract

16.24 Beyond the forms of redress above (which are ruled by Decree Law No 198/93), the general principles of Portuguese civil law, mainly with regard to breach of contract, are applicable.

The basic principle is that the party who undertakes to fulfil an obligation is liable for the consequences of a failure of fulfilment of that obligation, if he has acted in fault against the law or contract. This failure may be definitive or merely temporary. In the first instance, the interest of the other party to the contract is not satisfied, and, in the second instance, there is a simple delay or defective fulfilment.

The party who has failed to accomplish the contract is liable if he acted with fault, the other party has suffered damages, and there is a link between these damages and the act or omission of the obliged party. Definitive breach entitles the innocent party to terminate the contract and to an indemnity. The consumer is not required to complain to a regulatory authority.

If no amicable settlement is agreed between the parties, the consumer must institute a legal action in the civil courts.

6. Forms of redress

16.25 Consumers entitled to claim damages, should claim in the first instance from the travel agency, which in turn will pass on the loss to the insurance company.

If the travel agency refuses responsibility or, for any reason, does not pass on the loss to the insurance company, then the consumer may institute court proceedings against the travel agency, and against the insurance company whenever it is possible (*i.e.*, when the identity of the insurance company is known).

7. Insurance requirements

16.26 There are no specific legal rules concerning insurance drawn up for clients of travel agencies and car rental companies.

Thus, in connection with sale contracts for organised trips, the agency is under a legal duty to inform the consumer, before the beginning of any trip, about the possibility of drawing up an insurance contract to cover expenses arising from cancellation by the consumer, or an assistance contract to cover repatriation expenses in the case of accident or illness. Generally, a life insurance contract is also drawn up. Usually these insurance policies are automatically drawn up, and their cost is included in the total price of the trip.

Concerning car rental, since the civil liability car insurance is obligatory, the cost of the insurance is compulsorily included in the rental price.

If any insurer wilfully does not fulfil the obligations arising from the insurance contract, the insured has no other alternative than to appeal to the courts.

8. Health and safety standards

The legal rules governing health and safety standards are the following: **16.27**

(i)   Holiday accommodation: Decree Law No 328/86, dated 29 September 1986 and *Decreto Regulamentar* (enactment) No 8/89, dated 21 March 1989.
(ii)   Bus transport: Decree No 39987, dated 22 December 1954 and Decree No 84/85, dated 8 February 1985.
(iii) Air transport: all the principal Conventions on health and safety are applicable in Portugal.
(iv)   Rail transport: Decree No 39780, dated 21 August 1954 and Decree Law No 156/81, dated 9 June 1981.
(v)   Sea transport: Decree Law No 349/86, dated 17 October 1986 and Decree Law No 415-A/86, dated 12 December 1986.

9. General consumer rights

The rights of the consumer, in addition to the specific regime covering   **16.28** travel agencies, are contained in the following general rules:

(i)   Decree Law No 330/90, dated 23 October 1990, concerning the prohibition of misleading advertising, which transposes into the internal legal system Directives 84/450/EEC and 89/552/EEC;
(ii)   Law No 29/81, dated 22 August 1981 concerning consumer protection; and
(iii) Decree Law No 446/85, dated 25 October 1985, concerning standard terms and conditions, which, as a general rule, considers every clause which is against the principle of good faith to be null and void.

10. Financial services

The attribution and use of credit cards are regulated by Administrative   **16.29** Regulation No 360/73, dated 23 May 1973, by Administrative Regulation

No 401/77, dated 4 July 1977, and by Decree Law No 45/79, dated March 1979.

Concerning traveller's cheques, as happens in most countries, there are no applicable written rules, so that trade practice is applied.

The bureaux de change regime is regulated by Decree Law No 3/94, dated 11 January 1994. It is important to point out that, although travel and tourism agencies are bound to carry out their activities in independent facilities, exclusively used for the agency's activities, they may carry out exchange operation services in their facilities.

11. Compensation for victims of crime

16.30 The rules concerning civil liability arising from crimes, are exactly the same as those mentioned above concerning the insurers' responsibility (restricted to civil liability). Nevertheless, when we accumulate both responsibilities, they are both tried together as a single case, which must be presented in a criminal court, not a civil court.

Thus, the general rules of the Civil and Penal Code shall be applied, and therefore, the damages shall be attributed by the criminal court.

12. Time share regulation

16.31 The time sharing legal regime was approved by Decree Law No 275/93, dated 5 August 1993.

The main purposes of this legal instrument are, to improve the quality and the performance of tourist facilities working in the time sharing regime, and to reinforce the protection of the purchasers. In relation to the last aspect, the following issues are noted:

(i)   only 60% of the lodging units may be exploited in a time sharing regime;
(ii)   it is obligatory to give full information to the purchaser;
(iii)   the purchaser has the right to cancel the contract within 14 days after signature, without any penalty;
(iv)   heavy penalties apply for sellers who do not fulfil their legal obligations.

13. Passport and frontier control

16.32 Border controls and special entrance and stay regimes in Portuguese territory, on tourists coming from EC and EFTA countries, applicable in

Portugal, are the same as those in other EC countries. Thus Decree Law No 60/93, dated 3 March 1993, has special importance, since it transposes into the national legal system the following Directives: 68/360/EEC, dated 15 October 1968, 90/364/EEC, 90/365/EEC, 90/366/EEC, all dated 28 June 1990; 64/221/EEC, dated 25 February 1964; 68/360/EEC, dated 15 October 1968; 72/194/EEC, dated 18 May 1972; 73/148/EEC, dated 21 May 1973; and 75/34/EEC and 75/35/EEC, dated 17 December 1975.

Spain

Chapter 17
Spain

Héctor Díaz-Bastien and Paloma Pemán Domecq*
Díaz-Bastien & Truan, Madrid–Marbella–London

1. Regulatory authorities

From the time of the 1978 Constitution onward, the Spanish Public
Administration has been subject to a complex decentralisation process, a
process which is not yet considered to have concluded. This process
gave rise to the *Comunidades Autonomas*, which to a great extent coincide
geographically with the historical regions that made up the Kingdom of
Spain. As a result, the Spanish State today has a quasi-federal structure,
with a central government, a central parliament, and regional governments and parliaments.

17.1

According to the Constitution, the *Comunidades Autonomas* could
assume the promotion and regulation of tourism within their territories.[1]
As a result, the authorities that are currently competent in matters
related to tourism are usually the regional ones.

The regulatory bodies of the tourism industry may vary from one *Comunidad Autonoma* to another. Nevertheless, given the importance of
this industry in Spain, there is normally a *conserjería de turismo* (regional
ministry) whose functions include the promotion, legislation and regulation of the regional tourism sector. Authorities on a national level also
exist, whose competence includes supra-regional tourism, those powers
not assumed by the *Comunidades Autonomas*, or by Ceuta and Melilla,
Spanish cities in northern Africa that are not part of any *Comunidad
Autonoma*.

17.2

Diversity of the regulations of the *Comunidades Autonomas* is greatest in
matters involving health and safety standards, as General Health Act No
14/1986, of 25 April 1986, assigns regulatory powers to the city councils.

These observations indicate that in some matters which are the objects

17.3

---

* Díaz-Bastien & Truan Abogados was set up in 1978 in Madrid. Héctor Díaz-Bastien was one of
 its founder members. Paloma Pemán Domecq joined the firm in 1985. Notwithstanding the
 fact that the firm offers a full range of legal services, the areas where the firm mainly concen-
 trates its activities are Company and Commercial Law, Intellectual Property Law, Publishing,
 Advertising and Entertainment Law, Bankruptcy and Insolvency, Mergers and Acquisitions,
 Joint Ventures, EC Law, Property and Planning Law, and Litigation related to other matters
 listed.
[1] Art 148, s18*a*. According to other sections of this article, the *Comunidades Autonomas* may also
 have powers in matters involving land transport within their territories (s5*a*), museums (s15*a*)
 and health and hygiene (s21*a*).

of this study, regional legislative diversity may exist. However, the following comments refer to national legislation generally applicable to all of Spain, either directly or as a basis for regional legislation.

2. Freedom of establishment

17.4 In Spain, general freedom of establishment to operate in the tourism sector exists. Although this freedom is a result of Spain's entry into the European Union (EU), the deregulation which was carried out was not limited to the EU Member States but also applies to any foreign country, (with the exception of the so-called "special areas" of activity, which include Gambling and Air Transport, as non-EU investors need administrative authorisation to invest in such areas).

Moreover, foreign governments and certain official entities other than EC bodies (including Public Companies and other companies in which a foreign Public Administration exercises effective control over them) require authorisation from the Cabinet of Ministers in order to invest in Spain, except when an international treaty establishes otherwise.

17.5 However, freedom of establishment does not imply the total absence of formalities, but rather that in order to establish a tourism company, even Spanish nationals must comply with the legally established requirements, some of which will be described later.

In addition, some remnants of the abolished Exchange Controls still exist, in relation to capital assigned to the company "from abroad" (when the investor is not a Spanish resident), which relates principally to major investments (over Pta 500 million) or to those that, even indirectly, come from countries listed as tax havens by Spanish law.

3. Legal requirements

17.6 In spite of the regional nature of the rules regulating tourist activity (see 1 *supra*,) both the Central Administration and the *Comunidades Autonomas* agreed at the Sectorial Conference on Tourism held in Madrid on 7 October 1987 upon the need to have a general set of rules to regulate the activities of travel agencies. The fruits of this agreement are: Royal Decree No 271/1988 of 25 March 1988, and the Order of the Ministry of Transport, Tourism and Communications of 14 April 1988, which together contain the current basic rules and regulations for travel agencies.

These rules provide that travel agencies must necessarily be *sociedades anónimas* or *sociedades de responsabilidad limitada* (the two classes of limited companies under Spanish law). This means that the company law provisions and regulations regarding capital and the protection of creditors are applicable to travel agencies for the benefit of consumers.

In addition, some special requirements are established in relation to the capital requirements of travel agencies: **17.7**

(i)   the capital of retail travel agencies must be at least Pta 10 million, fully paid-up;

(ii)   wholesale travel agencies require a minimum capital of Pta 20 million, fully paid-up; and

(iii) wholesale-retail travel agencies are required to have at least Pta 30 million in paid-up capital.

Compliance with the requirements regarding company type and minimum capital reserves, as well as others that will be discussed below, is controlled by the competent tourist authorities, through the granting and/or possibility of revoking operating licences.

4.   Special legal requirements

The first requirement (outlined in 3, *supra*) refers to the need for travel agencies to have a required minimum capital reserve, depending on the type of activity that they will carry out, *i.e.*, retail, wholesale or mixed. **17.8**

However, travel agencies must also comply with other requirements, which are set out below.

(i)   Objects

The objects of travel agencies must be exclusive in nature, that is, they may only carry out activities involving mediation and/or organisation of tourist-related services, even using their own facilities in the rendering of their services. **17.9**

The following objectives are established as characteristic of travel agencies, although transport providers, hotels and other tourist companies may contract their services directly with customers:[2]

(i)   mediation in the selling of tickets or reservations in all types of transport and in the reservation of rooms and other tourist services;

(ii)   organisation and sale of travel packages; and

(iii) acting as a representative of other travel agencies in the rendering of services to the customers thereof.

---

[2] Sales completed away from business premises, normally on the basis of a catalogue, is one of the subjects of Act 7/1996, of 15 January, on retail trade.

Travel agencies may also provide the following services to their customers:

(i)   tourist information, including by means of advertising;

(ii)   currency exchange and the sale and cashing of traveller's cheques:

(iii)   baggage delivery;

(iv)   entering into insurance policies in order to cover risks derived from trips booked by them;

(v)   rental of vehicles, with or without a driver;

(vi)   reservation, purchase and sale of tickets for shows, museums and monuments;

(vii) rental of sporting equipment and material; and

(viii) chartering of transport.

Spanish law differentiates between three types of travel agencies:

(i)   wholesale travel agencies – known internationally as tour operators – that may only offer their products to retail travel agencies, but never to consumers directly;

(ii)   retail travel agencies, which sell the products of wholesale travel agencies and/or their own products to consumers, but cannot sell these to other travel agencies; and

(iii)   wholesale-retail travel agencies, which can combine the activities of the two aforementioned types.

(ii) Insurance

17.10 Travel agencies must take out an insurance policy to cover their liabilities, being either primary or secondary insurance, depending upon whether the services are provided with their own means or by external ones, for:

(i)   public liability arising from the business operation;

(ii)   secondary liability; and

(iii)   liability for damage caused to property.

Cover for each of these areas must be at least Pta 25 million, and must cover accidents of all types: personal injury, material damage and financial losses. The policy must always be kept in force; a travel agency may have its licence revoked if the policy is not in effect.

This insurance is apparently only to cover third parties who are not consumers, such as suppliers, as consumers are provided with a specific guarantee (*infra*).

(iii) Guarantee

17.11 Travel agencies are also obligated to establish and keep in force a guarantee with the competent tourist authority. This guarantee may be provided in cash, by means of either a bank guarantee or an insurance policy, or through a deposit of government securities.

The law provides for two types of guarantees, single guarantees and collective ones. Single guarantees must be of:

(i)   Pta 10 million for retail travel agencies;
(ii)   Pta 20 million for wholesale travel agencies and branches of foreign travel agencies; and
(iii)   Pta 30 million for wholesale-retail travel agencies.

Collective guarantees imply that various travel agencies establish a **17.12** legally-incorporated association to make a joint and several compensation fund. This type of guarantee must be 50% of the sum of the single guarantees that each member travel agency should contribute individually. The minimum amount of the fund must be Pta 400 million for each association, whether it be regional or national in nature.

The above guarantees, which are minimum requirements, allow for the opening of up to six establishments. Each additional establishment requires that the guarantee be increased by Pta 2 million in the case of a single guarantee, and by Pta 1 million only if a collective guarantee is involved.

It is worth noting that, in practice, collective guarantees are not used, **17.13** because travel agency associations formed on a national level would face a problem: since each *Comunidad Autonoma* has the power to administer the guarantees of the travel agencies registered in its territory, the national travel agency association would have to split the guarantee among the authorities pro rata according to the number and type of their members, which would not be very practical. Furthermore, the minimum amount of the collective guarantees requires regional associations to be of a given size in order for them to be economically viable, and this is not easy to achieve.

This is unfortunate, considering that the joint and several nature of the fund means higher protection for consumers, as the coverage would not be limited to the contribution of the individual travel agency liable, but to the total fund instead.

It should be pointed out that this guarantee covers liabilities which **17.14** could be incurred by a travel agency when rendering services to the *final user or consumer*. Under previous legislation, which only mentioned *consumers*, it was understood that accommodation-providers were covered as well. Currently, there is no doubt that this is a specific and exclusive guarantee for consumers.

In principle, in order for liability to be settled with guarantee funds, it is required that it be either awarded by a final judgment, or by an arbitration of a special Tribunal set up in the *Comunidad Autonoma*, according to the provisions of the regulations on the guarantee scheme. These special Tribunals exist only in a few *Comunidades Autonomas*, such as Valencia and the Canary Islands. For this reason arbitration is normally carried out by the so-called Boards of Consumer Arbitration (*infra*).

If the guarantee fund is used, the travel agency – or the association, if a collective guarantee is involved – must replace or complete it up to the required amount. Furthermore, in the event of revocation or renunciation, or if the travel agency has ceased officially operating, it must wait a year before cancelling the guarantee. This must be taken into account when starting proceedings against a travel agency under those conditions; it would be advisable to request a cautionary embargo on the guarantee.

17.15   Non-fulfilment of the obligation to reinstate the guarantee could mean a loss of the licence. This in turn means that the business would have to cease because travel agencies cannot carry out any other activity, and to continue operating as an agency could be penalised as a crime. As a result, in practice when liability must be covered by the guarantee, the travel agency prefers to settle it directly, because reinstatement of the bank guarantee or insurance provided usually entails some extra cost.

5.   Consumer rights and safeguards

17.16   The consumer is protected by the general provisions on contractual liability, civil liability and consumer protection, found in the Civil Code, and the General Consumer and User Defence Act No 26/1984 of 19 July 1984,[3] the scope of which extends to services and not only to products,[4] and in the General Act on Advertising No 34/1988 of 11 November 1988, which implements Directive 84/450 on Misleading Advertisements.

A set of specific rules and regulations also exists on the contractual powers of travel agency services, contained in the Order of the Ministry of Transport, Tourism and Communications of 14 April 1988 on Travel Agencies.

17.17   Before these are explained, it is worth highlighting a few aspects of Spanish Consumer Protection Law:

(i)   the 1978 Constitution expressly establishes the protection of consumers and users as one of the guiding principles of social and economic policy, and in consequence, the 1988 Act was passed;

(ii)   the subjects protected thereby are those persons, either natural or legal, that acquire, use or enjoy goods, products and/or services as

---

[3] This Act is not entirely in accordance with the Directive on defective products (see "*The Comparative Law Yearbook of International Business*", Volume 15, chapter on "Product Liability in Spanish Civil Law", by Paloma Pemán Domecq (Graham & Trotman/Martinus Nijhoff)) though the Act mentioned in n3 had not been passed at the time this book was written. It should also be pointed out that several *Comunidades Autonomas* have their own Acts in this respect, as is the case of Cataluña and Andalucía.

[4] Act No 22/1994 of 6 July 1994, implementing EC Directive on liability for defective products.

their final consumers and/or users; in consequence, any consumption or use that takes place within a production process or professional activity is excluded;

(iii)   users are entitled to all elements typical of each service, as well as to the conditions and guarantees offered thereto, even though they do not appear on the contract or documents received, that is, those that may have been offered in the relevant promotion or advertising campaign;

(iv)   general terms and conditions are also subject to a protective regulation in favour of consumers, being the most vulnerable of the contracting parties. Interpretation will be made in their favour in the event of doubt, and clauses and conditions that do not comply with the said regulation[5] will be absolutely null and void.

The special rules and regulations related to the contracting of services with travel agencies establishes, among other consumer rights, the following: **17.18**

(i)   that the deposit to be paid when booking a trip cannot exceed 40% of the total estimated cost thereof;

(ii)   that contracts for package travel must include clauses related to possible liabilities and cancellations, and to the conditions of the trip;

(iii)   that, in cases where the price of a package tour increases by more than 15% (which may only be due to modifications in transport fares and to fluctuations in the exchange rate of currencies when these are expressly reserved in the contract), the customer may cancel the trip, and will be entitled to a refund of any amounts paid, excluding any administrative and cancellation expenses that the agency may incur;

(iv)   that the consumer may, at any time, cancel the trip and receive a refund of any amounts paid, subject to the obligation to compensate the travel agency for: administrative and cancellation expenses when individual services are involved; and a penalty in the case of package travel, the amount of which may vary between 5 and 25% of the total cost of the trip when cancellation takes place within 15 days prior to the start date of the trip. When certain special economic conditions exist, the cancellation expenses may be determined according to that agreed to in the relevant contract;

(v)   that cancellation of organised trips or package travel because of an inability to meet the required quota of travellers for the trip, must be communicated beforehand (at least 10 days). It is necessary that this quota has been specified in the conditions of the trip in order for a cancellation on these grounds to be possible;

---

[5]   The Unfair Terms in Consumer Contracts Directive 93/13/EC has not yet been transposed to Spanish Law. Nevertheless, the Spanish rules and regulations on the general conditions of said contracts makes this transplanting unnecessary.

(vi)   that a full refund of amounts paid be made, with the exception of agreed expenses, in the event of cancellation for reasons not attributable to the agency before commencement of the trip;

(vii)   that a return trip and a proportional refund of amounts paid be provided in the event that the continuation of the trip is not possible for reasons not attributable to the agency;

(viii)   if it is impossible to render the services according to the agreed conditions, the consumer may opt between reimbursement of the total amount paid and other services with similar characteristics in terms of category and quality. If the consumer opted for the latter and any of the services is found to be inferior to that contracted, the consumer has the right to receive a refund for the price difference.

17.19   Some of those provisions are similar to those of the Package Travel Directive 30/314/EC, and others are even stricter. However, this has been implemented by Act No 21/1995.

The most relevant aspects of this law in comparison with the Directive standards are:

(i)   that the brochure must include even the estimated price of optional excursions;

(ii)   the need to put the contract in writing;

(iii)   the minimum contents of the contract including any special request by the consumer accepted by the organiser or retailer;

(iv)   that assignment seems to have to be made for no consideration and must be reported in writing;

(v)   the minimum percentages on the total price in compensation to the consumer must depend on the time the non-fulfilment by either the organiser or the retailer takes place.;

(vi)   organisers and retailers will have to become travel agencies according to Spanish law and to establish and keep always in force a guarantee to cover their liabilities, especially in case of insolvency or bankruptcy.[6]

6.   Forms of redress

17.20   Article 31 of the 1984 General Consumer and User Defence Act commissioned the government to establish a specific system of arbitration in order to settle complaints or claims made by consumers and users. It had to be a system of arbitration without any special formalities, of voluntary

---

[6] Both aspects have still to be regulated.

application[7] and whose decisions would be binding and enforceable for the parties in question.

As a result of this mandate, the so-called Boards of Consumer Arbitration were set up in some parts of Spain. They were experimental in nature, but with the passage of time, it was deemed appropriate to implement the system all over the country, on the basis that the Boards were working quite satisfactorily.

In the interim, Act 36/1988 of 5 December 1988, on Arbitration, was passed in Spain. This Act, following EU recommendations, has made the Spanish regulation of arbitration procedures more flexible, so that its use may be more generalised. Consequently, the use of arbitration procedures in consumer-related matters has been growing in the last few years.

In accordance with the Arbitration Act, use of the consumer arbitration system must also be free of charge. **17.21**

Royal Decree number 636/1993 of 3 May 1993 finally regulated the so-called consumer arbitration system. This system is made up of a Board of Consumer Arbitration on a national level, (which will only handle arbitrations brought by consumer and user associations, whose scope is beyond the territory of a *Comunidad Autonoma*), and Boards of Consumer Arbitration at municipal, union of municipalities, provincial and regional levels, which the corresponding Public Administrations are still setting up.

Resort to this system is not allowed in the following cases:

(i)   those in which a final and definitive court decision already exists, except in relation to the execution thereof;

(ii) those matters which are inseparably united to others over which the parties in question have no capacity of disposition;

(iii) those in which the Public Prosecutions must intervene in order to represent and defend those lacking legal capacity to sue;

(iv) those involving intoxication, injury, death, or where there are reasonable indications of a crime.

7.   Insurance requirements

In Spain the so-called Compulsory Traveller's Insurance has existed since the latter part of the 1920s. It was created as just another measure of the policies forming part of tourist development policies of the time. **17.22**

Because of the protective nature of the requirements, very little margin of freedom in contracting is left to the parties in question. Nevertheless, at the end of the 1960s, compatibility with any other insurance a traveller might contract was established. The traveller may also sue the driver or transport company.

---

[7] The voluntary nature provided for this arbitration implies that the consumer or user has always the alternative of taking the matter to the standard Courts and Tribunals if he prefers these to protect his rights.

The purpose of the Compulsory Traveller's Insurance is to compensate passengers, or their heirs when the former have suffered bodily injuries or death, in an accident involving a Spanish means of collective public transport by land within Spanish territory or started the journey therein, or in the case of accidents involving Spanish ships, when the journey began in a national port.

17.23   All travellers holding a ticket, even though free of charge, are covered by this insurance, which the transporters are required to take out. Moreover, the Regulations on the Compulsory Traveller's Insurance[8] also provide for the possibility of assuming loss of the ticket when the circumstances of the accident make it plausible.

The coverage of such insurance extends to financial compensation – which amounts are legally established depending on the seriousness of the injuries suffered and on the cost of medical assistance required. It should be noted that this is only provided if the accident results in the passenger's death, permanent disability or, at least, temporary disability.

This compulsory insurance is compatible with any other insurance that the passenger may take out for the specific journey or any other covering it, as may be the case when fares are paid with a credit card. Furthermore, in any event it is stressed that the civil liability of the driver, transport company or third party who caused the accident, remains.[9]

17.24   On the other hand, public passenger transportation companies that use road, rail and cable, must have unlimited coverage on their civil liability for damage arising in the rendering of their transport service.[10] In this context, it is established that car rental companies must take out insurance providing unlimited civil liability coverage against third parties for damages that may arise from the use and circulation of their vehicles. This is a prerequisite to obtain the authorisation that each car needs to be used in this activity, similar to the requirement for travel agencies to deposit their guarantee in order to obtain their operating licences.

17.25   Air transport was for some time subject to the Compulsory Traveller's Insurance, but this is no longer the case. Today, a multilateral international agreement exists which treats the issue of the liability of air transport companies,[11] and in the case of domestic flights, the Air Navigation Act 48/1960 of 21 July 1960 regulates in detail the liability of the transport company in the event of an accident, especially those involving death, personal injury or other bodily damage, as well as the destruction,

---

[8] Royal Decree 1575/1989 of 22 December 1989.

[9] Directive 90/232/EEC on Insurance against Civil Liability in respect of the Use of Motor Vehicles has now been implemented by Act 30/1995, of 8 November, on private insurance. Coverage is extended to the whole EFTA, and even to that required by the law of the Member State where the accident took place or the vehicle was parked.

[10] Article 5–2 of the Regulations on Land Transportation contained in Royal Decree No 1211/1990 of 28 September 1990.

[11] The Warsaw Convention of 12 October 1929 for the Unification of certain rules related to international air transportation.

loss, damage or delay of checked-in baggage and hand baggage.[12] In addition, EU Council Regulation No 295/91 of 4 February 1991 sets out the form of compensation for cases involving denial of boarding on regular air transportation.

On the other hand, in order for an airline to be licensed, it is required to have taken out insurance to cover its liability in the event of an accident, especially with respect to passengers, baggage, cargo, mail and third parties.[13]

8. Financial services

The supply and use of credit cards and traveller's cheques in Spain, does not require any special formalities; on the contrary, obtaining a credit card is relatively easy. The only point of note is that the remnants of the supposedly abolished Exchange Controls require banks to communicate to the Bank of Spain their foreign transactions, such as the purchase and sale of traveller's cheques, for statistical reasons. **17.26**

In terms of use, the most common credit cards and traveller's cheques are accepted by the majority of shops, restaurants and hotels in tourist areas. However, it is possible to come across some establishments that do not take them, so it is advisable to carry some cash at all times. In any event, there are quite a few cash points, and these accept most major international cash cards.

The system established for the bureaux de change by the Bank of Spain Circular 8/1992 of 24 April 1992 is more complex. Any person, natural or legal, who wishes to carry out the activities of foreign currency exchange, must register himself as a bureau de change with the Bank of Spain. Foreign natural persons need to have a residency card if they come from an EU Member State, or a work permit if they come from a third country. **17.27**

Authorised transactions are: **17.28**

(i)   the purchase from residents, of foreign bank-notes and traveller's cheques drawn in a foreign currency, against pesetas not exceeding one million pesetas. In order to execute purchases for larger amounts, the Bank of Spain must approve the computer system used to register transactions;

(ii)   the purchase from non-residents, of foreign bank-notes and traveller's cheques drawn in a foreign currency against pesetas. If the amount to be exchanged exceeds the equivalent of one million pesetas, the non-resident must produce the statement he made to

---

[12] The compensation amounts were updated by Royal Decree 2333/1983 of 4 August 1983.

[13] According to the Order of the Public Works and Transportation Ministry of 29 December 1992 which develops EU Regulation 2407/1992 on the granting of operating licences.

the customs officials upon his arrival in Spain,[14] or certain proof of having received the money from a resident.[15] This is another important remnant of the Exchange Controls which could create, and in fact does cause quite a few inconveniences to those visitors to Spain who have not been duly advised about it;

(iii) to provide Spanish bank-notes to non-residents for expenses they may incur during their stay in Spain, for the equivalent of the amount received in their favour in a bank account held by the bureau de change. In order to carry out this activity, the bureau de change must register itself with the Balance of Payments Office of the Bank of Spain;

(iv) the sale of foreign bank-notes to residents and non-residents against domestic or foreign bank-notes. This activity also requires special registration with the Balance of Payments Office of the Bank of Spain; its concession is even more restricted than for the activity in (iii) *supra*.

9.   Compensation for victims of crime

(i) General

17.29   In the Spanish judicial system, criminal actions have priority over all others. Therefore, civil liability arising from a crime is a matter that is generally determined through criminal proceedings, although sometimes, as an independent part of the process, and regulated by the Criminal Code. Even in cases involving the death of the presumed offender, where the proceedings become civil ones, it is the regulations of the Criminal Code which are applicable.

The general rule that refers to civil liability of the criminal is contained in Article 19 of the Criminal Code, which states that *all persons criminally responsible for a crime, shall also be civilly liable.* There is also an entire section[16] in the Criminal Code that regulates civil liability derived from punishable offences. This regulation can be summarised by the concepts of scope, and of succession.

(ii) Scope

17.30   Civil liability for crimes extends not only to offenders, but also to their accomplices, and those who have financially benefited from the crime.

---

[14] A statement on the import of cash, bank drafts to bearer or gold for more than one million pesetas or its equivalent – per person and trip – has to be made by means of a form called "Modelo B-1".

[15] This refers to "Modelo B–3", which must be filled in when the cash or the amount of the bank drafts to bearer received exceeds one million pesetas or its equivalent.

[16] The 4th of Book 1.

Civil liability regulated by the Criminal Code entails the following obligations:

(i)   restitution of the object, if possible the same as that stolen, and payment for any damages that it may have suffered;

(ii)   repair of damage caused, which involves paying the price of the object at the time it was destroyed;

(iii)   compensation for material and mental damages incurred by the aggrieved party, his family or even a third party who is an outsider to the crime or its object.

(iii)   Succession

Civil liability for offences is transferred to the heirs of the responsible party. For example, if the responsible party were to die as a result of a traffic accident caused by his negligence, his estate would be liable for the civil liability determined by a court.   **17.31**

The action of the aggrieved party is also assigned to his heirs, so that if it were he who died in the above example, they could continue with the suit.

10.   Time sharing

Although it may seem surprising, given the great extent to which this variety of property has grown in practice in the most important Spanish tourist areas, there is no specific regulation for time share contracts in Spanish written law. In any event, they are a vehicle that is frequently used in the property industry and are recognised by the authorities; there has even been an attempt to legislate this matter. However, the Directive 94/47/EC on the protection of purchasers in contracts relating to the purchase of a right to utilise one or more immovable properties on a time share basis will have to be implemented in Spanish law.   **17.32**

However, Spain does have a specific set of rules and regulations on consumer protection, in terms of the information that must be provided to consumers in the purchase or rental of housing,[17] and which is applicable to the so-called *multipropiedad* or *propiedad a tiempo compartido*, which is how Spanish Law denominates time sharing.   **17.33**

These rules and regulations refer to the sale or renting by a company to individuals. In addition to establishing the obligation of veracity in the offer and in advertisements, it requires that the public have readily available ample information and documentation about the house/flat and

---

[17] Contained in Royal Decree 515/1989 of 21 April 1989.

the building or estate on which it is located, such as the planning permits and the name and address of the architect and builder. Unfortunately however, the developers and rental companies quite often do not comply with these obligations, while consumers are ignorant of the fact that they have the right to request such information.

11. Passport and frontier control

17.34 Although the Treaty on European Union has officially made the borders within the European Union disappear, in practice this is not yet a reality. However, Spain has also been one of the signatories of the Schengen Agreements[18] on the gradual elimination of controls at common borders, although Spanish borders are still important because most of them are exterior to the EU.

Under these circumstances, the basic legislation on this matter is Act 7/1985 of 1 July 1985 on the rights and liberties of foreigners in Spain, and its Regulations, passed by Royal Decree 1119/1986 of 26 May 1986. This Act and its Regulations govern the entry, stay, work and establishment of foreigners in Spain, but without prejudice to the rights established in the international treaties to which Spain is a signatory.

17.35 Thus, the Accession Treaty of Spain to the EU required that a special system be established for citizens of the other EU Member States. This is currently contained in Royal Decree 766/1992 of 26 June 1992. This system is also applicable to families of Spaniards and nationals of other Member States regardless of their nationalities. According to these rules and regulations, EU citizens on a tourist visit to Spain do not require a visa, but their family members who are nationals of third countries may require one, if no international treaty exists to exempt them.

Royal Decree 737/95 extends this privileged system to the citizens of those countries which form the so-called European Economic Area.[19]

In any event, Spain, which is pre-eminently a tourist country, tends to facilitate to the utmost the possibility for citizens of other countries to visit the country. Thus, for stays of less than 90 days, those under 14 years of age do not require a visa, nor do nationals of countries that have a treaty with Spain exempting them from visas, of which there are several.[20]

---

[18] The other signatories are Belgium, the Netherlands, Luxembourg, Germany, France, Italy, Portugal and Greece. The accession of Austria has already been started.

[19] Among the countries which have a Treaty of this type with Spain are Argentina, Brazil, Canada, Chile, Finland, Iceland, Japan, Morocco, Mexico, Norway, Singapore, Sweden and Venezuela.

[20] Currently Ireland and Liechtenstein, but regarding the latter not applicable until 1998.

12. Final remarks

In this chapter, the authors have aspired to provide a detailed representa- **17.36**
tion of the treatment that the tourism industry has in Spanish law, laying
special emphasis on those aspects which refer to the protection of
tourists as users of services. However, as has already been mentioned, its
content is not in the least exhaustive, given the profusion of rules and
regulations that exist on this subject in Spain.

CONTENTS OF CHAPTER 18

United Kingdom

Chapter 18

United Kingdom

Becket Bedford, *Barrister*,
Iain Taylor and David Parratt, *Bishop Robertson and Chalmers*,
Zahd Yaqub, *Barrister*
and June Turkington, *McKinty & Wright*

Section I*

Overview of UK Travel Law

Becket Bedford, *Barrister*

1. Introduction

(i) General
18.1

The UK tourism and travel industry had until recently never been made the subject of a distinctive legislative code. Nowhere were there set out in a systematic way the conditions for the incorporation of travel businesses and the sale of travel arrangements to the consumer. On the contrary, the travel industry was largely self-regulatory, and would have remained so, but for the intervention of Community law. There were previously no legal restrictions on the freedom to set up in business, save in the air travel industry. The terms on which the industry dealt with the public were governed by contract law and by statutory codes of general application. Following the implementation of the European Package Travel Directive[1] (the Directive) by the Package Travel Regulations 1992[2] (the regulations), there is now a specific legislative code to regulate the travel industry in the UK, and the conditions now exist for the emergence of a distinct body of law which may come to be known as tourism law. (Unless stated otherwise, the provisions referred to in this chapter apply also in Northern Ireland.)

(ii) ATOL
18.2

Prior to the Directive, independent regulation of the air travel industry

---

* The law relating to Northern Ireland was contributed by June Turkington, solicitor (Northern Ireland).

[1] Council Directive 90/314/EEC on package travel, package holidays and package tours, OJ.1990 L158/59.

[2] SI 1992/3288, Consumer protection, The Package Travel, Package Holidays and Package Tours Regulations 1992.

had existed since 1973, in limited form, by way of the creation of the Air Travel Organisers' Licensing (ATOL) system,[3] operated by the Civil Aviation Authority (CAA). ATOL regulates the provision of charter flight seats and gives threefold protection to holidaymakers who fly to their holiday destinations on flight tickets sold as part of their package holiday, or who book charter flights from licence holders.

18.3　　Firstly, entry to the industry is limited to persons who must be suitably qualified in terms of their fitness and financial worth. It is a criminal offence to operate as an air travel organiser without a licence.[4] Secondly, each licence holder is required to maintain a bond as a condition of his licence. The bonds are for distribution to out-of-pocket and stranded holidaymakers whose licensed tour operators have collapsed. The third level of protection provided by ATOL is a cash reserve, known as the Air Travel Reserve Fund. The Fund is to compensate travellers where individual bonds prove inadequate to the task.

(ii)　The Civil Aviation Authority

18.4　The CAA is the regulatory body charged with operating the ATOL system. The CAA's powers are limited to awarding and monitoring compliance with ATOL licences and to administering the Air Travel Trust Fund. The CAA also has an enforcement role and it will prosecute operators who trade without a licence or in breach of their licences. The CAA has no function in the resolution of holiday disputes and it has no power to regulate the terms on which the industry contracts with the public.

2.　The Package Travel Regulations 1992

(i)　General

18.5　The regulations implementing the Directive, extend the type of financial protection available under ATOL to the package travel industry generally, without introducing a licensing system of general application.

Most importantly, for the first time the regulations control the terms on which the package travel industry can sell to the public, by introducing a criminal as well as a civil code.

The regulations apply only to defined packages, namely any combination of transport, accommodation and/or other tourist service, accounting for a significant part of the package. The package must be for a duration of more than 24 hours or include an overnight stay.[5]

---

[3] SI 1972/ 223, The Civil Aviation (Air Travel Organisers' Licensing) regulations 1972.
[4] Regulation 2(1) and (5) SI 1973/223. Airlines and airline operators are exempted from the requirement to hold a licence.
[5] Regulation 2(1), SI 1992/3288.

(ii) Approved bodies for the purposes of bonding

Prior to the regulations the travel industry was largely free from regulation. **18.6**
However, the industry had always sought to regulate itself, and the various
trade associations which existed prior to the regulations survive today, and
what is more, they have also been given a vital role under the regulations.

The regulations require package sellers to make financial arrange- **18.7**
ments for the protection of the consumer in the event of insolvency
(*infra*).[6] The regulations allow package sellers to make the necessary
financial arrangements with their various trade associations. To this end,
the following trade associations have been approved to administer bonds
under the regulations:

(i)   The Association of British Travel Agents Limited (ABTA), which
        runs a bonding scheme under regulation 18.[7] (In order to bond
        with ABTA a package seller must be a member of ABTA.);

(ii)   The Association of Independent Tour Operators (AITO), which
        runs a bonding scheme under regulation 18.[8] (In order to obtain
        bonding with AITO a package seller must first become a member.);

(iii)   The Confederation of Passenger Transport (CPT), which runs a
        bonding scheme under regulation 18.[9] (Membership of the CPT is
        required for bonding. The CPT is a trade association which repre-
        sents coach travel operators.);

(iv)   The Federation of Tour Operators (FTO), which runs a bonding
        scheme under regulation 17.[10] (Membership is required for bond-
        ing purposes and the FTO limits membership to all but the very
        largest package sellers.);

(v)   The Passenger Shipping Association (PSA), which runs a bonding
        scheme under regulation 17.[11] (Membership is required for bond-
        ing purposes and is open to ferry and cruise operators.); and

(vi)   The Association of Bonded Travel Organisers Trust Limited
        (ABTOT), which is the only approved body which is not in itself a
        trade association, and as a result there is no requirement to
        become a member of ABTOT in order to obtain bonding. ABTOT
        runs a bonding scheme under regulation 18.[12]

(iii) Enforcement of criminal provisions

Trading Standards Officers operating from Local Weights and Measures **18.8**
Authorities or, in Northern Ireland, the Trading Standards Branch of the
Department of Economic Development, have primary responsibility for

---

[6] Regulation 16(1) and (2) *ibid*, see also paras 80 *et seq*.
[7] See para 77.
[8] *ibid*.
[9] *ibid*.
[10] Para 76.
[11] *ibid*.
[12] See n 7 *supra*.

enforcing the criminal provisions of the regulations. Their powers under the regulations complement those under the Trade Descriptions Act 1968 and the Consumer Protection Act 1987.[13]

(iv)   Criminal Code

18.9   It is a criminal offence to contract with members of the public for the sale of travel packages without the requisite financial cover.[14] The regulations prescribe the minimum steps which the industry must take in order to protect holiday makers against the insolvency of package travel providers.[15]

The regulations create new offences concerning the supply of brochures.[16] It is an offence not to supply certain stipulated information concerning visa requirements.[17] It is an offence not to supply certain other stipulated information regarding the itinerary in good time.[18]

The travel industry is already subject to existing offences concerning the giving of misleading descriptions of its services and misleading indications as to price under the Trade Descriptions Act 1968 and under the Consumer Protection Act 1987.

(v)   Civil Code

18.10   The regulations set out a civil code in respect of: misleading descriptive matter;[19] the binding nature of brochures;[20] the content and form of contracts;[21] transfer of bookings;[22] price revision;[23] a significant alteration to essential terms;[24] the rights of consumers in the event of cancellation;[25] where a significant proportion of services are not provided;[26] or where the contract is not properly performed.[27] Breaches of the civil code introduced by the regulations render package retailers and organisers liable in damages to individual consumers.

The Misrepresentation Act 1967,[28] the Unfair Contract Terms Act

---

[13] Part III of the Consumer Protection Act 1987, which deals with misleading price indications, does not apply in Northern Ireland, but Pt III of the Consumer Protection (Northern Ireland) Order 1987 (SI 1987/2049) is identical in substance.
[14] Regulation 16(3) SI 1992/3288.
[15] Regulation 16(2) *ibid.*
[16] Regulation 5(3) *ibid.*
[17] Regulation 7(3) *ibid.*
[18] Regulation 8(3) *ibid.*
[19] Regulation 4 *ibid.*
[20] Regulation 6 *ibid.*
[21] Regulation 9 *ibid.*
[22] Regulation 10 *ibid.*
[23] Regulation 11 *ibid.*
[24] Regulation 12 *ibid.*
[25] Regulation 13 *ibid.*
[26] Regulation 14 *ibid.*
[27] Regulation 15 *ibid.*
[28] The Misrepresentation Act 1967 does not apply in Northern Ireland. The equivalent there is the Misrepresentation Act (Northern Ireland) 1967.

1977, the Unfair Contract Terms Directive,[29] and the Supply of Goods and Services Act 1982, all govern the terms of consumer contracts.

3. Conditions for entry into the UK travel industry

Save for the air travel industry, at one time any enterprise wishing to sell **18.11** holiday arrangements in the United Kingdom could set up in business free from any legal restriction.

Today the position is dramatically changed. For the package travel industry, at least, clear restrictions limit entry to the travel industry to only those operators who can arrange cover for the protection of the consumer in the event of financial collapse.

Two regimes sit side by side regulating entry to the travel industry as a **18.12** whole. On the one hand a licensing system controls entry to the air travel industry, while the rest of the industry need only comply with the Package Travel regulations. As a result, a distinction is made in the United Kingdom between "licensable operations" and "non-licensable operations".

4. Licensable operations

(i) Provision of flight accommodation

The provision of air travel in the United Kingdom is a licensable operation **18.13** and an enterprise wishing to sell air flights on their own or as part of an inclusive package is required by the ATOL regulations to hold a licence.[30]

The Civil Aviation (Air Travel Organisers' Licensing) regulations 1972, as amended (the ATOL regulations), provide that it shall not be lawful for any person in the United Kingdom to make available flight accommodation anywhere in the world unless he is the holder of an ATOL licence.[31] Similarly the ATOL regulations require any person in the United Kingdom who holds himself out as person capable of providing flight accommodation to hold an ATOL licence.[32]

On the other hand, it is permissible to sell or to offer for sale, flight **18.14** accommodation without an ATOL licence, as the agent of another licence holder.[33] Further, airlines themselves and their agents are exempted from the requirement to hold a licence.[34]

Difficulty arises when determining whether a person selling flight accommodation does so on his own account, or as the agent of a licence holder or an airline. The distinction is crucial because in the former case the seller requires a licence to trade, and if he does not have one he

---

[29] The Unfair Contract Terms Directive has been implemented in Northern Ireland by regulations.
[30] Regulation 2, SI 1972/223 Civil Aviation, The Civil Aviation (Air Travel Organisers' Licensing) Regulations 1972.
[31] Regulation 2(1)(a) *ibid.*
[32] Regulation 2(1)(b) *ibid.*
[33] Regulation 2(2)(b) *ibid.*
[34] Regulation 2(1)(ii), (2)(a) and (b) *ibid.*

commits an offence under ATOL regulation 2(5), and is liable to criminal prosecution by the CAA.

The CAA has given the following guidance, but it stresses the need for any person about to begin operations, which may be licensable, to take careful legal advice.[35]

> Anyone who buys seats on an aircraft, whether on a scheduled or charter flight and re-sells them in his own name needs a licence.[36]
>
> Anyone other than an airline, who advertises himself as a person who is prepared to sell seats on an aircraft, whether as part of a package holiday or otherwise, needs a licence unless he is authorised to act as an agent of an airline or of an existing licence holder and makes it clear in his advertising that he is such.[37]
>
> Anyone who sells or advertises seats on an aircraft as agent for someone who is neither an airline nor an existing licence holder must have a licence.[38]
>
> Whether a person acts as an agent or on his own account depends on the contractual relationship between himself and the customer. If he enters into a contract under which he undertakes to the customer to provide a seat on an aircraft, he acts on his own account. If he merely acts as an intermediary in the making of a contract between an airline and the customer, he is an agent.[39]
>
> Particular difficulties may arise in determining whether seats on scheduled flights are sold by the airline through an agent to the public, or are sold by the airline to a travel organiser for resale to the public by the travel organiser as a principal. A simple test in practice is whether the airline will regard itself as responsible to the customer from the first moment that a booking is taken: if it does, and is willing to confirm that it does, then that is strong evidence that the travel organiser is selling as an agent and does not need to be licensed. On the other hand, if the airline does not regard itself as being responsible to the customer from the time of booking, the sales will probably need to be covered by a licence. Other factors which are likely to indicate a sale of seats to an organiser on his own account for resale are the existence of special fares not available to the public, and the existence of an allocation of seats, whether or not all or part of the allocation may be cancelled."[40]

(ii) ATOL licence applications

18.15 Any person, whether established in another Member State or in the United Kingdom, selling flights in the United Kingdom is required to hold a licence.[41] It is an offence to do so without a licence from the CAA.[42]

---

[35] Para 3, Application for an Air Travel Organiser's Licence: Explanatory Notes, Civil Aviation Authority April 1992, CAA Document No 221.

[36] *ibid.*

[37] *ibid.*

[38] *ibid.*

[39] *ibid.*

[40] *ibid.*

[41] By Regulation 2 of the Civil Aviation (Air Travel Organisers' Licensing) Regulations SI 1972/223 airlines and airline operators are exempted from the requirement to hold a licence.

[42] Section 2(1) and (5) *ibid.*

(iii)   Criteria for the award of licences

The CAA must consider applications from air travel organisers from other Member States on the same terms as domestic organisers. It cannot discriminate against enterprises according to the nationality of the management or shareholders. Applicants may be corporate bodies, with either limited or guaranteed liability, or they may be firms, partnerships or individuals.

The CAA has stated that there is no numerical limit on entry[43] and doubtless any such restriction would contravene Community freedoms of establishment to provide services and free movement of goods.   **18.17**

Successful applicants must show a level of "fitness" and financial strength appropriate to the scale of operations to be conducted under the licence.[44] The CAA can only base its grant or refusal of a licence on the fitness or financial resources of an applicant.

(iv)   Fitness

"Fitness" is not exhaustively defined in the regulations, but the CAA interprets it "as including both integrity and competence and it will consider whether in its view an applicant is likely to conduct his licensable operations in a proper manner if he is granted a licence."[45]   **18.18**

Regulation 3(2) provides that the CAA shall refuse a licence to an applicant unless satisfied that he:

> is a fit person to make available accommodation for the carriage of persons on flights (and in determining whether the applicant is a fit person the [CAA] shall have regard to his and his employees past activities generally and, where the applicant is a body corporate, to the past activities generally of the persons appearing to the Authority to control that body, but shall not be obliged to refuse a licence on the grounds that it considers the applicant has insufficient experience in making available accommodation for the carriage of persons on flights).

(v)   Financial resources

Regulation 3(2) provides that the CAA shall refuse a licence to an applicant unless satisfied that: **18.19**

> the resources of the applicant and the financial arrangements made by him are adequate for discharging his actual and potential obligations in respect of activities in which he is engaged (if any) and in which he may expect to engage if he is granted the licence.

In practice, the CAA will base its assessment of an applicant's financial strength on the latest accounts and the ratio between recoverable net

---

[43] CAA's Memorandum to HL European Select Committee July 1988.
[44] Section 3(2) SI 1972/223.
[45] Paragraph 11, CAA: Explanatory Notes, Document No 221, April 1992.

current assets and the projected turnover of both non-licensable and licensable operations. The CAA will further consider the financial position of related or parent companies. Entry conditions are more onerous for new applicants and individuals. Other factors which impinge on the financial assessment include level of overheads, the market sector, the extent of customer funds held at any one time, track record and general experience of management.

18.20   It is a condition of any licence granted by the CAA that the applicant has made satisfactory bonding arrangements. Thus, in the event of failure, the bond can be administered to repatriate and/or compensate stranded or disappointed holiday makers. The level of bonding is normally 10% of licensed turnover, rising to 15% for new entrants, and higher where failure will result in a high level of exposure.

Bonds must be lodged with the CAA and further, the bonds themselves must be provided by banks who are members of the British Bankers' Association and by insurance companies authorised under the Insurance Companies Act 1982.[46] There is a further qualification for bonds up to £1 million. The bond providers will have to be UK-regulated and domiciled banks, and insurance companies must have an issued share capital and reserves of a minimum of £50 million.[47]

18.21   It is submitted that a refusal by the CAA to accept a bond provided by a bank or insurance company regulated and domiciled in another Member State would be unlawful.

(vi)   Application procedure

18.22   The CAA controls entry to the air travel industry, and as the licensing authority under the ATOL system,[48] applications for licences are made to it.

Applications for a licence must be made at least six months before the commencement of the licence.[49]

Licences are granted for one year periods and are defined in the terms of the business which the operator may do under the licence expressed in the number of seats to be offered and in forecast revenue.[50]

It is for the applicant to define the terms of the licence which he seeks. However, the CAA has complete discretion to modify those terms or to refuse the licence.[51]

Further, the CAA has power to make provision in the licence for minimum charges, and to specify the goods and services which may be made available under the licence.[52]

---

[46] Para 26, *ibid.*
[47] *ibid.*
[48] Section 71 Civil Aviation Act 1982 and Regulation 3 SI 1972/223.
[49] Regulation 3(1) SI 1972/223.
[50] CAA's Memorandum to HL European Select Committee July 1988.
[51] Regulation 3(1) SI 1972/223.
[52] Regulation 3(3) *ibid.*

Licences, once granted, must be renewed three months before their **18.23** date of expiry.[53] A licence holder may, by giving the CAA six months notice, apply to revoke, suspend or vary a term of its licence. Further the CAA is obliged to revoke, suspend or vary a licence on three weeks notice, if it is satisfied that the licence holder is no longer "fit" or that his financial resources are no longer adequate.[54]

In a serious case a licence may be suspended by the CAA on 72 hours notice.[55] Where the CAA has granted a licence subject to its own schedule of terms,[56] the CAA may, by varying its schedule, and on giving three weeks notice to individual licensees, automatically incorporate the variation in all licences subject to the schedule.[57]

(vii) Refusal to grant a licence

There is provision in the regulations for a right of appeal to the county **18.24** court against a decision by the CAA to refuse a licence on the grounds that the applicant lacks "fitness" only.[58] The regulations do not provide for a right of appeal against a refusal on the grounds of insufficient financial resources.

It is submitted that an administrative action must lie by way of Judicial Review if a licence is unreasonably refused, or granted subject to unreasonable terms or restrictions which offend, for instance, against Community law.

5. Non-licensable operations

(i) Package travel business

A "non-licensable operation" describes all travel business except air **18.25** travel. It includes all package travel business where the transport element does not involve the provision of aircraft accommodation. Further, non-licensable operations include the provision of passenger transport services for rail, coach and sea by themselves. However, for the purposes of the present chapter, the latter do not fall to be considered in isolation, and will be dealt with only in so far as they relate to packages and the steps which must be taken before carrying on non-licensable operations in compliance with the Package Travel Regulations (SI 1992/3288).

There are no restrictions on the type of enterprises entitled to sell

---

[53] Regulation 3(4) *ibid.*
[54] Regulation 4 *ibid.*
[55] Regulation 6(2) *ibid.*
[56] Maintained under Regulation 7 *ibid.*
[57] *ibid.*
[58] Regulation 8 *ibid.*

packages in accordance with the Package Travel regulations. Thus companies whose liability is limited or guaranteed, partnerships and individuals, are all entitled to sell packages. Further, there are no restrictions affecting the ownership or management of companies entitled to sell packages.

18.26   In the United Kingdom there is complete freedom to sell package travel arrangements to the public, provided only that the financial arrangements required by regulation 16 of the Package Travel regulations are in place to protect the consumer in the event of insolvency. Failure to comply with regulation 16 is an offence, and will expose the entrepreneur to criminal prosecution by local trading standards officers.[59]

Regulation 16 provides that anybody who sells a package, other than occasionally to a consumer, shall at all times be able to provide sufficient evidence of security for the refund of money paid over and for the repatriation of the consumer in the event of insolvency. Moreover, the seller must ensure that he has in force one of a number of arrangements prescribed by the regulations for the protection of consumers against insolvency.

18.27   The arrangements are as follows:

(i)   bonding *simpliciter* with an approved body, guaranteeing payment up to a certain amount, calculated as either 25% of the turnover of expected package sales, or a sum equivalent to the maximum amount of all payments held by the seller at any one time in respect of unperformed package contracts;[60]

(ii)   bonding with an approved body with a reserve fund or insurance, guaranteeing payment of a sum equivalent to only 10% of expected sales turnover or the maximum amount of 100% of all payments held by seller at any one time;[61]

(iii)   the acquisition of insurance to indemnify consumers against the loss of money paid by them in respect of contracts in the event of insolvency;[62] and

(iv)   the establishment of a trust into which all monies payable by consumers in respect of contracts are held until the contracts are fully performed, so that in the event of insolvency the trust monies can be applied to meet the claims of consumers.[63]

(ii)   Obligations under regulation 16

18.28   Package sellers must comply with the twofold requirements of regulation 16. Firstly regulation 16(1) lays down a general requirement, namely that

---

[59] Regulation 16(3) SI 1992/3288.
[60] Regulation 17 *ibid.*
[61] Regulation 18 *ibid.*
[62] Regulation 19 *ibid.*
[63] Regulation 20 *ibid.* Further Regulation 21 provides for the establishment of a trust where the seller acts otherwise than in the course of business.

the package seller shall at all times be able to provide sufficient evidence of security for the refund of money paid over and for the repatriation of the consumer in the event of insolvency. Secondly, regulation 16(2) specifically requires package sellers to take certain minimum steps to protect consumers in the event of insolvency. In each case a failure to comply with either regulation 16(1) or (2) will result in criminal liability.

18.29   The difficulty is that the mere taking of one of the prescribed measures set out in regulation 16(2) will not necessarily render a seller immune from prosecution under regulation 16(1).

Consider the following case. A seller effects a bond which is equivalent to the maximum amount of all payments which he is likely to hold at any one time in accordance with regulation 17(4)(b). The seller collapses in peak season. Consumer claims for money paid over in respect of unperformed contracts are at their maximum. All the monies payable under the bond will be required to repay the consumers of unperformed contracts. Unfortunately, at the time of the collapse, a large number of the seller's customers are stranded abroad and the seller has no funds to pay for their repatriation. The seller will be liable to prosecution under regulation 16(1) even though he has complied with regulation 16(2), because he has not provided sufficient security for costs of repatriation.

18.30   Thus, potential package sellers are advised to take steps in addition to those prescribed by regulation 16(2), in order to protect the consumer in the event of insolvency.

A package seller is exempt from the requirement to have in force one of the minimum measures prescribed by regulation 16(2) if he has complied with the requirements for the protection of the consumer in the event of insolvency in another Member State, or if the package is one in respect of which the seller is required to hold an ATOL licence. However, irrespective of whether a seller has complied with the law of another Member State or whether he holds an ATOL licence, he will not escape criminal liability if the general requirement set out in regulation 16(1) is not met.

(iii)   Travel organiser and travel retailer

18.31   The regulations distinguish between "organisers" and "retailers" for the purposes of describing the sellers of package travel arrangements. An organiser is a person who organises packages and sells or offers them for sale, whether directly or through a retailer.[64] A retailer is a person who sells or offers for sale packages put together by an organiser.[65] Further, the regulations expressly contemplate that there may be conditions where both the organiser and the retailer are liable to the consumer under the same contract.[66]

---

[64] Regulation 2(1) *ibid.*
[65] *ibid.*
[66] *ibid,* cf. definition of "the other party to the contract".

The onerous conditions imposed by regulation 16 apply only to the person who enters into the contract with the consumer on his own account. As a result the application of regulation 16 raises similar difficulties to those posed by the application of regulation 2 of the ATOL regulations.[67]

18.32 A travel business which sells packages on behalf of some other person, as their agent, does not contract on its own account. Under the UK law of agency, the relationship between seller, agent and consumer is such that when the agent sells a package on behalf of the seller, he drops out of the picture and the consumer enters into a contract with the seller. As a result, provided one sells packages only in the capacity of agent for another, a travel business need not comply with regulation 16.

In the United Kingdom, packages are commonly sold by tour operators (organisers) through high street sales points known as a travel agencies (retailers). In each case, the question whether a travel agency or a person wishing to establish a travel agency in the United Kingdom will be required to comply with regulation 16, depends on whether (i) it is intended to conduct business as an agent properly so called, namely selling packages on behalf of some other person, for instance an organiser in return for a commission, or (ii) whether the agency intends to buy in packages from package organisers and sell them on its own account as a retailer.

6. Remedies in the event of insolvency of a travel organiser or travel retailer

(i) Reserve funds

18.33 A consumer will be without an effective remedy against a collapsed seller when the seller becomes insolvent, and is thus unable to meet the consumer's claims himself.

If a consumer is the customer of a seller which is bonded with an approved body with a reserve fund under regulation 18, and the seller's bond is inadequate to meet the customer's claim, the approved body will be obliged to pay any unmet claims, whether for money paid over in respect of unperformed contracts or repatriation expenses, out of its reserve fund.

Similarly, in the event that an ATOL licensee's bond is inadequate to meet the claims of its customers, the CAA is obliged to pay any unmet claims from the Air Travel Reserve Trust Fund.

---

[67] See para. 38 *et seq.*

(ii) Bonds and insurance

Approved bodies which do not maintain reserve funds and which admin- **18.34** ister bonds under regulation 17 are under a duty to ensure that they obtain bonds from sellers which may reasonably be expected to enable all sums paid over by consumers under or in contemplation of unperformed packages to be repaid. Thus, if a consumer cannot be so repaid due to the inadequacy of such a bond, the approved body may be liable to the consumer, who in turn, may have a right of action against the approved body for breach of statutory duty. However, any such claim could only be made for money paid over in respect of an unperformed contract.[68] A stranded holiday-maker would not be able to claim for his repatriation expenses.

Where a seller has sought to comply with regulation 16 by taking out insurance and the seller has under-insured, the consumer has no remedy against the insurer, since the insurer is liable only up to the amount which he has agreed to indemnify.

(iii) Trust funds

Where a seller has sought to comply with regulation 16 by establishing a **18.35** trust fund, a trustee may be liable to a consumer where he has deliberately or negligently paid trust money to the seller in circumstances where he is not empowered to do so under regulation 20(4). However, effectively, consumers will be deprived even of this remedy, in the event that the seller is himself the trustee. Moreover, consumers may well find themselves out-of-pocket and with no remedy against the trustee, if they have to meet their own repatriation expenses, or where the trust fund is simply not big enough to reimburse all monies which have been paid over in respect of unperformed contracts.

(iv) Lack of protection

As a result, it must be concluded that there may well be circumstances in **18.36** which consumers discover that they are not protected in the event of insolvency.

Certainly, this will be the case where package sellers deliberately flout the law and take no steps at all to provide security or where, in purported compliance with regulation 19, the seller under-insures.

Consumers face a theoretical risk of being unable to reclaim the costs of their own repatriation, where the seller is bonded with an approved body under regulation 17.[69] Such a risk becomes real where the con-

---

[68] Regulation 17(3) SI 1992/3288 only requires the approved body to calculate the size of the bond by reference to "all monies paid over by consumers under or in contemplation of contracts for relevant packages. . . ."

[69] See para 95.

sumer's security is in the form of a trust fund administered by the seller himself under regulation 20.

Furthermore, there is the possibility that a massive failure in the industry could deplete even the reserve funds of bodies approved under regulation 18, or the Air Travel Trust Fund of the CAA.

(v) EC Package Travel Directive

18.37 Given that under the UK Package Travel regulations, not every out-of-pocket holiday maker will be fully protected in the event of insolvency, it is a moot point whether there will be a right of action against the UK government under European Law for failure to implement fully the EC Package Travel Directive.

By Article 7 of the Directive[70] the government is required to take all necessary steps to ensure that package sellers "shall provide sufficient evidence of security for the refund of money paid over and for the repatriation of the consumer in the event of insolvency."

The government view is that it has fully complied with the Directive, since the Directive does not require the government to ensure that package sellers actually provide sufficient evidence of security before setting up in business, rather the Directive only obliges the government to enact rules requiring them to do so.

18.38 Thus, by a combination of enacting Article 7, word for word, as regulation 16(1); by prescribing measures under regulation 16(2) requiring sellers, at least, to provide security for money paid over; by requiring sellers to notify consumers of their protection in the event of insolvency;[71] and further by making non-compliance with those regulations a criminal offence; the government believes that the Directive has been properly implemented.

On the other hand, it may be asserted as follows:

Article 189 of the EC Treaty provides that a "directive shall be binding, as to the result to be achieved, upon each Member State to which it is addressed, but shall leave to the national authorities the choice of form and methods."

The binding result to be achieved by Article 7 of the Package Travel Directive is that package sellers "*shall provide sufficient evidence of security . . . .*" and not "*shall be required to provide. . . .*"

18.39 Thus, if the United Kingdom does not prevent package sellers from trading without their having provided "sufficient evidence of security. . .," the result of Article 7 of the Directive is not achieved. If the Directive has not been implemented properly and a consumer suffers loss as a result, he may have a right of action against the government under the principle in the case of *Francovich*.[72]

---

[70] Council Directive 90/314/EEC.
[71] Regulations 5 and 7, SI 1992/3288.
[72] *Francovich* v *Italy* [1993] 2 CMLR 66.

Section II*

UK Travel Law Provisions

1.   Introduction

The United Kingdom, comprised of Scotland, England, Northern Ireland **18.40**
and Wales, is represented by one Parliament at Westminster in London,
England. Scotland was an independent nation until 1707. By the Treaty
of Union of that year, Scotland and England became one country.
Pre–1707 Scotland had her own law and the Treaty of Union made provision
that this should remain so "in all time coming".

Parliament at Westminster has a legislative function. It passes Acts of
Parliament which are enforced throughout the United Kingdom, and
thus in Scotland. An Act of Parliament will override Scots common law if
the two conflict. The Act may explicitly provide that it does not apply to
Scotland, applies solely to Scotland, or is applicable throughout the
United Kingdom. Parliament also has the power to delegate authority to
government institutions and other bodies to create legislation. Again, this
legislation will be enforced over and above Scots common law, unless the
legislation provides that it does not apply to Scotland.

Since Direct Rule was introduced in Northern Ireland by the Northern
Ireland Act 1974, most Northern Ireland legislation has been made by
way of Order in Council, a form of delegated legislation. Northern Ireland statute law generally follows the substance of that in England and
Wales, but is often implemented by a separate Order in Council. There is
sometimes a delay of two to three years between implementation of legislation in England and Wales and implementation in Northern Ireland.
Northern Ireland common law is largely based on English common law
and English caselaw is frequently cited in the Northern Ireland Courts.

European Community Law takes precedence over both Parliament and **18.41**
Scots common law. The United Kingdom joined the EC in 1972 and by
an Act of Parliament, ceding sovereignty to the EC, undertook that laws
created by the Community would form part of the law of the United
Kingdom. However, not all Community law has direct effect. A Directive
issued by the EC must be implemented by a Member State within a certain time period. The Member State will implement the Directive by passing domestic legislation. (Any commentary in this text relating to
European Community law applies equally to Northern Ireland.)

---

* This section was contributed principally by Iain Taylor and David Parratt, both Scottish solicitors, as regards Scots law on travel. The material was reviewed and contributed to by Zahd
Yaqub, Barrister to provide the English law content. This section deals with England, Scotland
and Northern Ireland. Where differences appear, Scotland and Northern Ireland are treated
separately. As regards the Scots position, the law is stated as at 1 September 1994.

Thus, the EC Directive on package holidays (which has had probably the most profound impact on the tourism industry), was required to be implemented into UK law. This was done through the delegated legislation of The Package Travel, Package Holidays and Package Tours regulations 1992.[1]

2. Regulatory authorities

(i) The courts

18.42 In England, Acts of Parliament and European law relating to tourism will be enforced in the English courts and in Northern Ireland by the courts of Northern Ireland. In Scotland, matters relating to tourism will be enforced, *prima facie*, by the Scottish courts.

(ii) Statutory bodies

(a) Department of Trade and Industry (DTI)

18.43 The DTI is a government department. The Secretary of State of this Department is responsible for legislation and policy relating to consumer affairs *e.g.* fair trading; weights and measures; consumer safety. He is also responsible for monitoring restrictive practices, monopolies and mergers.

The DTI had responsibility for the implementation of the Package Travel Directive[2] and has overall responsibility for the enforcement of the Package Travel regulations. In England, local authority Trading Standards Departments are responsible for investigation and prosecutions. In Scotland, Trading Standards Departments[3] are responsible for investigation, but prosecutions are brought by the Procurator Fiscal. Prosecutions must be reported to the Office of Fair Trading.

The Department of Economic Development (DED) in Northern Ireland carries out similar functions to those of the DTI in England and Wales. The DED has overall responsibility for the implementation of the Package Directive in Northern Ireland and for the enforcement of the Package Regulations. Its Trading Standards Branch is also responsible for investigation and prosecutions, which are brought in conjunction with the Director of Public Prosecutions for Northern Ireland. Prosecutions in Northern Ireland must also be reported to the Office of Fair Trading.

(b) Office of Fair Trading (OFT)

18.44 The OFT was constituted by an Act of Parliament.[4] It is a government agency headed by a Director General. It reviews commercial activities in

---

[1] SI 1992/3288. The regulations came into force on 23 December 1992.
[2] Implemented by secondary legislation.
[3] These are departments of local authorities. They are sometimes referred to as Weights and Measures Departments.
[4] See Fair Trading Act 1973.

the United Kingdom relating to, *inter alia,* services supplied to consumers. The Director General of Fair Trading is appointed by the Secretary of State and has power to regulate practices which harm consumer interests. The Director may refer cases to the Consumer Protection Advisory Committee (CPAC), which may investigate consumer trade practices. The CPAC may make proposals to the Secretary of State, who may make an order, which will become law on being passed by Parliament. The Director may bring proceedings in the High Court in England or in the Sheriff Court in Scotland. The court may make an order which if breached, amounts to contempt of court resulting in sanctions.

The Office of Fair Trading has similar functions in Northern Ireland. The closest equivalent in Northern Ireland to the Consumer Protection Advisory Committee is probably the General Consumer Council. This Council can investigate consumer trade practices, issue reports and make recommendations.

(c)   Civil Aviation Authority (CAA)

The CAA is under the immediate supervision of the DTI, and carries out **18.45** the same functions in Northern Ireland. It is responsible for the administration of airlines operating in and flying to and from, airports in the United Kingdom. It has direct discretionary control over the granting of Air Travel Organiser's Licences (ATOLs).[5] Any person selling package holidays or any holiday with air travel as the primary method of transport is required to obtain an ATOL.

(d)   Monopolies and Mergers Commission (MMC)

The MMC is a government agency which can investigate anti-competitive **18.46** practices on a referral from the Director of Fair Trading.[6] It carries out the same functions in Northern Ireland.

(iii)   Voluntary associations

In addition to the statutory bodies which regulate the tourism industry, **18.47** and the courts which enforce the law governing travel and tourism, there are a number of voluntary bodies to which tour operators and travel agents may subscribe. Normally these bodies set strict entrance requirements, and members must abide by their rules of membership.[7] They have no power to impose criminal sanction or to bring judicial proceedings, but regulate the activities of their members and thus to some extent, practice within the travel and tourism industry. The following is not an exhaustive list.

---

[5] See *infra.*
[6] The MCC was constituted by The Fair Trading Act 1973.
[7] Some voluntary bodies also provide guidance as to the conduct of their members. See *infra.*

(a) Association of British Travel Agents (ABTA)

18.48 ABTA is the best known of the voluntary associations. It is a company limited by guarantee, comprised of tour operator and travel agent members who pay annual subscriptions. Members must abide by rules laid down in its articles of association and comply with its Codes of Conduct.

(b) Association of Independent Tour Operators (AITO)

18.49 AITO is also a company limited by guarantee. Members must abide by its Quality Charter[8] and must also have a "bond"[9] securing clients' money. AITO operates its own bonding scheme through AITO Trust Limited.

(c) Federation of Tour Operators (FTO)

18.50 The FTO (formerly known as the Tour Operators Study Group) provides a bonding system for its members, accepted by both ABTA and the CAA. It also examines the trade itself, and seeks to change practice and procedure to the benefit of both its members and consumers.

(d) Passenger Shipping Association (PSA)

18.51 The PSA has bonding requirements and Codes of Conduct which apply to all its members.

(e) Confederation of Passenger Transport UK

18.52 The Confederation is a trade association which regulates its coach and bus operator members.

3. Legal and professional rules

(i) The Package Regulations

18.53 The law applicable to tourism and travel has been profoundly influenced by The Package Travel, Package Holidays and Package Tours Regulations 1992, (The Package Regulations), which implement Council Directive 90/314/EEC. The EC recognised disparities in the national laws of Member States affecting tourism and package holidays, and, as part of its general aim to harmonise laws, implement the internal market and establish minimum standards relating to package travel, adopted the Directive on 13 June 1990.

18.54   The Directive and subsequent Package Regulations establish minimum requirements relating to package travel covering *inter alia*:

(i)   brochure requirements, their content and accuracy and other information to be provided to a consumer;

---

[8] Similar to the ABTA Codes of Conduct.
[9] A type of financial security.

(ii)   the circumstances in which a contract may be altered;

(iii)   liability relating to the performance of the contract; and

(iv)   measures for financial security in the event of insolvency.

Although the Directive relates only to package holidays, the scope of the Package Regulations which implement the Directive is sufficiently wide to embrace other elements of travel law, and thus have a bearing on *any* consideration of "tourism law".

A "package" is defined in regulation 2(1) as:

> the pre-arranged combination of at least two of the following components when sold or offered for sale at an inclusive price and when the service covers a period of more than 24 hours or includes overnight accommodation:
> (a)   transport;
> (b)   accommodation;
> (c)   other tourist services not ancillary to transport or accommodation and accounting for a significant proportion of the package.

It continues by stipulating that: **18.55**

> (1) The submission of separate accounts for different components shall not cause the arrangements to be other than a package.
> (2) Nothing in this definition shall cause a combination which is arranged at the request of the consumer and in accordance with his specific instructions (whether modified or not) to be treated as other than pre-arranged.

The regulations do not use the terms "tour operator" and "travel agent". They make reference to "organiser" and "retailer". For ease of reference, however, the terms "tour operator" and "travel agent" will be used throughout this chapter.

(ii)   Duties of the holiday provider

The provisions of the Directive and the Package Regulations do not   **18.56**
replace pre-existing GB or Northern Ireland statute or Scots, English or Northern Ireland common law principles and case law *in toto*. These continue in so far as they are consistent with the regulations. However, before the Package Regulations, no statute provided for the duties incumbent on a tour operator or the nature of the contract entered into between it and the holiday-maker. The regulations now impose comprehensive duties on tour operators and travel agents. Failure to fulfil these duties will in some circumstances expose a travel agent or tour operator to criminal liability, and in other circumstances will give a holiday-maker remedies in either delict or contract.

The Package Regulations impose strict liability on a tour operator for   **18.57**
the proper performance of obligations under the contract. Regulation 15(1) provides that the tour operator is:

liable to the consumer for the proper performance of the obligations under the contract, irrespective of whether such obligations are to be performed by that other party or by other suppliers of services, but this shall not affect any remedy or right of action which that other party may have against those other suppliers of services.

18.58 Regulation 15(2) further provides that the tour operator is liable to the consumer for any damage caused to him by failure to perform the contract or improper performance of the contract, unless the failure or improper performance is due neither to the fault of the tour operator nor that of another supplier of services because:

(a) it is attributable to the consumer;

(b) it is attributable to a third party unconnected with the provision of the services contracted for, and is unforeseeable or unavoidable; or

(c) it is due to:

(i) unusual or unforeseeable circumstances beyond the control of the tour operator, the consequences of which could not have been avoided even if all due care had been exercised; or

(ii) an event which neither the tour operator nor the supplier of services, even if all due care had been exercised, could foresee or forestall.

18.59 Liability may be limited in accordance with international conventions.[10] Damages other than for personal injury may be limited in terms of the contract, provided the limitation is not unreasonable.[11] In assessing what is reasonable, the courts will refer to the Unfair Contract Terms Act 1977, Schedule 2.

In the event of the circumstances described in paragraph (2)(b) and (c) of regulation 15 occurring, the tour operator is under a duty to provide prompt assistance to a holiday-maker in difficulty.[12] Further, if a holiday-maker makes a complaint about a defect in the performance of the contract, the tour operator or its local representative is under a duty to make prompt efforts to find appropriate solutions.[13] These duties are implied into every contract. A holiday-maker is required to communicate any failure to the tour operator or to the supplier of services in writing at the earliest opportunity.

18.60 Previously, the providers of holidays were not required to discharge such an onerous duty. The Package Regulations provide further duties on a tour operator to inform the holiday-maker of any changes to his holiday prior to his departure.

(iii) Cancellation, alteration and transfer

18.61 The Regulations specify in what circumstances a holiday or travel arrangement may be cancelled, altered or substituted. They also regulate

---

[10] The Package Travel, Package Holidays and Package Tours Regulations reg 15(3).

[11] *Ibid* reg 15(4).

[12] *Ibid* reg 15(7).

[13] *Ibid* reg 15(9).

the imposition of charges. The conditions of the contract will normally provide for the circumstances of withdrawal or cancellation. When booking, the customer is normally required to sign part of the form agreeing to abide by the conditions allowing him to withdraw from the contract, if desired, with a penalty or cancellation charge, calculated relative to the proximity of departure. There will also normally be a condition allowing the tour operator to cancel the holiday or to make alterations to it. These conditions will be subject to both the Package Regulations and the Unfair Contract Terms Act 1977.

Regulation 9 of the Package Regulations provides that there are compulsory details (which are specified in Schedule 2) which must be intimated to the customer. It is an implied term of the contract that these details are provided.[14] Failure to provide these details is a material breach of the contract, unless the time interval between booking and departure is so short that it is impracticable to do so.

(a) Transfer[15]

A customer may transfer a booking to another person if prevented **18.62** from proceeding with the package. This right is incorporated as an implied term and cannot be excluded.[16] The customer must give reasonable notice and meet the additional cost to the operator of the transfer. The booking conditions must make it clear that additional costs will arise.

(b) Alteration[17]

Where an organiser is constrained to "alter significantly" the package, **18.63** this must be intimated to the consumer as "quickly as possible". The consumer is entitled to withdraw, or to accept a rider to the contract specifying the alterations and their impact on the price, but must intimate his decision to the organiser as soon as possible.

(c) Cancellation[18]

Where the organiser cancels the package, and the customer is not at **18.64** fault, then the consumer is entitled: to take another package of equivalent or superior quality if this is available; to take an inferior package if available and obtain the difference in price; or to be repaid all the monies paid by him as soon as possible. He is entitled to compensation except where the cancellation is due to there being fewer than the minimum number of persons required and he has been informed in writing

---

[14] *Ibid* reg 9(3).
[15] *Ibid* reg 10.
[16] *Ibid* reg 10(1).
[17] *Ibid* reg 12.
[18] *Ibid* reg 13.

"within the period specified in the description of the package", or where the package is cancelled by reason of unusual and unforeseeable circumstances beyond the control of the organiser, which could not have been avoided with the exercise of all due care. Overbooking is not an unusual or unforeseen circumstance.

(d) Surcharges[19]

18.65 Any term in the contract specifying that the price may be revised is void unless the revisions made are solely due to variations in transport costs dues, taxes or fees charged for services at ports and airports, or to exchange rates applying to a particular package. A clause must be included specifying precisely how the revision will be calculated. Surcharges cannot be imposed within the 30 days prior to departure and the operator must meet the first two per cent of any increase in the price of the package.

4.   Freedom of establishment of travel agents

(i) Travel agency in England

18.66 In England, the law of agency describes the relationship that arises when one man is appointed to act as the representative of another.

Agents are employed by a principal to use their expertise to negotiate contracts on the principal's behalf. The parties involved are the principal, the agent, and the person who wishes to enter the contract with the principal. The agency relationship comes into existence because the principal and agent have agreed between themselves that the agent should use his expertise to perform certain jobs for the principal.

A contract made with a third party by an agent is enforceable both by and against the principal. The English doctrine is that an agent may make a contract for his principal which has the same consequences as if the latter had made it himself. The principal acquires the rights and liabilities. The agent drops out and ceases to be a party to the contract.

18.67 In the context of package travel, the tour operator is the principal who employs the travel agent to contract with clients on his behalf. This relationship is evidenced by a contract, the agency agreement.

The contract expressly appoints the travel agent to act as agent for the tour operator and to sell packages detailed in the tour operator's travel brochures. The third party uses the travel agent in order to book his holiday with the tour operator.

---

[19] *Ibid* reg 11.

(ii) Travel agency in Scotland

Any individual in Scotland may establish a travel agency or tour operator **18.68**
business. Council Directive 73/148/EEC[20] provides for the abolition of
restrictions preventing nationals of Member States wishing to establish
themselves in other Member States in order to provide services. Council
Directive 82/470/EEC[21] provides facilitation measures for the establishment of services incidental to transport and travel agencies. The Directive
provides for alternative acceptable standards of proof of repute and
financial standing required by any Member State.

A travel agent may be established in Scotland in the form of a sole
trader, partnership or private limited company. The travel agent must
comply with domestic law as to its formation, management, function and
operation.[22]

It must also comply with the Scots common law of agency. In general a
travel agent will sell the holidays of other organisations. It will display
brochures, take details of holidays requested by the public, confirm bookings and receive payment for holidays booked. It will perform these functions as an "agent" on behalf of the organisation promoting the holiday,
whose role in law is "principal". An agent has been described as "a person
having express or implied authority to act on behalf of another party,
who is called the principal".[23] The travel agent acts on behalf of the tour
operator, acting as agent for the principal with the principal's authority.
When a travel agent sells a holiday to a member of the public, he places
that member of the public in a direct contractual relationship with the
tour operator principal. Normally, if a member of the public brings legal
action he must do so against the tour operator, not the travel agent.[24]

The travel agent may enter into an "agency agreement" with a tour **18.69**
operator. There is no requirement in Scots law that this agreement be
written.[25] However, in accordance with modern commercial practice,
agency agreements are now normally written.[26] The agreement will stipulate the authority granted by the principal tour operator to the travel
agent, and will stipulate respective duties.[27]

---

[20] Abolition of Restrictions on Movement and Residence within the Community for Nationals of
Member States with regard to the Establishment and the Provision of Services. Adopted 21
May 1973.

[21] Directive to Facilitate the Exercise of Freedom of Establishment and Freedom to supply
services for the Self Employed.

[22] See Business Names Act 1985, Partnership Act 1890, and also the Companies Act 1985, as
amended by Companies Act 1989. The vast and complex scope of The Companies Acts pre-
cludes detailed analysis in this chapter.

[23] Bowstead, "*Agency*" p. 1.

[24] Unless the agent has acted outwith his authority and his acts have not been ratified by the
principal whereby he will be personally liable.

[25] An oral contract of agency is competent. *Pickin* v *Hawkes* (1878) 5R.676.

[26] In the event of dispute, the agreement can be interpreted by a court more easily if the duties
of either party are clearly ascertainable.

[27] A tour operator may enter Agency Agreements with various travel agents.

A travel agent will sell the holidays of a tour operator. A tour operator, however, may not prohibit a travel agent discounting the price of a holiday if the agent meets the cost of the discount itself. The Restriction on Agreements and Conduct (Tour Operators) Order 1987 provides that:

> it is unlawful for a tour operator to make an agreement which prohibits a travel agent from offering "inducements" to the public.[28]

18.70　An "inducement" is defined as a benefit, whether pecuniary or not, offered to a class or classes of persons, or to the public at large by a travel agent expressly on his own behalf as an incentive to that class or those classes of persons, or to the public at large, to acquire foreign package holidays through another.[29]

It is unlawful for a tour operator to withhold or to threaten to withhold orders for agency services from travel agents who offer inducements.[30] It is also unlawful for a tour operator to give preference to travel agents who do not offer inducements.

(iii)　Travel agency in Northern Ireland

18.71　The Northern Ireland law of agency is closely modelled on English law. The commentary at (i) above also summarises the position in Northern Ireland.

(iv)　Special legal requirements

18.72　There is no requirement for a travel agent to register with a national organisation nor to join any association. Such membership of organisations and associations is voluntary.

The best known of the voluntary organisations is the Association of British Travel Agents (ABTA). Membership criteria of ABTA are fairly stringent.

ABTA membership criteria

18.73　Before a travel agent may be affiliated to ABTA, it must satisfy the Travel Agents' Council of ABTA that:

(i)　　it is engaged in the business of a travel agent;

(ii)　　that, at any premises at which travel agency business is conducted, there is at least one person who within the last three years has had two years relevant practical experience; or has 18 months experience and has passed the Certificate of Travel Agency Competence Level I; or has one year of experience and has passed the Certificate of Travel Agency Competence Level II;

---

[28] Art 3(1)
[29] Art 2
[30] Art 5

(iii)   that its financial position is sound;

(iv)   that any directors, principal shareholders, or partners in the travel agency are of a respectable and honest character, that none are undischarged bankrupts, or have made compositions with their creditors, or have a history of conduct which in the opinion of the Council is in conflict with membership of ABTA;

(v)   that the travel agency is not trading under the name of or a name similar to a former member of the Association which has failed to meet any liabilities;

(vi)   membership entrance fee of £1,250 must be paid; and

(vii)   annual subscriptions must be met, which are calculated in accordance with the annual turnover of the individual travel agent.

5. Freedom of establishment of tour operators

(i) General business organisation

Any individual wishing to conduct business in the United Kingdom as a tour operator may do so either as a sole trader, or through the medium of a partnership or a limited company. As with the criteria required by law in establishing a travel agency, the formation, structure, function and operation of a tour operator must comply with UK statute and Scots, English or Northern Ireland common law.[31]   **18.74**

(ii) Special legal requirements

As with travel agents, there is no mandatory registration requirement with any national body or register. A number of organisations and associations for tour operators do exist, but membership of these is voluntary.   **18.75**

ABTA also regulates tour operator members. Membership criteria are also fairly stringent.

ABTA membership criteria

Before a tour operator may be affiliated to ABTA, it must satisfy the Tour Operators' Council that: **18.76**

(i)   it is engaged in the business of a tour operator as principal, organising and offering for sale to members of the public, tours, holidays or other travel arrangements comprising at least transportation and accommodation;

(ii)   that it publishes literature to market its tours and holidays;

(iii)   that its financial position is sound;

---

[31] See n 19 *supra.*

(iv)   that it has in force a bond of guarantee or other security securing its liability;

(v)   that it has contributed to the cost of the current insurance policy approved by the Tour Operators' Council, calculated in accordance with the annual turnover of the individual tour operator;

(vi)   that its directors, principal shareholders, partners or other persons employed in its management are of a respectable and honest character, that none are undischarged bankrupts, or have made compositions with their creditors, or have a history of conduct which in the opinion of the Council is in conflict with membership of ABTA; and

(vii)   that it is not trading or registered under the name of or a name similar to a former member of the Association which has failed to meet any of its liabilities.

(iii)   Financial requirements

(a)   The Package Regulations

18.77   The Package Regulations place an obligation on tour operators to arrange "financial protection" for their clients. The tour operator must ensure that clients' monies will be refunded and/or that clients will be repatriated, should the operator become insolvent and cease trading. Sufficient evidence of security of money paid over by a client must be provided by the tour operator. The Package Regulations stipulate three methods;

(i)   bond;

(ii)   insurance policy; and

(iii)   trust account.[32]

18.78   If tour operators fail to comply with these requirements, they will be guilty of a criminal offence. In Scotland both a partnership and a company have a separate legal *persona*. Regulation 25(2) and (4) provides that:

(i)   where a company is guilty of an offence, any "director, manager, secretary or other similar officer or any person who was purporting to act in such a capacity" shall be personally guilty of an offence if the offence was committed with his "consent or connivance";

(ii)   where a Scottish partnership is guilty of an offence, any individual "partner is guilty of the offence if the offence was committed with his consent or connivance";

(iii)   where the affairs of a body corporate are managed by its members, the provisions of (i) above shall apply in relation to the acts and

---

[32] Package Regulations 16–22 specify the financial requirements to be met by organisers.

defaults of a member in connection with his functions of management as if he were a director of the body corporate.

(b) Bond

Regulation 17 provides conditions that must be met where a bond is not   **18.79**
reinforced by insurance cover, or with a fund. Regulation 18 provides
conditions to be met where there is the added protection of insurance
cover or a reserve fund in addition to a bond.

The bond must be entered into by an "authorised institution" which
binds itself to pay to an "approved body" a certain sum.[33] The bond must
not be expressed to be in force for a period exceeding 18 months.[34] An
"approved body" is defined as a body which is for the time being
approved by the Secretary of State for this purpose.[35] Regulation 18(6)
states that a body may not be approved for the purposes of regulation 18
unless it has a reserve fund or insurance cover with an authorised insurer
of an amount designated to enable all monies paid by consumers to be
repaid, in the event of the insolvency of the tour operator.

In terms of regulation 17, the sum must be sufficient as to "reasonably   **18.80**
be expected to enable all monies paid over by the consumers under or in
contemplation of contracts for relevant packages which have not been
fully performed to be repaid".[36] The minimum sum must be either not
less than 25% of all payments received by the tour operator in a 12
month period from the date the bond enters into force, or alternatively
the maximum amount the tour operator expects to hold at any one time
in respect of contracts not fully performed, whichever is the smaller.[37]

In terms of regulation 18, the sum must be the lesser of the maximum
amount of all payments which the tour operator expects to hold at any
one time in respect of contracts not fully performed, or a sum "not less
than 10% of all payments which the tour operator estimates he will
receive under or in contemplation of contracts for relevant packages in
the 12 month period" from the date the bond enters into force.[38]

(c) Insurance

A tour operator may meet the financial security requirements of regula-   **18.81**
tion 16 by taking out insurance cover. The approved method of doing so
is determined by regulation 19. The cover may be under one or more
policies, but for each policy the insurer must agree that in the event of
the insolvency of the tour operator, it will indemnify consumers as
"insured persons" against loss of money paid by them in contemplation
of contracts or package holidays.[39]

---

[33] *Ibid* reg 17(1).
[34] *Ibid* reg 17(2).
[355] *Ibid* reg 17(7).
[36] *Ibid* reg 17(3).
[37] *Ibid* reg 17(4).
[38] *Ibid* reg 18(3) and (4).
[39] *Ibid* reg 19(1).

The insurer is not entitled to avoid indemnity due to omissions of the tour operator. In the event of insolvency of the tour operator, "the consumer acquires the benefit of the policy".[40]

(d) Trust

18.82 A tour operator may satisfy regulation 16: financial security requirements, by protecting a holiday-maker's money in a trust account.

Regulation 20 specifies that money paid by a particular consumer must be held by a trustee in the United Kingdom until there is either performance of the contract, cancellation of the contract, or repayment to the consumer.

The tour operator bears the cost of administering the trust, but is entitled to any interest. The trustee may only release monies when the tour operator produces a statement signed by him specifying that the contract has been performed, cancelled (resulting in forfeiture of monies), or that the sum of money paid by the consumer as specified in the statement, has been repaid.

In the event of insolvency of the tour operator, monies held by the trustee in trust will form part of the estate of the insolvent. If monies held by the trustee are insufficient, claims shall be met *pari passu.*

18.83 Regulation 21 provides for the situation where an organiser of a package acts "otherwise than in the course of business". Schools, associations and clubs will often arrange holidays. As it is unrealistic for such bodies to comply with the onerous obligations in regulations 16–20, regulation 21 expressly provides for their obligations. An organiser is entitled to pay for the holiday with the holiday-maker's money prior to performance, cancellation or repayment. Regulation 21 does not apply to tour operators organising package holidays.

(e) Exceptions to the regulation 16 rule

18.84 There are two exceptions to the requirement of tour operators to provide "financial protection" for their clients' money. Regulation 16(2) provides that a tour operator is exempt where the holiday:

(i) is covered by measures adopted or retained by the Member State where it is established for the purposes of implementing Article 7 of the Directive" *i.e.* the tour operator is established in another Member State which has in force protective legislation.

(ii) is one in respect of which it is required to hold a licence under Civil Aviation (Air Travel Organisers Licensing) Regulations 1972 or is covered by the arrangements it has entered into for the purposes of those Regulations.

(f) Breach of Financial Requirements

18.85 Regulation 22 specifies that a breach of the financial regulations in regulations 16–22 is a criminal offence. If found guilty, the party in breach is

---

[40] *Ibid* reg 19(2).

liable to a fine (not exceeding level five on the standard scale on summary conviction, and to an unlimited fine on conviction on indictment).

(iv) Licence requirements: ATOL

The requirement of a tour operator to obtain an ATOL is regulated by the Civil Aviation Act 1982[41] and by the Civil Aviation (Air Travel Organisers Licensing) Regulations 1972 as amended.   **18.86**

ATOLs are regulated by the Civil Aviation Authority (CAA) which is under the ultimate supervision of the Department of Trade.

The Act specifies that:

> No person in the United Kingdom is entitled to make available accommodation on aircraft for flights in any part of the world, or hold himself out as being entitled to do so, unless he is either the operator of the relevant aircraft or he holds an Air Travel Organisers Licence and complies with its terms.[42]

A tour operator who sells a holiday with air travel as the principal means of transport, is required to hold a licence (ATOL) obtainable from the CAA.[43] The tour operator must comply with the provisions of the ATOL licence.

The tour operator must apply to the CAA in writing for the grant of a licence, which may be granted in the terms of the application, or modified as the CAA "thinks fit" or refused.[44] An application must be accompanied by the appropriate fee and must be submitted to the authority not less than six months prior to the date from which the licence is proposed to take effect. The CAA shall refuse to grant a licence unless it is satisfied that: **18.87**

(i)   the applicant is a fit person to make available accommodation for the carriage of persons on flights, having regard to the past activities of an applicant and his employees;[45]

(ii)   the resources of the applicant and financial arrangements made by him are adequate for discharging his ATOL obligations and potential obligations in respect of the activities in which he is engaged and in which he may be expected to engage.[46]

The granting of a licence is subject to the condition that the holder has entered into a "satisfactory agreement" whereby a specified sum of money will be available, (in the event of failure) to a trustee and shall be applied towards repatriating stranded passengers and reimbursing any of   **18.88**

---

[41] See Civil Aviation Act 1982 s 71(1).
[42] S 71 1982 Act and Civil Aviation (Air Travel Organiser's Licensing) Regulations 1972 reg 1.
[43] Civil Aviation (Air Travel etc) Regulations 1972 reg 2.
[44] *Ibid* reg 3.
[45] *Ibid* reg 3(2)a.
[46] *Ibid* reg 3(2)b.

the holder's customers who have paid, in whole, or in part, for a flight or a holiday that has not yet taken place.[47]

Some of the voluntary associations operate their own bonding requirements for members. Bonds granted in favour of ABTA or the FTO are accepted by the CAA in lieu of their own bonding requirements. However, the licence will not be granted, until the CAA has received notification that the individual tour operator has fulfilled the respective bonding requirements of ABTA or the FTO. If an ATOL holder does not belong to either association, it must grant a bond in favour of the CAA, which will be called up and administered in the event of the holder ceasing to trade.[48]

18.89   The ATOL is granted in such terms as the CAA "thinks fit". Appeal lies to the Sheriff Court,[49] in Scotland, and the High Court in England. "Standard Terms" are incorporated into all ATOLs.[50]

An airline or air operator is not required to hold an ATOL. Neither is an agent of an airline or authorised agent of an ATOL holder. Thus, a travel agent need not obtain an ATOL when selling tickets or holidays on behalf of ATOL-holding airlines or tour operators.[51] However, where a travel agent is relying on this exception, it is required to disclose its status as an agent who is making accommodation available.[52]

(a)   Categories of ATOL

18.90   There are three types of ATOL holder:[52a]

– a four-digit ATOL number in form ATOL 9999 denotes an ATOL holder authorised to sell air packages and charter and discounted scheduled flights;
– a five-digit ATOL number prefixed "7" 9999 denotes an ATOL holder authorised to sell discounted scheduled tickets. Air packages may *not* be organised;
– a five-digit ATOL number prefixed "8" 9999 denotes an agency ATOL holder authorised to sell discounted scheduled tickets for airlines that have provided deeds of undertaking. An airline may only deal with this type of ATOL holder if it has provided the CAA with a deed of undertaking. Air packages may *not* be organised.

Pursuant to regulation 1(2) of the Civil Aviation (Air Travel Organisers' Licensing) Regulations 1995, an ATOL receipt shall be a document issued by the authorised agent of a licence holder and shall contain:

---

[47] See CAA Explanatory Notes April 1994 "Application for an Air Travel Organiser's Licence".
[48] *Ibid* reg 8(2)a.
[49] See Air Travel Organiser's Licence Schedule of Standard Terms.
[50] *E.g.* Standard Term One specifies that an ATOL holder must state its exact company name, and ATOL number in all publicity material, booking forms, brochures and confirmation of booking forms.
[51] Reg 2(2) as amended by SI 1981/314.
[52] See *Gimblett* v *McGlashen* 1986 IS&B AvR IV/77 QB DC.
[52a] CAA information, 1996.

- the name of the agent and the fact that he is acting in the capacity of agent;
- the name of the licence holder, the number of his ATOL and the licence holder's booking reference;
- where the licence holder intends to make available flights as an agent of an airline, and has provided to the CAA a deed of undertaking from that airline, the name of the airline that will provide the flight;
- the name of the persons making the booking and the number of persons covered by it;
- the date, origin and destination of each flight booked;
- an indication of whether the booking is for a package, and of any elements in addition to a flight included in the contract price; and
- the amount of payment accepted by the agent on the licence holder's behalf and the total amount payable under the contract.

6. Consumer rights and safeguards

(i) European consumer protection

The European Community has supplemented UK legislation relating to consumer protection introducing Directives establishing common levels of protection for the consumer. **18.91**

Tourism will always involve the provision of services. EC Directives provide consumers with increased remedies for injury or loss suffered as a result of badly provided services, or where the contract is not fulfilled by the supplier. The Directives also relate to the marketing of these services.

(a) Unfair terms in consumer contracts

The Unfair Terms in Consumer Contracts Directive 93/13/EEC was adopted by the Council of Ministers in April 1993. The United Kingdom has implemented this Directive from 1 July 1995. **18.92**

The Directive must be considered alongside the Unfair Contract Terms Act 1977. The Act deals primarily with exclusion clauses in consumer contracts.[53]

The Directive imports into UK contract law for the first time a general concept of "fairness". It specifies that a contractual term which has not been individually negotiated is to be regarded as unfair if, contrary to the requirement of good faith, it causes a significant imbalance in the parties' rights and obligations arising under the contract, to the detriment of the consumer. In determining good faith, regard must be had to the strength of the bargaining position of the parties, whether the consumer was given an inducement to agree, whether the goods or services were **18.93**

---

[53] See *infra*.

sold or supplied to the special order of the consumer, and the extent to which the seller or supplier takes into account the legitimate interests of the other parties. Terms of a contract drafted in advance are always to be regarded as having not been individually negotiated, even if a single term, or certain aspects of it have been.

Where a contract is offered to a consumer in writing, a seller or supplier is under an obligation to ensure that the terms are drafted in plain, intelligible language. If there is doubt as to the meaning of a term, it will be interpreted in the manner most favourable to the consumer.

(b) Misleading advertising

18.94 The Misleading Advertising Directive 84/450/EEC was implemented in the United Kingdom by the Control of Misleading Advertisements Regulations 1988.[54]

There is a proposal for a Council Directive concerning comparative advertising which would enable consumers to make easier and more informed comparisons between products by allowing firms to practise comparative advertising under certain conditions. It is proposed that comparative advertising will be permitted if it is not misleading, does not cause confusion between trademarks, does not discredit the advertiser's competitors, and if the comparison is objective and verifiable.

(c) Distance selling

18.95 A proposal for a Council Directive on the protection of consumers in respect of contracts negotiated at a distance (distance selling)[55] as amended[56] was submitted to the Commission on 7 October 1994. The proposal seeks to make it easier to compare products and services by regulating some distance-selling techniques employed by firms in Member States. Distance selling covers any agreements solicited and concluded without the supplier and consumer being simultaneously present, by using a means of communication at a distance, such as fax, electronic mail, telephone or automatic calling units.

18.96 The proposed Directive would require that consumers should have a seven day cooling-off period in which to cancel agreements without penalty. At the time of solicitation, the consumer should be provided with clear and unambiguous information as to the identity of the seller, the main characteristics of the product, the service, the price and quantity of transport charges, as well as VAT charges, payment, delivery and performance arrangements, and the period for which the solicitation remains valid. The consumer should be given similar information in writing no later than at the time of delivery and in the language used at the time of the solicitation.

---

[54] SI 1988/915.
[55] COM(92) 11.
[56] COM(93) 396.

If no time limit for performance is stipulated in the contract, performance should begin not more than thirty days after the order is received by the supplier. The proposed Directive would cover the supply of all goods and services (with a number of exceptions).[57]

(d) Contracts negotiated away from business premises

The Contracts Negotiated Away From Business Premises Directive 85/577/EEC is implemented into UK law by The Consumer Protection (Cancellation of Contracts Concluded away from Business Premises) Regulations 1987 and 1988. Where goods or services are supplied to a consumer by a trader during an unsolicited visit to a consumer's home; or to the home of another person; or to the consumer's place of work; there is no enforceable contract against the consumer unless the trader has delivered a notice in writing to him indicating his right to cancel the contract within a period of seven days. The notice must be easily legible and must be afforded at least the same prominence as other terms in the contract document. If, within a period of seven days, the consumer serves a notice of cancellation in writing on the trader, the notice shall operate to cancel the contract and any sum paid by the consumer shall become repayable.

18.97

The regulations do not apply to the supply of goods or services where the terms of the contract are contained in a trader's catalogue which is readily available to the consumer before the conclusion of the contract. Neither do they apply where the parties to the contract intend that there shall be maintained continuity of contract, and the catalogue and contract contain a prominent notice indicating the consumer has a right of return within seven days.

18.98

The United Kingdom has long-standing consumer protection statutes in respect of false or misleading information given to a consumer.

(ii) Trade Descriptions Act 1968

(a) Section 14

Section 14(1) provides that:

It shall be an offence for any person[58] in the course of any trade or business:

18.99

    (a)   to make a statement which he knows to be false;

    (b)   recklessly to make a statement which is false as to any of the following matters, that is to say:

---

[57] The proposed exceptions being: automatic vending machines, made-to-measure products, services with a reservation (transport, accommodation, catering and entertainment) and contracts for the supply of foodstuffs, beverages or other goods and services intended for current consumption.

[58] This includes bodies corporate. The company's directors and principal officers would also be liable for commission of the offence.

(i) the provision in the course of any trade or business of any services, accommodation or facilities;

(ii) the nature of any services, accommodation or facilities provided in the course of any trade or business;

(iii) the time at which, manner in which or persons by whom any services, accommodation are so provided;

(iv) the examination, approval or evaluation by any person of any services, accommodation or services so provided.

For the purposes of the section:

(a) anything (whether or not a statement as to any of the matters specified in the preceding subsection) likely to be taken for such a statement as to any of those matters as would be false, shall be deemed to be a false statement as to that matter; and

(b) a statement made regardless of whether it is true or false shall be deemed to be made recklessly, whether or not the person making it had reasons for believing that it might be false.

18.100   In this section "false" means false to a material degree,[59] and "services" does not include anything done under a contract of service.

Section 14 of the Act makes it a criminal offence to make statements which are known to be false or are made recklessly. If found guilty, in summary proceedings, there is a maximum fine of £5,000, and an unlimited fine for conviction on indictment.

Section 14 is enforced by local authorities through their Trading Standards Departments. Any prosecutions brought under the Act must be reported to the Office of Fair Trading. An individual may bring a private prosecution under the Act. A prosecution does not however preclude civil proceedings.

Section 14 is enforced in Northern Ireland by the Trading Standards Branch of the Department of Economic Development. Any prosecutions under the Act must be reported to the Office of Fair Trading.

(b)   A statement made by a person "which he knows to be false"

18.101   A tour operator which publishes a brochure advertising a holiday containing false information, which it knows to be false, is guilty of an offence.

If a tour operator prints brochures for distribution to travel agents containing information which subsequently becomes false due to a change in circumstances, then on discovery of the false information the tour operator must take immediate steps to correct this, and to ensure that all outlets displaying the incorrect brochures are notified of the change in circumstances.

If a customer subsequently purchases a holiday on the basis of an uncorrected brochure, who is responsible – the travel agent who was advised by the tour operator of the changes but did not draw these to the customer's attention, or the tour operator?

---

[59] Trade Descriptions Act 1968 s 14(4).

The House of Lords in *Wings* v *Ellis*[60] (on English appeal) *held* that a tour operator would be in breach of section 14(1)(a) if a brochure published by it: **18.102**

(i)   contained false information which was relied upon by a customer, and
(ii)   at that time the tour operator knew the pre-printed brochure contained false information.

The tour operator will be liable irrespective of any steps taken by it to intimate the changes to its agents displaying the brochures, unless it can invoke one of the statutory defences.

(c)   Recklessness

The meaning of 'reckless' as used in section 14 was considered by the English Court of Appeal in *MFI Warehouses Limited* v *Nattrass*[61] where it was held that the prosecution need only show that an advertiser did not have regard to the truth or falsity of the advertisement, irrespective of any dishonest intention on his part.[62] **18.103**

(d)   Enforcement

Enforcement of section 14 is the duty of Trading Standards Officers[63] working in association with the Office of Fair Trading and the Department of Prices and Consumer Protection. Any prosecutions must be reported to the OFT. In Scotland, a prosecution will be brought by the Procurator Fiscal. **18.104**

(e)   Defences

Section 24(1) provides a defence. It is a defence:

(i)   that the commission of the offence was due to a mistake or to the reliance on information supplied to the individual or to the act or default of another person, an accident or some other cause beyond his control; and **18.105**
(ii)   that he took all reasonable precautions and exercised all due diligence to avoid the commission of such an offence by himself or any person under his control.

---

[60] [1985] AC 272, [1984] 3 All ER 577, [1984] 3 WLR 965.
[61] [1973] 1 All ER 762.
[62] Both *Wings* v *Ellis* and *MFI Warehouses Limited* v *Nattrass* were English cases, in the House of Lords and Court of Appeal respectively. A Court in Scotland would not be bound by precedent, but would find them highly persuasive. The authors have only been able to find one Scottish case relative to s 14 examining recklessness in providing a false trade description relating to holiday arrangements: see *Herron* v *Lunn Poly (Scotland) Limited* 1972 SLT (Sh.Ct)2. In Northern Ireland, decisions of the House of Lords on Appeal from England are binding, whilst decisions of the Court of Appeal or High Court in England are of persuasive authority only. The level of persuasiveness of any decision will often depend on the composition of the Court which gave that decision. There must usually be some fairly compelling reason for the Northern Ireland Courts to depart from a well-established line of authority of the English Courts.
[63] Weights and Measures Act 1985 s 69(3).

(iii) Consumer Protection Act 1987[64]

(a) Section 20

18.106 Section 20(1) provides that:

> a person shall be guilty of an offence if, in the course of any business of his, he gives (by any means whatever) to any consumers an indication which is misleading as to the price at which any goods, services, accommodation or facilities are available (whether generally or from particular persons).

"Price" is described as the total sum to be paid[65] (including VAT). It is immaterial how the price is indicated to the consumer.

18.107 Section 20(2) further states that a person shall be guilty of an offence if:

> in the course of any business of his, he has given an indication to any consumers which, after it was given, has become misleading, and some or all of those customers might reasonably be expected to rely on the indication, and he fails to take all such steps as are reasonable to prevent those customers from relying on the indication.

It is necessary that some or all of these consumers might reasonably be expected to rely on it at a time after it became misleading.

(b) Code of Practice

18.108 The Act provides for a Code of Practice, some of which applies to the travel industry.

It specifies that tour operators must make the correct price clear when a holiday is being booked. This must be done before the holiday-maker has entered into the contract. If the price indication becomes misleading while the brochure is in existence, the consumer must be advised. Travel agents so advised must ensure that the correct price is made clear to the holiday-maker.

The Code of Practice provides guidance as to the interpretation of the 1987 Act. A breach of the Code is not a criminal offence, nor will civil liability be incurred, but the breach may be used as evidence of a tour operator's failure.

(c) Defences

18.109 The Act provides various defences for prosecutions brought under section 20.[66] It is a defence if:

---

[64] The Act was brought into force, along with the associated Price Indications Regulations and Code of Practice, on 1 March 1989. The equivalent provision in Northern Ireland is art 14 of the Consumer Protection (Northern Ireland) Order 1987 Defences are set out in art 17, and the defence of due diligence appears at art 30.

[65] S 20(6).

[66] The defences are contained in s 24.

(i)   the price indication received by the individual was published in any book, newspaper, magazine, film or radio, television broadcast or cable programme, and the indication was not contained in an advertisement;[67]

(ii)   the individual, in the course of business, publishes advertisements and at the time of publication he was unaware or had no reason to suspect that in publishing the advertisements he would commit an offence;[68]

(iii)   the price indication did not relate to the availability from him of any goods, services, accommodation or facilities.[69]

Section 39 provides a general defence. If the individual shows that all reasonable steps were taken and all due diligence was exercised to avoid the commission of the offence, then he is not guilty of the offence.

(d)   Enforcement

The Act is enforced by Trading Standards Officers, by referral from the Director General of Fair Trading. A conviction on indictment may be punished by an unlimited fine, and on summary conviction by a maximum fine of £5,000. An action may be time-barred if not brought within three years from the commission of the actual offence or one year from its discovery.   **18.110**

In Northern Ireland the Act is enforced by the Trading Standards Branch of the Department of Economic Development. Trading Standards Officers will often use "test purchases" as a method of investigation.

(iv)   The Package Regulations 1992

The Package Regulations also provide for criminal liability in respect of misleading information.   **18.111**

Regulation 5 stipulates that:

(i)   No organiser shall make available a brochure to a possible consumer unless it indicates in a legible, comprehensive and accurate manner the price and adequate information about matters specified in Sch 1 of the regulations in respect of the packages offered for sale in the brochure to the extent that those matters are relevant to the packages so offered.

(ii)   No retailer shall make available to a possible consumer a brochure which he knows or has reasonable cause to believe does not comply with the requirements of para (i).

An "organiser" who contravenes 5(i) and a "retailer" who contravenes 5(ii) is guilty of a criminal offence, and liable on summary conviction to a   **18.112**

---

[67] *Ibid* s 24(2).
[68] *Ibid* s 24(3).
[69] *Ibid* s 24(4).

fine not exceeding level five on the Standard Scale (currently £5,000), and on conviction on indictment to an unlimited fine.

18.113   "Brochure" is defined as any brochure in which packages are offered for sale.[70] Where a brochure was first made available to consumers before 31 December 1992 no liability arises, or in respect of identical brochures being made available to consumers at any time.[71]

The liability imposed by regulation 5 is not absolute. Regulation 24 provides for defences.[72] Schedule 1 specifies the information which must be included in a brochure. This includes *inter alia*: the price; the destination; means of transport; type of accommodation and its location, category and main features; whether meals are included; itinerary; information in respect of passport and visa requirements for British citizens; health formalities; the amount of money or percentage of the price to be paid on account and the timetable for payment of the balance; whether a minimum number of persons are required for the package to proceed and the deadline for informing consumers that the package will not proceed; delay arrangements which apply at outward or homeward points of departures and arrangements for the security of money paid over; and repatriation arrangements in the event of insolvency.

18.114   The particulars in the brochure[73] constitute implied terms in the contract.[74] This has the effect of ensuring that the particulars become binding terms in the contract. Breach of these terms by the other party to the contract will give the holiday-maker a remedy. Breach of contract entitles him to damages if he can prove he suffered loss or injury as a result of the breach.

There are however two exceptions:

(i)   if the brochure contains an express statement that changes may be made before a contract is concluded and the changes are clearly communicated to the consumer before the contract is concluded,[75] and

(ii)   the consumer and the organiser agree on conclusion of the contract that all or some of the particulars contained in the brochure should not form part of the contract;

then an offence shall not have been committed.

18.115   Regulation 7 stipulates that before a contract is made, the tour operator must provide certain information "in writing or some other appropriate form to an intending consumer." It must specify general information

---

[70] Package Regulations 1992, reg 2(1).
[71] *Ibid* reg 5(4).
[72] See *infra*.
[73] (whether or not required by reg 5(1)).
[74] This is subject to two exceptions. See *supra*.
[75] The exceptions are contained in s 6(2).

about passport and visa requirements which apply to British citizens purchasing the package, and the likely length of time required to obtain a passport and relevant visa. It must also provide information about health formalities and arrangements for the security of monies paid and (where applicable), the repatriation of the consumer in the event of insolvency.

Regulation 7 covers the situation where a tour operator may sell holidays through the medium of a brochure, and affords the consumer the same protection as regulation 5.

If an intending consumer is not provided with the required information, then the tour operator is guilty of an offence and liable to a fine not exceeding level five on the Standard Scale on summary conviction, and on indictment to an unlimited fine. **18.116**

Regulation 8 provides that the following information shall be supplied to the consumer by the tour operator in good time prior to the commencement of the journey:[76]

(a) the times and places of the intermediate stops, transport connections and particulars of the place to be occupied by the traveller (*e.g.* cabin or berth on ship, sleeper compartment on train);

(b) (i)   the name, address and telephone number of the representative of the tour operator in the locality of where the consumer is to stay or, where there is no representative, an agency in the locality which can be relied on by the consumer for assistance in the event of difficulty, or, where there is no agency or representative, a telephone number or other information which will enable the consumer to contact the tour operator;

(ii) in respect of a journey or stay abroad by a child under 16 years on the day the journey or stay is due to commence, information enabling direct contact to be made with the child or person responsible at the place where he is to stay;

(iii) information about an insurance policy which the consumer may, if he wishes, take out in respect of the insured risks of the costs of cancellation, assistance including repatriation, accident or illness (except where an insurance policy is required to be taken out as a term of the contract).

A breach of regulation 8 is punishable by a fine on summary conviction up to level five on the Standard Scale, and on indictment by an unlimited fine. **18.117**

(a)   Defences for Breach of Regulations 5, 7 and 8

Regulations 5, 7, and 8 do not impose strict liability. **18.118**

Regulation 24(1) provides the following defence:

---

[76] *Ibid* reg 8(1).

567

Subject to the following provisions of this regulation, in proceedings against any person for an offence under Regulations 5, 7, 8, 16 and 22, it shall be a defence for that person to show that he took all reasonable steps and exercised all due diligence to avoid committing the offence.

18.119 This defence is similar to those available under the Trade Descriptions Act and the Consumer Protection Act. Where a tour operator or travel agent, relying on regulation 24(1), alleges that the commission of the offence was due to the act or default of another or reliance on information given by another, in order to be entitled to rely on the defence, regulation 24(2) specifies that intimation must be made to the prosecution at least seven clear days before the trial date.

The tour operator or travel agent is not entitled to rely on the defence by reason of reliance on information supplied by another, unless he can show that it was reasonable, in all the circumstances, to rely on the information. Particular attention must be paid to the steps which are taken or those that might reasonably be taken by the tour operator or travel agent to verify the information, and whether they might have any reason to disbelieve that information.

(v) Civil liability for false and misleading statements

(a) The Package Regulations

18.120 Regulation 4 of the Package Regulations stipulates that:

(i) No organiser or retailer shall supply to a consumer any descriptive matter concerning a package, the price of a package or any other conditions applying to the contract which contains misleading information.

(ii) If an organiser or retailer is in breach of paragraph (1) he shall be liable to compensate the consumer for any loss which the consumer suffers as a consequence.

As seen above, the Trade Descriptions Act 1968 and the Consumer Protection Act 1987 impose *criminal* liability for false and misleading information supplied knowingly or recklessly. Regulation 4 imposes *civil* liability in respect of "misleading" information. It need not be supplied knowingly or recklessly. The holiday-maker relying on regulation 4, need only show he suffered loss as a result of the misleading information. The regulations do not require him to show that he relied on the information.

Thus a tour operator or travel agent may incur civil liability for misrepresentation.

18.121 A misrepresentation has been described as:

an inaccurate statement of past or present fact made expressly or impliedly, by assertion or concealment, or by failure to disclose in circumstances where there was a positive duty to disclose, prior to or at the time of contracting, by one party to the other, which is a material factor in inducing the other party to contract on the terms on which he did.[77]

The misrepresentation may give rise to actions based either in contract or delict.

(b)   Contract misrepresentation

The misrepresentation must produce "error" in the mind of the party **18.122** challenging the contract. The consumer will not have grounds for an action where he was unaware of the misrepresentation and was not deceived, or where he knew that a representation was incorrect and did not challenge it.

Misrepresentation may be:

(i)   innocent;
(ii)   negligent; or
(iii)   fraudulent.

A misrepresentation is innocent if the maker honestly but mistakenly believed what he asserted, and did not intend to deceive, but ought to have taken and did not take reasonable care in the circumstances to ascertain the correctness of his representation.

A misrepresentation is negligent if the maker failed to take reasonable **18.123** care and was duty bound to do so.

A misrepresentation is fraudulent if the maker intended to deceive, or had no honest belief in the accuracy of his representation, or knowingly or recklessly made the statement not caring whether it was true or false.

If an individual is induced to enter a contract by a misrepresentation, the extent of his remedy will depend on the nature of the misrepresentation. If innocent, he may only rescind the contract. If fraudulent or negligent, he is entitled to an additional remedy of damages.

(vi)   Remedies for breach of contract

A party to a contract may be in breach of that contract in a number of **18.124** ways. The remedies available to the party not in breach will vary according to how the "guilty" party has breached the contract.[78]

(a)   Repudiation

Where a party to the contract fails to fulfil his obligations – relating to a **18.125** matter going to the "root of the contract"[79] he will have repudiated the contract. Repudiation will not *per se* terminate the contract. The innocent

---

[77] See Walker, '*Principles of Scottish Private Law*' 4th Ed., Vol II, p. 75.

[78] Northern Ireland contract law closely follows the equivalent English law principles, and the commentary in this section relating to England is equally applciable to Northern Ireland..

[79] See *Woodar Investments Development Limited* v *Wimpey Construction (UK) Ltd* [1980] 1 All ER 571 per Lord Wilberforce on 576.

party is entitled to "rescind" the contract, *i.e.* to withdraw from the contract. His decision to withdraw must be in response to the repudiation.

(b) Anticipatory breach[80]

18.126 Where performance of the contract takes place at a future date, one party may intimate to the other that he will be unable to fulfil his obligations under the contract. He repudiates the contract before he is due to perform his obligations. This is an "anticipatory breach" of the contract. The innocent party may:

(i)   rescind the contract and sue for damages;

(ii)   wait until the time period within which the other party must perform his obligations has elapsed and sue for damages; or

(iii) perform his own obligations under the contract, and then take action against the other party in breach.

(c) Action for payment

18.127 Where the contract price is not paid, the innocent party may raise an action to recover the money due to him. He is entitled to interest calculated according to the terms of the contract.

(d) Specific Implement in Scotland

18.128 The innocent party in breach of contract may raise proceedings to compel the other party to fulfil his obligations. Implement is the primary remedy in Scots law. If such an action is unenforceable, the innocent party may bring an action for damages.

(e) Damages

18.129 Every breach of contract gives rise to damages.[81]

Damages awarded in contract seek to restore the innocent party to the position they would have been in had the contract been performed. There must be proof however, that a breach has occurred, and that there is a direct causal connection between that breach and the loss suffered.

The party in breach is not held to be responsible for all the consequences of the breach – only those which may be "reasonably foreseeable". They will not be liable for losses which are too remote. The case of *Hadley* v *Baxendale*[82] provides a two stage test for assessing damages:

(i)   the consequence of the breach was a normal one which anyone would have appreciated;

---

[80] This will often be of importance in situations where individuals enter into contracts with tour operators or other providers of tourist services, where they pay over their money and the operator or business subsequently becomes insolvent and ceases trading before providing the service to the individual. At the point of declaring itself insolvent, the insolvent party will be in anticipatory breach of the contract.

[81] *E.g.* see *Webster* v *Cramond Iron Co* 1875 2R 752.

[82] 9 Exch 341. Although an English case, the two-step test is often referred to by Scottish Courts.

(ii)   if special circumstances pertained to the contract and both parties
       were aware of them, then damages from the breach would be those
       ordinarily resulting from the breach of contract in the special cir-
       cumstances.

The case of *Victoria Laundry (Windsor) Limited* v *Newman Industries Limited*[83]
refined the test, holding that the damages recoverable would be those
damages a reasonable person would view as likely to result from the
breach.

Damages for non-pecuniary loss

If a breach of contract occurs, it is possible to claim for damages for non-   **18.130**
pecuniary or non-monetary loss. Thus, where a holiday brochure mis-
describes a holiday, the holiday-maker is entitled to damages for his
disappointment.[84]

Mitigation of loss

An innocent party must take all reasonable steps to minimise his loss   **18.131**
when faced with a breach of contract. If he does not and could have
avoided the loss by doing so, he is not entitled to damages. The onus of
proof rests with the contract-breaker to prove what steps a reasonable
person would have taken.

(f)   Delictual misrepresentation in Scotland

If a tour operator or travel agent makes a representation to a holiday-   **18.132**
maker then the holiday-maker may have, in addition to an action in contract, an action in delict.

The misrepresentation must have been a material factor in inducing
the consumer to contract and he must have suffered the loss as a consequence. If the misrepresentation is made innocently, no delictual
remedy exists.

If the misrepresentation is made fraudulently, then the holiday-maker
may recover damages in delict. In the event that a tour operator or travel
agent makes a misrepresentation, then the operator and agent are liable
for all losses arising directly from the fraudulent conduct.

If the misrepresentation is negligent, section 10 of the Law Reform   **18.133**
(Miscellaneous Provisions) (Scotland) Act 1985 provides that:

> A party to a contract who has been induced to enter into it by negligent
> misrepresentation made by or on behalf of another party to the contract,
> shall not be disentitled, by reason only that the misrepresentation is not
> fraudulent, from recovering damages from the other party in respect of any
> loss or damage he has suffered as a result of the misrepresentation. Any
> rule of law that such damages cannot be recovered unless fraud is proved
> shall cease to have effect.

---

[83] [1949] 2 KB 528.
[84] *Jarvis* v *Swan's Tours Limited* [1973] 2 QB 233.

The consumer, however, must prove that a "duty of care" existed between himself and the tour operator or travel agent.

18.134 A travel agent will have an incumbent duty to a client to exercise reasonable skill and care. If he fails in that duty and causes pecuniary loss to a client which is due to the failure, then he is liable for the loss caused.[85] The travel agent owes a duty of care to holiday-makers for representations made by him. The duty arises because the travel agent knows, or ought to know, that the representation is intended, or is likely, to be relied on by the client.

The travel agent has a special knowledge or skill on which an intending holiday-maker will rely. The agent exercises this in the ordinary course of his business. The holiday-maker is entitled to place reliance on such information or opinion, and the travel agent ought to know that the consumer will do so and will suffer loss if the information is incorrect or inaccurate.[86]

Delict and damages

18.135 Whereas damages in contract seek to place an innocent party in the position he would have been had the breach not occurred, damages in delict seek to place an injured party (in so far as possible) in the position he would have been in had the delictual conduct never occurred. This area of law is complex but the major principles are that:

(i)   there must exist a duty of care, owed by one party to the other;

(ii)   that duty of care must have been breached;

(iii)   and the breach resulted in the loss.[87]

A travel agent or tour operator will owe a duty of care to a member of the public wishing advice on which holiday to take.

(g)   Causation

18.136 A breach of a duty of care may result in loss, injury or damage. The breach must be the effective cause, which if proven, will entitle the injured party to damages. If another party also owes the individual a duty of care and is also in breach of that duty, resulting in loss, injury or damage, then both parties may simultaneously be liable in damages. The Law Reform (Miscellaneous Provisions) (Scotland) Act 1940 section 3 provides:

(i)   where in any action of damages in respect of loss or damage arising from any wrongful acts or negligent acts or omissions two or more persons are . . . found jointly and severally liable in damages or expenses, they shall be liable *inter se* to contribute to such damages or expenses in such proportions as a jury or the court . . . may deem just . . . and;

---

[85] See *Hedley Byrne* v *Heller and Partners* [1964] AC 465.

[86] *John Kenway* v *Orcantic* 1979 SLT 46.

[87] The classic case on duty of care is *Donoghue* v *Stevenson* 1932 SC (HL) 31, 1932 SLT 317.

(ii) Where any person has paid any damages or expenses . . . he shall be entitled to recover from any other person who, if sued, might also have been held liable in respect of the loss or damage on which the action was founded, such contribution, if any, as the court may deem just.

7. Rights against transport operators

Regulation 15(3) of the Package Regulations provides that compensation for damage arising from the non-performance or improper performance of the services involved in the package may be limited in accordance with international conventions governing such services. A number of international conventions regulate travel by sea, rail, road and air. It is important to note that these conventions will not apply solely to package holidays.

18.137

(i) Carriage by sea

The Athens Convention 1974 regulates the international carriage of passengers and their luggage by sea. Its terms are incorporated into the law of the United Kingdom by section 14 of The Merchant Shipping Act 1979. This Act only regulates "international" carriage by sea, *i.e.* where the points of departure and arrival are in two different states, or, if in a single state, there is an intermediate stopover in another state. It covers carriage of passengers and their baggage by ship. If, in the course of carriage, a passenger suffers death or personal injury, or his baggage is lost or damaged, the shipping company may be liable. The loss, injury or damage must occur during carriage and must have occurred as a result of the fault or negligence of the shipping company, its employees acting within the scope of their employment, or its servants acting within their authority.

18.138

The burden of proving quantum of damage and loss that occurred during the course of carriage, rests with the person seeking to claim compensation.[88] There is a ceiling for damages in respect of death or personal injury, of 100,000 Special Drawing Rights.[89] For damage to or loss of cabin baggage, there is a ceiling of 833,000 Special Drawing Rights.[90] For other baggage there is a ceiling of 12,000 Special Drawing Rights.[91]

(ii) Carriage by rail

The Berne Convention of 1970 governs international carriage by rail. It is incorporated into UK law by the International Transport Conventions

18.139

---

[88] Where however the loss, injury or damage occurs as a result of ship wreck, explosion, fire, a defect in the ship, collision or standing, the burden of proof will be transferred to the carrier or person defending the claim.

[89] Approximately £110,000.

[90] Approximately £900.

[91] Approximately £1,300.

Act 1983.[92] The railway is liable for death or personal injury to a passenger caused by an accident arising out of the operation of the railway, or while the passenger was in, embarking or disembarking from railway vehicles. It is impossible for a railway to contract out of liability for personal injury and death. The railway is further liable for loss of or damage to a passenger's hand baggage. If a passenger wishes to raise an action he or she must do so within three years from the day after the accident or his or her personal representatives must do so within three years from the date of death of the passenger.[93]

(iii)   Carriage by road

18.140   The Geneva Convention of 1973 governs the international carriage of passengers and luggage by road. The United Kingdom is not yet a contracting party to the convention. The Carriage of Passengers by Road Act 1974, as yet not in force, provides for the implementation of the convention into UK law on its ratification. The convention provides that the carrier by road will be liable for any loss or damage resulting from the death or personal injury to a passenger, caused by an accident occurring whilst the passenger was in, entering or alighting from a vehicle. The carrier will also be liable for loss or damage to baggage during its loading, unloading and carriage.

(iv)   Carriage by air

18.141   The Warsaw Convention of 1929, as amended by The Hague Protocol of 1985, governs international carriage by air. It is incorporated into UK law by the Carriage by Air Act 1961.

In any international carriage of passengers, a ticket must be provided containing information indicating points of departure and destination, the name and address of the carrier, and a statement to the effect that carriage is subject to the rules of liability contained in the convention. The carrier will be liable in damages for the death or injury of a passenger by accident on board or in embarking or disembarking. It will further be liable for loss or injury to registered baggage or cargo if sustained during carriage by air, *i.e.* whilst in its charge. It will also be liable for any delay in the carriage of passengers, baggage or goods.

18.142   Liability may be avoided if the carrier can prove that itself, its agents or servants, took all "necessary measures" to avoid the damage, or that it was impossible for them to take such measures.

If there is contributory negligence on the part of the passenger, liability may be limited to 250,000 gold francs[94] for death and personal injury;

---

[92] SI 1985/612.
[93] This is subject to a maximum time-bar of five years for any actions raised.
[94] Approximately £13,500.

5,000 gold francs[95] for loss of or damage to hand baggage and 250 gold francs[96] per kilogram for loss or damage to registered baggage.

8. Forms of redress

(i) Arbitration

If the holiday-maker cannot obtain redress to his satisfaction directly from a tour operator, there is usually provision, either in the contract or by taking the matter to one of the tour operator/travel agents' voluntary associations, to take the matter to arbitration.   **18.143**

ABTA and AITO both operate arbitration schemes.

ABTA's codes of conduct, for both travel agents and tour operators, impose an obligation on them to take all possible steps to resolve complaints as quickly and as amicably as possible. Where the complaint cannot be resolved, the holiday-maker may contact ABTA for assistance. He will be invited by ABTA to apply for resolution to the Chartered Institute of Arbitration, together with an application fee. Once the holiday-maker has applied, he must accept the decision of the arbiter. The procedure is by documents alone. There is no provision for personal appearance. The application must be submitted within nine months of the date of return from the unsatisfactory holiday.

(ii) Court action

(a) England

A holiday claim in England may be raised in the small claims court, part of the county court (there are 270 in the country) for monetary claims for less than £3,000.   **18.144**

In exceptional circumstances, where the case raises a difficult question of law, or facts of exceptional complexity are involved, then the claim falls to the court (CCR Ord 19 r 3(2)).

The procedure is conducted by a district judge, without the need for lawyers. The costs are therefore restricted to the costs which are stated on the summons, and any enforcement costs.

(b) Scotland

A holiday claim case may be raised in the Sheriff Court under either the Small Claims procedure, Summary Cause, or Ordinary Cause, or in the Outer House of the Court of Session. As small sums of money are usually involved and very complex issues of law rarely arise, most claims are dealt with through the Small Claims procedure or by Summary Cause actions.

Small claims[97]

Actions which may be brought under Small Claims procedure are: **18.145**

---

[95] Approximately £270.
[96] Approximately £13.50 per kilogram.
[97] The small claims procedure is fairly recent. It limits the use of court time for cases concerning relatively small sums of money.

(i)   actions of payment of money not exceeding £750, exclusive of interest and expenses;

(ii)   actions *ad factum praestandum* and actions for the recovery of possession of movable property, where there is an alternative claim for payment of a sum not exceeding £750, exclusive of interest and expenses; and

(iii) actions under (i) and (ii) above which are excluded only because they mention money limits, if the parties so agree.[98]

Summary Cause procedure

Summary Cause procedure generally deals with actions of monetary value of not less than £750, but not exceeding £1,500.

Northern Ireland

A holiday claim for less than £1,000 may be taken to the Small Claims Court in Northern Ireland. This is a simplified procedure which is designed to be used by members of the public, without legal representation. Costs are not allowed in the Small Claims Court. Any holiday claim for more than £1,000 is likely to be taken in the County Court. The jurisdiction of the County Court extends to claims up to £15,000.

(iii)   Compensation for criminal injuries

(a)   Criminal Injuries Compensation Authority[99]

18.146   The Criminal Injuries Compensation Authority makes provision for the award of *ex gratia* monetary payments as compensation for individuals who have sustained personal injury directly attributable to a crime of violence. Any individual of any nationality may apply. Application is not restricted to UK nationals or residents.

An applicant may apply where personal injury was directly attributable to a crime of violence, to an offence of trespass on a railway, to the apprehension or attempted apprehension of an offender or suspected offender, or prevention or attempted prevention of an offence, or to the giving of assistance to any Police Constable engaged in any such activity.

18.147   The personal injury must be sustained in Great Britain[100] or on a British aircraft, hovercraft or ship, or under or above an installation in a designated area[101] or any waters within 500 metres of such an installation, or in a lighthouse off the coast of Great Britain.

There is no requirement for the offender or person causing the criminal injury to have been convicted of a criminal act. Compensation, however, is not payable where the injury sustained was accidental.

---

[98] Small Claims (Scotland) Order 1988, SI 1988.

[99] A non-statutory state scheme established in August 1964. It has subsequently been modified and is now replaced by a Tariff Scheme implemented on 1 April 1994.

[100] Includes that part of the Channel Tunnel designated part of Great Britain by the Channel Tunnel Act 1987.

[101] Within the meaning of s 1(7) of the Continental Shelf Act 1964.

Applications must be received by the Authority within one year of the incident which gave rise to injury. In exceptional cases the Authority may waive this requirement.

The Authority may withhold or reduce an award, if it considers the applicant failed to take all reasonable steps to inform the Police, or to co-operate with the Police or the Authority. Further, the conduct and character of the applicant may be taken into account by the Authority in withholding or reducing an award.

(iv) Compensation for victims of crime

The new Criminal Injury Compensation Authority, which came into being on 1 April 1996, will keep the old systems in place until all outstanding costs have been decided, and this could continue for about two years. The new scheme is based on a "tariff" under which standard amounts of compensation will be paid to eligible applicants depending upon the nature and severity of the injury. The applicant's age, sex and other circumstances will have no bearing on this standard amount of compensation. More than 300 injuries are specified in the tariff with levels of awards varying between, for example, £1,000 for temporary partial deafness to £250,000 for permanent serious brain damage. Maximum award will be half a million pounds. The time limit for submitting an application is two years. **18.148**

This scheme has not been implemented in Northern Ireland.

Awards made by the Authority reflect the severity of injury sustained in accordance with a tariff of awards. There is a minimum award of £1,000. If injuries are sustained, which in the Authority's view do not qualify for at least the minimum award, then there is no provision for an award. The maximum award available is £250,000. Review and appeal procedures are available for contesting an Authority decision. **18.149**

(b) Compensation orders in England

The courts have powers under the Powers of Criminal Courts Act 1973, sections 35–38, (as amended), to make an order: (1) to pay compensation for any personal injury, loss or damage resulting from the offence, or any offence taken into consideration on sentence, or where no loss, damage or insurer can be shown, no compensation order, or, (2) to make payments for funeral expenses or bereavement in respect of a death resulting from any such offence, other than a death due to an accident arising out of the presence (the maximum amount which may be awarded for bereavement is £7,500) of a motor vehicle on a road. The rules require that before an order is made the judge must: **18.150**

(i)   satisfy himself that injury, loss or damage has resulted from the offence of which the offender has been convicted, or is having taken into consideration;

577

(ii)   settle the amount of the injury, loss or damage which the offender may be required to pay;

(iii)   consider the means of the offender (Morrish and McLean *Crown Court Index*, 15th Edition, Longmans).

(c)   Compensation Orders in Scotland

18.151   There is provision for the compensation of victims of crime in Scotland through Part IV of the Criminal Justice (Scotland) Act 1980. A Sheriff or Senator of Justice may incorporate as part of a sentence, a monetary payment to be made to a victim by an offender. On indictment, an unlimited sum as compensation may be imposed. The Compensation Order may be made for personal injury, loss or damage caused, directly or indirectly, by the acts which constituted the offence. It cannot be made in respect of fear and alarm in the absence of injury, or injury, loss or damage resulting from any road accident (except in the case of damage to a stolen vehicle).

This remedy is incorporated in the criminal law sentencing procedure, and it is therefore necessary that the offender must be apprehended and convicted, before a Sheriff may consider a Compensation Order for any loss, injury or damage caused.

(d)   Compensation in Northern Ireland

18.152   A person who has suffered a criminal injury in Northern Ireland may apply to the Compensation Agency, an executive agency of the Northern Ireland Office, for compensation. The definition in the Criminal Injuries (Northern Ireland) Order 1977 of a criminal injury is similar to that applicable in England. There are strict time limits for submission of the relevant application forms for compensation. There is no strict tariff system applicable, although payment will be related to the seriousness of the injuries. If the Compensation Agency is satisfied that the claim for compensation has been made out, the Agency will make an offer of compensation. This is often subject to negotiation between the Agency and the Applicant's advisers. If a settlement can be agreed, then a payment will be made to the Applicant and he will also receive a contribution towards his costs. If the Applicant is not prepared to accept the offer of compensation made by the Agency, he has a right of appeal to the county court.

A Compensation Order may also be made in certain circumstances by a criminal court.

9.   The Tourist Boards

18.153   The Development of Tourism Act 1969, established four bodies known respectively as the British Tourist Authority (BTA); the English Tourist Board; the Scottish Tourist Board; and the Welsh Tourist Board.[102]

---

[102] (c. 51) s 1(1).

The chairman and board members of the BTA are appointed by the Secretary of State for National Heritage and various advisory committees drawn from the public and private sectors.

The BTA's role is to promote Britain overseas as a tourist destination and to help strengthen the performance of the industry, by encouraging improvement and provision of tourist amenities in Britain. It is also responsible for advising the government and public bodies on tourism.

(i) English Tourist Board

The overall mission of the English Tourist Board (ETB) is to increase tourism spending in England and to underpin the BTA's work in attracting tourists from overseas.

18.154

To achieve that end, the ETB's priorities are to give advice and leadership to the tourism industry, and to help improve product quality and England's competitiveness.

The responsibility for operating domestic tourism marketing development and quality standards programmes has been assumed by England's regional tourism boards (who also conduct their own marketing, research, training and information activities).

Major activities carried out by the ETB are:

18.155

(i)   setting up national classification and grading schemes for holiday accommodation – such as the crown scheme for serviced accommodation;

(ii)   forming and co-ordinating the National Tourist Board Information Centre networks;

(iii) stimulating suitable local tourism development and management through a series of local partnership initiatives linking public and private interests and other agencies.

In 1983, the BTA's and the ETB's structures were amended to streamline activities, improve efficiency and to avoid possible duplication. A joint head office was established and a number of service departments combined.

In 1989, following further reviews, the ETB began devolving more resources and responsibilities to the regional tourist boards. The same review suspended government financial aid (formerly made under Section 4 of the 1969 Act) for tourism developments in England. It was retained in Scotland and Wales.

(ii) Scottish Tourist Board

The Scottish Tourist Board (STB) consists of a chairman and not more than six other members appointed by the Secretary of State for Scotland.[103] Its function is to encourage people to visit Scotland, people living

18.156

---

[103] *Ibid.* s 1(3).

in Great Britain to take their holidays in Scotland, and to encourage the provision and improvement of tourist amenities and facilities in Scotland.

The STB has particular powers *inter alia*:

(i)   to promote and undertake publicity in any form;

(ii)   to provide advisory and information services;

(iii) to undertake and promote research;

(iv)   to establish committees to advise the Board in respect of its functions; and

(v)   to contribute or to reimburse expenditure incurred by any other person or organisation carrying out any activity which the Board has power to carry on.

18.157   There is provision for financial assistance to be given to tourist projects.[104] In particular the STB has power to provide financial assistance for any project which, in the opinion of the Board, will provide or improve tourist amenities and facilities in Scotland.

The Tourism (Overseas Promotion) (Scotland) Act 1984 provided the STB with an additional power: to carry on any activities outside the United Kingdom for the purpose of encouraging people to visit Scotland.[105] The STB must exercise the power only with the consent of the Secretary of State, acting in consultation with the BTA.[106]

18.158   The STB has recently been subject to re-structuring following a "Review of Support Arrangements for the Tourism Industry in Scotland" announced by the Scottish Office in October 1992 by the Secretary of State for Scotland. From 1 April 1994, the STB has responsibility for marketing the whole of Scotland.[107] It also now has the responsibility for funding and controlling the Area Tourist Board network. There are at present 32 Area Tourist Boards which will be greatly reduced through the Local Government (Scotland) Bill. The new ATB network is intended to be operational by 1 April 1996. The Board hopes that the present re-structuring will lead to increased global competition in the tourism market.

(iii)   Northern Ireland Tourist Board

18.159   The Northern Ireland Tourist Board (NITB) was established by the Development of Tourist Traffic Act (Northern Ireland) 1948. The Mission Statement of the Northern Ireland Tourist Board states that it is "to develop and present Northern Ireland as a quality competitive destination within the international market-place; to promote domestic tourism; and to

---

[104] *Ibid.* s 3.

[105] *Ibid.* s 1(1).

[106] *Ibid.* s 1(2).

[107] Including the Highlands and Islands area previously promoted by Highlands and Islands Enterprise (HIE).

maximise the tourist industry's potential to become a significant creator of wealth and jobs in Northern Ireland". The Northern Ireland Tourist Board carries out the following activities:

(i) quality assurance – the NITB grades accommodation and awards NITB approval;

(ii) it has established a network of tourism information centres, with 24 local centres throughout Northern Ireland;

(iii) encouraging partnership between the public and private sectors to develop tourism in the province, including the setting up of a tourism task force.

10. Regulation of time share agreements

The Time Share Act 1992 provides rights of cancellation in respect of time share accommodation agreements. "Time Share Accommodation" is defined as any living accommodation in the United Kingdom or elsewhere, used or intended to be used wholly or partly for leisure purposes, by a class of persons all of whom have rights to use that accommodation for intermittent periods of short duration.[108] "Time Share Agreement" is defined as an agreement under which time share rights are conferred or purported to be conferred on any person.[109]   **18.160**

An individual in the course of his business must not offer to provide a time share agreement unless he provides a document setting out the terms of the agreement and a notice setting out rights of cancellation.[110] The cancellation period must be not less than 14 days after the day on which the agreement is entered into.[111] If the agreement is cancelled, the offeror has no further rights or obligations, but is entitled to recover any sums paid under or in contemplation of the agreement.[112]

Contravention of section 1 of the Time Share Act is a criminal offence. A person found guilty of this offence is liable on summary conviction to a fine not exceeding the statutory maximum, and on conviction on indictment to an unlimited fine.   **18.161**

There are at present ongoing proposals for a Council Directive concerning the protection of purchasers in contracts relating to the utilisation of immovable property on a time share basis.[113]

The proposed Directive also provides for a cooling-off period of 14   **18.162**

---

[108] *Ibid.* s 1(1)a.
[109] *Ibid.* s 1(4).
[110] *Ibid.* s 2(1).
[111] *Ibid.* s 2(2)a.
[112] *Ibid.* s 2(2)b.
[113] For the most recent proposals see: "Amended proposal for a Council Directive on the protection of purchasers in contracts relating to the purchase of a right to utilise one or several immovable properties on a time share basis" COM(93) 487 final OJ 1993 C222 p5.

days, from the signature of the contract. It alternatively provides a cooling-off period of at least 28 days from the date of signature of the contract, where the right of time share can be exercised in a country other than the one where the purchaser has his normal residence. A vendor must also provide a full information document, the terms of which are to be incorporated into the contract.

Member States will be required to implement provisions governing reimbursement of advance payment in the event of non-completion of the property. Reimbursement requirements will also apply to cases where the right of withdrawal is exercised, in so far as there is no element of unjust enrichment for either party. The Council is close to adopting this Directive. It is proposed that Member States will then have a two year period to implement it.

11. Hotels in England, Scotland and Northern Ireland

18.163 The law in Scotland regulating hotels and hotel-keepers originates in Scottish Parliamentary enactments of the fifteenth century. A hotel-keeper was then obliged to provide a traveller with ale and bread and other foods, all at a reasonable price.[114] The law in both Scotland and England is now regulated mostly by the Hotel Proprietors Act 1956 (c. 62)

Section 1(3) of the 1956 Act specifies that an hotel is an establishment held out by the proprietor as offering food, drink and, if required, sleeping accommodation, to any traveller able and willing to pay a reasonable sum for the facilities and services, and who is in a fit state to be received.

There is a common law duty on a hotel-keeper to receive and accommodate guests, but such guests must be "travellers".[115]

A traveller is an individual who comes to the hotel to utilise the facilities and services and accommodation such as it provides, and who is willing to pay for them. There is no requirement that he stay for a night. In law, the length of time the traveller remains a guest of the hotel is a question of fact. If he stays for a considerable length of time he will no longer be deemed to be a guest, but a "lodger".

18.164 The hotel-keeper is under a general duty to receive all travellers presenting themselves and willing to pay "without favour".[116] He is bound to supply reasonable refreshment to any traveller willing to pay for it and is bound to take in not only the traveller, but also his baggage,[117] *i.e.* whatever the traveller brings with him.

The right of the traveller to be received is not absolute. He may be

---

[114] Innkeepers Act 1424.
[115] *Lamond* v *Richard and Gordon Hotels Limited* [1897] 1 QB 541.
[116] See for example: *Rothfield* v *North British Railway Co* 1920 SC 805, 1920 SLT 269.
[117] *Robins & Co* v *Gray* [1985] 2 QB 501 CA.

refused if there are no vacancies, if he is not in a fit state to be received, if his presence would endanger other guests, if he is unwilling to pay a reasonable price, or if he is accompanied by objectionable friends or savage or unsuitable animals.[118]

The hotel-keeper is obliged to reject an alien who fails to provide a statement as to his name, date of arrival, passport number, address and nationality.[119]

The price for overnight accommodation must be displayed at an estab-   **18.165**
lishment where there are no fewer than four bedrooms or eight beds.[120] The price must state the maximum and minimum prices available, and VAT must be shown separately or inclusive with a calculation, and also whether meals are included in the price.

General principles of contract apply between hotel-keeper and guest. The contract may be concluded at the reception desk. Any booking formalities or conditions brought subsequently to a guest's attention will not be incorporated in the contract. If a hotel-keeper seeks to exclude liability, then a clause to that effect in the contract will be subject to the Unfair Contract Terms Act 1977.[121] The guest and the hotel-keeper are parties to the contract. If the hotel-keeper does not fulfil his obligations, he is in breach of contract, and the guest will have a remedy in damages.

A guest may, however, seek to recover damages from the hotel-keeper   **18.166**
for loss of enjoyment for both himself and his family, even though it is only himself and the hotel-keeper who are parties to the contract.

In England, the Occupier's Liability Acts 1957 and 1984 impose a duty on those who occupy premises, *i.e.* on those who have possession and control of, land and buildings. The duty of care in section 2 (2) is:

> a duty to take care as in all the circumstances of the case is reasonable, to see that the visitor will be reasonably safe in using the premises for the purposes for which he is invited or permitted by the occupier to be there.

The duty is aimed at the visitor rather than the premises.

The Occupier's Liability (Scotland) Act 1960, applies in relation to   **18.167**
hotels in Scotland. The occupier, (normally the hotel-keeper) is under a duty of care to take reasonable steps to prevent the occurrence of loss, injury or damage to persons or their property on the premises. Scots law does not distinguish between a guest and an individual trespassing in the premises. A hotel-keeper may owe a duty of care to an individual who has no lawful right to be on the premises and who suffers loss or injury.

The Northern Ireland Tourist Board carries out two important regulatory functions in relation to hotels. Firstly, it certifies an hotel as having reached a certain standard, using the familiar star type grading system.

---

[118] *R* v *Rymer* [1877] 2QBD 136.
[119] Immigration (Hotel Records) Order 1972 SI 1972/689 Art 4
[120] Tourism (Sleeping Accomodation Price Display) Order 1977.
[121] See *supra.*

Secondly, a liquor licence cannot be granted to an hotel unless it has been certified by the Tourist Board as reaching an acceptable standard.

18.168 The proprietor's liability to visitors in Northern Ireland is governed by the Occupier's Liability Act (Northern Ireland) 1957 and the Occupier's Liability (Northern Ireland) Order 1957.[122] Section 2 of the 1957 Act sets out the duty of care.

There is an international convention relating to the liability of hotel-keepers. The Paris Convention 1962 was ratified by the United Kingdom in July 1963. Property, belonging to a guest (staying at a hotel)[123] which is damaged or lost, is the liability of the hotel-keeper, who will be liable up to a maximum of 3,000 gold francs[124] for the loss or damage. If property is specifically handed to the hotel-keeper for safe-keeping, there is no limit in compensation for any resultant loss or damage.

12. Damage claims by consumers

(i) Holiday booking

Clarke and Greenwood v *Airtours* (Current Law, April 1995)

18.169 The plaintiffs, two families of four, booked a holiday to Tenerife for two weeks with the defendant at a cost of £2,058.25. Whilst they had requested and booked 3-star (or 3 A) hotel rooms, on half board, to be allocated on arrival, they were in fact given self-catering apartments. The apartments were situated on several floors, thus separating the parents from their children. The rooms, which were stark and uninviting, were infested with cockroaches. Wild dogs roamed freely over the grounds, the restaurant facility was not cleared, with staff allowing cats to eat food left on the tables, and the food served was of a very poor standard. The area around the apartments was scruffy; the outside walls of the complex were covered in graffiti and broken glass around the swimming pool caused cuts to one of the infant plaintiff's feet. Despite the plaintiff's numerous complaints, both to the local representative and the head office on the island, and several telephone calls to the defendant and their agents in England, the defendant failed to remedy the situation or to deal with the plaintiffs in a humane way. Three of the plaintiffs accepted an offer of another apartment within the complex, but both of the two subsequent rooms were also infested with cockroaches. The plaintiffs demanded to return home, but were told that they would have to meet the cost of such journey themselves.

---

[122] SI 1987/1280 (NI).

[123] This is not defined in the convention.

[124] Neither the convention nor indeed UK statute provides for the conversion of gold francs to pounds sterling.

Held, judgment being entered for all eight plaintiffs, that damages   **18.170**
awarded would be: £500 per family in respect of expenses incurred in
eating elsewhere during the holiday; and £800 per plaintiff in respect of
general damages for distress and disappointment. Total damages
awarded were £8,040. Interest on special damages was awarded from the
date the holiday began.

Causby v *Portland Holidays* (Current Law, April 1995)

The two plaintiffs, husband and wife, booked a 14-night holiday to   **18.171**
Majorca in August 1993 at a cost of £802. At the time of booking Mr
Causby requested a hotel which was quiet and relaxing, on level ground,
and near to the sea and beach. This was important because he suffered
from arthritis and diabetes, and also had problems with breathlessness
and walking. For the first three days there were no problems and it was a
good start to the holiday. On the fourth day the plaintiffs decided to walk
to the beach. It took them one-and-a-half hours coming back, aggravating
Mr Causby's problems of breathlessness and associated problems with his
leg. In the hotel itself their holiday was marred by the arrival of new
occupants and with them a great deal of noise, both from their children
who seemed to be uncontrollable, and from the pool table beneath their
bedroom window where people played pool at all hours and as late as
11.45pm. Furthermore, there was noise from two building sites nearby
from 8am to lunchtime and from 3.30pm to 6.30pm. When the wind
blew, dust from the site blew into the hotel and on to their bedroom
balcony. Mr Causby made a complaint to his courier on three occasions
which was not followed up. The plaintiffs accepted that the flight and
facilities of the hotel plus the food were excellent. Mr Causby was
awarded general damages for loss of enjoyment of £220. Mrs Causby was
awarded general damages for loss of enjoyment of £110. Total award was
£330 plus court fee of £60.

(ii) Loss of enjoyment

Kelly v *Airtours* (Current Law, December 1995)

The plaintiff booked a two-week holiday in Orlando, Florida in June   **18.172**
1994, for himself, his wife and three children. The price of the holiday
was £1,884.70, and the flight to and from Florida was by way of the defendant's own chartered flight. There were two hotels called Holiday Inn in
Orlando, Florida. The booking was made over the telephone, and while
the description given by the agent was of the first hotel, the plaintiff and
his family were booked into the latter which was of a lesser standard in
terms of size of accommodation and facilities offered. This breach of contract was aggravated by two factors: the defendant's representative was
"worse than useless"; and on the tenth day of the holiday the hotel was
transformed by the arrival of 600 "fanatical" Dutch football supporters,
and the restaurant prices were increased. The supporters were extremely

noisy, interfering with the sleep of the plaintiff's family, and it was no longer appropriate for the plaintiff's children to use the hotel swimming pool.

18.173 *Held*, that damages would be awarded in the sum of £950 for diminution in the value of the holiday, together with £1,850 by way of general damages and £100 for special damages. The district judge also awarded the sum of £30, which represented the cost of the earphones which the plaintiff and his family were required to hire to make use of the entertainment facilities on the flight, on the grounds that notice of this additional cost ought to have been given in the brochure.

Rebello v *Leisure Villas* (Current Law, October 1995)

18.174 The plaintiff booked a private detached holiday villa for herself and her husband for a 14-night holiday in Corfu at a total cost of £1,448.60, inclusive of £179 car hire. The villa turned out to be a very small studio apartment, whose only sitting area was outside on the patio. The patio was used by an elderly lady who spent each day stoning olives, and was also used day and night as a thoroughfare by the occupiers of an apartment downstairs. In addition, the view from the patio was partially obscured by several television aerials, and the shower was always either too hot or too cold. The plaintiff's holiday was not a disaster, but, as her principle holiday of the year, it proved very disappointing.

Held, that damages of £650 in respect of a 50% diminution in value (car hire not included) and £450 in respect of distress and disappointment be awarded, plus interest.

Clarke and Greenwood v *Suntours* [1995] 4 C2 132

18.175 The plaintiffs, two young women, were awarded almost £3,000 compensation against their holiday company for sexual harassment by the hotel waiters.

18.176 The Court held that holiday makers who are mugged abroad can sue their package tour operator if the firm fails to warn them that they are in an area where such crimes are a high risk. The Court ruled that firms are obliged to provide information about the danger of being robbed or attacked, because these are details which the customer might have difficulty in obtaining for themselves.

(iii) Case study

Wong Mee Wan v *(1) Kwan Kin Travel Services Ltd (2) China Travel Services Co (3) Pak Tan Lake Travel Services Co*

18.177 In August 1988 Miss Ho Shui Lee, a resident of Hong Kong, was drowned whilst on holiday in the People's Republic of China. Her mother brought proceedings against the first defendants, whose registered office was in

Hong Kong, and against the second and third defendants, both of which carried on business in China.

Miss Ho contracted to take a package tour offered by the first defendant to Pak Tang Lake. As far as the border the group was accompanied by a tour leader employed by the first defendant, but beyond the border was accompanied by an employee of the second defendant (a Mr Ho). Due to various delays at the border, the party was late arriving at the guest house where they were to spend the first night, and when they arrived at the lake side, Mr Ho told them that the ferry had already gone, and that there was no alternative but to cross the lake in a speedboat. The speedboat was driven by an employee of the third defendant. Since the boat took only eight people, three trips were needed. The employee refused to make the third trip, and a volunteer – another employee of the third defendant – was found to drive the boat. On this trip the boat went very fast and hit a fishing junk, and the occupants were thrown into the water. Two were drowned, though the others were taken to safety.

The trial judge found that since the group had no practical alternative **18.178** but to take the speedboat across the lake, the trip by speedboat was an integral part of the guided tour provided by the first defendant. Accordingly, the first defendants, who owed Miss Ho "a primary and contractual duty to take reasonable care for her safety" were negligent in not providing a safe system of operation for the speedboat.

On appeal it was found that Miss Ho's death was caused by negligence on the part of the second and third defendants. The issue turned on whether the first defendants undertook themselves to *provide* the services – in which case (subject to any exemption clause) there would be an implied term that they would carry out those services with reasonable care and skill, or whether they merely undertook to *arrange* for services to be provided by others acting as their agents – where they would be under a duty to use reasonable care and skill in selecting those other persons.

On appeal to the Privy Council, their Lordships considered several English cases concerned with the provision of package tours:

In the case of *Craven* v *Strand Holidays (Canada) Ltd* ((1982) 40 OR 186), **18.179** the plaintiffs claimed damages for personal injury when the bus in which they were travelling in Colombia overturned due to the negligence of the driver. The driver was not an employee of the defendant, but the bus trip had been arranged as part of a package tour sold by the defendant to the plaintiffs. The Court held that the defendant had only contracted to arrange for the performance of that service, and accordingly would only be liable if it had been negligent in the selection of the bus operator.

The case of *Stewart* v *Reavell's Garage* ([1952] 2 QB 545) seems to follow a different reasoning. The plaintiff took his car to the defendant's garage to have the braking system repaired, and agreed, on the recommendation of the defendants, that the work would be carried out by specialists. The work carried out by the specialists was faulty, and in finding for the plaintiff, Sellers J found that that was the defendants' duty ". . . to provide good workmanship, materials of good quality and a braking system reasonably fit for its purpose, and this they failed to do . . ."

18.180   In *Rogers* v *Night Riders* ([1983] RTR 324 (a case argued in tort) the Court of Appeal considered a case where the plaintiff had telephoned the defendants, a mini-cab company, to ask for a car to take her to Euston station. The defendants had not sent one of their own cars, but contacted an owner-driver of a mini-cab, to whom the defendants rented a car radio. The plaintiff was injured when the door of the car opened without warning. The Court found that the defendants had undertaken to provide a car and driver to take the plaintiff to her destination, and accordingly, that they owed a duty to take care to ensure that the vehicle was safe.

The Court of Appeal in *Jarvis* v *Swan Tours* ([1973] QB 233) found that although some of the services to be provided as part of a holiday package were not provided by the defendants themselves, the defendant travel agents had on the terms of their brochure undertaken to provide a holiday of a "certain quality", and that since they had failed to provide a holiday of the standard contracted for, they were liable in damages.

18.181   In *Wilson* v *Best Travel Ltd* [1993] 1 All ER 353, the judge held that the duty of care owed by a tour operator to its customers (as a supplier of services for the purposes of s 13 of the Supply of Goods and Services Act 1982), was a duty to "exclude from the accommodation offered any hotel the characteristics of which were such that guests could not spend a holiday there in reasonable safety".

Their lordships also considered the decision in *Wall* v *Silver Wing* (unrep). The plaintiffs in this case were injured when they had to jump from a hotel bedroom because the means of escape otherwise available had been barred by the locking of a gate which was usually open – it had been open when the defendants visited the hotel. Hodgson J here rejected the plaintiff's argument that there was an implied term in the contract that the plaintiffs should be reasonably safe in using the hotel, holding that it would be unreasonable to saddle a tour operator with an obligation to ensure the safety of all the components of a package, including those over which he had no control.

18.182   The Court of Appeal in the present case had agreed with the reasoning in *Wall* – finding that it would impose an "intolerable burden" on tour operators if they were to be held liable for the negligence of transport operators in another country. The duty of the first defendant in providing the package tour to Miss Ho did include "seeing that the transportation which it was aware would be used was supplied by reputable organisations", but, on a careful analysis of the facts, Penlington JA found that the first defendant could not reasonably have anticipated that the third defendant would use a speedboat driven by an inexperienced and negligent employee – especially given that the defendant "was not aware that speedboats might be used at all during the tour".

In deciding whether, as a matter of construction, the contract between Miss Ho and Kwan Kin Travel was one which obliged the defendants to provide services, or only to arrange for those services to be provided, their Lordships referred to the first defendant's brochure – which was accepted to contain the terms of the contract – and to the reality of the situation. Although it was apparent that parts of the tour would be carried out by others, taking the contract as a whole their Lordships considered that the first defendants undertook to provide and not merely to arrange all the services included in the programme. In their Lordships' view it was an implied term of the contract that those services would be carried out with reasonable care and skill; that term did not mean, to use the words of Hodgson J in *Wall* that the first defendant undertook to ensure "the safety of all the components of the package" – only that reasonable care and skill would be used in rendering the services to be provided under the contract.

Recognising the concern of the Court of Appeal to avoid imposing an **18.183** "intolerable" burden on package tour operators, their Lordships pointed out that the tour operator does have the opportunity to protect himself against claims – either by negotiating suitable contractual terms with those who are to perform the services, or by taking out insurance cover. In discussing whether an unreasonable burden would be imposed if the contract were held to contain a term that reasonable care and skill would be used, their Lordships also referred to the provisions of the Package Travel Regulations, in particular regulation 15(1) which specifically provides that although the liability of the organiser or retailer of a package tour to the consumer subsists irrespective of whether such obligations are to be performed by the organiser or retailer or by other suppliers of services, that liability does not interfere with any remedy or right of action which the organiser or retailer may have against the suppliers of those services.

Their Lordships accordingly decided that where the tour operator agrees that services will be supplied – whether by him or by others on his behalf – to imply a term that those services will be carried out with reasonable care and skill is not imposing an "intolerable" burden on the tour operator, and held the first defendant liable for breach of contract as found by the trial judge.

Part III

Appendices

CONTENTS OF APPENDICES

Council Directive 82/470/EEC

of 29 June 1982

on measures to facilitate the effective exercise of freedom of establishment and freedom to provide services in respect of activities of self-employed persons in certain services incidental to transport and travel agencies (ISIC Group 718) and in storage and warehousing (ISIC Group 720)

A1.1 THE COUNCIL OF THE EUROPEAN COMMUNITIES,

Having regard to the Treaty establishing the European Economic Community, and in particular Articles 49, 57 and 66 thereof,

Having regard to the proposal from the Commission,[1]

Having regard to the opinion of the European Parliament,[2]

Having regard to the opinion of the Economic and Social Committee,[3]

Whereas, pursuant to the Treaty, all discriminatory treatment based on nationality with regard to nourishment and provision of services is prohibited as from the end of the transitional period; whereas the principle of such treatment based on nationality applies in particular to the right to join professional organizations where the professional activities of the person concerned necessarily involve the exercise of this right.

Whereas, moreover, Article 57 of the Treaty provides that in order to make it easier for persons to take up and pursue activities as self-employed persons, directives are to be issued for the mutual recognition of diplomas, certificates and other evidence of formal qualifications and for the coordination of the provisions laid down by law, regulation or administrative action in Member States;

Whereas, in the absence of mutual recognition of diplomas and of immediate coordination, it nevertheless appears desirable to facilitate the attainment of freedom of establishment and freedom to provide services in respect of the activities falling within ISIC Groups 718 and 720 by the adoption of measures intended primarily to avoid causing exceptional difficulties for nationals of Member States in which the taking up of such activities is not subject to any conditions;

Whereas, in order to prevent such difficulties arising, the main object of the measures should be to allow, as sufficient qualification for taking up the activities in question, excluding transport activities proper, in host Member States which have rules governing the taking up of such activities, the fact that the activities have been pursued in the country of provenance for a reasonable period of time, such period being, in cases where no previous training is required, sufficiently recent to ensure that the person concerned possesses professional knowledge equivalent to that required of the host country's own nationals; **A1.2**

Whereas the activity in question must have been pursued and any vocational training received in the same branch of trade as that in which the beneficiary wishes to establish himself in the host Member State, where the latter country imposes this requirement on its own nationals;

Whereas, in accordance with the general principles of the Treaty as to equal-

---

[1] OJ No 73, 23. 4. 1966, p. 1099/66.
[2] OJ No 201, 5. 11. 1966, p. 3475/66.
[3] OJ No 17, 28. 1. 1967, p. 284/67.

ity of treatment and with the judgments of the Court of Justice on this matter, the freedom to provide services in each Member State is exercised on the same terms as such State imposes in its laws and regulations on its own nationals engaged in the same activity; whereas it is incumbent on Member States, when they adopt the measures necessary to comply with this Directive, to ensure equivalence of conditions for their own nationals and nationals of other Member States as regards their freedom to engage in the activities concerned, with particular reference to operating conditions and financial guarantees required;

Whereas, in so far as in Member States the taking up or pursuit of the activities referred in this Directive is also dependent in the case of employed persons on the possession of general, commercial or professional knowledge and ability, this Directive should also apply to this category of persons in order to remove an obstacle to the free movement of workers and thereby to supplement the measures adopted in Council Regulation (EEC) No 1612/68 of 15 October 1968 on freedom of movement for workers within the Community;[1]

Whereas, for the same reason, the provisions relating to proof of good repute and proof of no previous bankruptcy should also apply to employed persons,

A1.3 HAS ADOPTED THIS DIRECTIVE:

Article 1

1. Member States shall adopt the measures set out in this Directive in respect of establishment or provision of services in their territories by natural persons and companies or firms covered by Title I of the General Programmes[2] (hereinafter called 'beneficiaries') in

---

[1] OJ No L 257, 19. 10. 1968, p. 2.
[2] OJ No 2, 15. 1. 1962, pp. 32/62 and 36/62.

the sector of activities coming within Article 2.

2 This Directive shall also apply to nationals of Member States who, as provided in Regulation (EEC) No 1612/68, wish to pursue as employed persons activities coming within Article 2 of this Directive.

Article 2

This Directive shall apply to the activi- **A1.4** ties appearing in Annex I of the General Programme for the abolition of restrictions on freedom of establishment, ISIC Groups 718 and 720.

These activities shall comprise in particular:

A. (a) acting as an intermediary between contractor for various methods of transport and persons who dispatch or receive goods and who carry out various related activities:

    (aa) by concluding contracts with transport contractors, on behalf of principals:

    (bb) by choosing the method of transport, the firm and the route considered more profitable for the principal;

    (cc) by arranging the technical aspects of the transport operation (e.g. packing required for transportation); by carrying out various operations incidental to transport (e.g. ensuring ice supplies for refrigerated wagons);

    (dd) by completing the formalities connected with the transport such as the drafting of way bills; by assembling and dispersing shipments;

    (ee) by coordinating the various stages of transportation, by ensuring transit, reshipment, transhipment and other terminal operations;

(ff) by arranging both freight and carriers and means of transport for persons dispatching goods or receiving them;

(b) assessing transport costs, and checking the detailed accounts;

(c) hiring railway cars or wagons for transporting persons or goods;

(d) taking certain temporary or permanent measures in the name of and on behalf of a shipowner or sea transport carrier (with the port authorities, ship's chandlers, etc);

(e) acting as an intermediary in the sale, purchase or hiring of ships;

B. (a) organizing, offering for sale and selling, outright or on commission, single or collective items (transport, board, lodging, excursions, etc) for a journey or stay, whatever the reason for travelling;

(b) arranging, negotiating and concluding contracts for the transport of emigrants;

C. (a) receiving all objects and goods deposited, on behalf of the depositor, whether under customs control or not, in warehouses, general stores, furniture depots, coldstores, silos, etc;

(b) supplying the depositor with a receipt for the object or goods deposited;

(c) providing pens, feed and sales rings for livestock being temporarily accommodated while awaiting sale or while in transit to or from the market;

D. (a) carrying out inspection or technical valuation of motor vehicles;

(b) measuring, weighing and gauging goods.

Article 3

In respect of the activities listed in Article 2, the usual titles current in Member States are given below for guidance:

A1.5

Belgium

A. Commissionnaire de transport
Vervoercommissionair
Courtier de transport
Vervoermakelaar
Commissionnaire-expéditeur au transport
Commissionair-expediteur bij het vervoer
Commissionnaire affréteur
Commissionair-bevrachter
Commissionnaire-affréteur routier
Commissionair-wegbevrachter
Affréteur routier
Wegbevrachter
Affréteur fluvial
Binnenvaartbevrachter of rivierbevrachter
Affréteur maritime
Scheepsbevrachter
Agent maritime
Scheepsagent
Courtier de navires
Scheepsmakelaar

B. Agent de voyages
Reisagent
Agent d'émigration
Emigratieagent

C. Entrepositaire
Depothouder

D. Expert en automobiles
Deskundige inzake auto's
Peseur — mesureur — jaugeur juré
Beëdigde wegers, meters en ijkers

Germany

A. Spediteur
Abfertigungsspediteur
Güterkraftverkehrsvermittler
Schiffsmakler
Vermieter von Eisenbahnwagen und Eisenbahnwaggons

B. Reisebürounternehmer
Auswanderungsagent

C. Lagerhalter

D. Kraftfahrzeugsachverständiger
Wäger

597

Denmark

A. Speditør
Skibsagent

B. Rejsebureau

C. Opbevaring

D. Vejer og måler
Bilinspektør og bilassistent

A1.6 *France*

A. Commissionnaire de transport
Courtier de fret routier
Dépositaire de colis
Courtier de fret de navigation
intérieure
Agent maritime
Agent consignataire de navires

B. Agent de voyage

C. Entrepositaire
Exploitant de magasin général

D. Expert en automobiles
Peseur — mesureur juré

Greece

A. Πράκτοαζ μεταφορῶν
Ναυτικός πράκτοραζ
Ἐφοδιαστής πλοίων
Ναυλομεσίτηζ ἐπαγγελματικῶν
τουριστικῶν
πλοίων καί πλοιαρίων
Ναυλομεσίτεζ πλοίων

B. Πράκτοραζ γιά ἐπιβατικά
ἀκτοπλοϊκά πλοῖα Τουριστικά
γραφεῖα:
1. Γενικοῦ τουρισμοῦ
2. Ἐσωτερικοῦ τουρισμοῦ
3. Tour operator
Πράκτορεζ μεταναστευσεωζ καί
ἀντιπρόσωποί τουζ

Γ. Γενικέζ ἀποθῆκεζ

Λ. Πραγματογνώμονεζ ἐπί τροχαίων
ἀτυχημάτων

Ireland

A. Forwarding agent
Shipping and forwarding agent
Shipbroker
Freight agent
Shipping agent
Air freight agent
Road haulage broker

B. Travel agent
Tour operator

Air broker
Air travel organizer

C. Bonder
Warehouseman
Market or lairage operator

D. Motor vehicle examiner

Italy

A. Spedizioniere (commissionario)
Mediatore
Agente marittimo raccomandatario
Mediatore marittimo

B. Agente di viaggio e turismo
Mandatario di vettore di emigrante

C. Esercenti depositi in magazzini
doganali di proprietà privata
Esercenti magazzini generali
Esercenti depositi franchi

D. Stimatore e pesatore pubblico

Luxembourg

A. Commissionnaire de transport
Commissionnaire expéditeur au
transport

B. Agent de voyage
Agent d'émigration

C. Entrepositaire

D. Expert en automobiles
Peseur

Netherlands

A. Expediteur
Bevrachter
Scheepsmakelaar
Scheepsagent
Verhuren van spoorrijtuigen en
spoorwagens

B. Reisbureaubedrijf
Reisagentschap
Emigratieagent

C. Douane-entrepot (publiek,
particulier, fictief)
Gewone opslagplaatsen

D. Technische inspectie van
motorrijtuigen
Meter, wagen en ijken

598

United Kingdom

A. Freight forwarder
   Shipbroker
   Air cargo agent
   Shipping and forwarding agent

B. Tour operator
   Travel agent
   Air broker
   Air travel organizer

C. Storekeeper
   Livestock dealer
   Market or lairage operator
   Warehousekeeper
   Wharfinger

D. Motor vehicle examiner
   Master porter
   Cargo superintendent

Article 4

A1.7 1. Where a host Member State requires of its own nationals wishing to take up one of the activities coming within Article 2 proof of good repute and proof that they have not previously been declared bankrupt, or proof of either one of these, that State shall accept as sufficient evidence, in respect of nationals of other Member States, the production of an extract from the 'judicial record' or, failing this, of an equivalent document issued by a competent judicial or administrative authority in the country of origin or of provenance showing that these requirements have been met.

2. Where a host Member State imposes on its own nationals wishing to take up one of the activities referred to in Article 2 (B) certain requirements as to good repute, and evidence that such requirements are satisfied cannot be obtained from the document referred to in paragraph 1, that State shall accept as sufficient evidence, in respect of nationals of other Member States, a certificate issued by a competent judicial or administrative authority in the country of origin or in the country of provenance, indicating that the requirements in question have been met. Such certificate shall relate to the specific facts regarded as relevant by the host country.

3. Where the country of origin or the country whence the foreign national comes does not issue the document referred to in paragraph 1 or the certificate referred to in paragraph 2, furnishing proof of good repute or proof of no previous bankruptcy, such proof may be replaced by a declaration on oath – or, in States where there is no provision for declaration on oath, by a solemn declaration – made by the person concerned before a competent judicial or administrative authority, or where appropriate a notary, in the country of origin or the country whence that person comes; such authority or notary will issue a certificate attesting the authenticity of the declaration on oath or solemn declaration. The declaration in respect of no previous bankruptcy may also be made before a competent professional or trade body in the said country.

Notwithstanding the foregoing, the host Member State may also take into account specific information which it has acquired through its own means.

4. Where in the host Member State proof of financial standing is required, that State shall regard certificates issued by banks in other States as equivalent to certificates issued in its own territory.

5. Documents issued in accordance with paragraphs 1, 2, 3 and 4 shall not be produced more than three months after their date of issue.

6. Member States shall, within the time limit laid down in Article 8, designate the authorities and bodies competent to issue the documents referred to above and shall forthwith inform the other Member States and the Commission thereof.

Article 5

Member States in which the taking up or pursuit of any activity referred to in Article 2 is subject to possession of cer- **A1.8**

599

tain qualifications shall ensure that any beneficiary who applies therefor be provided, before he establishes himself or before he begins to pursue any activity on a temporary basis, with information as to the rules governing the activity which he proposes to pursue.

Article 6

A1.9 1. Where, in a Member State, the taking up or pursuit of any activity coming within Article 2 (A) (a), (b) or (d) is dependent on the possession of general, commercial, or professional knowledge and ability, that Member State shall accept as sufficient evidence of such knowledge and ability the fact that the activity in question has been pursued in another Member State for any of the following periods:

(a) five consecutive years in an independent capacity or in a managerial capacity; or

(b) either:

two consecutive years in an independent capacity or in a managerial capacity, where the beneficiary proves that for the activity in question he has received previous training lasting at least three years, attested by a certificate recognized by the State, or regarded by the competent professional or trade body as fully satisfying its requirements; or

three consecutive years either in an independent capacity or in a managerial capacity, where the beneficiary proves that for the activity in question he has received previous training lasting at least two years, attested by a certificate recognized by the State, or regarded by the competent professional or trade body as fully satisfying its requirements; or

(c) two consecutive years in an independent capacity or in a managerial capacity, where the beneficiary proves that he has pursued the activity in question for at least three

years in a non-independent capacity; or

(d) three consecutive years in a non-independent capacity where the beneficiary proves that for the activity in question he has received at least two years of previous training, attested by a certificate recognized by the State or regarded by the competent professional or trade body as fully satisfying its requirements.

2. Where, in a Member State, the taking up or pursuit of any activity coming within Article 2, point A (c) or (e), point B (b), point C or D is dependent on the possession of general, commercial, or professional knowledge and ability, that Member State shall accept as sufficient evidence of such knowledge and ability the fact that the activity in question has been pursued in another Member State for any of the following periods: **A1.10**

(a) three consecutive years in an independent capacity or in a managerial capacity; or

(b) two consecutive years either in an independent capacity or in a managerial capacity, where the beneficiary proves that for the activity in question he has received previous training, attested by a certificate recognized by the State, or regarded by the competent professional or trade body as fully satisfying its requirements; or

(c) two consecutive years in an independent capacity or in a managerial capacity, where the beneficiary proves that he has pursued the activity in question for at least three years in a non-independent capacity; or

(d) three consecutive years in a non-independent capacity where the beneficiary proves that for the activity in question he has received previous training, attested by a certificate recognized by the State or regarded by the competent professional or trade body as fully satisfying its requirements.

A1.11 3. Where, in a Member State, the taking up or pursuit of the activities coming within Article 2 (B) (a) is dependent on the possession of general, commercial, or professional knowledge and ability, that Member State shall accept as sufficient evidence of such knowledge and ability the fact that the activity in question has been pursued in another Member State for any of the following periods:

(a) six consecutive years in an independent capacity or in a managerial capacity; or

(b) either:

three consecutive years either in an independent capacity or in a managerial capacity, where the beneficiary proves that for the activity in question he has received previous training lasting at least three years, attested by a certificate recognized by the State, or regarded by the competent professional or trade body as fully satisfying its requirements; or

four consecutive years either in an independent capacity or in a managerial capacity, where the beneficiary proves that for the activity in question he has received previous training lasting at least two years, attested by a certificate recognized by the State, or regarded by the competent professional or trade body as fully satisfying its requirements; or

(c) three consecutive years in an independent capacity or in a managerial capacity, where the beneficiary proves that he has pursued the activity in question for at least five years in a non-independent capacity; or

(d) either:

five consecutive years in a non-independent capacity where the beneficiary proves that for the activity in question he has received previous training lasting at least three years, attested by a certificate recognized by the State or regarded by the competent professional or trade body as fully satisfying its requirements; or

six consecutive years in a non-independent capacity where the beneficiary proves that for the activity in question he has received previous training lasting at least two years, attested by a certificate recognized by the State or regarded by the competent professional or trade body as fully satisfying its requirements.

4. The host Member State may require of nationals of other Member States, in so far as it so requires of its own nationals, that the activity in question should have been pursued and vocational training received in the same branch of trade as that in which the beneficiary wishes to establish himself in the host Member State.

5. In the cases referred to in paragraphs 1 (a) and (c), 2 (a) and (c) and 3 (a) and (c), pursuit of the activity shall not have ceased more than ten years before the date on which the application provided for in Article 7 (3) is made. However, where a shorter period is laid down in a Member State for its own nationals, that period may also be applied in respect of beneficiaries.

Article 7

1. A person shall be regarded as having **A1.12**
pursued an activity in a managerial capacity within the meaning of Article 6 (1) and (2) if he has pursued such an activity in an undertaking in the occupational field in question:

(a) as manager of an undertaking or manager of a branch of an undertaking; or

(b) as deputy to the proprietor or to the manager of an undertaking, where such post involves responsibility equivalent to that of the proprietor or manager represented; or

(c) in a managerial post with duties of a commercial nature and with responsibility for at least one department of the undertaking.

2. A person shall be regarded as having pursued an activity in a managerial capacity within the meaning of Article 6 (3) if he has pursued such an activity in an undertaking in the occupational field in question:

(a) as manager of an undertaking; or

(b) as deputy to the proprietor or to the manager of an undertaking or manager of a branch of an undertaking, where such post involves responsibility equivalent to that of the proprietor or manager represented; or

(c) in a managerial post with duties of a commercial nature and with responsibility for at least one department of the undertaking.

3. Proof that the conditions laid down in Article 6 are satisfied shall be established by a certificate issued by the competent authority or body in the Member State of origin or Member State whence the person concerned comes, which such person shall submit in support of his application for authorization to pursue the activity or activities in question in the host country.

4. Member States shall, within the time limit laid down in Article 8, designate the authorities and bodies competent to issue the certificates referred to in paragraph 3 and shall forthwith inform the other Member States and the Commission thereof.

Article 8

Member States shall adopt the measures necessary to comply with this Directive within 18 months of its notification and shall forthwith inform the Commission thereof.

A1.13

Article 9

Member States shall communicate to the Commission the texts of the main provisions of national law which they adopt in the field covered by this Directive.

A1.14

Article 10

This Directive is addressed to the Member States.

A1.15

Done at Brussels, 29 June 1982.

For the Council
The President
P de KEERSMAEKER

Council Directive 84/450/EEC

of 10 September 1984

relating to the approximation of the laws, regulations and administrative provisions of the Member States concerning misleading advertising

A2.1

THE COUNCIL OF THE EUROPEAN COMMUNITIES,

Having regard to the Treaty establishing the European Economic Community, and in particular Article 100 thereof,

Having regard to the proposal from the Commission,[1]

Having regard to the opinion of the European Parliament,[2]

Having regard to the opinion of the Economic and Social Committee,[3]

Whereas the laws against misleading advertising now in force in the Member States differ widely; whereas, this advertising reaches beyond the frontiers of individual Member States, it has a direct effect on the establishment and the functioning of the Common Market;

Whereas misleading advertising can lead to distortion of competition within the Common Market;

Whereas advertising, whether or not it induces a contract, affects the economic welfare of consumers;

Whereas misleading advertising may cause a consumer to take decisions prejudicial to him when acquiring goods or other property, or using services, and the differences between the laws of the Member States not only lead, in many cases, to inadequate levels of consumer protection, but also hinder the execution of advertising campaigns beyond national boundaries and thus affect the free circulation of goods and provision of services;

Whereas the second programme of the European Economic Community for a consumer protection and information policy[4] provides for appropriate action for the protection of consumers against misleading and unfair advertising;

Whereas it is in the interest of the public in general, as well as that of consumers and all those who, in competition with one another, carry on a trade, business, craft or profession, in the Common Market, to harmonize in the first instance national provisions against misleading advertising and that, at a second stage, unfair advertising and, as far as necessary, comparative advertising should be dealt with, on the basis of appropriate Commission proposals;

A2.2

Whereas minimum and objective criteria for determining whether advertising is misleading should be established for this purpose;

Whereas the laws to be adopted by Member States against misleading advertising must be adequate and effective;

Whereas persons or organizations regarded under national law as having a legitimate interest in the matter must have facilities for initiating proceedings against misleading advertising, either before a court or before an administrative authority which is competent to decide upon complaints or to initiate appropriate legal proceedings;

Whereas it should be for each Member State to decide whether to enable the courts or administrative authorities to require prior recourse to other estab-

[1] OJ No C 70, 21. 3. 1978, p. 4.
[2] OJ No C 140, 5. 6. 1979, p. 23.
[3] OJ No C 171, 9. 7. 1979, p. 43.

[4] OJ No C 133, 3. 6. 1981, p. 1.

lished means of dealing with the complaint;

Whereas the courts or administrative authorities must have powers enabling them to order or obtain the cessation of misleading advertising;

A2.3 Whereas in certain cases it may be desirable to prohibit misleading advertising even before it is published; whereas, however, this in no way implies that Member States are under an obligation to introduce rules requiring the systematic prior vetting of advertising;

Whereas provision should be made for accelerated procedures under which measures with interim or definitive effect can be taken;

Whereas it may be desirable to order the publication of decisions made by courts or administrative authorities or of corrective statements in order to eliminate any continuing effects of misleading advertising;

Whereas administrative authorities must be impartial and the exercise of their powers must be subject to judicial review;

Whereas the voluntary control exercised by self-regulatory bodies to eliminate misleading advertising may avoid recourse to administrative or judicial action and ought therefore to be encouraged;

Whereas the advertiser should be able to prove, by appropriate means, the material accuracy of the factual claims he makes in his advertising, and may in appropriate cases be required to do so by the court or administrative authority;

Whereas this Directive must not preclude Member States from retaining or adopting provisions with a view to ensuring more extensive protection of consumers, persons carrying on a trade, business, craft or profession, and the general public,

HAS ADOPTED THIS DIRECTIVE:

Article 1 — A2.4

The purpose of this Directive is to protect consumers, persons carrying on a trade or business or practising a craft or profession and the interests of the public in general against misleading advertising and the consequences thereof.

Article 2 — A2.5

For the purposes of this Directive:

1 'advertising' means the making of a representation in any form in connection with a trade, business, craft or profession in order to promote the supply of goods or services, including immovable property rights and obligations;

2 'misleading advertising' means any advertising which in any way, including its presentation, deceives or is likely to deceive the persons to whom it is addressed or whom it reaches and which, by reason of its deceptive nature, is likely to affect their economic behaviour or which, for those reasons, injures or is likely to injure a competitor.

3 'person' means any natural or legal person.

Article 3 — A2.6

In determining whether advertising is misleading, account shall be taken of all its features, and in particular of any information it contains concerning

(a) the characteristics of goods or services, such as their availability, nature, execution, composition, method and date of manufacture or provision, fitness for purpose, uses, quantity, specification, geographical or commercial origin or the results to be expected from their use, or the results and material features of tests or checks carried out on the goods or services;

(b) the price or the manner in which the price is calculated, and the conditions on which the goods are supplied or the services provided;

(c) the nature, attributes and rights of

the advertiser, such as his identity and assets, his qualifications and ownership of industrial, commercial or intellectual property rights or his awards and distinctions.

Article 4

1. Member States shall ensure that adequate and effective means exist for the control of misleading advertising in the interests of consumers as well as competitors and the general public.

Such means shall include legal provisions under which persons or organizations regarded under national law as having a legitimate interest in prohibiting misleading advertising may:

a) take legal action against such advertising; and/or

b) bring such advertising before an administrative authority competent either to decide on complaints or to initiate appropriate legal proceedings.

It shall be for each Member State to decide which of these facilities shall be available and whether to enable the courts or administrative authorities to require prior recourse to other established means of dealing with complaints, including those referred to in Article 5.

2. Under the legal provisions referred to in paragraph 1, Member States shall confer upon the courts or administrative authorities powers enabling them, in cases where they deem such measures to be necessary taking into account all the interests involved and in particular the public interest:

to order the cessation of or to institute appropriate legal proceedings for an order for the cessation of, misleading advertising, or

if misleading advertising has not yet been published but publication is imminent, to order the prohibition of, or to institute appropriate legal proceedings for an order for the prohibition of, such publication,

even without proof of actual loss or damage or of intention or negligence on the part of the advertiser.

Member States shall also make provision for the measures referred to in the first subparagraph to be taken under an accelerated procedure:

either with interim effect, or

with definitive effect,

on the understanding that it is for each Member State to decide which of the two options to select.

Furthermore, Member States may confer upon the courts or administrative authorities powers enabling them, with a view to eliminating the continuing effects of misleading advertising the cessation of which has been ordered by a final decision:

to require publication of that decision in full or in part and in such form as they deem adequate,

to require in addition the publication of a corrective statement.

3. The administrative authorities referred to in paragraph 1 must:

(a) be composed so as not to cast doubt on their impartiality;

(b) have adequate powers, where they decide on complaints, to monitor and enforce the observance of their decisions effectively;

(c) normally give reasons for their decisions.

Where the powers referred to in paragraph 2 are exercised exclusively by an administrative authority, reasons for its decisions shall always be given. Furthermore in this case, provision must be made for procedures whereby improper or unreasonable exercise of its powers by the administrative authority or improper or unreasonable failure to exercise the said powers can be the subject of judicial review.

Article 5

This Directive does not exclude the voluntary control of misleading advertising by self-regulatory bodies and recourse to these bodies or organisations referred to in Article 4 if proceedings before such bodies are in addition to the court or administrative proceedings referred to in that Article.

A2.9

Article 6

Member States shall confer upon the courts or administrative authorities powers enabling them in the civil or administrative proceedings provided for in Article 4:

(a) to require the advertiser to furnish evidence as to the accuracy of factual claims in advertising if, taking into account the legitimate interests of the advertiser and any other party to the proceedings such a requirement appears appropriate on the basis of the circumstances of the particular case; and

(b) to consider factual claims as inaccurate if the evidence demanded in accordance with (a) is not furnished or is deemed insufficient by the court or administrative authority.

Article 7

A2.10

This Directive shall not preclude Member States from retaining or adopting provisions with a view to ensuring more extensive protection for consumers, persons carrying on a trade, business, craft or profession, and the general public.

Article 8

A2.11

Member States shall bring into force the measures necessary to comply with this Directive by 1 October 1986 at the latest. They shall forthwith inform the Commission thereof.

Member States shall communicate to the Commission the text of all provisions of national law which they adopt in the field covered by this Directive.

Article 9

A2.12

This Directive is addressed to the Member States.

Done at Brussels, 10 September 1984.

For the Council
The President
P O'TOOLE

Council Directive 85/577/EEC

of 20 December 1985

to protect the consumer in respect of contracts negotiated away from business premises

A3.1

THE COUNCIL OF THE EUROPEAN COMMUNITIES,

Having regard to the Treaty establishing the European Economic Community, and in particular Article 100 thereof,

Having regard to the proposal from the Commission,[1]

Having regard to the opinion of the European Parliament,[2]

Having regard to the opinion of the Economic and Social Committee,[3]

Whereas it is a common form of commercial practice in the Member States for the conclusion of a contract or a unilateral engagement between a trader and consumer to be made away from the business premises of the trader, and whereas such contracts and engagements are the subject of legislation which differs from one Member State to another;

Whereas any disparity between such legislation may directly affect the functioning of the Common Market; whereas it is therefore necessary to approximate laws in this field;

Whereas the preliminary programme of the European Economic Community for a consumer protection and information policy[4] provides *inter alia*, under paragraphs 24 and 25, that appropriate measures be taken to protect consumers against unfair commercial practices in respect of doorstep selling; whereas the second programme of the European

Economic Community for a consumer protection and information policy[5] confirmed that the action and priorities defined in the preliminary programme would be pursued;

Whereas the special feature of contracts concluded away from the business premises of the trader is that as a rule it is the trader who initiates the contract negotiations, for which the consumer is unprepared or which he does not accept; whereas the consumer is often unable to compare the quality and price of the offer with other offers; whereas this surprise element generally exists not only in contracts made at the doorstep but also in other forms of contract concluded by the trader away from his business premises;

A3.2

Whereas the consumer should be given a right of cancellation over a period of at least seven days in order to enable him to assess the obligations arising under the contract;

Whereas appropriate measures should be taken to ensure that the consumer is informed in writing of this period for reflection;

Whereas the freedom of Member States to maintain or introduce a total or partial prohibition on the conclusion of contracts away from business premises, inasmuch as they consider this to be in the interest of consumers, must not be affected;

HAS ADOPTED THIS DIRECTIVE:

Article 1

A3.3

1. This Directive shall apply to contracts under which a trader supplies

---

[1] OJ No C 22, 29. 1. 1977, p. 6; OJ No C 127, 1. 6. 1978, p. 6.
[2] OJ No C 241, 10. 10. 1977, p. 26.
[3] OJ No C 180, 18. 7. 1977, p. 39.
[4] OJ No C 92, 25. 4. 1975, p. 2.

[5] OJ No C 133, 3. 6. 1981, p. 1.

goods or services to a consumer and which are concluded:

during an excursion organized by the trader away from his business premises, or

during a visit by a trader

(i) to the consumer's home or to that of another consumer;

(ii) to the consumer's place of work;

where the visit does not take place at the express request of the consumer.

2. This Directive shall also apply to contracts for the supply of goods or services other than those concerning which the consumer requested the visit of the trader, provided that when he requested the visit the consumer did not know, or could not reasonably have known, that the supply of those other goods or services formed part of the trader's commercial or professional activities.

3. This Directive shall also apply to contracts in respect of which an offer was made by the consumer under conditions similar to those described in paragraph 1 or paragraph 2 although the consumer was not bound by that offer before its acceptance by the trader.

4. This Directive shall also apply to offers made contractually by the consumer under conditions similar to those described in paragraph 1 or paragraph 2 where the consumer is bound by his offer.

A3.4
Article 2

For the purposes of this Directive:

"consumer" means a natural person who, in transactions covered by this Directive, is acting for purposes which can be regarded as outside his trade or profession;

"trader" means a natural or legal person who, for the transaction in question, acts in his commercial or professional capacity, and anyone acting in the name or on behalf of a trader.

Article 3
A3.5

1. The Member States may decide that this Directive shall apply only to contracts for which the payment to be made by the consumer exceeds a specified amount. This amount may not exceed 60 ECU.

The Council, acting on a proposal from the Commission, shall examine and, if necessary, revise this amount for the first time no later than four years after notification of the Directive and thereafter every two years, taking into account economic and monetary developments in the Community.

2. This Directive shall not apply to:

(a) contracts for the construction, sale and rental of immovable property or contracts concerning other rights relating to immovable property.

Contracts for the supply of goods and for their incorporation in immovable property or contracts for repairing immovable property shall fall within the scope of this Directive;

(b) contracts for the supply of foodstuffs or beverages or other goods intended for current consumption in the household and supplied by regular roundsmen;

(c) contracts for the supply of goods or services, provided that all three of the following conditions are met:

(i) the contract is concluded on the basis of a trader's catalogue which the consumer has a proper opportunity of reading in the absence of the trader's representative,

(ii) there is intended to be continuity of contact between the trader's representative and the consumer in relation to that or any subsequent transaction,

(iii) both the catalogue and the contract clearly inform the consumer of his right to return goods to the supplier within a period of not less than seven days of receipt or otherwise to cancel the contract within that period without obligation of any kind other than to take reasonable care of the goods;

(d) insurance contracts;

(e) contracts for securities.

3. By way of derogation from Article 1 (2), Member States may refrain from applying this Directive to contracts for the supply of goods or services having a direct connection with the goods or services concerning which the consumer requested the visit of the trader.

A3.6

Article 4

In the case of transactions within the scope of Article 1, traders shall be required to give consumers written notice of their right of cancellation within the period laid down in Article 5, together with the name and address of a person against whom that right may be exercised.

Such notice shall be dated and shall state particulars enabling the contract to be identified. It shall be given to the consumer:

(a) in the case of Article 1 (1), at the time of conclusion of the contract;

(b) in the case of Article 1 (2), not later than the time of conclusion of the contract;

(c) in the case of Article 1 (3) and 1 (4), when the offer is made by the consumer.

Member States shall ensure that their national legislation lays down appropriate consumer protection measures in cases where the information referred to in this Article is not supplied.

A3.7

Article 5

1. The consumer shall have the right to renounce the effects of his undertaking by sending notice within a period of not less than seven days from receipt by the consumer of the notice referred to in Article 4, in accordance with the procedure laid down by national law. It shall be sufficient if the notice is dispatched before the end of such period.

2. The giving of the notice shall have the effect of releasing the consumer from any obligations under the cancelled contract.

Article 6   **A3.8**

The consumer may not waive the rights conferred on him by this Directive.

Article 7   **A3.9**

If the consumer exercises his right of renunciation, the legal effects of such renunciation shall be governed by national laws, particularly regarding the reimbursement of payments for goods or services provided and the return of goods received.

Article 8   **A3.10**

This Directive shall not prevent Member States from adopting or maintaining more favourable provisions to protect consumers in the field which it covers.

Article 9   **A3.11**

1. Member States shall take the measures necessary to comply with this Directive within 24 months of its notification.[1] They shall forthwith inform the Commission thereof.

2. Member States shall ensure that the texts of the main provisions of national law which they adopt in the field covered by this Directive are communicated to the Commission.

Article 10   **A3.12**

This Directive is addressed to the Member States.

Done at Brussels, 20 December 1985.

For the Council
The President
R KRIEPS

---

[1] This Directive was notified to the Member States on 23 December 1985.

609

Council Directive 90/314/EEC

of 13 June 1990

on package travel, package holidays and package tours

THE COUNCIL OF THE EUROPEAN COMMUNITIES,

Having regard to the Treaty establishing the European Economic Community, and in particular Article 100a thereof,

Having regard to the proposal from the Commission,[1]

In co-operation with the European Parliament,[2]

Having regard to the opinion of the Economic and Social Committee,[3]

Whereas one of the main objectives of the Community is to complete the internal market, of which the tourist sector is an essential part;

Whereas the national laws of Member States concerning package travel, package holidays and package tours, hereinafter referred to as 'packages', show many disparities and national practices in this field are markedly different, which gives rise to obstacles to the freedom to provide services in respect of packages and distortions of competition amongst operators established in different Member States;

Whereas the establishment of common rules on packages will contribute to the elimination of these obstacles and thereby to the achievement of a Common Market in services, thus enabling operators established in one Member State to offer their services in other Member States and Community consumers to benefit from comparable conditions when buying a package in any Member State;

Whereas paragraph 36 (b) of the Annex to the Council resolution of 19 May 1981 on a second programme of the European Economic Community for a consumer protection and information policy[4] invites the Commission to study, *inter alia*, tourism and, if appropriate, to put forward suitable proposals, with due regard for their significance for consumer protection and the effects of differences in Member States' legislation on the proper functioning of the Common Market;

Whereas in the resolution on a Community policy on tourism on 10 April 1984[5] the Council welcomed the Commission's initiative in drawing attention to the importance of tourism and took note of the Commission's initial guidelines for a Community policy on tourism;

Whereas the Commission communication to the Council entitled 'A New Impetus for Consumer Protection Policy', which was approved by resolution of the Council on 6 May 1986,[6] lists in paragraph 37, among the measures proposed by the Commission, the harmonization of legislation on packages;

Whereas tourism plays an increasingly important role in the economies of the Member States; whereas the package system is a fundamental part of tourism; whereas the package travel industry in Member States would be stimulated to greater growth and productivity if at least a minimum of common rules were adopted in order to give it a Community dimension; whereas this would not only produce

[1] OJ No C 96, 12. 4. 1988, p. 5.
[2] OJ No C 69, 20. 3. 1989, p. 102 and OJ No C 149, 18. 6. 1990.
[3] OJ No C 102, 24. 4. 1989, p. 27.

[4] OJ No C 165, 23. 6. 1981, p. 24.
[5] OJ No C 115, 30. 4. 1984, p. 1.
[6] OJ No C 118, 7. 3. 1986, p. 28.

benefits for Community citizens buying packages organized on the basis of those rules, but would attract tourists from outside the Community seeking the advantages of guaranteed standards in packages;

A4.3 Whereas disparities in the rules protecting consumers in different Member States are a disincentive to consumers in one Member State from buying packages in another Member State;

Whereas this disincentive is particularly effective in deterring consumers from buying packages outside their own Member State, and more effective than it would be in relation to the acquisition of other services, having regard to the special nature of the services supplied in a package which generally involve the expenditure of substantial amounts of money in advance and the supply of the services in a State other than that in which the consumer is resident;

Whereas the consumer should have the benefit of the protection introduced by this Directive irrespective of whether he is a direct contracting party, a transferee or a member of a group on whose behalf another person has concluded a contract in respect of a package;

Whereas the organiser of the package and/or the retailer of it should be under obligation to ensure that in descriptive matter relating to packages which they respectively organise and sell, the information which is given is not misleading and brochures made available to consumers contain information which is comprehensible and accurate;

Whereas the consumer needs to have a record of the terms of contract applicable to the package; whereas this can conveniently be achieved by requiring that all the terms of the contract be stated in writing or such other documentary form as shall be comprehensible and accessible to him, and that he be given a copy thereof;

Whereas the consumer should be at liberty in certain circumstances to transfer to a willing third person a booking made by him for a package;

Whereas the price established under the contract should not in principle be subject to revision except where the possibility of upward or downward revision is expressly provided for in the contract; whereas that possibility should nonetheless be subject to certain conditions;

A4.4 Whereas the consumer should in certain circumstances be free to withdraw before departure from a package travel contract;

Whereas there should be a clear definition of the rights available to the consumer in circumstances where the organizer of the package cancels it before the agreed date of departure;

Whereas if, after the consumer has departed, there occurs a significant failure of performance of the services for which he has contracted or the organiser perceives that he will be unable to procure a significant part of the services to be provided; the organiser should have certain obligations towards the consumer;

Whereas the organiser and/or retailer party to the contract should be liable to the consumer for the proper performance of the obligations arising from the contract; whereas, moreover, the organiser and/or retailer should be liable for the damage resulting for the consumer from failure to perform or improper performance of the contract unless the defects in the performance of the contract are attributable neither to any fault of theirs nor to that of another supplier of services;

Whereas in cases where the organiser and/or retailer is liable for failure to perform or improper performance of the services involved in the package, such liability should be limited in accordance with the international conventions governing such services, in particular the Warsaw Convention of 1929 on International Carriage by Air, the Berne Convention of 1961 on Carriage by Rail, the Athens Convention of

1974 on Carriage by Sea and the Paris Convention of 1962 on the Liability of Hotel-keepers; whereas, moreover, with regard to damage other than personal injury, it should be possible for liability also to be limited under the package contract provided, however, that such limits are not unreasonable;

Whereas certain arrangements should be made for the information of consumers and the handling of complaints;

Whereas both the consumer and the package travel industry would benefit if organisers and/or retailers were placed under an obligation to provide sufficient evidence of security in the event of insolvency;

Whereas Member States should be at liberty to adopt, or retain, more stringent provisions relating to package travel for the purpose of protecting the consumer,

HAS ADOPTED THIS DIRECTIVE:

A4.5
Article 1
The purpose of this Directive is to approximate the laws, regulations and administrative provisions of the Member States relating to packages sold or offered for sale in the territory of the Community.

A4.6
Article 2
For the purposes of this Directive:

1. "package" means the pre-arranged combination of not fewer than two of the following when sold or offered for sale at an inclusive price and when the service covers a period of more than 24 hours or includes overnight accommodation:

   (a) transport;

   (b) accommodation;

   (c) other tourist services not ancillary to transport or accommodation and accounting for a significant proportion of the package.

   The separate billing of various com-

ponents of the same package shall not absolve the organiser or retailer from the obligations under this Directive;

2. "organiser" means the person who, other than ocasionally, organises packages and sells or offers them for sale, whether directly or through a retailer;

3. "retailer" means the person who sells or offers for sale the package put together by the organiser;

4. "consumer" means the person who takes or agrees to take the package ("the principal contractor"), or any person on whose behalf the principal contractor agrees to purchase the package ("the other beneficiaries") or any person to whom the principal contractor or any of the other beneficiaries transfers the package ("the transferee");

5. "contract" means the agreement linking the consumer to the organiser and/or the retailer.

Article 3
A4.7
1. Any descriptive matter concerning a package and supplied by the organiser or the retailer to the consumer, the price of the package and any other conditions applying to the contract must not contain any misleading information.

2. When a brochure is made available to the consumer, it shall indicate in a legible, comprehensible and accurate manner both the price and adequate information concerning:

(a) the destination and the means, characteristics and categories of transport used;

(b) the type of accommodation, its location, category or degree of comfort and its main features, its approval and tourist classification under the rules of the host Member State concerned;

(c) the meal plan;

(d) the itinerary;

(e) general information on passport and visa requirements for nationals of the Member State or States concerned and health formalities required for the journey and the stay;

(f) either the monetary amount or the percentage of the price which is to be paid on account, and the timetable for payment of the balance;

(g) whether a minimum number of persons is required for the package to take place and, if so, the deadline for informing the consumer in the event of cancellation.

The particulars contained in the brochure are binding on the organiser or retailer, unless:

changes in such particulars have been clearly communicated to the consumer before conclusion of the contract, in which case the brochure shall expressly state so,

changes are made later following an agreement between the parties to the contract.

Article 4

A4.8

1. (a) The organiser and/or the retailer shall provide the consumer, in writing or any other appropriate form, before the contract is concluded, with general information on passport and visa requirements applicable to nationals of the Member State or States concerned and in particular on the periods for obtaining them, as well as with information on the health formalities required for the journey and the stay;

(b) The organiser and/or retailer shall also provide the consumer, in writing or any other appropriate form, with the following information in good time before the start of the journey:

(i) the times and places of intermediate stops and transport connections as well as details of the place to be occupied by the traveller, *e.g.* cabin or berth on ship, sleeper compartment on train;

(ii) the name, address and telephone number of the organiser's and/or retailer's local representative or, failing that, of local agencies on whose assistance a consumer in difficulty could call.

Where no such representatives or agencies exist, the consumer must in any case be provided with an emergency telephone number or any other information that will enable him to contact the organiser and/or the retailer;

(iii) in the case of journeys or stays abroad by minors, information enabling direct contact to be established with the child or the person responsible at the child's place of stay;

(iv) information on the optional conclusion of an insurance policy to cover the cost of cancellation by the consumer or the cost of assistance, including repatriation, in the event of accident or illness.

2. Member States shall ensure that in relation to the contract the following principles apply: **A4.9**

(a) depending on the particular package, the contract shall contain at least the elements listed in the Annex;

(b) all the terms of the contract are set out in writing or such other form as is comprehensible and accessible to the consumer and must be communicated to him before the conclusion of the contract; the consumer is given a copy of these terms;

(c) the provision under (b) shall not preclude the belated conclusion of last-minute reservations or contracts.

3. Where the consumer is prevented from proceeding with the package, he may transfer his booking, having first given the organiser or the retailer reasonable notice of his intention before departure, to a person who satisfies all the conditions applicable to the package. The transferor of the package and the transferee shall be jointly and severally liable to the organiser or retailer party to the contract for payment of the balance due and for any additional costs arising from such transfer.

4. (a) The prices laid down in the contract shall not be subject to revision unless the contract expressly provides for the possibility of upward or downward revision and states precisely how the revised price is to be calculated, and solely to allow for variations in:

transportation costs, including the cost of fuel,

dues, taxes or fees chargeable for certain services, such as landing taxes or embarkation or disembarkation fees at ports and airports,

the exchange rates applied to the particular package.

(b) During the 20 days prior to the departure date stipulated, the price stated in the contract shall not be increased.

5. If the organiser finds that before the departure he is constrained to alter significantly any of the essential terms, such as the price, he shall notify the consumer as quickly as possible in order to enable him to take appropriate decisions and in particular:

either to withdraw from the contract without penalty,

or to accept a rider to the contract specifying the alterations made and their impact on the price.

The consumer shall inform the organiser or the retailer of his decision as soon as possible.

6. If the consumer withdraws from the contract pursuant to paragraph 5, or if, for whatever cause, other than the fault of the consumer, the organiser cancels the package before the agreed date of departure, the consumer shall be entitled: **A4.10**

(a) either to take a substitute package of equivalent or higher quality where the organiser and/or retailer is able to offer him such a substitute. If the replacement package offered is of lower quality, the organiser shall refund the difference in price to the consumer;

(b) or to be repaid as soon as possible all sums paid by him under the contract.

In such a case, he shall be entitled, if appropriate, to be compensated by either the organiser or the retailer, whichever the relevant Member State's law requires, for non-performance of the contract, except where:

(i) cancellation is on the grounds that the number of persons enrolled for the package is less 'than the minimum number required and the consumer is informed of the cancellation, in writing, within the period indicated in the package description; or

(ii) cancellation, excluding overbooking, is for reasons of *force majeure*, i.e. unusual and unforeseeable circumstances beyond the control of the party by whom it is pleaded, the consequences of which could not have been avoided even if all due care had been exercised.

7. Where, after departure, a significant proportion of the services contracted for is not provided or the organiser perceives that he will be unable to procure a significant proportion of the services to be provided, the organiser shall make suitable alternative arrangements, at no extra cost to the con-

sumer, for the continuation of the package, and where appropriate compensate the consumer for the difference between the services offered and those supplied.

If it is impossible to make such arrangements or these are not accepted by the consumer for good reasons, the organiser shall, where appropriate, provide the consumer, at no extra cost, with equivalent transport back to the place of departure, or to another return-point to which the consumer has agreed and shall, where appropriate, compensate the consumer.

Article 5

A4.11 1. Member States shall take the necessary steps to ensure that the organiser and/or retailer party to the contract is liable to the consumer for the proper performance of the obligations arising from the contract, irrespective of whether such obligations are to be performed by that organiser and/or retailer or by other suppliers of services without prejudice to the right of the organiser and/or retailer to pursue those other suppliers of services.

2. With regard to the damage resulting for the consumer from the failure to perform or the improper performance of the contract, Member States shall take the necessary steps to ensure that the organiser and/or retailer is/are liable unless such failure to perform or improper performance is attributable neither to any fault of theirs nor to that of another supplier of services, because:

the failures which occur in the performance of the contract are attributable to the consumer,

such failures are attributable to a third party unconnected with the provision of the services contracted for, and are unforeseeable or unavoidable,

such failures are due to a case of *force majeure* such as that defined in Article 4 (6), second subparagraph (ii), or to an event which the organiser and/or retailer or the supplier of services, even

with all due care, could not foresee or forestall.

In the cases referred to in the second and third indents, the organiser and/or retailer party to the contract shall be required to give prompt assistance to a consumer in difficulty.

In the matter of damages arising from the non-performance or improper performance of the services involved in the package, the Member States may allow compensation to be limited in accordance with the international conventions governing such services.

In the matter of damage other than personal injury resulting from the non-performance or improper performance of the services involved in the package, the Member States may allow compensation to be limited under the contract. Such limitation shall not be unreasonable.

3. Without prejudice to the fourth subparagraph of paragraph 2, there may be no exclusion by means of a contractual clause from the provisions of paragraphs 1 and 2.

4. The consumer must communicate any failure in the performance of a contract which he perceives on the spot to the supplier of the services concerned and to the organiser and/or retailer in writing or any other appropriate form at the earliest opportunity.

This obligation must be stated clearly and explicitly in the contract.

Article 6 **A4.12**

In cases of complaint, the organiser and/or retailer or his local representative, if there is one, must make prompt efforts to find appropriate solutions.

Article 7 **A4.13**

The organiser and/or retailer party to the contract shall provide sufficient evidence of security for the refund of money paid over and for the repatriation of the consumer in the event of insolvency.

615

A4.14

Article 8

Member States may adopt or return more stringent provisions in the field covered by this Directive to protect the consumer.

A4.15

Article 9

1. Member States shall bring into force the measures necessary to comply with this Directive before 31 December 1992. They shall forthwith inform the Commission thereof.

2. Member States shall communicate to the Commission the texts of the main provisions of national law which they adopt in the field governed by this Directive. The Commission shall inform the other Member States thereof.

Article 10

A4.16

This Directive is addressed to the Member States.

Done at Luxembourg, 13 June 1990.

For the Council
The President
D J O'MALLEY

ANNEX

A4.17 Elements to be included in the contract if relevant to the particular package:

(a) the travel destination(s) and, where periods of stay are involved, the relevant periods, with dates;

(b) the means, characteristics and categories of transport to be used, the dates, times and points of departure and return;

(c) where the package includes accommodation, its location, its tourist category or degree of comfort, its main features, its compliance with the rules of the host Member State concerned and the meal plan;

(d) whether a minimum number of persons is required for the package to take place and, if so, the deadline for informing the consumer in the event of cancellation;

(e) the itinerary;

(f) visits, excursions or other services which are included in the total price agreed for the package;

(g) the name and address of the organizer, the retailer and where appropriate the insurer;

(h) the price of the package, an indication of the possibility of price revisions under Article 4 (4) and an indication of any dues, taxes or fees chargeable for certain services (landing, embarkation or disembarkation fees at ports and airports, tourist taxes) where such costs are not included in the package;

(i) the payment schedule and method of payment;

(j) special requirements which the consumer has communicated to the organiser or retailer when making the booking, and which both have accepted;

(k) periods within which the consumer must make any complaint concerning failure to perform or improper performance of the contract.

Council Decision 92/421/EEC

of 13 July 1992

on a Community action plan to assist tourism

A5.1

THE COUNCIL OF THE EUROPEAN COMMUNITIES,

Having regard to the Treaty establishing the European Economic Community, and in particular Article 235 thereof,

Having regard to the proposal from the Commission,[1]

Having regard to the opinion of the European Parliament,[2]

Having regard to the opinion of the Economic and Social Committee,[3]

Whereas tourism occupies an important place in the economy of the Member States, with tourist activities representing a large potential source of employment;

Whereas tourism allows people of all kinds to gain a better knowledge of Europe's cultural roots and of the cultures and ways of life in the Member States, thus making a contribution to the progress of the idea of 'European citizenship';

Whereas the results of the European Year of Tourism should be taken into account;

Whereas, in view of the above, Community action regarding tourism should take the form of a strengthening of the horizontal approach to tourism in Community and national policies, and of the implementation of specific measures, and whereas that approach should also include coordination of the measures undertaken by Commission departments which affect tourism; whereas certain Community policies, in particular transport policy, have a major impact on tourism in the various regions of the Community;

Whereas the Community can contribute to improving the quality and competitiveness of the Community's tourism services on offer, by encouraging a joint approach to the medium-term problems facing European tourism, by promoting the development of the tourist industry and the diversification of tourist activity and the development of transnational measures, and by developing the promotion of European tourism on the main markets of third countries;

A5.2

Whereas tourism can make an effective contribution to achieving economic and social cohesion in the Community and whereas it can promote in the Community a harmonious development of economic activity, continuous and balanced expansion, a higher standard of living and closer relations between the States which it links;

Whereas the measures to be implemented under the action plan must comply with certain criteria in particular the need to comply with the subsidiarity principle;

Whereas tourism in the Community will have to show consideration for local populations and for the natural and cultural environment in order to improve the quality of services offered;

Whereas free competition should be preserved in the sector, both for the benefit of consumers and in order to promote small and medium-sized enterprises (SMEs);

Whereas it is necessary to encourage not only better integration of tourism into the various Community policies but also close cooperation between all public and private bodies in the sector,

A5.3

[1] OJ No C 120, 12. 5. 1992, p. 13.
[2] OJ No C 67. 16. 3. 1992, p. 235.
[3] OJ No C 49, 24. 2. 1992, p. 43.

including representatives of tourist regions, and whereas the implementation at Community level of a number of specific measures, complementary to those taken at national level, is the best way of achieving such cooperation, while avoiding any distortion of competition which may be caused;

Whereas statistics on tourism should be developed and forward analysis of new types of tourism carried out;

Whereas a plan of three years' duration is called for;

Whereas an amount of ECU 18 million is deemed necessary to implement this plan;

Whereas the amounts to be committed for the financing of the plan will have to come within the Community financial framework in force;

Whereas procedures should be laid down for the exercise of the powers for implementing this plan conferred on the Commission pursuant to Decision 87/373/EEC;[1]

Whereas the Treaty does not provide for any powers for the adoption of this Decision other than those mentioned in Article 235,

HAS DECIDED AS FOLLOWS:

A5.4

Article 1

A Community action plan to assist tourism shall be drawn up. The measures forming the subject of this plan are contained in the Annex.

A5.5

Article 2

1. The duration of the action plan shall be three years 1 from January 1993.

2. The Community financial resources deemed necessary for its implementation amount to ECU 18 million and shall fall within the Community financial framework in force.

3. The budget authority shall deter-

[1] OJ No L 197, 18. 7. 1987, p. 33.

mine the appropriations available for each financial year, taking into account the principles of sound management referred to in Article 2 of the Financial Regulation applicable to the general budget of the European Communities.

Article 3

A5.6

1. The Commission shall put the action plan into operation. In order to fulfil the objectives of the plan, it may undertake measures other than those set out in the Annex, where, exceptionally, additional action is required in order to carry out one of the measures in full. Such additional action shall be assessed in relation both to existing priorities and to available financial resources. The Commission shall coordinate the action with the various Community policies, and through the various Directorates-General concerned, in accordance with current procedures.

The Commission shall refer to the committee referred to in paragraph 2 and the Council those initiatives adopted in the framework of Community policies which have a major effect on tourism.

2. The Commission shall be assisted in implementing the action plan by a committee composed of representatives of the Member States and chaired by the representative of the Commission.

The representative of the Commission shall submit to the committee a draft of the measures to be taken. The committee shall deliver its opinion on the draft within a time limit which the chairman may lay down according to the urgency of the matter. The opinion shall be delivered by the majority laid down in Article 148 (2) of the Treaty in the case of decisions which the Council is required to adopt on a proposal from the Commission. The votes of the representatives of the Member States within the committee shall be weighted in the manner set out in that Article. The chairman shall not vote.

The Commission shall adopt measures which shall apply immediately. However, if these measures are not in accordance with the opinion of the committee, they shall be communicated by the Commission to the Council forthwith. In that event the Commission shall defer application of the measures which it has decided for a period of two months from the date of communication.

The Council, acting by a qualified majority, may take a different decision within the time limit referred to in the previous paragraph.

A5.7

Article 4

1. The measures must be consistent with the principle of subsidiarity.

2. A selection shall be made, for the different measures proposed, by reference to the following criteria:

(a) the measures must be cost-effective and make a significant impact on the Community tourist industry;

(b) they must facilitate the development of the tourist industry with particular reference to small and medium-sized businesses;

(c) they must help improve the quality of Community tourist services;

(d) they must encourage competition within the Community and increase the competitiveness of Community tourist services on the world market;

(e) they must be conducive to preserving and protection the quality of the natural environment, the cultural heritage and the integrity of local populations;

(f) they must be conducive to improving the provision of information and services and to the protection of tourists.

3. The measures shall be implemented through co-ordination with the national authorities and, if necessary, with the regional or local authorities as well, so as to take account of the importance of tourism for regional development.

Article 5   **A5.8**

Every year from the date of adoption of the action plan, the Commission, in a report to the European Parliament and the Council, shall evaluate the Community's activities which affect tourism.

Article 6   **A5.9**

The Commission shall regularly evaluate the results of the action plan. This evaluation will include wherever power measurable outputs of the plan and be in accordance with the criteria in Article 4. The committee will be informed by the Commission of the latter's evaluation of the plan, and of the results thereof. No later than 30 June 1995, the Commission will submit a report on this evaluation to the European Parliament and the Council. On the basis of that report, the Council shall decide, in accordance with the provisions of the Treaty, whether or not to extend the plan for a further period.

Done at Brussels, 13 July 1992.

For the Council
The President
J GUMMER

ANNEX 1.

I.   Community measures to assist tourism

A5.10   **1. Improving knowledge of the tourist industry and ensuring greater consistency of Community measures**

Community action is intended to improve the consistency of the measures taken to assist tourism by increasing knowledge of its characteristics, components and development.

This will be carried out by means of the following measures:

(a) development of Community statistics on tourism;

(b) detailed studies aimed at improving knowledge of tourism as an activity, assessment of the impact of current Community policies to assist tourism, forward analysis of new types of tourism, and the preparation of strategies adapted to keep pace with demand;

(c) consultation of tourism professionals within the Community.

A5.11   **2. Staggering of holidays**

Community action is designed to promote a better seasonal distribution of tourism.

This will be carried out by means of the following measures:

(a) support for the setting-up of an international framework whose purpose would be to exchange information and monitor the activities of governments and the tourist industry;

(b) support for measures aimed at coordinating actions and strategies to encourage the use of tourism infrastructure and facilities outside the peak season.

3. Transnational measures   A5.12

Community action is designed to promote transnational tourist development initiatives covering many different specialist sectors of the industry.

This will be carried out by means of the following measures:

(a) support for cooperation between border regions;

(b) support for transnational initiatives contributing to the improvement of tourist information, in particular those using new technology;

(c) development of tourist cooperation with Central and Eastern Europe and the Maghreb through the transfer of know-how on training and the implementation of strategies for promotion, as well as on marketing and the creation of small and medium-sized tourist enterprises;

(d) support for tourist and technical cooperation in the context of partnership between towns;

(e) support for pilot projects aimed at cooperation between the public and private sectors for the development of traditional tourist regions in decline as well as less developed rural regions.

4. Tourists as consumers   A5.13

Community action aims to support initiatives which improve the information of tourists and their protection, in areas such as existing classification systems, signposting symbols, timeshare arrangements, overbooking and procedures for redress.

A5.14

5. Cultural tourism

Community action is designed both to highlight the importance of the cultural heritage for tourism and to promote a greater knowledge of the cultures, traditions and ways of life of Europeans.

This will be carried out by means of the following measures:

(a) support for initiatives to develop new European cultural tourism routes, in cooperation with the Member States, regions and local authorities concerned, and to disseminate information on these routes by means of brochures and publications;

(b) support for the exchange of experience in the field of visitor management techniques;

(c) promotion and assistance in the use of European networks enabling tourist operators and cultural institutions to exchange experience, especially as regards highlighting the value of cultural heritage.

A5.15

6. Tourism and the environment

The aim of Community action in the area of the interaction between tourism and the environment is to ensure that the environment is more fully taken into account.

This will be carried out by means of the following measures:

(a) support for initiatives aimed at informing and increasing the awareness of tourists and suppliers of services about the interaction between tourism and the environment and in particular through the creation of a European environmental prize;

(b) support for innovative pilot projects to reconcile tourism and nature protection at local or regional level, in particular coastal and mountain areas,

nature parks and reserves, *e.g.* by measures for the guidance of visitors;

(c) support for the development of networks involving transnational exchanges of experience, including experience of environmental problems and their possible solution through visitor management at sites;

(d) support for initiatives encouraging forms of environment-friendly tourism.

7. Rural tourism

A5.16

Community action in this field is designed to develop tourist activities in a rural environment, notably farm tourism, small family-run hotels or facilities set up by associations or local authorities.

This will be carried out by means of the following measures:

(a) support for partnership initiatives between operators at local, regional, national or European level, to facilitate exchanges of experience and the transfer of good practice through the organisation of visits, seminars, exchanges of experts and the development of transnational pilot schemes, in particular in the field of vocational training;

(b) improved information for rural operators and better access for them to the various Community aid schemes available for rural tourism, in particular through the publication of documents for mass circulation and the publication of an operator's manual;

(c) encouragement for improving the quality of rural tourism supply and support for measures to facilitate access to tourism in a rural environment.

A5.17   **8. Social tourism**

Community activity in this field seeks to facilitate access to tourism by groups of people who, for various reasons, but especially for social or health reasons, have difficulty in taking holidays.

This will be carried out by means of the following measures:

(a) shared information at Community level between public and private sector partners concerning the various methods used in the Member States to encourage holiday-taking by certain categories of tourists;

(b) support for the coordination between Member States of measures aimed at eliminating barriers to the development of tourism for the disabled, and for the exchange of information in this field.

A5.18   **9. Youth tourism**

Community action in this field is, through support for existing Community policies, aimed both at promoting young people's knowledge of cultures and lifestyles in the various Member States and at making it easier for young people to take holidays.

This will be carried out by means of the following measures:

(a) a feasibility study into establishing links between 'youth cards';

(b) support for research into the need to create a network of exchanges with regard to 'European classes' (school travel for pupils from several Member States).

A5.19   **10. Training**

Community action in this field is aimed, through support for existing Community policies, at making the tourist industry in the Community more competitive through support for increased professionalism in Community tourism.

This will be carried out by means of the following measures:

(a) dissemination of information among young people on tourist resources and profession;

(b) support for ongoing measures to draw up professional profiles for the industry and improvement of mutual information on the qualifications attained in the various Member States;

(c) encouragement of the participation of tourist businesses and their employees in existing Community training programmes and measures;

(d) support for transnational cooperation projects between universities, tourism schools, tourism professionals, or the authorities concerned, especially for training in the fields of rural, cultural and environmental tourism;

(e) support for networks aimed at improving the quality of vocational training so as to raise the quality of tourism services.

11.   Promotion in third countries   **A5.20**

Community action in this field is directed at making Europe a more attractive destination for tourists from distant countries.

This will be carried out by means of measures confined to pilot projects to promote Europe as a tourist destination on the markets of distant countries, particularly North America and Japan, whose growth is likely to have an impact on tourism within the Community.

II. Timetable of priorities

When implementing measures in accordance with the procedure laid down in Article 3, priority will be given for 1993 to the following measures.

These priorities may be modified for the financial years 1994/95 according to the procedure referred to in Article 3 (2).

Priority measures for 1993:

A5.21 1. **Improving knowledge of the tourist industry and ensuring greater consistency of Community measures:**

    (a) development of Community statistics on tourism;

    (b) detailed studies aimed at improving knowledge of tourism as an activity, assessment of the impact of current Community policies to assist tourism, forward analysis of new types of tourism and the preparation of strategies adapted to keep pace with demand;

    (c) consultation of tourism professionals within the Community.

A5.22 2. **Staggering of holidays:**

    (a) support for the setting-up of an international framework whose purpose would be to exchange information and monitor the activities of governments and the tourist industry.

A5.23 3. **Transnational measures:**

    (a) support of co-operation between border regions;

    (b) support for transnational initiatives contributing to the improvement of tourist information, in particular those using new technology;

    (c) development of tourist co-operation with Central and Eastern Europe and the Maghreb through the transfer of know-how on training and the implementation of strategies for promotion, as well as on marketing and the creation of small and medium-sized tourist businesses.

4. **Tourists as consumers:**   **A5.24**

Community action aims to support initiatives which improve the information of tourists and their protection, in areas such as existing classification systems, signposting symbols, time-share arrangements, over-booking and procedures for redress.

5. **Cultural tourism:**   **A5.25**

    (a) support for initiatives to develop new European cultural tourism routes, in cooperation with the Member States, regions and local authorities concerned, and to disseminate information on these routes by means of brochures and publications;

    (b) support for the exchange of experience in the field of visitor management techniques.

6. **Tourism and the environment:**   **A5.26**

    (a) support for initiatives aimed at informing and increasing the awareness of tourists and suppliers of services about the interaction between tourism and the environment and in particular through the creation of a European environmental prize;

    (b) support for innovative pilot projects to reconcile tourism and nature protection at local or regional level, in particular coastal and mountain areas, nature parks and reserves, e.g. by measures for the guidance of visitors;

    (c) support for the development

of networks involving trans-national exchanges of experi-ence, including experience of environmental problems and their possible solution through visitor management at sites;

(d) support for initiatives encourag-ing forms of environment-friendly tourism.

A5.27 **7. Rural tourism:**

(b) improved information for rural operators and better access for them to the various Community aid schemes available for rural tourism, in particular through the publication of documents for mass circulation and the publication of an operators's manual;

(c) encouragement for improving the quality of rural tourism sup-ply and support for measures to facilitate access to tourism in a rural environment.

A5.28 **8. Social tourism:**

(b) support for the co-ordination between Member States of measures aimed at eliminating barriers to the development of tourism for the disabled, and for the exchange of information in this field.

A5.29 **9. Youth tourism:**

Community action in this field is, through support for existing Com-munity policies, aimed both at pro-moting young people's knowledge of cultures and lifestyles in the vari-ous Member States and at making it easier for young people to take holi-days.

This will be carried out by means of the following measures:

(a) a feasibility study into establish-ing links between 'youth cards';

(b) support for research into the need to create a network of exchanges with regard to 'Euro-pean classes' (school travel for pupils from several Member States).

10. Training: **A5.30**

(b) support for ongoing measures to draw up professional profiles for the industry and improve-ment of mutual information on the qualifications attained in the various Member States;

(c) encouragement of the participa-tion of tourism businesses and their employees in existing Community training pro-grammes and measures;

(d) support for transnational co-operation projects between universities, tourism schools, tourism professionals, or the authorities concerned, espe-cially for training in the fields of rural, cultural and environmen-tal tourism.

11. Promotion in third countries: **A5.31**

Pilot projects to promote Europe as a tourist destination on the mar-kets of distant countries, particu-larly North America and Japan, whose growth is likely to have an impact on tourism within the Com-munity.

Council Directive 93/13/EEC

of 5 April 1993

on unfair terms in consumer contracts

A6.1 THE COUNCIL OF THE EUROPEAN COMMUNITIES,

Having regard to the Treaty establishing the European Economic Community, and in particular Article 100 A thereof,

Having regard to the proposal from the Commission,[1]

In cooperation with the European Parliament,[2]

Having regard to the opinion of the Economic and Social Committee,[3]

Whereas it is necessary to adopt measures with the aim of progressively establishing the internal market before 31 December 1992; whereas the internal market comprises an area without internal frontiers in which goods, persons, services and capital move freely;

Whereas the laws of Member States relating to the terms of contract between the seller of goods or supplier of services, on the one hand, and the consumer of them, on the other hand, show many disparities, with the result that the national markets for the sale of goods and services to consumers differ from each other and that distortions of competition may arise amongst the sellers and suppliers, notably when they sell and supply in other Member States;

Whereas, in particular, the laws of Member States relating to unfair terms in consumer contracts show marked divergences;

Whereas it is the responsibility of the Member States to ensure that contracts concluded with consumers do not contain unfair terms;

[1] OJ No C 73, 24. 3. 1992, p. 7.
[2] OJ No C 326, 16. 12. 1991, p. 108 and OJ No C 21, 25. 1. 1993.
[3] OJ No C 159, 17. 6. 1991, p. 34.

Whereas, generally speaking, consumers do not know the rules of law which, in Member States other than their own, govern contracts for the sale of goods or services; whereas this lack of awareness may deter them from direct transactions for the purchase of goods or services in another Member State;

Whereas, in order to facilitate the establishment of the internal market and to safeguard the citizen in his role as consumer when acquiring goods and services under contracts which are governed by the laws of Member States other than his own, it is essential to remove unfair terms from those contracts;

Whereas sellers of goods and suppliers of services will thereby be helped in their task of selling goods and supplying services, both at home and throughout the internal market; whereas competition will thus be stimulated, so contributing to increased choice for Community citizens as consumers;

Whereas the two Community programmes for a consumer protection and information policy[4] underlined the importance of safeguarding consumers in the matter of unfair terms of contract; whereas this protection ought to be provided by laws and regulations which are either harmonized at Community level or adopted directly at that level;

Whereas in accordance with the principle laid down under the heading 'Protection of the economic interests of the consumers', as stated in those programmes: 'acquirers of goods and services should be protected against the

A6.2

[4] OJ No C 92, 25. 4. 1975, p. 1 and OJ No C 133, 3. 6. 1981, p. 1.

abuse of power by the seller or supplier, in particular against one-sided standard contracts and the unfair exclusion of essential rights in contracts';

A6.3 Whereas more effective protection of the consumer can be achieved by adopting uniform rules of law in the matter of unfair terms; whereas those rules should apply to all contracts concluded between sellers or suppliers and consumers; whereas as a result *inter alia* contracts relating to employment, contracts relating to succession rights, contracts relating to rights under family law and contracts relating to the incorporation and organization of companies or partnership agreements must be excluded from this Directive;

Whereas the consumer must receive equal protection under contracts concluded by word of mouth and written contracts regardless, in the latter case, of whether the terms of the contract are contained in one or more documents;

Whereas, however, as they now stand, national laws allow only partial harmonization to be envisaged; whereas, in particular, only contractual terms which have not been individually negotiated are covered by this Directive; whereas Member States should have the option, with due regard for the Treaty, to afford consumers a higher level of protection through national provisions that are more stringent than those of this Directive;

Whereas the statutory or regulatory provisions of the Member States which directly or indirectly determine the terms of consumer contracts are presumed not to contain unfair terms; whereas, therefore, it does not appear to be necessary to subject the terms which reflect mandatory statutory or regulatory provisions and the principles or provisions of international conventions to which the Member States or the Community are party; whereas in that respect the wording 'mandatory statutory or regulatory provisions' in

Article 1 (2) also covers rules which, according to the law, shall apply between the contracting parties provided that no other arrangements have been established;

Whereas Member States must however **A6.4** ensure that unfair terms are not included, particularly because this Directive also applies to trades, business or professions of a public nature;

Whereas it is necessary to fix in a general way the criteria for assessing the unfair character of contract terms;

Whereas the assessment, according to the general criteria chosen, of the unfair character of terms, in particular in sale or supply activities of a public nature providing collective services which take account of solidarity among users, must be supplemented by a means of making an overall evaluation of the different interests involved; whereas this constitutes the requirement of good faith whereas, in making an assessment of good faith; particular regard shall be had to the strength of the bargaining positions of the parties, whether the consumer had an inducement to agree to the term and whether the goods or services were sold or supplied to the special order of the consumer; whereas the requirement of good faith may be satisfied by the seller or supplier where he deals fairly and equitably with the other party whose legitimate interest he has to take into account;

Whereas, for the purposes of this Directive, the annexed list of terms can be of indicative value only and, because of the cause of the minimal character of the Directive, the scope of these terms may be the subject of amplification or more restrictive editing by the Member States in their national laws;

Whereas the nature of goods or services should have an influence on assessing the unfairness of contractual terms;

Whereas, for the purposes of this Directive, assessment of unfair character shall not be made of terms which describe the main subject matter of the contract nor the quality/price ratio of the goods or services supplied; whereas the main subject matter of the contract and the price/quality ratio may nevertheless be taken into account in assessing the fairness of other terms; whereas it follows, *inter alia*, that in insurance contracts, the terms which clearly define or circumscribe the insured risk and the insurer's liability shall not be subject to such assessment since these restrictions are taken into account in calculating the premium paid by the consumer;

A6.5 Whereas contracts should be drafted in plain, intelligible language, the consumer should actually be given an opportunity to examine all the terms and, if in doubt, the interpretation most favourable to the consumer should prevail;

Whereas Member States should ensure that unfair terms are not used in contracts concluded with consumers by a seller or supplier and that if, nevertheless, such terms are so used, they will not bind the consumer, and the contract will continue to bind the parties upon those terms if it is capable of continuing in existence without the unfair provisions;

Whereas there is a risk that, in certain cases, the consumer may be deprived of protection under this Directive by designating the law of a non-Member country as the law applicable to the contract; whereas provisions should therefore be included in this Directive designed to avert this risk;

Whereas persons or organizations, if regarded under the law of a Member State as having a legitimate interest in the matter, must have facilities for initiating proceedings concerning terms of contract drawn up for general use in contracts concluded with consumers, and in particular unfair terms, either before a court or before an administrative authority competent to decide upon complaints or to initiate appropriate legal proceedings; whereas this possibility does not, however, entail prior verification of the general conditions obtaining in individual economic sectors;

Whereas the courts or administrative authorities of the Member States must have at their disposal adequate and effective means of preventing the continued application of unfair terms in consumer contracts,

HAS ADOPTED THIS DIRECTIVE:

Article 1   A6.6

1. The purpose of this Directive is to approximate the laws, regulations and administrative provisions of the Member States relating to unfair terms in contracts concluded between a seller or supplier and a consumer.

2. The contractual terms which reflect mandatory statutory or regulatory provisions and the provisions or principles of international conventions to which the Member States or the Community are party, particularly in the transport area, shall not be subject to the provisions of this Directive.

Article 2   A6.7

For the purposes of this Directive:

a) 'unfair terms' means the contractual terms defined in Article 3;

b) 'consumer' means any natural person who, in contracts covered by this Directive, is acting for purposes which are outside his trade, business or profession;

c) 'seller or supplier' means any natural or legal person who, in contracts covered by this Directive, is acting for purposes relating to his trade, business or profession, whether publicly owned or privately owned.

Article 3   A6.8

1. A contractual term which has not been individually negotiated shall be

627

regarded as unfair if, contrary to the requirement of good faith, it causes a significant imbalance in the parties' rights and obligations arising under the contract, to the detriment of the consumer.

2. A term shall always be regarded as not individually negotiated where it has been drafted in advance and the consumer has therefore not been able to influence the substance of the term, particularly in the context of a pre-formulated standard contract.

The fact that certain aspects of a term or one specific term have been individually negotiated shall not exclude the application of this Article to the rest of a contract if an overall assessment of the contract indicates that it is nevertheless a pre-formulated standard contract.

Where any seller or supplier claims that a standard term has been individually negotiated, the burden of proof in this respect shall be incumbent on him.

3. The Annex shall contain an indicative and non-exhaustive list of the terms which may be regarded as unfair.

A6.9

Article 4

1. Without prejudice to Article 7, the unfairness of a contractual term shall be assessed, taking into account the nature of the goods or services for which the contract was concluded and by referring, at the time of conclusion of the contract, to all the circumstances attending the conclusion of the contract and to all the other terms of the contract or of another contract on which it is dependent.

2. Assessment of the unfair nature of the terms shall relate neither to the definition of the main subject matter of the contract nor to the adequacy of the price and remuneration, on the one hand, as against the services or goods supplied in exchange, on the other, in so far as these terms are in plain intelligible language.

Article 5

A6.10

In the case of contracts where all or certain terms offered to the consumer are in writing, these terms must always be drafted in plain, intelligible language. Where there is doubt about the meaning of a term, the interpretation most favourable to the consumer shall prevail. This rule on interpretation shall not apply in the context of the procedures laid down in Article 7 (2).

Article 6

A6.11

1. Member States shall lay down that unfair terms used in a contract concluded with a consumer by a seller or supplier shall, as provided for under their national law, not be binding on the consumer and that the contract shall continue to bind the parties upon those terms if it is capable of continuing in existence without the unfair terms.

2. Member States shall take the necessary measures to ensure that the consumer does not lose the protection granted by this Directive by virtue of the choice of the law of a non-Member country as the law applicable to the contract if the latter has a close connection with the territory of the Member States.

Article 7

A6.12

1. Member States shall ensure that, in the interests of consumers and of competitors, adequate and effective means exist to prevent the continued use of unfair terms in contracts concluded with consumers by sellers or suppliers.

2. The means referred to in paragraph 1 shall include provisions whereby persons or organizations, having a legitimate interest under national law in protecting consumers, may take action according to the national law concerned before the courts or before competent administrative bodies for a decision as to whether contractual terms drawn up for general use are unfair, so that they can apply appropriate and effective means to prevent the continued use of such terms.

3. With due regard for national laws, the legal remedies referred to in paragraph 2 may be directed separately or jointly against a number of sellers or suppliers from the same economic sector or their associations which use or recommend the use of the same general contractual terms or similar terms.

A6.13

Article 8

Member States may adopt or retain the most stringent provisions compatible with the Treaty in the area covered by this Directive, to ensure a maximum degree of protection for the consumer.

A6.14

Article 9

The Commission shall present a report to the European Parliament and to the Council concerning the application of this Directive five years at the latest after the date in Article 10 (1).

A6.15

Article 10

1. Member States shall bring into force the laws, regulations and administrative provisions necessary to comply with this Directive no later than 31 December 1994. They shall forthwith inform the Commission thereof.

These provisions shall be applicable to all contracts concluded after 31 December 1994.

2. When Member States adopt these measures, they shall contain a reference to this Directive or shall be accompanied by such reference on the occasion of their official publication. The methods of making such a reference shall be laid down by the Member States.

3. Member States shall communicate the main provisions of national law which they adopt in the field covered by this Directive to the Commission.

Article 11

A6.16

This Directive is addressed to the Member States.

Done at Luxembourg, 5 April 1993.

For the Council
The President
N HELVEG PETERSEN

ANNEX

Terms referred to in Article 3 (3)

A6.17

1. **Terms which have the object or effect of:**

(a) excluding or limiting the legal liability of a seller or supplier in the event of the death of a consumer or personal injury to the latter resulting from an act or omission of that seller or supplier;

(b) inappropriately excluding or limiting the legal rights of the consumer *vis-à-vis* the seller or supplier or another party in the event of total or partial non-performance or inadequate performance by the seller or supplier of any of the contractual obligations, including the option of off-setting a debt owed to the seller or supplier against any claim which the consumer may have against him;

(c) making an agreement binding on the consumer whereas provision of services by the seller or supplier is subject to a condition whose realization depends on his own will alone;

(d) permitting the seller or supplier to retain sums paid by the consumer where the latter decides not to conclude or perform the contract, without providing for the consumer to receive compensation of an equivalent amount from the seller or supplier where the latter is the party cancelling the contract;

(e) requiring any consumer who fails to fulfil his obligation to pay a disproportionately high sum in compensation;

(f) authorizing the seller or supplier to dissolve the contract on a discretionary basis where the same facility is not granted to the consumer, or permitting the seller or supplier to retain the sums paid for services not yet supplied by him where it is the seller or supplier himself who dissolves the contract;

(g) enabling the seller or supplier to terminate a contract of indeterminate duration without reasonable notice except where there are serious grounds for doing so;

(h) automatically extending a contract of fixed duration where the consumer does not indicate otherwise, when the deadline fixed for the consumer to express this desire not to extend the contract is unreasonably early;

(i) irrevocably binding the consumer to terms with which he had no real opportunity of becoming acquainted before the conclusion of the contract;

(j) enabling the seller or supplier to alter the terms of the contract unilaterally without a valid reason which is specified in the contract;

(k) enabling the seller or supplier to alter unilaterally without a valid reason any characteristics of the product or service to be provided;

(l) providing for the price of goods to be determined at the time of delivery or allowing a seller of goods or supplier of services to increase their price without in both cases giving the consumer the corresponding right to cancel the con-

tract if the final price is too high in relation to the price agreed when the contract was concluded;

(m) giving the seller or supplier the right to determine whether the goods or services supplied are in conformity with the contract, or giving him the exclusive right to interpret any term of the contract;

(n) limiting the seller's or supplier's obligation to respect commitments undertaken by his agents or making his commitments subject to compliance with a particular formality;

(o) obliging the consumer to fulfil all his obligations where the seller or supplier does not perform his;

(p) giving the seller or supplier the possibility of transferring his rights and obligations under the contract, where this may serve to reduce the guarantees for the consumer, without the latter's agreement;

(q) excluding or hindering the consumer's right to take legal action or exercise any other legal remedy, particularly by requiring the consumer to take disputes exclusively to arbitration not covered by legal provisions, unduly restricting the evidence available to him or imposing on him a burden of proof which, according to the applicable law, should lie with another party to the contract.

2. Scope of subparagraphs (g), (j) and (l) A6.18

(a) Subparagraph (g) is without hindrance to terms by which a supplier of financial services reserves the right to terminate unilaterally a contract of indeterminate duration without notice where there is a valid reason, provided that the supplier is required to inform the other contracting party or parties thereof immediately.

(b) Subparagraph (j) is without hindrance to terms under which a supplier of financial services reserves the right to alter the rate of interest payable by the consumer or due to the latter, or the amount of other charges for financial services without notice where there is a valid reason, provided that the supplier is required to inform the other contracting party or parties thereof at the earliest opportunity and that the latter are free to dissolve the contract immediately.

Subparagraph (j) is also without hindrance to terms under which a seller or supplier reserves the right to alter unilaterally the conditions of a contract of indeterminate duration, provided that he is required to inform the consumer with reasonable notice and that the consumer is free to dissolve the contract.

(c) Subparagraphs (g), (j) and (l) do not apply to:

transactions in transferable securities, financial instruments and other products or services where the price is linked to fluctuations in a stock exchange quotation or index or a financial market rate that the seller or supplier does not control;

contracts for the purchase or sale of foreign currency, traveller's cheques or international money orders denominated in foreign currency;

(d) Subparagraph (l) is without hindrance to price-indexation clauses, where lawful, provided that the method by which prices vary is explicitly described.

Proposed Convention
Com(93) 684 Final

Proposal for a decision, based on Article K.3 of the Treaty on European Union establishing the Convention on the crossing of the external frontiers of the Member States

(Submitted by the Commission on 10 December 1993)

A7.1 THE COUNCIL OF THE EUROPEAN UNION,

Having regard to the Treaty on European Union, and in particular Article K.3 (2) thereof,

Having regard to the proposal from the Commission,

Having regard to the opinion of the European Parliament,

Whereas the rules governing crossings by persons at the external frontiers of the Member States and the exercise of controls on such crossings are, by virtue of Article K.1 of the Treaty on European Union and without prejudice to the powers of the European Community, matters of common interest which may be the subject of cooperation under Title VI;

Whereas the rules governing crossings at the external frontiers of the Member States by citizens of the Union and other persons entitled under Community law fall within the scope of the Treaty establishing the European Community; whereas this Convention primarily defines the rules applicable to persons not entitled under Community law; whereas controls on crossings at external frontiers must cover all persons arriving at a frontier to the extent necessary to distinguish those entitled under Community law from other persons;

Whereas Article 7a of the Treaty establishing the European Community sets the common objective of an area without internal frontiers in which the free movement of persons is ensured;

Whereas attainment of this objective requires effective controls, in line with common criteria, on persons at the external frontiers of those States and closer cooperation on implementing a common visa policy;

Whereas the controls on persons con- **A7.2** ducted by each Member State at its external frontiers must be carried out according to rules which should be adopted in common, with due regard for the interests of all Member States;

Whereas the aim of such controls is to enable threats to public policy and public security to be eliminated in the Member States of the European Union and to combat illegal immigration, while preserving the openness of those States to the rest of the world and their intensive exchanges with other countries, particularly in the cultural, scientific and economic spheres;

Whereas the introduction of a system of controls at external frontiers requires that particular attention be paid to the questions of infrastructure and frontier surveillance on the part of countries which, because of their geographical position and configuration, are exposed to increased migratory pressure;

Whereas the Member States intend to conduct these controls in compliance with their common international commitments, in particular the European Convention for the Protection of Human Rights and Fundamental Freedoms of 4 November 1950 and the Geneva Convention of 28 July 1951, as amended by the New York Protocol of 31 January 1967, relating to the status of refugees as well as with more favourable constitutional provisions on asylum,

HAS DECIDED AS FOLLOWS:

A7.3

Article 1

1. It is recommended that the Member States adopt the Convention on controls on persons crossing external frontiers established by this Decision, the text of which is annexed hereto, in accordance with their respective constitutional requirements by 31 December 1994.

2. The Member States shall notify the General Secretariat of the Council of the instruments attesting completion of the procedures for the adoption of the Convention in accordance with their respective constitutional requirements, and deposit them with it.

A7.4

Article 2

1. The Convention shall enter into force on the first day of the second month following the deposit of the instrument of adoption with the General Secretariat of the Council by the last Member State to take that step.

The provisions concerning the adoption of measures in implementation of the Convention shall apply from the date of its entry into force. The other provisions shall apply from the first day of the third month following that date.

2. The Secretary-General of the Council shall inform the Member States of the date of entry into force of this Convention.

Article 3

A7.5

This Decision shall enter into force on the day of its publication in the *Official Journal of the European Communities.*

Convention

on controls on persons crossing external frontiers

TITLE I

GENERAL

A7.6

Article 1

Definitions

1. For the purposes of this Convention:

(a) 'persons entitled under Community law' means:

  (i) citizens of the Union within the meaning of Article 8 (1) of the Treaty establishing the European Community;

  (ii) members of the family of such citizens who are nationals of a third State and have the right of entry and residence in a Member State by virtue of an instrument enacted under the Treaty establishing the European Community;

  (iii) nationals of third States who, by agreement between the European Community and its Member States and such countries, have rights of entry and residence in a Member State which are identical with those enjoyed by citizens of the Union, and members of the family of such persons who are nationals of a third State and have the right of entry and residence in a Member State under any such agreement;

(b) 'residence permit' means any authorization issued by the authorities of a Member State authorizing a person not entitled under Community law to stay in its territory, with the exception of visas and the provisional residence permit referred to in Articles 8 and 15;

(c) 'entry visa' means authorization or decision by a Member State, given in accordance with decisions adopted under Article 100c of the Treaty establishing the European Community, to enable a person to enter its territory who is required to hold a visa to do so, subject to other entry conditions being fulfilled;

A7.7　(d) 'transit visa' means authorization or decision by a Member State, given in accordance with decisions adopted under Article 100c of the Treaty establishing the European Community, to enable a person to transit through its territory or through the transit zone of a port or airport who is required to hold a visa to do so, subject to other transit conditions being fulfilled; the time taken to transit shall not exceed five days;

(e) 're-entry visa' means authorization by a State enabling a person who is not a national of that State and who is present in the territory of that State to re-enter within a specified period without re-obtaining an entry visa to that State;

(f) 'uniform visa' means entry, transit or re-entry visa of the uniform format provided for in Article 100c (3) of the Treaty establishing the European Community, issued under the rules specified in Articles 19 to 22 of this Convention;

(g) 'short stay' means an uninterrupted stay or successive stays in the territories of the Member States the length of which does not exceed three months, calculated over six months from the date of first entry;

(h) 'external frontiers' means:

(i) a Member State's land frontier which is not contiguous with a frontier of another Member State, and maritime frontiers;

(ii) airports and seaports, except where they are considered to be internal frontiers for purposes of instruments enacted under the Treaty establishing the European Community;

(i) 'local frontier traffic' means the movement, within a limited geo-graphical area defined in a convention concluded by a Member State with a contiguous State which is not a member of the European Communities, of persons who come within the scope of that convention and are thereby entitled to cross the external land frontier of the Member State concerned under special conditions.

2. This Convention applies, except where there is an express statement to the contrary, to all persons other than those entitled under Community law.

TITLE II
GENERAL PRINCIPLES

Article 2
A7.8
Crossing external frontiers

1. All persons crossing the external frontiers shall do so at authorized crossing points permanently controlled by the Member States.

2. Persons crossing external frontiers at any point other than authorized crossing points shall be liable to penalties as determined by each Member State.

3. Each Member State shall determine the location and opening conditions of authorized crossing points on its external frontiers and shall communicate this information and any changes thereto to the General Secretariat of the Council, which shall inform the other Member States accordingly. Crossing at crossing points outside their opening hours shall not be permitted.

4. By way of exception, as provided in Article 1 (2), this Article also applies to persons entitled under Community law who cross the external frontiers, unless otherwise stipulated in the law of the Member State concerned.

5. The exceptions and specific rules applying to particular categories of maritime traffic for the crossing of external frontiers, and the arrangements for local frontier traffic, shall be determined by measures to give effect to this Convention.

A7.9

Article 3
Surveillance of external frontiers

External frontier stretches other than authorized crossing points shall be kept under effective surveillance by mobile units or by other appropriate means. Member States undertake to provide surveillance yielding similarly effective results along all their external frontiers; their surveillance agencies shall consult and cooperate to that end.

A7.10

Article 4
Controls at external frontiers

The crossing of external frontiers shall be subject to control by the competent authorities of the Member State concerned. Controls shall be carried out in accordance with national law, with due regard for the provisions of this Convention.

A7.11

Article 5
Nature of controls at external frontiers

1. When crossing an external frontier upon entering or leaving the territories of the Member States, all persons shall be subject to a visual control under conditions which permit their identity to be established by examination of their travel documents.

2. Upon entry, persons shall also be subject to a control to ensure that they fulfil the conditions set out in Article 7. By way of exception, as provided in Article 1 (2), persons entitled under Community law who are third-country nationals shall be subject to the condition in Article 7 (1) (b) if they are required to hold a visa by virtue of instruments enacted under Article 100c of the Treaty establishing the European Community.

3. Detailed rules for applying the controls shall be determined by measures to give effect to this Convention.

4. Certain controls may, exceptionally, be relaxed, due regard being had for any conditions that may be laid down by measures to give effect to this Convention.

Controls upon entry shall take precedence over controls upon departure.

5. Without prejudice to Community provisions regulating controls on baggage carried by travellers and on their vehicles, controls on persons and their vehicles and baggage may be performed where necessary for the purposes of:

detecting and preventing threats to national security and public policy, or

combating illegal immigration.

6. When effecting these controls, Member States shall take account of the interests of the other Member States.

Article 6
Specific arrangements for airports

A7.12

1. Member States shall ensure that passengers on flights from third States who transfer onto internal flights will be subject to an entry control at the airport at which the external flight arrives. Passengers on internal flights who transfer onto flights bound for third States will be subject to a departure control at the airport from which the external flight departs.

2. Paragraph 1 is without prejudice to Community baggage inspection measures.

3. Member States shall also take any measures necessary to ensure that:

passengers who embark in a Member State on a flight coming from a third State which is bound for a destination in a Member State are subject at the airport of destination to the controls specified for passengers coming from third countries,

passengers who embark in a Member State on a flight bound for a destination in a third State and who disembark in another Member State are subject at the airport of embarkation to the controls specified for passengers going to third countries,

passengers who embark in a Member State to go to another Member State on

635

a flight coming from and bound for one or more third States are subject at the airports of the Member States to the controls specified for passengers coming from or bound for third countries, depending on whether they are departing from or arriving in a Member State.

TITLE III

CONTROL ARRANGEMENTS AT EXTERNAL FRONTIERS

A7.13

Article 7
Controls on persons not entitled under Community law

1. Any person may be authorized to enter the territories of the Member States for a short stay provided that he meets the following requirements:

(a) that he present a valid travel document which authorizes the crossing of frontiers; a list and description of such documents shall be drawn up by measures to give effect to this Convention;

(b) where applicable, that he be in possession of a visa valid for the length of stay envisaged;

(c) that he does not represent a threat to the public policy, national security or international relations of Member States and, in particular, that his name does not appear on the joint list provided for in Article 10;

(d) that he produce, if necessary, documents justifying the purpose and conditions of the intended stay or transit, in particular the required work permits if there is reason to believe that he intends to work;

(e) that he have sufficient means of subsistence, both for the period of the intended stay or transit and for him to return to his country of origin or travel to a third State into which he is certain to be admitted, or be in a position to acquire such means lawfully.

2. Any person may also be refused entry:

(a) if his name appears on the national list of persons who are not to be admitted to the Member State to which he seeks entry;

(b) in all the circumstances in which a national of a Member State may be refused entry to another Member State.

Article 8
Crossing of external frontiers by third-country nationals residing in a Member State

A7.14

1. A Member State shall not require a visa of a person who wishes to enter its territory for a short stay or to transit through it, provided that that person:

(a) fulfils the conditions in Article 7, except that in paragraph 1 (b); and

(b) holds a residence permit issued by another Member State permitting him to reside in that State, the period of validity of which, at the time of entry, still has more than four months to run.

2. In exceptional cases, paragraph 1 may also apply to persons who hold a provisional residence permit issued by a Member State and a travel document issued by that Member State.

3. Member States shall, under conditions determined by measures to give effect to this Convention, take back any person to whom they have issued a residence permit or provisional residence permit within the meaning of paragraphs 1 and 2 and who is illegally resident in the territory of another Member State.

4. In exceptional cases, a Member State may depart from the provisions of paragraphs 1 and 2 for urgent reasons of national security, but must take into consideration the interests of the other Member States. The Member State concerned shall inform the other Member States in an appropriate manner, deter-

mined by measures to give effect to this Convention.

Such measures shall be used only to the extent that and for as long as is strictly necessary to achieve the purposes referred to in the first subparagraph.

5. For the purposes of implementing this Article,

a list of the residence permits and provisional residence permits referred to in paragraphs 1 and 2 which shall be accepted as equivalent to visas, and

an indicative list of the exceptional circumstances in which Member States' authorities shall accept the provisional residence permits and the travel documents referred to in paragraph 2 as equivalent to visas

shall be drawn up by measures to give effect to this Convention.

A7.15

Article 9
Stays other than for a short time

Persons who propose to stay in a Member State other than for a short time shall enter that State under the conditions laid down in its national law. In that case access shall be restricted to the territory of that State.

TITLE IV

NOTIFICATIONS FOR REFUSING ENTRY

A7.16

Article 10
List of persons to be refused entry

1. A joint list of persons to whom the Member States shall refuse entry to their territories shall be drawn up on the basis of national notifications by measures to give effect to this Convention.

2. The list, which shall be continually updated, shall contain the names submitted for this purpose by each Member State.

3. The decision to put a person on the joint list shall be based on the threat which that person may represent to the public policy or national security of a Member State. It shall be based on a decision taken with due regard for the rules of procedure laid down by national law by the administrative or competent judicial authorities of the Member States on account of:

a custodial sentence of one year or more in the Member State concerned, or

information to the effect that the person concerned has committed a serious crime, or

serious grounds for believing that he is planning to commit a serious crime or that he represents a threat to the public policy or national security of a Member State, or

a serious offence or repeated offences against the law relating to the entry and residence of foreigners.

4. Detailed rules for applying the criteria set out in paragraph 3 shall be determined by measures to give effect to this Convention.

Article 11
Issue of residence permit

A7.17

1. Where a person whose name is on the joint list provided for in Article 10 applies for a residence permit, the Member State to which application is made shall first consult the Member State which entered the name on the list and shall take into account the interests of that State; the residence permit shall be issued for substantive reasons only, notably on humanitarian grounds or by reason of international commitments.

If the residence permit is issued, the Member State which entered the name on the joint list shall delete the entry.

2. If it becomes apparent that the name of a person who is in possession of a valid residence permit issued by one of the Member States is on the joint list, the Member State which entered the name and the Member State which issued the residence permit shall consult each other in order to

determine whether there are sufficient grounds for withdrawing the residence permit.

If the residence permit is not withdrawn, the Member State which made the entry shall delete it.

3. Detailed rules for the application of this Article shall be determined by measures to give effect to this Convention.

A7.18

Article 12
Refusal of entry to a Member State

1. Entry into the territories of the Member States shall be refused to persons who fail to fulfil one or more of the conditions set out in Articles 7 (1) and 9.

2. A Member State may, however, on humanitarian grounds or in the national interest or by reason of international commitments, allow persons who fail to fulfil those conditions to enter its territory. In such a case, permission to enter shall be restricted to the territory of the Member State concerned, which, if the person concerned is on the joint list, shall inform the other Member States in an appropriate manner, determined by measures to give effect to this Convention.

A7.19

Article 13
Exchange of information

1. The exchange of information on data contained in the joint list shall be computerized.

2. The creation, organization and operation of this computerized system will be the subject of the Convention on the European Information System. The Convention will include guarantees for the protection of individuals with regard to the processing of personal data.

3. The joint list may be consulted by the competent authorities of the Member States which, in accordance with their national laws, are concerned with:

processing visa applications,

frontier controls,

police checks,

the admission and regulation of the stay of persons who are not nationals of a Member State.

4. Each Member State shall inform the Commission and the other Member States of the agencies authorized, pursuant to this Article, to consult the joint list.

TITLE V

ACCOMPANYING MEASURES

Article 14
Responsibilities of carriers

A7.20

1. Without prejudice to Article 27 and instruments enacted under the Treaty establishing the European Community, the Member States undertake to incorporate in their national legislation measures relating to airlines and shipping companies and to public-service international carriers transporting groups overland by coach, with the exception of local frontier traffic.

2. The purpose of such measures will be:

to oblige the carrier to take all necessary measures to ensure that persons coming from third countries are in possession of valid travel documents and of the necessary visas, and to impose appropriate penalties on carriers failing to fulfil this obligation,

to oblige the carrier, where required by the control authorities, to assume responsibility without delay (this may include covering the costs of accommodation until departure), and to return to the State from which he was transported or to the State which issued his passport or to any State to which he is certain to be admitted, a person coming from a third country who is refused admission at the first control on entry into Community territory.

A7.21

Article 15
Illegal crossing of an external frontier

1. A person who illegally crosses an external frontier without a residence permit or who does not fulfil, or no longer fulfils, the conditions of residence in a Member State shall normally be required to leave the territory of the Member State without delay, unless his stay is regularized.

If such a person holds a valid residence permit or provisional residence permit issued by another Member State, he shall go to the territory of that Member State without delay, unless he is authorized to go to another country to which he is certain to be admitted.

2. Where such a person has not left voluntarily or where it may be assumed that he will not so leave or if his immediate departure is required for reasons of national security or public policy, he shall be expelled as laid down in the legislation of the Member State in which he was found. He shall be expelled from the territory of that Member State to his country of origin. He may equally be expelled to any other country to which he may be admitted, notably under the relevant provisions of readmission agreements between Member States.

3. A list of the residence permits or provisional residence permits issued by the Member State shall be drawn up by measures to give effect to this Convention.

4. Should one of them so request, Member States shall conclude bilateral agreements between themselves on the readmission of persons who are not entitled under Community law.

A7.22

Article 16
Compensation for financial imbalances

Subject to determination of the appropriate criteria and practical arrangements by measures to give effect to this Convention, Member States shall compensate each other for any financial imbalances which may result from the obligation to expel provided in Article 15 where such expulsion cannot be effected at the expense of the person concerned or of a third party.

TITLE VI

VISAS

Article 17
Common visa policy

A7.23

Member States undertake to harmonize their visa policies progressively, without prejudice to decisions adopted under Article 100c of the Treaty establishing the European Community.

Article 18
Uniform visa

A7.24

A Member State shall not require a visa issued by its own authorities of a person applying to stay for a short time within its territory who holds a uniform visa.

Article 19
Conditions for issue of uniform visa

A7.25

1. A uniform visa may be issued only where a person fulfils the conditions for entry laid down in Article 7 (1), except that in subparagraph (b).

2. Uniform visas shall be issued on the basis of the following common conditions and criteria:

travel documents presented upon application for a visa must be checked to ensure that they are in order and authentic,

the expiry date of the travel document must be at least three months later than the final date for stays stated on the visa, account being taken of the time within which the visa must be used,

the travel document must be recognized by all Member States,

the travel document must be valid in all Member States,

the travel document must allow for the return of the traveller to his country of origin or his entry into a third country,

the existence and validity of an authorization or a re-entry visa for the traveller to return to the country of departure must be checked if such formalities are required by the authorities of that country. The same shall apply to any authorization required for entry to a third country.

Article 20
Prior consultation of central authorities

1. Where in certain cases a Member State makes the issue of visas subject to prior consultation of its central authorities and where it wishes to be consulted on the issue, in such cases, of a uniform visa by another Member State, this visa shall not be issued unless the central authorities of the Member State concerned have been consulted in advance and have expressed no objection.

The absence of a reply from these authorities within a period to be determined by measures to give effect to this Convention shall be regarded as indicating that there is no objection to the issue of a visa. The period shall be 14 days at most.

If there is an objection, or if the consultation procedure referred to in the first subparagraph has not been implemented for reasons of urgency, only a national visa with restricted territorial validity shall be issued.

2. Rules for implementing this Article shall be determined by measures to give effect to this Convention, having particular regard for Member States' security; they may specify cases in which the issue of a uniform visa must be made subject to prior consultation of the central authorities of the Member State or States requiring such consultation, but this shall be without prejudice to Member States' option to hold prior consultations with their own central authorities in other cases.

Article 21
Multiple-entry uniform visa

1. The uniform visa may be a visa valid for one or more entries. Neither the length of any continuous stay nor the total length of successive stays may exceed three months in a six-month period starting on the date of entry.

2. The conditions and criteria for issuing multiple-entry uniform visas shall be determined by measures to give effect to this Convention.

Article 22
Issue of uniform visa

1. The uniform visa shall be issued by the diplomatic and consular authorities of the Member States or, in exceptional cases, by other authorities determined in accordance with national legislation.

2. The Member State which is the main destination shall normally be responsible for issuing the visa. If it is not possible to determine that destination, the Member State of first entry shall be responsible.

3. The principles stated in this Article shall be implemented by measures to give effect to this Convention.

Article 23
Extension of stay

A Member State may, if necessary, issue a visa the validity of which is restricted to its own territory to the holder of a uniform visa in the course of any one six-month period.

A Member State may also authorize a person holding a uniform visa to remain in its territory for more than three months.

Article 24
National visas

1. Member States may issue visas valid only in their respective territories in the cases provided for in Articles 20, 23 and 25.

2. In addition, a Member State may, on

humanitarian grounds or in the national interest or by reason of international commitments, issue a person who does not meet any or some of the conditions laid down in Article 7 (1) (a), (c), (d) and (e) with a visa valid only in its own territory.

3. A Member State which has issued a person with a visa pursuant to paragraph 2 shall so inform the other Member States if that person is on the joint list or if the State consulted pursuant to Article 20 has objected. This information shall be supplied in accordance with the procedures established under Article 12 (2) in accordance with the measures to give effect to this Convention.

4. Visas issued in accordance with paragraphs 1 and 2 shall indicate their distinct nature and be different in appearance from the uniform visa.

A7.31

Article 25
Long-stay visas

Visas for stays of more than three months shall be national visas issued by each Member State in accordance with its national law.

The issue of such visas shall be subject to consultation of the joint list.

TITLE VII

IMPLEMENTATION

A7.32

Article 26
Implementing measures

Decisions needed to give effect to this Convention, other than those expressly provided therein, shall be adopted by the Council, acting unanimously on a proposal from the Commission or on the initiative of a Member State.

A7.33

Article 27
Primacy of instruments

1. This Convention shall be subject to the European Convention for the Protection of Human Rights and Fundamental Freedoms of 4 November 1950 and to the Geneva Convention of 28 July 1951, as amended by the New York

Protocol of 31 January 1967, relating to the status of refugees and without prejudice to more favourable constitutional provisions of Member States on asylum.

2. This Convention shall not affect bilateral conventions on local frontier traffic.

Article 28
Relations with third States

A7.34

1. A Member State which envisages conducting negotiations on frontier controls with a third State shall inform the other Member States and the Commission accordingly in good time.

2. No Member State shall conclude with one or more third States agreements simplifying or removing frontier controls without the prior agreement of the Council.

This paragraph does not apply to agreements on local frontier traffic where such agreements conform to the arrangements laid down pursuant to Article 2 and is without prejudice to Article 27 (2).

Article 29
Jurisdiction of the Court of Justice

A7.35

The Court of Justice of the European Communities shall have jurisdiction:

to give preliminary rulings concerning the interpretation of this Convention; references shall be made as provided in the second and third paragraphs of Article 177 of the Treaty establishing the European Community,

in disputes concerning the implementation of this Convention, on application by a Member State or the Commission.

TITLE VIII

FINAL PROVISIONS

Article 30
Extent

A7.36

(text to be inserted later)

Directive 94/47/EEC of the European Parliament and the Council

of 26 October 1994

on the protection of purchasers in respect of certain aspects of contracts relating to the purchase of the right to use immovable properties on a timeshare basis

A8.1 THE EUROPEAN PARLIAMENT AND THE COUNCIL OF THE EUROPEAN UNION,

Having regard to the Treaty establishing the European Community, and in particular Article 100a thereof,

Having regard to the proposal from the Commission,[1]

Having regard to the opinion of the Economic and Social Committee,[2]

Acting in accordance with the procedure laid down in Article 189b of the Treaty,[3]

1.   Whereas the disparities between national legislations on contracts relating to the purchase of the right to use one or more immovable properties on a time share basis are likely to create barriers to the proper operation of the internal market and distortions of competition and lead to the compartmentalization of national markets;

2.   Whereas the aim of this Directive is to establish a minimum basis of common rules on such matters which will make it possible to ensure that the internal market

operates properly and will thereby protect purchasers; whereas it is sufficient for those rules to cover contractual transactions only with regard to those aspects that relate to information on the constituent parts of contracts, the arrangements for communicating such information and the procedures and arrangements for cancellation and withdrawal; whereas the appropriate instrument to achieve that aim is a Directive; whereas this Directive is therefore consistent with the principle of subsidiarity;

3.   Whereas the legal nature of the rights which are the subject of the contracts covered by this Directive varies considerably from one Member State to another; whereas reference should therefore be made in summary form to those variations, giving a sufficiently broad definition of such contracts, without thereby implying harmonization within the Community of the legal nature of the rights in question;

4.   Whereas this Directive is not **A8.2** designed to regulate the extent to which contracts for the use of one or more immovable properties on a time share basis may be concluded in Member States or the legal basis for such contracts;

5.   Whereas, in practice, contracts relating to the purchase of the right to use one or more immovable properties on a time share basis differ from tenancy agreements; whereas that difference can be seen from, *inter alia*, the means of payment;

---

1   OJ No C 299, 5. 11. 1993, p. 8
2   OJ No C 108, 19. 4. 1993, p. 1.
3   Opinion of the European Parliament of 26 May 1993 (OJ No C 176, 28.6. 1993, p. 95 and OJ No C 225, 20. 9. 1993, p. 70) confirmed on 2 December 1993 (OJ No C 342, 20. 12. 1993, p. 3); Council common position of 4 March 1994 (OJ No C 137, 19. 5. 1994, p. 42) and decision of the European Parliament of 4 May 1994 (OJ No C 205, 25. 7. 1994). Join[t] text of the Conciliation Committee of 22. 9. 1994.

6. Whereas it may be seen from the market that hotels, residential hotels and other similar residential tourist premises are involved in contractual transactions similar to those which have made this Directive necessary;

7. Whereas it is necessary to avoid any misleading or incomplete details in information concerned specifically with the sale of the rights to use one or more immovable properties on a time share basis; whereas such information should be supplemented by a document which must be made available to anyone who requests it; whereas the information therein must constitute part of the contract for the purchase of the right to use one or more immovable properties on a time share basis;

8. Whereas, in order to give purchasers a high level of protection and in view of the specific characteristics of systems for using immovable properties on a time share basis, contracts for the purchase of the right to use one or more immovable properties on a time share basis must include certain minimal items;

A8.3

9. Whereas, with a view to establishing effective protection for purchasers in this field, it is necessary to stipulate minimum obligations with which vendors must comply *vis-à-vis* purchasers;

10. Whereas the contract for the purchase of the right to use one or more immovable properties on a time share basis must be drawn up in the official language or one of the official languages of the Member State in which the purchaser is resident or in the official language or one of the official languages of the Member State of which he is a national which must be one of the official languages of the Community; whereas, however, the Member State in which the purchaser is resident may require that the contract be drawn up in its language or its languages which must be an official language or official languages of the Community; whereas provision should be made for a certified translation of each contract for the purposes of the formalities to be completed in the Member State in which the relevant property is situated;

11. Whereas to give the purchaser the chance to realize more fully what his obligations and rights under the contract are he should be allowed a period during which he may withdraw from the contract without giving reasons since the property in question is often situated in a State and subject to legislation which are different from his own;

12. Whereas the requirement on the vendor's part that advance payments be made before the end of the period during which the purchaser may withdraw without giving reasons may reduce the purchaser's protection; whereas, therefore, advance payments before the end of that period should be prohibited; **A8.4**

13. Whereas in the event of cancellation of or withdrawal from a contract for the purchase of the right to use one or more immovable properties on a time share basis the price of which is entirely or partly covered by credit granted to the purchaser by the vendor or by a third party on the basis of an agreement concluded between that third party and the vendor, it should be provided that the credit agreement should be cancelled without penalty;

14. Whereas there is a risk, in certain cases, that the consumer may be deprived of the protection provided for in this Directive if the law of a non-Member State is specified as the law applicable to the contract; whereas this Directive should therefore include provisions intended to obviate that risk;

15. Whereas it is for the Member States

to adopt measures to ensure that the vendor fulfils his obligations,

HAVE ADOPTED THIS DIRECTIVE:

A8.5

Article 1

The purpose of this Directive shall be to approximate the laws, regulations and administrative provisions of the Member States on the protection of purchasers in respect of certain aspects of contracts relating directly or indirectly to the purchase of the right to use one or more immovable properties on a time share basis.

This Directive shall cover only those aspects of the above provisions concerning contractual transactions that relate to:

information on the constituent parts of a contract and the arrangements for the communication of that information,

the procedures and arrangements for cancellation and withdrawal.

With due regard to the general rules of the Treaty, the Member States shall remain competent for other matters, *inter alia* determination of the legal nature of the rights which are the subject of the contracts covered by this Directive.

A8.6

Article 2

For the purposes of this Directive:

'contract relating directly or indirectly to the purchase of the right to use one or more immovable properties on a timeshare basis', hereinafter referred to as 'contract', shall mean any contract or group of contracts concluded for at least three years under which, directly or indirectly, on payment of a certain global price, a real property right or any other right relating to the use of one or more immovable properties for a specified or specifiable period of the year, which may not be less than one week, is established or is the subject of a transfer or an undertaking to transfer,

"immovable property" shall mean any building or part of a building for use as

accommodation to which the right which is the subject of the contract relates,

'vendor' shall mean any natural or legal person who, acting in transactions covered by this Directive and in his professional capacity, establishes, transfers or undertakes to transfer the right which is the subject of the contract,

'purchaser' shall mean any natural person who, acting in transactions covered by this Directive, for purposes which may be regarded as being outwith his professional capacity, has the right which is the subject of the contract transferred to him or for whom the right which is the subject of the contract is established.

Article 3
A8.7

1. The Member States shall make provision in their legislation for measures to ensure that the vendor is required to provide any person requesting information on the immovable property or properties with a document which, in addition to a general description of the property or properties, shall provide at least brief and accurate information on the particulars referred to in points (a) to (g), (i) and (l) of the Annex and on how further information may be obtained.

2 The Member States shall make provision in their legislation to ensure that all the information referred to in paragraph 1 which must be provided in the document referred to in paragraph 1 forms an integral part of the contract.

Unless the parties expressly agree otherwise, only changes resulting from circumstances beyond the vendor's control may be made to the information provided in the document referred to in paragraph 1.

Any changes to that information shall be communicated to the purchaser before the contract is concluded. The contract shall expressly mention any such changes.

3. Any advertising referring to the immovable property concerned shall

644

indicate the possibility of obtaining the document referred to in paragraph 1 and where it may be obtained.

A8.8

Article 4

The Member States shall make provision in their legislation to ensure that:

the contract, which shall be in writing, includes at least the items referred to in the Annex,

the contract and the document referred to in Article 3 (1) are drawn up in the language or one of the languages of Member State in which the purchaser is resident or in the language or one of the languages of the Member State of which he is national which shall be an official language or official languages of the Community, at the purchaser's option. The Member State in which the purchaser is resident may, however, require that the contract be drawn up in all cases in at least its language or languages which must be an official language or official languages of the Community, and

the vendor provides the purchaser with a certified translation of the contract in the language or one of the languages of the Member State in which the immovable property is situated which shall be an official language or official languages of the Community.

A8.9

Article 5

The Member States shall make provision in their legislation to ensure that:

1. in addition to the possibilities available to the purchaser under national laws on the nullity of contracts, the purchaser shall have the right:

to withdraw without giving any reason within ten calendar days of both parties' signing the contract or of both parties' signing a binding preliminary contract. If the tenth day is a public holiday, the period shall be extended to the first working day thereafter,

if the contract does not include the information referred to in points (a), (b), (c), (d)(1), (d)(2), (h), (i), (k), (l) and (m) of the Annex, at the time of both parties' signing the contract or of both parties' signing a binding preliminary contract, to cancel the contract within three months thereof. If the information in question is provided within those three months, the purchaser's withdrawal period provided for in the first indent, shall then start,

if by the end of the three-month period provided for in the second indent the purchaser has not exercised the right to cancel and the contract does not include the information referred to in points (a), (b), (c), (d)(1), (d)(2), (h), (i), (k), (l) and (m) of the Annex, to the withdrawal period provided for in the first indent from the day after the end of that three-month period;

2. if the purchaser intends to exercise the rights provided for in paragraph 1 he shall, before the expiry of the relevant deadline, notify the person whose name and address appear in the contract for the purpose by a means which can be proved in accordance with national law in accordance with the procedures specified in the contract pursuant to point (l) of the Annex. The deadline shall be deemed to have been observed if the notification, if it is in writing, is dispatched before the deadline expires;

A8.10

3. where the purchaser exercises the right provided for in the first indent of paragraph 1, he may be required to defray, where appropriate, only those expenses which, in accordance with national law, are incurred as a result of the conclusion of and withdrawal from the contract and which correspond to legal formalities which must be completed before the end of the period referred to in the first indent of paragraph 1. Such expenses shall be expressly mentioned in the contract;

4. where the purchaser exercises the right of cancellation provided for in the second indent of paragraph 1 he shall not be required to make any defrayal.

A8.11

Article 6

The Member States shall make provision in their legislation to prohibit any advance payments by a purchaser before the end of the period during which he may exercise the right of withdrawal.

A8.12

Article 7

The Member States shall make provision in their legislation to ensure that:

if the price is fully or partly covered by credit granted by the vendor, or

if the price is fully or partly covered by credit granted to the purchaser by a third party on the basis of an agreement between the third party and the vendor,

the credit agreement shall be cancelled, without any penalty, if the purchaser exercises his right to cancel or withdraw from the contract as provided for in Article 5.

The Member States shall lay down detailed arrangements to govern the cancellation of credit agreements.

A8.13

Article 8

The Member States shall make provision in their legislation to ensure that any clause whereby a purchaser renounces the enjoyment of rights under this Directive or whereby a vendor is freed from the responsibilities arising from this Directive shall not be binding on the purchaser, under conditions laid down by national law.

A8.14

Article 9

The Member States shall take the measures necessary to ensure that, whatever the law applicable may be, the purchaser is not deprived of the protection afforded by this Directive, if the immovable property concerned is situated within the territory of a Member State.

Article 10 **A8.15**

The Member States shall make provision in their legislation for the consequences of non-compliance with this Directive.

Article 11 **A8.16**

This Directive shall not prevent Member States from adopting or maintaining provisions which are more favourable as regards the protection of purchasers in the field in question, without prejudice to their obligations under the Treaty.

Article 12 **A8.17**

1. Member States shall bring into force the laws, regulations and administrative provisions necessary for them to comply with this Directive no later than 30 months after its publication in the *Official Journal of the European Communities*. They shall immediately inform the Commission thereof.

When Member States adopt those measures, they shall include references to this Directive or shall accompany them with such references on their official publication. The Member States shall lay down the manner in which such references shall be made.

2. The Member States shall communicate to the Commission the texts of the provisions of national law which they adopt in the field governed by this Directive.

Article 13 **A8.18**

This Directive is addressed to the Member States.

Done at Strasbourg, 26 October 1994.

For the European Parliament,
The President
K HÄNSCH

For the Council
The President
J EEKHOFF

ANNEX

A8.19 **Minimum list of items to be included in the contract referred to in Article 4**

(a) The identities and domiciles of the parties, including specific information on the vendor's legal status at the time of the conclusion of the contract and the identity and domicile of the owner.

(b) The exact nature of the right which is the subject of the contract and a clause setting out the conditions governing the exercise of that right within the territory of the Member State(s) in which the property or properties concerned relates is or are situated and if those conditions have been fulfilled or, if they have not, what conditions remain to be fulfilled.

(c) When the property has been determined, an accurate description of that property and its location.

(d) Where the immovable property is under construction:

(1) the state of completion;

(2) a reasonable estimate of the deadline for completion of the immovable property;

(3) where it concerns a specific immovable property, the number of the building permit and the name(s) and full address(es) of the competent authority or authorities;

(4) the state of completion of the services rendering the immovable property fully operational (gas, electricity, water and telephone connections);

(5) a guarantee regarding completion of the immovable property or a guarantee regarding reimbursement of any payment made if the property is not completed and, where appropriate, the conditions

governing the operation of those guarantees.

(e) The services (lighting, water, maintenance, refuse collection) to which the purchaser has or will have access and on what conditions. **A8.20**

(f) The common facilities, such as swimming pool, sauna, etc, to which the purchaser has or may have access, and, where appropriate, on what conditions.

(g) The principles on the basis of which the maintenance of and repairs to the immovable property and its administration and management will be arranged.

(h) The exact period within which the right which is the subject of the contract may be exercised and, if necessary, its duration; the date on which the purchaser may start to exercise the contractual right.

(i) The price to be paid by the purchaser to exercise the contractual right; an estimate of the amount to be paid by the purchaser for the use of common facilities and services; the basis for the calculation of the amount of charges relating to occupation of the property, the mandatory statutory charges (for example, taxes and fees) and the administrative overheads (for example, management, maintenance and repairs).

(j) A clause stating that acquisition will not result in costs, charges or obligations other than those specified in the contract.

(k) Whether or not is is possible to join a scheme for the exchange or resale of the contractual rights, and any costs involved should an exchange and/or resale scheme be organised by the vendor or by a third party designated by him in the contract.

A8.21 (l) Information on the right to cancel or withdraw from the contract and indication of the person to whom any letter of cancellation or withdrawal should be sent, specifying also the arrangements under which such letters may be sent; precise indication of the nature and amount of the costs which the purchaser will be required to defray pursuant to Article 5(3) if he exercises his right to withdraw; where appropriate, information on the arrangements for the cancellation of the credit agreement linked to the contract in the event of cancellation of the contract or withdrawal from it.

(m) The date and place of each party's signing of the contract.

Council Regulation (EC) No 1683/95

of 29 May 1995

laying down a uniform format for visas

THE COUNCIL OF THE EUROPEAN UNION,

A9.1 Having regard to the Treaty establishing the European Community, in particular Article 100c (3) thereof,

Having regard to the proposal from the Commission,

Having regard to the opinion of the European Parliament,

Whereas Article 100c (3) of the Treaty requires the Council to adopt measures relating to a uniform format for visas before 1 January 1996;

Whereas the introduction of a uniform format for visas is an important step towards the harmonization of visa policy; whereas Article 7a of the Treaty stipulates that the internal market shall comprise an area without internal frontiers in which the free movement of persons is ensured in accordance with the provisions of the Treaty; whereas this step is also to be regarded as forming a coherent whole with measures falling within Title VI of the Treaty on European Union;

Whereas it is essential that the uniform format for visas should contain all the necessary information and meet very high technical standards, notably as regards safeguards against counterfeiting and falsification; whereas it must also be suited to use by all the Member States and bear universally recognizable security features which are clearly visible to the naked eye;

Whereas this Regulation only lays down such specifications as are not secret; whereas these specifications need to be supplemented by further specifications which must remain secret in order to prevent counterfeiting and falsification and which may not include personal data or references to such data; whereas powers to adopt further specifications should be conferred on the Commission;

Whereas, to ensure that the information referred to is not made available to more persons than necessary, it is also essential that each Member State should designate not more than one body having responsibility for printing the uniform format for visas, with Member States remaining free to change the body, if need be; whereas, for security reasons, each Member State must communicate the name of the competent body to the Commission and the other Member States;

Whereas, to be effective, this Regulation should apply to all visas covered by Article 5; whereas Member States should be free also to use the uniform visa format for visas which can be used for purposes other than those covered by Article 5 provided differences visible to the naked eye are incorporated to make confusion with the uniform visa impossible;

Whereas, with regard to the personal data to be entered on the uniform format for visas in accordance with the Annex hereto, compliance should be ensured with Member States' data-protection provisions as well as with the relevant Community legislation,

HAS ADOPTED THIS REGULATION:

Article 1

Visas issued by the Member States in conformity with Article 5 shall be produced in the form of a uniform format (sticker). They shall conform to the specifications set out in the Annex.

A9.2

Article 2

A9.3 Further technical specifications which render the visa difficult to counterfeit or falsify shall be laid down in accordance with the procedure set out in Article 6.

Article 3

A9.4 1. The specifications referred to in Article 2 shall be secret and not be published. They shall be made available only to bodies designated by the Member States as responsible for printing and to persons duly authorized by a Member State or the Commission.

2. Each Member State shall designate one body having responsibility for printing visas. It shall communicate the name of that body to the Commission and the other Member States. The same body may be designated by two or more Member States for this purpose. Each Member State shall be entitled to change its designated body. It shall inform the Commission and the other Member States accordingly.

Article 4

A9.5 1. Without prejudice to the relevant more extensive provisions concerning data protection, an individual to whom a visa is issued shall have the right to verify the personal particulars entered on the visa and, where appropriate, to ask for any corrections or deletions to be made.

2. No information in machine-readable form shall be given on the uniform format for visas unless it also appears in the boxes described in points 6 to 12 of the Annex, or unless it is mentioned in the relevant travel document.

Article 5

A9.6 For the purposes of this Regulation a 'via' shall mean an authorization given by or a decision taken by a Member State which is required for entry into its territory with a view to:

– an ·intended stay in that Member State or in several Member States of no more than three months in all,
– transit through the territory or airport transit zone of that Member State or several Member States.

Article 6

1. Where reference is made to the procedure defined in this Article, the following provisions shall apply. **A9.7**

2. The Commission shall be assisted by a committee composed of the representatives of the Member States and chaired by the representative of the Commission.

The representative of the Commission shall submit to the committee a draft of the measures to be taken. The committee shall deliver its opinion on the draft within a time limit which the chairman may lay down according to the urgency of the matter. The opinion shall be delivered by the majority laid down in Article 148 (2) of the Treaty in the case of decisions which the Council is required to adopt on a proposal from the Commission. The votes of the representatives of the Member States within the committee shall be weighted in the manner set out in that Article. The chairman shall not vote.

3. (a) The Commission shall adopt the measures envisaged if they are in accordance with the opinion of the committee.
   (b) If the measures envisaged are not in accordance with the opinion of the committee, or if no opinion is delivered, the Commission shall, without delay, submit to the Council a proposal relating to the measures to be taken. The Council shall act by a qualified majority.

If, on the expiry of a period of two months, the Council has not acted, the proposed measures shall be adopted by the Commission, save where the Council has decided against the said measures by a simple majority.

Article 7

A9.8 Where Member States use the uniform visa format for purposes other than those covered by Article 5, appropriate measures must be taken to ensure that confusion with the visa referred to in Article 5 is not possible.

Article 8

A9.9 This Regulation shall enter into force on the twentieth day following that of its publication in the *Official Journal of* the European Communities.

Article I shall become applicable six months after the adoption of the measures referred to in Article 2.

This Regulation shall be binding in its entirety and directly applicable in all Member States.

Done at Brussels, 29 May 1995.

For the Council
The President
H. de CHARETTE

ANNEX
Security features

A specimen visa is provided here in the Official Journal.

1. A sign consisting of nine ellipses in a fan-shape shall appear in this space.[1]

2. An optically variable mark ('kinegram' or equivalent) shall appear in this space. Depending on the angle of view, 12 stars, the letter 'E' and a globe become visible in various sizes and colours.

3. The logo consisting of a letter or letters indicating the issuing Member State (or 'BNL' in the case of the Benelux countries, namely Belgium, Luxembourg and the Netherlands) with a latent image effect shall appear in this space. This logo shall appear light when held flat and dark when turned by 90°. The following logos shall be used: A for Austria, BNL for Benelux, D for Germany, DK for Denmark, E for Spain, F for France, FIN for Finland, GR for Greece, I for Italy, IRL for Ireland, P for Portugal, S for Sweden, UK for the United Kingdom.

4. The word 'visa' in capital letters shall appear in the middle of this space in optically variable colouring. Depending on the angle of view, it shall appear green or red.

5. This box shall contain the number of the visa, which shall be pre-printed and shall begin with the letter or letters indicating the issuing country as described in point 3 above. A special type shall be used.

Sections to be completed

6. This box shall begin with the words 'valid for'. The issuing authority shall indicate the territory or territories for which the visa is valid.

7. This box shall begin with the word 'from' and the word 'until' shall appear further along the line. The issuing authority shall indicate here the period of validity of the visa.

---

[1] References to "this space" refer to the specimen printed in the Official Journal.

8.   This box shall begin with the words 'number of entries' and further along the line the words 'duration of stay' (i.e. duration of applicants' intended stay) and again 'days' shall appear.

9.   This box shall begin with the words 'issued in' and shall be used to indicate the place of issue.

10.   This box shall begin with the word 'on' (after which the date of issue shall be filled in by the issuing authority) and further along the line the words 'number of passport' shall appear (after which the holder's passport number shall appear).

11.   This box shall begin with the words 'type of visa'. The issuing authority shall indicate the category of visa in conformity with Articles 5 and 7 of this Regulation.

12.   This box shall begin with the word 'remarks'. It shall be used by the issuing authority to indicate any further information which is considered necessary, provided that it complies with Article 4 of this Regulation. The following two and a half lines shall be left empty for such remarks.

13.   This box shall contain the relevant machine-readable information to facilitate external border controls.

The paper shall be pastel green with red and blue markings.

The words designating the boxes shall appear in English and French. The issuing State may add a third official Community language. However, the word 'visa' in the top line may appear in any one official language of the Community.

Common Position (EC) No 19/95

adopted by the Council on 29 June 1995

with a view to adopting Directive 95/.../EC of the European Parliament and of the Council of . . . on the protection of consumers in respect of distance contracts

THE EUROPEAN PARLIAMENT AND THE COUNCIL OF THE EUROPEAN UNION,

A10.1 Having regard to the Treaty establishing the European Community, and in particular Article 100a thereof,

Having regard to the proposal from the Commission[1],

Having regard to the opinion of the Economic and Social Committee[2],

Acting in accordance with the procedure laid down in Article 189b of the Treaty[3],

1. Whereas, in connection with the attainment of the aims of the internal market, measures must be taken for the gradual consolidation of that market;

2. Whereas the free movement of goods and services affects not only the business sector but also private individuals; whereas it means that consumers should be able to have access to the goods and services of a Member State on the same terms as the population of that State;

3. Whereas cross-border distance selling could be one of the main tangible results of the completion of the internal market for consumers, as noted *inter alia* in the Commission communication to the Council entitled 'Towards a single market in distribution'; whereas it is indispensable for the proper functioning of the internal market that consumers should be able to apply to a business outside their country, even if it has a subsidiary in the consumer's country of residence;

4. Whereas the introduction of new technologies is multiplying the means available to consumers to have knowledge of the offers being made everywhere in the Community and to place orders; whereas some Member States have already taken different or diverging measures to protect consumers in respect of distance selling, with negative repercussions for competition between business in the single market; whereas it is therefore necessary to introduce a minimum set of common rules at Community level in this field;

5. Whereas paragraphs 18 and 19 of **A10.2** the Annex to the Council resolution of 14 April 1975 on a preliminary programme of the European Economic Community for a consumer protection and information policy[4] point to the need to protect the purchasers of goods or services against demands for payment for unsolicited goods and against high-pressure selling methods;

6. Whereas paragraph 33 of the Commission communication to the Council entitled 'A new impetus for consumer protection policy', approved by the Council resolution of 23 June 1986[5], states that the Commission will present proposals

---

[1] OJ No C 156, 23. 6. 1992, p. 14.
[2] OJ No C 19, 25. 1. 1993, p. 111.
[3] Opinion of the European Parliament of 26 May 1993 (OJ No C 176, 26. 6. 1993, p. 95), Council common position of . . . (not yet published in the Official Journal) and Decision of the European Parliament of . . . (not yet published in the Official Journal).

[4] OJ No C 92, 25. 4. 1975, p. 1.
[5] OJ No C 167, 5. 7. 1986, p. 1.

regarding the use of new information technologies enabling consumers to place orders with suppliers from their homes;

7. Whereas the Council resolution of 9 November 1989 on future priorities for relaunching consumer protection policy[1] calls upon the Commission to give priority to the areas referred to in the Annex to that resolution; whereas that Annex refers to new technologies involving teleshopping; whereas the Commission has responded to that resolution by adopting a three-year action plan for consumer protection policy in the European Economic Community (1990) to 1992); whereas that plan provides for the adoption of a Directive;

8. Whereas the languages used for distance contracts are a matter for the Member States;

A10.3 9. Whereas contracts negotiated at a distance involve the use of one or more means of communication at a distance; whereas the various means of communication are used as part of an organized distance sales or service-provision scheme not involving the simultaneous presence of the supplier and the consumer; whereas the ongoing evolution of those means of communication does not allow an exhaustive list to be compiled but requires the definition of principles valid even for those that are still little used;

10. Whereas the use of such means of communication must not lead to a reduction in the information provided to the consumer; whereas it is therefore necessary to determine the information that is required to be sent to the consumer whatever the means of communication used; whereas the information supplied must also comply with the other relevant Community rules, in particular those in Council Directive 84/450/EEC of 10 September 1984 relating to the approximation of the laws, regulations and administrative provisions of the Member States concerning misleading advertising[2];

11. Whereas information disseminated by certain electronic technologies often has an ephemeral character in so far as it is not received on a permanent medium; whereas the consumer must therefore receive written notice in good time of the information necessary for proper performance of the contract;

12. Whereas the consumer is not able in concrete terms to see the product or ascertain the service provided before concluding the contract; whereas provision should be made, where it is appropriate, for a right to withdraw from the contract; whereas it is for the Member States to determine the other conditions and arrangements following exercise of the right of withdrawal;

13. Whereas it is also necessary to prescribe a time limit for performance if this is not specified at the time of ordering;

14. Whereas the promotional technique involving the sending of a product or the provision of a service to the consumer in return for payment without a prior request from or the explicit agreement of the consumer cannot be permitted – unless what it involved is a replacement;

15. Whereas the principles set out in Articles 8 and 10 of the European Convention for the Protection of Human Rights and Fundamental Freedoms of 4 November 1950 apply; whereas the consumer's right to privacy, particularly as regards freedom from intrusion by certain particularly intrusive means

---

[1] OJ No C 294, 22. 11. 1989, p. 1.

[2] OJ No L 250, 19. 9. 1984, p. 17.

of communication should be recognized; whereas specific limits on the use of such means should therefore be stipulated;

16. Whereas Commission recommendation 92/295/EEC of 7 April 1992 on codes of practice for the protection of consumers in respect of contracts negotiated at a distance[1] stipulates that it is desirable that the minimum binding rules contained in this Directive should be supplemented by voluntary self-regulatory arrangements in the form of codes of practice;

A10.4

17. Whereas non-compliance with this Directive may harm not only consumers but also competitors; whereas provisions may therefore be laid down permitting public bodies, or their representatives, or consumer organizations which, under national legislation, have a legitimate interest in consumer protection, or professional organizations which have a legitimate interest in taking action, to monitor its application;

18. Whereas in the use of new technologies the consumer is not in control of the means of communication used; whereas it is therefore necessary to provide that the burden of proof may be on the supplier;

19. Whereas there is a risk that, in certain cases, the consumer may be deprived of protection under this Directive through designation of the law of a non-member country as the law applicable to the contract; whereas provisions should therefore be included in this Directive to avert that risk;

20. Whereas a Member State may ban, in the general interest, the marketing on its territory of certain goods and services through distance contracts; whereas that ban must

comply with Community rules; whereas there is already provision for such bans, notably with regard to medicinal products, under Council Directive 89/552/EEC of 3 October 1989 on the coordination of certain provisions laid down by law, regulation or administrative action in Member States concerning the pursuit of television broadcasting activities[2] and Council Directive 92/28/EEC of 31 March 1992 on the advertising of medicinal products for human use[3],

HAVE ADOPTED THIS DIRECTIVE:

Article 1
Object

The object of this Directive is to approximate the laws, regulations and administrative provisions of the Member States concerning distance contracts between consumers and suppliers.

A10.5

Article 2
Definitions

For the purposes of this Directive:

1. 'distance contract' means any contract concerning goods or services concluded between a supplier and a consumer as a consequence of an organized distance sales or service-provision scheme of the supplier, using, for this contract, exclusively one or more means of communication at a distance up to the conclusion of the contract and including the conclusion on the contract itself;

A10.6

2. 'consumer' means any natural person who, in contracts covered by this Directive, is acting for purposes which are outside his trade, business or profession;

3. 'supplier' means any natural or legal person who, in contracts

[1] OJ No L 156, 10. 6. 1992, p. 21.

[2] OJ No L 298, 17. 10. 1989, p. 23.
[3] OJ No L 113, 30. 4. 1992, p. 13.

covered by this Directive, is acting in his commercial or professional capacity;

4. 'means of communication at a distance' means any means which, without the simultaneous physical presence of the supplier and the consumer, may be used for the purposes of the conclusion of a contract between those parties. An indicative list of the means covered by this Directive is contained in Annex I;

5. 'operator of a means of communication' means any public or private natural or legal person whose trade, business or profession involves making one or more means of communication at a distance available to suppliers.

Article 3
Exemptions

A10.7 1. This Directive shall not apply to contracts:

– relating to financial services, a non-exhaustive list of which is given in Annex II,

– concluded by means of automatic vending machines or automated commercial premises,

– concluded with telecommunications operators through the use of public pay-phones;

– concluded for the construction and sale of immovable property or relating to other immovable property rights, except for rental,

– concluded at an auction.

2. Articles 4, 5, 6 and Article 7 (1) and (2) shall not apply:

– to contracts for the supply of foodstuffs, beverages or other goods intended for current consumption supplied to the home of the consumer, to his residence or to his workplace by regular roundsmen,

– contracts for the provision of services with respect to accommoda-

tion, transport, catering or leisure, where the supplier undertakes, when the contract is concluded, to provide these services at a specific date or within a specific period.

Article 4
Prior information

1. In good time prior to the conclusion of any distance contract, the consumer shall be provided with the following information: **A10.8**

(a) the identity of the supplier;

(b) the main characteristics of the goods or services;

(c) the price of the goods or services including all taxes;

(d) delivery costs, where appropriate;

(e) the arrangements for payment, delivery or performance;

(f) the existence of a right of withdrawal, except in the cases referred to in Article 6 (3);

(g) the cost of using the means of communication at a distance, where it is calculated at other than the basic rate;

(h) the period for which the offer or the price remains valid.

2. The information referred to in paragraph 1, the commercial purpose of which must be made clear, shall be provided in a clear and comprehensible manner in any way appropriate to the means of communication at a distance used, with due regard, in particular, to the principles of good faith in commercial transactions and those governing the protection of minors.

Article 5
Written confirmation of information

1. The consumer must receive written confirmation of the information referred to in Article 4 (1) (a) to (f), in   **A10.9**

good time during the performance of the contract and at the latest at the time of delivery, where goods are concerned, unless the information has already been given to the consumer prior to conclusion of the contract in writing or on another durable medium available to him.

In any event the following must be provided:

– written information on the conditions and procedures for exercising the right of withdrawal, within the meaning of Article 6, including the cases referred to in the first indent of Article 6 (3),

– the geographical address of the place of business of the supplier to which the consumer may address any complaints,

– information on after-sales services and guarantees which exist,

– the conditions for cancelling the contract, where it is of unspecified duration or a duration longer than one year.

2. Paragraph 1 shall not apply to services the performance of which is effected by the use of a means of communication at a distance, when they are supplied on only one occasion and are invoiced by the operator of the means of communication at a distance. Nevertheless, the consumer must in all cases be able to obtain the geographical address of the place of business of the supplier to which he may address any complaints.

Article 6
Right of withdrawal

A10.10 1. For any distance contract the consumer shall have a period of not less than seven days in which he may withdraw from the contract without penalty, without giving any reason.

The period for exercise of this right shall begin:

– for goods, from the day of receipt by the consumer where the obligations laid down in Article 5 have been fulfilled,

– for services, from the day of conclusion of the contract or from the day on which the obligations laid down in Article 5 were fulfilled if they are fulfilled after conclusion of the contract, on condition that this period does not exceed the three-month period referred to in the following subparagraph.

If the supplier has failed to fulfil the obligations laid down in Article 5, the period shall be three months. The period shall begin:

– for goods, from the day of receipt by the consumer,

– for services, from the day of conclusion of the contract.

If the information referred to in Article 5 is supplied within this three-month period, the consumer shall from that moment have available the seven-day period referred to in the first paragraph.

2. Where the right of withdrawal has been exercised by the consumer pursuant to this Article, the supplier shall be obliged to reimburse the sums paid by the consumer. Such reimbursement must be carried out as soon as possible.

3. Unless the parties have agreed otherwise, the consumer may not exercise the right of withdrawal provided for in paragraph 1 in respect of contracts:

– for the provision of services, if performance has begun, with the consumer's agreement, before the end of the seven-day period referred to in paragraph 1,

– for the supply of goods or services the price of which is dependent on fluctuations in the financial market which cannot be controlled by the supplier,

– for the supply of goods made to measure to the consumer's specifications or clearly personalized or which, by reason of their nature, cannot be returned, or are liable to deteriorate or expire rapidly,

– for the supply of audio or video recordings, records or computer software,

– for the supply of newspapers, periodicals and magazines,

– for gaming and lottery services.

4. The Member States shall make provision in their legislation to ensure that:

– if the price of goods or services is fully or partly covered by credit granted by the supplier,

or

– if that price is fully or partly covered by credit granted to the consumer by a third party on the basis of an agreement between the third party and the supplier,

the credit agreement shall be cancelled, without any penalty, if the consumer exercises his right to withdraw from the contract in accordance with paragraph 1.

Member States shall determine the detailed rules for cancellation of the credit agreement.

Article 7
Performance

A10.11 1. Unless the parties have agreed otherwise, the supplier must execute the order within a maximum of 30 days from the day following that on which the consumer forwarded his order to the supplier.

2. Where a supplier fails to perform his side of the contract on the grounds that the goods or services ordered are unavailable, the consumer must be informed of this situation and must be able to obtain a refund of any sums he has paid as soon as possible.

3. Nevertheless Member States may lay down that the supplier may provide the consumer with goods or services of equivalent quality and price provided this possibility was provided for prior to conclusion of the contract or when the contract was concluded or when the consumer was informed of the unavailability of his order. The cost of returning the goods following exercise of the right of withdrawal is, in this case, the liability of the supplier, and the consumer must be informed of this. In such cases the supply of goods or services may not be deemed to constitute inertia selling within the meaning of Article 9.

Article 8
Payment by card

Member States shall ensure that appropriate measures exist to allow a consumer: **A10.12**

– to request cancellation of a payment where fraudulent use has been made of his payment card within the context of distance contracts covered by this Directive,

– in the event of fraudulent use, to be recredited with the sums paid or have them returned.

Article 9
Inertia selling

Member States shall take the measures necessary to: **A10.13**

– prohibit the supply of goods or services to a consumer without being ordered by the consumer beforehand, where such supply involves a demand for payment,

– exempt the consumer from the performance of any consideration in cases of unsolicited supply, the absence of a response not constituting consent.

Article 10
Restrictions on the use of certain means of communication at a distance

A10.14 1. Use by a supplier of the following means requires the prior consent of the consumer:

– automated calling system without human intervention (automatic calling machine),

– facsimile machine (fax).

2. Member States shall ensure that means of communication at a distance, other than those referred to in paragraph 1, which allow individual communications may be used only where there is no clear objection from the consumer.

Article 11
Judicial or administrative redress

A10.15 1. Member States shall ensure that adequate and effective means exist to enforce compliance with this Directive in the interests of consumers.

2. The means referred to in paragraph 1 may include provisions whereby public bodies or their representatives or consumer organizations having a legitimate interest under national law in protecting consumers or professional organizations having a legitimate interest may take action under national law before the courts or before the competent administrative bodies to ensure that the provisions of this Directive are applied.

3. (a) Member States may stipulate that the burden of proof concerning the existence of prior information, written confirmation or compliance with time-limits or the consumer's consent can be placed on the supplier.

(b) Member States shall take the measures necessary to ensure that suppliers and operators of

means of communication, when they are able to do so, cease practices which do not comply with measures adopted pursuant to this Directive.

4. Member States may provide that voluntary supervision of compliance with the provisions of this Directive entrusted to self-regulatory bodies and recourse to such bodies to settle disputes are added to the means which Member States must provide to ensure compliance with the provisions of this Directive.

Article 12
Binding nature

1. The consumer may not waive the rights conferred on him by the transposition of this Directive into national law.   **A10.16**

2. The Member States shall take the measures necessary to ensure that the consumer does not lose the protection granted by this Directive by virtue of the choice of the law of a non-member country as the law applicable to the contract if the latter has a close connection with the territory of one or more Member States.

Article 13
Community rules

1. The provisions of this Directive shall apply in so far as there are no particular provisions in rules of Community law governing certain types of distance contracts in their entirety.   **A11.17**

2. Where specific Community rules on goods or services contain provisions governing aspects connected with:

– information prior to conclusion of the contract,

– written confirmation of the prior information,

– right of withdrawal,

– inertia selling,

– judicial or administrative redress,

659

– restrictions on the use of means of communication at a distance,

– payment by card,

– performance of the contract,

such provisions shall apply solely to distance contracts in respect of the aspects covered.

Article 14
Minimal clause

A10.18 Members States may introduce or maintain, in the area covered by this Directive, more stringent provisions compatible with the Treaty, to ensure a higher level of consumer protection. Such provisions shall, where appropriate, include the prohibition, in the general interest, of the marketing of certain goods or services, particularly medicinal products, in their territory by means of distance contracts, with due regard for the Treaty.

Article 15
Implementation

A10.19 1. Member States shall bring into force the laws, regulations and administrative provisions necessary to comply with this Directive no later than three years after it enters into force. They shall forthwith inform the Commission thereof.

2. When Member States adopt the measures referred to in paragraph 1, they shall contain a reference to this Directive or shall be accompanied by such reference on the occasion of their official publication. The procedure for such reference shall be laid down by Member States.

3. Member States shall communicate to the Commission the text of the provisions of national law which they adopt in the field governed by this Directive.

4. No later than six years after the entry into force of this Directive the Commission shall submit a report to the European Parliament and to the Council on the implementation of this Directive, accompanied if appropriate by a proposal for the revision of this Directive.

Article 16

This Directive shall enter into force on the day of its publication in the *Official Journal of the European Communities.* **A10.20**

Article 17

This Directive is addressed to the Member States. **A10.21**

Done at . . .

For the European *Parliament*	*For the Council*
The President	*The President*

ANNEX I

Means of communication covered by Article 2, point 4 **A10.22**

– Unaddressed printed matter

– Addressed printed matter

– Standard letter

– Press advertising with order form

– Catalogue

– Telephone with human intervention

– Telephone without human intervention (automatic calling machine, audiotext)

- Radio

- Videophone (telephone with screen)

- Videortex (microcomputer and television screen) with keyboard or touch screen

- Electronic mail

- Facsimile machine (fax)

- Television (teleshopping)

ANNEX II

Financial services within the meaning of Article 3 (1)   **A10.23**

- Investment services

- Insurance and reinsurance operations

- Banking services

- Operations relating to pension funds

- Services relating to dealings in futures or options

Such services include in particular:

- investment services referred to in the Annex to Directive 93/22/EEC[1]; services of collective investment undertakings,

- services covered by the activities subject to mutual recognition referred to in the Annex to Directive 89/646/EEC[2],

- operations covered by the insurance activities referred to in:

- Article 1 of Directive 73/239/EEC[3],

- the Annex to Directive 79/267/EEC[4],

- Directive 64/225/EEC[5],

- Directives 92/49/EEC[6] and 92/96/EEC[7].

---

[1] OJ No L 141, 11. 6. 1993, p. 27.
[2] OJ No L 386, 30. 12. 1989, p. 1. Directive as amended by Directive 92/30/EEC (OJ No L 110, 28. 4. 1992, p. 52).
[3] OJ No L 228, 16. 8. 1973, p. 3. Directive as last amended by Directive 92/49/EEC (OJ No L 228, 11. 8. 1992, p. 1).
[4] OJ No L 63, 13. 3. 1979, p. 1. Directive as last amended by Directive 90/619/EEC (OJ No L 330, 29. 11. 1990, p. 50).
[5] OJ No L 56, 4. 4. 1964, p. 878. Directive as amended by the 1973 Act of Accession.
[6] OJ No L 228, 11. 8. 1992, p. 1.
[7] OJ No L 360, 9. 12. 1992, p. 1.

STATEMENT OF THE COUNCIL'S REASONS

I. INTRODUCTION

A10.24 1. On 21 May 1992 the Commission submitted a proposal[1] for a Directive, based on Article 100a of the Treaty, on the protection of consumers in respect of distance contracts.

2. The European Parliament delivered its first-reading opinion[2] on 26 May 1993. Further to that opinion, the Commission submitted an amended proposal[3] on 7 October 1993.

The Economic and Social Committee delivered its opinion[4] on 24 November 1993.

3. The Council unanimously adopted its common position, in accordance with Article 189b of the Treaty, on 29 June 1995.

II. OBJECTIVE

A10.25 4. The purpose of the Commission proposal is to provide greater protection for consumers as regards distance contracts, particularly through better prior information on the features of the contract, through the introduction of a right of withdrawal and of means of judicial or administrative redress and through provisions governing performance of the contract. In this way the proposal contributes to the establishment of the internal market in this field.

III. ANALYSIS OF THE COMMON POSITION

General comments

A10.26 5. With a view to the objective outlined above and in the light of the swiftly developing technology and markets addressed by this proposal, the Council set out to ensure a high level of consumer protection by means of a set of provisions that in some cases establish stronger safeguards than those envisaged by the Commission or the European Parliament and that are as precise and easy to implement as possible. The Council accordingly endeavoured to allow the principle of subsidiarity to operate to the extent compatible with the requisite harmonization in this sector and bearing in mind that Member States may adopt more stringent provisions. This desire for workable arrangements prompted the Council to drop the approach based on contract solicitation, which upon scrutiny proved unsuited to the specific manner in which distance contracts are established.

6. On the basis of the above guidelines the Council was able to incorporate into its common position word for word, in substance or in part those European Parliament amendments included by the Commission in its amended proposal – except for amendments 10, 13, 15, 20, 29 (and 6 concerning the related recital) and 32 (and 9 concerning the related recital) – as well as amendment 30, which was not taken up in the amended proposal.

---

[1] OJ No C 156, 23. 6. 1992.
[2] OJ No C 176, 28. 6. 1993.
[3] OJ No C 308, 15. 11. 1993.
[4] OJ No C 19, 25. 1. 1993.

7. Specific comments

(Unless otherwise indicated, references below are to the text of the amended proposal.)   **A10.27**

In addition to the reordering of Articles in line with the successive stages leading up to the contract and its performance, the following amendments were made to the Commission's amended proposal by the Council and accepted by the Commission:

(i)   The dropping of the approach based on contract solicitation (see point 5) made it necessary to adjust Articles 1, 2, first indent and sixth indent (deletion), 4, 5, 6, 10, 11 (1) and 14 (3) and to adjust the preamble accordingly.

Similarly, since means of communication can be used actually to conclude a contract, the term 'distance contract' should be used throughout the Directive and not just 'contract negotiated at a distance'.

(ii) Article 2

Apart from the above adjustments, the definitions have been rationalized so as to avoid repetition and to align on the phraseology used in Community legislation. The definition of an 'order' has been deleted, with the term being used here in its ordinary sense, that of an 'operator' now covers only persons making means of communication available to suppliers since they are the ones whose practices need to be regulated.

Split performance of a contract is not covered by the text and is therefore, in the absence of any provisions on it, left to national legislation (see amendment 11).

(iii) Article 3

The Council wanted to restrict the extent of the exemptions since only some of the provisions will not apply to contracts for the supply of goods for current consumption or of services 'with reservation' (in particular, as Parliament wished, the right of withdrawal is not available for such services).

While recognizing the importance of consumer protection as regards distance contracts for financial services, the Council took the view, given the specific nature of financial services – which are already covered by Community legislation in many respects – and of immovable property (apart from rental) – where national laws still contain special arrangements – and as contracts for such services and such property are in large part already excluded from the right of withdrawal by the amended proposal (Article 12 (4), second and third indents), that it was better to exclude[1] them from the scope.

The practical arrangements for auction sales and the instant nature of the 'contract' represented by use of public pay-phones also warrant their exclusion from the scope.

(iv) Information (Articles 5, 6 and 11)   **A10.28**

Taking the view that consumer information is a key part of consumer protection, the Council wanted to clarify and restructure these Articles so as to distinguish between prior information (Article 4 of the common position) and written confirmation of information (Article 5 of the common position):

– with paragraphs 1 (g) and 2 of the new Article 4 taking over paragraphs 3[2] and 1 and 2 of Article 5,

---

[1] It should be noted, however, that credit agreements linked to a distance contract continue to be covered when the right of withdrawal is exercised in respect of the distance contract.

[2] In a tightened-up form since the cost of using the means of communication has to be stated.

663

 – with the new Article 5 taking over Article 11 and clarifying the term 'the supplier's most appropriate place of business' (to which the consumer may address any complaints).

(v) Restrictions on the use of means of communication (Article 4)

Article 10 of the common position makes Article 4 more precise so as not to hold out the illusion of protection that is unenforceable and accordingly applies only to means 'which allow individual communications'.

Taking the view that protection is already available for the telephone (ex-directory numbers) or electronic mail (access codes), that such means can 'be used only where there is no clear objection from the consumer' and that automatic calling machines are already covered by prior consent, the Council did not include the telephone (apart from automatic calling machines) or electronic mail among the means of communication requiring prior consent.

(vi) Provisions relating to performance (Articles 8, 9, 10 and 13)

The time limit for performance is set by Article 7 (1) of the common position more strictly than by the amended proposal (performance within 30 days after the order is forwarded and not performance to begin not more than 30 days after the order is received.

Unavailability of what was ordered and substitute supplies are covered by Article 7 (2) and (3) of the common position.

Article 9 of the common position deals with inertia selling, exempting the consumer from any obligation to the supplier, and excludes altogether goods supplied free of charge as referred to in Article 9 (4) of the amended proposal, the wording of which has therefore not been included.

As regards methods of payment, the Council – like the European Parliament – did not think it advisable to prohibit payment in advance, in view of the risks involved in such transactions for suppliers, and therefore did not include Article 8 of the amended proposal. On the other hand, it has required the supplier to 'reimburse the sums paid by the consumer' in the event of withdrawal (Article 6 (2) of the common position) and of failure to perform (Article 7 (2) of the common position) in line with the objective of amendment 30 while taking the view that the introduction of a guarantee scheme in case of supplier default is a broader issue of relevance to all of the supplier's obligations and should be dealt with as such.

Article 8 of the common position deals with payment by card (Article 13), taking a wider view of any kind of fraudulent use in the context of a distance contract, while leaving open the arrangements for the return of sums repayable; this could in particular allow the operation of a guarantee scheme, which was ruled out by the wording of Article 13 of the amended proposal.

A10.29   (vii) Right of withdrawal (Article 12)

It became clear to the Council that this Article needed to be clarified so that the provision of information (particularly on the right of withdrawal) could mesh more smoothly with the exercise of the right of withdrawal. The approach followed in the Directive of the European Parliament and of the Council on the

protection of purchasers in respect of certain aspects of contracts relating to the purchase of a right to use immovable properties on a timeshare basis proved to be a suitable model for the purpose and resulted in the wording of Article 6 (1) of the common position, based on a three-month period within which missing information can still be supplied and a withdrawal period proper of seven days.

The Council wanted to amend the scope of this Article, which now excludes contracts for:

– services if performance has begun with the consumer's agreement (and not all services if performance has begun),

– immovable property (and not all contracts concluded in the form of an authenticated document),

– audio or video recordings, records or computer software, since these may be copied almost immediately,

– newspapers, periodicals and magazines, since their contents are soon out of date,

– gaming and lottery services, in view of their special manner of operation.

The Council did not, however, think it advisable to exclude products for personal hygiene.

(viii) Judicial or administrative protection (Articles 14, 16 and 17)

In Article 11 of the common position, the Council basically sought to avoid over-specific wording which might not tally with all national systems of law, while retaining the substance of Article 14, in particular the possibility of action by professional or consumer organizations and the possibility of reversing the burden of proof or of self-regulation.

Article 12 (2) of the common position spells out the conditions for enjoying the protection afforded by this Directive to the consumer where the law of a non-member country has been chosen and Article 13 of the common position details the relationship of this Directive to existing Community legislation.

(ix) Final provisions (Articles 18 and 19)

The minimal clause (Article 14 of the common position) comprises *inter alia*, among the more stringent provisions, the prohibition of the marketing of medicinal products, without confining this to prescription drugs (amendment 36/rev.).

The common position had to set a transposition period as the date laid down in the Commission proposal had passed and it has opted here for a three-year period, comparable to that set for other consumer protection acts.

A reporting and revision clause has also been added (Article 15 (4) of the common position).

(x) Provisions not included

– amendment 20 (Article 7): it is not for this Directive to amend the conditions for implementation of Directive 89/552/EEC,

– amendment 29 (Article 12 (5)): this Directive makes provision only for failure to perform as a result of unavailability of the goods or services ordered,

– amendment 32 (Article 15): firstly, this provision comes under Member States' general duty to inform the public and, secondly, this Directive is not addressed to the 'organizations concerned'.

Proposed Directive COM (95) 276 Final

Proposal for a European Parliament and Council Directive on consumer protection in the indication of the prices of products offered to consumers

(Text with EEA relevance)

(Submitted by the Commission on 17 July 1995)

THE EUROPEAN PARLIAMENT AND THE COUNCIL OF THE EUROPEAN UNION,

A11.1 Having regard to the Treaty establishing the European Community, and in particular Article 129a (2) thereof,

Having regard to the proposal from the Commission,

Having regard to the opinion of the Economic and Social Committee,

Acting in conformity with the procedure provided for in Article 189b of the Treaty establishing the European Community,

1. Whereas consumers must be guaranteed a high level of protection; whereas the Community should contribute thereto by specific actions which provide for adequate information of consumers on the prices of products offered to them;

2. Whereas the Community's programmes for a consumer protection and information policy[1] provide for the establishment of common principles for indicating prices;

3. Whereas these principles have been established by Council Directive 79/581/EEC[2] of 19 June 1979 as amended by Directive 88/315/EEC[3] and Directive 88/314/EEC[4] concerning the indication of prices of foodstuffs and non-food products;

4. Whereas the obligation to indicate the selling price and the price per unit of measurement contributes substantially to improving consumer information by providing consumers with essential data in order to make reasoned choices;

5. Whereas, however, the mechanism adopted included a certain number of exceptions to the general obligation to indicate the unit price, notably when products are marketed in quantities or capacities corresponding to the values of the ranges adopted at Community level;

6. Whereas this link between indication of the unit price of products and standardization of packaging introduced rigidities into the implementation of the mechanism adopted, which has proven overly complex to apply; whereas it is thus necessary to abandon this link in the interests of simplification, without prejudice to the rules governing packaging standardization;

7. Whereas, therefore, account should be taken of all the difficulties encountered in implementing the mechanism provided for in the abovementioned Directives and a new and simplified mechanism proposed which will enable the main objective to be achieved more easily, namely adequate information of consumers;

8. Whereas indicating the selling price and the unit price is the

---

[1] OJ No C 92, 25. 4. 1975, p. 2 and OJ No C 133, 3. 6. 1981, p. 2.
[2] OJ No L 158, 26. 6. 1979, p. 19.
[3] OJ No L 142, 9. 6. 1988, p. 23.
[4] OJ No L 142, 9. 6. 1988, p. 19.

easiest way to enable consumers to evaluate and compare the nature and quality of products in an optimum manner and hence to make informed choices on the basis of simple comparisons;

9. Whereas, therefore, the general obligation to indicate both the selling price and the unit price for all products should be maintained except for products marketed in bulk, where the selling price cannot be determined until the final consumer indicates how much of the product he requires;

A11.2

10. Whereas only Community-level rules can ensure homogenous and transparent information that will benefit all consumers in the context of the internal market; whereas the new, simplified approach is both necessary and sufficient to achieve this objective;

11. Whereas, moreover, price transparency is a priority in the run-up to Economic and Monetary Union, and must therefore be significantly improved and arrangements made for its entry into effect in good time for the transition to the single currency;

12. Whereas introduction of the single currency will be greatly facilitated by providing consumers with simple yardsticks for comparing the prices of products;

13. Whereas there is a need to take into account the fact that certain products are widely and customarily sold in quantities different from the values of the base quantity referred to in the Directive; whereas it is thus advisable to allow Member States, in certain cases, to authorize that the unit price be indicated in relation to the quantity value which custom has enshrined;

14. Whereas Member States must be free to adapt the obligation to indicate the unit price for certain trades or forms of trade, and also to determine that such indication

is not necessary for a certain number of products, when it does not provide useful information for consumers;

15. Whereas Member States should also remain free to waive the obligation to indicate the unit price in the case of products for which such price indication would not be meaningful or would be liable to cause confusion; whereas this is the case notably when indication of the quantity is not a relevant particular for price comparison purposes, or when different products are marketed in the same packaging;

16. Whereas in the case of non-food products, Member States, with a view to facilitating application of the mechanism implemented, are free to draw up a list of products or categories of products for which the obligation to indicate the unit price remains applicable;

17. Whereas trends in distribution methods must be taken into consideration; whereas solutions must be found to permit optimum information of consumers on product prices at the lowest possible marginal cost;

18. Whereas a variable adaptation period should be provided for depending on the economic operators concerned in order to enable them to make the detailed arrangements for indicating unit prices;

19. Whereas particular attention should be paid to the adaptations required in small retail business, notably taking into account technological trends and the envisaged timetable for the introduction of the single currency; whereas to this end the Commission shall present an evaluation report on the situation two years before the final deadline for the general application of the mechanism,

HAVE ADOPTED THIS DIRECTIVE:

Article 1

A11.3 The purpose of this Directive is to stipulate indication of the selling price and the price per unit of measurement of products offered by traders to final consumers, so as to facilitate comparison of prices, wherever such comparison is relevant.

Article 2

A11.4 For the purpose of this Directive:

(a) 'selling price' means the price for a given quantity of the product;

(b) 'unit price' means the price for one kilogram, one litre, one metre, one square metre or cubic metre of the product or any other quantity which is widely and customarily used in the Member States in the marketing of specific products;

(c) 'products sold in bulk' means products which are not pre-packaged and/or are not measured or weighed except in the presence of the final consumer.

Article 3

A11.5 1. The selling price and the unit price shall be indicated for all products referred to in Article 1, subject to the provisions of Article 6.

2. For products sold in bulk, the unit price must be indicated for all products referred to in Article 1, since the selling price cannot be determined prior to the request expressed by the final consumer.

Article 4

A11.6 1. The selling price and the unit price must be unambiguous, easily identifiable and clearly legible.

2. The selling price and the unit price shall relate to the final price of the product under the conditions laid down by the Member States.

3. The unit price shall refer to the quantity declared, in accordance with national and Community provisions, and notably net quantities of products.

Article 5

A11.7 Member States shall lay down the detailed rules for indicating prices, notably as regards prices applying to quantities that are widely and customarily used, referred to in Article 2 (b).

Article 6

A11.8 1. Member States may waive the obligation to indicate the unit price of products for which such indication would not be meaningful because of the products' nature or purpose, and products for which such indication would not provide the consumer with adequate information or would be liable to create confusion.

2. Member States may waive the obligation to indicate the unit price of products for which indication of length, mass or volume is not required by national or Community provisions. This applies in particular to products sold by individual item or singly.

3. With a view to implementing the provisions set out in paragraphs 1 and 2 above, the Member States may, in the case of non-food products, establish a list of the products or product categories to which the obligation to indicate the unit price shall remain applicable.

Article 7

A11.9 Member States may provide that the obligation to indicate the unit price of products other than those marketed in bulk which are sold by certain small retail businesses shall apply at the latest by 6 June 2001, if the obligation to indicate the unit price from 7 June 1997

– is likely to constitute an excessive burden for these businesses, or

– is impracticable because of the number of products on sale, the sales area, the nature of the place of sale or specific conditions applicable to certain forms of business, such as certain types of itinerant trade.

Article 8

A11.10 Member States shall lay down penalties for infringements of national provisions adopted in application of this Directive, and shall take all necessary measures to ensure that these are enforced. These penalties must be effective, proportionate and dissuasive.

Article 9

A11.11 Council Directive 79/581/EEC, as amended by Directive 88/315/EEC and Directive 88/314/EEC shall be repealed with effect from 7 June 1997.

Article 10

A11.12 1. Member States shall bring into force the laws, regulations and administrative provisions necessary to comply with this Directive by 6 June 1997 at the latest. They shall forthwith inform the Commission thereof. The provisions adopted shall be applicable as of 7 June 1997.

2. When Member States adopt these provisions, these shall contain a reference to this Directive or shall be accompanied by such a reference at the time of their official publication. The procedure for such reference shall be adopted by the Member States.

3. Member States shall communicate to the Commission the text of the provisions of national law which they adopt in the field governed by this Directive. In particular, they shall indicate the rules adopted pursuant to Articles 5, 6 and 7, and any later amendments thereto.

4. Member States shall communicate the provisions governing the penalties provided for in Article 8, and any later amendments thereto.

Article 11

1. The Commission shall, not more **A11.13** than two years after the date referred to in Article 10 (1), submit to the European Parliament and the Council an initial report on the application of the provisions of Article 7.

2. The Commission shall, not more than four years after the date referred to in Article 10 (1), submit to the European Parliament and the Council global report on the application of this Directive.

Article 12

This Directive is addressed to the Member States. **A11.14**

Proposed Directive COM (95) 346 Final

Proposal for a Council Directive on the right of third-country nationals to travel in the Community

(Text with EEA relevance)

(Submitted by the Commission on 24 August 1995)

THE COUNCIL OF THE EUROPEAN UNION,

A12.1 Having regard to the Treaty establishing the European Community, and in particular Article 100 thereof,

Having regard to the proposal from the Commission,

Having regard to the opinion of the European Parliament,

Having regard to the opinion of the Economic and Social Committee,

Having regard to the opinion of the Committee of the Regions,

Whereas Article 7a of the Treaty for the establishment of an internal market, which is to comprise an area without internal frontiers in which the free movement of goods, persons, services and capital is ensured in accordance with the provisions of the Treaty;

Whereas in order to achieve this objective Member States will have to allow third-country nationals who are lawfully in the territory of another Member State to enter their territories for short stays; whereas if there were no such right to travel each Member State would have to consider the fact that there were people in other Member States who were not entitled to enter its territory, which might be an argument for maintaining controls at internal frontiers;

Whereas the approximation of Member States' laws on this question directly affects the establishment and functioning of the internal market;

Whereas the issue of a residence permit by a Member State to a third-country national, whereby the latter is authorized to live in that State, is an act surrounded by sufficient safeguards for the other Member States no longer to need to subject the person concerned to the requirement that he obtain a visa in advance from their own authorities and hence for them to grant him the right to travel; whereas, in any event, each Member State may expel the person concerned to the Member State which issued the residence permit, which is obliged to readmit him, if he stays unlawfully in its territory, if he does not fulfil the conditions governing the right to travel, or if he represents a threat to public order or public security in that State, or to its international relations;

Whereas, where a third-country **A12.2** national who is not resident in the Community is in possession of a visa issued by a Member State which permits him to cross the external frontiers of all the Member States by virtue of its being valid throughout the Community and mutually recognized by the Member States for that purpose, each Member State enjoys sufficient safeguards for it to grant the person concerned the right to travel; whereas the same right must *a fortioti* be granted to third-country nationals who may cross the external frontiers without being subject to a visa requirement; whereas, in any event, each Member State is entitled to expel a third-country national if he does not fulfil the conditions governing the right to travel or if he represents a threat to public order or public security in that State, or to its international relations;

Whereas persons who exercise the right to travel should not become a burden on the social assistance system in the

Member States they visit; whereas the right should therefore be subject to the condition that such persons have sufficient resources to undertake the trip;

Whereas this Directive forms part of a general body of Community and national provisions governing the legal position of third-country nationals in the Member States; whereas the scope of this Directive should accordingly be precisely defined,

HAS ADOPTED THIS DIRECTIVE:

Article 1

A12.3 1. Member States shall grant third-country nationals who are lawfully in a Member State the right to travel in the territories of the other Member States in accordance with this Directive.

2. This Directive shall be without prejudice to rights

- which Community law confers on third-country nationals who are members of the families of citizens of the Union,

- which are granted to third-country nationals and to members of their families irrespective of nationality where, under an agreement between the Community, its Member States and the relevant third country, they enjoy rights of entry and residence in a Member State identical to those of citizens of the Union.

3. This Directive shall not affect provisions of Community or domestic law on

- stays other than for a short time, and

- access to employment and the taking-up of activities as a self-employed person

applicable to third-country nationals.

Article 2

For the purpose of this Directive:

A12.4 1. **'right to travel'** means the right to cross internal Community borders and to remain in the territory of a Member State for a short stay, or to travel onward, without the person concerned being required to obtain a visa from the Member State or States in whose territory the right is exercised;

2. **'residence permit'** means any document or authorization issued by the authorities in a Member State which permits a person to reside in that Member State, and which appears on the list referred to in Article 3 (4);

3. **'visa within the meaning of point (3) of Article 2'** means a visa which is valid throughout the Community and which is mutually recognized for the purpose of crossing the external frontiers of the Member States;

4. **'third-country national'** means any person who is not a citizen of the Union within the meaning of Article 8 (1) of the Treaty establishing the European Community.

Article 3

1. Member States shall grant the right   **A12.5** to travel to third-country nationals who hold a valid residence permit issued by another Member State.

Any such person may travel in the territories of the other Member States for a continuous period of not more than three months provided that he meets the following requirements:

- he must be in possession of a valid residence permit and a valid travel document.

- he must have sufficient means of subsistence, both to cover the period of the intended stay or transit and to enable him to return to the Member State which issued the residence permit, or to travel to a third country into which he is certain to be admitted.

2. Member States shall, in accordance with the conditions laid down in the Annex, readmit any person to whom they have issued a residence permit and

who is unlawfully resident in the territory of another Member State, even if the validity of that permit has expired.

3. A third-country national who holds a residence permit issued by a Member State and who is exercising the right to travel may be expelled if he does not meet the requirements laid down in paragraph 1 or if he represents a threat to public order or public security in the Member State in which he is exercising the right to travel, or to its international relations.

4. Member States shall provide the Commission and the other Member States with a list of the documents they issue which are treated as equivalent to residence permits for the purposes of this Article, updating it as and when necessary.

The Commission shall publish the lists and any updates in the *Official Journal of the European Communities.*

Article 4

A12.6 1. Member States shall grant the right to travel to third-country nationals who hold a visa within the meaning of point (3) of Article 2.

Such persons may travel in the territories of the Member States during the period of stay permitted by the visa, provided that they are in possession of a travel document bearing the valid visa and meet the requirement laid down in the second indent of Article 3 (1).

2. Member States shall confer the right to travel on third-country nationals who are exempted from visa requirements by all the Member States.

Such persons may travel in the territories of the Member States for a total of no more than three months within a period of six months from the date of first entry in the territory of one of the Member States, provides that they are in possession of valid travel documents and meet the requirement laid down in the second indent of Article 3 (1).

3. Paragraph 2 shall also apply to

third-country nationals who are subject to a visa requirement in a number of Member States.

However, the right to travel shall in their case be restricted to the territories of such Member States as have exempted nationals of the relevant third country from the obligation to hold a visa, unless they do hold a visa within the meaning of point (3) of Article 2.

In the latter event, the period of stay in the territories of the Member States which require a visa shall be limited to the period permitted by the visa.

4. The provision of this Article shall not prevent any Member State from authorizing the stay in its territory of a third-country national beyond three months.

5. A third-country national allowed to enter the Community for a short stay who is exercising the right to travel may be expelled if he does not satisfy the conditions in paragraphs 1 or 2, according to whether or not he is subject to a visa requirement, or if he represents a threat to public order or public security in the Member State in which he is exercising the right to travel, or to its international relations.

Article 5

A12.7 Member States may require persons exercising the right to travel to report their presence in their territories.

Article 6

A12.8 Member States shall bring into force the laws, regulations and administrative provisions necessary to comply with this Directive by 31 December 1996. They shall immediately inform the Commission thereof.

When Member States adopt these provisions, these shall contain a reference to this Directive or shall be accompanied by such reference at the time of their official publication. The procedure for such reference shall be adopted by Member States.

A12.9

Article 7

This Directive shall enter into force on the 20th day following its publication in the *Official Journal of the European Communities*.

Article 8

This Directive is addressed to the Member States.

A12.10

ANNEX

Conditions for the readmission by the Member States of third-country nationals who are unlawfully resident in a Member State but who hold a residence permit for another Member State (Article 3 (2) of the Directive)

1. These provisions on readmission are applicable to third-country nationals who hold a residence permit within the meaning of point (2) of Article 2 and who are exercising the right to travel but who are unlawfully resident in the territory of another Member State.

   The provisions do not affect Member States' obligations under the Dublin Asylum Convention to readmit applicants for asylum who are unlawfully resident in another Member State.

2. Where a person covered by point 1 has entered one Member State from another Member State for the purposes of a short stay or transit under Article 3 (1) and is unlawfully resident there, that person must go without delay to the Member State for which he holds a residence permit unless he is authorized to go to another country to which he is certain to be admitted.

   If a third-country national wishes to go to another country, he must provide documentary evidence that he may be admitted to that country, e.g. in the form of an entry permit or valid visa, and that he is in possession of the necessary resources, e.g. in the form of a ticket or other documentation that allows him to travel, and cash or a bank deposit in order to secure his transportation and his residence in the country to which he may be admitted.

3. If a third-country national unlawfully resident in the territory of a Member State refuses to leave voluntarily, Member States are required to readmit him in accordance with the guidelines set out below.

   If the person holds a valid residence permit for another Member State, the Member State which has issued the permit is required to readmit him.

   Moreover, Member States must readmit a third-country national in accordance with Article 3 (2) within a period of up to two months after the expiration of the validity of the residence permit.

   The obligation to readmit him is subject to the condition that a request for readmitting him shall be lodged within one month by the authorities becoming aware of the person's unlawful presence in the Member State

4. The person is to be readmitted after a request has been made by the competent authorities in the requesting Member State showing that the person in question holds a valid residence permit for the readmitting Member State.

   A Member State receiving a request in accordance with point 3 must reply to the request within eight days. If the Member State does not respond within that time, it will be deemed to have agreed to readmission, unless it has expressly requested a non-week extension of that time limit.

The Member State to which the request was addressed is required to take in, within a month at most, the person it has agreed to take back. That time limit may be extended by agreement between the two Member States concerned, upon submission by the requesting Member State of an explicit and justified application.

Member States are to exchange lists of authorities competent to consider requests for readmission and of points at borders where readmission can take place.

5. The financial costs entailed by readmission are to be met by the person concerned. Where the person is unable to meet the expenses, the expenses up to the point of readmission are as a rule to be met by the Member State requesting readmission.

Proposed Directive COM (95) 347 Final

Proposal for a Council Directive on the elimination of controls on persons crossing internal frontiers

(Text with EEA relevance)

(Submitted by the Commission on 24 August 1995)

THE COUNCIL OF THE EUROPEAN UNION,

A13.1 Having regard to the Treaty establishing the European Community, and in particular Article 100 thereof,

Having regard to the proposal from the Commission,

Having regard to the opinion of the European Parliament,

Having regard to the opinion of the Economic and Social Committee,

Having regard to the opinion of the Committee of the Regions,

Whereas Article 7a of the Treaty provides for the establishment of the internal market, which is to comprise an area without internal frontiers in which the free movement of goods, persons, services and capital is ensured in accordance with the provisions of the Treaty;

Whereas the establishment of the internal market consequently calls for the abolition of all controls and formalities for persons crossing internal frontiers; whereas, in this context, seaports and airports stand apart, as they serve both traffic with other Member States and traffic with non-member countries; whereas application of the freedom-of-movement principle should nevertheless result in the elimination of controls and formalities for persons taking an intra-Community flight or making an intra-Community sea crossing;

Whereas the Community and the Member States have decided to take the measures they deem essential for eliminating the underlying reasons for the application of frontier controls and formalities under national law;

Whereas the relevant accompanying measures have been introduced satisfactorily;

Whereas, in order to fulfil the clear and unconditional obligation enshrined in Article 7a, and in the interest of legal certainty, it is necessary in these circumstances to confirm that frontier controls and formalities within the Community are to be abolished;

Whereas this Directive should relate both to controls or formalities applied by public authorities and to those applied by other persons under national rules;

Whereas it is necessary to stipulate the conditions in which a Member State may temporarily reinstate controls at internal frontiers in the event of a serious threat to public policy or public security,

HAS ADOPTED THIS DIRECTIVE:

Article 1

1. All persons, whatever their nationality, shall be able to cross Member States' frontiers within the Community at any point, without such crossing being subject to any frontier control or formality. **A13.2**

2. The elimination of controls and formalities for persons crossing internal frontiers shall not affect the exercise of the law-enforcement powers conferred on the competent authorities by the legislation of each Member State over the whole of its territory, nor any obligations to possess and carry documents which are laid down by its legislation.

Article 2

A13.3 1. A Member State may, in the event of a serious threat to public policy or public security, reinstate controls at its frontiers within the Community for a period of not more than 30 days. Any Member State taking such action shall immediately notify the Commission and the other Member States, supplying them with all the appropriate information.

2. Where the serious threat to public policy security lasts longer than 30 days, the Member State concerned may maintain the controls at its frontiers within the Community for renewable periods of not more than 30 days. Each renewal shall be decided after the other Member States and the Commission have been consulted.

At the Member State's request, the Commission and the other Member States shall treat in confidence the information it supplies to justify maintaining these controls.

3. The controls referred to in paragraphs 1 and 2 and the length of the period during which they are applied shall not exceed what is strictly necessary to respond to the serious threat.

Article 3

A13.4 For the purposes of this Directive:

1. **'a Member State's frontier within the Community'** means:

   - the Member States' common land frontiers, including the rail or road terminals for links by bridge or tunnel between Member States,

   - their airports for intra-Community flights,

   - their seaports for intra-Community sea crossings;

2. **'intra-Community flight'** means the movement of an aircraft between two Community airports, without any stopovers, and which does not start from or end at a non-Community airport;

3. **'intra-Community sea crossing'** means the movement between two Community ports, without any intermediate calls, of a vessel plying regularly between two or more specified Community ports;

4. **'frontier control or formality'** means:

   - any control applied in connection with or on the occasion of the crossing of an internal frontier, by the public authorities of a Member State or by other persons, under the national legislation of a Member State,

   - any formality imposed on a person in connection with the crossing of an internal frontier and to be fulfilled on the occasion of such crossing.

Article 4

No later than two years after implementation of this Directive, and every three years thereafter, the Commission shall report on its application to the European Parliament, the Council, the Economic and Social Committee and the Committee of the Regions.   **A13.5**

Article 5

Member States shall bring into force the laws, regulations and administrative provisions necessary to comply with this Directive not later than 31 December 1996. They shall immediately inform the Commission thereof and shall also transmit to it a table showing the correlation between each of the provisions of this Directive and the relevant provisions of national law, irrespective of whether these predate this Directive or are approved for the specific purpose of transposing it.   **A13.6**

When Member States adopt these provisions, these shall contain a reference to this Directive or shall be accompanied by such reference at the time of their official publication. The procedure for such reference shall be adopted by Member States.

Article 6

A13.7 This Directive shall enter into force on the 20th day following its publication in the *Official Journal of the European Communities.*

Article 7

This Directive is addressed to the **A13.8** Member States.

Council Regulation (EC) No 2317/95

of 25 September 1995

determining the third countries whose nationals must be in possession of visas when crossing the external borders of the Member States

THE COUNCIL OF THE EUROPEAN UNION,

A14.1   Having regard to the Treaty establishing the European Community,

Having regard to the proposal from the Commission[1],

Having regard to the opinion of the European Parliament[2],

Whereas Article 100c of the Treaty requires the Council to determine the third countries whose nationals must be in possession of a visa when crossing the external borders of the Member States;

Whereas the drawing up of the common list annexed to this Regulation represents an important step towards the harmonization of visa policy; whereas the second paragraph of Article 7a of the Treaty stipulates in particular that the internal market shall comprise an area without internal frontiers in which the free movement of persons is ensured in accordance with the Treaty; whereas other aspects of the harmonization of visa policy, including the conditions for the issue of visas, are matters to be determined under Title VI of the Treaty on European Union;

Whereas risks relating to security and illegal immigration should be given priority consideration when the said common list annexed hereto is drawn up; whereas, in addition, Member States' international relations with third countries also play a role;

Whereas the principle that a Member State may not require a visa from a

person wishing to cross its external borders if that person holds a visa issued by another Member State which meets the harmonized conditions governing the issue of visas and is valid throughout the Community or if that person holds an appropriate permit issued by a Member State is a matter that should be determined under Title VI of the Treaty on European Union;

Whereas this Regulation shall not prevent a Member State from deciding under what conditions nationals of third countries lawfully resident within its territory may re-enter it after having left the territory of the Member States of the Union during the period of validity of their permits;

Whereas, in special cases justifying an exemption where visa requirements would in principle exist, Member States may exempt certain categories of person in keeping with international law or custom;

Whereas since national rules differ on stateless persons, recognized refugees and persons who produce passports or travel documents issued by a territorial entity or authority which is not recognized as a State by all Member States, Member States may decide on visa requirements for that group of persons, where that territorial entity or authority is not on the said common list;

Whereas when adding a new entities to the list it is necessary to take account of diplomatic implications and guidelines adopted on the matter by the European Union; whereas, at all events

---

[1]   OJ No C 11, 15. 1. 1994, p. 15.
[2]   OJ No C 128, 9. 5. 1994, p. 350.

678

the inclusion of a third country on the common list is entirely without prejudice to its international status;

Whereas the determination of third countries whose nationals must be in possession of visas when crossing the external borders of the Member States should be achieved gradually; whereas Member States will constantly endeavour to harmonize their visa policies with regard to third countries not on the common list; whereas the present provisions must not prejudice the achievement of free movement for persons as provided for in Article 7a of the Treaty; whereas the Commission should draw up a progress report on harmonization after five years;

Whereas, with a view to ensuring that the system is administered openly and that the persons concerned are informed, Member States must communicate to the other Member States and to the Commission the measures which they take pursuant to this Regulation; whereas for the same reasons that information must also be published in the *Official Journal of the European Communities*;

Whereas the information provided for in Articles 2 (4) and 4 (2) must be published before the other provisions of this Regulation come into force; whereas Articles 2 (4) and 4 (2) must therefore become applicable one month before the other provisions of the Regulation,

HAS ADOPTED THIS REGULATION:

Article 1

A14.2 1. Nationals of third countries on the common list in the Annex shall be required to be in possession of visas when crossing the external borders of the Member States.

2. Nationals of countries formerly part of countries on the common list shall be subject to the requirements of paragraph 1 unless and until the Council decides otherwise under the procedure laid down in Article 100c of the Treaty.

Article 2

1. The Member States shall determine the visa requirements for nationals of third countries not on the common list.   **A14.3**

2. The Member States shall determine the visa requirements for stateless persons and recognized refugees.

3. The Member States shall determine the visa requirements for persons who produce passports or travel documents issued by a territorial entity or authority which is not recognized as a State by all Member States if that entity or territorial authority is not on the common list.

4. Within ten working days of the entry into force of this paragraph, Member States shall communicate to the other Member States and the Commission the measures they have taken pursuant to paragraphs 1, 2 and 3. Any further measures taken pursuant to paragraph 1 shall be similarly communicated within five working days.

The Commission shall publish the measures communicated pursuant to this paragraph and updates thereof in the *Official Journal of the European Communities* for information.

Article 3

Five years after the entry into force of this Regulation the Commission shall draw up a progress report of the harmonization of Member States' visa policies with regard to third countries not on the common list and, if necessary, submit to the Council proposals for further measures required to achieve the objective of harmonization laid down in Article 100c.   **A14.4**

Article 4

1. A Member State may exempt nationals of third countries subject to visa requirements under Article 1 (1) and (2) from those requirements. This shall apply in particular to civilian air and sea crew, flight crew and attendants on emergency or rescue flights and other helpers in the event of disas-   **A14.5**

ter or accident and holders of diplomatic passports, official duty passports and other official passports.

2. Article 2 (4) shall apply *mutatis mutandis.*

A14.6

Article 5

For the purposes of this Regulation, 'visas' shall mean an authorization given or a decision taken by a Member State which is required for entry into its territory with a view to:

– an intended stay in that Member State or in several Member States of no more than three months in all,

– transit through the territory of that Member State or several Member States, except for transit through the international zones of airports and transfers between airports in a Member State.

Article 6

This Regulation shall be without prejudice to any further harmonization between individual Member States, going beyond the common list, determining the third countries whose nationals must be in possession of a visa when crossing their external borders.

A14.7

Article 7

This Regulation shall enter into force six months after its publication in the *Official Journal of the European Communities* except for Articles 2 (4) and 4 (2) which shall enter into force on the day following publication.

A14.8

This Regulation shall be binding in its entirety and directly applicable in all Member States.

Done at Brussels, 25 September 1995.

For the Council
The President
J. A. BELLOCH JULBE

ANNEX

COMMON LIST REFERRED TO IN ARTICLE 1

I. States

Afghanistan	Ghana	Pakistan
Albania	Guinea	Papua New Guinea
Algeria	Guinea Bissau	Peru
Angola	Guyana	Philippines
Armenia	Haiti	Qatar
Azerbaijan	India	Romania
Bahrain	Indonesia	Russia
Bangladesh	Iran	Rwanda
Belarus	Iraq	Sao Tomé and Principe
Benin	Jordan	Saudi Arabia
Bhutan	Kazakhstan	Senegal
Bulgaria	Kyrgyzstan	Sierra Leone
Burkina Faso	Kuwait	Somalia
Burundi	Laos	Sri Lanka
Cambodia	Lebanon	Sudan
Cameroon	Liberia	Suriname
Cape Verde	Libya	Syria
Central African Republic	Madagascar	Tajikistan
Chad	Maldives	Tanzania
China	Mali	Thailand
Comoros	Mauritania	Togo

Congo
Côte-d'Ivoire
Cuba
Djibouti
Dominican Republic
Egypt
Equatorial Guinea
Eritrea
Ethiopia
Fiji
Gabon
The Gambia
Georgia

Mauritius
Moldova
Mongolia
Morocco
Mozambique
Myanmar
Nepal
Niger
Nigeria
North Korea
Oman

Tunisia
Turkey
Turkmenistan
Uganda
Ukraine
United Arab Emirates
Uzbekistan
Vietnam
Yemen
Zaire
Zambia

II. Entities and territorial authorities not recognized as States by all the Member States

Taiwan
Former Yugoslav Republic of Macedonia
Federal Republic of Yugoslavia (Serbia and Montenegro)

Council Directive 95/57/EC

of 23 November 1995

on the collection of statistical information in the field of tourism

THE COUNCIL OF THE EUROPEAN UNION,

A15.1 Having regard to the Treaty establishing the European Community, and in particular Article 213 thereof,

Having regard to the proposal from the Commission,

Whereas the Resolutions of the European Parliament of 11 June 1991[1] and 18 January 1994[2] stress that the Community has a major role to play in developing tourism statistics;

Whereas the elaboration of a Directive aimed at channelling efforts currently expended in a fragmented manner at national level has been approved by the Economic and Social Committee[3];

Whereas, under Decision 90/655/EEC[4], a Community methodological framework for the compilation of Community tourism statistics has been developed;

Whereas the results of the two-year programme (1991–1992) for developing Community tourism statistics under Decision 90/655/EEC highlight the needs of users in the private and public sector for reliable and comparable statistics on tourism demand and supply at Community level available at short notice;

Whereas the development of Community statistics on tourism was recognized as a priority by Council Decision 92/421/EEC of 13 July 1992 on a Community action plan to assist tourism[5];

Whereas the recognized role of tourism as a tool of development and socio-economic integration can be better ensured through knowledge of the basic related statistics, notably established at regional level;

Whereas, in order to assess the competitiveness of the Community tourist industry, it is necessary to gain greater knowledge of the volume of tourism, the characteristics thereof, the profile of the tourist and tourist expenditure;

Whereas monthly information is required to be able to measure the seasonal influences of demand on tourist accommodation capacity and thereby to assist public authorities and economic operators to develop more suitable strategies and policies for improving the seasonal spread of holidays and the performance of tourist activities;

Whereas further Community activity in **A15.2** this field must continue to be based on a pragmatic approach which is consistent with the principle of subsidiarity;

Whereas the necessary synergies between national, international and Community statistical projects impinging on tourism must be ensured in order to reduce the onus of collecting information;

Whereas methodological work developed in cooperation with other international organizations, such as the Organization for Economic Cooperation and Development and the World Tourism Organization, and the Recommendations adopted by the Statistical Commission of the United Nations in March 1993 should be taken into account in order to ensure better comparability of tourism statistics at world level;

Whereas reliable and efficient monitoring of the structure and evolution of

---

[1] OJ No C 183, 15. 7. 1991, p. 74.
[2] OJ No C 44, 14. 2. 1994, p. 61.
[3] OJ No C 52, 19. 2. 1994, p. 22.
[4] OJ No L 358, 21. 12. 1990, p. 89.
[5] OJ No L 231, 13. 8. 1992, p. 26.

tourism demand and supply can be significantly improved by establishing an appropriate recognized Community framework;

Whereas such a system may generate economies of scale, while producing information benefiting all Member States and parties concerned;

Whereas a Community instrument could facilitate the dissemination of comparable tourism statistics;

Whereas Council Decision 93/464/ EEC of 22 July 1993 on the framework programme for priority actions in the field of statistical information, 1993 to 1997[1] provides for the setting-up of an information system on tourism supply and demand;

Whereas a Council Directive can provide a common framework to maximize the benefits of the various actions which are being carried out at national level;

Whereas the statistical data compiled under a Community system must be reliable and appropriate to ensure comparability between Member States; whereas it is therefore necessary to establish jointly the criteria enabling these requirements to be met,

HAS ADOPTED THIS DIRECTIVE:

Article 1
Aim

A15.3 For the purpose of establishing an information system on tourism statistics at Community level, Member States shall carry out the collection, compilation, processing and transmission of harmonized Community statistical information on tourism supply and demand.

Article 2
Domain of information collection and basic definitions

A15.4 For the purposes of this Directive, the data to be collected shall relate to:

[1] OJ No L 219, 28. 8. 1993, p. 1.

(a) the capacity of collective tourist accommodation establishments

The types of collective accommodation in question are as follows:

1. hotels and similar establishments

2. other collective accommodation establishments, *inter alia*:

   2.1. tourist campsites

   2.2. holiday dwellings

   2.3. other collective accommodation;

(b) guest flows in collective accommodation establishments:

The collection shall cover internal tourism, i.e. domestic and inbound tourism; 'domestic tourism' shall mean residents of the given country travelling only within this country and 'inbound tourism' shall mean non-residents travelling within the given country;

(c) tourism demand:

The collection shall cover national tourism, i.e. domestic and outbound tourism; 'outbound tourism' shall mean residents of a country travelling in another country. The information on tourism demand shall concern trips the main purpose of which is holidays or business and which involve at least one or more consecutive nights spent away from the usual place of residence.

Article 3
Information collection characteristics

1. A list of data collection characteristics, showing their periodicity and their territorial breakdown appears in the Annex. **A15.5**

2. The definitions to be applied to the data collection characteristics and any adjustments to the list of data collection characteristics shall be

683

determined by the Commission in accordance with the procedure laid down in Article 12.

Article 4
Accuracy of statistical information

A15.6 1. The collection of the statistical information shall, where possible, ensure that the results meet the necessary minimum accuracy requirements. These requirements, and the procedures for ensuring the harmonized processing of systematic biases, shall be established by the Commission in accordance with the procedure laid down in Article 12. The minimum accuracy requirements shall be determined with particular reference to annual overnight stays at national level.

2. As regards the basis on which the information is collected, Member States shall take whatever measures they deem appropriate to maintain the quality and comparability of the results.

Article 5
Collection of statistical information

A15.7 1. Member States may, where appropriate, base the collection of the statistical information referred to in Article 3 on existing data, sources and systems.

2. For the characteristics with annual periodicity, the first reference period shall begin on 1 January 1996. For the characteristics relating to the columns on monthly and quarterly data appearing in sections B and C respectively of the Annex, the first reference period shall begin on 1 January 1997.

Article 6
Processing of data

A15.8 Member States shall process the information collected under Article 3 in accordance with the accuracy requirements stipulated in Article 4 and the

detailed rules adopted in accordance with the procedure laid down in Article 12. The regional level shall be in accordance with the Nomenclature of Territorial Units (NUT) of the Statistical Office of the European Communities.

Article 7
Transmission of data

1. Member States shall transmit the **A15.9** data processed in accordance with Article 6, including the information declared confidential by Member States pursuant to domestic legislation or practice concerning statistical confidentiality, and in accordance with the provisions of Council Regulation (Euratom, EEC) No 1588/90 of 11 June 1990 on the transmission of data subject to statistical confidentiality to the Statistical Office of the European Communities[1]. The said Regulation governs the confidential treatment of information.

2. The transmission of provisional annual data shall take place within six months of the end of the reference period, and the revised annual results shall be transmitted within a maximum period of 12 months following the end of the reference period. The transmission of provisional monthly and quarterly data shall take place within three months of the end of the corresponding reference period, and the revised monthly and quarterly results shall be transmitted within a maximum period of six months following the end of the corresponding reference period.

3. Acting in accordance with the procedure laid down in Article 12, the Commission may, for the purpose of facilitating the task of the parties responsible for providing information, establish, standardized data transmission procedures and create the conditions for increased use of automatic data processing and electronic data transmission.

---

[1] OJ No L 151, 15. 6. 1990, p. 1.

Article 8
Reports

A15.10 1. Member States shall provide the Commission at its request with all information necessary to evaluate the quality, comparability and completeness of the statistical information. Member States shall also provide the Commission with details of any subsequent changes in the methods used.

2. The Commission shall present to the European Parliament, the Council and the Economic and Social Committee a report on the experience acquired in the work carried out pursuant to this Directive after data have been collected over a period of three years.

Article 9
Dissemination of the results

A15.11 The arrangements for the dissemination of the data by the Commission shall be determined pursuant to the procedure laid down in Article 12.

Article 10
Transition period

A15.12 1. Without prejudice to Article 13, Member States shall take all the measures necessary to make the Community information system operational during a transition period, which shall end three years after entry into force of this Directive for monthly and annual data, and five years after entry into force of this Directive for quarterly data.

2. During the transition period, the Commission may, in accordance with the procedure laid down in Article 12, accept derogations from the provisions of this Directive, in so far as the national statistical systems require adaptations in the field of tourism.

Article 11
Committee

A15.13 As regards the procedures for implementing this Directive, and any measures for adjustment to economic and technical developments, concerning in particular:

- the definitions to be applied to the information collection characteristics and any adjustments to the list of data collection characteristics (Article 3), in so far as these adjustments do not make the collection process more onerous,

- accuracy requirements and the harmonized processing of systematic biases (Article 4),

- processing of data (Article 6), data transmission procedures (Article 7) and dissemination of the results (Article 9),

- the derogations from the provisions of this Directive during the transition period (Article 10),

the Commission shall be assisted, in accordance with the provisions laid down in Article 12, by the Statistical Programme Committee established by Decision 89/382/EEC, Euratom[1], hereinafter referred to as the 'Committee'.

Article 12
Procedure

A15.14 1. The representative of the Commission shall submit to the Committee a draft of the measures to be taken. The Committee shall deliver its opinion on the draft within a time-limit which the chairman may lay down according to the urgency of the matter. The opinion shall be delivered by the majority laid down in Article 148 (2) of the Treaty in the case of decisions which the Council is required to adopt on a proposal from the Commission. The votes of the

_____
[1] OJ No L 181, 28. 6. 1989, p. 47.

representatives of the Member States within the committee shall be weighted in the manner set out in that Article. The chairman shall not vote.

2. (a) The Commission shall adopt measures which shall apply immediately.

(b) However, if these measures are not in accordance with the opinion of the committee, they shall be communicated by the Commission to the Council forthwith. In that event:

– the Commission shall defer application of the measures which it has decided for a period of three months from the date of communication,

– the Council, acting by a qualified majority, may take a different decision within the time-limit referred to in the first indent.

Article 13
Implementation of the Directive

Member States shall bring into force the laws, regulations and administrative provisions necessary to comply with this Directive before 23 November 1996.

A15.15

Article 14
Entry into force

This Directive shall enter into force on the 20th day following its publication in the *Official Journal of the European Communities.*

A15.16

Article 15
Final provision

This Directive is addressed to the Member States.

A15.17

Done at Brussels, 23 November 1995.

For the Council
The President
C. WESTENDORP y CABEZA

Common Position (EC) No 32/95

adopted by the Council on 4 December 1995

with a view to adopting Directive 95/.../EC of the European Parliament and of the Council of . . . on cross-border credit transfers

THE EUROPEAN PARLIAMENT AND THE COUNCIL OF THE EUROPEAN UNION,

A16.1 Having regard to the Treaty establishing the European Community, and in particular Article 100a thereof,

Having regard to the proposal from the Commission[1],

Having regard to the opinion of the Economic and Social Committee[2],

Having regard to the opinion of the European Monetary Institute,

Acting in accordance with the procedure laid down in Article 189b of the Treaty[3],

(1) Whereas the volume of cross-border payments is growing steadily as the completion of the internal market and the progressive move towards full economic and monetary union lead to greater trade flows and movement of people throughout the Community; whereas cross-border credit transfers account for a substantial part of the volume and the value of cross-border payments;

(2) Whereas it is of paramount importance for individuals and businesses, especially small and medium-sized enterprises, to be able to make credit transfers rapidly, reliably and cheaply from one part of the Community to another; whereas greater competition in the market for cross-border credit transfers should lead to improved services and reduced prices;

(3) Whereas this Directive intends to follow up the progress made towards the completion of the internal market, in particular towards the liberalization of capital movements with a view to the implementation of economic and monetary union; whereas its provisions should apply to credit transfers in the currencies of the Member States and in ecus;

(4) Whereas the European Parliament, in its resolution of 12 February 1993[4], called for a Council Directive to lay down rules in the area of transparency and performance of cross-border payments;

(5) Whereas the issues covered by this Directive must be dealt with separately from the systemic issues which remain under consideration within the Commission; whereas it may be necessary to make a further proposal to cover these systemic issues, particularly the problem of settlement finality;

(6) Whereas the purpose of this Directive is to improve cross-border credit transfer services and thus assist the European Monetary Institute (EMI) in its task of promoting the efficiency of cross-border payments with a view to the preparation of the third

---

[1] OJ No C 360, 17. 12. 1994, p. 13. OJ No C 199, 3. 8. 1995, p. 16.

[2] OJ No C 236, 11. 9. 1995, p. 1.

[3] Opinion of the European Parliament of 19 May 1995 (OJ No C 151, 19. 6. 1995, p. 370), Council common position of . . . (not yet published in the Official Journal) and Decision of the European Parliament of . . . (not yet published in the Official Journal).

---

[4] OJ No C 72, 15. 3. 1993, p. 158.

stage of economic and monetary union;

A16.2

(7) Whereas, in line with the objectives set out in the second recital, this Directive should apply to any credit transfer of an amount less than ECU 25 000; whereas that amount should be increased to ECU 30 000 two years after the final implementation date for this Directive;

(8) Whereas, having regard to the third paragraph of Article 3b of the Treaty, and with a view to ensuring transparency, this Directive lays down the minimum requirements needed to ensure an adequate level of customer information both before and after the execution of a cross-border credit transfer; whereas this Directive lays down minimum execution requirements, in particular in terms of performance, which institutions offering cross-border credit transfer services should adhere to, including the obligation to execute a cross-border credit transfer in accordance with the customer's instructions; whereas this Directive fulfils the principles set out in Commission recommendation 90/109/EEC of 14 February 1990 on the transparency of banking conditions relating to cross-border financial transactions[1]; whereas this Directive is without prejudice to Council Directive 91/308/EEC of 10 June 1991 on prevention of the use of the financial system for the purpose of money laundering[2];

(9) Whereas, this Directive should contribute to reducing the maximum time taken to execute a cross-border credit transfer and encourage those institutions which already take a very short time to do so to maintain that practice;

(10) Whereas, in the report it will submit to the European Parlia-

ment and the Council within two years of implementation of this Directive, the Commission should particularly examine the time limit to be applied in the absence of a time limit agreed between the originator and his institution, taking into account both technical developments and the situation existing in each Member State;

(11) Whereas there should be an obligation upon institutions to refund in the event of non-execution of a credit transfer; whereas the obligation to refund imposes a contingent liability on institutions which might, in the absence of a limit, have a prejudicial effect on the solvency requirement; whereas that obligation to refund should therefore be applicable up to ECU 10 000;

(12) Whereas Article 8 does not affect the general provisions of national law whereby an institution is responsible to the originator when a cross-border credit transfer has not been completed because of an error committed by that institution;

(13) Whereas it is necessary to distinguish, among the circumstances with which institutions involved in the execution of a cross-border credit transfer may be confronted, including circumstances relating to insolvency, those caused by *force majeure*; whereas for that purpose the definition of *force majeure* given in Article 4 of Directive 90/314/EEC of 13 June 1990 on package travel, package holidays and package tours[3] should be taken as a basis;

(14) Whereas there need to be adequate and effective means in the Member States for the settlement of possible disputes between customers and institutions,

HAS ADOPTED THIS DIRECTIVE:

---

[1] OJ No L 67, 15. 3. 1990, p. 39.
[2] OJ No L 166, 28. 6. 1991, p. 77.

[3] OJ No L 158, 23. 6. 1993, p. 59.

SECTION I
Scope and definitions

Article 1
Scope

A16.3 1. The provisions of this Directive shall apply to cross-border credit transfers ordered by persons other than those covered by Article 2 (a), (b) and (c) and executed by credit institutions and other institutions.

2. Until . . .*, this Directive shall apply to cross-border credit transfers in the currencies of the Member States and in ecus of amounts less than ECU 25 000. After that date, this Directive shall apply to cross-border credit transfers in the currencies of the Member States and in ecus of amounts less than ECU 30 000.

Article 2
Definitions

For the purposes of this Directive:

A16.4 (a) **'credit institution'** means an institution as defined in Article 1 of Council Directive 77/780/EEC[4], and includes branches, within the meaning of the third indent of that Article and located in the Community, of credit institutions which have their head offices outside the Community and which by way of business execute cross-border transfers;

(b) **'other institution'** means any natural or legal person, other than a credit institution, that by way of business executes cross-border credit transfers;

(c) **'financial institution'** means an institution as defined in Article 4 (1) of Council Regulation (EC) No 3604/93 of 13 December 1993

specifying definitions for the application of the prohibition of privileged access referred to in Article 104a of the Treaty[5];

(d) **'institution'** means a credit institution or other institution; for the purposes of Articles 6, 7 and 8, branches of one credit institution situated in different Member States which participate in the execution of a cross-border credit transfer shall be regarded as separate institutions;

(e) **'intermediary institution'** means an institution which is neither that of the originator nor that of the beneficiary and which participates in the execution of a cross-border credit transfer;

(f) **'cross-border credit transfer'** means a transaction carried out on the initiative of an originator via an institution or its branch in one Member State, with a view to making available an amount of money to a beneficiary at an institution or its branch in another Member State; the originator and the beneficiary may be one and the same person;

(g) **'cross-border credit transfer order'** means an unconditional instruction in any form, given directly by an originator to an institution to execute a cross-border credit transfer;

(h) **'originator'** means a natural or legal person that orders the making of a cross-border credit transfer to a beneficiary;

(i) **'beneficiary'** means the final recipient of a cross-border credit transfer for whom the corresponding funds are made available in an account to which he has access;

(j) **'customer'** means the originator or the beneficiary, as the context may require;

---

* Two years after the date of implementation of this Directive.
[4] OJ No L 322, 17. 12. 1977, p. 30. Directive as last amended by Directive 95/26/EC (OJ No L 168, 18. 7. 1995, p. 7).

---

[5] OJ No L 332, 30. 12. 1993, p. 4.

(k) **'reference interest rate'** means an interest rate representing compensation and established in accordance with the rules laid down by the Member State in which the establishment which must pay the compensation to the customer is situated;

(l) **'date of acceptance'** means the date of fulfilment of the institution's conditions as to the execution of the cross-border credit transfer order and relating to the availability of adequate financial cover and the information required to execute that order.

SECTION II
Transparency of conditions for cross-border credit transfers

Article 3
Prior information on conditions for cross-border credit transfers

A16.5 Member States shall ensure that institutions make available to their actual and prospective customers in writing, including where appropriate by electronic means, and in a readily comprehensible form, information on conditions for cross-border credit transfers. This information shall include at least:

– an indication of the time needed, in execution of a cross-border credit transfer order given to the institution, for the funds to be credited to the account of the beneficiary's institution; the point from which that time runs must be clearly indicated,

– an indication of the time needed, upon receipt of a cross-border credit transfer, for the funds credited to the account of the institution to be credited to the beneficiary's account,

– the manner of calculation of any commission fees and charges payable by the customer to the institution, including where appropriate the rates,

– the value date, if any, applicable by the institution,

– an indication of the complaint and redress procedures available to the customer and the method of gaining access to them,

– an indication of the reference exchange rates used.

Article 4
Information subsequent to a cross-border credit transfer

Member States shall ensure that institutions supply their customers, unless the latter expressly forgo this, subsequent to the execution or receipt of a cross-border credit transfer, with clear information in writing, including where appropriate by electronic means, and in a readily comprehensible form. This information shall include at least: **A16.6**

– a reference enabling the customer to identify the cross-border credit transfer,

– the original amount of the cross-border credit transfer,

– the amount of all charges and commission fees payable by the customer,

– the value date, if any, applied by the institution.

Where the originator has specified that the charges for the cross-border credit transfer are to be wholly or partly borne by the beneficiary, the latter shall be informed thereof by his own institution.

Where any amount has been converted, the institution which converted it shall inform its customer of the exchange rate used.

SECTION III
Minimum obligations of institutions in respect of cross-border credit transfers

Article 5
Specific undertakings by the institution

A16.7 Unless it does not wish to deal with that customer, an institution must at a customer's request, for a cross-border credit transfer with stated specifications, give an undertaking concerning the time needed for execution of the transfer and the commission fees and charges payable, apart from those relating to the exchange rate used.

Article 6
Obligations regarding time taken

A16.8 1. The originator's institution shall execute the cross-border credit transfer in question within the time limit agreed with the originator.

Where the agreed time limit is not complied with or, in the absence of any such time limit, where, at the end of the fifth banking business day following the date of acceptance of the cross-border credit transfer order, the funds have not been credited to the account of the beneficiary's institution, the originator's institution shall compensate the beneficiary's institution.

Compensation shall comprise the payment of interest calculated by applying the reference rate of interest to the amount of the cross-border credit transfer for the period from:

- the end of the agreed time limit or, in the absence of any such time limit, the end of the fifth banking business day following the date of acceptance of the cross-border credit transfer order, to

- the date on which the funds are credited to the account of the beneficiary's institution.

Similarly, where non-performance of the cross-border credit transfer within the time limit agreed or, in the absence of any such time limit, before the end of the fifth banking business day following the date of acceptance of the cross-border credit transfer is attributable to an intermediary institution, that institution shall be required to compensate the institution from which the order originated.

2. The beneficiary's institution shall make the funds resulting from the cross-border credit transfer available to the beneficiary within the time limit agreed with the beneficiary.

Where the agreed time limit is not complied with or, in the absence of any such time limit, where, at the end of the banking business day following the day on which the funds were credited to the account of the beneficiary's institution, the funds have not been credited to the beneficiary's account, the beneficiary's institution shall compensate the beneficiary.

Compensation shall comprise the payment of interest calculated by applying the reference rate of interest to the amount of the cross-border credit transfer for the period from:

- the end of the agreed time limit or, in the absence of any such time limit, the end of the banking business day following the day on which the funds were credited to the account of the beneficiary's institution, to

- the date on which the funds are credited to the beneficiary's account.

3. No compensation shall be payable pursuant to paragraphs 1 and 2 where the originator's institution or, as the case may be, the beneficiary's institution, can establish that the delay is attributable to the originator or, as the case may be, the beneficiary.

4. Paragraphs 1, 2 and 3 shall be entirely without prejudice to the other

rights of customers and institutions that
have participated in the execution of a
cross-border credit transfer order.

Article 7
Obligation to execute the cross-border transfer in accordance with the instructions

A16.9 1. The originator's institution, any
intermediary institution and the beneficiary's institution, after the date of
acceptance of the cross-border credit
transfer order, shall each be obliged to
execute that credit transfer for the full
amount thereof unless the originator
has specified that the costs of the cross-
border credit transfer are to be borne
wholly or partly by the beneficiary.

The first subparagraph is without
prejudice to the possibility of the
beneficiary's institution levying a
charge on the beneficiary relating to
the administration of his account, in
accordance with the relevant rules and
customs. However, such a charge may
not be used by the institution to avoid
the obligations imposed by the said
subparagraph.

2. Without prejudice to any other
claims, where the originator's institution or an intermediary institution has
made a deduction from the amount of
the cross-border credit transfer in
breach of paragraph 1, the originator's
institution shall, when requested by the
originator, credit, free of all deductions
and at its own cost, the amount so
deducted to the beneficiary unless the
originator has requested that this
amount be credited to him.

Any intermediary institution which has
made a deduction in breach of paragraph 1 shall credit the amount so
deducted, free of all deductions and at
its own cost, to the originator's institution or, if the originator's institution so
requests, to the beneficiary of the cross-
border credit transfer.

3. Where a breach of the duty to
execute the cross-border credit transfer
order in accordance with the origina-

tor's instructions has been caused by
the beneficiary's institution, and without prejudice to any other claim which
may be made, the beneficiary's institution shall be liable to credit to the beneficiary, at its own cost, any sum
wrongly deducted.

Article 8
Obligation upon institutions to refund in the event of non-execution of transfers

1. If, after a cross-border credit A16.10
transfer order has been accepted by
the originator's institution, the relevant
amounts are not credited to the
account of the beneficiary's institution,
without prejudice to any other claim
which may be made, the originator's
institution shall credit the originator,
up to ECU 10000, with the amount of
the cross-border credit transfer plus:

– interest calculated by applying the
  reference interest rate to the
  amount of the cross-border credit
  transfer for the period between the
  date of the cross-border credit
  transfer order and the date of the
  credit, and

– the charges related to the cross-
  border credit transfer paid by the
  originator.

These amounts shall be made available
to the originator within 14 banking
business days following the date of his
request, unless the funds corresponding to the cross-border credit transfer
have in the meantime been credited
to the account of the beneficiary's
institution.

Such request may not be made before
expiry of the time limit agreed between
the originator's institution and the
originator for the execution of the
cross-border credit transfer order or, in
the absence of any such time limit,
before expiry of the time limit laid
down in the second subparagraph of
Article 6 (1).

Similarly, each intermediary institution which has accepted the cross-border credit transfer order likewise owes an obligation to refund at its own cost the amount of the credit transfer, including related costs and interest, to the institution which instructed it. If the cross-border credit transfer was not completed because of errors or omissions given by that institution, the intermediary institution shall endeavour as far as possible to refund the amount of the transfer.

2. By way of derogation from paragraph 1, if the cross-border credit transfer was not completed because of its non-execution by an intermediary institution chosen by the beneficiary's institution, the latter institution shall be obliged to make the funds corresponding to the amount of the transfer available to the beneficiary.

3. By way of derogation from paragraph 1, if the cross-border credit transfer was not completed because of an error or omission in the instructions given by the originator to his institution or because of non-execution of the cross-border credit transfer by an intermediary institution expressly chosen by the originator, the originator's institution and the other institutions involved shall endeavour as far as possible to refund the amount of the transfer.

Where the amount has been recovered by the originator's institution, it shall credit it to the originator subject to a deduction of costs arising from the recovery.

Article 9
Situation of *force majeure*

A16.11 Without prejudice to the provisions of Directive 91/308/EEC, institutions participating in the execution of a cross-border credit transfer order shall be released from the obligations laid down in this Directive where they can adduce reason of *force majeure*, namely abnormal and unforeseeable circumstances beyond the control of the person

pleading *force majeure*, the consequences of which would have been unavoidable despite all efforts to the contrary, which are relevant to its provisions.

Article 10
Settlement of disputes

Member States shall ensure that there are adequate and effective means for the settlement of disputes between an originator and his institution or between a beneficiary and his institution. **A16.12**

SECTION IV
Final provisions

Article 11
Implementation

1. Member States shall bring into force the laws, regulations and administrative provisions necessary to comply with this Directive by . . . * at the latest. They shall forthwith inform the Commission thereof. **A16.13**

When Member States adopt these provisions, they shall contain a reference to this Directive or shall be accompanied by such reference on the occasion of their official publication. The methods of making such reference shall be laid down by Member States.

2. Member States shall communicate to the Commission the text of the main laws, regulations or administrative provisions which they adopt in the field governed by this Directive.

Article 12
Report to the European Parliament and the Council

No later than two years after the date of implementation of this Directive, the Commission shall present a report to **A16.14**

---

* Thirty months after the date this Directive enters into force.

the European Parliament and the Council on the application of this Directive, accompanied where appropriate by proposals for its revision.

This report shall, in the light of the situation existing in each Member State and of the technical developments that have taken place, deal particularly with the question of the time limit set in Article 6 (1).

Article 13
Entry into force

A16.15 This Directive shall enter into force on the date of its publication in the *Official Journal of the European Communities*.

Article 14
Addressees

This Directive is addressed to the Member States. **A16.16**

Done at . . .

For the European Parliament

The President

For the Council

The President

STATEMENT OF THE COUNCIL'S REASONS

I. INTRODUCTION

1. On 18 November 1994 the Commission forwarded to the Council the above proposal for a Directive, based on Article 100a of the EC Treaty.

   The Economic and Social Committee and the European Parliament delivered their opinions on 1 June 1995 and 19 May 1995 respectively. The European Monetary Institute gave its opinion on 20 March 1995.

   Following these opinions, the Commission submitted an amended proposal on 7 June 1995.

2. On 4 December 1995, the Council adopted its common position pursuant to Article 189b of the Treaty.

II. OBJECTIVE

The aim of the Directive is to improve cross-border credit transfer services for individuals as well as businesses, especially small and medium-sized enterprises, by introducing:

– a minimum standard for the information of customers both prior and subsequent to the cross-border credit transfer,

– time limits within which, in the absence of agreement between bank and customer, the institutions of the originator and the beneficiary are required to execute the transfer (five days and one day respectively),

– an obligation to execute the transfer in accordance with the instructions contained in the payment order (double-charging ban),

– in the event of non-execution of transfers, without prejudice to any other claim which may be made, an obligation to refund the amount of the transfer up to ECU 10 000 plus interest and charges paid,

– an obligation for Member States to ensure that adequate and effective means exist for the settlement of any disputes between a bank and its customer.

The Directive forms part of a series of measures aimed at facilitating cross-border payments of which cross-border credit transfers account for a substantial part both in terms of volume and of value. The original proposal accompanied a Commission communication in the European Parliament, the Council, the European Monetary Institute and the Economic and Social Committee on 'EU funds transfers: transparency, performance and stability'.

III. ANALYSIS OF THE COMMON POSITION

a. Scope (Article 1)

Compared to the amended Commission proposal the common position:

- excludes credit transfers ordered by large professional financial establishments, which in the sense of the Directive are those institutions defined in Article 2 (a), (b) and (c). This limitation is introduced because of the professional nature of these institutions,

- does not explicitly define the scope of the Directive with reference to credit transfers within the European Union since this could give the misleading impression that all credit transfers within the Union and not just cross-border credit transfers were covered and since such a definition could exclude transfers involving an intermediary institution in a third country. The amendments proposed by the European Parliament relating to such a definition of the scope, in particular amendment No 1, are consequently not followed in the common position,

- applies the Directive to credit transfers of less than ECU 25000 for a period of two years after the date of implementation and to transfers of less than ECU 30000 after this period. In determining the scope of the Directive by reference to transfers of a certain amount the common position follows the approach of amendment No 5 proposed by the European Parliament,

- adapts for the sake of further precision and textual coherence the drafting of Paragraph 1.

In following the amended Commission proposal regarding the limitation of the scope to cross-border credit transfers in the currencies of the Member States and in ecus, the common position includes part of amendment No 5 proposed by the European Parliament.

b. Definitions (Article 2)

With a view to making the drafting of the Directive more precise, the common position amends the drafting of the definitions set out in the amended Commission proposal. In particular the definitions of the terms 'payment'. 'crossborder payment' and 'credit transfer' have been merged into the new term 'cross-border credit transfer' which has implications for the title of the Directive.

The common position further:

- changes the term 'payment order' to 'cross-border credit transfer order', the term 'acceptance' to 'date of acceptance' and the term 'interest' to 'reference interest rate'. In amending the definition of the term 'reference interest rate' to cover a more flexible rate, in line with the approach of the Commission's amended proposal, the common position takes account of amendment No 7 proposed by the European Parliament,

- introduces a definition of the term 'financial institution',

- deletes as unnecessary, in view of the amended drafting of the definitions and of the following Articles, the definitions of the terms: 'person', *force majeure* (which is, however, defined in a separate Article 9), 'value date', 'completion' and 'business day'. As a consequence of the deletion of the definition of 'completion', the common position does not include amendment No 8 proposed by the European Parliament,

– keeps with certain adaptations and clarifications the definitions of the terms: 'credit institution', 'other institution', 'institution', 'intermediary institution', 'originator', 'beneficiary' and 'customer'. In keeping the main part of definition of 'intermediary institution' as it was set out in the amended Commission proposal, the common position largely includes amendment No 9 proposed by the European Parliament.

c. Transparency (Articles 3 and 4)

The common position maintains all the essential features of the amended Commission proposal for Articles 3 and 4 and in so doing follows the major part of amendment No 10, and follows, albeit in a slightly different wording, amendment No 11 proposes by the European Parliament. The last subparagraph of amendment No 10 is not included in Article 3 of the common position since the Council finds it important to allow for a certain degree of flexibility as to the exact manner in which the information is communicated to the customer.

The drafting is amended, by comparison with the amended Commission proposal, in order to indicate the obligations of the institutions in a more precise manner. With a view to greater transparency, the common position further stipulates that the information to be given subsequent to the credit transfer (Article 4) must include

– in all cases, the original amount of the cross-border credit transfer,

– an indication of the exchange rate used, where any amount has been converted.

d. Minimum obligations of institutions (Articles 5 to 10)

Regarding the minimum obligations of institutions the common position maintains all the fundamental features of the amended Commission proposal, but amends the drafting with a view to describing more succinctly the rights and obligations of the originator, the beneficiary and the institutions involved, including any intermediate institutions. In particular the common position gives precise guidelines as to the calculation and payment of any compensation or reimbursement.

A new Article 5 is introduced which obliges an institution to give an undertaking to a customer regarding the terms applicable to a specific cross-border credit transfer.

In two new recitals, the ninth and the 10th, the common position makes clear that one of the principal aims of the Directive is to reduce the maximum time taken to effect a cross-border credit transfer and urges the Commission to re-examine this question in the report it will submit in accordance with Article 12. The common position thus takes account of amendment No 12 proposed by the European Parliament, although the enacting terms of the Directive has not been amended as proposed.

In making clear in Article 6 (1) (4) the obligations of an intermediary institution, the common position follows in substance amendment No 13 proposed by the European Parliament.

The common position stipulates in Article 6 (2) and (3) that the beneficiary's institution must compensate the beneficiary if the funds have not been credited to his account within the time limits set out in the Directive, unless the delay is attributable to the beneficiary. The common position thus covers the substance of amendment No 14 proposed by the European Parliament, and in fact goes further towards protecting the client.

The common position follows the amended Commission [amended] proposal in incorporating amendment No 15 proposed by the European Parliament. In making the beneficiary the first recipient of any wrongly deducted costs, Article 7 (2) of the common position, in line with the amended Commission proposal, largely follows the substance of amendment No 16 proposed by the European Parliament, although the question of reimbursement within the chain of involved institutions is treated in the manner set out in the Commission's original proposal.

The common position largely follows the amended Commission proposal for Article 8 in including a ceiling for reimbursement and by making the reimbursement dependent upon a request by the originator. The deadline for reimbursement is fixed at 14 banking business days after the request is made. In line with the amended Commission proposal the ceiling is fixed at ECU 10 000. The common position thus partially follows amendment No 18 proposed by the European Parliament, while it does not incorporate amendment No 28 proposed by the European Parliament.

In limiting any refund in case of defective instructions given by the originator to the amount of the transfer; the common position follows in substance amendment No 19 proposed by the European Parliament.

In line with the amended Commission proposal the rules relating to *force majeure* are set out in a separate Article 9. This provision applies to the Directive as a whole and it sets out in full a definition of *force majeure* corresponding to that included in Directive 90/314/EEC. The common position thus follows the substance of amendments Nos 6 and 21 proposed by the European Parliament.

In line with the amended Commission proposal the common position includes an Article 10 relating to the settlement of disputes. Although drafted in a more general manner, the common position follows the spirit of amendment No 22 proposed by the European Parliament.

e. Implementation

Compared to the amended Commission proposal, Article 11 of the common position fixes the date of implementation by reference to date of entry into force of the Directive (30 months after the entry into force). The date of presentation of the Commission's report (Article 12) is brought forward by one year compared to the amended Commission proposal, to no later than two years after the date of implementation.

f. Recitals

The recitals have been adopted following the changes made to the amended Commission proposal. Amendments Nos 3 and 4 proposed by the European Parliament have been followed to the extent that the corresponding amendments proposed to the enacting terms have been incorporated into the text of the common position. In adapting the third recital without changing the essential thrust of the text compared to the Commission's amended proposal, the common position further takes account of amendment No 2 proposed by the European Parliament.

IV. CONCLUSIONS

The Council considers that all amendments to the amended Commission proposal, including the determination of the scope, are in accordance with the aims of the Directive, namely to make it possible for individuals and businesses, especially small and medium-sized enterprises, to make cross-border credit transfers rapidly, reliably and cheaply from one part of the Community to another. The changes to the text aim primarily at ensuring the transparency and legal certainty for both the customers and the institutions concerned, and do not change the essential thrust of the amended Commission proposal.

697

Council Recommendation 96/C 5/01

of 22 December 1995

on harmonizing means of combating illegal immigration and illegal employment and improving the relevant means of control

THE COUNCIL OF THE EUROPEAN UNION,

A17.1 Having regard to the Treaty on European Union, and in particular K.3 (2) thereof,

Having regard to the initiative submitted by the French Republic on 22 December 1994,

Having regard to the recommendation of the Ministers of the Member States of the European Communities with responsibility for immigration of 1 June 1993 concerning checks on, and expulsion of, third-country nationals residing or working without authorization,

Having regard to the recommendation of the Ministers of the Member States of the European Communities with responsibility for immigration of 30 November 1992 regarding practices followed by Member States on expulsion,

Whereas, pursuant to Article K.1 (2) and (3) of the EC Treaty, policy regarding nationals of third countries and in particular combating unauthorized immigration, residence and work are matters of common interest and therefore fall within the areas for cooperation between Member States referred to in Title VI of the Treaty;

Whereas the Member States, faced with an increase in illegal immigration, have already adopted specific measures to ensure better control of population flows and to avoid the continued unlawful presence in their territories of foreign nationals who have entered or are residing without authorization;

Whereas, however, the efficiency of that action implies the implementation of coordinated and consistent measures;

Whereas, although recommendations laying down guiding principles for practice with regard to expulsion have already been adopted, that effort at alignment needs to be reinforced by recommending Member States to comply with a number of principles designed to ensure a better check on the situation of foreign nationals present within their territories;

Whereas this recommendation is in keeping with Community legislation, the Convention for the Protection of Human Rights and Fundamental Freedoms of 4 November 1950, and in particular Articles 3 and 14 thereof, and the Geneva Convention of 28 July 1951 relating to the Status of Refugees, as amended by the New York Protocol of 31 January 1967,

HEREBY RECOMMENDS Member States to **A17.2** harmonize further the means for checking on foreign nationals to verify that they fulfil the conditions laid down by the rules applicable to entry, residence and employment on the basis of the following guidelines:

1. This recommendation does not extend to citizens of the European Union or to nationals of EFTA member countries party to the Agreement on the European Economic Area, or to members of their families entitled under Community law.

2. Where an identity check is carried out on a foreigner in accordance with national law, at least where a person appears to be residing in the country unlawfully, his residence situation should be verified. This may apply in particular in the following cases:

– identity checks in connection with the investigation or prosecution of offences,

– identity checks to ward off threats to public order or security,

– identity checks in order to combat illegal entry or residence in certain areas (e.g. frontier areas and ports, airports and railways stations handling international traffic), without prejudice to border controls.

3. Third-country nationals should be in a position, according to national law, to present to the competent authorities confirmation, for example by way of papers or documents by virtue of which they are so authorized, of their authority to reside within the territory of the Member State where they are.

4. Where national law regards the residence or employment situation as a prerequisite for foreign nationals to qualify for benefits provided by a public service of a Member State in particular in the area of health, retirement, family or work, that condition cannot be met until it has been verified that the residence and employment situation of the person concerned and his or her family does not disqualify them from the benefit. Verification of residence or employment status is not required where intervention by a public authority is necessary on overriding humanitarian grounds.

Such verifications are carried out by the services providing the benefits, with the assistance, if necessary, of the authorities responsible in particular for issuing residence or work permits, in accordance with national law relating, in particular, to data protection.

Member States should inform the central or local authorities responsible for dispensing benefits to

foreign nationals of the importance of combating illegal immigration in order to encourage them to report to the competent authorities, in accordance with national law, such cases of breaches of the residence rules as they may detect in the course of their work.

The attention of the authorities responsible for issuing residence permits should also be drawn to the risk of marriages of convenience.

5. Employers wishing to recruit foreign nationals should be encouraged to verify that their residence or employment situations are in order by requiring them to present the document(s) by virtue of which they are authorized to reside and work in the Member State concerned. Member States could stipulate that employers may, if necessary, under the conditions laid down by national law relating, in particular, to data protection, check with the authorities responsible in particular for issuing residence and work permits; the said authorities may communicate the relevant information under procedures which guarantee confidentiality in the transmission of individual data. **A17.3**

6. Any person who is considered, under the national law of the Member State concerned, to be employing a foreign national who does not have authorization should be made subject to appropriate penalties.

7. The authorities competent to authorize residence should be empowered to take measures to check that persons who have been refused authorization to reside within the territory of the Member State have left that territory of their own accord.

8. Each Member State should consider setting up a central file of

foreign nationals containing information on the administrative situation of foreign nationals with regard to residence, including any refusal of authorization to reside and any expulsion measures. Any file thus set up will operate in compliance with the standards laid down in Council of Europe Convention 108 of 28 January 1981 for the Protection of Individuals with regard to Automatic Processing of Personal Data.

9. Member States should satisfy themselves that residence documents issued to foreign nationals are adequately secured against forgery and fraudulent use – particularly by colour photocopying – and, should, if necessary, amend them accordingly.

A17.4 10. Member States should take the measures necessary to reinforce and improve means of identifying foreign nationals who are not in a lawful position and who have no travel documents or other documents by which they can be identified.

Where a foreign national who is not in a lawful position is, or is likely to be, detained under the circumstances provided for in Chapter II of the recommendation of 30 November 1992 of the Ministers of the Member States of the European Communities with responsibility for immigration

regarding practices followed by Member States on expulsion, the period of detention should be used in particular to obtain the necessary travel documents for expelling foreign nationals who have no documents. The consular authorities of the country of origin or the country of the nationality of the foreign national concerned should be encouraged to make additional identification efforts to obtain travel documents.

Foreign nationals who have deliberately brought about their illegal position, particularly by refusing to supply travel documents, should be subject to penalties. In appropriate cases, such penalties may fall under criminal law.

Member States will review the follow-up to Chapter III.2 of the recommendation of 30 November 1992 of the Ministers of the Member States of the European Communities with responsibility for immigration regarding practices followed by Member States on expulsion.

The Council will review regularly, for example once a year, the progress made on harmonization in the fields covered by this recommendation.

Done at Brussels, 22 December 1995.

For the Council
The President
L ATIENZA SERNA

Council Recommendation 96/C 5/02

of 22 December 1995

on concerted action and cooperation in carrying out expulsion measures

THE COUNCIL OF THE EUROPEAN UNION,

A18.1 Having regard to the recommendation of the Ministers of the Member States of the European Communities responsible for immigration of 30 November 1992 concerning transit for the purposes of expulsion and the addendum thereto of 1 and 2 June 1993,

Whereas Article K.1 (3) (c) of the Treaty on European Union stipulates that combating unauthorized immigration, residence and work by nationals of third countries on the territory of Member States are matters of common interest;

Whereas the Council has already adopted specific measures to secure better control of migratory flows and to prevent third-country nationals entering Member States' territory unauthorized and remaining there illegally;

Whereas expulsion measures in respect of third-country nationals whose presence is unauthorized cannot be carried out owing to the absence of travel or identity documents;

Whereas, in order to achieve the effective carrying-out of expulsion measures, recommendations addressed to the Member States of the European Union and aimed at better coordination of those measures should be adopted at Council level;

Whereas the provisions of this recommendation are without prejudice to the European Convention for the Protection of Human Rights and Fundamental Freedoms of 4 November 1950 of to the Geneva Convention of 28 July 1951 relating to the Status of Refugees, as amended by the New York Protocol of 31 January 1967,

HEREBY RECOMMENDS MEMBER STATES' GOVERNMENTS:

to apply the principles set out below: **A18.2**

with a view to cooperation in the procurement of the necessary documentation

1. to implement specific mechanisms to improve the procurement of the necessary documentation from the consular authorities of the third State to which third-country nationals are to be expelled when they lack travel or identity documents;

2. where member States experience repeated difficulties with certain third States in the matter of procuring documentation:

   (a) to make a particular effort to arrange for persons to be expelled to be identified by the consular authorities;

   (b) to issue repeated invitations to consular authorities to visit centres in which third-country nationals are being held, where appropriate, in order to identify them for the purpose of providing documentation;

   (c) to urge the same authorities to issue travel documents with a period of validity sufficient for expulsion to be carried out;

3. in the first instance to make use of the provisions on presumption of nationality of the standard readmission agreement adopted by the Council on 30 November 1994;

4. to issue, where it is not possible to obtain the necessary travel documents by using the above means, the standard travel document adopted by the Council on 30 November 1994;

with a view to cooperation in carrying out transit for expulsion purposes

A18.3 5. to cooperate to facilitate transit for expulsion purposes when the decision has been adopted by another Member State on the basis of the principles set out herein:

(a) In accordance with the Ministers' recommendation of 30 November 1992 concerning transit for the purposes of expulsion and the addendum thereto of 1 and 2 June 1993, which are annexed hereto, any member State may, at the request of another Member State, authorize the transit of a third-country national across its territory for expulsion purposes.

(b) The Member State requesting the transit shall notify the requested State whether it considers it essential for the person being expelled to have an escort.

(c) The requested State shall be free to decide on the transit procedures; whether the escort is to be provided by the Member State which decided on the expulsion, whether it will provide the escort itself during transit or whether escort during transit will be arranged jointly with the State which decided on the expulsion.

(d) In the case of unescorted transit, the Member State which adopted the expulsion measure may, giving sufficient notice, request the State which has authorized transit to take the necessary measures in order to ensure departure to the place of destination.

(e) In the event of a third-country national's refusal to embark in the transit Member State, the Member States concerned may consider, in accordance with their laws and lest expulsion prove impossible to carry out, the possibility of availing themselves of, or seeking to establish, the appropriate legal machinery for enforcing expulsion.

(f) The transit Member State may return the third-country national to the territory of the Member State which adopted the expulsion measure if, for any reason whatsoever, the expulsion measure cannot be carried out.

(g) Member States may determine bilaterally the circumstances in which it may be possible to forego the refunding of costs on a case-by-case basis and replace it with an annual settlement of expenses occasioned by expulsion operations at either party's request;

with a view to concerted action in carrying out expulsions

6. to carry out expulsions, in appropriate instances, as a concerted effort with other Member States on the basis of the following principles: **A18.4**

(a) the Member State which adopts the expulsion measure shall assume responsibility for carrying out measures for the expulsion of a third-country national it has itself adopted and shall use the resources available on the air transport market or, if necessary, resources it has organized itself.

(b) The Member State which adopts the expulsion measure may request cooperation from another Member State to locate seats available to carry out the expulsion by air.

(c) The Member State whose cooperation has been requested for carrying out an expulsion measure by air shall be entitled to refuse to allow expulsion to be carried out from its territory.

(d) With a view to coordinating the carry-out of expulsion measures, each Member State shall inform other Member States which authority in its territory shall be responsible for:

– centralizing information on seats available on flights for expulsion purposes,

– contracting the competent authorities in the other Member States with a view to using seats available on flights,

– requesting authorization from other Member States to use seats available on flights departing from them,

– exchanging information with the authorities in other Member States in relation to carrying out expulsions by air,

with a view to monitoring the implementation of this recommendation

the Council shall regularly review the progress achieved in relation to the practical application of the cooperation and concerted action measures covered by this recommendation.

A18.5

Done at Brussels, 22 December 1995.

For the Council
The President
L ATIENZA SERNA

ANNEX I
RECOMMENDATION

concerning transit for the purposes of expulsion

(approved by the Ministers on 30 November 1992)

The ministers with responsibility for immigration,

CONSIDERING Member States' practices regarding transit for the purposes of expulsion;

WHEREAS it is appropriate to standardize such practices with a view to their harmonization;

WHEREAS the measures to be applied should meet the criteria of speed, efficiency and economy,

RECOMMEND that the following guidelines be applied:

I

For the purposes of this recommendation 'transit' means the transit of a person who is not a national of a Member State through the territory or the transit zone of a port or airport of a Member State.

II

A Member State which has decided to expel a third-country national

– to a third country should in principle do so without the person transiting through the territory of another Member State,

– to another Member State should in principle do so without the person transiting through the territory of a third Member State.

III

1. Where there are special reasons to justify this and, in particular, in the interests of efficiency, speed and economy, Member States may ask another Member State to authorize entry into its territory or transit through its territory of third-country nationals who are the subject of an expulsion measure.[1]

2. The State which has adopted the expulsion measure shall prove, before such a request is made, that the expellee's right to continue his journey and to enter the country of destination are guaranteed in the normal way.

3. The State to which the request is made shall deal with it without prejudice to the cases referred to in section VI.

IV

The State taking the expulsion measure shall notify the transit State whether the person being expelled needs to be escorted. The transit State may:

–   authorize the State which adopted the expulsion measure to provide the escort itself,

–   decide to provide the escort itself, or

–   decide to provide the escort in cooperation with the State which adopted the expulsion measure.

V

1. Requests for transit for purposes of expulsion must include information concerning:

    –   the identity of the third-country national being expelled,

    –   the State of final destination,

    –   the nature and date of the expulsion decision, and the authority which took the decision,

    –   factors enabling a judgment to be made as to whether the third-country national can be admitted to the country of final destination or the second transit country,

    –   the travel documents or other personal documents in the possession of the person concerned,

    –   the identification of the department making the request,

    –   the conditions of transit through the requested State (timetable, route, means of transport, etc.),

    –   whether an escort is required, and the details thereof.

2. Requests for transit for expulsion purposes must be submitted as soon as possible in accordance with the domestic legislation of the requested State to the authorities responsible for expulsion, who must reply to the request at the earliest opportunity.

VI

Cases in which transit for expulsion purposes may be refused:

–   where the third-country national who is the subject of a request for overland transit constitutes a threat to public order, national security or the international relations of the transit State,

–   where the information referred to in Section V (3) is not considered satisfactory.

---

[1]   Statement *re* Section III:
'Reasons of efficiency, speed and economy as referred to in Section III will include, *inter alia*, obligations resulting from the geographical situation of the Grand Duchy of Luxembourg.'

VII

If for some reason the expulsion measure cannot be carried out, the State through which transit is to take place may return the expellee, without any formalities, to the territory of the requesting State.

VIII

Where expulsion cannot be carried out at the expense of the third-country national or a third party, the requesting State shall be liable for:

– travel and other expenses, including escort costs, up until the departure from the territory of the Member State of transit of a third-country national whose transit has been authorized,

– the costs involved in any return/

IX

These recommendations shall not preclude closer cooperation between two or more Member States.

X

Member States which propose to conduct negotiations with another Member State or with a third State on transit for purposes of expulsion shall inform the other Member States in due time.

XI

This recommendation shall not contravene the provisions of the European Convention for the Protection of Human Rights and Fundamental Freedoms of 4 November 1950, nor those of the Convention on the Status of Refugees of 28 July 1951.

This recommendation shall not contravene the provisions of international conventions currently in force concerning extradition and extradition in transit.

This recommendation shall not replace extradition and transit extradition procedures by the transit procedure for expulsion purposes.

ANNEX II
ADDENDUM

to the recommendation concerning transit for the purposes of expulsion

(approved by the Ministers on 1 and 2 June 1993)

1. With a view to meeting the criteria of efficiency, speed and economy in connection with transit for purposes of expulsion a distinction may be made between the different expulsion measures, by air, sea or land, applied by the Member States.

2. Expulsion by air accompanied by transit through the transit zone of an airport should be excluded from the provisions requiring an entry and transit authorization (see Section III of the recommendation), so that in such cases it will be sufficient to notify the country of transit.

3. Notification of transit for expulsion purposes by air should contain the information required for transit requests indicated in Section V of the recommendation.

4. In the case of expulsion by land or sea, requests for and notifications of entry into the territory of a State or transit through that State shall be addressed to a

central contact body designated by the transit State, in accordance with the recommendations set out in the recommendation.

If, in the case of expulsion by air, the transit State does not grant permission, that information must be communicated to the requesting State within 24 hours of the notification of transit.

5. Member States shall draw up a joint list of contact bodies.

In the case of expulsion by air, it would be desirable to contact directly the competent official(s) of the transit airport concerned or, in accordance with national procedures, any other competent official, provided that the 24-hour rule is observed (see point 4 above).

Proposed Directive COM 95/712

Proposal for a European Parliament and Council Directive on injunctions for the protection of consumers' interests

(Text with EEA relevance)

COM(95) 712 final – 96/025 (COD)

(Submitted by the Commission on 16 February 1996)

THE EUROPEAN PARLIAMENT AND THE COUNCIL OF THE EUROPEAN UNION,

Having regard to the Treaty establishing the European Community, and in particular Article 100a thereof,

Having regard to the proposal from the Commission,

A19.1 Having regard to the opinion of the Economic and Social Committee,

Acting in accordance with the procedure referred to in Article 189b of the Treaty,

Whereas certain Community directives, listed in the schedule annexed to this Directive, lay down rules with regard to protection of the economic interests of consumers;

Whereas current mechanisms available both at national and at Community level for ensuring compliance with those directives do not always allow the effects of infringements of their provisions to be corrected in good time to protect consumers' interests;

Whereas, as far as the restraint of unlawful practices is concerned, the efficacy of national measures transposing those Directives is thwarted when those practices have their effects in a Member State other than the country in which they originate;

Whereas those difficulties can disrupt the smooth functioning of the internal market, their consequence being that it is sufficient to move the source of an unlawful practice in order to place it out of reach of all forms of redress;

whereas this constitutes a distortion of competition that is harmful to the great majority of firms which comply with the provisions of national law;

Whereas those difficulties are likely to diminish consumer confidence in the internal market and may have discriminatory effects on organizations representing consumers adversely affected by a practice that infringes Community law;

Whereas those practices often extend **A19.2** beyond the frontiers of the Member States, which is, indeed, the reason for approximating the systems of substantive law in question;

Whereas, there is thus an urgent need for some degree of coordination of national provisions designed to enjoin the cessation of the abovementioned unlawful practices, so that the existing means of redress can take effect, irrespective of the country in which the unlawful practice has had its effects;

Whereas the objective of the action envisaged can only be attained by the Community legislature; whereas it is therefore incumbent on the Community legislature to act;

Whereas the third paragraph of Article 3b of the Treaty makes it incumbent [of] the Community not to go beyond what is necessary to achieve the objectives of the Treaty; whereas, in accordance with that Article, the specific features of certain national legal systems must be respected; whereas that condition can be met by leaving Member States free to choose between different options having equivalent effect;

A19.3 Whereas one option should consist in requiring an independent public body, specifically responsible for the protection of consumer interests and/or competition matters, to exercise the rights of action set out in this Directive;

Whereas the other option should provide for the exercise of those rights by organizations which have a legitimate interest in protecting consumers, or by organizations representing firms, in accordance with criteria laid down by national law;

Whereas Member States should be able to combine those two options;

Whereas Member States should designate at national level the bodies and/or organizations qualified for the purposes of this Directive; whereas the principle of mutual recognition. Should be applied to the bodies and/or organizations thus certified by Member States;

Whereas it is incumbent on the Member States to communicate to the Commission the list of bodies and/or organizations thus qualified for the purposes of this Directive, as well as any changes to these national lists; whereas it is the business of the Commission to ensure their publication in the *Official Journal of the European Communities*;

Whereas this Directive should be without prejudice to the rules of private international law and the conventions in force between the Member States;

Whereas Member States should be able to require that a prior notification be issued by the party that intends to bring an action for an injunction, in order to give the defendant an opportunity to bring the contested infringement to an end;

Whereas the application of this Directive should not prejudice the application of Community competition rules,

HAVE ADOPTED THIS DIRECTIVE:

Article 1
Scope

1. The purpose of this Directive is to **A19.4** coordinate the laws, regulations and administrative provisions of Member States relating to certain remedies designed to protect consumers' interests, so as to ensure the smooth functioning of the internal market.

2. For the purposes of this Directive an infringement shall mean any act contrary to the directives listed in the Annex and transposed into the internal legal order of the Member States which harms consumers' interests.

Article 2
Actions for an injunction

1. Member States shall designate the **A19.5** court or authority competent to rule on the proceedings commenced by the qualified entities within the meaning of Article 3, and seeking:

(a) an order, given at very short notice, and where appropriate by way of summary procedure, requiring the cessation of any act that is to be regarded as an infringement;

(b) where appropriate, adoption of the measures needed to rectify the effects of the infringement, including publication of the decision;

(c) an order against the losing party for payment to the plaintiff, in the event of failure to comply with the decision within a time-limit specified by the authority, of a fixed amount for each day's delay or any other amount provided for in national legislation, with a view to ensuring compliance with the decisions.

2. When the action may, pursuant to a convention, be brought in a Member State other than the one whose legislation has allegedly been infringed, the competent authority hearing the case

shall take the same measures as are laid down for infringements of national legislation.

Article 3
Entities qualified to bring an action

A19.6 1. For the purposes of this Directive, a 'qualified entity' means any body or organization which, according to national law, has a legitimate interest in ensuring that the provisions referred to in Article 1 are complied with, in particular:

(a) an independent public body, specifically responsible for protecting consumer interests, in Member States in which such bodies exists; and/or

(b) organizations with a legitimate interest in protecting consumer interests, as well as organizations representing firms or federations of firms, in accordance with the criteria laid down by their national law.

2. For the purposes of this Directive, and without prejudice to the rights granted to other entities under national legislation, each Member State shall draw up at national level a list of entities qualified to bring an action under Article 2. The bodies and organizations included in that list shall receive a document certifying their right to appear before the relevant courts or authorities.

3. The lists drawn up in accordance with paragraph 2, as well as any changes thereto, shall be communicated by the Member States to the Commission and shall be published in the C Series of the *Official Journal of the European Communities.*

Article 4
Intra-Community infringements

A19.7 1. Member States shall take the measures necessary to ensure that any qualified entity whose interests are affected by an infringement originating in another Member State may seise the court or competent authority referred to in Article 2, on presentation of the document provided for in Article 3 (2).

2. Member States may provide that direct seisure referred to in paragraph 1 shall be sought only after a prior seisure of the qualified entity of the Member State having territorial jurisdiction, with a view to ensuring that it brings the action provided for in Article 2; in such case Member States shall give the qualified national entities a reasonable time-limit within which to react.

Article 5
Prior notification

1. Member States may introduce or maintain in force a requirement that the party that intends to seek an injunction shall issue a prior notification to the defendant; Member States which rely on this option shall ensure that the rules governing prior notification shall permit an action for an injunction within a reasonable time-limit. **A19.8**

2. The rules governing prior notification adopted by Member States shall be notified to the Commission and shall be published in the C Series of the *Official Journal of the European Communities.*

3. The limitation period shall cease to run once the prior notification has been issued.

Article 6
Reports

Every three years and for the first time no later than 31 December 2000 the Commission shall present the European Parliament and the Council with a report on the application of this Directive. **A19.9**

Article 7
Provisions for wider actions

This Directive shall not prevent Member States from adopting or maintain- **A19.10** ing in force provisions designed to grant representative organizations of consumers or professionals and/or public bodies and any other person concerned more extensive rights to bring action at national level/

Article 8
Implementation

A19.11 1. Member States shall bring into force the laws, regulations and administrative provisions necessary to comply with this Directive by 31 December 1997. They shall immediately inform the Commission thereof.

When Member States adopt these provisions, these shall contain a reference to this Directive or shall be accompanied by such reference at the time of their official publication. The procedure for such reference shall be adopted by Member States.

2. Member States shall communicate to the Commission the provisions of national law which they adopt in the field covered by this Directive.

Article 9
Entry into force

This Directive shall enter into force on the twentieth day following that of its publication in the *Official Journal of the European Communities*. A19.12

Article 10
Addressees

This Directive is addressed to the Member States. A19.13

ANNEX
List of Directives covered by Article 1 (2)

- Council Directive 84/450/EEC of 10 September 1984 (misleading advertising); OJ No L 250, 19. 9. 1984, p. 17;

- Council Directive 85/577/EEC of 20 December 1985 (contracts negotiated away from business premises); OJ No L 372, 31. 12. 1985, p. 31;

- Council Directive 87/102/EEC of 22 December 1986 – OJ No L 42, 12. 2. 1987, p. 48, as amended by Council Directive 90/88/EEC of 22 February 1990 (consumer credit) (OJ No L 61, 10. 3. 1990, p. 14);

- Council Directive 89/552/EEC of 3 October 1989 (on the pursuit of television broadcasting activities): Articles 10 to 23; OJ No L 298, 17. 10. 1989, p. 23;

- Council Directive 90/314/EEC of 13 June 1990 (package travel, package holidays and package tours); OJ No L 158, 23. 6. 1990, p. 59;

- Council Directive 92/28/EEC of 31 March 1992 (advertising of medicinal products for human use); OJ No L 113, 30. 4. 1992, p. 13;

- Council Directive 93/13/EEC of 5 April 1993 (unfair terms in consumer contracts); OJ No L 95, 21. 4. 1993, p. 29;

- European Parliament and Council Directive 94/47/EC of 26 October 1994 (protection of purchasers in respect of certain aspects of contracts relating to the purchase of the right to use immovable properties on a time-share basis); OJ No L 280, 29. 10. 1994, p. 83;

- European Parliament and Council Directive . . . of . . . (contracts negotiated at a distance).

ANNEX REPORT

Actions for an injunction in regard to the protection of the collective interest of consumers in the Member States of the European Union (status: 31 March 1995)

Countries	Source	Causa petendi	Qualified entity
Belgium	1 Act of 14/7/91 (MB 29/8/91) 2 Act of 12/6/91 (MB 9/7/91) 3 Act of 4/12/90 (MB 22/8/90) 4 Act of 21/10/92 (MB 17/11/92) 5 Act of 16/2/94 (MB 1/4/94)	1 All infringements of the law on commercial practices, including misleading advertising 2 Consumer credit 3 Financial services 4 Advertising for the liberal professions 5 Package holidays	All associations whose purpose is to protect consumers' interests and which have legal personality, provided they are represented on the Consumer Council or approved by the Minister for Economic Affairs
Denmark	Marketing Practices Act 1975 (last amendment: 1 June 1994)	All infringements of the law on commercial practices	The consumers' ombudsmen
Germany	1 UWG 1909 (as amended in 1965 and 1987) 2 AGB 1976	1 All infringements covered by Articles 1, 3, 4, 6, 7, 8 of the Competition Act 2 Unfair terms	Associations having legal capacity whose task, as set out in their articles of association, includes protection of consumers' interests by providing information, by providing advice (UWG); + members must include active associations or associations whose membership includes at least 75 natural persons (AGB)
Greece	Act No 2000/91 (ETK 24/12/91) as amended by Act No 2251/94 (ETK 16/11/94)	Any unlawful practice affecting the general interests of consumers (Act No 2251/94 contains a non-exhaustive list of infringements)	Consumers' associations with at least 500 active members which have been registered for at least two years in the relevant register
Spain	1 Act No 34/1998 of 11/11/88 (BOE 14/11/88) 2 Act No 3/1991 of 10.1.91 (BOE 11/1/91)	1 Illegal advertising 2 Any act which is directly in breach of good faith (clausula general: Article 5)	Associations whose purpose, according to their articles of association, is to protect consumers, provided the "act of unfair competition directly affects consumer interests" Article 19)
France	Act No 88-14 of 5/1/1988 (OJ 6/1/88) (for the collective protection of individual rights: Act No 92-60 of 18/1/1992)	Direct or indirect harm to the collective of consumers Unlawful actions or unfair terms	Approved associations (see Decree 88-586 of 6 May 1988)
Ireland	Consumer Information Act	"Practices that are, or are likely to be, misleading to the public"	Director of Consumer Affairs

ANNEX REPORT (continued)

Countries	Source	Causa petendi	Qualified entity
Italy tions	1 Legislative Decree of 25.1.1992 No 74 2 Act 549 of 28.12.93	1 Misleading advertising 2 Protection of the ozone layer and the environment	1 All consumers and consumer organiza-tions 2 All consumer organizations or enviromental protection organizations
Luxembourg	1 Act of 25/8/83 2 Act of 27/11/86	1 Unfair terms 2 Unfair commercial practices	Consumer associations represented at the Luxembourg Price Commission
Netherlands	1 Article 6:196 of the Civil Code (BW) 2 Article 6:240 of the Civil Code (BW) 3 Wet persoons-registratie 4 Articles 3:305a and 3:305b of the BW (Act of 6/4/1994; entry into force, 1/7/1994)	1 Misleading advertising 2 Unfair terms 3 Protection of privacy (rectification of files) 4 "General" action	Associations having legal personality whose tasks include promotion of consumer interests
Austria tion)	1 Consumentenschutzgesetz 1979 (§§28 and 29) 2 UWG (Act on unfair competition)	1 Unfair terms 2 Unfair advertising, unfair competition	1 VKI (Verein für Konsumenteninforma-tion and "Chambers of the Social Partners" 2 "Chambers of the Social Partners (consumers being represented in the "Bundesarbeitskammer")
Portugal	Decree No 446/85 of 25/10/1985	Unfair terms	Representative associations of consumers under the terms of the relevant legislation
Finland	Consumer Ombudsman Act	Any practice which infringes provisions designed to protect the collective interest of consumers	Consumer Ombudsman
Sweden	Consumer Ombudsman Act	Any practice which infringes provisions designed to protect the collective interest of consumers	Consumer Ombudsman
United Kingdom	Fair Trading Act 1973	Any practice which is detrimental to consumer interests in the United Kingdom and must be regarded as unfair to the consumer	Director General of Fair Trading

Common Position (EC) No 29/96

adopted by the Council on 19 March 1996

with a view to adopting Directive 96/.../EC of the European Parliament and of the Council amending Directive 84/450/EEC concerning misleading advertising so as to include comparative advertising

THE EUROPEAN PARLIAMENT AND THE COUNCIL OF THE EUROPEAN UNION

A20.1 Having regard to the Treaty establishing the European Community, and in particular Article 100a thereof,

Having regard to the proposal from the Commission[1],

Having regard to the opinion of the Economic and Social Committee[2],

Acting in accordance with the procedure referred to in Article 198b of the Treaty[3],

(1) Whereas one of the Community's main aims is to complete the internal market' whereas measures must be adopted to ensure the smooth running of the said market; whereas the market comprises an area which has no internal frontiers and in which goods, persons, services and capital can move freely;

(2) Whereas the completion of the internal market will mean an ever wider range of choice; whereas, given that consumers can and must make the best possible use of the internal market, and that advertising is a very important means of creating genuine outlets for all goods and services throughout the

Community, the basic provisions governing the form and content of comparative advertising should be uniform and the conditions of the use of comparative advertising in the Member States should be harmonized; whereas this will help demonstrate the merits of the various comparable products; whereas comparative advertising can also stimulate competition between suppliers of goods and services to the consumer's advantage;

(3) Whereas the laws, regulations and administrative provisions of the individual Member States concerning comparative advertising differ widely; whereas advertising reaches beyond the frontiers and is received on the territory of other Member States; whereas the acceptance or non-acceptance of comparative advertising according to the various national laws may constitute an obstacle to the free movement of goods and services and create distortions of competition; whereas, in particular, firms may be exposed to forms of advertising developed by competitors to which they cannot reply in equal measure; whereas the freedom to provide services relating to comparative advertising should be assured; whereas the Community is called on to remedy this situation;

(4) Whereas the sixth recital of Council Directive 84/450/EEC of 10 September 1984 relating to the approximation of laws, regulations and administrative provisions of

---

[1] OJ No C 180, 11.7.1991, p. 14.
[2] OJ No C 49, 24.2.1992, p. 35.
[3] Opinion of the European Parliament of 18 November 1992 (OJ No C 337, 21.12.1992, p. 142), common position of the Council of . . . (not yet published in the Official Journal) and Decision of the European Parliament of . . . (not yet published in the Official Journal).

the Member States concerning misleading advertising[1] states that, after the harmonization of national provisions against misleading advertising, "at a second stage . . ., as far as necessary, comparative advertising should be dealt with, on the basis of appropriate Commission proposals";

A20.2 (5) Whereas point 3 (d) of the Annex to the Council resolution of 14 April 1975 on a preliminary programme of the European Economic Committee for a consumer protection and information policy[2] includes the right to information among the basic rights of consumers; whereas this right is confirmed by the Council Resolution of 19 May 1981 on a second programme of the European Economic Community for a consumer protection and information policy[3], point 40 of the Annex, which deals specifically with consumer information; whereas comparative advertising, when it compares relevant, verifiable and representative features and is not misleading, is a legitimate means of informing consumers of their advantage;

(6) Whereas it is desirable to provide a broad concept of comparative advertising to cover all modalities of comparative advertising;

(7) Whereas conditions of permitted comparative advertising, as far as the comparison is concerned, should be established in order to determine which practices relating to comparative advertising may distort competition, cause damage to competitors and have an adverse effect on consumer choice; whereas such conditions of permitted advertising should include criteria of objective comparison of the features of goods and services;

(8) Whereas the comparison of the price only of goods and services should be possible if this comparison respects certain conditions, in particular that it shall not be misleading;

(9) Whereas, in order to prevent **A20.3** comparative advertising being used in an anti-competitive and unfair manner, only comparisons between competing goods, and services meeting the same needs or intended for the same purpose should be permitted;

(10) Whereas the conditions of comparative advertising should be cumulative and respected in their entirety; whereas this shall not prevent Member States from defining modalities of implementation for each of the conditions, in order to find the appropriate solution in each case;

(11) Whereas these conditions should include, in particular, consideration of the provisions resulting from Council Regulation (EEC) No 2081/92 of 14 July 1992 on the protection of geographical indications and designations of origin for agricultural products and foodstuffs[4], and in particular Article 13 thereof, and of the other Community provisions adopted in the agricultural sphere;

(12) Whereas Article 5 of First Council Directive 89/104 of 21 December 1988 to approximate the laws of the Member States relating to trade marks[5] confers exclusive rights on the proprietor of a registered trade mark, including the right to prevent all third parties from using, in the course of trade, any sign which is identical with, or similar to, the trade mark in relation to identical goods or services

---

[1] OJ No L 250, 19.9.1984, p. 17.
[2] OJ No C 92, 25.4.1975, p. 1.
[3] OJ No C 133, 3.6.1981, p. 1.

[4] OJ No L 208, 24.7.1992, p. 1.
[5] OJ No L 40, 11.2.1989, p. 1. Directive as last amended by Decision 92/10/EEC (OJ No L 6, 11.1.1992, p. 35).

or even, where appropriate, other goods;

(13) Whereas it may, however, be indispensable, in order to make comparative advertising effective, to identify the goods or services of a competitor, making reference to a trade mark or trade name of which the latter is the proprietor;

(14) Whereas such use of another's trade mark, trade name or other distinguishing marks does not breach this exclusive right in cases where it complies with the conditions laid down by this Directive, the intended target being solely to distinguish between them and thus to highlight differences objectively;

(15) Whereas provisions should be made for the legal and/or administrative means of redress mentioned in Articles 4 and 5 of Directive 84/450/EEC to be available to control comparative advertising which fails to meet the conditions laid down by this Directive; whereas Article 6 applies to unpermitted comparative advertising in the same way;

(16) Whereas Article 7 of Directive 84/450/EEC allowing Member States to retain or adopt provisions with a view to ensuring more extensive protection for consumers, persons carrying on a trade, business, craft or profession, and the general public, should not apply to comparative advertising, given that the objective of amending the said Directive is to establish conditions under which comparative advertising is permitted;

(17) Whereas a comparison which presents goods or services as an imitation or a replica of goods or services bearing a registered trade mark shall not be considered to fulfil the conditions to be met by permitted comparative advertising;

(18) Whereas this Directive in no way affects Community provisions on advertising for specific products and/or services or restrictions or prohibitions on advertising in particular media; **A20.4**

(19) Whereas if a Member State, in compliance with the provisions of the Treaty, prohibits advertising regarding certain goods or services, this ban may, whether it is imposed directly or by a body or organization responsible under the law of that Member State for regulating the exercise of a commercial, industrial, craft or professional activity, be extended to comparative advertising;

(20) Whereas Member States shall not be obliged to permit comparative advertising for goods or services on which they maintain or introduce bans, including bans as regards marketing methods or advertising which targets vulnerable consumer groups;

(21) Whereas regulating comparative advertising is, under the conditions set out in this Directive, necessary for the smooth running of the internal market and whereas action at Community level is required; whereas the adoption of a Directive is the appropriate instrument because it lays down uniform general principles while allowing the Member States to choose the form and appropriate method by which to attain these objectives; whereas it is in accordance with the principle of subsidiarity.

HAVE ADOPTED THIS DIRECTIVE:

Article 1

Directive 84/450/EEC is hereby amended as follows: **A20.5**

1. the title shall be replaced by the following:

'Council Directive of 10 September 1984 concerning misleading and comparative advertising';

2. Article 1 shall be replaced by the following:

"Article 1
The purpose of this Directive is to protect consumers, persons carrying on a trade or business or practising a craft or profession and the interests of the public in general against misleading advertising and the unfair consequences thereof and to lay down the conditions under which comparative advertising is permitted.";

3. the following point shall be inserted in Article 2:

"2 (a): 'comparative advertising' means any advertising which explicitly or by implication identifies a competitor or goods or services offered by a competitor;";

A20.6 4. the following Article shall be added:

"Article 3a
1. Comparative advertising shall, as far as the comparison is concerned, be permitted when the following conditions are met:

(a) it is not misleading according to Articles 2 (2), 3 and 7 (1);

(b) it compares goods or services meeting the same needs or intended for the same purpose;

(c) it objectively compares one or more material, relevant, verifiable and representative features of those goods and services, which may include price;

(d) it does not create confusion in the market place between the advertiser and a competitor or between the advertiser's trade marks, trade names, other distinguishing marks, goods or services and those of a competitor;

(e) it does not discredit or denigrate the trade marks, trade names,

other distinguishing marks, goods, services or activities of a competitor;

(f) for products with designation of origin, it relates in each case to products with the same designation;

(g) it does not take unfair advantage of the reputation of a trade mark, trade name or other distinguishing marks of a competitor or of the designation of origin of competing products.

2. Any comparison referring to a special offer shall indicate in a clear and unequivocal way the date on which the offer ends or, where appropriate, that the special offer is subject to the availability of the goods and services, and, where the special offer has not yet begun, the date of the state of the period during which the special price or other specific conditions shall apply.";

5. the first and second subparagraphs **A20.7** of Article 4 (1) shall be replaced by the following:

"1. Member States shall ensure that adequate and effective means exist for the control of misleading advertising and for the compliance with the provisions on comparative advertising in the interests of consumers as well as competitors and the general public.

Such means shall include legal provisions under which persons or organizations regarded under national law as having a legitimate interest in prohibiting misleading advertising or regulating comparative advertising may:

(a) take legal action against such advertising;

and/or

(b) bring such advertising before an administrative authority competent either to decide on complaints or to initiate appropriate legal proceedings.";

6. Article 4 (2) is hereby amended as follows:

    (a) the indents in the first subparagraph shall be replaced by the following:

"– to order the cessation of, or to institute appropriate legal proceedings for an order for the cessation of, misleading or unpermitted comparative advertising, or

– if the misleading or unpermitted comparative advertising has not yet been published but publication is imminent, to order the prohibition of, or to institute appropriate legal proceedings for an order for the prohibition of, such publication,";

    (b) the introductory wording to the third subparagraph shall be replaced by the following:

"Furthermore, Member States may confer upon the courts or administrative authorities powers enabling them, with a view to eliminating the continuing effects of misleading or unpermitted comparative advertising, the cessation of which has been ordered by a final decision";

A20.8 7. Article 5 shall be replaced by the following:

"*Article 5*
This Directive does not exclude the voluntary control of misleading or comparative advertising by self-regulatory bodies and recourse to such bodies by the persons or organizations referred to in Article 4 if proceedings before such bodies are in addition to the court or administrative proceedings referred to in that Article.";

A20.9 8. Article 7 shall be replaced by the following:

"*Article 7*
1. This Directive shall not preclude Member States from retaining or adopting provisions with a view to ensuring more extensive protection, with regard to misleading advertising, for consumers, persons carrying on a trade, business, craft or profession, and the general public.

2. Paragraph 1 shall not apply to comparative advertising as far as the comparison is concerned.

3. The provisions of this Directive shall apply without prejudice to Community provisions on advertising for specific products and/or services or to restrictions or prohibitions on advertising in particular media.

4. The provisions of this Directive concerning comparative advertising shall not oblige Member States which, in compliance with the provisions of the Treaty, maintain or introduce advertising bans regarding certain goods or services, whether imposed directly or by a body or organization responsible, under the law of the Member States, for regulating the exercise of a commercial, industrial, craft or professional activity, to permit comparative advertising regarding those goods or services. Where these bans are limited to particular media, the Directive shall apply to the media not covered by these bans.".

Article 2

1. Member States shall bring into force **A20.10** the laws, regulations and administrative provisions necessary to comply with this Directive at the latest 30 months after its publication in the *Official Journal of the European Communities*. They shall forthwith inform the Commission thereof.

2. When Member States adopt these measures, they shall contain a refer-

ence to this Directive or shall be accompanied by such reference on the occasion of their official publication. The methods of making such reference shall be laid down by Member States.

3. Member States shall communicate to the Commission the text of the main provisions of domestic law which they adopt in the field governed by this Directive.

Article 3

This Directive is addressed to the Member States.

Done at . . .

For the Council
The President

STATEMENT OF THE COUNCIL'S REASONS

I. INTRODUCTION

1. On 28 May 1991, the Commission sent the Council a proposal, based on Article 100a of the EC Treaty, on comparative advertising and amending Directive 84/450/EEC on misleading advertising.
2. The European Parliament and the Economic and Social Committee delivered their opinions on 18 November 1991[1] and 24 February 1992[2] respectively.
3. On 21 April 1994, the Commission forwarded an amended proposal to the Council.
4. On 18 March 1996, the Council adopted its common position in accordance with Article 189b of the Treaty.

II. OBJECTIVE

The proposal is designed to harmonize conditions for comparative advertising with a view to accomplishing the internal market, contributing to improving the information of consumers and stimulating competition. To realize this objective, it appears appropriate to amend Directive 84/450/EEC on misleading advertising.

III. ANALYSIS OF THE COMMON POSITION

(The references concern, if not otherwise indicated, the text of the common position.)

– *Article 2 (2) (a) of the amended Directive*

The Council has dropped the term "of the same kind" in the definition and completed instead the list of conditions in Article 3 (a) (1b). The definition has thus been made more general in order to ensure a high degree of harmonization and to avoid the coexistence of Community and national rules in this field.

– *Article 1 and 3 (a) (1), introductory sentence*

The Council has replaced the term "allowed" by "permitted" to make it clear that authorization is not implied.

– *Article 2 (a) introductory sentence*

The Council has added the terms "as far as the comparison is concerned" to ensure that stricter national consumer protection in this field is not put into question.

---

[1] OJ No C 337 21.12.1992, p. 142.
[2] OJ No C 49, 24.2.1992, p. 35.

718

– *Article 2 (a) (1) points (a), (b) and (f)*

The Council has:

– (a): foreseen a more accurate reference to the provisions on misleading advertising relevant in this context,

– (b): replaced the criterion of "same kind" by a more appropriate wording,

– (f): added an indent on products with designation or origin.

– *Article 7*

Article 7 of the mother Directive has been completed by three new paragraphs (paragraphs 2 to 4):

– paragraph 2 provides for a maximum harmonization in order to ensure that given the possibility for Member States to provide for more extensive protection with regard to misleading advertising under paragraph 1 of this Article, there remains a reasonable scope for comparative advertising;

– paragraph 3 provides for the necessary precision regarding other Community legislation on advertising.

– paragraph 4 ensures that Member States may maintain or introduce bans regarding certain goods or services meant to protect the consumer.

– *Deadline for implementation (Article 2 of the common position text)*

The Council wishes a deadline of 30 months, as in the case of Directive 94/47/EC of the European Parliament and the Council on "timeshare".

– *Other provisions*

Articles 1, 4 (1), 4 (2) and 5 of the mother Directive have, for the sake of the clarity and coherence of the text, been completed or adapted to cover comparative advertising also.

– *Preamble*

The Council has adapted the recitals to the text as modified and inserted, in particular, recital Nos 8, 11, 17 and 20.

Proposed Council Regulation (EC)

on air carrier liability in case of accidents

THE COUNCIL OF THE EUROPEAN UNION,

A21.1 Having regard to the Treaty establishing the European Community, and in particular Article 84(2) thereof,

Having regard to the proposal from the Commission,[1]

Acting in accordance with the procedure set out in Article 189c, in co-operation with the European Parliament,[2]

Having regard to the opinion of the Economic and Social Committee,[3]

Whereas the rules on liability in case of accidents are governed by the Convention for the Unification of Certain Rules Relating to International Carriage by Air, signed at Warsaw on 12 October 1929, or that Convention as amended at The Hague on 28 September 1955, whichever may be applicable; whereas the Warsaw Convention is applied worldwide for the benefit of both passengers and air carriers, and must be preserved;

Whereas the rules on the nature and limitation of liability in the event of death, wounding or any other bodily injury suffered by a passenger form part of the terms and conditions of carriage in the air transport contract between carrier and passenger; whereas Council Regulation (EEC) No 2407/92,[4] Regulation (EEC No 2408/92,[5] as amended by the Act of Accession of Austria, Finland and Sweden, and Regulation (EEC) No 2409/92[6] have created an internal aviation market wherein it is appropriate that the rules on the nature and limitation of liability should be harmonized.

Whereas the limit set on liability by the Warsaw Convention is too low by today's economic and social standards; whereas in consequence Member States have variously increased the liability limit, thereby leading to different terms and conditions of carriage in the Community;

Whereas in addition the Warsaw Convention only applies to international transport; whereas in the internal aviation market the distinction between national and international transport has been eliminated; whereas it is therefore appropriate to have the same level and nature of liability in both national and international transport;

Whereas the present low limit of liability often leads to lengthy legal actions which damage the image of air transport;

Whereas Community action in the field of air transport should also aim at a high level of protection for the interests of users;

Whereas in order to provide harmonized conditions of carriage in respect of liability of air carrier and, further, in order to ensure a high level of effective protection of air users, action, regard being had to the principle of subsidiarity, can best be addressed at Community level;

Whereas it is appropriate to remove all limits of liability in the event of death, wounding or any other bodily injury suffered by a passenger;

Whereas, in order to avoid situations where victims of unpreventable accidents remain uncovered, carriers should not, with respect to any claim arising out of the death, wounding or other bodily injury of a passenger

---

1

2

3

[4] OJ No L 240, 24. 8. 1992, p. 1.
[5] OJ No L 240, 24. 8. 1992, p. 8.
[6] OJ No L 240, 24. 8. 1992, p. 25.

under Article 17 of the Warsaw Convention, avail themselves of any defence under Article (20)§1 thereof up to the sum of ECU 100000;

Whereas passengers or next-of-kin should receive a lump sum as soon as possible in order to face immediate needs;

Whereas persons entitled to compensation should have the benefit of legal clarity in the event of an accident; whereas they should be fully informed beforehand of the applicable rules; whereas it is necessary to avoid lengthy litigation or claims processes; whereas it is appropriate in addition to give the person entitled to compensation the option of taking action in the courts of the Member States in which the passenger has his domicile or permanent residence;

Whereas it is desirable in order to avoid distortion of competition that third-country carriers adequately inform passengers of their conditions of carriage;

Whereas the improvement of the situation for luggage and cargo is currently taken care of at International Civil Aviation Organisation (ICAO) level and does not require the same urgent treatment as the passengers' situation;

Whereas it is appropriate and necessary that the values expressed in this Regulation be increased in accordance with economic developments; whereas it is appropriate to empower the Commission, after consultation of an advisory committee, to decide upon such increases,

HAS ADOPTED THIS REGULATION:

Article 1

A21.2 This Regulation defines the obligations of Community air carriers to cover liability in the event of accidents to passengers.

Article 2

A21.3 1. For the purpose of this Regulation:

    (a) **"air carrier"** means an air transport undertaking with a valid operating licence;

    (b) **"Community air carrier"** means an air transport undertaking within the meaning of Council Regulation (EEC) No 2407/92;

    (c) **"persons entitled to compensation"** means the victims and/or persons who, in the light of the applicable law, are entitled to represent the victims in accordance with a legal provision, a court decision or in accordance with a special contract;

    (d) **"lump sum"** means an advance payment to the person entitled to compensation to enable him to meet his most urgent needs, without prejudice to the speediest settlement of full compensation;

    (e) **"ECU"** means the unit of account adopted in drawing up the general budget of the European Communities in accordance with Articles 207 and 209 of the Treaty.

    (f) **"Warsaw Convention"** means the Convention for the Unification of certain Rules relating to International Carriage by Air, signed in Warsaw on 12 October 1929, together with all international instruments which build on and are associated with it;

2. Concepts contained in this Regulation which are not defined in paragraph 1 shall be equivalent to those used in the Warsaw Convention.

Article 3

1. The liability of a Community air carrier for damages sustained in the event of the death, wounding or any other bodily injury suffered by a passenger shall not be subject to any statutory or contractual limits.   **A21.4**

2. For any damages up to the sum of ECU 100000 the Community air carrier shall not exclude or limit his liability by proving that he and

his agents have taken all necessary measures to avoid the damage or that it was impossible for him or them to take such measures.

Article 4

A21.5 1. The carrier shall without delay, and in any event not later than ten days after the event during which the damage occurred, pay to or make available to the person entitled to compensation a lump sum of up to ECU 50 000 in proportion to the injury sustained and in any event a sum of ECU 50 000 in case of death.

2. The lump sum may be offset against any subsequent sum to be paid in respect of the liability of the Community air carrier, but is not returnable under any circumstances.

Article 5

A21.6 1. The provisions contained in Articles 3 and 4 shall be included in the Community air carrier's conditions of carriage

2. Adequate information on the provisions contained in Articles 3 and 4 shall on request be given to passengers at the Community carrier's agencies, travel agencies and check-in counters, and a summary of the requirements shall be made on the ticket document.

3. Air carriers established outside the Community and not subject to the obligations referred to in Articles 3 and 4 shall expressly and clearly inform the passengers thereof, at the time of purchase of the ticket at the carrier's agencies, travel agencies, or check-in counters located in the territory of a Member State. Air carriers shall on request provide the passengers with a form setting out their conditions. The fact that the limit is indicated on the ticket document shall not constitute sufficient information.

Article 6

A21.7

Once a year Members States' authorities shall notify the list of third country air carriers not subject to the rules of this Regulation to the Air Transport User Organizations concerned and to the Commission, which shall make that list available to the other Member States.

Article 7

A21.8

A person entitled to compensation in the case of accidents involving Community air carriers may, in addition to the rights conferred by Article 28 of the Warsaw Convention, bring an action for liability before the courts of the Member State where the passenger has his domicile or permanent residence.

Article 8

A21.9

The Commission may, in accordance with the procedure laid down in Article 9(1), decide by regulation to increase as appropriate the values set out in Article 3 and 4 if economic developments indicate the necessity of such measures.

Article 9

A21.10

1. The Commission shall be assisted by a committee of an advisory nature composed of the representatives of the Member States and chaired by the representative of the Commission.

The representative of the Commission shall submit to the committee a draft of the measures to be taken. The committee shall deliver its opinion on the draft, within a time-limit which the chairman may lay down according to the urgency of the matter, if necessary by taking a vote.

The opinion shall be recorded in the minutes; in addition, each Member State shall have the right to ask to have its position recorded in the minutes.

The Committee shall take the utmost account of the opinion delivered by the committee. It shall inform the committee of the manner in which its opinion has been taken into account.

2. Furthermore, the Committee may be consulted by the Commission on any other question concerning the application of the Regulation.

Article 10

This Regulation shall enter into force six months after the date of its publication in the Official Journal of the European Communities.

This Regulation shall be binding in its entirety and directly applicable in all Member States.

Done at Brussels,

For the Council
The President

A21.11

ANNEX I

LIABILITY LIMITS IN EC COUNTRIES[1]

W/H:	Limits of Warsaw/The Hague, as converted following national rules (or raised as indicated)[2]

A21.12

AUSTRIA: Liability under the contract of carriage up to AS 430000 per person Obligatory passenger accident insurance AS 550000 per passenger SDR 100 000 on the national carrier

BELGIUM: W/H applied to all services
No domestic services
SDR 100 000 on Sabena and affiliates – US$ 58000 for charters and air taxis

DENMARK: SDR 100000 applied to all air services
Limits for damages other than death and injury are different for domestic and international air services

FINLAND: W/H applied to international services. If the country of destination is not party to the W/H the limits of MP3 apply (SDR 100000)
SDR 100000 for domestic services
SDR 100000 on Finnair on international services

FRANCE: SDR 100000 applied to all services
Limits other than death and injury are W/H on all air services

GERMANY: W/H applied to international air services, based on law on conversion rates (e.g. Francs Poincaré 250000 = DM 53600)
DM 150 000 for Lufthansa
DM 320 000 on domestic air services

GREECE: W/H applied to all services
In absence of law on conversion rates, some court decisions are contradictory

---

[1] Sven Brise's study, see footnote 3 (Explanatory Memorandum). The study did not examine the situations existing in Austria, Finland and Sweden.

[2] For all limits (except Portugal on domestic carriage), carriers can avail themselves of the defence of Article 20§1 of WC.

National legislation specifies a limit of DRS 4 000 000 applied to domestic air services (may not be exceeded if damages are awarded in the form of periodic payments) in the case of death or injury

IRELAND: W/H applied to all services
SDR 100 000 on Aer Lingus (international air services)
Same amount for other Ireland registered operators

ITALY: W/H as converted by law into SDR (international) and LIT (domestic) applied to all services. Limits specified are:
SDR 100 000 international air services
LIT 195 000 000 domestic air services
N.B. It should be noted that foreign airlines operating to Italy are subject to the law imposing the international limit of SDR 100 000

LUXEMBOURG: W/H applied to all air services
No domestic services
SDR 100 000 on all Luxembourg registered passenger carriers

NETHERLANDS: W/H applied to all air services
SDR 100 000 (all Netherlands registered major carriers)

PORTUGAL: liability without fault (domestic services)
on all services: Escudos 12 000 000 per passenger; baggage as per The Hague

SPAIN: on all services: PTS 3 500 000 per passenger; baggage as per The Hague

SWEDEN: SDR 100 000 on international and domestic services

UK: W/H applied to all air services, raised to SDR 100 000.

ANNEX II

A21.13
IATA INTER-CARRIER AGREEMENT ON PASSENGER LIABILITY

Whereas: The Warsaw Convention system is of great benefit to international air transportation; and

Noting that: The Convention's limits of liability, which have not been amended since 1955, are now grossly inadequate in most countries and that international airlines have previously acted together to increase them to the benefit of passengers.

The undersigned carriers agree:

1. to take action to waive the limitation of liability on recoverable compensatory damages in Article 22 paragraph 1 of the Warsaw Convention as to claims for death, wounding or other bodily injury of a passenger within the meaning of Article 17 of the Convention, so that recoverable compensatory damages may be determined and awarded by reference of the law of the domicile of the passenger;

2. to reserve all available defences pursuant to the provisions of the Convention; nevertheless, any carrier may waive any defence, including the waiver of any defence up to a specified monetary amount of recoverable compensatory damages, as circumstances may warrant;

3. to reserve their rights of recourse against any other person, including rights of contribution or indemnity, with respect to any sums paid by the carrier;

4. to encourage other airlines involved in the international carriage of passengers to apply the terms of this Agreement to such carriage;

5. to implement the provisions of this Agreement no later than 1 November 1996 or upon receipt of requisite government approvals, whichever is later;

6. that nothing in this Agreement shall affect the rights of the passenger or the claimant otherwise available under the Convention;

7. that this Agreement may be signed in any number of counterparts, all of which shall constitute one Agreement. Any carrier may become a party to this Agreement by signing a counterpart hereof and depositing it with the Director General of the International Air Transport Association (IATA);

8. that any carrier party hereto may withdraw from this Agreement by giving twelve (12) months' written notice of withdrawal to the Director-General of IATA and to the other carriers parties to the Agreement.

INTER-CARRIER AGREEMENT ON PASSENGER LIABILITY
IATA explanatory note

The Inter-carrier Agreement is an "umbrella accord"; the precise legal rights and **A21.14** responsibilities of the signatory carriers with respect to passengers will be spelled out in the applicable Conditions of Carriage and tariff filings.

The carriers signatory to the Agreement undertake to waive in accordance with the Agreement such limitations of liability as are set out in the Warsaw Convention (1929), The Hague Protocol (1955), the Montreal Agreement of 1966 and/or limits they may have previously agreed to implement or were required by governments to implement.

Such waiver by a carrier may be made to the extent required to permit the law of the domicile of the passenger to govern the determination and award of the recoverable compensatory damages under the Inter-carrier Agreement. But this is an option. Should a carrier wish to waive the limits of liability but not insist on the law of the domicile of the passenger governing the calculation of the recoverable compensatory damages, or not be so required by a governmental authority, it may rely on the law of the court to which the case is submitted.

The Warsaw Convention system defences will remain available, in whole or in part, to the carriers signatory to the Agreement, unless a carrier decides to waive them or is so required by a governmental authority.

Proposed European Parliament and Council Directive

establishing a mechanism for the recognition of qualifications in respect of the professional activities covered by the Directives on liberalization and transitional measures and supplementing the general systems for the recognition of qualifications

THE EUROPEAN PARLIAMENT AND THE COUNCIL OF THE EUROPEAN UNION,

A22.1 Having regard to the Treaty establishing the European Community, and in particular Articles 49 and 57(1), the first and third sentences of Article 57(2), and Article 66 thereof,

Having regard to the proposal from the Commission,[1]

Having regard to the opinion delivered by the Economic and Social Committee,[2]

Acting in accordance with the procedure laid down in Article 189b of the Treaty,

(1) Whereas. pursuant to the Treaty, all discriminatory treatment based on nationality with regard to establishment and provision of services is prohibited as from the end of the transitional period; whereas, therefore, certain provisions of the Directives applying to this subject have become redundant as regards the implementation of the rule of national treatment, since this rule is established, with direct effect, by the Treaty itself;

(2) Whereas, however, certain of the Directives' provisions that facilitate the effective exercise of the right of establishment and the freedom to provide services should be retained, particularly where they usefully lay down how obligations under the Treaty are to be discharged;

(3) Whereas, in order to facilitate the exercise of the freedom of establishment and the freedom to provide services in respect of a number of activities, Directives introducing transitional measures have been adopted pending mutual recognition of qualifications; whereas those Directives allow, as sufficient qualification for taking up the activities in question in Member States which have rules governing the taking-up of such activities, the fact that the activity in question has been pursued for a reasonable and sufficiently recent period of time, in the Member State from where the foreign national comes;

(4) Whereas the main provisions of the said Directives should be replaced in line with the conclusions of the European Council in Edinburgh on 11 and 12 December 1992, regarding subsidiarity, the simplification of Community legislation and, in particular, the reconsideration by the Commission of the relatively old directives dealing with professional qualifications; whereas the directives in question should therefore be repealed;

(5) Whereas appropriate procedures need to be introduced for updating the categories of professional experience and the lists of professional activities to which those categories refer;

(6) Whereas Council Directive 89/48/EEC of 21 December 1988 on a general system for the recognition of higher-education diplo-

---

[1] OJ No C . . . .
[2] OJ No C . . . .

mas awarded on completion of professional education and training of at least three years' duration[3] and Council Directive 92/51/EEC of 18 June 1992 on a second general system for the recognition of professional education and training to supplement Directive 89/48/EEC,[4] as last amended by Commission Directive 95/43/EC,[5] do not apply to certain professional activities covered by the Directives applying to this subject-matter; whereas recognition machinery in respect of qualifications should, therefore, be introduced for those professional activities not covered by Directives 89/48/EEC and 92/51/EEC;

(7) Whereas Member States should also be required, under the general system, to recognize certificates of sound financial standing issued by banks in other Member States and certificates of insurance against the financial consequences of professional liability issued by insurance undertakings in other Member States;

(8) Whereas Directives 89/48/EEC and 92/51/EEC should be amended in order to facilitate the free movement of nurses who do not hold any of the qualifications listed in Article 3 of Directive 77/452/EEC of 27 June 1977 concerning the mutual recognition of diplomas, certificates, and other evidence of the formal qualifications of nurses responsible for general care, including measures to facilitate the effective exercise of the right of establishment and freedom to provide services,[6] as last amended by the Act of Accession of Austria, Finland and Sweden;

(9) Whereas this Directive should require regular reports to be drawn

up on its implementation;

(10) Whereas this Directive should be without prejudice to the application of Articles 48(4) and 55 of the Treaty.

HAVE ADOPTED THIS DIRECTIVE:

TITLE I

Article 1
Scope

1. Member States shall adopt the measures defined in this Directive in respect of establishment or provision of services in their territories by natural persons and companies or firms covered by Title I of the General Programmes[7] (hereinafter called "beneficiaries") and wishing to pursue the activities listed in Annex A. **A22.2**

2. This Directive shall apply to nationals of Member States who wish to pursue in the host Member State, in a self-employed or employed capacity, the activities listed in Annex A.

Article 2

Member States in which the taking-up or pursuit of any activity referred to in Annex A is subject to possession of certain qualifications shall ensure that any applicant beneficiary is provided, before he establishes himself or before he begins to pursue any activity on a temporary basis, with information as to the rules governing the occupation which he proposes to pursue. **A22.3**

TITLE II

Article 3
Additional measure on the recognition of qualifications

1. Without prejudice to Article 4, a Member State may not, on the grounds of inadequate qualifications, refuse to permit a national of **A22.4**

---

[3] OJ No L 19, 24. 1. 1989, p. 16/
[4] OJ No L 209, 24. 7. 1992, p. 25.
[5] OJ No L 184, 3. 8. 1995, p. 21.
[6] OJ No L 176, 15. 7. 1977, p. 1.

[7] OJ No 2, 15. 1. 1962, pp. 32/62 and 36/62.

another Member State to take up or pursue any of the activities listed in Part One of Annex A on the same conditions as apply to its own nationals, without having first compared the skills certified by the qualifications obtained by the applicant with a view to pursuing the same activity elsewhere in the Community with those required under its own national rules. Where the comparative examination shows that the knowledge and skills certified by a qualification awarded by another Member State correspond to those required by the national rules, the host Member State cannot refuse the holder the right to pursue the activity in question. Where, however, the comparative examination shows only partial correspondence, the host Member State shall give the applicant the opportunity to demonstrate that he has acquired the knowledge and skills which were lacking.

2. Applications for recognition within the meaning of paragraph 1 shall be examined within the shortest possible time, and the competent authority in the host Member State shall state its reasons when giving a decision, which shall be taken no later than four months from the date on which the application and comprehensive supporting documentation were submitted. There shall be a right to appeal under national law against a decision, or against the absence of such decision.

TITLE III

Article 4

Recognition of professional qualifications on the basis of professional experience acquired in another Member State

A22.5 Where, in a Member State, the taking-up or pursuit of any activity listed in Annex A is subject to possession of general, commercial or professional knowledge and ability, that Member State shall accept as sufficient evidence of such knowledge and ability the fact that the activity in question has been pursued in another Member State. This must be done where the activity is mentioned in Annex A:

1. In the case of the activities in List I:

    (a) six consecutive years in either a self-employed or a managerial capacity; or

    (b) three consecutive years in a self-employed or managerial capacity, where the beneficiary proves that for the activity in question he has received at least three years' previous training attested by a certificate recognized by the State or regarded by a competent professional or trade body as fully satisfying its requirements; or

    (c) three consecutive years in a self-employed capacity, where the beneficiary proves that he has pursued the activity in question for at least five years in an employed capacity; or

    (d) five consecutive years in a managerial capacity of which at least three years were spent in technical posts with responsibility for one or more departments of the undertaking, where the beneficiary proves that for the activity in question he has received at least three years' previous training attested by a certificate recognized by the State or regarded by a competent professional or trade body as fully satisfying its requirements.

In the cases referred to at (a) and (c), pursuit of the activity shall not have ceased more than ten years before the date on which the application under Article 6 is made.

2. In the case of the activities in List II:

   (a) six consecutive years in either a self-employed or a managerial capacity; or

   (b) three consecutive years in a self-employed or managerial capacity, where the beneficiary proves that for the activity in question he has received at least three years' previous training attested by a certificate recognized by the State or regarded by a competent professional or trade body as fully satisfying its requirements; or

   four consecutive years in a self-employed or managerial capacity, where the beneficiary proves that for the activity in question he has received at least two years' previous training attested by a certificate recognized by the State or regarded by a competent professional or trade body as fully satisfying its requirements; or

   (c) three consecutive years in a self-employed or managerial capacity, where the beneficiary proves that he has pursued the activity in question for at least five years in an employed capacity; or

   (d) five consecutive years in an employed capacity, where the beneficiary proves that for the activity in question he has received at least three years' previous training attested by a certificate recognized by the State or regarded by a competent professional or trade body as fully satisfying its requirements; or

   six consecutive years in an employed capacity, where the beneficiary proves that for the activity in question he has received at least two years' previous training attested by a certificate recognized by the State or regarded by a compe-

tent professional or trade body as fully satisfying its requirements.

In the cases referred to at (a) and (c), pursuit of the activity shall not have ceased more than ten years before the date on which the application provided for in Article 6 is made.

3. In the case of the activities in List III:

   (a) six consecutive years in either a self-employed or a managerial capacity; or

   (b) three consecutive years in a self-employed or managerial capacity, where the beneficiary proves that for the activity in question he has received at least three years' previous training attested by a certificate recognized by the State or regarded by a competent professional or trade body as fully satisfying its requirements; or

   (c) three consecutive years in a self-employed capacity, where the beneficiary proves that he has pursued the activity in question for at least five years in an employed capacity.

In the cases referred to at (a) and (c), pursuit of the activity shall not have ceased more than ten years before the date on which the application provided for in Article 6 is made.

4. In the case of the activities in List IV: **A22.6**

   (a) five consecutive years in either a self-employed or managerial capacity; or

   (b) two consecutive years in a self-employed or managerial capacity, where the beneficiary proves that for the activity in question he has received at least three years' previous training attested by a certificate recognized by the State or regarded by a competent professional or trade body as fully satisfying its requirements; or

729

(c) three consecutive years in a self-employed or managerial capacity, where the beneficiary proves that for the activity in question he has received at least two years' previous training attested by a certificate recognized by the State or regarded by a competent professional or trade body as fully satisfying its requirements; or

(d) two consecutive years in a self-employed or managerial capacity, where the beneficiary proves that he has pursued the activity in question for at least three years in an employed capacity; or

(e) three consecutive years in an employed capacity, where the beneficiary proves that for the activity in question he has received at least two years' previous training attested by a certificate recognized by the State or regarded by a competent professional or trade body as fully satisfying its requirements.

5. In the case of the activities in List V:

(a) three years in a self employed or managerial capacity, provided that pursuit of the activity in question did not cease more than two years before the date on which the application provided for in Article 6 is made, unless the host Member State permits its nationals to interrupt their pursuit of that activity for a longer period; or

(b) three years in a self-employed or managerial capacity, provided that pursuit of the activity in question did not cease more than two years before the date on which the application provided for in Article 6 is made.

6. In the case of the activities in List VI:

(a) three consecutive years in either a self-employed or a managerial capacity; or

(b) two consecutive years in a self-employed or managerial capacity, where the beneficiary proves that for the activity in question he has received previous training attested by a certificate recognized by the State or regarded by a competent professional or trade body as fully satisfying its requirements; or

(c) two consecutive years in a self-employed or managerial capacity, where the beneficiary proves that he has pursued the activity in question for at least three years in an employed capacity; or

(d) three consecutive years in an employed capacity, where the beneficiary proves that for the activity in question he has received previous training attested by a certificate recognized by the State or regarded by a competent professional or trade body as fully satisfying its requirements.

In the cases referred to at (a) and (c), pursuit of the activity shall not have ceased more than ten years before the date on which the application provided for in Article 6 is made.

Article 5

A person shall be regarded as having pursued an activity in a managerial capacity within the meaning of Article 4 if he has pursued such an activity in an industrial or commercial enterprise in the occupational field in question: **A22.7**

(a) as manager of an undertaking or manager of a branch of an undertaking; or

(b) as deputy to the proprietor or to the manager of an undertaking where such post involves responsibility equivalent to that of the proprietor or manager represented; or

(c) in a managerial post with duties of a commercial nature and with responsibility for at least one department of the undertaking.

Article 6

Proof that the conditions laid down in Article 4 are satisfied shall be established by a certificate issued by the competent authority or body in the home Member State or in the Member State from where the applicant comes and which the applicant shall submit in support of his application for authorization to pursue the activity or activities in question in the host Member State.

TITLE IV

Article 7

Recognition of other professional qualifications obtained in another Member State

A22.8

1. Where a host Member State requires its own nationals wishing to take up any activity referred to in Article 1(2) to furnish proof of good character and proof that they have not previously been declared bankrupt, or proof of either of these, it shall accept as sufficient evidence, in respect of nationals of the other Member States, the production of an extract from the "judicial record" or, failing this, of an equivalent document issued by a competent judicial or administrative authority in the home Member State or in the Member State from where the applicant comes showing that these requirements have been met.

2. Where a host Member State imposes on its own nationals wishing to take up any activity referred to in Article 1(2) certain requirements as to good character and requires them to prove that they have not previously been declared bankrupt and have not previously been the subject of professional or administrative disciplinary measures (for example, withdrawal of the right to hold certain offices, suspension from practice or striking-off), but proof cannot be obtained from the document referred to in paragraph 1, it shall accept as sufficient evidence in respect of nationals of other Member States a certificate issued by a competent judicial or administrative authority in the home Member State or in the Member State from where the applicant comes attesting that the requirements have been met. Such certificate shall relate to the specific facts regarded as relevant by the host Member State.

3. Where the home Member State or the Member State from where the applicant comes does not issue the documents referred to in paragraphs 1 and 2, such documents shall be replaced by a declaration on oath – or, in those Member States where there is no provision for such declaration on oath, by a solemn declaration – made by the person concerned before a competent judicial or administrative authority or, where appropriate, a notary in that Member State; such authority or notary shall issue a certificate attesting the authenticity of the declaration on oath or solemn declaration. The declaration of no previous bankruptcy may also be made before a competent professional or trade body in that Member State.

4. Where the host Member State requires proof of financial standing, it shall regard certificates issued by banks in the home Member State or in the Member State from where the applicant comes as equivalent to those issued in its own territory.

5. Where a Member State requires its own nationals wishing to take up or pursue any activity referred to in Article 1(2) to furnish proof that they are insured against the financial risks arising from their professional liability, it shall accept certificates issued by the insurance undertakings of other Member States as equivalent to those issued in its own territory. Such certificates shall state that the insurer has complied with the laws and regulations in force in the host Member State regarding the terms and extent of cover.

731

6. The documents referred to in paragraphs 1, 2, 3 and 5 may not be produced more than three months after their date of issue.

TITLE V

Article 8

Supplement to the general system for the recognition of diplomas

A22.9 1. Directive 89/48/EEC is amended as follows:

(a) the following paragraph is added to Article 2:

"Notwithstanding the preceding paragraph, where a nurse who does not hold one of the qualifications listed in Article 3 of Directive 77/452/EEC* wishes to pursue in another Member State the activities of a nurse responsible for general care as defined in Article 1 of Directive 77/452/EEC, the provisions of this Directive shall apply."

(b) the following paragraphs 5 and 6 are added to Article 6:

"5. Where proof of financial standing is required in order to take up or pursue a regulated profession in the host Member State, that Member State shall regard certificates issued by banks in the Member State of origin or in the Member State from where the foreign national comes as equivalent to those issued in its own territory.

6. Where the competent authority of the host Member State requires of its own nationals wishing to take up or pursue a regulated profession proof that they are insured against the financial risks arising from their professional liability, that Member State shall accept certificates issued by insurance undertakings of other Member

States as equivalent to those issued in its own territory. Such certificates shall state that the insurer has complied with the laws and regulations in force in the host Member State regarding the terms and extent of cover. They may not be produced more than three months after their date of issue."

2. Directive 92/51/EEC is amended as follows:

(a) the following paragraph is inserted into Article 2:

"Notwithstanding the preceding paragraph, where a nurse who does not hold one of the qualifications listed in Article 3 of Directive 77/452/EEC* wishes to pursue in another Member State the activities of a nurse responsible for general care as defined in Article 1 of Directive 77/452/EEC, the provisions of this Directive shall apply.

(b) the following paragraphs 5 and 6 are added to Article 10:

"5. Where proof of financial standing is required in order to take up or pursue a regulated profession in the host Member State, that Member State shall regard certificates issued by banks in the Member State of origin or in the Member State from where the foreign national comes as equivalent to those issued in its own territory.

6. Where the competent authority of the host Member State requires of its own nationals wishing to take up or pursue a regulated profession proof that they are insured against the financial risks arising from their professional liability, that Member State shall accept certificates issued by insurance undertakings of other Member States as equivalent to those issued in its own territory. Such

---

* "OJ No L 176, 15. 7. 1977, p. 1."

* "OJ No L 176, 15. 7. 1977, p. 1."

certificates shall state that the insurer has complied with the laws and regulations in force in the host Member State regarding the terms and extent of cover. They may not be produced more than three months after their date of issue."

TITLE VI
Procedural provisions

Article 9

A22.10 The provisions of Article 4 and the lists shown in Annex A may be amended in accordance with the procedure set out in Article 10.

Article 10

A22.11 The Commission shall be assisted by the committee set up pursuant to Article 15(3) of Directive 92/51/EEC, composed of representatives of the Member States and chaired by a representative of the Commission.

The representative of the Commission shall submit to the committee a draft of the measures to be taken. The committee shall deliver its opinion on the draft within a time-limit which the chairman may lay down according to the urgency of the matter. The opinion shall be delivered by the majority laid down in Article 148(2) of the Treaty in the case of decisions which the Council is required to adopt on a proposal from the Commission. The votes of the representatives of the Member States within the committee shall be weighted in the manner set out in that Article. The chairman shall not vote.

The Commission shall adopt measures which shall apply immediately. However, if these measures are not in accordance with the opinion of the committee, they shall be communicated by the Commission to the Council forthwith. In that event, the Commission shall defer application of the measures which it has decided for a period to be laid down in each act

adopted by the Council, but which may in no case exceed three months from the date of communication.

The Council, acting by a qualified majority, may take a different decision within the time limit referred to in the third paragraph.

Article 11

1. Member States shall designate, **A22.12** within the period stipulated in Article 14, the authorities and bodies responsible for issuing the certificates referred to in Articles 6 and 7(1), (2) and (3) and shall communicate this information forthwith to the other Member States and to the Commission.

2. The coordinating group set up under Article 9(2) of Directive 89/48/EEC shall also be responsible for:

   – facilitating the implementation of this Directive;

   – collecting all useful information for its application in the Member States.

TITLE VII
Final provisions

Article 12

1. The Directives listed in Annex B are **A22.13** hereby repealed.

2. References to the repealed Directives shall be construed as references to this Directive.

Article 13

As from 1 January 1999, Member States **A22.14** shall communicate to the Commission every two years a report on the application of the system introduced.

In addition to general remarks, this report shall contain a statistical summary of the decisions taken and a description of the main problems arising from the application of this Directive.

Article 14

A22.15 1. Member States shall bring into force the laws, regulations and administrative provisions necessary to comply with this Directive before 1 January 1999. They shall immediately inform the Commission thereof.

When Member States adopt these provisions, these shall contain a reference to this Directive or shall be accompanied by such reference at the time of their official publication. The procedure for such reference shall be adopted by Member States.

2. Member States shall communicate to the Commission the text of the main provisions of national law which they adopt in the field covered by this Directive.

Article 15

This Directive shall enter into force on the twentieth day following that of its publication in the Official Journal of the European Communities. **A22.16**

Article 16

This Directive is addressed to the Member States. **A22.17**

Done at Brussels,

For the European Parliament   *For the Council*

The President   *The President*

ANNEX A

PART ONE

A22.18   **Activities related to categories of professional experience**

List I

(Major Groups covered by Directives: 64/427/EEC, as amended by Directive 69/77/EEC; 68/366/EEC, 75/368/EEC, 75/369/EEC)

1

Directive 64/427/EEC
(corresponding liberalization Directive: 64/429/EEC)
NICE Nomenclature (corresponding to ISIC Major Groups 23–40)

Major Group 23		Manufacture of textiles
	232	Manufacturing and processing of textile materials on woollen machinery
	233	Manufacturing and processing of textile materials on cotton machinery
	234	Manufacturing and processing of textile materials on silk machinery
	235	Manufacturing and processing of textile materials on flax and hemp machinery
	236	Other textile fibre industries (jute, hard fibres, etc.) cordage
	237	Manufacture of knitted and crocheted goods
	238	Textile finishing
	239	Other textile industries
Major Group 24		Manufacture of footwear, other wearing apparel and bedding
	241	Machine manufacture of footwear (except from rubber or wood)

	242	Manufacture by hand and repair of footwear
	243	Manufacture of wearing apparel (except furs)
	244	Manufacture of mattresses and bedding
	245	Skin and fur industries
Major Group 25		Manufacture of wood and cork, except manufacture of furniture
	251	Sawing and industrial preparation of wood
	252	Manufacture of semi-finished wood products
	253	Series production of wooden building components including flooring
	254	Manufacture of wooden containers
	255	Manufacture of other wooden products (except furniture)
	259	Manufacture of straw, cork, basketware, wicker-work and rattan products; brush-making
Major Group 26	260	Manufacture of wooden furniture
Major Group 27		Manufacture of paper and paper products
	271	Manufacture of pulp, paper and paperboard
	272	Processing of paper and paperboard, and manufacture of articles of pulp
Major Group 28	280	Printing, publishing and allied industries
Major Group 29		Leather industry
	291	Tanneries and leather finishing plants
	292	Manufacture of leather products
ex Major Group 30		Manufacture of rubber and plastic products, man-made fibres and starch products
	301	Processing of rubber and asbestos
	302	Processing of plastic materials
	303	Production of man-made fibres
ex Major Group 31		Chemical industry
	311	Manufacture of chemical base materials and further processing of such materials
	312	Specialized manufacture of chemical products principally for industrial and agricultural purposes (including the manufacture for industrial use of fats and oils of vegetable or animal origin falling within ISIC Group 312)
	313	Specialized manufacture of chemical products principally for domestic or office use (excluding the manufacture of medicinal and pharmaceutical products (ISIC ex Group 319)
Major Group 32	320	Petroleum industry
Major Group 33		Manufacture of non-metallic mineral products
	331	Manufacture of structural clay products
	332	Manufacture of glass and glass products
	333	Manufacture of ceramic products, including refractory goods
	334	Manufacture of cement, lime and plaster
	335	Manufacture of structural materials, in concrete, cement and plaster
	339	Stone working and manufacture of other non-metallic mineral products

Major Group 34		Production and primary transformation of ferrous and non-ferrous metals
	341	Iron and steel industry (as defined in the ECSC Treaty, including integrated steelworks-owned coking plants)
	342	Manufacture of steel tubes
	343	Wire-drawing, cold-drawing, cold-rolling of strip, cold-forming
	344	Production and primary transformation of non-ferrous metals
	345	Ferrous and non-ferrous metal foundries
Major Group 35		Manufacture of footwear, other wearing apparel and bedding
	351	Forging, heavy stamping and heavy pressing
	352	Secondary transformation and surface-treatment
	353	Metal structures
	354	Boilermaking, manufacture of industrial hollow-ware
	355	Manufacture of tools and implements and finished articles of metal (except electrical equipment)
	359	Ancillary mechanical engineering activities
Major Group 36		Manufacture of machinery other than electrical machinery
	361	Manufacture of agricultural machinery and tractors
	362	Manufacture of office machinery
	363	Manufacture of metal-working and other machine-tools and fixtures and attachments for these and for other powered tool
	364	Manufacture of textile machinery and accessories, manufacture of sewing machines
	365	Manufacture of machinery and equipment for the food-manufacturing and beverage industries and for the chemical and allied industries
	366	Manufacture of plant and equipment for mines, iron and steel works foundries, and for the construction industry manufacture of mechanical handling equipment
	367	Manufacture of transmission equipment
	368	Manufacture of machinery for other specific industrial purposes
	369	Manufacture of other non-electrical machinery and equipment
Major Group 37		Electrical engineering
	371	Manufacture of electric wiring and cables
	372	Manufacture of motors, generators, transformers, switchgear, and other similar equipment for the provision of electric power
	373	Manufacture of wearing apparel (except furs)
	374	Manufacture of mattresses and bedding
	375	Skin and fur industries
	376	Manufacture of electric appliances for domestic use
	377	Manufacture of lamps and lighting equipment
	378	Manufacture of batteries and accumulators
	379	Repair, assembly and specialist installation of electrical equipment

ex Major Group 38		Manufacture of transport equipment
	383	Manufacture of motor vehicles and parts thereof
	384	Repair of motor vehicles, motorcycles and cycles
	385	Manufacture of motorcycles, cycles and parts thereof
	389	Manufacture of transport equipment not elsewhere classified
Major Group 39		Miscellaneous manufacturing industries
	391	Manufacture of precision instruments and measuring and controlling instruments
	392	Manufacture of medico-surgical instruments and equipment and orthopaedic appliances (except orthopaedic footwear)
	393	Manufacture of photographic and optical equipment
	394	Manufacture and repair of watches and clocks
	395	Jewellery and precious metal manufacturing
	396	Manufacture and repair of musical instruments
	397	Manufacture of games, toys, sporting and athletic goods
	399	Other manufacturing industries
Major Group 40		Construction
	400	Construction (non-specialized); demolition
	401	Construction of buildings (dwellings or other)
	402	Civil engineering; building of roads, bridges, railways, etc.
	403	Installation work
	404	Decorating and finishing

2
Directive 68/366/EEC
(liberalization Directive 68/365/EEC)
NICE Nomenclature

Major Group 20A	200	Industries producing animal and vegetable fats and oils	**A22.19**
20B		Food manufacturing industries (excluding the beverage industry)	
	201	Slaughtering, preparation and preserving of meat	
	202	Milk and milk products industry	
	203	Canning and preserving of fruits and vegetables	
	204	Canning and preserving of fish and other sea foods	
	205	Manufacture of grain mill products	
	206	Manufacture of bakery products, including rusks and biscuits	
	207	Sugar industry	
	208	Manufacture of cocoa, chocolate and sugar confectionery	
	209	Manufacture of miscellaneous food products	
Major Group 21		Beverage industry	
	211	Production of ethyl alcohol by fermentation, production of yeast and spirits	
	212	Production of wine and other unmalted alcoholic beverages	
	213	Brewing and malting	
	214	Soft drinks and carbonated water industries	
ex Major Group 30		Manufacture of rubber products, plastic materials, artificial and synthetic fibres and starch products	
	304	Manufacture of starch products	

3

Directive 75/368/EEC: activities listed in Article 5(1)
ISIC Nomenclature

A22.20

ex Major Group 04		Fishing
	043	Inland water fishing

ex Major Group 38		Manufacture of transport equipment
	381	Shipbuilding and repairing
	382	Manufacture of railroad equipment
	386	Manufacture of aircraft (including space equipment)

ex Major Group 71 — Activities allied to transport and activities other than transport coming under the following groups:

- ex 711 Sleeping- and dining-care services; maintenance of railway stock in repair sheds; cleaning of carriages
- ex 712 Maintenance of stock for urban, suburban and interurban passenger transport
- ex 713 Maintenance of stock for other passenger land transport (such as motor cars, coaches, taxis)
- ex 714 Operation and maintenance of services in support of road transport (such as roads, tunnels and toll-bridges, goods depots, car parks, bus and tram depots)
- ex 716 Activities allied to inland water transport (such as operation and maintenance of waterways, ports and other installations for inland water transport; tug and piloting services in ports, setting of buoys, loading and unloading of vessels and other similar activities, such as salvaging of vessels, towing and the operation of boathouses)

Major Group 73 — Communication: postal services and telecommunications

ex Major Group 85 — Personal services

- 854 Laundries and laundry services, dry-cleaning and dyeing
- ex 856 Photographic studios: portrait and commercial photograph except journalistic photographers
- ex 859 Personal services not elsewhere classified (maintenance and cleaning of buildings or accommodation only)

4

Directive 75/369/EEC

A22.21

(Article 6: where the activity is regarded as being of an industrial
or small-craft nature)
ISIC Nomenclature

The following itinerant activities:

(a) the buying and selling of goods:

- by itinerant tradesmen, hawkers or pedlars (ex ISIC Group 612);

- in covered markets other than from permanently fixed installations and in open-air markets;

(b) activities covered by transitional measures already adopted that expressly exclude or do not mention the pursuit of such activities on an itinerant basis.

List II

Directive 82/470/EEC Article 6(3)　　　　　　　　　　　　　**A22.22**
(Groups 718 and 720 of the ISIC Nomenclature

The activities comprise in particular:

– organizing, offering for sale and selling, outright or on commission, single or collective items (transport, board, lodging, excursions, etc.) for a journey or stay whatever the reasons for travelling (Article 2(B)(a)).

List III

Directive 82/489/EEC　　　　　　　　　　　　　　　　　　**A22.23**

ex Major Group 855　Hairdressing, excluding services of chiropodists and professional beauticians' and hairdressers' training schools

List IV

Directive 82/470/EEC, Article 6(1)　　　　　　　　　　　　**A22.24**
(Groups 718 and 720 of the ISIC Nomenclature

The activities comprise in particular:

– acting as an intermediary between contractors for various methods of transport and persons who dispatch or receive goods and who carry out related activities:

   (aa)　by concluding contracts with transport contractors, on behalf of principals;

   (bb)　by choosing the method of transport, the firm and the route considered most profitable for the principal;

   (cc)　by arranging the technical aspects of the transport operation (e.g. packing required for transportation); by carrying out various operations incidental to transport (e.g. ensuring ice supplies for refrigerated wagons);

   (dd)　by completing the formalities connected with the transport such as the drafting of way bills; by assembling and dispersing shipments;

   (ee)　by coordinating the various stages of transportation, by ensuring transit, reshipment, transshipment and other termination operations;

   (ff)　by arranging both freight and carriers and means of transport for persons dispatching goods or receiving them;

– assessing transport costs and checking the detailed accounts;

– taking certain temporary or permanent measures in the name of and on behalf of a shipowner or sea transport carrier (with the port authorities, ship's chandlers, etc.)

(The activities listed under Article 2(A)(a), (b) and (d))

List V

Directives 70/523/EEC and 64/222/EEC　　　　　　　　　**A22.25**

(a)

Directive 70/523/EEC
(activities of self-employed persons in the wholesale coal trade and activities of intermediaries in the coal trade: ex Group 6112, ISIC Nomenclature)

739

(b)

Directive 64/222/EEC
(liberalization Directive 64/224/EEC)

1. professional activities of an intermediary who is empowered and instructed by one or more persons to negotiate or enter into commercial transactions in the name of and on behalf of those persons;

2. professional activities of an intermediary who, while not being permanently so instructed, brings together persons wishing to contract directly with one another or arranges their commercial transactions or assists in the completion thereof;

3. professional activities of an intermediary who enters into commercial transactions in his own name on behalf of others;

4. professional activities of an intermediary who carries out wholesale selling by auction on behalf of others;

5. professional activities of an intermediary who goes from door to door seeking order[s];

6. provision of services, by way of professional activities, by an intermediary in the employment of one or more commercial, industrial or small craft undertakings.

List VI

A22.26   Directives 68/364/EEC, 68/368/EEC, 75/368/EEC, 75/369/EEC, 82/470/EEC

1

Directive 68/364/EEC
(liberalization Directive 68/363/EEC)

ISIC ex Group 612 Retail trade

Excluded activities:

012	Letting-out for hire of farm machinery
640	Real estate, letting of property
713	Letting-out for hire of automobiles, carriages and horses
718	Letting-out for hire of railway carriages and wagons
839	Renting of machinery to commercial undertakings
841	Booking of cinema seats and renting of cinematograph films
842	Booking of theatre seats and renting of theatrical equipment
843	Letting-out for hire of boats, bicycles, coin-operated machines for games of skill or chance
853	Letting of furnished rooms
854	Laundered linen hire
859	Garment hire

2

68/368/EEC
(liberalization Directive 68/367/EEC)
ISIC Nomenclature

ISIC ex Major Group 85:

1. Restaurants, cafés, taverns and other drinking and eating places (ISIC Group 852)

2. Hotels, rooming houses, camps and other lodging places (ISIC Group 853)

3
75/368/EEC (Article 7)

All the activities listed in the Annex to Directive 75/368/EEC, except those referred   **A22.27**
to in Article 5 of the Directive (List I, No 3 of this proposal).
ISIC Nomenclature

ex 62   Banks and other financial institutions

ex 620   Patent buying and licensing companies

ex 71   Transport

    ex 713   Road passenger transport, excluding transportation by means of motor vehicles

    ex 719   Transportation by pipelines of liquid hydrocarbons and other liquid chemical products

ex 82   Community services

    827   Libraries, museums, botanical and zoological gardens

ex 84   Recreation services

    843   Recreation services n.e.c.:

        – sporting activities (sports grounds, organizing sporting fixtures, etc.), except the activities of sports instructors
        – games (racing stables, areas for games, racecourses, etc.)
        – other recreational activities (circuses, amusement parks and other entertainments)

ex 85   Personal services

    ex 851   Domestic services

    ex 855   Beauty parlours and services of manicurists, excluding services of chiropodists and professional beauticians' and hairdressers' training schools

    ex 859   Personal services not elsewhere classified, except sports and paramedical masseurs and mountain guides, divided into the following groups

        – disinfecting and pest control
        – hiring of clothes and storage facilities
        – marriage bureaux and similar services
        – astrology, fortune-telling and the like
        – sanitary services and associated activities
        – undertaking and cemetery maintenance
        – couriers and interpreter-guides

4
75/369/EEC (Article 5)

The following itinerant activities: **A22.28**

(a) the buying and selling of goods:

    – by itinerant tradesmen, hawkers or pedlars (ex ISIC Group 612);
    – in covered markets other than from permanently fixed installations and in open-air markets;

(b) activities covered by transitional measures already adopted that expressly exclude or do not mention the pursuit of such activities on an itinerant basis.

741

5
82/470/EEC (Article 6(2))

(Activities listed in Article 2(A)(c) and (e), (B)(b), (C) and (D)) These activities comprise in particular:

- hiring railway cars or wagons for transporting persons or goods;
- acting as an intermediary in the sale, purchase or hiring of ships;
- arranging, negotiating and concluding contracts for the transport of emigrants;
- receiving all objects and goods deposited, on behalf of the depositor, whether customs control or not, in warehouses, general stores, furniture depots, colds silos, etc.
- supplying the depositor with a receipt for the object or goods deposited;
- providing pens, feed and sales rings for livestock being temporarily accommodated while awaiting sale or while in transit to or from the market;
- carrying out inspection or technical valuation of motor vehicles;
- measuring, weighing and gauging goods.

ANNEX B
REPEALED DIRECTIVES
A22.29
Part One: Liberalization Directives

63/261/EEC: Council Directive of 2 April 1963 laying down detailed provisions for the attainment of freedom of establishment in agriculture in the territory of a Member State in respect of nationals of other countries of the Community who have been employed as paid agricultural workers in that Member State for a continuous period of two years

63/262/EEC: Council Directive of 2 April 1963 laying down detailed provisions for the attainment of freedom of establishment on agricultural holdings abandoned or left uncultivated for more than two years

63/607/EEC: Council Directive of 15 October 1963 implementing in respect of the film industry the provisions of the General Programme for the abolition of restrictions on freedom to provide services

64/223/EEC: Council Directive of 25 February 1964 concerning the attainment of freedom of establishment and freedom to provide services in respect of activities in wholesale trade

64/224/EEC: Council Directive of 25 February 1964 concerning the attainment of freedom of establishment and freedom to provide services in respect of activities of intermediaries in commerce, industry and small craft industries

64/428/EEC: Council Directive of 7 July 1964 concerning the attainment of freedom of establishment and freedom to provide services in respect of activities of self-employed persons in mining and quarrying (ISIC Major Groups 11–19)

64/429/EEC: Council Directive of 7 July 1964 concerning the attainment of freedom of establishment and freedom to provide services in respect of activities of self-employed persons in manufacturing and processing industries falling within ISIC Major Groups 23–40 (industry and small craft industries)

742

65/1/EEC: Council Directive of 14 December 1964 laying down detailed provisions for the attainment of freedom to provide services in agriculture and horticulture

65/264/EEC: Second Council Directive of 13 May 1965 implementing in respect of the film industry the provisions of the General Programmes for the abolition of restrictions on freedom of establishment and freedom to provide services

66/162/EEC: Council Directive of 28 February 1966 concerning the attainment of freedom of establishment and freedom to provide services in respect of activities of self-employed persons engaging in the provision of electricity, gas, water and sanitary services (ISIC Division 5)

67/43/EEC: Council Directive of 12 January 1967 concerning the attainment of freedom of establishment and freedom to provide services in respect of activities of self-employed persons concerned with: 1. Mattes of "real estate" (excluding 6401) (ISIC Group ex 640); 2. The provision of certain "business services not elsewhere classified" (ISIC Group 839)

67/530/EEC: Council Directive of 25 July 1967 concerning the freedom of nationals of a Member State established as farmers in another Member State to transfer from one holding to another

67/531/EEC: Council Directive of 25 July 1967 concerning the application of the laws Member States relating to agricultural leases to farmers who are nationals other Member States

67/532/EEC: Council Directive of 25 July 1967 concerning freedom of access cooperatives for farmers who are nationals of one Member State and established in another Member State

67/654/EEC: Council Directive of 24 October 1967 laying down detailed provisions for the attainment of freedom of establishment and freedom to provide services in respect of activities of self-employed persons in forestry and logging

68/192/EEC: Council Directive of 5 April 1968 concerning freedom of access to the various forms of credit for farmers who are nationals of one Member State and established in another Member State

68/363/EEC: Council Directive of 15 October 1968 concerning the attainment of freedom of establishment and freedom to provide services in respect of activities of self-employed persons in retail trade (ISIC ex Group 612)

68/365/EEC: Council Directive of 15 October 1968 concerning the attainment of freedom of establishment and freedom to provide services in respect of activities of self-employed persons in the food manufacturing and beverage industries (ISIC Major Group 20 and 21)

68/367/EEC: Council Directive of 15 October 1968 concerning the attainment of freedom of establishment and freedom to provide services in respect of activities of self-employed persons in the personal services sector (ISIC ex Major Group 85); 1. Restaurants, cafes, taverns and other drinking and eating places (ISIC Group 852); 2. Hotels, rooming houses, camps and other lodging places (ISIC Group 853)

68/369/EEC: Council Directive of 15 October 1968 concerning the attainment of freedom of establishment in respect of activities of self-employed persons in film distribution

68/415/EEC: Council Directive of 20 December 1968 concerning freedom of access to the various forms of aid for farmers who are nationals of one Member State and established in another Member State

69/82/EEC: Council Directive of 13 March 1969 concerning the attainment of freedom of establishment and freedom to provide services in respect of activities of self-employed persons engaging in exploration (prospecting and drilling) for petroleum and natural gas (ISIC ex Major Group 13)

70/451/EEC: Council Directive of 29 September 1970 concerning the attainment of freedom of establishment and freedom to provide services in respect of activities of self-employed persons in film production

70/522/EEC: Council Directive of 30 November 1970 concerning the attainment of freedom of establishment and freedom to provide services in respect of activities of self-employed persons in the wholesale coal trade and activities of intermediaries in the coal trade (ISIC ex Group 6112)

71/18/EEC: Council Directive of 16 December 1970 laying down detailed provisions for the attainment of freedom of establishment in respect of self-employed persons providing agricultural and horticultural services

Part Two: Directives that provide for transitional measures

64/222/EEC: Council Directive of 25 February 1964 laying down detailed provisions concerning transitional measures in respect of activities in wholesale trade and activities of intermediaries in commerce, industry and small craft industries

64/427/EEC: Council Directive of 7 July 1964 laying down detailed provisions concerning transitional measures in respect of activities of self-employed persons in manufacturing and processing industries falling within ISIC Major Groups 23–40 (Industry and small craft industries), as amended by Council Directive 69/77/EEC of 4 March 1969

68/364/EEC: Council Directive of 15 October 1968 laying down detailed provisions concerning transitional measures in respect of activities of self-employed persons in retail trade (ISIC ex Group 612)

68/366/EEC: Council Directive of 15 October 1968 laying down detailed provisions concerning transitional measures in respect of activities of self-employed persons in the food manufacturing and beverage industries (ISIC Major Groups 20 and 21)

68/368/EEC: Council Directive of 15 October 1968 laying down detailed provisions concerning transitional measures in respect of activities of self-employed persons in the personal services sector (ISIC ex Major Group 85); 1. Restaurants, cafes, taverns and other drinking and eating places (ISIC Group 852); 2. Hotels, rooming houses, camps and other lodging places (ISIC Group 853)

70/523/EEC: Council Directive of 30 November 1970 laying down detailed provisions concerning transitional measures in respect of activities of self-employed persons in the wholesale coal trade and in respect of activities of intermediaries in the coal trade (ISIC ex group 6112)

75/368/EEC: Council Directive of 16 June 1975 on measures to facilitate the effective exercise of freedom of establishment and freedom to provide services in respect of various activities (ex ISIC Division 01 to 85) and, in particular, transitional measures in respect of those activities

75/369/EEC: Council Directive of 16 June 1975 on measures to facilitate the effective exercise of freedom of establishment and freedom to provide services in respect of itinerant activities and, in particular, transitional measures in respect of those activities

82/470/EEC: Council Directive of 29 June 1982 on measures to facilitate the effective exercise of freedom of establishment and freedom to provide services in respect of activities of self-employed persons in certain services incidental to transport and travel agencies (ISIC Group 718) and in storage and warehousing (ISIC Group 720)

82/489/EEC: Council Directive of 19 July 1982 laying down measures to facilitate the effective exercise of the right of establishment and freedom to provide services in hairdressing

Proposed Council Directive

on the elimination of controls on persons crossing internal frontiers

THE COUNCIL OF THE EUROPEAN UNION,

A23.1 Having regard to the Treaty establishing the European Community, and in particular Article 100 thereof,

Having regard to the proposal from the Commission,

Having regard to the opinion of the European Parliament,

Having regard to the opinion of the Economic and Social Committee,

Having regard to the opinion of the Committee of the Regions,

Whereas Article 7a of the Treaty provides for the establishment of the internal market, which is to comprise an area without internal frontiers in which the free movement of goods, persons, services and capital is ensured in accordance with the provisions of the Treaty;

Whereas the establishment of the internal market consequently calls for the abolition of all controls and formalities for persons crossing internal frontiers; whereas, in this context, seaports and airports stand apart, as they serve both traffic with other Member States and traffic with non-member countries; whereas application of the freedom-of-movement principle should nevertheless result in the elimination of controls and formalities for persons taking an intra-Community flight or making an intra-Community sea crossing;

Whereas the Community and the Member States have decided to take the measures they deem essential for eliminating the underlying reasons for the application of frontier controls and formalities under national law;

Whereas the relevant accompanying measures have been introduced satisfactorily;

Whereas, in order to fulfil the clear and unconditional obligation enshrined in Article 7a, and in the interest of legal certainty, it is necessary in these circumstances to confirm that frontier controls and formalities within the Community are to be abolished;

Whereas this Directive should relate both to controls or formalities applied by public authorities and to those applied by other persons under national rules;

Whereas it is necessary to stipulate the conditions in which a Member State may temporarily reinstate controls at internal frontiers in the event of a serious threat to public policy or public security,

HAS ADOPTED THIS DIRECTIVE:

Article 1

1. All persons, whatever their nationality, shall be able to cross Member States' frontiers within the Community at any point, without such crossing being subject to any frontier control or formality. **A23.2**

2. The elimination of controls and formalities for persons crossing internal frontiers shall not affect the exercise of the law-enforcement powers conferred on the competent authorities by the legislation of each Member State over the whole of its territory, nor any obligations to possess and carry documents which are laid down by its legislation.

Article 2

1. A Member State may, in the event of a serious threat to public policy or public security, reinstate controls at its frontiers within the **A23.3**

Community for a period of not more than thirty days. Any Member State taking such action shall immediately notify the Commission and the other Member States, supplying them with all the appropriate information.

2. Where the serious threat to public policy or public security lasts longer than thirty days, the Member State concerned may maintain the controls at its frontiers within the Community for renewable periods of not more than thirty days. Each renewal shall be decided after the other Member States and the Commission have been consulted.

   At the member State's request, the Commission and the other Member States shall treat in confidence the information it supplies to justify maintaining these controls.

3. The controls referred to in paragraphs 1 and 2 and the length of the period during which they are applied shall not exceed what is strictly necessary to respond to the serious threat.

Article 3

A23.4 For the purpose of this Directive:

1. **"A Member State's frontier within the Community"** means:

   – the member States' common land frontiers, including the rail or road terminals for links by bridge or tunnel between Member States;

   – their airports for intra-Community flights;

   – their seaports for intra-Community sea crossings:

2. **"Intra-Community flight"** means the movement of an aircraft between two Community airports, without any stopovers, and which does not start from or end at a non-Community airport;

3. **"Intra-Community sea crossing"** means the movement between two Community ports, without any intermediate calls, of a vessel plying regularly, between two or more specified Community ports;

4. **"Frontier control or formality"** means:

   – any control applied, in connection with or on the occasion of the crossing of an internal frontier, by the public authorities of a Member State or by other persons, under the national legislation of a Member State;

   – any formality imposed on a person in connection with the crossing of an internal frontier and to be fulfilled on the occasion of such crossing.

Article 4

No later than two years after implementation of this Directive, and every three years thereafter, the Commission shall report on its application to the European Parliament, the Council, the Economic and Social Committee and the Committee of the Regions. **A23.5**

Article 5

Member States shall bring into force the laws, regulations and administrative provisions necessary to comply with this Directive not later than 31 December 1996. They shall immediately inform the Commission thereof and shall also transmit to it a table showing the correlation between each of the provisions of this Directive and the relevant provisions of national law, irrespective of whether these predate this Directive or are approved for the specific purpose of transposing it. **A23.6**

When Member States adopt these provisions, these shall contain a reference to this Directive or shall be accompanied by such reference at the time of their official publication. The procedure for such reference shall be adopted by Member States.

Joined Cases C–178/94, C–179/94, C–188/94, C–189/94 and C–190/94

Erich Dillenkofer and Others v Federal Republic of Germany

Law governing the institutions　　　　　　　　　　　　8 October 1996

PRELIMINARY RULING

(Directive 90/314/EEC on package travel, package holidays and package tours – non-transposition – liability of Member State and its obligations to make reparation) Full Court

By orders of 6 June 1994, received at the Court on 28 June 1994 in Cases C–178/94 and C–179/94 and on 1 July 1994 in Cases C–188/94, C–189/94 and C–190/94, the *Landgericht* Bonn referred to the Court for a preliminary ruling 12 questions on the interpretation of Council Directive 90/314/EEC of 13 June 1990 (hereinafter "the Directive").　　**A24.1**

The questions have been raised in the course of actions for which Erich Dillenkofer, Christian Erdmann, Hans-Jürgen Schulte, Anke Heuer and Werner, Torsten and Ursula Knor (hereinafter "the plaintiffs") have brought against the Federal Republic of Germany for damage they suffered because the Directive was not transposed within the prescribed period.

Conditions under which a Member State incurs liability (Questions 8, 9, 10, 11 and 12)

The crux of these questions is whether a failure to transpose a Directive within the prescribed period is sufficient *per se* to afford individuals who have suffered injury a right to reparation or whether other conditions must also be taken into consideration. In order to reply to those questions, reference must first be made to the Court's case law on the individual's right to reparation of damage caused by a breach of Community law for which a Member State can be held responsible.　　**A24.2**

The Court has held that the principle of State liability for loss and damage caused to individuals as a result of breaches of Community law for which the State can be held responsible is inherent in the system of the Treaty (*Francovich, Brasserie du Pêcheur and Factortame, British Telecommunications, Hedley Lomas*). Furthermore, the Court has held that the conditions under which State liability gives rise to a right to reparation depend on the nature of the breach of Community law giving rise to the loss and damage.

When the Court held that the conditions under which State liability gives rise to a right to reparation depended on the nature of the breach of Community law causing the damage, that meant that those conditions are to be applied according to each type of situation.

On the one hand, a breach of Community law is sufficiently serious if a Community institution or a Member State, in the exercise of its rule-making powers, manifestly and gravely disregards the limits on those powers. On the other hand, if, at the time when it committed the infringement, the Member State in question was not called upon to make any legislative choices and had only considerably reduced, or even no, discretion, the mere infringement of Community law may be sufficient to establish the existence of a sufficiently serious breach.

So where, as in *Francovich*, a Member State fails, in breach of the third paragraph of Article 189 of the Treaty, to take any of the measures necessary to achieve the result prescribed by a Directive within the period it lays down, that Member State manifestly and gravely disregards the limits on its discretion.

Consequently, such a breach gives rise to a right to reparation on the part of individuals if the result prescribed by the Directive entails the grant of rights to them, the content of those rights is identifiable on the basis of the provisions of the Directive and a causal link exists between the loss and damage suffered by the injured parties: no other conditions need be taken into consideration.

In particular, reparation of that loss and damage cannot depend on a prior finding by the Court of an infringement of Community law attributable to the State, nor or the existence of intentional fault or negligence on the part of the organ of the State to which the infringement is attributable.

Grant to individuals of rights whose contents is sufficiently identifiable (Questions 1 and 2)

A24.3   By its first two questions, the national court asks whether the result prescribed by Article 7 of the Directive entails the grant to package travellers of rights guaranteeing the refund of money paid over and repatriation in the event of the insolvency of the travel organiser and/or the retailer party to the contract (hereinafter "the organiser"), and whether the content of those rights can be sufficiently identified. The question whether the result prescribed by Article 7 of the Directive entails the grant of rights to individuals must be examined first.

According to the actual wording of Article 7, this provision prescribes, as the result of its implementation, an obligation for the organiser to have sufficient security for the refund of money paid over and for the repatriation of the consumer in the event of insolvency.

Since the purpose of such security is to protect consumers against financial risks arising from the insolvency of package travel organisers, the Community legislature has placed operators under an obligation to offer sufficient evidence of such security in order to protect consumers against such risks.

In that connection, the German and United Kingdom governments' argument that the Directive, which is based on Article 100a of the Treaty, is aimed essentially at ensuring freedom to provide services and, more generally, freedom of competition cannot be valid.

First, the recitals in the preamble to the Directive repeatedly refer to the purpose of protecting consumers. Secondly, the fact that the Directive is intended to assure other objectives cannot preclude its provisions from also having the aim of protecting consumers.

Similarly, the German and United Kingdom governments' argument that the actual wording of Article 7 shows that this provision simply requires package travel organisers to provide sufficient evidence of security and that its lack of reference to any right of consumers to such security indicates that such a right is only an indirect and derived right must be rejected.

In that regard, it suffices to point out that the obligation to offer sufficient evidence of security necessarily implies that those having that obligation must actually take out such security. Indeed, the obligation laid down in Article 7 would be pointless in the absence of security actually enabling money to be paid over to be refunded or the consumer to be repatriated, should occasion arise.

The next point to be examined is whether the content of the rights in question are identifiable on the basis of the provisions of the Directive alone.

The persons having rights under Article 7 are sufficiently identified as consumers, as defined by Article 2 of the Directive. The same holds true of the content of those rights. Those rights consist in a guarantee that money paid over by purchasers of package travel will be refunded and a guarantee that they will be repatriated in the event of the insolvency of the organiser. In those circumstances, the purpose of Article 7 of the Directive must be to grant to individuals rights whose content is determinable with sufficient precision.

That conclusion is not affected by the fact that the Directive leaves the Member States considerable latitude as regards the choice of means for achieving the result it seeks. The fact that states may choose between a wide variety of means for achieving the result prescribed by a Directive is of no importance if the purpose of the Directive is to grant to individuals rights whose content is determinable with sufficient precision.

The measures necessary for proper transposition of the Directive (Questions 3, 4, 5, 6 and 7)

Questions 3 and 4

By questions 3 and 4, the national court is essentially asking the Court to specify what "necessary measures" the Member States should have adopted in order to comply with Article 9 of the Directive.

First of all, according to settled case law, the provisions of a Directive

A24.4

751

must be implemented with unquestionable binding force and with the specificity, precision and clarity required in order to satisfy the requirement of legal certainty.

Secondly, in providing that the Member States were to bring into force the measures necessary to comply with the Directive before 31 December 1992, Article 9 required the Member States to adopt all the measures necessary to ensure that the provisions of the Directive were fully effective and so guarantee achievement of the prescribed result.

It follows that Article 7 would not have been fully implemented if, within the prescribed period, the national legislature had done no more than adopt the necessary legal framework for requiring organisers by law to provide sufficient evidence of security.

Question 5

A24.5   By its fifth question, the national court asks whether the objective of consumer protection pursued by Article 7 of the Directive is satisfied if the Member State allows the travel organiser to require a deposit of up to 10% towards the travel price, with a maximum of DM 500, before handing over to his customer documents which the national court describes as "documents of value", namely documents evidencing the consumer's right to the provision of the various services included in the travel package (by airlines or hotel companies).

By this question the national court is seeking to ascertain in substance whether it is in conformity with Article 7 for the national legislature to make the consumer bear the risk relating to such a deposit so that the deposit is left uncovered by the security mentioned in that provision.

The purpose of Article 7 of the Directive is to protect the consumer against the risks defined in that provision arising from the insolvency of the organiser. It would be contrary to that purpose to limit that protection by leaving any deposit payment uncovered by the security for a refund or repatriation. The Directive contains no basis for any such limitation of the rights guaranteed by Article 7.

Question 7

A24.6   By Question 7(b) the national court asks whether the security of which organisers must "provide sufficient evidence", in accordance with Article 7 of the Directive, is lacking even if, on payment of the travel price, travellers have documents of value.

According to the German government, the protection guaranteed by Article 7 is not lacking if the traveller has documents guaranteeing a direct right against the actual provider of services (the airline company or the hotelier).

That argument cannot be accepted. The protection which Article 7 guarantees to consumers could be impaired if they were made to enforce credit vouchers against third parties who are not, in any event, required to honour them and who are likewise themselves exposed to the risks consequent on insolvency.

In Question 7(a) the national court asks whether the Federal Republic of Germany could have omitted altogether to transpose Article 7 of the Directive in view of the *Bundesgerichtshof's* "advance payment" judgment.

Since the aim of Article 7 is to protect the consumer against the risks set out in that provision, arising from the organiser's insolvency, a judgment such as the *Bundesgerichtshof's* advance payment judgment cannot satisfy the requirements of the Directive if it requires the consumer to bear the risk of the organiser's insolvency as regards the deposit required and also the risk that, when the consumer has received documents of value, the actual provider of the services might not honour them or might become insolvent.

Question 6

By Question 6 the national court asks whether the Directive requires   **A24.7**
Member States to adopt specific measures to protect package travellers against their own negligence.

First, neither the objective of the Directive nor its specific provisions require the Member States to adopt specific provision in relation to Article 7 to protect package travellers from their own negligence.

Secondly, according to the Court's case law, in determining the loss or damage for which reparation may be granted, the national court may always inquire whether the injured person showed reasonable care so as to avoid the loss or damage or to mitigate it.

The Court ruled:

1   Failure to take any measure to transpose a Directive in order to   **A24.8**
    achieve the result it prescribes within the period laid down for that
    purposes constitutes *per se* a serious breach of Community law and
    consequently gives rise to a right of reparation for individuals suffer-
    ing injury if the result prescribed by the Directive entails the grant to
    individuals of rights whose content is identifiable and a causal link
    exists between the breach of the State's obligation and the loss or
    damage suffered.

2   The result prescribed by Article 7 of Council Directive 90/314/EEC
    of 13 June 1990 on package travel, package holidays and package
    tours entails the grant to package travellers of rights guaranteeing a
    refund of money paid over and their repatriation in the event of
    the organiser's insolvency; the content of those rights is sufficiently
    identifiable.

3   In order to comply with Article 9 of Directive 90/314, the Member
    State should have adopted, within the period prescribed, all the

measures necessary to ensure that, as from 1 January 1993, individuals would have effective protection against the risk of the insolvency of the organiser and/or retailer party to the contract.

4　If a Member State allows the package travel organiser and/or retailer party to a contract to require payment of a deposit of up to 10% towards the travel price, with a maximum of DM 500, the protective purpose pursued by Article 7 of Directive 90/314 is not satisfied unless a refund of that deposit is also guaranteed in the event of the insolvency of the package travel organiser and/or retailer party to the contract.

5　Article 7 of Directive 90/314 is to be interpreted as meaning that the "security of which organisers must offer sufficient evidence is lacking even if, on payment of the travel price, travellers are in possession of documents of value and that the Federal Republic of Germany could not have omitted altogether to transpose Directive 90/314 on the basis of the *Bundesgerichtshof's* "advance payment" judgment of 12 March 1987.

6　Directive 90/314 does not require Member States to adopt specific measures in relation to Article 7 in order to protect package travellers against their own negligence.

Reproduced with the kind permission of the Information Office of the Court of Justice of the European Communities.

Index